REEFER MOVIE MADNESS

The statements made by the individuals interviewed in this book reflect their individual viewpoints and should not be construed as the views of the publisher. The material contained in this book is presented only for informational purposes. The publisher and the authors do not condone or advocate in any way the use of prohibited substances or illegal activity of any kind.

Editor: David Cashion
Photo Editor: Meg Handler
Designer: Danielle Young
Production Manager: Ankur Ghosh

Cataloging-in-Publication data has been applied for and is available from the Library of Congress.
ISBN: 978-0-8109-0312-8

Printed and bound in China
10 9 8 7 6 5 4 3 2 1

Abrams Image books are available at special discounts when purchased in quantity for premiums and promotions as well as fundraising or educational use. Special editions can also be created to specification. For details, contact specialmarkets@abramsbooks.com or the address below.

THE ART OF BOOKS SINCE 1949

115 West 18th Street
New York, NY 10011
www.abramsbooks.com

REEFER MOVIE MADNESS

THE ULTIMATE STONER FILM GUIDE

SHIRLEY HALPERIN & STEVE BLOOM

ABRAMS IMAGE, NEW YORK

CONTENTS

Introduction

Marijuana and movies go together like bong hits and the munchies. For more than forty years, films have been an integral part of pot culture, helping shape individual interests and fashions, and igniting imagination, chatter, and passion. We share with marijuana enthusiasts countless esoteric references stemming from the movies—films like *Up in Smoke* or *Dazed and Confused*, both of which any self-respecting stoner should be able to recite by heart; *Friday*, a must-see for hip-hop–loving potheads; or *Easy Rider*, an essential primer to the outsider cinema of the late sixties and early seventies. These films are as much a part of the stoner psyche as Bob Marley and Bambus. They're also the inspiration for *Reefer Movie Madness*.

As longtime tokers, we've been immersed in the movies that shape pot culture since well before we began our careers as entertainment journalists. One of us was very much a product of the eighties, but the pivotal film that kick-started it for her was 1967's *The Graduate*. Its trippy, seamless transitions and mellow Simon & Garfunkel soundtrack transformed a preppy high school kid into a full-fledged hippie. For the other, growing up in the sixties and seventies, it was *Easy Rider* that stoked his stoner imagination. Since those formative teenage years, we've both remained acutely aware of pot's progression into popular culture, especially in the world of film.

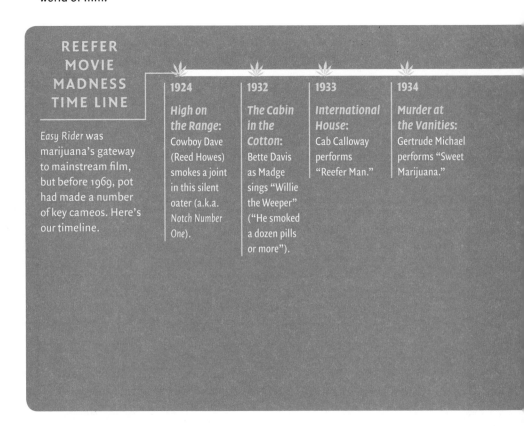

REEFER MOVIE MADNESS TIME LINE

Easy Rider was marijuana's gateway to mainstream film, but before 1969, pot had made a number of key cameos. Here's our timeline.

1924	1932	1933	1934
High on the Range: Cowboy Dave (Reed Howes) smokes a joint in this silent oater (a.k.a. *Notch Number One*).	*The Cabin in the Cotton*: Bette Davis as Madge sings "Willie the Weeper" ("He smoked a dozen pills or more").	*International House*: Cab Calloway performs "Reefer Man."	*Murder at the Vanities*: Gertrude Michael performs "Sweet Marijuana."

Until the late seventies, marijuana had usually shown up in dramas, rom-coms, and action flicks. Then along came Cheech & Chong with *Up in Smoke* in 1978. This was the first stoner comedy—Cheech and Chong created the genre. Two guys getting high all the time. One guy stonier than the other. Long on high jinks and hilarity, short on plot-production quality.

But credit for the genre also goes to *Animal House*, released in 1978 as well. Where *Up in Smoke* is entirely about marijuana, *Animal House* is a party movie with one great pot scene. The tentacles of both movies can be seen throughout this book.

These days, between the *Harold & Kumar* franchise and the Judd Apatow library, big-budget studio films are being written for and directly marketed to stoners and setting box-office records. And in the indie world, movies like *The Wackness*, *Smiley Face*, and *Super High Me* have made their mark at the festivals and beyond.

Outside of obvious bait like *Pineapple Express*, *Half Baked*, or *How High*, there are literally hundreds of movies with psychedelic overtones, trippy animated content, or party-fueled antics. And you couldn't even start counting the number of silly, cheesy, over-the-top comedies that suddenly seem funnier once you're high. Everybody has that one random movie that they consider a stoner treasure while others simply view it as a kind-of-funny, B-grade guilty pleasure. You'll find a few of these examples in *Reefer Movie Madness*, from popular go-tos like *Anchorman*, *Airplane*, and *Fletch*, to the lesser-knowns like *Waiting...* and *Wet Hot American Summer*.

1936	1937	1942	1945	1949
Reefer Madness: Government antidrug film shows young people smoking "reefers," dancing wildly, laughing hysterically, and making out until police bust the joint.	*Marihuana, the Weed with Roots in Hell!:* Burma (Harley Wood) looks directly into the camera as she smokes and inhales her first joint—her face contorts and then she bursts into laughter.	*Assassin of Youth:* Straitlaced Joan (Luana Walters) busts a high school pot-smoking ring that includes her dealer cousin, Linda (Fay McKenzie).	*Devil's Harvest:* In this cousin of *Reefer Madness*, joints are smoked before all hell breaks loose!	*The Woman in Green:* Hypnotist Lydia (Hillary Brooke) attempts to sedate Sherlock Holmes (Basil Rathbone) with a pill containing "Cannabis Japonica," which she says will make him drowsy. Holmes substitutes it with "a drug of my own," then captures his nemesis, Moriarty (Henry Daniell).	*Wild Weed:* Chorus girl Anne Lester (Lila Leeds) starts smoking pot with the help of dealer Markey (Alan Baxter) and gets busted in this exploitation film.

We aimed to cover it all—from wacky, raunchy comedies and out-there sci-fi or fantasy flicks to sixties artifacts, intense indie dramas, and action-packed studio blockbusters. And like our previous effort, *Pot Culture: The A–Z Guide to Stoner Language and Life*, *Reefer Movie Madness* is presented in an easy-to-follow, alphabetical format broken down into seven sections: comedies; dramas; sci-fi, fantasy, and horror; action and sports; animated; music; and documentaries. There are lots of stony sidebars and celebrity interviews. Actors Tommy Chong, Cheech Marin, Taryn Manning, Jay Chandrasekhar, Adrianne Curry, Andy Milonakis, and Danneel Harris offer behind-the-scenes insight. And musicians like Snoop Dogg, B-Real, Method Man, Redman, Jason Mraz, Melissa Etheridge, Kings of Leon's Nathan Followill, and The Flaming Lips's Wayne Coyne helped clue us to a wider array of films from off the beaten path, each more mind-bending than the next.

In case you're wondering, there is a method to the madness presented here. Our starting point, of course, is *Reefer Madness*, the 1936 antimarijuana exploitation classic that preceded the government's prohibition of marijuana by a year. However, the original plan to include 420 movies (for obvious stoner reasons) ballooned to more than seven hundred. We used a set of criteria to eliminate films that are super cool, respected, award-winning, or generally awesome, from the ones we consider vital to the stoner library. That criteria is: Marijuana or other drugs are central to the story, or the movie is particularly fun to watch stoned. With that in mind, *Reefer*

1951	1958		1959		1960
Alice in Wonderland: Blue caterpillar smokes a hookah. *Drug Addiction:* Marty (John Gavarro) smokes pot with a friend then moves on to heroin.	*High School Confidential!:* Joan (Diane Jergens) smokes "sticks" provided by hepcat Tony (Russ Tamblyn), who's actually a narc. *The Cool and the Crazy:* Juvenile delinquent Jackie (Richard Bakalyan) turns all the square kids on to pot.	*Touch of Evil:* Mexican gang member to Susie (Janet Leigh): "You know what marijuana is, don't you? You know what Mary Jane is?" The motel manager (Dennis Weaver) finds a half-smoked joint in Susie's room.	*The Gene Krupa Story:* Sal Mineo as the jazz drummer smokes a joint with singer Dorissa Dinell (Susan Oliver). "Don't diddle it, go on," she says. "Put your miseries out to pasture." Krupa gets arrested for reefers and goes to jail.	*Pull My Daisy:* Cool cats smoke pot while playing jazz in Robert Frank's experimental short narrated and written by Jack Kerouac.	*Key Witness:* Gang member Cowboy (Dennis Hopper) pays Muggles (Joby Baker) with a bag of weed and of course Muggles smokes it.

Movie Madness's central mission is to catalog every movie in which pot is the star—from Cheech & Chong's monster spliffs and *How High*'s killer hydro to the ditch weed of *Dazed and Confused* and the Ivy League buds of Harold & Kumar.

For movies where marijuana is not essential to the plot but contain a key scene, line, or character that smokes, deals, or otherwise encourages its use, we included those too. So you'll find a film like *The Breakfast Club*, which offers little in terms of visual stimuli but features pot in a pivotal turning-point scene, or *Nine to Five*, in which three underappreciated secretaries toke up and dream up ways of offing their chauvinistic boss, or the simple exchange of a joint between Ben Stiller and Cameron Diaz in *There's Something About Mary*. If marijuana shows up in a movie, it's generally there for good reason.

Still, casting an even wider net, *Reefer Movie Madness* also lists movies with distinct drug themes that reach beyond pot and all its derivatives (hash, brownies, and whatnot). You'll find a fair amount of hallucinogens represented—everything from mushrooms (*Fresh Cut Grass*) and acid (*Flirting with Disaster*), to peyote (*Natural Born Killers, The Doors*) and Ecstasy (*Go*), to cocaine (*Scarface, Blow*) and pills (*Drugstore Cowboy*), and even heroin (*The French Connection, Requiem for a Dream*). Why bother with hard drugs in a guide for stoners? Because in film form, any screen portrayal of a mind-altering substance is stony. Plus, how could we not include movies like *Scarface* and *GoodFellas*, both of which countless potheads have watched so many times and know by heart?

1961	1962	1966		1967	
West Side Story: In "Gee, Officer Krupke!" Action (Tony Mordente) sings, "My parents treat me rough / With all their marijuana / They won't give me a puff."	*Sweet Bird of Youth:* Paul Newman as Chance and Geraldine Page as actress Alexandra Del Lago smoke a joint in a hotel room. "This is high-class pot," Chance says. "Where'd you get it?"	*Blow-Up:* Joints are smoked in a party scene at a Parisian rock club. "Here, have a drag," says Ron (Peter Bowles). *Chappaqua:* William S. Burroughs as the perfectly named Opium Jones smokes a joint in France. *Hallucination Generation:* Hipsters get high on hash and acid.	*The Wild Angels:* Heavenly Blues (Peter Fonda) and Loser (Bruce Dern) smoke joints. "Yeah, I'd like to get high," Loser says, then dies.	*The Love-Ins:* Patricia (Susan Oliver) imagines she's Alice in Wonderland during an LSD trip and smokes from a hookah. At the Love-In in San Francisco's Golden Gate Park, there's a sign that reads: PLEASE DON'T SMOKE THE GRASS.	*Hell's Angels on Wheels:* Poet (Jack Nicholson) smokes a roach. Bikers pass joints around. *The Trip:* Max (Dennis Hopper) rolls a joint, and several are passed around in Roger Corman's LSD exposé.

No matter how much we wanted to, we obviously couldn't continue to add movies to the main review sections past our publisher's deadline. And despite our monumental effort to uncover every possible entry for this book—we searched high and low and spent countless hours listening to friends and acquaintances tell us every possible movie that should be included—we may have forgotten a few. With more than seven hundred movies referenced in this guide, almost all of the movies we hoped to squeeze in made it in, in one form or another. But let us know what you think, and keep up with the latest *Reefer Movie Madness* news at www.reefermoviemadness.com.

In the end, was it a fruitful experiment? Absolutely. And educational to boot. Spending countless hours watching movies and researching this fascinating subject was like a crash course in film history without having to go to school. We started out marijuana experts and turned into movie geeks. We hope you enjoy our stoner-film odyssey.

1968

Wild in the Streets:
Daphne (Shelley Winters) puffs a pipe, and joints are smoked by Max's band of merry pranksters.

I Love You, Alice B. Toklas!:
Hippie chick Nancy (Leigh Taylor-Young) bakes "groovy brownies," inspired by Alice B. Toklas. Harold (Peter Sellers), Joyce (Joyce Van Patten), and Harold's parents all sample the brownies.

Maryjane:
High school students smoke joints and party while school officials and the police try to rain on their pot parade. Fabian (Phil Blake) stars as a sympathetic teacher who gets caught up in the controversy.

The Hooked Generation:
Sadistic smugglers smoke joints and a hookah.

Skidoo:
Hippies in a psychedelic bus pass a joint using a roach clip.

Psych-Out:
Stoney (Jack Nicholson) opens the movie taking a hit of a joint and asking, "What is it? Gold?" (referring to Colombian Gold). Later, after another puff, Stoney exclaims, "Pretty good grass!"

Barbarella:
Jane Fonda as Barbarella joins the party in the "place of pleasure" in Sogo, inhaling "essence of man" out of a gigantic hookah.

1969

Easy Rider:
Wyatt (Peter Fonda), George (Jack Nicholson), and Billy (Dennis Hopper) smoke joints around the campfire. "You've got to hold it in your lungs longer, George," Billy instructs.

Alice's Restaurant:
Joints are passed around during the singing of "Amazing Grace."

Bob & Carol & Ted & Alice:
Ted (Elliott Gould) and Alice (Dyan Cannon) take hits from Bob's wooden peace pipe. "Is this Acapulco Gold?" Ted asks. "Ah, no," Bob (Robert Culp) replies, "this is beautiful downtown Burbank."

☙ REEFER MOVIE MADNESS KEY ☙

Sometimes it's a pipe, more often a joint. You might see a plant, a blunt, or a bong. One of the characters may do a line of coke, a shot of tequila, or eat mushrooms. Does all this mean there's a formula to the stoner-friendly flick? In a word: Yes. Some combination of the above (or below) are commonly found elements in the seven hundred–plus films listed in *Reefer Movie Madness*, and we've painstakingly combed through them all so you know exactly what you're in for. Just refer to the *Reefer* key.

 Acid (or LSD)

 Joint

 Blunt

 Marijuana plant

 Bong (or hookah)

 Mushrooms

 Booze

 Nudity (male/female)

 Cocaine (or crack)

 Pipe

 Crystal meth

 Pills

 Ecstasy

 Tobacco

 Heroin (or opium)

Adventureland (2009)

🌿 🌿 🌿 🌿 Brainy but virginal, James Brennan (Jesse Eisenberg) has just graduated college and is intent on spending the summer traveling Europe before attending grad school in New York City. But when he learns his father has been downsized at work, James is forced to spend the summer of 1987 at home in Pittsburgh, with only a plastic bag full of prerolled joints, gifted by his dormmate, to distract him. Discouraged to discover that his comparative literature degree qualifies him for absolutely nothing, James ends up getting a job working the games at Adventureland, the local amusement park. There he meets a colorful cast of characters, including the darkly alluring Em Lewin (Kristen Stewart); the park's resident married lothario Mike Connell (Ryan Reynolds); alienated, pipe-smoking intellectual Joel (Martin Starr of *Freaks and Geeks*); his goofy childhood friend Tommy Frigo (Matt Bush), who's constantly pranking him; and the requisite disco-dancing temptress Lisa P (Margarita Levieva). The main plot complication occurs when James finds out that Em, with whom he's having a chaste but promising relationship, is actually carrying on an affair with the married Mike behind his back.

All the clichés of young romance are covered here, but the key to the movie's success are its knowing nods to pop culture, with the Replacements's "Bastards of Young" and "Unsatisfied" framing the action, and the film's central romance between James and Em spiked with their mutual love of hip cult acts like Big Star, Lou Reed, and Eno. A key plot point revolves around repairman Mike's insistence he once jammed with Lou Reed, though James gently offers a correction when he overhears him trying to impress a gaggle of young girls by quoting the lyrics to "Satellite of Love" as "shine a light on love." (Can you say "douchebag"?) Ultimately, what gives *Adventureland* its pot culture cred is that plastic baggie of rolled joints prompting several thoughtful stoned revelations and the cookies Em makes out of them, which leads to a very stoned bumper car ride. No wonder it gets compared to *Dazed and Confused*.

> "Hey James, you still have any of those baby joints?"
>
> **—Mike**

🌿 DIRECTOR'S TAKE: GREG MOTTOLA 🌿

Greg Mottola directed *Superbad* (2007), which, despite its party theme, was surprisingly dry on the weed front, but his follow-up, *Adventureland* (2009), starring Kristen Stewart and Jesse Eisenberg, more than made up for it. The director explains the movie's pot influence.

Reefer Movie Madness: Would you consider *Adventureland* a stoner movie? James isn't your stereotypical pothead, or is he?

Greg Mottola: To me, the baggie of joints that's gifted to James is a currency for a very uncool guy to be cool—briefly, at times. Pot was such a part of life [back in 1987]. I grew up in the suburbs, and the drinking age was eighteen in New York, so we were just drinking and smoking pot.

RMM: When making a movie with a central pot theme, do you have to get in the right head space, as it were?

GM: I stop partying when I make a movie, but I've never been a huge stoner because my brain chemistry is terrible on marijuana. I'm the kind of stoner that needs to get into one of those altered states—hydropods or one of those isolation chambers—and play Miles Davis's *Kind of Blue* over and over again. I can't be around people when I'm stoned—unlike Seth Rogen, who can write five movies and be stoned the entire time. I'm sure there was a lot of pot smoking happening on *Adventureland*, and I just wasn't privy to it.

Airplane! (1980)

Disaster movies were all the rage in the seventies—*Poseidon Adventure, Earthquake,* and *Airport* to name a few—but none did impending catastrophic doom as hilariously as 1980's *Airplane!,* the movie that launched a dozen copycats, including the *Naked Gun* series, B-movie classic *Top Secret!,* and its own not-nearly-as-funny sequel in outer space. As a pioneering force (or farce) in this slapstick sub-genre, *Airplane!* is all about laugh-out-loud humor, whether that involves punching out Hare Krishnas, making lewd sexual comments to a seven-year-old kid, or having a matronly, composed older white woman translate jive—all absurdities are welcome on this trip. As for the plot, it's a love story, first and foremost. Former pilot Ted Striker's (Robert Hays) postwar trauma is driving his stewardess girlfriend, Elaine (Julie Hagerty), away. To get her back, he overcomes his fear of flying (though not his drinking problem) and boards the flight she's working on. But when the passengers and most of the crew eat some bad fish and suffer a severe case of food poisoning, Striker has to take over the plane and face not just his phobia, but his wartime nemesis, Rex Kramer (Robert Stack). Of course, that's all secondary to minute after minute of brilliant dialogue. There's not a single dud, and too many rib-bursting lines to mention, but here's just a few: "Joey, do you like movies about gladiators?"; "Roger, Roger. What's our vector, Victor?" "I am serious . . . and don't call me Shirley." Actually, this one time you can! (Look on the cover, stoner.)

Ali G Indahouse (2002)

Four years before *Borat* became an international sensation, Sacha Baron Cohen's breakthrough character Ali G had his own TV show and movie, which was only released in England. After being picked up by HBO, *Da Ali G Show* developed a cult following in the U.S., leading fans to discover this movie about the faux hip-hopper who shakes up parliamentary politics with his "Keepin' It Real" message. Part Monty Python, part stoner slapstick, and very, very British, Baron's first film is distinguished by its bawdy sense of humor and affection for all things cannabis. Invited to inspect the "Confiscation Room," Ali eyes thirty kilos of pot. "Is there any skunk?" he asks. Next, he and his buds are smoking a two-foot spliff and watching pornos. In another scene, Ali quells an argumentative meeting of world leaders by dumping one of the "confiscated" weed bags into an urn. "Big up to herbal tea, a'ight!" he declares. Oh, and just in case you ever wondered what Ali G stands for—it's Alistair Graham.

Alice's Restaurant (1969)

Two years after his groundbreaking *Bonnie and Clyde,* director Arthur Penn adapted Arlo Guthrie's nineteen-minute song about a hippie church-turned-café, the Vietnam draft, and a littering bust. Guthrie plays himself—a folk-singing minstrel like his famous father, Woody (Joseph Boley), who is hospitalized and passes away but not before Arlo and Pete Seeger serenade him with "Let's Go Riding in My Car." Arlo does a lot of that in the movie, hitchhiking cross-country and zipping around in his red VW bus. He settles down for a while in Western Massachusetts, where Alice (Patricia Quinn) and Ray Block (James Broderick) convert the church into a counterculture scene, with huge dinners, musical jamborees, plenty of pot and lots of "free love." Alice "makes it" with Ray and junkie Shelley (Michael McClanahan), leading to a conflict that almost ruins the "scene." The lighter subplots of Arlo's garbage-dumping bust and his experience with the draft board provide some laughs. But Penn goes deeper, exploring schisms within the hippie community that might prevent it from seizing the moment when even local police appear to be on their side.

Anchorman: The Legend of Ron Burgundy (2004)

Ron Burgundy (Will Ferrell) is not your ordinary newsman—more like a San Diegoan superhero. The women love him. His news team members worship him. The man can play jazz flute like a pro and communicate with his own dog (sing along: "Oh Baxter, you are my little gentleman / I'll take you to foggy London town"). But when Channel 4 News hires female reporter Veronica Corningstone (Christina Applegate), the same foxy lady Ron tried to impress with his talk of leather-bound books at one of his famous pool parties, the good old days of this boys' club soon become a thing of the past. Of course, not before Ron, field reporter Brian Fantana (Paul Rudd), weatherman Brick Tamland (Steve Carell), and sportscaster Champ Kind (David Koechner) make her life a living hell. But Veronica is a fighter and a lover (soon after she starts working, but before being promoted to coanchor, she and Ron have a passionate, but short-lived love affair), and rather than bow to their sexist cracks, she slips the F-bomb into Ron's teleprompter and he ends up getting fired. The downward spiral continues when his beloved dog Baxter is punted into the ocean by a snarly biker (Jack Black)—prompting one of the greatest lines in the movie, "I'm in a glass cage of emotion!"— and in no time, Ron's wandering the streets like a hobo drinking warm milk. The news wars, meanwhile, continue as rival stations scramble to cover the birth of a baby panda at the San Diego Zoo. And these competing anchormen (including Ben Stiller, Vince Vaughn, and Luke Wilson) aren't above sabotage, like when the NPR anchor (played by Tim Robbins) pushes Veronica into a nearby bear cage. And you can guess who saves the day and thereby redeems his San Diego hero status.

As the Judd Apatow (and Ferrell) library goes, *Anchorman* is a shining example of comedy perfection, down to the tiniest seventies detail. But it's no one-man show—Rudd, Carell, SNL's Fred Willard and Chris Parnell, and Vaughn as Wes Mantooth deserve equal credit, as does Applegate and that "absolutely breathtaking heiney." We wanna be friends with it, too.

☘ WILL FERRELL MOVIES TO WATCH STONED ☘

By Andrew McMahon, singer of Jack's Mannequin

Zoolander (2001): "I saw *Zoolander* on my first Warped Tour and came away thinking I hated that movie. Until I noticed we started quoting it all the time and having these *Zoolander*-esque conversations. After that, I think I watched it every day for a year straight."

Old School (2003): "This is one of those movies that you can watch sober and it's just as funny. I'd take Will Ferrell as Frank the Tank in any direction, but stoned is probably a better way."

Wedding Crashers (2005): "Will Ferrell has a short but sweet cameo as Chazz, the dude who invented wedding crashing, which may be one of his best roles ever. At least, it's pretty high on my list."

Talladega Nights: The Ballad of Ricky Bobby (2006): "There's been some debate about whether or not *Talladega Nights* is a good movie. Some argue there's not really a script and Will Ferrell and John C. Reilly just riff in whatever clothes they're wearing. With that said, I'm into it!"

Anchorman: The Legend of Ron Burgundy (2004): "The best thing about *Anchorman* is Ron Burgundy's lines: 'Milk was a bad choice.' 'Scotchy, scotch, scotch. I love scotch.' 'I wanna be in you.' They're endless. And I grew up not far from San Diego, and still travel through there enough with the band where we always refer to it as 'a whale's vagina.' It's our permanent perception of San Diego now."

Animal House (1978)

🪶 🍸 🌿 👓

🌿🌿🌿🌿🌿 The combination of *National Lampoon* wit and *Saturday Night Live* slapstick produced the greatest comedy of the seventies, one whose impact is still felt in the films of Judd Apatow, the Farrelly brothers, Kevin Smith, Ben Stiller, and Will Farrell. Often copied (*PCU, Orange County, How High, Van Wilder*) but never equaled, director John Landis assembled a young, mostly unknown cast for his hilarious take on college life, with warring frats and a deranged dean threatening the dreaded "double secret probation." Pinto (Tom Hulce) and Flounder (Stephen Furst) join Delta House, home to Faber College campus rebels Otter (Tim Matheson), Bluto (John Belushi), Boon (Peter Riegert), and D-Day (Bruce McGill), while the right-wing Omega House and Dean Wormer (John Vernon) conspire against the Deltas, known for boisterous toga parties featuring Otis Day & the Nights ("Shout"). Along the way, there are famous scenes like "Food Fight," "Road Trip," and the classic sesh with Professor Jennings (Donald Sutherland): "Would anybody like to smoke some pot?" Pinto, Boon, and Katy (Karen Allen) all puff with the Prof, but it's Pinto who has the best line: "Could I buy some pot from you?" Delta's revenge is a well-choreographed takeover of the town parade, complete with D-Day's Deathmobile plowing into the grandstand. No one gets hurt, but it's clear the divisions from the sixties had not been healed by 1978.

Bluto: "Christ, seven years of college down the drain."

Annie Hall (1977)

🪶 🌿 🥄

🌿🌿🌿🌿🌿 Ah, to be in love in New York City—one of the few places on earth where a neurotic, pseudo-intellectual Jew and a freethinking, fashion-forward Wisconsin transplant can date and make no apologies for it. That's what *Annie Hall* is about: a love story, involving two unlikely participants who at times seem so dramatically different that there's no way they could bear each other for an afternoon, let alone a few years. Case in point: Before having sex, Annie, played by Diane Keaton, likes taking a couple hits off a joint to, you know, get in the mood. But the uptight Alvy (Woody Allen), who always says exactly what's on his mind, disapproves. "Grass, the illusion that it will make a white woman more like Billie Holiday," he says in one of the film's pivotal scenes. Later in their relationship, Alvy commits the ultimate faux pas by sneezing directly into a pile of cocaine and scattering it everywhere, to the annoyance of Annie and her hipster friends. Needless to say, what ensues is an emotional tug-of-war that spans two coasts, several Manhattan apartments, countless coffee chats, and awkward moments. But it's the combination of Alvy's nerdiness and Annie's inherent cool factor that makes this story so endearing and, at points, laugh-out-loud funny.

> "Have you ever made love high?"
> —**Annie**
>
> "Me, no. If I have grass or alcohol or anything I get unbearably wonderful; I get too wonderful for words."
> —**Alvy**

On the heady front, long takes of conversational dialogue require serious concentration, some might even say patience, but not in a Kevin Smith way. After all, the movie came out in the late seventies and is very much of that era (even Paul Simon scored a bit part, as a sleazy music-business executive). In fact, *Annie Hall* won Best Picture in 1977 (one of four

Oscars it took that year), beating out *Star Wars*. Indeed, it might be far from hyperspeed, but as one of Woody Allen's most popular films, *Annie Hall* is one hell of a roller-coaster ride. *La di da, la di da, la la.*

Banger Sisters, The
(2002)

You can take the girl out of the Sunset Strip, but you can't take the Sunset Strip out of the girl—that's the basic premise of *The Banger Sisters*, which reunites former groupies Suzette (Goldie Hawn) and Lavinia (Susan Sarandon) after twenty years of estrangement. Suzette, still a party girl, has just gotten fired from her job as a bartender at the Whisky-A-Go-Go, while Lavinia, or "Vinnie," is an uptight mother of two teenaged girls who's put her wild days behind her. The duo reconnects under auspicious circumstances. Suzette is crashing with Harry (Geoffrey Rush), an anxiety-ridden

author she picked up at a Phoenix hotel where she sees Vin's daughter Hannah (Erika Christensen) drunk and tripping on acid after the prom. Suzette takes Hannah, the school valedictorian, home, and when the two pals get together the next day, she sees how grim and joyless Vinnie's life has turned out to be. Determined to unleash the spirit of their youth, Suzette eventually manages to break through

Vinnie's icy exterior and the two hit the clubs, share a joint, and reminisce about the many rock stars they banged back in the day. Vinnie's family members, especially daughter Ginger (played by Sarandon's real-life daughter Eva Amurri), are in a state of utter shock when the person they knew as mom suddenly chops her hair, starts wearing skin-tight pleather, describes Jim Morrison as if she knew him, and later divulges her groupie past and the "rock cocks" collection she had hidden in the basement. Vin rediscovers her former self and this tale of two cougars wraps up neatly at Hannah's graduation the next day. But for all the mentions of what "a blast" they had in the good old days, the adult Banger sisters, and this uninspired, predictable movie, are more like a drag.

Suzette: "See that bathroom? Jim Morrison passed out in there one night, with me underneath him."

Beerfest (2006)

Potheads have Cheech & Chong, and brew enthusiasts have *Beerfest*, the ultimate movie about drinking. The fourth offering of the comedy canon of party kings Broken Lizard, the writing team behind *Super Troopers* and *Club Dread*, stars Jay Chandrasekhar (who also directs), Kevin Heffernan, Steve Lemme, Paul Soter, and Erik Stolhanske as competitors at the top-secret Beerfest, a drinking tournament in the heart of Germany run by Baron Wolfgang von Wolfhausen. American brothers Jan and Todd Wolfhouse (Soter and Stolhanske) are also descendants of the von Wolfhausens, but when their grandfather took off for the States with the secret family beer recipe, the clan was essentially disowned and their grandmother Gam Gam (Cloris Leachman) was deemed a whore (which, in fact, she was). To reclaim their grandparents' honor and their rightful inheritance, the von Wolfhausen brewery in Bavaria, the brothers put together an all-star team of players, including down-on-his-luck male prostitute Barry (Chandrasekhar), Jewish scientist and chemistry expert Finkelstein (Lemme), and Landfill (Heffernan), an extra-large tank of a man still bitter over being fired from a brewery. The guys train for a year straight, during which they find the secret recipe and start producing the delicious brew they dub Schnitzengiggle. But in their constant state of intoxication, they don't realize there's a spy in the midst, posing as Gam Gam's maid, Cherry (Mo'Nique). Undeterred, they make the trek to Deutschland and use the Trojan keg method to sneak into the competition. Their rivalry with the funny-talking Germans is tense, and includes rounds of quarters, beer pong, upside-down shots, and tests of volume, depth, and height.

Why include a drinking movie in a book for stoners? Aside from Willie Nelson's cameo in the last scene, which opens the door to a possible sequel called *Potfest*, *Beerfest* is an endless barrage of laughs, especially when-

> "Holy crap, Willie Nelson! What are you doing here?"
>
> **—Fink**
>
> "Well, it's kind of a funny story. I was invited over here for this big secret international pot smoking competition and my teammates Cheech and Chong chickened out on me—they wouldn't fly on my biodiesel airplane—and the smoke-out's in thirty minutes and I don't wanna get disqualified. You guys don't want to be my teammates, do you?"
>
> **—Willie**

ever Chandrasekhar, Will Forte, or Eric Christian Olsen enter the picture. As for the message—you can ingest in excess day in, day out with zero consequences—can't we all relate to that?

Better Off Dead (1985)

Lane Meyer (John Cusack) would rather die than live without his girlfriend, Beth (Amanda Wyss), the one who dumped him for the school ski-team captain with these parting words: "I really think it's in my best interest if I went out with someone more popular. Better looking. Drives a nicer car." But for all his fruitless attempts to off himself—by hanging, jumping off a bridge, carbon monoxide poisoning, and setting himself on fire— Lane comes close, but can't seem to go through with it. As dreary as life in Greendale, California, may be (you "can't even get real drugs here," says his dopey bud Charles, played by Curtis Armstrong, who looks for cheap highs in everything from whipped cream to snow), things start looking up when Monique (Diane Franklin), a cute-as-a-button French foreign-exchange student, moves in next door, and, in her attempt to escape the clutches of the man-sized turd that is neighbor Ricky Smith (Dan Schneider), be-friends Lane and helps him tackle the dreaded K-12 ski run.

It's fitting that Lane is not only a decent skier, but also a skilled illustrator since every character in *Better Off Dead* is like a living cartoon, from his annoyingly clueless parents (his father's how-to manual is titled *Youth and the Drug Explosion*), to the relentless paperboy who chases his ass all over town, to his little brother who fashions a rocket out of household items and orders a book on how to pick up trashy women, and, of course, to his Asian rivals, the fresh-off-the-boat brothers who learned English watching *Wide World of Sports*. But the greatest caricature is Lane himself, a precursor to Cusack's future roles in *Say Anything* and *One Crazy Summer*, who does eighties teen angst better than just about anybody.

Charles De Mar: "This is pure snow! It's everywhere. Have you any idea what the street value of this mountain is?"

Big Lebowski, The
(1998)

🐛 🍸 🎷 👀

🌿 🌿 🌿 🌿 🌿 Jeff Bridges portrays sixties radical Jeffrey "The Dude" Lebowski in the Coens' brilliant farce about a pot-smoking slacker with a special fondness for bowling. Brought to you by Joel Coen—the absurdist auteur who along with his co-writer brother, Ethan, is also responsible for *Raising Arizona* and *Fargo*—*Lebowski* begins with a long shot of The Dude in bathrobe and slippers at the local Ralph's supermarket, sniffing a carton of half-and-half. He's quickly mistaken for another Jeffrey Lebowski and suffers the indignity of having his rug peed on. The Dude teams up with fellow bowlers Walter (John Goodman) and Donny (Steve Buscemi). A Vietnam vet with anger issues, Walter's hilarious: He promises a "world of pain" to anyone who crosses him, and he refuses to bowl on the Sabbath, even though he's not Jewish. The impressive cast includes artist Maude (Julianne Moore), toadie Brandt (Philip Seymour Hoffman), bowling rival Jesus (John Turturro), and Tara Reid as Bunny Lebowski. In the film, which is based on the life of Jeff Dowd, The Dude smokes pot prodigiously—in his car, bathtub, by a fireplace and in bed with Maude (and twice with roach clips). He's a baby boomer who loves Creedence and White Russians, and hates the Eagles and authority figures, man. An event known as Lebowski Fest celebrating this cult classic regularly travels around the country.

Maude Lebowski: "What do you do for recreation?"

The Dude: "Oh, the usual. I bowl. Drive around. The occasional acid flashback."

🌿 FIVE MORE BY THE COEN BROTHERS 🌿

Raising Arizona (1987): In the Coens' breakthrough film, Nicolas Cage and Holly Hunter play H.I. and Edwina, a couple so desperate to start a family that they steal a baby from a brood of quintuplets. With a reward offered by the newborn's father, local furniture mogul Nathan Arizona, the hunt is on as a motley crew of characters led by John Goodman's Gale Snoats search for little Nathan Jr. and attempt to corner his kidnappers.

Barton Fink (1991): A curious look at the machinations of moviemaking weaves together this surrealistic story about a Broadway playwright who's transitioning to Hollywood. Complicating matters more for Barton (John Turturro)—but curing his writer's block—is next-door-neighbor Charlie's (John Goodman) involvement in a murder. Influenced by the work of Alfred Hitchcock, Roman Polanski, and William Faulkner, *Fink* is as heady as film noir gets.

Fargo (1996): An Oscar-winning caper that keeps in line with the Coens' recurring themes of kidnapping, blackmail, and crime gone wrong, it features Frances McDormand as local police chief Marge, who's hot on the snowy Minnesota trail of two-bit cons Carl (Steve Buscemi) and Gaear (Peter Stormare), and their conspirator, car dealer Jerry (William H. Macy).

No Country for Old Men (2007): Set in the barren desert of West Texas, the Coens' second Oscar winner is a spine-chilling thriller about a botched drug deal and its ensuing fallout. Javier Bardem plays the menacing Chigurh, whose thirst for money and blatant disregard for human life puts everyone within eyesight in harm's way. Woody Harrelson, Josh Brolin, and Tommy Lee Jones costar in this intense adaptation of the Cormac McCarthy novel.

A Serious Man (2009): Nominated for a Best Picture and Best Original Screenplay Oscar, this is the Coen brothers' stoniest movie since *The Big Lebowski*. Set in late sixties Minnesota, it's the story of a troubled Jewish family in which the marijuana use of the movie's youngest protagonist, thirteen-year-old Danny (Aaron Wolff), is a running gag. After smoking a joint before his bar mitzvah, he delivers the highest haftorah in film history.

☙ Q & A: THE BIG LEBOWSKI'S REAL DUDE ☙

Reefer Movie Madness sat down with Jeff "The Dude" Dowd, the California slacker and film producer who inspired Jeff Bridges's character in *The Big Lebowski*, for his take on the stoner classic.

Reefer Movie Madness: It's been said that The Dude has struck a generational chord, like John Belushi in *Animal House*. What's his appeal?

Jeff Dowd: The Dude is like the holy fool or the court jester, like Charlie Chaplin or Jon Stewart or Chris Rock—goofy people who somehow go for the truth, or at least a different look at the illusion. That's the appeal of The Dude: People like a guy who tells it like it is.

RMM: *The Big Lebowski* wasn't seen as a success initially, but it's since attracted this massive cult following. Why do you think that is?

JD: The movie really makes people feel better— it's very powerful. For instance, there's a guy who's a paramedic in New York and he lost a lot of friends on 9/11. After that, he checked out entirely—just sat on his couch every day, went to therapists, doctors, took every kind of pill— like a zombie. About six months later, he's sitting around all bummed out and sees *The Big Lebowski* on his

shelf. So he puts it on, and he said that for the first time in months, "I started to smile, then I smiled more, then I started to laugh, and laugh, and laugh harder." His wife, Dee, says it just brought him out of it entirely, like a miracle treatment. And from then on, he was totally back.

RMM: What do you think is the best line in the script?

JD: "Fuckin' A," that never gets old.

RMM: The Dudeism about hating the Eagles, true or false?

JD: The Dude is beyond hate. The Dude is into reconciliation and moving on. My heart's in a good place.

RMM: You appear at Lebowski Fests all over the country, and you're constantly being interviewed about the movie. How much of your day-to-day life involves being The Dude?

JD: It's not every day. I check the Facebook page and reply to people, because people feel special when you reply.

RMM: The Coen brothers are acclaimed for directing Academy Award–winning movies like *Fargo* and *No Country for Old Men*, but how do you think they handle the countless stoners who foist praise only on *Lebowski*? Is it a thorn in their side?

JD: No. These fucking guys, these Oscar winners, they're no different than Muhammad Ali—everybody loses a couple fights. But career-wise, it turned out for these guys. I think they're proud of it.

✿ BEST BUDS ✿

Ten stony duos that take friendship to a higher level

1. Cheech & Chong: Starring in no fewer than eight movies together, Tommy Chong and Cheech Marin are the original comedy stoners who set the bar high for all dopey duos to follow. Now that the slurring Chong and the wisecracking Marin have returned to live performing, one more movie vehicle (and an animated twist on their classic skits) is on the horizon.

2. Harold and Kumar: As the unlikeliest odd couple in film history (and the first Korean and Indian to play lead stoner roles), Harold (John Cho) and Kumar (Kal Penn) go from a relatively pedestrian munchies run to high-risk high jinks like sneaking a bong onto an airplane, escaping from Guantanamo Bay, and puffing with the president.

3. Silas and Jamal (*How High*): Hip-hop heavyweights Method Man and Redman cashed in as Silas and Jamal in *How High*. Like Cheech & Chong, they first performed on stage before taking their act to the screen and their cannabis-fueled chemistry shows. *How High 2*, anyone?

4. Craig and Smokey (*Friday*): Chris Tucker is pothead instigator Smokey in *Friday*, who urges Ice Cube's Craig to get high "because it's Friday, you ain't got no job, and you ain't got shit to do!" Tucker is high-larious. For the sequels, Mike Epps takes the lead, but never hits the sweet spots of the original.

5. Saul and Dale (*Pineapple Express*): Seth Rogen's stoner résumé was pretty solid before *Pineapple Express*, but no one saw James Franco's dealer dude Saul coming. When Rogen's Dale wants to buy his weed and split, Saul cajoles him into sticking around and sharing the amazing cross joint. Who knew a dealer and one of his customers would become such BFFs?

6. Thurgood and Brian (*Half Baked*): Dave Chappelle's manic Thurgood and Jim Breuer's heavy-lidded Brian proved to be a perfect match in *Half Baked*. This was the first black-and-white "best buds" pairing, and when you add Guillermo Díaz's Scarface to the mix, you have a true stoner rainbow coalition.

7. Jay and Silent Bob: One's a fat mute (Kevin Smith), the other a shit-talking troublemaker (Jason Mewes). Together, New Jersey's stoner slackers take comic book geekdom to new heights in Smith's *Clerks*, *Clerks II*, *Mallrats*, *Dogma*, and, of course, their pothead peak, *Jay and Silent Bob Strike Back*.

8. Ricky and Julian (*Trailer Park Boys*): Canada's dopiest duo—played by Robb Wells and John Paul Tremblay—are the definition of white trash, forced to scam their dope, smokes, and pepperoni out of people dumber than themselves—the residents of Sunnyvale trailer park. Seven TV seasons and one feature film later, and it never gets old.

9. Tenacious D: From HBO to the concert stage to the silver screen, the inspired madness of JB (Jack Black) and KG (Kyle Gass) reaches exalted heights in *Tenacious D in The Pick of Destiny*. Chatterbox Black and dumbfounded Gass have so much chemistry it almost hurts.

10. Wyatt and Billy (*Easy Rider*): As the original movie stoners, Peter Fonda and Dennis Hopper practically created the drug-movie genre with their depictions of Wyatt (a.k.a. Captain America) and Billy in *Easy Rider*. Stoic like his father, Fonda moves in strange ways, while Hopper's Billy is all nervous, staccato, marijuana-fueled energy. They also appeared together in *The Trip* and *Cheech & Chong's Next Movie*.

Bill & Ted's Excellent Adventure (1989)

🍸 ✏️

🌿 🌿 🌿 🌿 The tagline says it all: "History is about to be rewritten by two guys who can't spell." Bill S. Preston, Esq. (Alex Winter), and Ted Theodore Logan (Keanu Reeves), two dudes from San Dimas, California, are given an ultimatum by their history teacher—either ace their final presentation or fail the class. The assignment: What would key historical figures think of San Dimas? And what better way is there to answer that question than to cruise through time in a phone booth with Rufus (George Carlin), their trusty guide from the future, picking up history's legends so they can tell their own stories? The clueless duo hijack notorious warlord Napoléon (Terry Camilleri), famous gunslinger Billy the Kid (Dan Shor), the misunderstood Joan of Arc (Jane Wiedlin), and the mind-blowing philosopher Socrates (Tony Steedman), among others, and bring their friends along on a series of fun adventures. In the process, they all learn from each other. Who knew Napoléon would be such a good bowler? Or that Abraham Lincoln (Robert Barron) would love Icees? The transplanted crew heads to the San Dimas mall, where they rewrite history—Beethoven (Clifford David) shreds on a synthesizer, Joan of Arc teaches an aerobics class, and Genghis Khan (Al Leong) goes wild at a sporting goods store with a skateboard and some football gear. Once Bill and Ted finally arrive (late) to their presentation at school, they get by with help from their new pals and manage to graduate high school. Totally excellent! Now that the film feels like an eighties time capsule, it's hard to get past the obvious lack of pot in Bill & Ted's Excellent Adventure (likely a sacrifice for the PG rating). Then

again, these guys are so dense, they're almost an insult to stoners. Still, there's no denying classic lines like, "Strange things are afoot at the Circle-K," and the whacked-out premise that society in the year 2688 is based entirely around Bill and Ted as legendary leaders in their own right. As Rufus says, "Don't worry, it'll all make sense." Even more so if you're baked.

Bill: "Okay, Ted, George Washington. One: the father of our country."

Ted: "Two: born on Presidents' Day."

Bill: "Three: the dollar bill guy."

Ted: "Bill, you ever made a mushroom out of his head?"

Black Sheep (1996)

✏️ 🍸 ✏️

🌿 🌿 🌿 🌿 This incredibly silly yet sometimes very funny David Spade–Chris Farley vehicle follows a formula that will feel like a familiar flashback to anyone who's seen *Tommy Boy*. Farley plays Mike Donnelly, the well-meaning doofus brother of aspiring politician Al (*Animal House* star Tim Matheson), and Spade is Steve Dodds, the guy Al hires to make sure that his brother doesn't ruin his career. *Black Sheep* is essentially a series of madcap adventures (Mike's accused of setting a rec center on fire; the duo escape to the woods, where the cabin they crash in is destroyed by a storm; Farley smokes pot with a reggae band at a Rock the Vote concert; they're both completely high on nitrous oxide while driving a police car, etc). Throughout, they're sabotaged by Al's dirty opponent, Governor Tracy (Christine Ebersole). Oh yeah—Gary Busey also shows up, playing a totally whacked-out Vietnam vet. Just roll with it and roll one up—it's clear that Farley did, since his eyes are half-closed throughout, though that somehow doesn't get in the way of his always-genius comedic timing.

> "What the heck is that?"
> —Steve Dodds (spotting a bat)

> "It's Ozzy Osbourne!"
> —Mike Donnelly

Blazing Saddles (1974)

🌿 🍸 🌿

🌿 🌿 🌿 🌿 What happens when you introduce 1974 slang, fashion, and pop culture to the American Old West circa 1874? A classic Mel Brooks absurdist comedy that, in just over ninety minutes, parodies several decades of gun-toting, cattle-herding, Indian-fighting cowboys while simultaneously making heady commentary on modern-day racism. It all takes place in the frontier town of Rock Ridge, where crooked Attorney General Hedley Lamarr (Harvey Korman) names a spunky railroad worker the town's first black sheriff. Lamarr and cross-eyed Governor William J. Le Petomane (played by Brooks) hope for a quick lynching so that train tracks can be built directly through the town, but Black Bart (Cleavon Little) is no dummy. In little time, he wins over the townspeople (all of whom share the last name Johnson) and, with the help of his smoking buddy the "Waco Kid" Jim (Gene Wilder), pledges to protect them against an attack by a rogue gang of "rustlers, cutthroats, murderers, bounty hunters, desperadoes, mugs, pugs, thugs, nitwits, half-wits, dimwits, vipers, snipers, con men, Indian agents, Mexican bandits, muggers, buggerers, bushwhackers, hornswagglers, horse thieves, bull dykes, train robbers, bank robbers, ass kickers, shit kickers, and Methodists" (as per Lamarr's recruitment instructions). It all culminates in a massive rumble that spills out of the movie set and onto the Warner Bros. lot (the late Dom DeLuise makes a cameo as an uber-gay director), thoroughly blurring the line between cinema as entertainment and the business of making movies.

Indeed, *Blazing Saddles* was a trailblazer in its time. It featured the first audible fart in a major movie (acted out as a virtual ballet of gassy campfire thugs), tossed around the n-word no less than seventeen times, offended Jews, Blacks, Native Americans, the Irish, Germans, and everyone in between, and in one fell swoop (and three Oscar nominations) it turned John Wayne–era machismo into a thing of the past. But in the end, it's about the gags—Indians speaking Yiddish, prostitute and lounge singer Lili Von Shtupp (Madeline Kahn) marveling at Bart's natural "gift," Count Basie and his orchestra playing along to their own score—and breaking down stereotypes. After all, if a black sheriff and a white gunslinger can share a joint, can't we all get along?

> "My mind is aglow with whirling, transient nodes of thought careening through a cosmic vapor of invention."
>
> —**Hedley Lamarr**

Blume in Love (1973)

🍸 🌿 👓

🌿 🌿 🌿 Pot often makes for strange bedfellows, like the unlikely threesome of Stephen Blume (George Segal), his ex-wife Nina (Susan Anspach), and her boyfriend Elmo (Kris Kristofferson), who share a joint, some laughs, and, soon after, the promise of a lifelong bond. Told as a series of recollections, some from Stephen's therapist's office, others from a jaunt to Europe, it's clear that he's a troubled soul—especially when it comes to relationships, because almost as soon as this divorce attorney signs his own separation papers, he falls head-over-heels back in love with Nina. And while you might think Stephen's an impulsive kind of

dude (he dabbles in swinging, meditation, Triscuits, and any number of popular early seventies fads), this longing and pining for his ex is surprisingly consistent, not to mention relentless. In time, he befriends her new man, Elmo, a musician and all-around good guy, and the three become close, until Stephen crosses the line. But even that doesn't turn out badly in this story, where positive vibes trump all feelings of jealousy, bitterness, and guilt. To that end, *Blume in Love* is a raw look at the sanctity of marriage—and the aftershocks of divorce—that's shot beautifully and told eloquently, but at two-and-a-half-hours long and teeming with deep, introspective thoughts, it can be one giant snoozer if you're not up for some serious concentration.

Bob & Carol & Ted & Alice (1969)

After Bob (Robert Culp) and Carol (Natalie Wood) spend a weekend at the New Age resort "The Institute," the two realize they're a completely different married couple. No more cop-outs, no more holding back emotions—even if it means they want to stray. The Californians only share the truth with each other and everyone around them. This naturally includes their best friends, Ted (Elliott Gould) and Alice (Dyan Cannon), who are a bit more uptight when it comes to work and home and, predictably, frigid when it comes to sex. But Bob and Carol's newfound ways begin to influence their besties, and some swingin' notions really hit home with Ted and Alice after some strong pulls from Bob's wooden peace pipe. "Is this Acapulco Gold?" Ted asks. "Ah, no," Bob replies. "This is beautiful downtown Burbank." That's the night that Carol lets her friends know that she and Bob are experimenting with an open relationship. Director Paul Mazursky (*Down and Out in Beverly Hills*) lets

> "Well, I am completely and totally zonked out of my skull."
>
> **—Carol**

the marital-troubled conversations play out beautifully in this groovy flick.

Bongwater (1997)

This stoner rom-com directed by Richard Sears and adapted from Michael Hornburg's novel stars Luke Wilson (David) as a pot dealer/painter and Alicia Witt (Serena) as his wannabe girlfriend. It takes all movie long for them to get together, but along the way his house in Portland burns down, she runs off to New York, David picks mushrooms with Mary (the late Brittany Murphy), gay lovers Tony (Andy Dick) and Robert (Jeremy Sisto) argue, and David, Mary, and a bunch of hippies take acid provided by Devlin (Jack Black) in the woods. While in New York, Serena gets raped by a sleazy club owner, but never tells, not even BF Jennifer (Amy Locaine). A bundle of wild-woman energy and attitude, flame-haired Serena returns to Oregon slightly humbled and finally falls for easygoing David.

David: "I don't sell nickel bags—spread the word!"

Borat: Cultural Learnings of America for Make Benefit Glorious Nation of Kazakhstan (2006)

Borat made a star out of Sacha Baron Cohen, inspired an entire country to protest, and showed theater upon packed theater of innocents what a really, really fat guy looks like when he's naked—and pissed. And if that alone doesn't give you an uncontrollable case of the giggles, you're probably just not high enough. This mockumentary (the protagonist and a couple of other players are character actors—and everyone else is just reacting to their insanity) features Cohen as Borat Sagdiyev, a TV reporter in the far-off nation of Kazakhstan, where, in a prolonged, gut-busting intro, we learn that men make out with their sisters, the town rapist is a venerated man, and people are generally happy despite their country's problems—namely, "economic, social, and Jew." To learn a bit more about the rest of the world, Borat makes a pilgrimage to America, where he encounters a driving instructor who's appalled when he takes a slug from a fifth of vodka while behind the wheel, a group of high-society women who somehow disapprove of the hooker he's invited to dinner, and a slew of party boys who think it would be dandy if we all had our own slaves—not to mention a run-in with real-life Pamela Anderson, who's less than pleased when Borat tries to force her into becoming Mrs. Borat. But what's amazing about *Borat* isn't just how well Cohen slips into character, but his bravery in exposing stereotypes while putting himself in harm's way, whether it's via a bunch of unhappy rednecks at a rodeo (Borat sings the Kazakhstani national anthem to the tune of the "Star-Spangles Banner"), or when he's getting crushed by his "producer," Azamat Bagatov (the understated and overweight Ken Davitian). Just take a bong rip, and be glad you're in on the joke: the country of Kazakhstan itself obviously wasn't, or they never would have taken out a four-page ad in the *New York Times* condemning the movie.

Bottle Shock (2008)

🔦 🍸 ✂️

🌿 🌿 🌿 🌿 Consider this true story set in California's wine country as *Sideways* for the stoner crowd—and what a victorious tale it is. Back in 1976, Napa Valley was the joke of the wine industry, which had, for centuries, been ruled by the French. But all that changed when Paris-based sommelier Steven Spurrier (Alan Rickman) gave the little-known vineyards a chance to compete in a prestigious blind taste test in France. Among the best that Cali had to offer was Chateau Montelena's Chardonnay, which vintner Jim Barrett (Bill Pullman) labored over for years until the barrels reached perfection. At the same time, he mortgaged his vineyard to the gills. With little help from his long-haired stoner son, Bo (Chris Pine), who spends most of his time chasing girls and palling around with field workers Gustavo (Freddy Rodríguez) and the always-blazed Shenky (Hal B. Klein), Jim is at the end of his rope. But Bo is determined to get Napa noticed as well as impress his father, and after several tense squabbles, the two come together ever so tenderly—unlike the French judges when they realize they've voted the American wines as winners, both red and white. Wine, like pot, requires a certain level of connoisseurship to truly appreciate the nuances of a particular vintage, which is one reason *Bottle Shock*, which also features a bong rip in the first three minutes, stands out as a stoner-friendly flick. Add in some amazing music of the era and long, sweeping pans of miles upon miles of grapes growing on the mountainside, and it's simply divine.

Jim: "Do you have any ambition at all?"

Bo: "Uh, I don't know—to see the Dead live at the Cow Palace?"

Boys & Girls Guide to Getting Down, The (2006)

✏️ 🔦 🔍 🍸 ✂️ ⊙⊙

🌿 🌿 🌿 This might have been better titled, "To Live and Get High in L.A." A large cast of unknown actors portrays partiers who basically smoke pot, snort coke, drink, and hope to get lucky by the end of the night. In the film's sixteen chapters, we learn more about drug-taking and mating rituals than we do about the characters themselves, none of whom are particularly memorable. The "Merits of Marijuana" chapter is slightly out of touch: "There are two types of weed: dirt weed or shake and skunk weed, also known as kind bud, chronic, and the good shit. Dirt weed is great in the morning and at work." C'mon, who smokes schwag in Los Angeles? But the riff on dealers is smarter: "Their concept of time is different from regular people." When Tony (Juan Pacheco) has a bad reaction to a coke-Viagra combo, he's hospitalized and prescribed medical marijuana by a doctor who orders him to "smoke this twice a day before meals and complete the full course of treatment." What the flick lacks in storytelling, it makes up with clever animation and graphics.

Breakfast Club, The
(1985)

🌿🌿🌿🌿🌿 Among the greatest teen movies of all time, The Breakfast Club paints a spot-on portrait of high school life—where cliques divide and stereotypes rule—told through five unique voices: a brain, an athlete, a princess, a criminal, and a basket case. The unlikely cohorts are stuck together in Saturday detention, left with a full school day's worth of time to toil away in the library, and what transpires is not only some of the best and most insightful back-and-forth student banter ever written for the screen, but also gripping emotions you can't deny and the sense that high school, no matter how far in the past it may be, never really leaves you behind. Not to get too bogged down in its serious overtones, however, because Breakfast Club delivers plenty of laughs (mostly at the expense of tightwad guidance counselor/school overlord Vernon, played by Paul Gleason), including one giggle-inducing smoking scene. During a quick escape from the library, the five misfits—Bender (Judd Nelson), Claire (Molly Ringwald), Brian (Anthony Michael Hall), Andrew (Emilio Estevez), and Allison (Ally Sheedy)—make a run for the hallway where Bender has some weed stashed in his locker. But a close call with Vernon forces Bender to ditch the group, leaving his dope in nerd Brian's underpants. Later, when Bender sneaks back into the library, he entices all to partake in what is undoubtedly a dirty bag of schwag (mid-eighties, Midwest, what else could it be?), but a joint does the trick as each player's lighter side comes out.

The session is not a long scene, but it is a pivotal one, as pot proves to be the ultimate icebreaker for these five opposite characters. And its inclusion is curious (did the late director John Hughes, who was also responsible for beloved teen flicks like Pretty in Pink and Sixteen Candles occasionally puff?), but considering most of the movie takes place in one static location and spans a mere morning to afternoon, it goes to show that stoners worth their movie-watching salt don't necessarily have the attention span of a fly. Give us some good dialogue—the kind worth memorizing (and, trust us, we have)—no sex, and little action, and we're down for a day of detention, as long as it's as awesome as The Breakfast Club.

Vernon: "What if your home, what if your family, what if your dope was on fire?"

Bender: "Impossible, sir, it's in Johnson's underwear."

Broken Flowers (2005)

🌿🌿🌿🌿 From Rushmore to Lost in Translation to The Life Aquatic with Steve Zissou, Bill Murray has specialized in playing depressed characters with a wry outlook on life. In this Jim Jarmusch film, Murray's Don Johnston receives an anonymous letter informing him that he has a son the same day his girlfriend (Julie Delpy) moves out. Jamaican neighbor Winston (Jeffrey Wright) turns him on and recommends that Don revisit old girlfriends to find out who might be the mother of his illegitimate child. Don's tour is relatively uneventful—he sleeps with Laura (Sharon Stone) and is punched out by another girlfriend, Penny's old man—providing few answers during his reluctant search. Long shots, awkward pauses, and dissolves—all Jarmusch trademarks—make for interesting viewing, but the existential nature of the storyline is intended to leave you wondering whether Don will ever find true happiness.

Caddyshack (1980)

🌿 🌿 🌿 🌿 After co-writing *Animal House* (1978) and *Meatballs* (1979), Harold Ramis got behind the camera for this light farce about the denizens of Bushwood Country Club's golf course. The young caddies, headed by Danny (Michael O'Keefe), generally get into trouble while club owner Judge Smails (Ted Knight) declares war on an arrogant real-estate developer, Al Czervik (a hyperactive Rodney Dangerfield).

Danny and Ty (Chevy Chase) have sex with loose Lacey Underall (Cindy Morgan), and Carl (Bill Murray) fights off an army of gophers ("My enemy is an animal"). In one of the classic stoner scenes, Carl smokes out Ty with a "big Bob Marley joint" of "Carl Spackler's Bent"— a combination of Kentucky Bluegrass, Featherbed Bent, and Northern California Sinsemilla. "It'll get you stoned as the bejesus," Carl claims. "Thanks for the dope," Ty says as he staggers out of Carl's trashed-out pad.

Lacey to Danny: "Hey, Cary Grant, you wanna get high?"

Cannonball Run, The (1981)

🌿 🌿 🌿 🌿 Back in the seventies, long before there was TV's *Amazing Race* (or any reality shows, for that matter), a couple dozen vagabond speedsters would take off in groups of two on a contest to see who could make it from Connecticut to California in the least amount of time. The rules? There weren't any. Drive any car you wanted at any speed, but the fines were on your dime. The prize? It's not entirely clear in the movie version, but certainly bragging rights is a big part of the Cannonball's appeal and this is one competitive, all-or-nothing bunch. You have former racecar driver J. J. McClure (Burt Reynolds) and his mechanic partner Victor (Dom DeLuise), who race in an ambulance, hire a deranged-looking proctologist to support their cover and kidnap a gorgeous, tree-loving photojournalist they call "Beauty" (the always braless Farrah Fawcett) to pose as the patient. There's the Japanese team, led by Jackie Chan, who zips around in a state-of-the-art Subaru complete with night vision, rocket launcher, computer system, and a VCR to watch porn with. Rat Packers Sammy Davis Jr. and Dean Martin pose as a couple of alcoholic priests driving a Ferrari—every line of their dialogue is an absolute gem. Daniel Craig's predecessor Roger Moore, perhaps having trouble disassociating from the James Bond he played for twelve years, also joins in the high-speed fun as half-actor–half-character with a hilariously Jewish mother. There's a gazillionaire sheikh, two hot spandex bodysuit–wearing chicks, a couple of stuttering drunks, and "Him"—Victor's alter ego, Captain Chaos, whose sole purpose is to help those in need (at often inopportune times). No doubt there was plenty of weed on the actual Cannonball Run, which was held five times between 1971 and 1979, though none is seen in the movie. Still, it's good stony fun: Not only are cops called Smokeys, but Little Miss "I'm into trees" takes a nitrous hit in the ambulance, Peter Fonda makes a cameo as the leader of a biker gang, and the blooper reel as the credits roll is a colossal gigglefest. And the best part: You get the adrenaline rush, but never have to leave the couch.

Charlie Bartlett (2007)

🌿 🌿 When spoiled, rich-as-hell brat Charlie Bartlett (Anton Yelchin) gets kicked out of his prestigious private school for ID fraud, his life of leisure gets turned upside down. Thrown into the gauntlet of the public school system under the cynically alcoholic principal Nathan Gardner (Robert Downey Jr.), Charlie doesn't quite fit in. That is until he teams up with fellow student Murphey Bivens (Tyler

Hilton) and becomes the unofficial school psychologist, imparting advice to anxiety-ridden students and handing out antidepressant drugs to his classmates. But Charlie has his own demons, including a stay in prison, an emotionally unstable mother (Hope Davis), and a blossoming romance with the principal's daughter Susan (Kat Dennings). Fans of Wes Anderson's *Rushmore* will notice slight similarities in this box-office bomb, but *Charlie Bartlett* fails to deliver both in style and substance. Charlie is likable enough, but the character, and circumstances surrounding him, are trite, unoriginal, and too serious toward the end. There's even an ever-so-subtle antidrug and alcohol message, and who needs that?

Charlie Bartlett: "Oh, trust me doc, bringing psychiatric drugs and teenagers together is like opening a lemonade stand in the desert."

Cheech & Chong's Next Movie (1980)

They didn't call it a sequel, but this is basically *Up in Smoke 2*. Tommy Chong takes over the director's chair from Lou Adler, but the movie remains pretty much the same. It opens with Cheech Marin and Chong smoking out in a low-rider (the car blows up). Chong plays some ear-blistering acid-rock guitar solos and Cheech sings his now classic plaint "Mexican Americans" (to which Chong answers, "Beaners!"). And for the last quarter of the movie, Chong continually puffs a huge bomber joint. What sets this apart from its predecessor is Marin's double role as Paco and his

Texas cousin Red, who grows pot and carries around a duffel bag full of the stuff, and the introduction of Paul Reubens's Pee-wee Herman character (he plays the snooty hotel clerk). In a nod to *Close Encounters of the Third Kind*, the duo gets sucked up by a spaceship, which zooms into an animated joint, at the end. While it's hard to top *Up in Smoke*, this followup holds its own as the second phase of Cheech and Chong's stoner-comedy revolution.

Chong: "I figure it this way: Dope's gonna be legal in a few years. Then it'll be a legitimate job. All the other dudes won't be ready for it and I'll know how to do it. Then I'll have a job."

Cheech & Chong's The Corsican Brothers (1984)

A sendup of the 1941 swashbuckler, Cheech & Chong's sixth film—their only one sans marijuana—is more along the lines of a Mel Brooks spoof. Set during the French Revolution, twins Lucien (Chong) and Luis (Cheech) are separated at birth but reunite as adults. While Lucien attempts to lead the Revolution, Luis focuses his attention on Princess II (Cheech's actual wife, Rikki Marin; Princess I is played by Chong's wife, Shelby). After escaping the guillotine, Lucien and Luis scheme to break into the castle occupied by the Evil Fuckaire (a heavily made-up Roy Dotrice). The final fight scene with Lucien wielding stale French loaves as épées puts an exclamation point on this nutty comedy.

The kings of stoner comedy reminisce about the good old days when Hollywood gave them lots of money to make movies about marijuana.

Reefer Movie Madness: Which are your favorite Cheech & Chong movies?

Tommy Chong: *Up in Smoke* is my number one favorite.

Cheech Marin: It was the most fun to make. Any time you make your first movie, it's like the first time you make love. You're like, I finally got in! Oh man, there's nothing like it. I knew for the first Cheech & Chong movie, we could run backward with Japanese subtitles and we would find an audience, because I knew they were there.

RMM: What about *Next Movie*?

Cheech: We were involved in a lawsuit with the producer after *Up in Smoke* came out, so that allowed us a couple of years to get it together and try to do something else that was new. They weren't really Cheech & Chong movies to us, they were "day in the life" movies. Watching a movie of two guys trying to roll a joint.

RMM: In the *Stripes* DVD, Ivan Reitman says it was originally written as "Cheech & Chong Go to the Army." What do you recall about that?

Chong: We were in the middle of shooting *Next Movie* when Bill Murray, who was in the middle of *Stripes*, started yelling at us in the commissary at Universal:

"You guys fucked up, you should have done *Stripes!*" I remember the execs at Universal mentioning something about us doing *Stripes*, but we were already shooting our movie. I wouldn't have done it if we were free. I would never put Cheech & Chong in the army and, besides, I think *Next Movie* is a better movie.

RMM: Pee-wee Herman is in *Next Movie*. How did you know him?

Cheech: We were looking around for people to be in our movie and play characters, and we got Paul Reubens (Herman), Phil Hartman, Edie McClurg, and Cassandra Peterson (Elvira). It was a character Paul was already doing, so we put it in the movie. We knew he was funny. He's a really good actor, that's the bottom line about him.

RMM: What's the most underrated Cheech & Chong movie?

Chong: *Things Are Tough All Over*. Unfortunately, I think the title did it in.

Cheech: I think *Still Smokin* is the most underrated. That came about because Tommy was hanging out with some guys in Amsterdam. It wasn't like a concert film, but it was our way of doing a concert.

RMM: You and Cheech played double roles in *Things Are Tough All Over*—was that difficult?

Chong: It was fun. But it's not the best idea, because the main characters disappear when you do double roles. I would have hired actors if I could do it over again.

Cheech: We always did a bunch of characters onstage. I was used to it. It was weird to just play one character in a movie.

RMM: How did your one non-stoner Cheech & Chong movie, *The Corsican Brothers*, come about?

Cheech: Every comedy duo, whether they started onstage or on the radio or in the movies, has one of these in their portfolio, because there's always a studio executive that wants to remake their favorite movie in a classical setting, and they'll pay you to do it. In this case, it was *The Corsican Brothers*. It had been made a bunch of times, but they thought hey, we'll put Cheech & Chong in *The Corsican Brothers*. The Marx Brothers had one of these deals, too.

RMM: Are you a fan of the Marx Brothers?

Chong: I'm a fan, but not a diehard. I was more into Dean Martin and Jerry Lewis movies. Harpo was my favorite.

RMM: How about Mel Brooks? Was he an inspiration? Who else inspired you to direct, write, and star in your own movies?

Chong: Mel Brooks inspired me with his fart joke in *Blazing Saddles*. I met him once and asked him to be in a small movie I was directing and he turned me down flat. He told me, "I only do my movies, Tommy—you know that!" I said, "I do now." Terry Malick, who directed *Badlands*—my all-time favorite movie—actually told me to direct my own movies after I tried to hire him for *Up In Smoke*. Terry said, "No one can really do justice to something that you have been living with for years."

RMM: Many comedies today are influenced by *Up in Smoke* and *Animal House*, which both came out in 1978. What was so special about that year?

Chong: It was ten years after The Beatles broke up. Film studios were searching for the next "youth movie," so they looked to the hot comic actors—Cheech & Chong and the *Animal House* gang filled the bill.

RMM: *Up in Smoke* was the first stoner comedy. What do think of the stoner-comedy genre today?

Chong: I love all stoner movies. Stoner movies are like pot. Even the bad ones will give you a buzz!

Cheech: They're making stoner movies for their generation. It used to be a small group that was getting stoned; now it's everybody. I think *Knocked Up* is the best of all of them.

Chong: *Knocked Up* is probably one of the best ever stoner movies because it showed non-stoner wives coping with the "lifestyle." *Knocked Up* really put stoner movies in the elite section.

RMM: What do you think of *Harold & Kumar*, *Pineapple Express*, *Half Baked*, and any other stoner-buddy comedies?

Chong: *Harold & Kumar*—love 'em. *Pineapple Express*—loved it, even if the violence was stupid stoner. *Half Baked*—I was in that one. I played a con, which I became in "real life."

> "Stoner movies are like pot. Even the bad ones will give you a buzz!"
>
> **—Tommy Chong**

Class Reunion (1982)

In 1972, Lizzie Borden High School student Walter (Blackie Dammett) gets fooled by one of the popular kids, Bob Spinnaker (Gerrit Graham), into receiving a handjob from his equally fugly sister. In turn, the traumatic moment sends Walter to the loony bin until, ten years later, he escapes to terrorize his high school reunion and kill everyone. What would have been an amazing premise for a classic eighties raunchfest unfortunately goes the way of kid-friendly cornball antics instead. Director John Hughes holds back on the sexual gratuity as Walter knocks off his alum. The class of '72's famed pair of potheads, Chip Hendrix (Barry Diamond) and Carl Clapton (Art Evans), steal what little show is left with an array of weedy shenanigans. Carl, in a quasi-Rasta getup, smokes four joints at a time, and Chip, sporting the typical slacker wear at a formal (the faux tuxedo tee), doesn't even know where he is. During a slideshow projection that offers class highlights, the two tokers are shown in a bushel of sticky-icky, described as the "experimental farm behind the football bleachers" they set up back in the day. They get high all night long—even during the serial killings when everyone is in a panic. Talk about a buzz kill.

Chip: "You wanna take a trip to bozo-land?"

Clerks (1994)

One of the more important indie movies of the nineties, *Clerks* introduces iconic wage slaves/best buds Dante Hicks (Brian O'Halloran) and Randal Graves (Jeff Anderson)— and the immortal Jay and Silent Bob (Jason Mewes and director Kevin Smith). Filmed in low-budget black-and-white (supposedly the music used in the film cost more than it did to finance the movie), *Clerks* take us through a day in the lives of two New Jersey clerks at neighboring convenience and video stores. Still pining for his previous love Caitlin (Lisa Spoonhauer), Dante argues with his girlfriend Veronica (Marilyn Ghigliotti), deals with a parade of ridiculous customers, and gets lectured by Randal (who also takes pleasure in insulting everyone within eyesight)—all the while complaining, "I'm not even supposed to be here today." Jay and Silent Bob irreverently deal weed in front of the establishment, a crusty old dude dies while masturbating in the bathroom, and Dante closes the store to play hockey on the roof, and again to attend the funeral of a former girlfriend. Existential questions and pop commentary litter the pair's not-so-mindless patter, Dante's love life blows up thanks to Randal, the two clerks eventually fight it out, and Caitlin accidentally has sex with the dead guy. Thankfully Dante and Randal reconcile before quitting time, leaving us ready to embrace the boys again in *Clerks II*. Still, Jay has the last word as he sings about "shmokin' weed."

Clerks II (2006)

Despite fanboy testimonials lauding Kevin Smith's indie classic *Clerks*, the sequel enjoyed a far bigger budget, better acting, smart dialogue, and two sexual taboos. Reviving and expanding the bromance between Dante Hicks (Brian O'Halloran) and Randal Graves (Jeff Anderson), the sequel immediately jumps from black-and-white to color as the pair's New Jersey Quick Stop/RST Video strip mall goes up in flames, resulting in new dead-end jobs at Mooby's burger joint. Just another day in the life of Dante and Randal, except now it's Dante's last shift before moving to Florida with fiancée Emma Bunting (Jennifer Schwalbach Smith) to run a carwash for Emma's dad. Naturally, the revival includes Jay (Jason Mewes) and Silent Bob (Kevin Smith)—out of rehab, staying straight, and preaching Jesus while still dealing dope and talking pussy. Mooby's manager is Becky Scott (Rosario Dawson), whose beguiling presence is an obvious temptation to Dante. This movie really belongs to Anderson, whose bitterly sarcastic Randal is both the romantic and comedic star as he relentlessly tortures Dante, Emma, Becky, Mooby's naïve underling Elias, and various oddball customers (including cameos by Jason Lee and Ben Affleck). *Clerks* references abound, as well as tributes to and indictments of other well-known films and directors. Whether staging a huge choreographed dance number or simulating interspecies erotica between man and donkey, Smith never relinquishes the hetero-love theme between Dante and Randal. Winding up back in the black-and-white world of a newly rehabbed Quick Stop, everyone seems happy leaving room for a potential *Clerks III*.

Club Dread (2004)

The second Broken Lizard film isn't what you'd expect from the comedy team responsible for the classic *Super Troopers*. The intentionally cheesy slasher film is set on Pleasure Island, a resort in Costa Rica owned by washed-up singer Coconut Pete (Bill Paxton), where the sole mission is to party—even the island cop is referred to as "the fun police." But as we soon find out, someone is also there to murder. Enter the local legend of the Machete Maniac: a resort staffer who was coaxed into the jungle by a corpse, and who grabbed a machete, chopped off his penis, and proceeded to shred the rest of the staff. Once employees start dropping like flies and the boats stop working and phone lines go dead, everyone on the island becomes a suspect, while Juan (Steve Lemme), Dave (Paul Soter), Lars the staff masseur (Kevin Heffernan), and Putman (director Jay Chandrasekhar) are all put to the survival test. *Club Dread* has more than its share of funny moments, and if the mindless plot doesn't keep your heart pounding, that tiny bit of paranoia starting to creep in certainly will.

Sam: "It's not a party until someone breaks the Jacuzzi."

Club Paradise (1986)

SCTV meets Robin Williams in Jamaica—or at least in the fictional St. Nicholas. Burned out from fighting fires in Chicago, Jack (Williams) travels to the Caribbean, where he meets Phillippa (Twiggy) and partners with Ernest (Jimmy Cliff) to revive a rundown resort. But in typical Harold Ramis fashion, a developer and corrupt government official scheme to grab the beachfront property. Tourists soon come; among them are SCTV

vets Andrea Martin (Linda), Rick Moranis (Barry), and Eugene Levy (Barry). The Barrys are two of the most bumbling stoners ever on film. To impress the babes, these wild and crazy dudes try to "cop some primo Cannabis sativa" so they can get "totally demented" and "stoned out of our gourds." Levy ultimately finds a huge bag of ganja, police besiege the club, and Jack and Ernest take a stand. Reggae fans will enjoy several live performances by Cliff ("You Can't Keep a Good Man Down") and the Cliff–Elvis Costello collaboration "Seven-Day Weekend" over the final credits.

Barry: "We're looking for Johnny—smoke, jays, joints, buzz."

Clueless (1995)

Clueless is anything but another teen movie. For one thing, it's a modern-day (or at least mid-nineties) interpretation of Jane Austen's 1816 novel *Emma*, about a spoiled rich girl, told through the lens of Amy Heckerling (*Fast Times at Ridgemont High*). That girl is Cher (Alicia Silverstone), a fashion-obsessed, privileged have-it-all who decides that she's going to save the world one Beverly Hills rich kid at a time. She starts with new girl in town Tai (Brittany Murphy), a rough-around-the-edges New Yorker in desperate need of a makeover. Under Cher's tutelage, Tai goes from outcast to most popular girl in school and makes Cher see that vanity isn't everything. With new purpose, Cher aims to better herself through charity, putting aside old prejudices (like thinking stoner Travis Birkenstock, played by Breckin Meyer, wasn't dateable) and, in the process, discovers a thing or two about herself (namely, a massive crush on her do-gooder stepbrother, Josh, played by the adorable Paul Rudd). The language might feel a little silly at times, but other than that and the shoe-sized cell phones, *Clueless* has aged wonderfully. Bottom line: It's rare that you feel empathy for a bunch of rich kids, but this movie truly transcends all scenes (look no further than the "Rollin' with the Homies" party, where all take a puff off of Travis's joint) and has such good heart that you can't help but bask in its glow.

Dazed and Confused
(1993)

In the annals of stoner comedy history, there are two defining points—peaks, as it were—when potheads caused the mainstream to take pause. The first was in 1978, when Cheech & Chong's *Up In Smoke* became an unexpected box-office hit and, as a result, America completely *went to dope*. The second moment came in 1993, when a little-known low-budget indie film called *Dazed and Confused* hit theaters and instantly birthed a new generation of weed devotees. It was far from a blockbuster, but over time, Richard Linklater's glimpse at high school life in Austin, Texas circa 1976 has become a beloved stoner classic—so often quoted and referenced that any self-respecting head should consider it a DVD collection must.

Why is it so special? In Linklater's slacker style, *Dazed and Confused* tells interweaving tales of nearly a dozen characters, including the loveable hippie Slater (Rory Cochrane), the disenchanted football star Pink (as in Floyd, played by Jason London), and the unforgettable former graduate, hot-rod nut, and ladykiller Wooderson (Matthew McConaughey). But the main story revolves around two incoming freshmen, Sabrina (Christin Hinojosa) and Mitch (Wiley Wiggins), struggling to survive the town's hazing ritual on the last day of junior high. Sabrina's nemesis is Darla (Parker Posey), a bitchy senior intent on making her life a living hell. Mitch's is paddle-bearing bully O'Bannion (Ben Affleck), who chases him and his runt friends all over town. What ensues is a night of pot- and beer-fueled debauchery, complete with clashing cliques (the nerd crew, in particular Adam "I wanna dance" Goldberg, provides more than its share of laughs), suburban pranks, reckless driving, and one killer party at the moontower that lasts until morning.

At every turn, brilliant dialogue and stellar performances—especially by McConaughey, who, in his first movie role, improvised several of Wooderson's now classic lines (chief among them: "That's what I love about these high school girls, man. I get older, they stay the same age")—bring to life a time long gone: when the drinking age was eighteen, joints were as common as cigarettes, and few things mattered more than scoring Aerosmith tickets.

> "Say, man, you got a joint?"
> —**Wooderson**
> "No, not on me, man."
> —**Mitch**
> "It'd be a lot cooler if you did."
> —**Wooderson**

☘ NATHAN FOLLOWILL'S STONY MOVIE PICKS ☘

How do four brothers cope with dreadfully long rides on the tour bus? Kings of Leon's Nathan Followill likes to indulge in a puff (preferably out of a vaporizer, to save his voice) and a late-night flick. Here, the drummer offers his personal high five.

Dazed and Confused (1993): "I would say *Dazed and Confused* is the greatest stoner movie of all time because everybody had their version of a party at the moontower. Like in school, you had that one spot, or somebody's house that had really cool parents—or really dumb ones who had no idea their kids were turning the couch into a bong in the basement. It's a great movie that's just so well written—you think how amazing it was when it wasn't such a big deal to smoke, where pot wasn't even considered a drug back then. I mean, they got in trouble a little, but not too much. And for us, who grew up either home-schooled or going to Christian schools, we were like, 'That's what high school's like! We missed out on so much! We could've been doing that shit every weekend!' So we get to live vicariously through *Dazed and Confused*, and imagine how high school would've been for us if we went."

This Is Spiñal Tap (1984): "We didn't see *Spiñal Tap* until we were actually a band, and we were like, 'Oh my God, this movie was made for us! We're the only band in the world that they're identical to!' Then we'd go on tour and talk to other bands about the movie, and we realized that's why it's such a cult movie—because they've nailed everything about a band that's silly and hilarious. I could not tell you how many times we've said 'Hello, Cleveland' at shows before."

Fear and Loathing in Las Vegas (1998): "I love *Fear and Loathing*, because no matter how fucked up you are, you're not nearly as fucked up as Hunter Thompson. Benicio Del Toro is absolutely amazing. I don't think I could watch it on acid or 'shrooms—

I might jump off of a balcony or something—but if you're smoking weed, maybe get too high and start to think you're losing control a bit, you watch it and say, 'This is nothing, I'm totally fine. I could go to Sunday school right now and be fine.' It's actually entertaining that way."

Three Amigos (1986): "Honest to god, I've seen *Three Amigos* at least five hundred times. It's probably one of my top three movies of all time and every one of us could sit there and tell you the whole movie, word for word. That was one of the rare movies we got to watch growing up. My grandma recorded it off the TV, so it had all the cursing bleeped out. But even in the cleaned-up version, what's not to love about that movie?"

Caddyshack (1980): "*Caddyshack* is a great movie because we're all golfers, and what better place to light up than on the golf course? Bill Murray is absolutely hilarious, Chevy Chase is one of my favorite actors of all time, and every town has that little municipal course where you can buy a dime sack from the caddies. It's a feel-good story, where you find yourself smiling the whole time you're watching it, even if they're not saying anything particularly funny."

Deconstructing Harry (1997)

✐ 🍸 👓

🍁 🍁 🍁 Woody Allen received an Academy Award nomination for *Deconstructing Harry*, a story about—you guessed it—a self-loathing, neurotic New York writer who isn't capable of being faithful to any of his three wives and ends up falling for a young, doe-eyed fan (Elisabeth Shue). But unlike the relatively nerdy Alvy in *Annie Hall*, Harry Block (Allen) is a proud pervert, with a taste for whores and S & M, and a disdain for the social niceties of a real relationship (this is evident in the first four minutes, during which Julia Louis-Dreyfus, playing the character Leslie, gives a blowjob to her brother-in-law while her sister is within earshot). Harry works his issues out in books by applying past experiences to thinly veiled characters, which infuriates the real subjects—people like his sister-in-law Lucy (Judy Davis), with whom he has a tumultuous affair, and his ex-wife Joan (Kirstie Alley), a therapist whom he also cheats on with one of her patients. He tells these tales through a series of vignettes, each featuring different players and representing specific times in this life. Tobey Maguire, for example, plays Harvey, a young version of Harry who's first discovering hookers. Among the more unexpected moments in the film is when Harry takes one prostitute, Cookie (Hazelle Goodman), on a drive to his alma mater, where he's being honored for his writing. On a pit stop, she sneaks a toke off a joint, but he declines. But that's not the only scene

🍁 FIVE MORE BY WOODY ALLEN 🍁

What's Up Tiger Lily? (1966): Who hasn't muted the TV set and added their own nonsense dialogue, *Mystery Science Theater 3000*–style? In 1966, a young Woody Allen made an entire movie that way by taking a series of Japanese spy thrillers, overdubbing all the dialogue, and releasing the final result as *What's Up Tiger Lily?* With characters like Teri Yaki, Shepherd Wong, and Wing Fat, the ridiculous becomes sublime in Allen's directorial debut, which includes a killer score by The Lovin' Spoonful.

Sleeper (1973): As the perfect bridge from Allen's earlier visually zany films to his more straightforward romantic comedies, this time-travel flick features a terrifically silly, low-budget interpretation of the year 2173 (Allen plays a health-food store owner who's accidentally frozen in 1973 and thawed two hundred years later) and one trippy toke session involving the passing of an ostrich egg–sized metal "Orb," which party guests fondle with Ecstasy-like results.

Annie Hall (1977): Endlessly re-watchable and regarded by many as Allen's greatest comedic work, *Annie Hall* also contains the most drug scenes of any Woody Allen film, including winning one-liners about grass ("I took a puff at a party and tried to take my pants off over my head") and coke ("Well, I'm sure it's a lot of fun because the Incas did it, and they were a million laughs"), and Diane Keaton's out-of-body experience after smoking a joint before having sex.

Stardust Memories (1980): Cinematically, *Stardust Memories* is Allen at his most Felliniesque, with stunning black-and-white cinematography and nonstop manipulation of diegetic time that's more suited for the artsy stoner or mood. Combine this with Allen's usual genius and intense focus on relationships, existentialism, success, art, and the meaning of life and you've got a gorgeous, if slightly anxious, winner.

Hannah and Her Sisters (1986): More suited to a joint and a cup of tea than, say, a gravity bong, *Hannah and Her Sisters* weaves the lives of its main protagonists, played by Allen, Michael Caine, Carrie Fisher, Mia Farrow, and others, through mundane marital life in Manhattan. Allen's use of flashbacks helps create a film that's elegant and seemingly effortless in its storytelling, and, along with 1989's *Crimes and Misdemeanors*, represents the peak of Allen's eighties output.

that's stony. There's also a running gag where one character (played by Robin Williams) is perpetually blurry, while everything around him is sharp as a tack. In typical Woody Allen form, scores of A-list actors take on smaller roles, among them Demi Moore, Billy Crystal, Amy Irving, Stanley Tucci—even *The Sopranos*'s Tony Sirico appears as the cop who busts Harry and Cookie for weed. But it all comes down to Woody's, er, Harry's demented mind—it's a very dark place.

Harry Block: "Every hooker I ever speak to tells me that it beats the hell out of waitressing. Waitressing's gotta be the worst fucking job in the world."

Detroit Rock City
(1999)

🌿 🔥 🍸 ✂ 🍄

🌿 🌿 🌿 Man, life as a high school kid circa 1978 Cleveland sure was grim. Look no further than the unlucky foursome of Hawk (Edward Furlong), Lex (Giuseppe Andrews), Jam (Sam Huntington), and Trip (James DeBello), whose sole mission is to attend a Kiss concert at Detroit's Cobo Hall. But when Jam's Bible-thumping mom, who dubs their favorite band Knights in Satan's Service, foils their plans and burns the tickets, the guys take off on a desperate quest to make the show—first breaking Jam out of Catholic boarding school (by spiking the priest's pizza with magic mushrooms) and later fighting off a couple of Trans Am–riding douchebags. Along the way, they pick up and smoke out Christine (Natasha Lyonne), a typical "Stella" (disco bitch) with a sharp tongue ("Gimme a hit off that J, will ya? That's some kick-ass shit!"). But when they arrive in Detroit, things go from bad to worse: Lex's mom's Volvo is stolen with Christine passed out in the back, Trip picks on the wrong little kid and gets his ass kicked, Jam gets caught by his mother, and Hawk humiliates himself by stripping (and hurling) for cougars in a local girls-only club (Gene Simmons's real-life wife, Shannon Tweed, plays his seductress). Is all that worth the price of admission in the end? A local scalper says it best when he tells Hawk: "The question you gotta ask yourself is: How badly do you wanna see the great-est fucking rock-and-roll show on the fucking earth? I'm talking Gene and Paul, live. I'm talking about the most voluptuous women hanging out in the audience. I'm talking big breastices in tight vestices, my friend. You're talking people passing around joints in the audience. You're talking about fuckin' Detroit Rock City, brother." Amen.

Jam's mom: "God forbid someday you have a son like you, Jeremiah—a boy who lies through his teeth, buys demonic records, and smokes the dope."

Deuce Bigalow: European Gigolo (2005)

🌿 🔥 🍯

🌿 🌿 🌿 Six years after the original *Deuce Bigalow*, starring Saturday Night Live's Rob Schneider as an incompetent "man whore," the sequel shifts to Amsterdam, where Deuce hangs with pimp daddy T.J. (Eddie Griffin). The nonsensical plot—someone's killing off Europe's top gigolos—is just an excuse for broad slapstick, the best of which is the coffeeshop scene where fish-out-of-water Deuce has no clue what's going on. At one point a Dutch cop strolls in, freaking Deuce out. "Now that joint looks loose," the cop says. "If you want, I'll roll the next one." Unwittingly, Deuce gets stoned on space cake (T.J.: "It's what the astronauts eat, like Tang") and ends up climbing into a painting. There are a few other pot gags, but the film's low IQ will probably have you pressing Stop before you get to them. By the way, the director's name is indeed Mike Bigelow.

> "You're in Amsterdam. If you want coffee, you go to a café. If you want marijuana, ganji, or some freaky deaky, you go to a coffee shop."
>
> —T.J.

Dick (1999)

🍸🔪

🌿🌿🌿 When fifteen-year-old ditzes Arlene (Michelle Williams) and Betsy (Kirsten Dunst) unknowingly witness the Watergate break-in, they become entangled in one of the biggest scandals in American history. But upon a chance meeting with President Richard "Dick" Nixon (Dan Hedaya) during a field trip to the White House, he makes sure to keep the girls on his side by hiring them as his official dog walkers and youth advisors. Inadvertently armed with a box full of pot cookies, the girls observe more suspicious White House activity, and think nothing of it, but when Dick starts to become, well, a dick, the girls switch sides and help the Washington Post's Woodward (Will Ferrell) and Bernstein (Bruce McCulloch) uncover the truth as the secret source "Deep Throat."

Unless you're a baby boomer or a Watergate junkie, many of the jokey seventies references in this sharp political comedy might fly right over your stoned head. Without the help of Betsy and Darlene's "Hello Dolly" cookies, Nixon wouldn't have ended the Vietnam War or signed a peace treaty with the Soviet Union ("I think your cookies just saved the world from nuclear annihilation," Nixon mumbles). The only true stoner of the film is Betsy's brother Larry (Devon Gummersall), who happens to hide his stash in the jar of walnuts the girls use to make cookies for the president. But Dunst and Williams are perfectly cast as a pair of naïve and unsuspecting hippies-in-training who get themselves into a heap of trouble.

Doctor Detroit (1983)

🌿🌿🌿 Chi-Town pimp Smooth (Howard Hesseman) is at his wit's end trying to come up with the $80K he owes bawdy kingpin Mom (scene-stealer Kate Murtagh), so he suckers the wonky Clifford Skridlow (Dan Aykroyd) into partnering up with him in the hustling business and, unknown to Skridlow, fronting the university professor as the man who shorted Mom of her loot. All it takes to get Skridlow on board with the gangster's operation is a night out on the town. Shotgunning jays in a limo with some of Smooth's girls, splish-splashing in a Jacuzzi, and drinking literally prescription cocktails (random capsules of god-knows-what float in Skridlow's vodka gimlets) all help Skridlow embrace the underworld, and transform him into the notorious Doctor Detroit. The script by Bruce Jay Friedman (The Heartbreak Kid, Splash) certainly has its dull moments, but the finale, in which the good Doctor has to give an acceptance speech at the annual player's ball and compete against Mom in a duel (not to mention follow up James Brown's live performance of "Get Up Offa That Thing"), is worth the rental alone.

Skridlow (amazed at the effects of the ganja): "I can feel my hair growing."

Dogma (1999)

🔪🍸🔪

🌿🌿🌿 Dogma is one of those late-night post-bong-hit ideas that never should have seen the light of day. The movie's premise is absurd—that fallen angels Bartleby (Ben Affleck) and Loki (Matt Damon) are banished from the kingdom of heaven and pursue a reign of terror on earth, while Jesus' last living relative, an abortion clinic employee played by Linda Fiorentino, is tasked with stopping them from entering a New Jersey church where all their sins (including, in Loki's case, smoking a joint on a train with stoner icons Jay and Silent Bob) will be forgiven (an act that will trigger the apocalypse). Still, stoner auteur Kevin Smith made a brilliant move in casting George Carlin—the comic genius behind the infamous "Seven Dirty Words"—to play

a Catholic cardinal in this comedic take on the ridiculousness of religion. But like most of Smith's films, *Dogma* is often convoluted, difficult to follow (especially if you're prone to nodding off post-toke), and loaded with odd (and not very funny) religious in-jokes. A top-rate ensemble, which includes Chris Rock, Salma Hayek, and Hans Gruber himself, Alan Rickman as Metatron (a.k.a. the voice of God), along with Smith regulars Jason Mewes, Jason Lee, and Ethan Suplee, make up the various muses and demons, all exhibiting comic timing that strictly follows Smith's distinctive rhythms, but it's God herself (Alanis Morissette) who steals the show. Too bad you have to wade through 115 minutes of theological drivel to get there.

Jay: "I feel like I'm Han Solo, and you're Chewie, and she's Ben Kenobi, and we're in that fucked-up bar."

Don't Be a Menace to South Central While Drinking Your Juice in the Hood (1996)

🌿 🌿 🌿 🌿 Long before the Wayans brothers parodied scary movies and dance flicks, they took on the hard 'hood movies of the nineties—*Boyz N the Hood, Menace II Society, Poetic Justice,* and *Dead Presidents,* to name a few—in the hilariously long-titled *Don't Be a Menace to South Central While Drinking Your Juice in the Hood.* Ashtray (Shawn Wayans) is the central character, who moves back to

the 'hood to live with his dad and learn to become a man (even though Pop is technically a couple years younger than him). After chores, Tray's first priority is to roll over to his aunt's house at 187 Drive By Boulevard, where his cousin Loc Dog (Marlon Wayans) and weed-smoking, low-rider-driving O.G. (original gangster) grandma (who unfortunately has arthritis in her trigger finger) also live. Loc is a real menace to society who has a deep passion for illegal weapons of all sizes and a mean sense of style (four pagers, pink bunny slippers, braids ornamented to look like dime bags, multiple pacifiers and at least one joint); his homies include wheelchair-bound Crazy Legs (Suli McCullough), who used to be the best dancer in the 'hood before a drive-by left him paralyzed from the waist down, and Preach (Chris Spencer), a confused black-power activist. All is good in the 'hood until some major beef gets started when Ashtray hooks up with Toothpick's ex-girl Dashiki (Tracey Cherelle Jones)—Swahili for doggy style—who entices Tray to leave the ghetto and help take care of her seven kids. Hilarious from beginning to end, it's a must-see for *Scary Movie* fans and every hip-hop, 'hood-loving stoner.

Ashtray's Mom: "Tray, I don't want you hangin' out in the streets. I want you to finish school, 'cause without an education the only kind of work you're gonna get is selling drugs, pimping women, or working security for Eddie Murphy."

Down & Out with the Dolls (2002)

🌿 🌿 🌿 It's a punk rock tale for the ages. Four feisty outcasts start an all-girl band in Portland, Oregon, and are primed to make it big, but once they move in together, the claws come out and their path to stardom is totally derailed. Of course, it's all the singer's fault. Fauna (Zoë Poledouris) is your typical egomaniac Courtney Love–wannabe who once fronted local buzz band the Snogs. She joins guitarist Kali (Nicole Barrett), bassist Lavender (Melody Moore), and drummer Reggie (Kinnie Starr) to form the Paper Dolls, who quickly get a record deal via a ringing endorsement from rock star

Levi (Coyote Shivers), a childhood friend of Kali's and frontman for local heroes the Suicide Bombers. Only problem is, the slightly overweight Kali has a mad crush on Levi, but Fauna's got her sights set on him, too. Meanwhile, bi-curious stoner Reggie, who brings her double-tube bong to the band's first photo shoot, is finding that fame (and adoring female fans) suits her, even if that means ditching her longtime boyfriend and lackey Mulder (Brendan O'Hara). Lavender tries to play mediator, as does the barely intelligible homeless Joe, played hilariously by Motorhead's Lemmy Kilmister, who's renting out a closet in "the Dollhouse," but the drama implodes during a raging, boozy party, which leaves one rocker dead. *Down & Out with the Dolls* came out in 2002, but with the Nirvana posters and all that rainy weather, feels more like 1992. While some of the dialogue feels passé, the tunes hold up nicely.

Kali: "I want this band to mean something. Wouldn't you agree, Reggie?"

Reggie: "I just wanna rock."

Drive Me Crazy (1999)

🌿 🌿 🌿 Your prototypical teen crush tale takes a deceptive turn when next-door neighbors and former friends Nicole Maris (Melissa Joan Hart) and Chase Hammond (Adrian Grenier) team up and conspire to make their exes jealous. They couldn't be more different: She's the school-spirit queen in charge of the Centennial Dance; he's the class rebel who screws with the school's sprinkler system. Nothing seems to mesh between these two—not their friends, fashion, or taste in music—after weeks of pretending they're a happy couple. *Drive Me Crazy* is as predictable as PG-13 gets (complete with soundtrack featuring Britney Spears and Backstreet Boys), and *Entourage*'s future Vincent Chase isn't much of a punk, but one of his school buds—perpetual jokester Ray Neeley (Kris Park), perhaps?—makes a bong out of a science lab beaker. We'll tip our pipe to that.

Principal: "I always forget, are the pupils supposed to be smaller or bigger?"

Ray Neeley: "Well, that all depends."

Duck Season [Tempirada de patas] (2004)

🌿 🌿 🌿 Three teenagers spend the day together in a high-rise apartment in Mexico City. One of the four main characters, Ulises (Enrique Arreola), delivers a pizza and never leaves. Rita (Danny Perea) bakes pot brownies for her birthday, and the quartet gets pleasantly stoned. Not a lot happens in this black-and-white film; with its dissolves and long takes, it's reminiscent of Jim Jarmusch's early work.

Flama's mom: "All this mess for brownies?"

Duck Soup (1933)

🌿 🌿 🌿 🌿 🌿 The fifth Marx Brothers movie is their best and arguably the greatest comedy of all time. Starring Groucho, Chico, Harpo, and Zeppo, *Duck Soup* features jokes that are rapid-fire, with Groucho as Rufus T. Firefly, the recently instated president of Fredonia, directing most of his zingers at aristocrat Mrs. Gloria Teasdale (Margaret Dumont) and rival Ambassador Trentino of Sylvania (Louis Calhern). Chicolini (Chico) and Pinky (Harpo), double-agent spies hired by Trentino, chew up the scenery with their impeccable timing and madcap energy. Despite several high-concept musical numbers, the pace moves along faster than most Marx Brothers films. It's one highlight after another—from Chicolini and Pinky's hysterical first meeting with Trentino to several confrontations between them and a lemonade vendor (Edgar Kennedy) to Chicolini's trial to the war that's sparked by the word "upstart" and a glove slap. Woody Allen has long noted his admiration for the Marx brothers' comic genius, but for the purpose of this book you need look no further than Cheech & Chong for a worthy comparison. Though this is not a stoner movie per se (just cigars are smoked), you will laugh your ass off watching it—high or not. It's that funny.

Rufus: "Go, and never darken my towels again."

Dude, Where's My Car? (2000)

🔨 🔑 🍺

🌿 🌿 🌿 If only Jesse (Ashton Kutcher) and Chester (Seann William Scott) could remember what they did last night, the universe wouldn't be at risk of instant annihilation. Such is the premise to *Dude, Where's My Car?*, featuring the dopiest duo to hit the screen since Bill and Ted. Their day after

goes something like this: Wake up with a hangover, fight with their pizza delivery boss, lose the car, apologize to twin girlfriends Wanda (Jennifer Garner) and Wilma (Marla Sokoloff) for screwing up their anniversary, run into extraterrestrial hot chicks on the street, and get accosted for money by a transsexual, kidnapped by space-cult worshippers of Zoltan (Hal Sparks), bullied by local douchebag Tommy (Charlie O'Connell), and finally confronted by alien Nordic dudes seeking a powerful and mysterious contraption called the Continuum Transfunctioner, which Jesse and Chester absconded with the night before.

While it's understood that Jesse and Chester are major potheads, neither are ever shown puffing and refer to weed only as "Shibby," a sacrifice made for the PG-13 rating, no doubt. On that tip, you can barely make out a bong on their kitchen table and the only pipe shown is one that's smoked by their neighbor's dog. Instead, you get a constant barrage of "stoner-bashing" threats by Tommy, which doesn't bode well on the positive vibes scale. Parts of the film are amusing, like the "dude" and "sweet" exchange and Jesse's spat with the Chinese take-out intercom lady. And then the laughs dry up like a cashed bowl.

Jesse: "Is it possible that we got so wasted last night that we bought a lifetime supply of pudding and totally forgot about it?"

Encino Man (1992)

🍺 🔪

🌿 🌿 🌿 When high school outcasts Dave Morgan (a young Sean Astin) and "Stoney" Brown (Pauly Shore) discover a frozen caveman buried in their neighborhood, they decide to thaw him out and introduce him to modern living in a California suburb. But while outfitting the dude they dub "Link" (Brendan Fraser) in early nineties grunge wear is easy, high school life gets more complicated than they ever imagined, especially when Link and Dave compete for the same prom date. Farfetched (yeah, prehistoric glaciers would naturally end up in Los Angeles, where the average temperature is 70 degrees—duh!) and occasionally funny, thanks mostly to Shore's nonsensical ramblings (and constant references to "nugs" and "melons,"

> "The only thing you ever cared about, Stoney, was nugs, chilling, and grinding!"
>
> —Dave

even if the film shows neither), *Encino Man* also has a message: Freak-dom is in the eye of the beholder, *buddy*. Now if they only made a movie about an ancient stash, that would be something.

Everything's Gone Green (2007)

🌱 🍾

🍁 🍁 🍁 Paolo Costanzo, who played *Road Trip*'s resident pothead, gets top billing in this dark Canadian comedy, and once again shares the screen with some green. But it's not just weed that plays a vital role in this story—there's the color of money

and of jealousy, both of which twentysomething slacker Ryan is grappling with as he starts a new job with the British Columbia lottery photographing and interviewing winners. Indeed, life couldn't be weirder for this Vancouver son. He meets his unrequited love Ming (Steph Song) when a dead whale rolls up on the shore, and later teams up with her scam-artist boyfriend Bryce (J. R. Bourne), and the Japanese mob to extort prize money from lotto winners. His friend Spike (Gordon Michael Woolvett), a professional pot grower and aspiring franchiser, has enlisted Ryan's entrepreneurial parents to maintain a grow-op in their basement. His brother Kevin (Peter Kelamis) is a successful real estate agent with cash pouring in. It's no wonder Ryan gets

sucked into a life of excess, only to realize that age-old adage: Money doesn't equal happiness.

But for all the criminal tendencies throughout this film, there's an unwavering positivity to the characters' outlook on life, no matter how many times they get knocked down. And while Ryan is never shown smoking, there's no doubt this dude's a stoner—how else do you explain buying multiple econo-sized boxes of Pocky, those delectable Chinese chocolate sticks? Costanzo's performance is nuanced and subtle, like the film itself, which is visually stunning (right down to Ryan's apartment accessories, which include an awesomely colorful display of empty laundry detergent canisters). And while the pacing feels a little off at times, a killer soundtrack featuring a slew of Canada's finest indie rockers makes for a more-than-pleasant ride.

Ryan: "Dad, you have a grow-op in your basement. You could go to jail!"

Ryan's dad: "Oh, you're being so melodramatic. Besides, we're growing some of the finest bud in the Pacific Northwest. Come look at the buds on this one. Her name is Angelina."

Extract (2009)

🍸 🍾 💊

🍁 🍁 🍁 The latest offbeat comedy by Mike Judge (*Office Space, Beavis and Butt-Head Do America*) stars Jason Bateman as Joel, the disenchanted owner of a vanilla extract factory. Though sex is constantly on his mind, Joel and his wife, Suzie (Kristen Wiig), rarely have any, which bums him out to no end, and his work life isn't faring much better—one of his employees suffers a debilitating on-the-job injury, while the rest of the staff has grown disgruntled and demanding. Enter Cindy (Mila Kunis), a foxy con artist who shamelessly flirts with Joel, while also seducing the ball-less staffer Step (Clifton Collins Jr.) and encouraging him to sue the company. Mesmerized by Cindy and frustrated with Suzie, Joel turns to his best bud Dean (Ben Affleck), a bartender at the local Marriott and self-described "spiritualist and healer," whose advice is to drink, take drugs (namely Xanax), and hire a male gigolo to screw Suzie so Joel can carry on with Cindy guilt-free.

After a little Special K and one monstrous six-foot-bong hit, this plan makes perfect sense to Joel, and he forges ahead with the deception. Indeed, it's a demented Mike Judge world, and those who bemoaned the lack of weed in *Office Space* will be satisfied with *Extract*'s one outrageous pot scene. But with the exception of Dean, this group of food additive lifers is pretty lifeless.

> "It's not a drug, it's a flower. It has healing properties. Stress is a killer."
>
> —Dean

> "I get paranoid when I smoke pot."
>
> —Joel

> "Not if you smoke a little, bro."
>
> —Dean

The Family Stone (2005)

🔑 🍸

🍁 🍁 🍁 With an A-list ensemble cast that includes Diane Keaton, Sarah Jessica Parker, Luke Wilson, Rachel McAdams, Dermot Mulroney, and Claire Danes, it's no wonder this Christmastime romantic comedy oozes sap, even as it tries to ride a slightly edgier line. And by "edgy" we mean tragic and painful to sit through. The main offender is the uptight career-driven Meredith (Parker) who's dating Everett (Mulroney), one of six Stone children gathering with their parents, Sybil (Keaton) and Kelly (Craig T. Nelson), for the holidays. Meredith is instantly despised by his family, and brash younger sister Amy (McAdams) is especially cruel, so much so that Meredith recruits her own sister Julie (Danes) to the Stone home for backup. But pothead brother Ben (Wilson), who bonds with his dad over a bowl, takes pity on Meredith, gets her drunk, and complicates matters even more when she wakes up in his bed. Everett, meanwhile, falls for Julie, making the twisted sibling swap complete. Moving this tearjerker along are your clichéd ancillary storylines—Mom's dying of an unspecified disease, deaf and gay son Thad (Ty Giordano) wants to adopt a baby with his partner—and an ending fit to be tied in a shiny, red bow. It's as predictable as Hollywood gets.

Sybil: "You and Daddy have fun getting stoned?"

Fandango (1985)

✏️ 🍸 🖋️

🍁 🍁 🍁 🍁 Set during the Vietnam War, five guys who call themselves the "Groovers" graduate college in Texas and have big decisions to make when several of them receive draft notices and another is scheduled to get married. What to do? Road trip! Spirited by Gardner Barnes (Kevin Costner, in his first major role), they decide to dig up a buried treasure of theirs near the Mexican border. However, tensions arise when Gardner takes liberties with Phil's classic blue Cadillac, and soon Phil (Judd Nelson) has to prove his mettle by skydiving out of a plane. The gone-to-seed Pecos Valley Parachute School is run by hippie-dippie Truman Sparks (Marvin J. McIntyre) and his "old lady" Trelis (Glenne Headley). So it should come as no surprise when Truman offers Phil a joint while they're up in the air. "You might want to take a couple of hits of this before you go out the door," he advises. "It makes the trip down real interesting." Phil declines and barely survives the jump. After much consternation, the wedding is hastily planned, and then the guys go their separate ways, unclear what the future holds. References to James Dean and *Giant* tip the well-intentioned film's hand, but another Texas classic comes to mind: *The Last Picture Show*.

Far Out Man (1990)

✏️ 🖋️ 📏

🍁 🍁 🍁 In this family affair, Tommy Chong (minus Cheech Marin) provides the comic ridiculousness he's known for with the help of his wife Shelby (Tree), daughter Rae Dawn (herself), and son Paris (Kyle). Far Out Man (Chong) is a dimwit who reconnects with Tree after ten years apart. Martin Mull, C. Thomas Howell, Judd Nelson, Paul Bartel, and even Cheech are all participants in the madness that includes a trip to the animated Hippieland and Chong (who also directs) reuniting with his former bandmate Bobby Taylor of the Vancouvers. Funniest of all is Far Out Man constantly calling the sexy Tree "Man." But the film is a long way from Chong's best work.

Far Out Man: "I thought you were a reporter from *High Times*. I was waiting for my little gift."

Fast Times at Ridgemont High (1982)

🖊 🔥 🍸 👀

🍁 🍁 🍁 🍁 "What are you people on, dope?!" One simple line delivered by the crustiest history teacher to ever enter a classroom makes *Fast Times at Ridgemont High* quite possibly the greatest high school movie of all time. Not just because the infamous Mr. Hand is chiding surfer-slacker-stoner Jeff Spicoli (Sean Penn); he's admonishing a whole generation of burnouts wasting away in California's suburbs and beaches circa 1982—a time when Cheap Trick ruled, Pat Benatar dictated fashion, and kids sniffed Xeroxed handouts in class for a quick high— kids like Brad (Judge Reinhold) and his younger sister Stacy (Jennifer Jason Leigh), who both toil away

at pointless jobs while trying to keep their hormones in check; Mike Damone (Robert Romanus), student by day, scalper by night, who ends up fooling around with his best friend's girl; and Linda (Phoebe Cates), the resident hottie who imparts her sexual wisdom to anyone who'll listen. But by far the most memorable character is Spicoli—the kind of guy who rolls up to school in a smoke-filled VW bus, orders pizza during class, strolls into a fast-food franchise shirtless ("No shirt, no shoes, no dice") and spends every waking moment talking or fantasizing about surfing. And while Spicoli doesn't say all that much, every line he delivers in *Fast Times* is a priceless zinger, right down to the epilogue, which notes that, after Spicoli saves Brooke Shields from drowning, he blows the reward money hiring Van Halen to play his birthday party.

> "All I need are some tasty waves, a cool buzz, and I'm fine."
> —Jeff Spicoli

But *Fast Times* goes deeper than your typical high school romp of a movie. After all, the screenplay based on the book written by Cameron Crowe, which chronicled the year he spent undercover in a San Diego high school, is perfectly directed by Amy Heckerling (*Clueless*). Also look for Nicolas Cage, Eric Stoltz, and Anthony Edwards in early stoner roles.

Feeling Minnesota (1996)

🖊 🍸 ✂

🍁 🍁 🍁 This is one of those insanely dark comedies where the characters ride a fine line between seeming ironic and pathetically flawed. It's the tale of two degenerate brothers, Sam (Vincent D'Onofrio) and Jjaks (Keanu Reeves), and the local slut, Freddie (Cameron Diaz), who is forced to marry Sam as a reward for some shady money dealings. Freddie and Jjaks start an affair on her wedding day, and within days, conspire to escape town together. But hothead Sam foils their plans when he follows the couple to a motel, ends up shooting Freddie, and

☘ CISCO ADLER'S STONY MOVIE PICKS ☘

Rocker Cisco Adler knows a thing or two about stoner movies—his dad, Lou Adler, directed *Up in Smoke* and produced *The Rocky Horror Picture Show*, and was the brains behind *Monterey Pop*. Here, Malibu's proudest pothead (and one half of Shwayze) offers his personal high five:

***The Big Lebowski* (1998):** "Let's call it number one of all time. You can watch *Big Lebowski* a hundred times and find something new. The first time I saw it, I was sleeping over at my cousin's house and we went to see it. I remember he didn't like it at all, and I was so taken aback by it that I had an actual breakdown and called my father. I told my dad that I couldn't sleep in the same house as my cousin because he didn't like *The Big Lebowski*. A couple years later, my cousin came to me and said, 'I don't know what I was thinking.' Whether you consider it a stoner movie or not, it's just brilliant visually and the writing is amazing. 'In the parlance of our times.' That one always makes its way back around."

***Easy Rider* (1969):** "*Easy Rider* was one of those films that helped me figure out my parents' generation and where they were coming from. And even though it defined their generation, it also applies to every generation after. I watched it a year or two ago and really soaked it in. It's a classic."

***Up in Smoke* (1978):** "I was born in 1978 and it's funny to think that in that year, two things came out of my dad's work: one was me and the other was *Up in Smoke*. [Laughs] But that movie has always been a stamp that my dad is cool—like he's not just a producer, he worked on *Up in Smoke*!—and the hill that my house is on is actually where a lot of those shots of Malibu were taken, so I live and breathe the smoke."

***Fast Times at Ridgemont High* (1982):** "Another amazing movie that defines every generation—it doesn't matter that they're wearing seventies clothing or listening to seventies music in *Fast Times*, my high school was exactly like that. I'm a beach dude, so that movie—and the bit at the end about Spicoli's birthday party—definitely resonated."

***Grandma's Boy* (2006):** "I hadn't seen *Grandma's Boy* until about a year ago, and it was such an amazing experience. That movie is funny as fuck. [Dealer Dante] orders a lion as security, he has some African tribesman who brings him the grass and speaks to him by clicking, it's hilarious! We've been playing a lot of colleges and it seems like every kid has that movie locked in the vault."

frames his brother for it. The situation worsens once a crooked local cop, played by Dan Aykroyd, comes into the picture, and it's revealed that everyone involved is trying to blackmail someone else. In the end, you don't know whether to laugh or cry. On the plus side, the soundtrack featuring local indie rock heroes the Replacements, along with songs by Johnny Cash and Los Lobos, is pretty outstanding, as is the opening scene showing Sam and Jjaks's mom (played by Tuesday Weld) hitting a joint. And the final message, that everything happens for a reason, leaves you feeling pretty upbeat about *Feeling Minnesota*, despite its overall downer vibe.

Ferris Bueller's Day Off (1986)

🍃🍃🍃🍃 The comedy classic *Ferris Bueller's Day Off* may be the ultimate cinematic example of just about everyone's high school fantasy: On one crazy day, senior Ferris Bueller (Matthew Broderick) decides to play hooky, roping in his Eeyore-like friend Cameron (Alan Ruck) and his hottie girlfriend Sloane (Mia Sara) to share in the delinquency/fun, all the while avoiding his dad (Lyman Ward), his sister (a pre–*Dirty Dancing* Jennifer Grey), and his bumbling principal (Jeffrey Jones). While the PG-13 movie contains no mention of herb, it's got plenty of what-would-I-do-with-a-day-off highdeas (both good and bad), including stealing a parent's prized Ferrari, sneaking into a hoity-toity restaurant, checking out a fine-art museum,

catching a baseball game, and becoming the center of attention at a city parade by singing "Twist and Shout"—directly underneath his father's office—with Bueller all the while pontificating directly to the camera about major life choices: what to do about college, whether he should get married, what kind of trouble he can get into next. Though he's not a stoner, per se, Ferris Bueller is certainly a stoner icon: a boy-man who uses his power of persuasion to live a life full of leisure, and still emerges the coolest kid in school.

🍃 FOUR MORE BY JOHN HUGHES 🍃

Sixteen Candles **(1984):** The be-all and end-all of teen movies, Hughes's directorial debut is arguably his finest dissection of high school misery, as told through the eyes of sixteen-year-old Samantha Baker and a host of unforgettable ancillary characters—Jake Ryan, Farmer Ted, Long Duk Dong. Subtle yet hysterical, painful at times, but exultant at the end, there hasn't been a movie that's felt this good in the twenty-five years since.

The Breakfast Club **(1985):** A brain, an athlete, a princess, a basket case, and a criminal share a joint and society's walls come crashing down—now that's not just another teen movie. Hughes's Saturday detention masterpiece broke ground by going light on scenery and heavy on dialogue, but there's not a dull moment in any of its ninety-two minutes.

Weird Science **(1985):** Two nerds' dreams are realized when they use their computer to create the perfect woman. But what Gary Wallace and Wyatt Donnelly gain in popularity, they lose in self-respect when Lisa turns the tables on her creators. Craving a brainy buzz? Strap a bra on your head and step into the world of cheesy eighties special effects.

Pretty in Pink **(1986):** Hughes gives a distinct voice to kids from the other side of the tracks in this tear-jerking high school love story, which he also wrote. It's the classic battle of the haves versus the have-nots—Andie Walsh and Duckie Dale are the school freaks, while Blane McDonough and Steff (the ultimate preppy pothead), are privileged and popular—with no clear victor to declare.

Flashback (1990)

🍸 ✂️ 👅

🌿🌿 As counterculture icons go, Dennis Hopper ranks among the very best for breaking ground in films like *Easy Rider* and *Apocalypse Now*. But when it comes to his starring turn in 1990's *Flashback*, let's just say it wasn't his finest moment. Hopper plays fugitive sixties radical Huey Walker, who, after twenty years on the run, has finally been nabbed by the FBI. Young agent John Buckner (Kiefer Sutherland) is ordered to escort him by train from San Francisco to Spokane—only along the way, Huey pulls a number on his captor, convincing John he'd spiked his mineral water with LSD and that only massive amounts of alcohol will work as an antidote. Once John passes out, Huey does a quick change and passes himself off as the agent while turning John over to the authorities. The mix-up is sorted out, but when John is put on the other side of a gun barrel, the two team up and escape through the woods—the same terrain, it turns out, where John grew up on a hippie commune and was named "Free." In no time, the uptight copper drops his guard, throws on a tie-dye, and gets weepy watching old family movies. He resolves to drop out with Huey, but with the fuzz still on their trail, things go awry time and time again. With its casual mentions of sixties-era rallying cries (including Hopper's own reference to *Easy Rider*), *Flashback* feels like a hokey made-for-TV movie that's all talk—you won't see a joint or even a real tab of acid, but you will get your fill of clichés, right down to a screeching, corner-bending psychedelic Further bus. For the sake of its hippie spirit, here's hoping it was a replica.

> "Acid! LSD I scored back in the slam, man. Hey, don't you worry, I'm not gonna let you trip alone. I dropped a couple of tabs myself."
>
> —Huey

Fletch (1985)

🍸 ✂️ 💉

🌿🌿🌿🌿 Chevy Chase plays Los Angeles newspaper reporter Irwin M. Fletcher, who's posing as a beach bum while investigating a local drug ring. But when mysterious rich guy Alan Stanwyk (Tim Matheson) offers the Lakers-obsessed journo $50K to kill him, the story takes a new direction and, in getting to the bottom of it, Fletch takes on about a dozen alternate identities—Mr. Poon, Don Corleone, Harry S. Truman, and Dr. Rosenpenis, to name a few. He also beds Alan's hot wife, Gail (Dana Wheeler-Nicholson), charges a fortune to the Underhill's country club bill, and, on the police chief's orders, winds up in jail—all in the name of journalism. It's a smart mystery, based on the popular novel by Gregory McDonald, but the brilliance of *Fletch* lies in its gut-splitting zingers, line for line, scene by scene, all eternally quotable. Credit Chase, who ad-libbed much of this starring role, which many consider his funniest—and that's saying a lot with his résumé. It should come as no surprise that the sequel, *Fletch Lives*, doesn't even come close to the original, and a rumored forthcoming prequel will probably suffer the same fate. What would Fletch say about a modern-day, Internet-savvy version of himself—who might even be a blogger? No, never, never.

Gail Stanwyck: "What are you doing here?"

Fletch: "I ordered some lunch."

Gail Stanwyck: "You ordered it here?"

Fletch: "Well, I knew this is where my mouth would be."

Flirting with Disaster (1996)

🍸 💊 👅

🌿🌿🌿🌿🌿 The quintessential road story takes many twisted turns in this dark comedy about a guy who goes on a cross-country search for his biological parents. Ben Stiller plays Mel Coplin, a New Yorker and new father who enlists an adoption specialist (Téa Leoni) to accompany him and his wife, Nancy (Patricia Arquette), to San Diego to meet his real mother. Only when he gets there, he's met by the cackle of six-foot-plus blondes (the supposed mom and her two volleyball star daughters), relations who seem biologically impossible. So the journey continues to snowy Michigan, where a truck driver is deemed his dad. Not quite, as it turns out. And when Mel crashes the guy's big rig into a post office, and is subsequently taken in for questioning by two ATF agents (Josh Brolin and Richard Jenkins), things get even hairier. The group—including the agents—head to New Mexico to meet the Schlichting family. Living out in the middle of nowhere, Richard and Mary Schlichting (Alan Alda and Lily Tomlin) are former acid dealers who did indeed give up a son for adoption. Their other son, Lonnie (Glenn Fitzgerald), however, is anything but a cheery hippie and shows some serious resentment toward the guests—so much so that he doses Mel's meal with high-intensity liquid blotter. Only problem is, ATF agent Paul (Jenkins) eats it instead.

What happens next is a mind-blowing comedy of errors, where Paul starts tripping balls and takes off on a naked sprint through the desert; the Schlichtings freak out upon discovering his badge; Mel and Nancy spat; his adoptive parents, played brilliantly by Mary Tyler Moore and George Segal, show up, and it all ends in a car crash on a deserted road. Sound morose? It is, but hilariously so, and as one of Ben Stiller's earlier efforts, Flirting with Disaster is the perfect precursor to Meet The Parents with just as many awkward moments, laughs, and unbelievable highs.

Mary Schlichting: "How do you feel?"

Agent Paul: "Vivid. I'm seeing colors I don't want to see."

Forgetting Sarah Marshall (2008)

Yð (oʘ)

🍁 🍁 🍁 🍁 Written by beloved Judd Apatow associate Jason Segel (TV's How I Met Your Mother), Forgetting Sarah Marshall is a smart romantic comedy with a great ensemble cast set mostly in the lush greenery of Hawaii. When hot TV actress Sarah Marshall (Kristen Bell) breaks up with her longtime boyfriend and show's music composer, Peter Bretter (Segel), Peter goes into a rapid tailspin that includes lots of alcohol, crying jags, and sex with strangers. Encouraged by his stepbrother Brian (Bill Hader) to take a vacation, Peter ends up at the same Hawaii hotel as Sarah and her new boyfriend, the narcissistic English rock star Aldous Snow (Russell Brand). Peter is depressed and drinking but he bonds with several hotel employees, especially the lovely concierge Rachel Jansen (Mila Kunis), who helps him loosen up and have some real fun. Characters like the Aldous-worshipping, pot-dealing maître d' Matthew van der Wyk (Jonah Hill) and the stoner surf instructor Kunu (Paul Rudd) add some absurdist levity, but it's the incredibly zany Brand who provides the coolest comedic counterpoint to Segel's mope-ridden character. Sarah, Aldous, Peter, and Rachel eventually have a dinner together, where their emotional tensions are fueled by booze and morph into a full-fledged couples' competition. Segel's notorious Muppet obsession is also in view here, and his puppet-rock musical based on the Dracula story is both hilarious and crucial to the film's romantic conclusion, as are his full-frontal exposures that bookend this clever flick.

Matthew (on the phone at the restaurant): "Well, I would love to sell you some weed, Jeremy, but I'm at my fucking job right now. Obviously, because you called me at work, you know that I'm at my place of work, so I can't just leave here and sell you some weed. I can sell you some weed when I'm done."

40-Year-Old Virgin, The (2005)

🖊 🔧 🪕 Yð

🍁 🍁 🍁 🍁 🍁 Andy Stitzer (Steve Carell) is a nebbishy loner who collects vintage superhero toys, likes to watch Everybody Loves Raymond, doesn't own a car, and works in the stockroom at Smart Tech, a local electronic store. Not surprisingly, he's also never been laid. But unlike your typical dorky dude, Andy's not only brainy, he's kind of cute, sensitive, and prime for molding. So his store buds, Cal (Seth Rogen), David (Paul Rudd), and Jay (Romany Malco), take him on as a makeover project, showing Andy the way, not to a woman's heart, but into her pants. That involves some painful manscaping, binge drinking, and smooth talking, none of which sits well with Andy the teetotaler, but that doesn't stop his buds from trying. One of the film's best montages involves stockroom stoner Cal passing an apple pipe to Andy—one cough and he's off! (On the DVD's extended cut, there's also a scene where Smart Tech manager Paula, played brilliantly by Jane Lynch, asks Cal to score her weed.) But once Andy meets Trish (Catherine Keener), the hunt is over. She's a cool single mom divorcée (and technically a GILF—as in, grandma), and he falls hard. Only Andy can't bring himself to tell her that his cherry has yet to be popped and the anticipation nearly derails their relationship.

Beyond the quaint love story, however, are the film's most pants-splitting scenarios—Andy's drive with a drunk girl (played by Apatow's wife, Leslie Mann), the speed-dating round (Cal likes former lesbian Gina, pronounced jahy-na), Cal and David's "you know how I know you're gay?" banter, and, of course, the chest waxing scene, which, as production notes tell it, was the real deal and explains why everyone in the background is laughing uncontrollably. That, or they were high.

Cal: "How much have you had to drink, man?"

Andy: "Oh, how much have I had to drink? Hey, how many pots have you smoken?"

Four Rooms (1995)

All hell breaks loose in the Mon Signor Hotel on New Year's Eve. Bellhop Ted (Tim Roth) is featured in the four storylines and mini-movies that comprise this film, which is directed by Quentin Tarantino, Robert Rodriguez, Allison Anders, and Alexandre Rockwell. After the animated credits and retro swing theme song by Combustible Edison, Elspeth (Madonna) convenes a coven of witches in the Honeymoon Suite. The gag in Anders's segment is that the ladies need some jism for a potion and Ted's just the man to provide it. The next two segments, by Rockwell and Rodriguez, are less interesting and star-studded. Tarantino's finale, however, is worth waiting for. The director plays Chester, a narcissistic Hollywood player surrounded by sycophants Leo (Bruce Willis) and Norman (Paul Calderon). As Leo tokes off a roach clip, Chester orchestrates a bet involving a lighter, a hatchet, and Norman's pinkie. Several interludes spice up the movie, particularly the one with Margaret (Marisa Tomei) puffing on a pipe while her stony girlfriends play video games.

Friday (1995)

With a nod to Cheech & Chong, the first of three Friday films came straight outta Compton—home to Southern California's hip-hop culture. Starring Ice Cube (Craig) and Chris Tucker (Smokey) as the co-leads. Gray's tribute to the 'hood doesn't stray very far beyond Craig's front porch. "I'm gonna get you high today," Smokey promises, "because it's Friday . . . and you ain't got shit to do." Craig is recently unemployed and Smokey sells weed, but since he gets high on his own supply, Smokey can't afford to pay back Big Worm (Faizon Love), who threatens them both. Between Big Worm and neighborhood bully Deebo (Tiny Lister), they have plenty to contemplate while

> "There ain't nothin' wrong with smokin' weed. Weed is from the Earth. God put it there for me and you. Take advantage, man—take advantage!"
>
> —Smokey

Smokey keeps speed-rolling and inhaling joints. There's a love interest too: Craig has the hots for Debbie (Nia Long), whom he defends when she sasses Deebo. Unlike the more serious *Boyz N the Hood* and *Higher Learning*, we get to see the lighter side of L.A. gangsta life in this genre-defining, must-see flick.

Friday After Next
(2002)

🌿 🌿 🌿 The third and last installment of Ice Cube's *Friday* franchise is the least compelling. It's Christmas Eve, and all through the 'hood a sneaky Santa is ripping off homes chock-full of holiday presents. Cousins Craig (Cube) and Day-Day (Mike Epps) now live and work together after a short stay in Rancho Cucamonga (*Next Friday*). The thin plot involves catching the red-suited robber and the leads' usual money problems, culminating in a rent party. Except for the animated credits and a breakout supporting role for Katt Williams as pimpin' Money Mike, this delivery is mostly schwag.

> "Let me hit that before Willie bring his square ass out here."
>
> —Uncle Elroy

Friends with Money
(2006)

🌿 🌿 🌿 In a reversal of her role in *The Good Girl*, Jennifer Aniston plays the stoner in this slow-moving, dialogue-heavy dark comedy about a group of girlfriends and their messed-up lives. Christine (Catherine Keener) and her husband, David (Jason Isaacs), are writing partners on the verge of divorce; Franny (Joan Cusack) and Matt (Greg Germann) are a well-off couple desperate for a sense of purpose;

Jane (Frances McDormand) is menopausal and her husband, Aaron (Simon McBurney), is sexually ambiguous; while Olivia (Aniston) is single, depressed, and barely scraping by as a maid. Franny tries to fix up Olivia with her personal trainer Mike (Scott Cann), and things look promising initially. But when he starts tagging along on Olivia's jobs (and asking for a cut of her fee), she feels more discouraged than ever. Enter Marty (Bob Stephenson), an overweight, unemployed slob of a client who, in all his awkwardness, manages to charm Olivia. The two attend a fundraiser together, where Marty impresses Olivia's judgmental friends, and later share a joint back at his place. Lesson learned? Appearances can be deceiving.

Mike: "Do you smoke it?"

Olivia: "What? Their pot? No, I smoke my own."

Garage Days (2003)

🌿 🌿 This Australian production is one of those cheese-tastic, over-accessorized "rock-and-roll" movies that make you wonder, why did they bother? With cartoony effects and camerawork that comes across like some weird Nickelodeon series, it all feels made-for-TV. The story is about a loser metal band from Sydney that has never played a single gig (but inexplicably has a rehearsal space and a manager) and their lame attempts to try and "make it." They're up against evil, successful rival band Sprimp, and singer Freddy (Kick Gurry) pins his hopes on impressing their manager, Shad Kern (Marton Csokas), with all kinds of pathetic schemes. There's weed smoking backstage and a boy-falls-for-bandmate's-girlfriend subplot, but it feels like watered-down nonsense. The few interesting moments come with the racy sex scenes and a sequence titled "Fun with Drugs 2," which depicts a liquid acid–fueled dinner with the bass player's parents.

Shad Kern: "The best things about this playpen are the drugs and the women, and the worst things about this playpen—"

Freddy: "Are the drugs and the women."

Garden State (2004)

*This coming-of-age comedy is atypical for many reasons—not the least of which is that it boasts Zach Braff, star of silly TV show *Scrubs*, as its unlikely auteur. He plays Andrew Largeman, a twenty-six-year-old, pharmaceutically stunted struggling actor/waiter in Los Angeles who gets an unexpected phone call that his mother's passed away. He returns to his family home in suburban New Jersey for the first time in nearly a decade to attend the funeral. Afterward, Largeman parties with a few old friends—some Ecstasy, a little weed, a make-out sesh—but his glassy-eyed disposition tells the truth: None of this really affects him. In fact, he knows he's stunted, and then he meets Sam, a quirky girl gorgeously played by Natalie Portman, who, through a variety of psuedo-dates (including the inspection of a massive rock quarry) helps Largeman finally discover that, despite his numbness and the fact that he barely knows himself, he's still capable of love. *Garden State* is funny, but it's also surprisingly thoughtful. And if the grim New Jersey rain isn't heavy enough for you, dive into the soundtrack. As Sam famously says, the Shins's "New Slang" "will change your life."

Mark: "I'm okay with being unimpressive. I sleep better."

Get Out of My Room (1985)

*Cheech & Chong's last eighties production strings together four videos featuring Marin and documentary interviews with the duo. This would be their final project together until reuniting in 2008. Chong is clearly bored as Marin pushes his musical agenda. But "Born in East L.A." stands out and two years later became a feature movie, also directed by Marin. For Cheech completists only.

Chong: "Ever since I heard Nancy Reagan talk, I don't do drugs anymore—she's a real inspiration on me."

Good Luck (1996)

*Handicapped buddies Bernie (Gregory Hines) and Ole (Vincent D'Onofrio) decide to enter a white-water raft race in Oregon. The fact that Bernie is wheelchair-bound and Ole is blind (he suffers a football injury in the opening scene) doesn't stop them. Their road trip is full of heart-to-hearts and humorous adventures. When they arrive in Coos Bay, Farmer John (Max Gail) and the Southern Oregon Growers Association sponsor them at the race. Farmer John grows marijuana, but we never see his plants (though he does smoke a joint). After a bad practice run, Bernie and Ole get the hang of the rapids and triumphantly finish the race—dead last.

Farmer John's son: "We may be pot growers, but that doesn't mean we're not Americans."

Grandma's Boy (2006)

*Video games and pot culture intersect in this off-the-wall film from Adam Sandler's Happy Madison Productions. Alex (Allen Covert) tests video games at Brainasium, home to games like *Eternal Death Slayer*. He and his co-workers suffer from arrested development—for instance, Jeff (Nick Swardson) lives with his parents and sleeps in a bed shaped like a car. Alex gets evicted and moves in with Grandma Lilly (Doris Roberts of *Everybody Loves Raymond*) and her two female friends. He's a regular pot smoker, but hides it from Lilly, who finds his stash and, thinking it's tea, brews a potful and gets stoned with Grace (Shirley Jones) and Bea (Shirley Knight). At the office, self-proclaimed "genius" programmer J.P. (Joel Moore) is the butt of jokes due to his robotic antics, but when he steals Alex's game idea, the competition goes to another "level." At first, Mr. Cheezle (Kevin Nealon), the company's New Age boss, sides with J.P., who's been practicing at home, proves him wrong and exposes J.P. Funniest of all is Dante (Joe Dante)—one of the most outrageous movie dealers of all time. He hangs with an African tribesman, a Chinese martial artist, and a monkey, and fashions a Cheech & Chong–sized spliff when Alex asks him to "take the Frankenstein shit, the Deer shit, the Green Monster, the Bling and the Bling Bling and roll it all into one joint." Wasted, Alex and Dante need help getting to the office, so the chimp gets behind the wheel. Alex not only hits the high score, he gets the girl—Samantha (Linda Cardellini), who proves she can party with the game boys.

Alex: "I don't care what it's called. I just want a bag of fucking weed!"

Grosse Point Blank (1997)

It's not hard to see John Cusack's hitman-in-therapy Martin Q. Blank as a postgrad version of *Better Off Dead*'s Lane Meyer, or a renegade doppelganger for *Say Anything*'s Lloyd Dobler. Veering between deadpan one-liners and zany violence, he sits firmly within the Cusackian canon of somewhat dazed, overly sensitive dudes trying to sort out how to deal with the world when they're stuck on this one girl. In the case of assassin-for-hire Martin, he's ready to hang up his sniper rifle but has one last job to execute in his hometown, where he's destined to confront Debi (Minnie Driver), the long-lost girlfriend he abandoned on prom night. (She's a radio DJ, naturally, so they can easily work in dope music from the eighties and maintain Cusack's muso cred.) Timing is everything, and Martin's trip home happens to coincide with his ten-year high school reunion, which complicates his assassination assignment, but allows the opportunity to catch up with old friends. People like stoner-turned-Realtor Paul (Jeremy Piven), who sucks down a joint while pounding on the steering wheel in disbelief and yelling, "Ten years! Ten years! TEN YEARS!" In truth, every character is on fire in this comedic thriller—from Martin's assistant, Marcella (played by Cusack's sister, Joan), who delivers a killer one-liner every twenty seconds, to his analyst Dr. Oatman (Alan Arkin), to his manic enemy Grocer (Dan Aykroyd), which all makes for one action-packed head rush.

Half Baked (1998)

One of the funniest stoner comedies ever made (directed by Tamra Davis and written by Dave Chappelle and Neal Brennan), it features a multi-culti trio of stoners who start a pot delivery service to raise money to spring their friend Kenny (Harland Williams) from jail. Chappelle doubles as sweet-talking janitor Thurgood and gangster rapper Sir Smoke-a-lot. His perpetually high buds are Brian (Jim Breuer) and Scarface (Guillermo Díaz). When Thurgood meets straitlaced Mary Jane (Rachel True), the story takes a romantic turn for the worse. Thurgood is so smitten he promises not to smoke or sell weed. Meanwhile, business is booming—with cool buyer cameos from Snoop Dogg and Willie Nelson to Jon Stewart. In prison, Kenny's being protected by Squirrel Master (Tommy Chong). And rival dealer Samson (Clarence Williams III) wants a piece of Thurgood's action, setting off a climactic Batman-style rumble. To win Mary Jane back, Thurgood ultimately throws his last joint away, sadly confessing, "I love weed, but not as much as I love pussy." This cop-out ending—and the predictable male-female sparring about pot—diminishes an otherwise hilarious movie.

Jon Stewart: "Did you ever see the back of a dollar bill—on weeeeeed?"

Hangover, The (2009)

🍸💊

♨️ ♨️ ♨️ ♨️ What does it mean when you're in Vegas for a bachelor party and wake up the next morning not remembering a single thing? That you had a really good time, or that someone slipped you a roofie? In the case of The Hangover, a bit of both is to blame. Doug (Justin Bartha) and his best friends Phil (Bradley Cooper) and Stu (Ed Helms), along with his soon-to-be brother-in-law Alan (Zach Galifianakis) decide to rage on Doug's last night of freedom. After a couple of Jäger toasts, the guys wake up in their trashed $4K-a-night hotel suite, unable to explain where the groom is and why there's a tiger in the bathroom, not to mention a baby in the closet. The three retrace their steps in search of Doug, using clues that lead them to a hospital and a wedding chapel, where they discover that Stu married a stripper named Jade (Heather Graham) and gave her his grandmother's ring, the same one he was planning to propose with to his ultra-controlling girlfriend. The plot thickens when the guys are informed by eccentric wannabe-gangster Mr. Chow that they'll have to pay back the $80K that went missing from his man purse if they ever want to see Doug again. They also need to return that tiger to its rightful owner—boxing champ Mike Tyson. Can they do it all and make it to the wedding in one day? Hungover or not, best buds stick together. And you know what they say—what happens in Vegas stays in Vegas, even if you can't remember what happened at all.

Stu: "You do know counting cards is illegal, right?"

Alan: "Counting cards isn't illegal. It's frowned upon like masturbating on an airplane."

Phil: "I'm pretty sure that's illegal, too."

Alan: "Maybe since 9/11 when everyone got so damn sensitive. Thanks a lot, bin Laden!"

♨️ FOUR MORE BY TODD PHILLIPS ♨️

Road Trip (2000): The kooky college flick centered around a sex-tape fiasco has more than its share of stony antics, most courtesy of brainy pothead—and future weed innovator—Rubin (Paolo Costanzo) and the stoner left behind, seventh year undergrad Barry (Tom Green), who entertains endlessly as the University of Ithaca's tour guide and storyteller.

Bittersweet Motel (2000): One of three documentaries Phillips directed, Bittersweet Motel chronicles the band Phish on tours of the U.S. and Europe in 1997 and 1998, culminating in their three-day, 60,000-strong festival, the Great Went. Live footage interspersed with backstage snippets, rehearsal sessions, and candid interviews with band members tell the story, but it's all about the music and the vibes, beautifully captured for our future grandchildren to see.

Old School (2003): Featuring a trifecta of A-list funnymen, Phillips brings to life every man's fantasy—a frat house for grown-ups. Vince Vaughn leads the pack as pledge leader Beanie, while Mitch (Luke Wilson) follows apprehensively, and Frank the Tank (Will Ferrell) regresses completely. The enemy dean is played by Jeremy Piven, who joins Ellen Pompeo, Craig Kilborn, Juliette Lewis, Leah Remini, and Sean William Scott in the all-star comedy cast. Look for cameos by Artie Lange and the director himself.

Starsky & Hutch (2004): Spoofing the popular seventies cop series, Ben Stiller (Starsky) and Owen Wilson (Hutch) take on a major drug ring led by Jewish kingpin Feldman (Vince Vaughn). With help from convicted con man Big Earl (Will Ferrell), jive-talking informant Huggy Bear (Snoop Dogg), and Starsky's beloved Gran Torino, they bust up a golf course and a bat mitzvah in their quest to bring the crime lords down.

Harold & Kumar Go to White Castle (2004)

🌿🌿🌿🌿🌿 Turning the table on the stoner formula, Harold Lee (John Cho) and Kumar Patel (Kal Penn) are anything but your stereotypical potheads. For one thing, Harold is Korean and Kumar is Indian. They're also highly intelligent young professionals—one a future doctor, the other a financial analyst—not the kind of guys you'd expect to see sucking down bong hits and vegging in front of the TV. Yet that's exactly what Harold and Kumar do, and when they get a craving for White Castle burgers, they'll go to any lengths to satiate their appetites. On this particular Friday evening, they head to a White Castle in southern New Jersey and encounter more than their share of obstacles, like repeatedly losing their weed, butting heads with a pack of "extreme"-minded bullies, getting arrested for jaywalking, and, oddly enough, giving a ride to a jacked-up Neil Patrick Harris on the prowl for pussy, only to have him steal their car.

Along the way, their desperate drive to replenish their supply never dies—they try to procure medical marijuana at the hospital where Kumar's father and brother work, Kumar buys an eighty-dollar bag off a hippie undergrad at Princeton and later steals the dealer's entire stash from the police (following a brilliant fantasy sequence where he imagines a long and fruitful life with his bag-to-be, Weedie). There are weed-centric laughs at every turn of this wacky adventure—from the smoking cheetah to Goldstein and Rosenberg's shofar bong to Harold's concussion-induced dream of animated dancing burgers and pot leaves (not to mention the Ecstasy-fueled NPH, who steals the show)—all of which make *Harold &*

Kumar essential viewing for any self-respecting stoner. Only one bit of advice: Make your munchies plan ahead of time, whether carnivore or vegetarian, you will get hungry.

Harold & Kumar Escape from Guantanamo Bay (2008)

🌿🌿🌿🌿 More successful theatrically than its predecessor by about $20 million, the sequel starring Asian American

> "I just got a quarter of the finest herb in New York City and I'm not smoking that shit alone, OK? So you need to just chill the fuck out and prepare to get blazed, because in the next couple hours I expect both of us to be blitzed out of our skulls, got it?"
>
> —Kumar

Stoners in their element: the pot capital of the world

Still Smokin: Cheech & Chong's fifth movie is set entirely in Amsterdam, where they gorge on a gourmet canal-side feast that includes menu items like cream of hash soup, fungus mungus, and a wide assortment of space cakes.

Ocean's Twelve: On day one of their European jaunt, three of *Ocean's Twelve*'s team hit popular Amsterdam coffeeshop De Dampkring, where Danny (George Clooney) and Rusty (Brad Pitt) get the giggles while Linus (Matt Damon) can only manage to recite lyrics from Led Zeppelin's "Kashmir."

Harold & Kumar Escape from Guantanamo Bay: After an exhausting whirlwind trip to Texas by way of Washington, D.C., Gitmo, Florida, and Alabama, the Jersey stoners and their new girlfriends finally make it to Amsterdam, where the couples take in the sights and all that the magical city has to offer—toking along the canal, the red-light district, coffee shops, and the marijuana museum.

Beerfest: After winning the beer tournament in Germany, the American team travels to Amsterdam and runs into Willie Nelson, who tells them he's in town for an international pot competition, but his teammates Cheech and Chong chickened out.

Deuce Bigalow: European Gigolo: The former gigolo (Rob Schneider) escapes Malibu for Amsterdam, where his ex-pimp T. J. (Eddie Griffin) is living. But after scarfing a pot brownie in a coffee shop, Deucey imagines a hot windmill girl begging him to kiss her chest and in his dreamlike trance, inadvertently grabs his pal's nipples. Says T. J.: "No more space cakes for you!"

---

stoners Harold (John Cho) and Kumar (Kal Penn) has more on its mind than just a case of the munchies. Kumar, racially profiled at the airport, is accused of being a terrorist on a plane to Amsterdam when he attempts to smoke out of a bong that's mistaken by a hysterical passenger for a bomb. They're shipped to the Cuban prison, where they stay about a minute before escaping. Kumar's mission, besides lighting up whenever possible, is to thwart the marriage of his college sweetheart Vanessa (Danneel Harris) to the wrong guy, right-wing operative Colton (Eric Winter)—just like Benjamin in *The Graduate*. (It's a fairly standard plot device.) Meanwhile, Harold pines for Maria (Paula Garcés), whom he blew it with in the original. After floating back to the States on a raft with Cuban refugees, Harold and Kumar make stops at a "bottomless party" (lots of bush here), a KKK bonfire, and, best of all, the Western White House (lots of Bush there). They literally drop in via parachute on George W. (James Adomian), who treats his guests to joints "laced with blow so it knocks you out and keeps you goin' at the same

time." Flabbergasted, Kumar asks, "You get high and then put other people who smoke weed in jail? That's so hypocritical!" To which G.W. responds, "Shut the fuck up and smoke my weed." Hard-partying Neil Patrick Harris returns for more high jinks, scarfing down a bagful of magic mushrooms as he drives the guys past a roadblock and straight to a bordello run by Sally (Beverly D'Angelo), where he's serviced by the extremely large-breasted Tits Hemmingway (Echo Valley), and then chased out of the joint for bad behavior. Left for dead, Harris rises in the last scene (after the credits), presumably so he can return in part three for another round of debauchery. Oh, and of course, Harold and Kumar do finally make it to Amsterdam.

> **"Can't you wait until we get to Amsterdam? It's the weed capital of the world!"**
>
> **—Harold**

You could say actress Danneel Harris is a key figure in stoner movie history. After all, she played the girl who got Kumar high for the very first time! As Vanessa in *Harold & Kumar Escape from Guantanamo Bay*, Harris earns her pothead cred by sneaking a toke on her wedding day, and in one of the film's raunchier scenes, jumping headfirst into a threesome with Kumar and Weedie, leaving us all to wonder: What's in store for H & K 3?

Reefer Movie Madness: Were you a fan of the original *Harold & Kumar Go to White Castle*?

Danneel Harris: Yeah. And I just had to audition for the sequel. I think [director-writers Jon Hurwitz and Hayden Schlossberg] wanted Isla Fisher [for the role], but when I went in to read, my hair was really red, and they were probably high and thought I was her.

RMM: Vanessa has the doobie-ous distinction of introducing Kumar to pot. It all starts there, right?

DH: That's what I like best about her. Jon and Hayden were like, "You're the girl who's gonna bring weed into their lives." And she teaches the characters. Kumar wasn't into that, and I don't think Harold was either; he was all emo in the library. That scene is my favorite in the movie.

RMM: Were you smoking the fake stuff when you shotgunned that joint?

DH: At that point, yeah, we had done it so many times. But in Amsterdam . . . let's just say it's legal there, you know?

RMM: That's the thing about *Escape from Guantanamo Bay*; most of the movie is like a bad trip, but those last five minutes in Amsterdam with the credits rolling, you all look like you're having so much fun.

DH: You know on the boat when it pans over to that random guy smoking weed? I don't remember that happening at all. The best thing is, we finished shooting that scene, and I was in a weird place, so I was like, "You know what? Just drop me off. I just wanna walk home." So they pulled over in the middle of Amsterdam, let me out, and I walked around for a good hour and a half. Somehow I found the hotel, and there were, like, twenty million messages. OK, maybe it was longer than an hour and a half. Everyone was like, "Where are you?!" [laughs] That was such a fun trip.

RMM: And who can forget the ménage à trois with Weedie?

DH: They did right with that. I mean, it's obviously really funny. For everyone else on set, it was their favorite scene because it was just hard not to laugh. And the giant weed thing doesn't really move by itself. There was a person in the one that moves, so that's a costume. The one we were using to have sex with, it's just a big bag with wire arms and legs. Not to ruin the fantasy for everyone, but that was not real. We'd have to make it do what it was doing while filming, so it was awkward. We were like, "Does it look like it's really, you know, eating me out?" It was horribly funny and uncomfortable. Anyway, the crew guys, they stuck a lollipop in the bag so when I put my hand in there, they had to cut because I laughed really hard when I pulled it out. Then I ate it. I thought they should have left that in.

RMM: So it sounds like you didn't object to the raunch?

DH: No, because it's done for comedy. If it was a threesome with two guys, I'd have some questions about that. Because most movies now, especially all these "bro" comedies, it's all about making women look like idiots. Like, making the girl bend over . . . There's some of that in *Harold & Kumar*, but it still has this aura of comedy about it that's not as grody. And she does love weed, so it's a love story.

☙ DANNEEL HARRIS'S STONY MOVIE PICKS ❧

"My parents have the most interesting VHS collection," says Danneel Harris, whose favorite movies to smoke to all came out before she was even born.

Blazing Saddles (1974): "My parents absolutely loved *Blazing Saddles*, and that was one of those movies where they were like, 'You shouldn't watch this,' so of course, you're gonna watch it! I loved it. I laughed at all the right parts and my mom was like, 'OK, that was our first family film.' I do like that fact that, socially, it was groundbreaking. They were like, 'Here's racism, we're gonna laugh at it, and then maybe people will watch it and know that this is a problem.' Instead of beating you over the head with some boring documentary they show you in school, they should show this film in schools!"

Valley of the Dolls (1967): "It is the quintessential pill movie. It follows all these girls around—cute actresses, agents' wives— as they go back and forth from New York to Hollywood, but the entire time, all they do is take pills. I mean pills to wake up, pills to go to sleep, pills to go in the pool . . . You never really know exactly what they're taking because they just call them dolls. Everything is called dolls and it can make you high or sleepy. It's pretty funny because it was done in the sixties and it has all that music in it. Like, every time she reaches for a pill, it goes *bahm bahm bahm*. You're like, 'OK, she's gonna take the pill now . . .' It ends up being a whole mess."

Shampoo (1975): "I love Warren Beatty. He's sexy. It's the swinging sixties, free sex and love and all that, but apparently the women he's with—there's, like, seventeen of them—aren't into that. There's this scene at a really tripped-out hippie party. He's having sex with one girl when all these other girls show up, and then there's this huge, high, drug-induced chase where you're seeing the party through other people's eyes."

Everything You Ever Wanted to Know About Sex* (*But Were Afraid to Ask) (1972): "This was a movie that my mom said I could absolutely not watch, and I was like, 'I am definitely watching this one!' It's awesome. It's like a how-to movie with a whole bunch of vignettes where each one answers a question. There's one about loving animals that Gene Wilder is in that's called "What Is Sodomy?" The best part is the giant set of tits that roam the earth—they're as big as dinosaurs! It's the longest title in the world, and [director] Woody Allen is such a weirdo—in a great way."

Myra Breckinridge (1970): "There's some weird things going on in this movie, but it's amazing cinema. Everyone's in drag and dressing up and getting into these fantastical situations. I'm a huge Raquel Welch fan and she's the hottest tranny ever. She gets into all these crazy scenarios because of her alter ego . . . it's just a funny thing. This is a good movie for gay stoners."

Head Office (1985)

🖊 🍸 💉 👀

🌿🌿🌿 A fundamentally good guy, Jack Issel (Judge Reinhold) just so happens to have been born into a world of greed and corruption—from the household he grew up in headed by his pretentious father (a U.S. senator), to the Ivy League schools he slacked his way through, to his most recent venture: Corporate America. The insanely depraved conglomerate INC hires the college boy for an entry-level position, but, after a series of mishaps and backstabbings, the usual office politics have the partier shoot straight to the top. There Jack befriends the only colleagues he can trust—exec Max (Richard Masur) and limo driver Sal (Don Novello, a.k.a. Father Guido Sarducci), who all get buzzed on the job and smoke out in a company car en route to several happy hours. Unfortunately, director Ken Finkleman (*Airplane 2: The Sequel*) doesn't deliver what he promises with Issel's booze- and bud-infused rebel character. This silly satire distracts way too much with shtick.

High Society: A Pot Boiler (2009)

🖊 🍶 🍸 💉

🌿🌿🌿 Three male roommates receive a visit from two women and the high jinks begin. With little action to speak of, the focus is on budding relationships and bong-hitting skills. Scatological to a fault, Kristian Davies's script will make you howl, just not often enough. Davies's brother Erik (Trajan) is the center of attention—a sharp-witted cynic who can't seem to close the deal with the willing Sophie (Stephanie Ann Davies—Erik's real-life wife). The highlight scene comes when the foursome all spark up tulip joints constructed by Gavin (Peter Alton). Ballsy and often out of control, this is the kind of offbeat stoner comedy Seth Rogen wishes he could make.

Trajan: "I'm a fuckin' hero, a marijuana hero. Someone should make an action figure of me—you know, a figure that comes with a bong."

High Times' Pot Luck (2002)

🖊 🍶 🌱 🍸 🔪 👀

🌿🌿🌿 The Sopranos meets Cheech & Chong in this stoner gangster comedy directed by Alison Thompson. After mob soldier Frank (Frank Adonis of *GoodFellas* and *True Romance*) rescues punk-rocker Jade (Theo Kogan of the Lunachicks) from a street assault, she repays him with a shotgun hit. Frank had just lifted a suitcase containing twenty pounds of pot from thieves Mickey (Leif Riddell) and Ryan (Nick Iacovino). The suitcase changes hands numerous times (a hyper Jason Mewes of Jay and Silent Bob fame plays one of the dealers) before Frank ultimately gives it to Jade. All parties converge at the "reefer rally" in lower Manhattan, where Tommy Chong plays, smokes out of and raffles off the Chronicaster guitar pipe. But it's the contents of the suitcase that really gets the crowd excited. From the opening scene inside a grower's barn to the many close-ups of *High Times* quality kind bud, most of the marijuana displayed is real, a rarity in the wacky world of stoner movies.

History of the World: Part 1 (1981)

🖊 🌱 🔪

🌿🌿🌿🌿 Already famous for *The Producers* and *Blazing Saddles*, Mel Brooks went way back in time to tell the story of numerous epochs in history, from the Stone Age to the French Revolution. Playing various roles (Moses, Comicus the Standup Philosopher, King Louis XVI), Brooks is at the peak of his comic genius. No stone or stoner is left unturned, such as when Josephus (Gregory Hines) discovers a patch of "Roman Red" as he and his men are being chased. "I smell something familiar," he says. "The nose knows." Using a scroll, Josephus rolls up the largest joint in movie history, lights it and their chariot takes off, leaving a cloud of smoke that throws off their pursuers. In another druggy scene, Brooks, as Louis XI, snorts coke and asks the sexy Mademoiselle Rimbaud (Pamela Stephenson), "Care for a little toot?" When she declines, he says, "More for me."

How High (2001)

Part Cheech & Chong, part *Animal House*, Method Man (Silas P. Silas) and Redman (Jamal King) star in *How High*, one of the most raucous stoner movies of all time. The duo ar-rive at Harvard with blunts hanging out of their mouths and street attitude to spare. Thanks to a strain of weed that makes them smarter—and which Silas grows—they join the freshman class, turning the campus upside down. Silas competes with straight-arrow Bart (Chris Elwood) for good-girl Lauren (Lark Voorhies), setting up the romantic subplot. Like Dean Wormer in *Animal House*, Dean Cain

(Obba Babatundé) obsesses about Silas and Jamal's antisocial antics and places them on probation when their grades suddenly slip. In several nods to the *Friday* series, Anna Maria Horsford plays Jamal's mom and Mike Epps shows up for the requisite campus party as Baby Powder, a pimp who slaps people with a handful of powder supplied by his assistant pimp (Dublin James). The funky soundtrack opens with "Hits from the Bong" and includes a party performance of "Cisco Kid" by Cypress Hill.

Jamal: "I figure if I study high and take the test high, I'll get high scores, right?"

🍁 Q & A: METHOD MAN AND REDMAN 🍁

What's that age-old college myth? Study stoned, take the test stoned, and you'll do just as well, if not better? As full-time potheads Silas and Jamal in *How High*, Method Man and Redman prove the theory true when they ace the THC exam and end up at Harvard. How did the stoner classic come to be, and will there ever be a sequel? The rappers fill us in.

Reefer Movie Madness: *How High* was directed by Bob Dylan's son, Jesse, who later teamed with will.i.am for the "Yes We Can" video. How was working with him?

Method Man: I liked Jesse a lot. He had this deadpan thing going.

Redman: He was cool as fuck. He's the one that pulled it out of us and made it funny. I'd love to work with him again.

RMM: What movies influenced *How High*?

Meth: *Dazed and Confused, Fast Times at Ridgemont High, Reality Bites, Drugstore Cowboy, Requiem*

for a Dream... Did I say *Dazed and Confused*? That was all right. Had Ben Affleck and a lot of good characters.

Red: Also *Half Baked, Friday* 1 and 2, and *Animal House*, that's the one we really built *How High* from.

RMM: It's been a decade since the movie came out, will there ever be a *How High* 2?

Meth: I gotta give Dustin Abraham, the guy who wrote the first one, a swift kick in his ass. And the people at the studio, too. We gotta make this movie, but I don't think we can do *How High* 2 [as a sequel]. We'd do another stoner flick, but call it something else.

Igby Goes Down
(2002)

🖋 🍸 ⚗️ 💊 💉 👀

🌿 🌿 🌿 🌿 Throughout the course of his adolescence, rich Manhattanite teenager Igby Slocumb (Kieran Culkin) watched his father deteriorate under the pressures of upper-class life and schizophrenia. Now seventeen and armed with a battery of sarcasm and ennui, he wages a Holden Caulfield–style war on his pill-popping mother, Mimi (Susan Sarandon), Republican-in-training brother (Ryan Phillippe), and the throngs of socialites that surround his every move. He returns from military school to his dysfunctional life and, as in any other coming-of-age story, must decide which road to take. Igby finds drug and sex partners in a pair of older women—college student and part-time caterer Sookie (Claire Danes) and his uncle's (Jeff Goldblum) smack-addicted mistress Rachel (Amanda Peet)—and while he contemplates moving to sunny California, he learns that leaving everything he knows is much harder than it seems. A smart script, sassy characters, and superb acting all around make this one a must for the intellectual pothead. Igby and the blue bloods that orbit him turn on, tune in, and drop out, while quoting philosophers and grumbling about the existential crisis of the upper crust. While Igby really goes through the ringer, it's shamelessly fun to watch.

I Love You, Alice B. Toklas! (1968)

🖋 🍸 👅

🌿 🌿 🌿 🌿 One of the truly essential counterculture films of the sixties stars Peter Sellers as Harold Fine, a lawyer who leaves the "straight" world behind to become a hippie. When Harold meets Nancy (Leigh Taylor-Young), his life changes dramatically. She rolls and smokes a joint, and bakes up a batch of "Alice B. Toklas" brownies. (*The Alice B. Toklas Cookbook*, published in 1954, contains a recipe for "Haschich Fudge" that includes cannabis.) Unwittingly, Harold, his girlfriend Joyce (Joyce Van Patten), and his parents (Jo Van Fleet and Salem Ludwig) all get high on the space cakes. Deciding he's in love with Nancy, Harold leaves Joyce at the altar, and invites Nancy and her "groovy" friends to crash at his pad. But headbanded Harold is too possessive for Nancy; when she calls him "unhip," he fires back, "I've got pot, I've got acid, I've got LSD cubes. I'm so hip it hurts. It's very unhip of you to tell me I'm unhip." He goes back to Joyce, but can't manage to say "I do" the second time around. In cool Los Angeles locales such as Venice Beach and Laurel Canyon, Harold hits the street, exclaiming, "There's got to be something beautiful out there. There's got to be."

I'm Not Rappaport
(1996)

🖋 ⚗️

🌿 🌿 🌿 "Old friends sat on the park bench like bookends." This line from a Simon & Garfunkel song predates the play *I'm Not Rappaport* by nearly twenty years, but it describes the tale of two Central Park old-timers to a tee. In the movie version, Walter Matthau plays Nat, a stodgy geezer whose vivid imagination spurs elaborate storytelling, to the annoyance of his African American buddy Midge (Ossie Davis), who knows full well that it's all fiction. Indeed, Nat makes George Constanza's web of lies look downright childlike, and it's his big mouth that gets him, and by association, Midge, into a heap of trouble. You could blame the pot, which Nat is prescribed for his glaucoma. Only after the two share a joint, a merry-go-round ride, and uncontrollable fits of laughter do things start heading downhill. But between knife fights with drug dealers, legal wrangling with Midge's employer, and one cockamamie story about Nat's shtetl dalliance and subsequent love child living in Israel, the two learn to appreciate life—and each other—rather than just waiting for it to end. "Nostalgia comes around once a year, like Groundhog Day," says Nat in one of his more poignant rants. And while his constant chatter may feel like a heap of blab, this film touches all the right sensory buttons, especially the glorious sights and sounds of Central Park and the city that surrounds it.

Nat: "First you must control and calm yourself. Here, this'll do the trick. Here is some government grass, official legal dope from Uncle Sam. Doctor prescribes, the government pays—two ounces a month for the glaucoma dilates the capillaries, relieves the pressure everywhere."

In the Soup (1992)

A baby-faced Steve Buscemi plays down-on-his-luck loser Adolpho Rollo, an aspiring filmmaker with big dreams who's broke and facing a beat-down by slumlords for being behind on his rent. To scrounge up cash, he sells his script, the dense, unshootable five-hundred-page opus *Unconditional Surrender*, to a shady minor-league gangster and playboy named Joe (we never do learn his last name), played by Seymour Cassel, who promises that he'll finance the project. There's only one catch: Adolpho has to assist in Joe's criminal enterprise, which includes dealing drugs, in order to collect the cash. As an insecure good guy, Adolpho struggles with his new identity, even if he does like the perks, but when his next-door neighbor Angelica (Jennifer Beals) comes into the picture as a potential love interest on screen and in real life, Adolpho

feels an obligation to protect her from Joe's slimy ways and things get ugly. It all culminates in a smoke- and booze-heavy party (during which Joe's much younger girlfriend shotguns a hit off a joint into Adolpho's mouth) followed by one last alley deal involving a dude in a gorilla costume and a midget and a final confrontation between the two characters. Beautifully shot in black-and-white, this is one heady indie flick, and a Sundance winner at that, but pair any Buscemi movie with bong hits and you really can't go wrong.

Joe: "You'll see a gorilla, you'll see a midget. You'll say to that midget, 'Joe Blow from Kokomo.' He gives you something and that's it."

International House (1933)

This slapstick Marx Brothers–style musical comedy stars the infamously tipsy W. C. Fields (Professor Henry Quail), George Burns and Gracie Allen (essentially as themselves), Bela Lugosi (General Petronovich), and Cab Calloway, who provides the musical highlight with a swinging big-band rendition of his viper anthem "Reefer Man." Quail arrives in the town of "Woo Hoo" in China, where Dr. Wong (Edmund Breese) is demonstrating his pre-TV invention called the Radioscope. There's some intrigue as Quail and Petronovich compete for Dr. Wong's attention. But mostly Fields quips his way through the 72-minute film, cigar and drink virtually always in his mouth and hand. In one scene, he smokes the cigar via a long pipelike holder. The musical acts (Rudy Vallee, Baby Rose Marie) appear on the kinescope-quality monitor, sort of a film within the film. Calloway is saved for last, and he aces the tune ("Have you ever met that funny reefer man?"), pushing it to a fever pitch. Also look for the "Girls in Cellophane" dance number featuring thirty female dancers dressed in risqué outfits.

Calloway: "If he trades you dimes for nickels / And calls watermelons pickles / Then you know you're talkin' to that reefer man."

It Runs in the Family
(2003)

🖊 🍾 🌿 🍸 🔪

🌿 🌿 🌿 Three generations of Douglases come together for this feel-good flick about a family with long-festering issues. The Gromberg patriarch, Mitch (Kirk Douglas), and his son Alex (Michael Douglas) constantly bicker, while the younger sons, Asher (Cameron Douglas) and Eli (Rory Culkin), simply don't talk to their parents. Your typical relationship rifts are on full display—Alex occasionally cheats on his wife, Rebecca (Bernadette Peters), Asher is a perpetual screwup who dabbles in DJ-ing, growing and selling pot (in real life, Douglas was busted for selling meth)—and when grandma Evelyn (played by Michael Douglas's real-life mom, Diana Douglas) dies, the chasm grows deeper. Rebecca finds out about her husband's infidelity, Asher and his would-be girlfriend Peg (Michelle Monaghan) are arrested, and Eli starts hanging with the wrong crowd. But as the old saying goes, Daddy knows best and all is forgiven. As sappy family portraits go, this seemingly ultra-liberal clan (judging by their Tribeca apartment and Alex's pro bono legal work) paints a loving picture, but the movie squashes all good vibes with one excessively harsh dorm room bust. To its credit, however, Alex's surprisingly calm reaction to picking up his son from jail is inspiring.

Rebecca: "Do you think Asher was stoned?"

Alex: "No. I don't know, it's hard to tell, isn't it? He's always like that."

Jay and Silent Bob Strike Back (2001)

🖊 🍸 🔪

🌿 🌿 🌿 🌿 A stonerrific road-trip movie that's surprisingly funnier than it deserves to be, *Jay and Silent Bob Strike Back* brings back Kevin Smith's iconic convenience-store dealer buddies (Smith himself as Silent Bob, and sidekick Jason Mewes as Jay) with a convoluted, self-referential plot that manages to wrangle cameos from just about every actor Smith ever directed—from George Carlin (who plays a blow-jobbing hitchhiker) to Matt Damon (as the badass version of himself, blowing people away with a shotgun in the parody movie-within-a-movie *Good Will Hunting II: Hunting Season*). Though the story's secondary to the overall ridiculousness, it boils down to this: Jay and Silent Bob find out the comic book that's inspired by them, Bluntman and Chronic, has been adapted into a movie, currently shooting in L.A. Worried that the film will tarnish their good name and thereby prevent them from getting laid, they head West to shut the production down by any means necessary. Along the way, they get high with Scooby Doo, meet super-sexy leather-clad diamond thieves (played by Shannon Elizabeth and Eliza Dushku), run into Tracy Morgan (playing a fellow member of the duo's drug-dealer's union), kidnap a chimpanzee named Suzanne, get chased down by a pratfalling Will Ferrell, and go tête-à-tête with Luke Skywalker himself, Mark Hamill, using light sabers that double as bongs. High jinks aside, *Jay and Silent Bob* is a movie geek's paradise; even through the smoky haze, catching references to everything from *Star Wars* to *Mission: Impossible* to *The Fugitive* is a trip.

> "The Internet is a communication tool used the world over where people can come together to bitch about movies and share pornography with one another."
>
> —Holden

Kentucky Fried Movie, The (1977)

🖊 🔪 👀

🌿 🌿 🌿 🌿 More a collection of skits than a proper film, *Kentucky Fried Movie* was the brainchild of comedy trio David Zucker, Jerry Zucker, and Jim Abrahams (the guys behind slapstick classics like *Airplane!*, *Top Secret!*, and the *Naked Gun* movies), which means it's all about cheap laughs, pop culture potshots, and outrageous physical satire. In the vein of *Saturday Night Live*, but raunchier than the show ever got (even in its John Belushi heyday), an assorted cast of mostly unknowns brave every racial stereotype and sexual taboo as they poke fun at courtroom-TV dramas, 1970s game shows, blaxploitation flicks, newscasts, commercials, PSAs, and the dull-as-hell science films many kids of the seventies and eighties were forced to sit through in junior high school. Every vignette is roll-on-the-floor hilarious, from the Foxy Brown–inspired "Cleopatra Schwartz" to "High Adventure," a talk show featuring a microphone with a brain to the self-explanatory "Catholic High School Girls in Trouble," but perhaps the movie's best-known bit is its longest, "A Fistful of Yen," which spoofs the popular kung fu movie *Enter the Dragon* and features ridiculous characters with names like Hung Well and Long Wang. Another stony highlight is the "Feel-A-Round" theater sketch, which takes sensory overload to a whole new level. The 1987 film *Amazon Women on the Moon* has a similar format and features slightly updated sketches performed by a slew of A-listers, but there's nothing quite like the pioneering original, which never seems to get old.

Kicked in the Head
(1997)

When Redmond (Kevin Corrigan) fails to deliver a package of cocaine, he's in "deep doo-doo," just like his petty-thief uncle, Sam (James Woods). Redmond claims to be "on a spiritual quest, a voyage of self-discovery, a search for the truth." A fortune cookie prophecy somehow leads him to flight attendant Megan (Linda Fiorentino), whom he has absolutely nothing in common or chemistry with. His gun-wielding friend, Stretch (Michael Rapaport), puts him up and hosts a party where they do lines, smoke joints, and drink cans of Schaefer beer. Interspersed footage of the Hindenburg disaster is supposed to serve as some sort of metaphor for Redmond's life going up in flames. But somehow he manages to survive several shootouts and an attempted overdose on pills. Overacted to a fault (even Woods lays the New Yawk accent on way too thick), you'll feel like you were kicked in the head after watching this nonsensical drug caper.

Stretch (passing a joint): "You, burn this shit down."

Kingpin (1996)

In the Farrelly brothers' inconsistently funny follow-up to the much more raucous *Dumb and Dumber*, Woody Harrelson plays Roy Munson, a bowler who would have been the world's best were it not for his rival, Ernie McCracken (Bill Murray). Early in the film, McCracken throws Munson under the bus as they try to hustle some money by rolling strikes at a shady bowling alley. Years after his career's been ruined due to a destroyed hand that's left him with a hook for a hand, Munson solicits a hot young bowler, Ishmael (played by an up-for-anything Randy Quaid), as his ticket back into the glamorous world of pro bowling. Problem is, Ishmael's Amish. And so, a fish-out-of-Pennsylvania-back-country-water comedy is born, in two distinctive parts—first, when Munson visits the farm to convince Ishmael to join him (and ends up milking a "cow" with only one udder with his mouth) and later, when Ishmael gives in and goes on the road with Munson to earn money to save his family's land, breaking every Amish law along the way (including taking bong rips in the back of moving cars). In typical Farrelly fashion, following the plot can be challenging, depending on your state of mind, but story aside, there are plenty of laughs that don't strain the attention span—Quaid's inane-looking bowl-cut hairdo, for one.

Knocked Up (2007)

🌿🌿🌿🌿🌿 Arguably director Judd Apatow's second-finest film moment (right behind *The 40-Year-Old Virgin*), *Knocked Up* launched stoner poster boy Seth Rogen into the movie star stratosphere as the most unlikely leading man in a romantic comedy. Rogen plays Ben Stone, an overweight and under-motivated Canadian who lives in Los Angeles (illegally, technically) with his four movie-geek roommates (Jonah Hill, Jason Segel, Martin Starr, and Jay Baruchel) and spends his days smoking weed and dreaming up a Web site called "Flesh of the Stars" (never realizing, in typical pothead fashion, that Mr. Skin already exists). He meets Alison Scott (Katherine Heigl), a career-driven E! Entertainment reporter, at a club one night, they get completely sloshed, have sex, and she gets pregnant. Reality sets in swiftly, and their incompatibility becomes a nine-month tug-of-war with brief moments of genuine affection. Meanwhile, Alison's sister, Debbie (played by Apatow's real-life wife Leslie Mann), is going through her own relationship pains as she and husband, Pete (Paul Rudd), come to terms with the daily grind of parenthood. It's a good thing Ben is around to whisk Pete off to Vegas for an eye-opening night of 'shrooms and Cirque Du Soleil.

> **"Why don't you go fuck your fucking bong?"**
>
> **—Alison**
>
> **"I will! I'll do it doggy style, too, for once!"**
>
> **—Ben**

But the unlikely love story and typical Apatowian bromance aside, *Knocked Up* delivers perhaps the most realistic portrayal of stoners in their natural element—pontificating endlessly about movies (*ahem*), doing gas mask hits, making sure to save the bong during an earthquake—and also the most juvenile (look no further than the guys' beard-growing contest and pillow fart challenge). However, the film never lingers in immaturity for too long. Rather, it's smart, sassy, endlessly funny, and unlike most big studio rom-coms, doesn't lose its edge toward the end—the baby delivery scene is proof of that (even though he puts the pot aside for the girl). Throw in cameos by Ryan Seacrest, James Franco, and Steve Carell, along with parents played by Harold Ramis (Ben's dad) and *Growing Pains*'s Mrs. Seaver herself, Joanna Kerns (Alison's mom), and the subversive meets the suburban—you couldn't ask for a more winning stoner combination.

Last Detail, The (1973)

🌿🌿🌿🌿 After building his reputation as a B-movie actor in the sixties, Jack Nicholson became an A-list star in the early seventies on the strength of his roles in *Easy Rider*, *Five Easy Pieces*, and *Carnal Knowledge*. Playing dicks (not cops) became Nicholson's forte, and this Hal Ashby vehicle was a perfect opportunity to ply this stock in trade as a Navy MP. Ordered to deliver a prisoner from Norfolk, Virginia, to the brig in Portsmouth, Maine, Billy "Badass" Buddusky (Nicholson) and "Mule" Mulholl (Otis Young) decide to show Larry Meadows (Randy Quaid) a good time before he's locked up for eight years on a petty robbery charge. Both officers clearly don't like the assignment (Mule moans, "I hate this motherfucking, chickenshit detail") and think Meadows has been railroaded. In New York, the sound of chanting draws the trio into a Buddhist ceremony (Gilda Radner is one of the chanters!). They're invited to a Greenwich Village party, where Buddusky smokes a joint and cigar at the same time, and Meadows brags, "Hey, I smoked grass!" In Boston, Meadows gets laid by a young hooker played by Carole Kane. But the inexorable delivery to Portsmouth is a constant bummer—for everyone involved and the movie. You hope for a surprise ending where the MPs let their captive run free, but sadly, this doesn't happen.

Buddusky: "Heineken's the finest beer in the world, kid. President Kennedy used to drink it."

Last of the Red Hot Lovers (1972)

🌿 🍸 ✂

🌿 🌿 🌿 Alan Arkin plays Barney Cashman, a forty-five-year-old restaurant manager in the midst of a midlife crisis. His wife, Thelma (shown only as a big lump of bedding), bores him. His job leaves him smelling like the fish he handles all week. He's depressed, lonely, and often talks to himself, saying things like, "I read the obituaries every day just for the satisfaction of not seeing my name there." But when a beautiful customer propositions him one day, Barney considers indulging his wild side and having an affair. He brings Elaine (Sally Kellerman), a chain-smoking habitual adulterer, back to his mom's studio apartment, but despite her advances, he can't go through with it. Instead, they bicker, analyze, discuss, but never make it to pillow talk. Barney then meets long-legged aspiring actress Bobbi (Paula Prentiss), a transplant from California who loves to smoke weed and claims she has a doctor's prescription for it (in 1972!). Back at his mom's pad, Bobbi not only gets Barney high for the first time, but walks him through every step of the process ("You're letting it out too quickly, let me see you hold it in your lungs"). He gets wasted off her "quality pot," starts freaking out and yelling, "I hear my eyes blinking!" But even in his stony haze, he figures out that she's a bit of a psycho. Barney's third failed conquest is his wife's friend Charlotte (Sandy Balson), who also gets a private tour of his mom's apartment, but that, too, degenerates into a meltdown. Based on the 1968 play by Neil Simon, the film is as much a statement about "guiltless society" ("you can do anything you want, as long as you're honest about it") as it is a witty New York comedy, and a heady one at that. But in the words of Bobbi the stoner: "Don't fight it, honey. Hang it out for the world to see."

> "I just have to take a few drags before I face the world again. Doctor's orders."
>
> **—Bobbi**

Last Resort (1986)

🌿 🍸 ✂ 🍄 👓

🌿 🌿 A poor man's version of *National Lampoon's Vacation* (or, hell, even Carl Reiner's knee-slapper *Summer Rental*), Zane Buzby's first attempt in the director's chair proves as cheap and agonizing to watch as her bit part in 1982's *Class Reunion*. The leads are just as bad. Chicago chair salesman George Lollar (Charles Grodin) gets suckered into taking his fam to Club Sand, a shitty beach resort in a nebulous location where the showers spew out rusty water, the children get sequestered behind barbed wire, and games like "Show Us Your Breasts" are played by overweight vacationers. Luckily, some of the "resort" staff help George and his wife, Sheila (Robin Pearson Rose), unwind with the Club Sand Special Blend. "You are stoned," George tells his better half. "Oh, thank God," replies Sheila, who further embraces the drug culture on the island by ingesting some 'shrooms (we don't see her take them) and, in turn, makes horse noises for two days. Buzby focuses too much on characters' silly accents and slip-on-the-banana-peel-type gags, and not enough of more relatable (i.e., funny) vacation misadventures to play out.

George (after his first tug off a Special Blend joint): "It's good, it's good."

Life Aquatic with Steve Zissou, The (2004)

🌿 🔫 🍸 ✂ 👓

🌿 🌿 🌿 🌿 Twenty-four years after *Caddyshack* and *Where the Buffalo Roam*, Bill Murray was still smokin' as the title character in this offbeat Wes Anderson comedy inspired by the underwater adventures of Jacques Cousteau. Murray plays an oceanographer searching for the mythical jaguar shark, and is joined on the fantastic voyage by his long-lost son Ned Plimpton (Owen Wilson), a reporter (Cate Blanchett), and his nutty red-capped crew led by the insecure Klaus (Willem Dafoe). An aging stoner, Steve routinely smokes pot, as Ned fills his own pipe with tobacco and Steve's ex, Eleanor

(Anjelica Huston), puffs brown cigarillos. While a variety of conflicts arise, none are too consequential until Ned plunges into the sea. The underwater "Yellow Submarine" finale is colorful, even psychedelic, as their spotted prey circles the vessel. Decades removed from his spectacularly funny early films. Murray's maturity pays off, despite a shortage of belly laughs.

Steve: "Now if you'll excuse me, I'm going to go on an overnight drunk, and in ten days I'm going to set out to find the shark that ate my friend and destroy it. Anyone who wants to tag along is more than welcome."

Love Liza (2002)

Y🍷

🍁🍁🍁 Three years before he won the Academy Award for *Capote*, character actor Philip Seymour Hoffman took center stage as the downward bound Wilson in director Todd Louiso's somber first feature. As Wilson grieves over the suicide of his wife, Liza, he discovers gas fumes can help. Soon he's huffing day and night, hustling gas stations for high-octane petrol. Attempting to hide his new habit, Wilson buys a radio-control-operated model plane that uses its own special fuel. But the walls close in on Wilson, who snarls at his mother-in-law, Mary (Kathy Bates), his friend Denny (Jack Kehler), and gas attendants who refuse his irrational requests. Wilson spends much of the movie on the ground or floor or simply nodding out. He has just about no redeeming qualities. When Wilson's fired, he sets his house ablaze and drives away, presumably looking for his next gas fix.

Mallrats (1995)

🌱 🍷 👓

🍁🍁🍁 There's nothing quite like a trip to the mall to mend a broken heart. That's where life-long buds T.S. (Jeremy London) and Brodie (Jason Lee) retreat in search of camaraderie, cheap thrills and revenge after their girlfriends Brandi (Claire Forlani) and Rene (Shannen Doherty) dump them.

In the process, they wax philosophic about everything from the food court to superheroes, and even succeed in sabotaging a dating show that's staged in the mall (and features Brandi as the eligible suitorette) by enlisting *Star Wars*–obsessed pothead pals Jay (Jason Mewes) and Silent Bob (Kevin Smith) to knock out two of the contestants (by getting them stoned, 'natch).

Half slacker–romantic comedy, half comic-book fan fest (featuring an appearance by none other than comic-book legend Stan Lee), *Mallrats* feels like Smith's teenage movie fantasy realized. But as the follow-up to fan favorite *Clerks* (and an early vehicle for *My Name Is Earl* cohorts Lee and Ethan Suplee), it pales in comparison. While there's plenty of heady pontification, a staple in Smith's films, and an authenticity that comes with the sheer Jersey-ness of it all, much of the plot feels half-baked, and the set looks surprisingly low rent. And the most annoying constant in the movie: excessive yelling, which offers little more than a headache. On the plus side, as a post-script to his role in *Dazed and Confused*, Ben Affleck as Shannon, manager of Fashionable Male, plays another colossal douchebag brilliantly.

Jay to Silent Bob: "OK, lunch box, let's try this again. We tie you to the roof and you jump off and sail like a spitfire passing right over the arch-nemesis La Fours. You then swing up to the stage and knock out the pin. And when that's gone, the stage is trashed and we go smoke a bowl. You got it? Now get your fat ass up there! And dude, don't forget your helmet. Snoogens."

Martin & Orloff (2002)

✏️ 🥄 Y🍷 💉 👓

🍁🍁🍁 Upright Citizens Brigade members Ian Roberts (Martin) and Matt Walsh (Dr. Orloff) star in this zany stoner comedy, which also features UCB's Amy Poehler (Patty) and Matt Besser (Ron). When Martin arrives at Orloff's office for his psychiatry appointment, the fun begins. They head to a softball game, after which Orloff and Keith (Jon Benjamin) share a joint. Patty and Orloff's girlfriend, Kashia (Kim Raver), are strippers; they all attend a play by Dan (David Cross) starring Tina Fey,

Janeane Garofolo, and Rachel Dratch (in cameos). Martin creates characters like Sammy the Sparerib and Eddie the Eggroll at Marketing Force. After Eddie the Eggroll's tragic death, Martin attempts to commit suicide, leading him to Orloff, whose methods are clearly unsound—much like the film's plot, which is as absurd as it gets.

M.A.S.H. (1970)

🌿 🌿 🌿 Any movie that has a dentist named Painless, military doctors mixing cocktails as if in a chemistry lab rather than a pup tent, and football players toking on a jade while on the sidelines can't be all bad. In fact, M.A.S.H., the hysterical 1970 classic by Robert Altman, may be the best antiwar movie ever made. Set in Korea in the early fifties, M.A.S.H. portrays "Hawkeye" Pierce (Donald Sutherland) and "Trapper" John McIntyre (Elliott Gould) as two wartime surgeons with a sense of humor as dry as their martinis. They are the anti-authority, anti-war "pros from Dover" whose banter is unmatched (save Redford and Newman's banter perhaps) in film history. The film's opening scene of copters unloading wounded soldiers would be somber if not for the movie's Oscar Award–winning theme, "Suicide

🌿 FIVE MORE BY ROBERT ALTMAN 🌿

The Long Goodbye (1973): The gaggle of half-naked girls next door are the ones always zonked on pot brownies, but Elliott Gould's mumbling Philip Marlowe in Altman's loose adaptation of Raymond Chandler's twist-laden tale certainly seems like he's been on a perpetual high since 1953. An anachronism in the thick of L.A. at its weirdest, he eventually solves a case involving an alcoholic novelist (Sterling Hayden), his trophy wife (real-life baroness Nina Van Pallandt), a vicious gangster (director Mark Rydell) with Arnold Schwarzenegger as his silent thug, and a once-loyal friend (former Yankees pitcher Jim Bouton), who may or may not have committed suicide.

Nashville (1975): Country music takes center stage as twenty-four characters (some inspired by real-life singers) and multiple story lines converge at a political rally in the heart of Music City. The "Replacement Party" candidate is never shown, but nearly three hours of drama and quality tunes delivered by the likes of Keith Carradine, Shelley Duvall, and Altman-regular Lily Tomlin brighten the screen from beginning to end.

Popeye (1980): For decades, stoners have claimed Popeye's "spinach" was code for weed, and Altman's musical, non-animated version of the comic book classic (starring Robin Williams) may be proof. The seaside town of Sweethaven is a trippy complex of caves and cliff-side shacks surrounded by crystal blue waters with a mysterious creature lurking deep in the sea. Popeye tap-dances and high-kicks his way to Olive Oyl's heart, and kicks Bluto's ass in the process. Was it the green leaf or that pipe he's always smoking?

The Player (1992): In this ultimate Hollywood whodunit, Altman exposes the ugliness of a major film studio when one of its own is suspected of murder. Tim Robbins, Whoopi Goldberg, Fred Ward, Peter Gallagher, and country singer Lyle Lovett propel a cleverly woven plot that results in a movie within a movie about making movies. Pay attention.

A Prairie Home Companion (2006): Altman's last film (released five months before his death) pays tribute to the long-running public radio program by interweaving the show's real-life stars (host Garrison Keillor, sound-effects whiz Tom Keith) with Hollywood A-listers like Virginia Madsen, Meryl Streep, Kevin Kline, Tommy Lee Jones, and Lindsay Lohan. A highlight: Woody Harrelson and John C. Reilly as Lefty and Dusty, singing cowboys with a dopey shtick.

Is Painless," playing over it. In typical Altman fashion, a great ensemble cast—Tom Skerrit as "Duke," Sally Kellerman as the strident "Hot Lips" Houlihan, Robert Duvall as the smarmy Major Burns, and Gary Burghoff's memorable Corporal "Radar" O'Reilly—perform the selfless duties of military surgery interspersed with wacky bits of almost Marx Brothers–like antics. When "regular army" Major Burns hooks up with Hot Lips, a microphone under their cot broadcasts their tryst to the entire camp; when Hot Lips heads to the shower, the playful surgeons and nurses gather round as if in a theater and pull up the tent cover to reveal her in all of her naked glory; and in one of the funniest scenes, precluded by a Last Supper–style send-off, the well-endowed dentist "Painless" (John Schuck), who thinks he has gone gay because he can't get it up, is bedded by gorgeous Lieutenant "Dish" (Jo Ann Pflug), who "saves" him. (Her smile as she flies off in a helicopter the next morning is pure comic genius.) M.A.S.H. would become a hit TV series and may have been the precursor to all of those hospital dramas that came later. When the surgeons enter their tented hospitals, they are all business, great surgeons somehow caught up in the terror of war, and the only way to make sense of it (a la Catch-22) is to make fun. The movie culminates in a football game between two surgical divisions where, in order to win, the M.A.S.H. unit drugs the opposing team's star player. All in all, it is one bit of fun after another that makes you forget the horrors of war.

Meet Bill (2007)

Meet Bill (Aaron Eckhart), a banker who works for his wife's (Elizabeth Banks) father and hates his life. He's an executive vice president, a trophy title and job that nobody really respects, but Bill has more to offer, and on a chance meeting with the principal of his old private school, he's roped into becoming a mentor to a student. It just so happens it's someone he met while in the bathroom, The Kid (played by Logan Lerman), who came in to dump his weed and avoid getting busted by that same principal. Bill covered for him, and it's no surprise in this predictable film that the two seem destined for deep bonding. Meanwhile, Bill's wife is cheating on him, which destroys the life he's known. To regain some self-esteem, Bill starts swimming and improving his health, he cuts back on the candy bars, and starts smoking weed. It really does mellow him out and he finds the courage to quit his job and grow up. A super hot clerk (Jessica Alba) who works at a lingerie store in the mall also helps Bill realize that the small things are what really count, like knowing what kind of underwear a girl likes, prompting the weirdly wise-beyond-his-years Kid to point out: "The only way to get the old one back, is to get a new one."

Bill: "They hate that I'm working at their bank. I hate that I'm working at their bank."

Meet the Parents (2000)

In what seems like a never-ending barrage of faux pas upon faux pas, *Meet the Parents* is one of the most uncomfortable films to sit through, stoned or sober. It's likely because the story, which pits boyfriend against future father-in-law, is your worst nightmare played out turn by torturous turn. Greg Focker (Ben Stiller) is a male nurse planning to propose to his girlfriend, Pam (Teri Polo), but not without the blessing of her ex-CIA dad, Jack Byrnes (Robert De Niro)—a guy whose motto is "Under my roof it's my way or the Long Island Expressway." Indeed, a trip to the Byrneses' home goes from bad to worse almost as soon as Greg pulls up in a green rental (they say geniuses pick green—but Greg didn't pick the car), but it's his string of complicated ridiculous lies (that he pumped milk from a cat, for example) and

plain old bad decisions (like leaving an engagement ring in his checked luggage, which the airline loses) that eventually do him in. He gets along with a little help from ancillary characters like Pam's former boyfriend Kevin (Owen Wilson), an investment banker who models his life after Jesus', and her pot-smoking little brother Denny (Jon Abrahams), whose pipe Jack finds but blames on Greg. (Following a cringe-worthy exchange about the true meaning of "Puff the Magic Dragon," this all makes perfect sense.) There's little relief from Greg's carnival of misery, but plenty of laughs throughout, which is something that can't be said for the movie's sequel, *Meet the Fockers* (starring Dustin Hoffman and Barbra Streisand as Greg's parents). Stick with the original, which is a true classic and one of De Niro's finest (and certainly funniest) performances.

> "It's a sculpture I found in Greg's jacket."
>
> **—Denny**

> "This is no sculpture, Denny. This is a device for smoking marijuana."
>
> **—Jack**

Men Who Stare at Goats, The (2009)

What if the Army let its macho guard down and allowed for free thought? You'd have the New Earth Army, which is the focus of Grant Haslov's oddball comedy starring George Clooney, Ewan McGregor, Jeff Bridges, and Kevin Spacey. Part *Catch-22*, part *Jacob's Ladder*, *Goats* follows newsman Bob Wilton (McGregor) on a remarkable journey that begins in Kuwait, where he meets Lyn Cassady (Clooney), a retired New Earther. In flashbacks, we learn how Bill Django (Bridges) founded the division largely utilizing Zen concepts of mind power by training soldiers to be "warrior monks" and Jedis who could literally walk through walls. This theme is often played for laughs, with numerous pratfalls, as Bridges channels his inner "Dude." But when a young recruit commits suicide after being heavily dosed with LSD by Django's rival Larry Hooper (Spacey), Django is drummed out of the ranks. Lyn and Bob head to Iraq, where they're kidnapped, but ultimately find Hooper's base (and Django) in the desert, complete with a barn full of goats. Lyn and Django spike the camp's powdered eggs and water with acid, setting off much hilarity and wackiness, and ultimately saving the day and this trippy movie.

Modern Times (1936)

🌿🌿🌿🌿🌿 The last hurrah of Charlie Chaplin's legendary Little Tramp character, this film helped convince the House Un-American Activities Committee that Chaplin, the director and star, was a Communist, because of its obviously subversive sentiments: sympathy for the needy, support for organized labor, and its not-so-implicit critique of a system that, as described by Anatole France, "prohibits the wealthy as well as the poor from sleeping under the bridges, from begging in the streets, and from stealing bread." What the red-baiters apparently didn't mind was Chaplin's perspective on blow: After the Tramp is imprisoned for inadvertently leading a Communist parade, he ends up in a prison mess, where a search is underway for smuggled "nose powder" (as the title card puts it). After a fellow con furtively empties his coke into a salt shaker, the Tramp unknowingly sprinkles it all over his plate, bread, and neck. Wired, he walks in circles. And when other fellow cons take their guards hostage, the newly emboldened Tramp is able to overcome them and thwart the escape attempt. A hero, he's freed with a letter of commendation, which he uses to get a job at a shipyard, where he promptly sinks a massive ship. Always the ironist, Chaplin gave us the Tramp, who, when high, was a much more useful member of society.

Myra Breckinridge (1970)

🌿🌿🌿 You can't blame this campy, nonsensical flick on a bad acid trip. *Myra Breckinridge* was adapted from the popular Gore Vidal novel, which, at the time of its 1968 release, was hailed as a ground-breaking treatise on feminism and the sexual revolution. It was also deemed pornographic in some circles, and the film originally earned an X rating. That said, you won't see any full-frontal Raquel Welch, who plays tranny Myra (her goal: "the destruction of the last vestigial traces of traditional manhood"), or Mae West as Leticia or Farrah Fawcett as Mary Ann or Tom Selleck, who also makes his film debut, playing a guy simply known as "stud." What you do get is an assortment of raging parties—the kind where people sit around naked playing patty-cake, paint on each other, pass out in the bathroom—some fabulous dresses, ridiculous dialogue ("Where are my tits?"), lots of boob and ass shots, as well as quick cutaways to iconic scenes from Hollywood classics like *Something's Got to Give* and *The Pride of St. Louis*. As for the plot, good luck trying to follow it as the film moves from a stoned surgery to the Buck Loner acting academy to a supper club, the dentist's chair, and back to the creepy sex-change hospital (or getting that Shirley Temple song out of your head: "You've got to S-M-I-L-E to be H-A-double-P-Y!")

Naked in New York (1993)

🌿🌿🌿 Every college town has that guy who graduates but sticks around, not wanting to let go of what's familiar, convenient, and, perhaps most importantly, youthful. As Jake, an aspiring playwright who still lives in Cambridge, Massachusetts, Eric Stoltz is a guy stuck in a creative rut but thriving in the relationship department. That is, until his girlfriend Joanne (*Weeds* star Mary-Louise Parker) takes a job working for a hotshot photographer. Jake gets his big break, too, when his best friend Chris (Ralph Macchio) hands his play to an influential Broadway producer. But once he reaches New York, Jake learns the hard way that his words aren't precious, nor is his vision. Despite his objection, well-known actress Dana Coles (Kathleen Turner) is cast for the lead and, after she smokes him out, she puts the moves on Jake big time. Chris, whose homosexuality is obvious to everyone but Jake, also tries to plant one on his best friend, and the convergence of all these issues naturally derails the production and forces him to take a long look at himself. Much of the movie is told as narration through Jake's own recollections, with the occasional trippy daydream and flashback from infancy thrown in for good measure. And while the comedy may be dark, the film is robust and colorful, and that contradiction makes an otherwise predictable story slightly more interesting.

Napoleon Dynamite
(2004)

🌿🌿🌿🌿 Gloriously nerd-tastic from beginning to end, Jon Heder plays the uber-geeky protagonist, a friendless, moon boot–wearing, unicorn-obsessed loser who lives with his even dorkier brother, Kip (Aaron Ruell), at their grandmother's house in Preston, Idaho. Napoleon is the school joke, but when he befriends new kid Pedro (Efren Ramirez) and helps him run for class president, things start looking up—Napoleon amazes his classmates with a hip-hop number he learned by watching a VHS of *D-Qwon's Dance Grooves* and eventually connects with the equally awkward Deb (Tina Majorino), his only hope for a future girlfriend. Meanwhile, when Grandma takes a nasty spill on the sand dunes, the boys' uncle Rico (John Gries) comes to live with them and life gets just a little more miserable. There's not much plot to develop here; rather, *Napoleon Dynamite* feels like a series of absurdities—from their pet llama, Tina, to Kip's online relationship with the bootylicious La Fawnduh—each more hilariously painful than the next. No wonder this low-budget flick became an instant pop culture phenomenon and an unexpected box-office hit. And while many have said that the first viewing left them scratching their heads, it's since been widely embraced by stoners, mainly because of its constant references to food, be it Kip's nachos with a mound of cheese, Uncle Rico's steak, the Tater Tots Napoleon stashes in his pants side pocket, or Grandma's go-to quick fix, "a dang quesadilla," illa, illa.

🌿 SHWAYZE'S STONY MOVIE PICKS 🌿

SoCal rocker Shwayze doesn't recommend getting high for every movie. "Sometimes when you're so stoned, it can work against you," he says. "You get too critical and start thinking, 'That fool's overacting,' or 'That shit's fake.'" That said, comedies are usually a safe bet and here are Shwayze's top five.

Anchorman: The Legend of Ron Burgundy (2004): "*Anchorman*'s a classic for me because I went to college in San Diego and it's where I started smoking weed. Ron Burgundy is the sickest of all time. There are so many amazing scenes, like when they break into 'Afternoon Delight,' or the fight between the TV stations, and there's this one part—which may be a deleted scene—where they're all doing this gangsta walk down the stairs in slow motion and Ron sneezes. It's, like, the funniest thing ever."

Half Baked (1998): "Watching *Half Baked* stoned is pretty much a must. It's got Dave Chappelle and some great cameos. He does quit smoking weed in the end because it's either pot or the pussy, and I think if I were in that dilemma, I would have to make the same decision. I love being high, but I think the latter gets me higher."

The 40-Year-Old Virgin (2005): "*40-Year-Old Virgin* is classic Steve Carell, but my favorite scene is in the very beginning when he's trying to pee but he has a boner and can't get it in the bowl—every man can relate to that, trying to get that angle just right."

Napoleon Dynamite (2004): "The first time I saw *Napoleon Dynamite*, I didn't really like it. I went in there so baked, and I was like, this shit is so whack! I felt bad because my friends were saying it's the sickest, funniest movie ever. I think it was the hype, but now I love it."

Don't Be a Menace to South Central While Drinking Your Juice in the Hood (1996): "I love *Pootie Tang*, *White Chicks*, and *Undercover Brother*, but *Don't Be a Menace to South Central While Drinking Your Juice in the Hood* is amazing. Like *Scary Movie*, it's a parody, but of all those ghetto movies like *Boyz N the Hood* and *Menace II Society*. It's got all the Wayans—Shawn, Damon, Marlon, Keenan—and honestly, it's the funniest thing I've ever seen!"

National Lampoon's Senior Trip (1995)

🌿🌿 Those wacky folks at *National Lampoon* proved, yet again, why their brand of comedy is a teacher's worst nightmare with this late grunge-era high school caper. It all starts when class stoners Reggie (Rob Moore) and Dags (Jeremy Renner) throw a day party at Principal Moss's (Matt Frewer) house. Preppy ass-kisser Steve (Sergio Di Zio) ruins the fun by blabbing and the teens are given detention. Their punishment also includes an assignment: to write the president and tell him what's wrong with our educational system. Lo and behold, the letter gets his attention, and the whole motley crew is invited to Washington for a face-to-face with the leader of the free world. With a bus driver who goes by the name Red (Tommy Chong), likes to hit the bong on the highway, and provides the kids with horse tranquilizer to knock out Principal Moss, the trip turns into a nonstop party that doesn't let up once they reach their destination. Reg gets even more wasted when cops pull the bus over and he eats almost an ounce of weed. But as dumb as these slackers seem on the surface, they're smart enough to foil a sinister plot by their congressman to embarrass the president and push his own agenda. Endlessly silly, right down to Kevin McDonald's role as a psycho Trekkie hell-bent on sabotaging their senior trip, the troublemakers rule in this screwy flick. Now that's vindication.

Reggie: "Long live the dope king, man!"

National Lampoon's Stoned Age (2007)

🌿🌿🌿 Not to be confused with 1994's *The Stoned Age*, the National Lampoon film of the same name (also known as *Homo Erectus*), is a kooky, raunchy, boob-heavy prehistoric romp that tells the story (in today speak) of Ishbo (Adam Rifkind, who wrote and directed the movie), the tribe nerd and inventor, whose stud brother Thudnik "clubs" and marries Fardart (Ali Larter), the girl of Ishbo's dreams. David Carradine plays the boys' father and uncle in a double role, Talia Shire is Mom, and Ron Jeremy is tribesman Oog. But perhaps most hilarious is the duo of Zig (*Detroit Rock City's* Giuseppe Andrews) and Zog (Miles Dougal), the clan stoners, who "discovered a weed that when smoked, opened their minds to new levels of observation." They fashion a giant pipe out of tree bark that, when lit, gives new meaning to the term "torching the bowl." Gary Busey plays Krutz, a caveman from a rival tribe who incites war with the tribe and takes Fardart prisoner. Ishbo attempts to rescue her, only to be caught (and bathed) by a bikinied band of lesbian babes with names like Titsia, Ovaria, and Estrogena, and later rebuffed by his love and his tribe. Survivor-man, he's not, but as cavemen go, Ishbo's a brainy buffoon who's good for a laugh or two.

National Lampoon's Vacation (1983)

🌿🌿🌿🌿🌿 Nobody does physical comedy quite like Chevy Chase. Be it *Fletch*, *Caddyshack*, or the first installment of National Lampoon's *Vacation* series, he's the kind of actor that inspires crack-ups with a simple lift of the brow or turn of phrase. And it's as Clark W. Griswold, the classic clueless patriarch of America's most hapless family, that Chase's sheer comedic brilliance is put on full display. The Griswolds' disastrous road trip from Chicago to Los Angeles, where Wally World awaits, starts to go south before they even leave town. Clark gets gypped by a local car dealer (played by a young Eugene Levy) and the foursome has to settle for a subpar station wagon to trek the 2,400 miles. This is 1983, mind you; pre-GPS, Google maps, and cell phones, and even credit cards were still a novelty. So it's no wonder everything that could possibly go wrong, does:

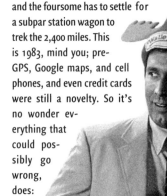

Aunt Edna and her equally stinky dog jump on board for a ride to Phoenix (neither makes it); wrong turns lead Clark, Ellen (Beverly D'Angelo), and their kids, Rusty (Anthony Michael Hall) and Audrey (Dana Barron), into the ghetto and leave them stranded in the middle of the desert; the family runs out of money; and desperation reaches its bitter end when they arrive to find Wally World closed. (Take a moment for another "Thank God we have Internet.") Of course, all the fun is in getting there. Number one: seeing Clark drool and babble over a babe in a Ferrari convertible (Christie Brinkley). Two: meeting Eddie, Clark's brother, and his clan of future rejects, especially the teenage bad-girl Vicki, who pulls out a shoebox full of fluffy green buds and later slips a joint to her cousin Audrey. Three: the dramatic finale—an amusement park taken hostage means all the roller-coaster rides your stomach can handle! Amazingly, even the future *Vacation* movies (*European*, *Christmas*, *Vegas*), which feature a revolving cast of Audreys and Rustys, aren't nearly as painful as most sequels. You can thank Chevy Chase for that rare pleasure, though we can't say the same of *Fletch Lives*.

Audrey: "Don't get offended, but being a farmer is not too cool, you know?"

Vicki: "Oh yeah, well, how cool is this?" (pulls out a shoebox full of pot)

Next Friday (2007)

 For the sequel to stoner-hit *Friday*, Craig (Ice Cube) moves on up to Rancho Cucamonga to live with his blunt-smoking Uncle Elroy (Don "D. C." Curry) and cousin Day-Day (Mike Epps). Smokey's in rehab and Craig's still jobless. Like the original, most of the action takes place in a small area—in this case, a standard-issue suburban cul-de-sac. Expecting to leave the crime and danger of South Central behind, Craig finds new problems—basically with the Hispanic gangbangers living across the street. It's Craig versus Joker (a hilarious Jacob Vargas) in an extended fight scene that includes Roach (Justin Pierce) subduing Chico the pit bull with a pot brownie. At the end, Craig and his dad (John Witherspoon) return home to the 'hood

for new adventures (see *Friday After Next*). While the new characters add to the family story line, Chris Tucker's Smokey is sorely missed.

Elroy: "I'm about to show you who the real Puff Daddy is!"

Nice Dreams (1981)

Cheech & Chong's third movie (directed by Tommy Chong) is just as zany as the first two. They sell pot-sicles out of an ice cream truck. Cops stake them out, but are too dumb to bust them. Sergeant Stedanko (Stacy Keach) is back from *Up in Smoke*, but he's too busy testing out weed and turning into a lizard to bother with police duties. In one scene, Chong fills up a huge bag of weed he takes from a grow room. In another, they do coke in a Chinese restaurant where Chong is mistaken for Jerry Garcia. Howie (Paul Reubens as Pee-wee Herman) takes their money. They follow him to Casa Del Wackos—an insane asylum run by Timothy Leary. Confined to a straitjacket and padded cell, Cheech Marin begs for the key. "You sure you want to be free?" Leary, playing himself, asks. "Stick out your tongue." He doses both of them, and Cheech imagines Hendrix playing "Purple Haze" and Chong becoming a cop and they end up as male dancers Maui and Wowie. Huh?

Stedanko: "The only way to catch a doper is when you yourself become a smoker. Your surest way to make them bleed is when you bust their ass and steal their weed."

Night Patrol (1984)

At best it's a poor man's *Naked Gun*, but stand-up hack Murray Langston pretty obviously co-wrote this gay- and fart-joke-filled script as a platform to exploit his *Gong Show* act, the Unknown Comic. Langston plays Melvin White, a piss-poor excuse for a Los Angeles cop who, after a series of on-the-job fuckups, gets paired with an oversexed partner (Pat Paulsen) for the agonizing overnight shift. They frequent filthy diners where roaches (bugs and marijuana butts) are everywhere and get fooled by suspects who distract the 5-o by getting them ripped and sending them off on a munchie bender. White moonlights at comedy clubs as the Unknown Comic, seeking fame and fortune. The movie is all over the place, which has both its charms and annoyances, but watch for a young Andrew Dice Clay, who cameos as a struggling comic named Tony Maroni.

Melvin (after taking a few pulls from a joint): "I don't feel a thing except maybe a little hungry."

Nine to Five (1980)

🌿🌿🌿🌿 The ultimate women's stoner movie stars Jane Fonda (Judy), Lily Tomlin (Violet), and Dolly Parton (Doralee) as secretaries at Consolidated Companies who plot against their male-chauvinist-pig boss Franklin Hart Jr. (Dabney Coleman) after having "an old-fashioned ladies pot party" in Doralee's apartment. Violet's son supplies that joint that has the co-workers giggling, munching, and conspiring to turn the tables on Hart. "This is really good pot—what did you say it was called?" Judy asks. "Maui Wowie," Violet informs. "Primo." Produced by Fonda (in 2009, Parton wrote new songs and produced a Broadway version of the movie), the game-changing feminist film succeeded by demanding equal rights for women in offices long dominated by male executives. They kidnap Hart and establish new policies that are praised by Hart's boss, Sterling Hayward, ultimately leading to Violet's long-awaited promotion. You go, girls!

Doralee: "Is that one of them marijuana cigarettes?"

Numb (2007)

🌿🌿🌿 Pot isn't for everybody, especially those prone to long bouts of depression and anxiety. Successful screenwriter Hudson (Matthew Perry)—the kind of guy whose idea of fun is watching the *Star Wars* trilogy with the commentary on—learns that firsthand when he takes one too many hits off a joint and unhinges "an already vulnerable brain" that's sent "into the bottom of the abyss."

> "My theory was simple: If smoking marijuana triggered my problem, smoking even more would reverse it, shocking my synapses back to normal. There's no science behind this, just gut feeling mixed with sheer desperation. Was I scared? Absolutely. Would it work? It had to."
>
> **—Hudson**

Hudson, plagued with inner turmoil stemming from difficult relationships with his mother and brother, is paralyzed by fear of an unknown future and left to wonder if he'll ever find somebody to love. Then along comes Sara (Lynn Collins), who seems up for the challenge of handling Hudson's acute depersonalization disorder, until he screws it all up. "She deserves a normal person, not a kleptomaniac freak show," he tells his best friend and writing partner, Tom (Kevin Pollak). The process of coming to terms with his debilitating detachment eventually leads Hudson back to weed, as he takes on a five-foot, six-tube bong in hopes that it will reverse his condition. "Is that all you got?" he screams following one monster hit that knocks him to the floor. With his brain chemistry sufficiently altered, Hudson soon finds some clarity (after another shoplifting experience and subsequent arrest) and new hope for a life with Sara. This guy's a downer, no doubt—as is the film.

Office Space (1999)

🌿 🌿 🌿 🌿 The first feature film by *Beavis and Butt-Head*–creator, Mike Judge, wasn't exactly a box-office smash when it came out, despite having *Friends*-era Jennifer Aniston in the lead female role, but in the decade since, it's gained enormous popularity as a cult hit. Its statement on the monotony of an unfulfilling cubicle job, and one employee's sudden pang of rebelliousness, provides a taste of liberation that few, if any of us, will experience in our lifetime. Peter Gibbons (Ron Livingston) despises his irksome boss at Initech, decides that he

just doesn't give a shit about his software position, and conspires with two laid-off staffers to embezzle money from the company in tiny increments. He fights the evil corporation in other ways, too—like beating the fax machine to a pulp with a baseball bat. But when his unfiltered sit-down with the efficiency experts gets him promoted, things take an unexpected turn for the better. That's what makes *Office Space* so instantly endearing—that, despite its grim setting, it's astoundingly Zen. So why don't you go ahead and pack that bowl, and try taking a hit

every time Lumbergh says "TPS reports." You'll be spaced out in no time.

Peter Gibbons: "So I was sitting in my cubicle today, and I realized, ever since I started working at Initech, every single day of my life has been worse than the day before it. So that means that every single day that you see me, that's on the worst day of my life."

Out-of-Towners, The (1999)

🍷 👅

🌿 🌿 🌿 In this modern-day retelling of Neil Simon's 1970 comedy (which starred Jack Lemmon and Sandy Dennis), Steve Martin plays Henry, an advertising executive from Ohio who travels to New York for a job interview. His wife Nancy (Goldie Hawn) tags along at the last minute for what turns out to be a frustrating trip. The airline loses their luggage, they get mugged, thrown out of their hotel, and are forced to spend the night in Central Park, where Henry is arrested for relieving himself. Nancy blackmails the hotel manager (played by John Cleese in a virtual reprise of his *Fawlty Towers* role) into paying her husband's bail and comping the presidential suite. While in lockup, a fellow inmate offers Henry an "aspirin" to shut him up, which ends up being some sort of hallucinogen. With two hours to go before his big interview, Henry prances around singing *Hair*'s "Aquarius/Let the Sunshine In" then heads to the appointment, but finds himself paralyzed in the elevator. Fortunately, Nancy is there to hold his hand and he soon realizes that their trying twenty-four hours together reaffirmed more than twenty years of marriage. Ultimately, it's an uplifting love story accented by Martin's quirky brand of physical comedy, but the laughs are few and far in between.

Henry: "Is there a playground or something nearby, say maybe with swings or monkey bars?"

Outside Providence
(1999)

🌿 🌿 🌿 🌿 🌿 After Tim (Shawn Hatosy) crashes his smoke-filled car, Dunphy (Alec Baldwin as Tim's dad) ships him off to boarding school. Tim is not the brightest bulb, but he manages to catch the attention of Brown-bound Jane (Amy Smart). Their relationship is stony sweet (he gives her dental roach clips for her birthday!). Back home in Pawtucket, Rhode Island, Tim's buds party on without him. Drugs Delaney (Jon Abrahams) is the leader of the pothead pack, but he also get into car accidents, the last of which proves fatal. Early on, Tim drops a plastic bong on the kitchen floor while Dunphy and his Archie Bunker–like friends are playing cards. "What in the world is this contraption?" Dunphy asks. Tim's wheelchair-bound little brother Jackie (Tommy Bone) tries to cover for him: "It's a horn." Dunphy's friend Joey (George Wendt of *Cheers*)—who later reveals he's gay to his shocked friends—shoots back: "OK, Satchmo, why don't you play us a few notes?" Tim turns the bong into a kazoo before Dunphy silences him: "All right, assbag, enough of that nonsense." At school, the stoners show Tim a novel way to get high using a ten-gallon drum, a huge industrial bowl, and a tube. Despite constant run-ins with school official Funderburk (Timothy Crowe), Tim manages to graduate. Written by Peter and Bobby Farrelly and set in 1974, this is the New England brothers' true stoner movie. Plus, the soundtrack rivals *Dazed and Confused*—not one song (from "No Matter What" to "Rock the Boat") hits a wrong note.

> "I always do better at studying when I'm stoned. It does something to my brain cells, really."
>
> **—Tim**

Owl and the Pussycat, The (1970)

Barbra Streisand stars as Doris, a yappy New York City call girl and wannabe actress who gets thrown out of her apartment and decides to attach herself to a neighbor, aspiring novelist Felix (George Segal). She barges into his pad at two in the morning, and out of annoyance (and perhaps a little pity), Felix allows her to stay over. When her incessant hollering gets them both thrown out of the building, they shack up (literally) at Felix's friend's place and then go their separate ways. But Felix can't seem to get Doris out of his mind, especially upon seeing her image on a poster advertising an X-rated movie called *Cycle Sluts*. The two reconnect at Felix's fiancée's parents' house, where Doris persuades Felix to smoke a joint and take a bath with her. Their stony serenity is interrupted, however, when the Weyderhauses unexpectedly come home. "They're really very understanding," Felix mumbles in the tub, baked out of his mind. "Just be yourself." Despite the chaos that ensues whenever these two are together, Doris and Felix drop their façades and fall for each other, proving that opposites really do attract.

> "I know what that is."
>
> **—Felix**
>
> "This will put you in a very good mood."
>
> **—Doris**
>
> "Yes, well, I don't want to be a party to this."
>
> **—Felix**
>
> "Oh, don't be such a tight-ass."
>
> **—Doris**

At the time of its release, *The Owl and the Pussycat* was deemed downright smutty, thanks to Doris's penchant for cursing, revealing lingerie, and overall sass. Credit comedy icon Buck Henry, who pushed the envelope with his adaptation of the Bill Manhoff play for the screen, and also Streisand, whose sassy performance, complete with that undeniable New Yawk accent, is surprisingly believable—if only all that shrieking weren't such a buzz kill.

Parenthood (1989)

Chronicling the intersecting day-to-day lives of four generations of the Buckman

family through good times and bad, *Parenthood* has all the sweetness of a kids' movie, but with distinct adult appeal. Case in point: The word (and concept) "amalgam" is whipped out in the first scene, at a baseball game no less! Granted, a film with such stellar credentials (it was written and directed by Ron Howard and stars Steve Martin) is bound to be smart and funny, but underneath the rated-G exterior are fully developed, ridiculously quirky characters that all seem to share a rebellious streak—whether that be jaded Aunt Helen (Dianne Wiest), who proudly declares she was at Woodstock, or overwhelmed dad Gil (Martin), who chastises his wife (Mary Steenburgen) for having smoked too much pot in college, or his bad-seed brother, Larry (Tom Hulce), a lifelong gambling addict who named his afro'd son Cool. Rounding out the all-star ensemble cast are: Rick Moranis as Gil's uptight brother-in-law, Jason Robards as the Buckman patriarch, and Keanu Reeves as a burn-out race-car driver who marries Helen's daughter Julie (Martha Plimpton) and breaks through to her confused younger brother, Garry (played by a very young Joaquin Phoenix, but credited as Leaf Phoenix). Even Grandma (Helen Shaw) kills it with more than her share of zingers. It's the quintessential feel-good movie complete with a Randy Newman soundtrack that, if it doesn't induce nausea by the umpteenth refrain of "I Love to See You Smile," is sure to spark some serious permagrin.

Gil Buckman: "She smoked grass!"

Karen Buckman: "Gil! I never smoked when I was pregnant."

Gil: "Yeah, but in college you were like a chimney. I thought you were gonna join a reggae band!"

Party Girl (1995)

✎ 🍸

🌿 🌿 🌿 *Party Girl* starts promisingly enough. During the opening credits, Mary (Parker Posey) takes a hit off a joint while handling door duties at an underground New York City party. She seems like a cool, chill chick—the cops don't faze her (she even throws out the medical-marijuana argument—a year before Proposition 215 was passed in California), neither does a brief stint in jail. But you soon realize that this smartass, attention-craving, fashion-savvy New Yorker is little more than your typical Generation-X slacker. She cares about one thing: partying (hence, the title). Things like paying the rent are annoying inconveniences in her world ("Life goes by so fast, what's the point?"). But there is a certain *je ne sais quoi* about Mary; the sweetness of an orphan perhaps (her mom died in a DWI accident, so Mary only takes public transportation), that prompts her godmother to give her a job at the library. Lo and behold, Mary's actually good at it (when she's not having after-hours sex among the stacks), to the surprise of her club-hopping, pot smoking friends, who throw her a massive birthday party toward the movie's end ("We still have

to hang that piñata and make the hash brownies"). The buzz kill, unfortunately, is in the film's lame dialogue, but it's worth sitting through just to get to the scene where Mary goes on a weed-fueled productivity binge in the library.

Mary: "I would like a nice, powerful, mind-altering substance. Preferably one that will make my unborn children grow gills."

PCU (1994)

🌿 🍸 ✂

🌿 🌿 🌿 This uninspired rip-off of *Animal House* was itself later copied by *Van Wilder*, proving that what goes around in stoner comedies, inevitably comes around. The Pit is Port Chester University's reigning party destination, home to top dog "Droz" (Jeremy Piven) and his rag-tag band of politically incorrect stoners. When the school prez (Jessica Walter) threatens the Pit (they owe $7,500), Droz decides it's time to party. George Clinton and Parliament Funkadelic tear the roof off the sucker, helping raise the funds and thus preventing conservative rival Rand (David Spade) from taking over the Pit. Jon Favreau (Gutter) and Jake Busey (Mersh) portray stereotypical waste-oid stoners, and there's a rare onscreen game of Frisbee golf.

> "Have a bong hit. Just one little binger can brighten up your day."
> —Mersh to Gutter

Pee-wee's Big Adventure (1985)

🍸 ✂

🌿 🌿 🌿 🌿 Tim Burton's feature film debut predated *Beetlejuice* by three years, but in many ways, it's just as wacky. Starring eighties Saturday morning icon Pee-wee Herman (Paul Reubens), who made skinny pants fashionable long before most emo kids were born, the story revolves around the eccentric man-child's cross-country search for his beloved bike. After the shiny red cycle, complete with James Bond–like add-ons, is stolen, Pee-wee visits a psychic who tells him it's at The Alamo in the basement, and so begins his hitch-hiking adventure. Along the way to San Antonio, he meets a host of random characters, including a waitress, a fugitive, and a biker gang, all of whom Pee-wee befriends with his quirky charm. He also has his share of scares, like a ride with ghostly truck driver Large Marge and one creepy dream of his bike being stripped and melted by scary clowns in doctors' jackets. But in Pee-wee's world, everything comes in vivid colors and hearty laughs, and there's plenty of both on his Big Adventure. Whether it's his stoner dream house full of toys, gadgets, and out-there tchotchkes, or watching the sunrise from inside the mouth of a tourist-stop dinosaur, his mad dash through the Warner Bros. film studios, or his dance atop the biker bar to the tune of "Tequila," Pee-wee will bring out the hee hee in even the most stodgy adult.

Pee-wee to Dottie: "You don't wanna get mixed up with a guy like me. I'm a loner, Dottie. A rebel."

Peggy Sue Got Married (1986)

"Reunions do funny things to people," Peggy Sue Kelcher (Kathleen Turner) says, foreshadowing her fate seconds before she faints in front of several hundred of her former classmates. Funny things like sending you twenty-five years into the past. In 1985, Peggy Sue is a soon-to-be-divorcée disillusioned with her life and cheating husband Charlie (Nicolas Cage), whom she married just out of high school. So when she wakes up in 1960, she grabs that do-over opportunity with all her contemporary-woman gusto. Peggy Sue hooks up with Michael Fitzsimmons (Kevin J. O'Connor), the brooding beatnik she used to swoon over (after the two smoke a joint under the stars), she makes nice with the class nerd she used to mock, and she imparts just enough modern-day wisdom to her naïve pre–JFK assassination friends to make a small but lasting impact. But it's a rekindled relationship with Charlie that throws Peggie Sue off track, and completely screws with her head. Directed by Francis Ford Coppola and nominated for three Academy Awards, this is a higher-level chick flick, complete with moody orchestral score and plenty of tear-jerking soliloquies. It's no Back to the Future, but for the girl's version, Peggy Sue is one good hang.

Walter: "The best thing about being a dentist: pure pharmaceutical grade. A couple lines of this and I could drill my own teeth."

☘ Q & A: CYPRESS HILL'S B-REAL ☘

Movies and comedy influence music, as is the case with L.A. hip-hop legends Cypress Hill, who took a few pages out of Cheech & Chong's scripts in order to create their pot-fueled group. Cypress Hill's frontman B-Real explains.

Reefer Movie Madness: Cypress Hill appeared on the *Scarface* video game. Did the movie have a big impact on you personally?

B-Real: Being of Cuban and Mexican descent, I can relate to the lifestyle because I've seen a lot of it. But *Scarface* is like an idea to a lot of kids that come up in hip-hop. Tony Montana [Al Pacino] started from nothing, he hustled his way to the top and he did what he had to do to get there. For a lot of rappers, that's how they feel. But it's also saying, be careful what you ask for. You gotta be accountable for the things you did to get there. Obviously at the end, Tony gets killed due to the shit he was doing. The underlying message to that story is: If you've got a hustler spirit and want to win, you'll go out there and work as hard as you have to work to get where you want to go. There's gonna be obstacles that you might have to go around, but you gotta keep pushin' forward no matter what. The dude was a drug dealer, he wasn't a positive role model, but people still took something positive from it, and that's cool.

RMM: What do Cheech and Chong mean to you?

B-Real: We tried to take the spirit they had going in their comedy shows and movies and bring it to our records. They have a chemistry— they were doing the kind of comedy nobody else would dare to do. They put their careers on the line for it. I'm sure that's eventually why Cheech [Marin] kind of broke away, because he wanted to be validated as an actor and didn't want the Cheech & Chong image hanging over his head. They took a lot of risks to do their comedy. What it did for them was make them legends and household names. People missed them while they were away, because there was nothing else like it. They were unique.

RMM: A host of stoner duos have come since *Up in Smoke*, from Redman and Method Man in *How High* to the Harold and Kumar movies to the *Friday* series. Can they all be traced back to *Up in Smoke*?

B-Real: It all comes from the Cheech & Chong thing. Method Man and Redman came and did a very good version of what today's Cheech & Chong would be and scored. That eventually influenced shit like *Half Baked* and *Harold & Kumar*—the list goes on. It's just different ethnic backgrounds, a different style of jokes, different writing. We took that and put it on record. Red and Method Man took it from our records and put it back on the screen. For Red and Meth to have the vision to do a Cheech & Chong–type flick, they're great representatives of our whole movement.

Pick-Up Summer
(1980)

🌿 🌿 Around the time of *Porky's*, *Meatballs*, *Ski School*, and other sex-romp comedies came the far tamer *Pick-Up Summer* (also known as *Pinball Summer*). It's the story of two horny Canadian high school buds, Greg (Michael Zelniker) and Steve (Carl Marotte), and their love of pinball, their pimped-out van, and a pair of hot sisters—not necessarily in that order. The foursome parade around an unspecified lakeside town, making daily stops at popular hangouts like O.J.'s Drive-In Theater and Pete's Arcade, where they scuffle regularly with a band of motorcycle-riding hoods led by the town jerk, Bert (Tom Kovacs). They also smoke a lot of weed (the bikers, too) in between pranks, parties, pinball, and make-out sessions. It's all about innocent fun projected through corny montages of the couples at the amusement park or frolicking in the lake, and also boobs, which there are plenty of (mostly braless and in wet T-shirts). Girls were called broads back then, pinball ruled (the movie's finale pits Greg against Bert at the arcade), and outside of those two things, not much else mattered—at least not that summer. Good times, average movie.

Counselor Frank Jelnick: "Have I got a surprise for you. Conned it out of Sergeant Stryker. It's called a joint! Got it from one of the kids at the O.J."

Secretary: "You're lighting it the wrong way, Frankie."

Pieces of April (2003)

🌿 🌿 🌿 🌿 Thanksgiving usually brings out the worst in families, and April Burns (Katie Holmes), your typical tattooed, pierced, Lower East Side punk rocker, is expecting an especially difficult holiday get-together, the first meal she's hosting at her tiny apartment. And with good reason: Joy (Patricia Clarkson), her mother, whom she never got along with, has cancer and only a short time to live. The family's drive from the suburbs into New York City is an expedition in itself. April's do-gooder sibling, Beth (Alison Pill), is so protective of her mom that she's seemingly taken over as the Burns matriarch, while brother Timmy (John Gallagher Jr.), an aspiring photographer documenting his mother's failing health, is the one who scores Joy a joint (the two sneak a toke in a rest-stop bathroom) to help ease her nausea. Meanwhile, April's stove isn't working, so she scrambles to find a tenant in her building willing to help out. The pressure is on for this "last supper" to be a positive and memorable experience for the whole family and an opportunity for April to prove that she's no longer the insolent, drug-taking rebel of her youth. Clarkson was nominated for an Oscar for her supporting role in *Pieces of April*, which features a stellar soundtrack supervised by The Magnetic Fields's Stephen Merritt, but it's Holmes who carries her awkward family frustrations so convincingly. Subtlety is key in this emotional indie flick, except when it comes to stuffing, roasting, basting, and transporting the turkey up and down a nasty East Village stairway. Vegetarians beware.

Joy: "Honey, roll it tighter next time."

Timmy: "Sorry, Mom."

Pineapple Express
(2008)

This best-buds comedy stars Seth Rogen as pothead subpoena-server Dale Denton and a shaggy, long-haired James Franco as his dealer Saul Silver—two guys whose lives are turned upside down when Denton inadvertently witnesses a murder at an address he was serving. Flustered and freaked out, he abandons the scene of the crime (after smashing into a police car), leaving behind a key piece of evidence: a roach of the super-rare strain Pineapple Express. As the duo tries to evade the would-be murderers now hot on their trail, hilariousness ensues: They try taking cover in the forest (Saul's first thought of a hiding spot: Quizno's), then meet up with middleman-turned-snitch (the constantly abused and herpes-ridden Red, played by Danny McBride) before stealing a cop car, going on a high-speed chase, and ending their evening in the most awkward meet-the-parents dinner ever. The movie pays homage not only to classic Cheech & Chong–style stoner comedies, but also B-grade action movies—from the looks of it, most of the budget went to over-the-top explosions toward the end. But it's the pothead banter that's laugh-out-loud funny as this dopey duo nails even the most subtle traits of stoner life—from a TV tuned in to 227 to the wonder at Franco's infamous two-person cross joint. But there's no doubt the best of *Pineapple* lies in the first half hour, starting with a black-and-white prequel, of sorts, where Bill Hader plays a willing participant in the government's top-secret pot research trials. It's all about pacing, so portion your stash accordingly for a very bumpy ride.

> "This is like if that Blue Oyster shit met that Afghan Kush I had—and they had a baby. And then, meanwhile, that crazy Northern Light stuff I had and the Super Red Espresso Snowflake met and had a baby. And by some miracle, those two babies met and fucked—this would be the shit that they birthed."
>
> —Saul

❧ STONER INVENTIONS AND INNOVATIONS ❧

D.I.Y. paraphernalia made by clever movie stoners

Gas Mask Pipe (*Knocked Up*): Ben (Seth Rogen) does his best Darth Vader "*Luke, I am your stoner*" while hot-boxing a gas mask pipe that delivers extra-potent hits.

Cross Joint (*Pineapple Express*): Saul (James Franco) demonstrates "the apex of the vortex of joint engineering" to Dale (Rogen)— a double joint that connects to form a cross. It takes two to light its three corners, but you get triple the high.

Shofar Bong (*Harold & Kumar Go to White Castle*): Harold and Kumar's Jewish neighbors Goldstein and Rosenberg toke out of a ceremonial Rosh Hashanah shofar (ram's horn), giving new meaning to the term "high holidays."

Rifle Hit (*Platoon*): Shotgunning in its most literal sense, Chris (Charlie Sheen) puffs out of an M16, thanks to his platoon leader Sergeant Elias (Willem Dafoe). Welcome to the Vietnamese jungle!

Pope (*The Wackness*): Psychiatrist Dr. Jeffrey Squires (Sir Ben Kingsley) likes to have his own sesh after he finishes with a patient. He lights up his sweet glass bong and blows out the smoke through a classic paper-towel-meets-air-freshener tube.

Smokeless Bong (*Harold & Kumar Escape from Guantanamo Bay*): It's only a six-hour flight from New York to Amsterdam, but Kumar (Kal Penn) can't wait that long so he tries to hit a double-tube smokeless bong in the bathroom. When a passenger mistakes the bong for a bomb, Harold (John Cho) and Kumar get shipped to the Cuban prison.

Belt Buckle Pipe (*Dazed and Confused*): Just before Wooderson (Matthew McConaughey) delivers his most famous line ("That's what I love about these high school girls. I get older, they stay the same age"), Pink (Jason London) sneaks a toke from his belt buckle, which doubles as a pipe.

Honey Bong (*True Romance*): Floyd (Brad Pitt) takes hits from a bong fashioned out of your typical bear-shaped plastic honey bottle, as menacing mobsters search for Clarence (Christian Slater), who's run off with their coke. He's so slacked out, Floyd even offers them a rip, which doesn't go over too well.

Jumper Cable Roach Clip (*Scary Movie*): Shorty (Marlon Wayans) forgets his standard roach clip, so he improvises with the greasy cables you generally find in the trunk of your car.

Fifty-five-Gallon Drum (*Outside Providence*): When Tim (Shawn Hatosy) arrives at prep school, he's initiated by his fellow stoner students, who cleverly adapt an oil drum with an industrial-sized bowl, a plastic tube, and a carburetor, natch.

President's Analyst, The (1967)

🍸

🍁 🍁 🍁 🍁 This sixties classic stars James Coburn as Sidney Schaefer, a New York psychiatrist who's selected to become "the president's analyst." He's transported to Washington and given the unenviable task of attending to the commander-in-chief's every whim. A red flashing light lets him know that he must stop whatever he's doing—sleeping, making love—and rush over to the White House. Sidney's followed everywhere by CEA and FBR agents and soon becomes so paranoid that he ditches D.C., setting up a long chase that dominates most of the movie. The best scene by far is when Sidney ducks into a hippie bus in Greenwich Village and takes off with some love children. He dons a wig, turtleneck, and vest, and plays gong in their rock band led by the Old Wrangler (Barry McGuire, famous for the 1965 antiwar song, "Eve of Destruction"). "You can sleep with me," hippie princess Snow White (Jill Banner) offers, and Sidney does, in a field of grass. When the Pudlians, a faux British band who are actually Canadian agents tailing Sidney, arrive, the Old Wrangler orchestrates a drug deal. "You wouldn't have some of that good Congo hash to trade me for some mighty fine LSD?" he inquires. Blue liquid in a vial is poured over ice and served at a club where the band plays. It's a fun, psychedelic scene until Sidney's kidnapped by the Pudlians. As it turns out, the real evildoers are not the CEA, FBR, or the sundry foreign agents, but TPC, a.k.a. the phone company. Locked inside a phone booth, Sidney is spirited away to TPC's futuristic headquarters run by human-looking robots. They plot to inject the "Cerebrum Communicator" into the brains of all Americans— "all you have to do is think the number of the person you wish to speak with and you are in instant communication with anyone in the world." Sounds pretty good, but Sidney thinks otherwise and, along with CEA spook Don Masters (Godfrey Cambridge) and KGB spy Kropotkin (Severn Darden), they shoot their way out and return to Washington.

Old Wrangler: "We're all fugitives here, we're all seekers. You can come explore with us— the lost innocence, the peaceful center."

Pretty in Pink (1986)

✏️ 🍸 🍷

🍁 🍁 🍁 🍁 As John Hughes movies go, Pretty in Pink is right up there with the greats— Sixteen Candles, The Breakfast Club—a teen flick with heart, smarts, and a message you can embrace: Freaks and geeks are people, too. Andie (Molly Ringwald) is one of those freaks—an outcast from the wrong side of the tracks (literally, an Amtrak passes right in front of the house she shares with her underemployed dad, played by Harry Dean Stanton) who takes some serious fashion risks, drives a pink beater, works at an indie record store and hangs with the school's New Wave burnout crowd. Her always-around guy pal is the dorky but lovable Duckie (Two and a Half Men's Jon Cryer) who's had a not-so-secret crush on her for years, but when one of the school's "richies," the BMW-driving Blane (Andrew McCarthy), crosses class lines and asks Andie to the prom, it drives a wedge in their friendship. It also causes problems for Blane when his best bud Steff (James Spader), a privileged prick who throws mas-

sive parties at his parents' mansion (he shows his joint-rolling skills the morning after), doesn't approve of the hookup and threatens to end their friendship over it. As for the prom, the three principals all suck it up and go stag (Andie fashions her own dress, natch), but there's resolution at the end, and it's a positive one.

It may take place in the eighties (back when kids smoked at school and computers looked downright prehistoric), but clique wars never change. Still, there's something about *Pretty in Pink*'s point of view that's especially harsh. Hughes hits all the right teenage emotions—pride, insecurity, conviction, exultation—with few cheap laughs (though there are a couple of good zingers, mostly courtesy of the Duck Man) and some great music. But in the end, it comes down to one key thought: As Otis Redding says, shouldn't we all "try a little tenderness"?

Steff to Blane: "This is my last serious party of my high school career. Hope you guys are gonna tough it out until Sunday at least, when my folks get home."

Prince of Pennsylvania, The
(1988)

🖋 ⛾

🌿 🌿 🌿 🌿 In one of his earliest roles, a pre–*Bill and Ted*'s Keanu Reeves took teen angst to new heights playing Rupert Marshetta, a Pennsylvania loner whose disinterest in school stems from being too smart for his own good. Besides caring for his older hippie girlfriend Carla Headlee (Amy Madigan), Rupert mostly lives in the clouds—imagining a better life for himself and his mom, who's basically a kept woman, lorded over by her hard-ass Vietnam vet husband, Gary (Fred Ward). Rupert never felt any connection to his supposed dad, so it comes as no surprise when he discovers his real father is actually Jack Sike (Jeff Hayenga), Gary's coworker at the coal mine. In a backward attempt to bond, Jack tells his son that he could sell Gary's land and make a fortune. A light goes off in his head and Rupert decides to kidnap his ex-dad and take him for everything he's got. Rupert's ridiculously awesome lopsided hair-

cut aside, Keanu Reeves's burgeoning talent shines through the dreary Pennsylvania landscape in this eighties sleeper, with endless scenes worthy of repeat viewing—like when Rupert and his punk friends drunkenly crash the school dance, making a mockery of the jocks. Inspiring you to look at the world with jaded innocence, *The Prince of Pennsylvania* lands somewhere in between comedy and drama, but never falls in the category of buzz kill.

Carla: "Most of the time you're in a fantasy world, Rupert."
Rupert: "Most of the time, you're stoned."
Carla: "I got my reasons."
Rupert: "Name twelve."

Private Benjamin
(1980)

🖋 ⛾ 🌿

🌿 🌿 🌿 Goldie Hawn plays shopping-obsessed have-it-all Judy Benjamin, a Jewish, eighties version of Jessica Simpson who decides to enlist in the army after her second husband (played by Albert Brooks) dies unexpectedly on their wedding night. She barely survives the first week of boot camp, especially once it's made clear that tightwad unit leader Captain Lewis (Eileen Brennan) has it in for her, but Private Benjamin is no bimbo (despite her famous line about army uniforms, "Is green the only color these come in?"). When she and her ragtag troupe of female misfits win a combat simulation (following a big bonfire smoke-out and giggle-fest while on guard duty the previous night), she gets the attention of a general who recommends her for an elite unit. G.I. Judy is eventually transferred to a base in France, where she reconnects with Henri (Armand Assante), a Parisian fling from an R & R weekend in New Orleans, and it's from this point on that the movie starts getting heady, venturing into deep relationship territory and tackling issues of infidelity and independence. A bold move for a comedy, and a bit of a bummer at that, but it did get the box-office hit three Oscar nominations, so the gamble paid off.

Captain Lewis: "You are not fit to wear that uniform!"
Private Benjamin: "No shit!"

Puff, Puff, Pass (2006)

🌿🌿🌿 Inspired by *Friday* and *Half Baked*, Mekhi Phifer's only film at the helm stars *That '70s Show*'s Danny Masterson (Larry) and Ronnie Warner (Rico)—he's also co-writer—as stoner buds who bumble around Los Angeles, but ultimately stumble into a sweet gig courtesy of Big Daddy (Phifer). Rico constantly sparks up spliffs, even in a rehab center, which they're kicked out of after one sex-filled night. The cast includes Terry Crews (*Friday After Next*) as wannabe-rapper Cold Crush, Darrell Hammond as Larry's older brother, Jonathan, and leggy blonde Ashley Scott as Big Daddy's girlfriend, Elise. Movie buffs will enjoy Larry and Rico's constant references to their favorite film, *The Shawshank Redemption*. As B stoner movies go, this one's pretty good, don't pass on *Puff, Puff, Pass*.

Larry: "Pot's the mainstay, you know, the baseline. An old friend."

Putney Swope (1969)

🌿🌿 In one of the great sixties farces (directed by Robert Downey Sr.), the title character (Arnold Johnson) takes over an advertising agency, installing a Black Power management style and a daring creative strategy (he refuses all ads for cigarettes, alcohol, and "war toys"). The raspy-voiced autocratic Swope runs Truth and Soul with the sensitivity of Fidel Castro. But his campaigns are inspired, especially the R-rated one for Lucky Airlines. Now we know where Robert Downey Jr. got his wacky sense of humor.

Mrs. Swope: "Swope, I'm gonna bend your Johnson."

Rancho Deluxe (1975)

🌿🌿🌿 Vegetarians may want to steer clear of this seventies tale of two cattle rustlers. Jeff Bridges plays Jack and *Law & Order*'s Sam Waterston is Cecil, longtime buds who thrive on riding horses, frolicking with the local girls—especially sharp-tongued sisters Mary (Maggie Wellman) and Betty Fargo (Patti D'Arbanville)—and profiting from poached cattle. They also like to share a joint on occasion, and marvel at that big Montana sky. But Jack and Cecil aren't the sharpest tools in the shed, and when a local cattle baron fixes on catching them red-handed, the hunt is on and the renegade cowboys end up on the losing side. But hell, it was a good ride. As far as pre-*Lebowski* Bridges goes, *Rancho Deluxe*, the name of a ranch that's actually a prison (massive penitentiary-run farms and ranches really did exist in Montana until 1979) is one of several Westerns he appeared in early in his career (*The Last Picture Show, Heaven's Gate*) and gives a good look at the beginnings of a future stoner hero. Giddyap.

Mary: "Betty's a dumb twat and I can't stand her. She flushed two lids down the toilet on me, smashed my black light when she was drunk, tore up half my posters, scratched my Humble Pie albums!"

Reality Bites (1994)

🌿🌿🌿 Like 1992's *Singles*, *Reality Bites* doubles as a document of Generation X told through the eyes of four friends struggling to find their own identities, respectable jobs, and love. Lelaina (Winona Ryder) just graduated from college as valedictorian and is filming a documentary while doubling as an assistant on a morning talk show. Troy (Ethan Hawke) is your typical book-smart slacker who likes to loaf around, smoke weed out of a can, and wax philosophic about everything under the sun. Vickie (Janeane Garofalo), a store manager at the Gap, is worried she might have AIDS thanks to her many hookups with random guys (including one played by Soul Asylum singer Dave Pirner). And Sammy (Steve Zahn) is an all-around good guy who's yet to come out of the closet to his mom. All share a deep bond and a love for pizza, pot, and music, but when Lelaina starts dating slick TV executive Mike (Ben Stiller), it causes a rift within the group, especially with BFF Troy, who realizes he's in love with her. Their relationship "evolves" into screaming brawls and insults, but each holds their

rooms instead. The guys, meanwhile, are all about the three Bs: beer, blunts, and babes. Potentially gay Eddie (Shahine Ezell) looks out for the hot-to-trot freshman girls, while Biz (Wesley Jonathan) and his cornrow cronies look to take advantage of them. A house party leads to a rock show and then to a kegger in the park (moontower-style) where many spliffs and cigarettes are smoked, and much beer is consumed, eventually prompting Charles, "Eddie's piss-wasted alter ego," to come out. With few adults and no cops entering the picture, it's teenage abandon to the highest degree. As their motto goes, "smoke, drink, don't think."

But as much as *Remember the Daze*, which was at one point called *The Beautiful Ordinary*, tries to be *Dazed and Confused* for the postmillennial crowd, it falls short in some key areas. For one thing, you don't feel empathy for these vapid characters, which, unlike *Dazed*'s Pink and Mitch, lack a sense of purpose. Where it does live up to its namesake is in the sheer quantity of pot smoked during its one hundred minutes of screen time. And that's a good thing.

own and eventually they come together. If it all feels like a bunch of nineties clichés wrapped up in a bow, it sort of is, and as Stiller's directorial debut, it's not particularly memorable. Still, *Reality Bites* has its moments: the "My Sharona" dance at the gas station, David Spade's bit role as the manager of a fast-food joint, and the opening scene of the foursome sharing a rooftop joint with a world of possibilities ahead.

Remember the Daze
(2007)

It's no coincidence that the word "daze" is used in the title of this movie, which chronicles the last day of school for a group of incoming seniors (and a couple of freshman) at Wilmington High in 1999—the kind of kids that blaze on their way to homeroom. Needless to say, sex, drugs, and debauchery are on the all-night agenda. Cheerleader Stacey (Marnette Patterson) is all about getting drunk as she considers breaking up with her boyfriend, Dylan (Khleo Thomas). Ditto for Lucy (*Pineapple Express*'s Amber Heard) who's totally over Pete (*Big Love*'s Douglas Smith). Friends and lesbian lovers Brianne (Melonie Diaz) and Dawn (Lyndsy Fonseca) are fighting, while besties Tori (*Gossip Girl*'s Leighton Meester) and Holly (Alexa Vega) sit out the parties to babysit and do mush-

> "I was looking at this brochure the other day for NYU, and my mom started flipping out saying that New York was all about sex and drugs! And I wanted to be like, you know what? I'm not a virgin, I already have a tattoo, and I do a ton of drugs here."
>
> —Julia

Reno 911!: Miami
(2007)

🌿🌿🌿🌿 With more punctuation than any movie title should ever be allowed to have, *Reno 911!: Miami* earns every minute of its R rating as the kooky troops of the Reno Sheriff's department graduate from the small screen to the big one. Lewd, crude, and perpetually clueless, Lieutenant Jim Dangle (Thomas Lennon) and his motley crew head to Miami for the American Police Convention, but when a chemical attack quarantines everyone inside, it's up to them to patrol the entire city of Miami. The situation worsens when acting mayor Jeff Spoder (Patton Oswalt) conspires with wannabe-gangsta Ethan (Paul Rudd doing his best Tony Montana impression) to steal the antidote. But thanks to their many screwups in the name of police duty, Reno's finest manage to foil the plot and come out as heroes.

Of course, the story is secondary to their typically wacky exploits, both individually and as a group. The whale detonation incident on the beach, the masturbation ballet at the motel, Clementine's (Wendy McLendon-Covey) mystery tattoo, Dangle's chat with the Aspen cops while in his civilian attire (pink bandanna and a Morrissey T-shirt), and the postscript where they mistake a rectal tool for a bong are just a few examples (though it is disappointing that we don't get to see Clemmy indulge her stoner side).

Then there's Dangle's candy thong, Trudy's (Kerri Kenney-Silver) granny panties, and Raineesha's (Niecy Nash) baseball mound of an ass, plus Paul Reubens's Pee-wee Herman as gay Terry's (Nick Swardson) dad—all brilliant. It came and went at the theater, but this treasure trove of laughs lives on—and maybe we'll even get the Scotland Yard sequel they hinted at.

Junior: "You know Reno's really a lot like Mayberry on the TV except everybody's on crystal meth and prostitution's legal."

Revenge of the Nerds
(1984)

🌿🌿🌿🌿 At Adams College, the Alpha Beta fraternity reigns supreme. Its rock-jock brethren chug beer out of trophies to bad hair-metal and treat women like objects. They even burn their frat palace to the ground after foolishly "fireballing" an unidentified hard liquor with a lighter. As a result, the university allots them the entire freshman dormitory for a temporary crash pad and, in turn, leaves the four-eyed Louis (Robert Carradine) and Gilbert (Anthony Edwards), and a handful of the school's social outcasts, with nowhere to reside. But when Lewis and Gilbert spearhead their Lambda Lambda Lambda chapter, chock-full of spastics, all with their own eclectic skill sets, the rag-tag team of misfits show the coeds how to throw down. The Tri-Lambs apply their schoolbook smarts to reinvent the Adams party scene and turn out the campus with antics that include their mush-mouthed Takashi (Brian Tochi) mastering a booze-infused tricycle race (he ingests a fictional prescriptive called "trichloromethylene" to counter any alcohol effects), their child prodigy Wormser (Andrew Cassese) installing an elaborate video surveillance system in the Pi Delta Pi sorority house, and their limp-wristed Lamar (Larry B. Scott) blaring Michael Jackson accompanied by the infamous "wonder joints," courtesy of Booger (Curtis Armstrong). A rowdy college classic on par with the kooky comedies of the time—*Meatballs, Police Academy, Porky's*—it still holds up more than twenty-five years later.

U. N. Jefferson: "This is some good shit."

Revenge of the Nerds II: Nerds in Paradise (1987)

While Louis (Robert Carradine), Booger (Curtis Armstrong), and the geeky gang may have triumphed over the neanderthal Alpha Betas back at Adams College, they have to prove themselves at a college convention in Ft. Lauderdale. Watered-down by its PG-13 rating, the sedated sequel doesn't deliver the booze or boobage like its classic predecessor, but manages to redeem itself in its final moments. After their douchebag nemeses ditch them on an unmarked Floridian island, the Tri-Lambs discover an endless jungle of cheeba that gives a whole new meaning to Booger's famed quip "We've got bush." The tropical crop not only expands the nerds' minds to help them figure a way off the island, but it also inspires a friendship between them and their former Alpha bully Frederick Palowakski, a.k.a. "The Ogre" (Donald Gibb), also left behind by the Alpha Betas. In the end, the Tri-Lambs are victorious at the convention and initiate Ogre into their clan with a heartfelt ceremony that requires his imbibing a jumbo-sized serving bowl of suicide punch.

Ogre: "What if C-A-T really spelled dog?"

Risky Business (1983)

With his parents away for a week, the first thing high school senior Joel Goodsen (Tom Cruise) does once he's home alone is pour a whiskey and Coke. His second act: the infamous dance in his tightie-whities to the tune of Bob Seger's "Old Time Rock & Roll." And for his third taste of freedom, he phones a call girl service and ends up with the luscious Lana (Rebecca De Mornay), who convinces him to turn his suburban Chicago house into a brothel just for a night. Dark, moody, and provocative, is it any wonder that Risky Business stands as one of the greatest teen fantasies to ever play out on a movie screen? The film was a star-making vehicle for a very young Cruise, who plays the clean-shaven college-bound Joel with such convinc-

ing naïveté that you almost forget it's the same guy from the Mission: Impossible movies. But Joel is also confident, even cocky; sporting the Ray-Ban sunglasses that became a pop culture fad, he and his friends Miles (Curtis Armstrong) and Barry (Bronson Pinchot) smoke joints, play poker, and eventually dream up the prostitution scheme, which has all their school buddies rushing to the bank to cash Grandma's gift bond. The party turns into a tailgate outside of his parents' house, while inside, the cash is rolling in. "You're one hotshit future enterpriser," Lana tells Joel before the two take off to do the deed on a train and forever cement the movie's sexiest moment. The next morning, however, things look bleak again as Lana's pimp Guido (Joe Pantoliano) steals everything in the Goodson home. The movie, like Joel's sheltered life, is a series of second guesses, but in the end, it comes down to one thing: that every now and then, you have to say, "What the fuck?"

> "You ever get high, Joel?"
>
> —Lana
>
> "Yeah, all the time."
>
> —Joel

Road Trip (2000)

🖋 🍶 🍸 👀

🌿🌿🌿🌿 In the tradition of *Animal House*, *Road Trip* meets all the requirements of your classic college movie: boobs, beer, weed, asshole authority figure, wacky roommate, underwear. Only difference is, much of this tale (directed by *Old School*'s Todd Phillips), happens off campus, but it's no less crass. Josh (Breckin Meyer) and his buds E.L. (Seann William Scott in a reprise of his Stiffler role from *American Pie*), the brainy stoner Rubin (Paolo Costanzo) and Kyle (D. J. Qualls) take off from Ithaca to Austin to intercept a videotape of Josh having

sex with the beautiful Beth (Amy Smart), which was accidentally mailed to his long-distance girlfriend in Austin. Along the 1,800-mile drive, they encounter their share of mishaps, not the least of which involves Kyle's car exploding, but there are good times, too, like when Kyle breaks out the Irish jig at an all-black fraternity party (and later scores— or "boinks," as he calls it—with a sista three times his size), and E.L. has an intimate encounter with a nurse at the sperm bank. Simultaneously, kooky dorm pal Barry Manilow (Tom Green), who's on his eighth year at the University of Ithaca and has seemingly never left New York State, tells Beth that Josh is headed to Boston to see his girlfriend, so she hops on a bus to confront the girl.

Whether it's the "Tiny Salmon" song, his obsession with Rubin's pet snake, or just his utter cluelessness, Barry steals every scene. But it's Rubin who puts *Road Trip* in the category of stoner classic. He smokes a joint with a grandfather and his dog, and ends up on the cover of *High Times* after discovering a strain of marijuana that's completely undetectable by any of today's standard drug tests.

E.L.: "Think about it, Josh, you're in college. The window of opportunity to drink and do drugs and take advantage of young girls is getting smaller by the day."

Rock Opera (1999)

🌿🌿🌿🌿 Austin's druggy rock-and-roll underground is the setting for Bob Ray's feature debut. Toe (Jerry Don Clark) leads the band Pigpoke, deals marijuana, and never saw a drug he wouldn't take. Fronted a quarter pound by Jarvis (Paul Wright), it mysteriously disappears after Stu (Steve Gurvich) shoots Toe in the butt with a tranquilizer dart. He trips out in psychedelic blues and reds. Jarvis sends Toe to Del Rio to pick up pills, and after a series of shootings and fights, Toe luckily captures the bag. In addition to directing, Ray appears as Bo, who blows up and sucks down a balloon of nitrous oxide. Another knowing scene is the demonstration of how to properly use a one-hitter. Nashville Pussy anchors a solid soundtrack of mostly local favorites. *Rock Opera* certainly does its part in keeping Austin's vibrant film scene weird.

> "I'm putting all the weed in aluminum foil, dude. People automatically assume it's a much more potent drug."
>
> —Tad

Rolling Kansas (2003)

🌿🌿 The Murphy brothers get a letter from their jailed hippie parents containing a map directing them to a "magical forest of marijuana" in Kansas. They take a break from studying for finals at their Texas college and head north in search of the weed. It's *Revenge of the Nerds* meets *Road Trip*. They get lost, go to a strip bar, almost hit a cow, need a tow, and meet Oldman (Rip Torn), who directs them to the plastic bud field. "There she is, that's Eve," Oldman says, pointing to the mother tree. "She's responsible for all of this." They chop down buds and stuff bags in the trunk, but never sample the stuff once, not even when Oldman offers them a joint. Heading back through Oklahoma, they stash the booty in a hay field rather than get busted at the checkpoint. When they return, the buds are gone. Instead, they manufacture T-shirts with the Kansas map on it. Feds, played by *Sideways'* Thomas Haden Church (he also directs) and Kevin Pollak swoop in and confiscate the shirts in exchange for a $500K government payment, which makes absolutely no sense. Oftentimes there's good reason why grade-B stoner movies go straight to DVD; this is one of them.

Agent Brinkley: "Are we clear, you less-than-cool disciple of Jim Morrison?"

Royal Tenenbaums, The (2001)

🌿🌿🌿🌿🌿 Most movies strive for the gentle magic that pervades *The Royal Tenenbaums*, a film that also accomplishes that rare feat where it plays like reading a book. It's a story about a family of authors abandoned by raconteur patriarch Royal Tenenbaum (Gene Hackman), who inexplicably abandons his flock of young prodigies. Royal is a huckster supreme who fakes an illness to return to the family home and derail his estranged wife's upcoming marriage, but at heart he longs to reconnect with his children—Chas (Ben Stiller), Margot (Gwyneth Paltrow), and Richie (Luke Wilson)—who have all also found themselves back at the family manse. They hate him, but begrudgingly love him, and being around each other brings up old issues in desperate need of sorting.

Tenenbaums is not your average family drama—it's the darkest of comedies with fully realized, heavily stylized, quirky characters, one of whom is the movie itself. Director Wes Anderson's vision is pervasive, every scene shot beautifully and highly detailed, like a movie told in miniature. Repeating literary motifs abound, only serving to focus your attention on what matters most: the interactions between people trying to deal with lives that didn't turn out the way that they had hoped. Heavy but also

> "I wish you'd've done this for me when I was a kid."
>
> —Eli
>
> "But you didn't have a drug problem then."
>
> —Richie
>
> "Yeah, but it still would've meant a lot to me."
>
> —Eli

gloriously funny (in a muted way), it often feels like a story you might recite to children, albeit one with overtones of incest and drug use. Owen Wilson's character, Eli Cash, the next-door neighbor who always wanted to be a Tenenbaum, is the culprit on the druggy front. He's seen with an unlit joint in his mouth, makes mentions of mescaline, and is later found in a room with nefarious characters cutting up some kind of powdery substance. His failures are just another facet of what it's like to lose yourself in what-could've-been, and when confronted with an intervention he gladly asks for help and then disappears. The next time you see him, it's with a face full of war paint hopped up on who-knows-what as he crashes his car into the front of the house, killing the family dog. Indeed, there's a sadness at the

☙ FIVE MORE BY WES ANDERSON ☙

Bottle Rocket **(1996):** Anderson's directorial debut was also a first for brothers Luke and Owen Wilson, who play two-bit crooks looking to upgrade their criminal endeavors while contending with a crew of incompetents. A pot bust is one of a series of bummers in this kooky Texas tale, which also includes a *My Name Is Earl*–like love story involving a motel maid who speaks no English.

Rushmore **(1998):** Jason Schwartzman takes center stage as Rushmore Academy's resident dork, Max Fischer, a kid so enraptured with a soft-spoken teacher that he's driven to attention-craving acts of desperation, many aimed at his frenemy Blume (Bill Murray). Rejected at every turn, Max's passion for extracurricular activities pays off when he stages an elaborate *Miss Saigon*–esque play to deliver his message.

The Life Aquatic with Steve Zissou **(2004):** Anderson's fantastic sea voyage follows once-revered oceanographer and documentary filmmaker Steve Zissou (Bill Murray) on a mission to find the mysterious jaguar shark that ate his best friend. Along for the ride is a reporter (played by Cate Blanchett) and Zissou's supposed son Ned (Owen Wilson), as well as a

gnarly crew that includes a Brazilian singer (Seu Jorge) who sings Bowie in Portuguese and good-natured German Klaus (Willem Dafoe), Zissou's loyal number two. With the look and feel of a seventies nature film, it's a deep, stony dive.

The Darjeeling Limited **(2007):** Owen Wilson goes five for five in Anderson's vibrant film (co-written with Jason Schwartzman and Roman Coppola) about three brothers (played by Wilson, Schwartzman, and Adrien Brody) traveling India by train on a journey of self-discovery. Bright colors and unspecified Indian painkillers accent zany scenes in train cars and markets while a quirky soundtrack leads the boys through abandonment issues and suicidal thoughts.

Fantastic Mr. Fox **(2009):** Opting for stop-motion animation instead of live action, Anderson created one of his most engaging films in years. George Clooney voices a charming thief of a fox and Meryl Streep is his long-suffering but loyal wife. Based on the 1970 Roald Dahl children's book, this offbeat adaptation scored an Oscar nomination for Best Animated Feature of the year.

core of *The Royal Tenenbaums*, and a soundtrack always ready with a sweet lamenting acoustic guitar just when it's needed (like during Richie's suicide scene set to Elliott Smith's "Needle in the Hay"). But in the end, all are forgiven, the bonds of this strange tribe stronger than any transgression.

Rude Awakening (1989)

As one of Cheech Marin's few solo stoner turns, *Rude Awakening* wasn't his finest moment. Blame the script, not the player. This eighties attempt to reawaken (or more like cash in on) the Woodstock spirit twenty years after the fact is painfully predictable. Jesus (Marin) and Fred (Eric Roberts) are two activist hippies wanted for draft dodging who escape to fictional Managuador and start a commune. But when they happen upon a dead American agent who's holding top secret papers, they decide to return to New York (Jesus' top priority: pastrami) and attempt to foil a secret government plot to incite a war in Central America. Of course, the time warp is a trip as the guys first learn about the ozone layer and are introduced to remote controls, VHS tapes, CD players, and other modern gizmos, but it's their reacquaintance with old hippie pals, who've all turned into loud and proud yuppies, that really bums them out. This is especially true of Fred's former flame, Petra (*Airplane*'s Julie Hagerty), and best friend Sammy (Robert Carradine), who has a money-hungry wife and a son that's taken to wearing tie-dyes. The situation gets stickier (and mildly amusing) when Jesus and Fred surprise Sammy with a visit, just as he and his wife (*Laverne & Shirley*'s Cindy Williams) are entertaining a couple of straitlaced co-op board members. Realizing the error of their greedy ways, the gang eventually reunites and takes over an NYU building, preaching peace to all who've gathered. Cameo appearances by counterculture heroes like Timothy Leary and David Peel, and a soundtrack that's heavy on Grateful Dead and other late-sixties classics, make *Rude Awakening* slightly more worthy of footnote status, but were it not for Jesus' hallucinations—sharing a cigar-size spliff with a fish, seeing doctors as adult-sized potato heads—this B movie would be utterly forgettable.

Saving Grace (2000)

Britain's key entry into the stoner comedy genre stars Brenda Blethyn as Grace—a down-on-her-luck widow who tries her hand at growing marijuana. Grace's gardener Matthew (Craig Ferguson—the Scottish-born, American late-night TV host, who co-wrote the script) gives her the grand idea. With her house up for sale and furniture being repossessed, Grace decides to use her green thumbs to make some quick cash. They build a greenhouse that lights up for all to see. This is clearly a gag, but one that can't help Grace's cause. When Grace tries pot for the first time ("I'm growing and selling it—I should know the effect it has"), she laughs, then succumbs, no match for the heavy weed. The same goes for Grace's friends Margaret (Phyllida Law) and Diana (Honey Chambers), who sample the "tea" and go completely cuckoo for Corn Flakes. While in London attempting to sell her weedy wares, Grace meets French dealer Jacques (Tcheky Karyo) in the film's most ludicrous scene. Matthew tries to help, but he's blindsided by his pregnant girlfriend, and decides that the illegal life is not for him. And when all parties converge on the greenhouse and Grace lights the three-foot pot pile afire, it's time to gag. What starts as an interesting premise goes up in smoke.

Grace: "We'll take cuttings from the mother plant, move the cuttings and grow them under lights hydroponically, go straight to budding—we can have the first harvest in a matter of weeks."

Scary Movie (2000)

Spoof-meister Keenan Ivory Wayans parodies *Scream* and *I Know What You Did Last Summer* in this spot-on first installment of the popular series. No one is safe as a psycho with a sickle terrorizes high schoolers. Cindy (Anna Faris) thinks it may be her boyfriend Bobby (Jon Abrahams), who spends most of the movie trying to get into her pants (beware the electric chastity

sized joint and smoked by a massive plant straight out of *Little Shop of Horrors*. "I'm sorry," he pleads, "I didn't mean to smoke your relatives." Buddy (Chris Masterson) comes to Shorty's rescue, tossing bags of Cheetos and Funyuns to the monster bud. Clearly out of ideas, Wayans passed on the next two sequels (directed by *Airplane*'s David Zucker).

Shorty: "Good night, little plant. You drink all this water up and you'll grow up to be a strong chronic plant. And then you'll be smoked by all the rappers and they'll do a lot of dumb shit that will fuck up their careers."

belt!). Or is it Ray (Shawn Wayans), who appears to like men more than women? Or mentally challenged Dookie (Trevor Roberts)? It can't be Shorty (Marlon Wayans)—he's too busy getting stoned. Shorty smokes blunts and wears a big pot-leaf T-shirt. When he forgets his roach clip, Shorty improvises with battery jumper cables. No gag is too raunchy for director Wayans: Drew (Carmen Electra) has her silicone breast slashed out in the opening scene and teacher Miss Mann is precisely that (she has the ball sack to prove it). At the end, Cindy cries out, "Noooooooo," then gets run over. Not to worry—Cindy appears, as does Brenda (Regina Hall), in all three sequels.

> "I got papers, blunts, bongs— all the ingredients to make a high nigga pie."
>
> **—Shorty**

Scary Movie 2 (2001)

🌿🌿🌿 Cindy (Anna Faris), Brenda (Regina Hall), Shorty (Marlon Wayans), and Ray (Shawn Wayans) return for another crack at this spoof formula with mixed results. They're all invited to spend the night at a haunted house run by Oldham (Tim Curry), Hanson (Chris Elliott), and the wheelchair-bound Dwight (David Cross). Shorty has the highlight scene when he's rolled up into a super-

Scooby-Doo (2002)

🌿🌿 After solving a particularly grueling case involving Pamela Anderson's toy factory, the Mystery, Inc., crew breaks up and goes their separate ways. Two years later, the gang has been reunited by Emile Mondavarious (Rowan Atkinson), the reclusive owner of Spooky Island, to solve a rather troubling mystery: College students have been arriving at the horror-themed island for spring break ready to party down, but by the time they leave, they've all turned into weird teetotaling assholes. During their hiatus, Daphne (Sarah Michelle Gellar) has become a black belt in karate, Fred (Freddie Prinze Jr.) is somehow really famous, Velma (Linda Cardellini) is working for NASA, and Scooby and Shaggy (Matthew Lillard) are the same as ever. While the idea of a horror-themed resort with brainwashed teenagers is frightening in and of itself, weird creatures that feast on human bodies to survive during the daylight makes this plot even creepier. But when Fred is brainwashed by these creatures and teams up with nineties pop band Sugar Ray to kidnap Scooby and Shaggy, things get downright ridiculous.

With that in mind, *Scooby-Doo* has long been considered stony, what with the characters' insatiable appetite for munchies like Scooby Snacks and Shaggy's overall cluelessness, and while this is a PG-rated kids' movie, it too has its share of subtle pot references. For instance, on the way to Spooky Island, Shaggy picks up a new girlfriend named Mary Jane (Isla Fisher), to which Shaggy declares, "Like, that is my favorite name!" And when we first see Scooby and Shaggy, smoke is pouring out of the Mystery Machine while "Pass the Dutchie" plays in the background. Inside the van, it's just the two of them roasting eggplant burgers, but again, there's that stony appetite—and a vegetarian menu, no less.

S.F.W. (1994)

🔪 🍸 ✂️ ◉◉

🌿 🌿 🌿 Twenty-year-old Cliff Spab (Stephen Dorff) and his best friend, Joe Dice (Jack Noseworthy), go to their local Fun Stop convenience store to pick up a sixer and end up being held hostage by the mysterious S.P.L.I.T. Image terrorist group. The captors' only demand is that the hostages' entire ordeal be videotaped and broadcast on national television. Confined with four other civilians, among them the adorable seventeen-year-old Wendy Pfister (Reese Witherspoon), we see the thirty-six-day standoff unfold through a series of trippy and violent flashbacks, with Cliff and Wendy as the only survivors. Cliff's devil-may-care attitude turns him into a hero and his catch phase, "So Fucking What," spurs a national movement including T-shirts, videos, an original GWAR song, and the TV movie *So Damn What*, starring Gary Coleman.

While much of the film feels like filler between the hostage crisis and its poignant ending, at least the ordeal is set to a good soundtrack which includes tracks by Radiohead and Soundgarden—the selection of "Teenage Whore" for the film's sole sex scene with Spab and Joe's sister Monica (Joey Lauren Adams) is particularly fitting. And stoners will appreciate Spab's mantra, which impresses a slacker disciple (played by a young Tobey Maguire), who's honored when he walks off with Spab's joint. But perhaps the most notable legacy of S.F.W. is in its statement on the potential dangers of reality TV, and to that end, the movie was way ahead of its time.

Shampoo (1975)

🔪 🍸 ✂️ ◉◉

🌿 🌿 It's 1968, the Nixon/Agnew ticket is about to sweep into the White House, and Vietnam is full blown, but Beverly Hills hairdresser to the stars George (Warren Beatty) couldn't care less about all the political upheaval. The opening scene sets the tone as two bedded figures go at it in heightened sexual passion. When all is said and done, Felicia (Lee Grant) lies back with a wondrously fulfilled sigh and lights a joint, while George hustles to meet his forlorn girlfriend, Jill (played brilliantly by the ever-sexy, giggly Goldie Hawn). Basically, that's the story. George jumps on his motorcycle, bouffant hair flying in the wind as he goes from girl to girl. George sighs a lot (you would be tired, too), but he is also disturbed—he wants a shop of his own and is befuddled. "Women are an occupational hazard," he says of his job. But, he can't keep his hands out of women's hair, so to speak.

In director Hal Ashby's trademark style, this is a screwball comedy with a strong sexual undercurrent: George's ex-girlfriend Jackie (the gorgeous Julie Christie) is shtupping Lester (Jack Warden), the rich husband of Felicia, and George is trying to get money out of Lester for the new shop. Along the way, George screws Tracy (Carrie Fisher), Felicia and George's daughter, and, eventually, Jackie. There is a classic seventies party scene where everyone gets buzzed as *Sgt. Pepper's Lonely Hearts Club Band* and Buffalo Springfield play in the background. In one of the funniest sequences, Jackie is asked what she wants and responds by pointing to George and saying, "I want to suck his cock," and then gets under the dinner table and proceeds to do just that. But George is Peter Pan and it's pretty apparent that he will never get his own shop or stick with one woman. Let's hear it for the sexual revolution—may it rest in peace.

Slacker (1991)

🍸🍶 🔪

🌿🌿🌿🌿 Richard Linklater, Austin's finest and stoniest director, made a great first impression with this talky and philosophical (Linklater's trademarks) tribute to the city's eccentric characters. It starts with the director arriving by cab in downtown Austin. The cab passes a station wagon that has just hit a woman. This is the last we see of Linklater and the beginning of a unique mosaic where characters walk in and out of scenes, never to return to the story line. Depending on your state of intoxication, following along may prove to be difficult, but the challenge to keep up with the characters is also fun. A beatnik hitchhiker (Charles Gunning) best expresses the movie's slacker ethic: "I may be living badly, but at least I don't have to work to do it. I'll get a job when I get the true call." Conspiracies like the JFK assassination get special lip service from the kooky cast. In one of the funnier segments, a burglar pulls a gun on the "Old Anarchist" (Louis Mackey), who disarms him with clever conversation. "This town has always had its share of crazies," he says. "I wouldn't want to live anywhere else."

Slackers (2002)

🍶 🔪 🍸🍶 🔪 👁️👁️

🌿🌿🌿 Any college comedy that kicks off with a classical rendition of The Who's 1971 teenage anthem "Baba O'Riley" warrants a closer look, and this one, like most Jason Segel vehicles, doesn't disappoint. Three best friends and roommates, Dave (Devon Sawa), Sam (Segel), and Jeff (Michael Maronna), are about to graduate from Holden University after four long years of majoring in cheating. But after Dave drops in on a class to steal the test questions, accidentally grabs a creepy dude's seat and hits on Angela (Jamie King), the object of self-named Cool Ethan's (Jason Schwartzman) obsession, Dave learns the hard way that he messed with the wrong nerd. Ethan threatens to expose their cheating schemes and blackmails the guys into helping him get Angela, who, naturally, has no interest in the annoying little creep. For the first time since high school, the guys are forced to study. Their subject: Angela. In one exploratory mission, Dave stops by Angela's house to gather information, but instead gets a very warm welcome by her cougar mom. No surprises here: Dave falls for Angela, and things fall apart when Ethan reveals their conspiracy. Dave reflectively wanders the campus in a montage set to a curiously rearranged "The Sign" by nineties dance-pop group Ace of Base, and comes up with a plan to win Angela back and save his friends.

As college flicks go, *Slackers* shines and rarely hacks, even in the face of blackmail and deceit. It also has its share of gross-out scenes and outrageous moments, but all in all, this film is about second chances and learning to tell the truth, even when the consequences are sometimes worse than the offense.

Sam: "You treat a hot girl like dirt, and she'll stick to you like mud."

SLC Punk (1998)

🔪 🕯️ 🍸🍶 🔪 👅

🌿🌿 Remember the annoying, mousy punk-rock poser kid from your high school? The one with the lame mohawk who spouted endlessly about anarchy and destroying the system? Imagine that for an hour and a half and you've got SLC Punk. Embodying the worst punk-rock poser tendencies, this film about Reagan-era misfits in Salt Lake City tries hard to be a black comedy, but misses on the comedy and even on the bleakness. Lacking a cohesive plot and marred by endless monologues about anarchy, the bad-acid-trip sequence that happens in the first twenty minutes is nearly the only thing worth watching. That's because it's hard to care about any of the characters, trying so desperately to be "different," but especially loathsome is Matthew Lillard's narrator Stevo, whose tiring exposition on his life and the "scene" do nothing but dare you to hit the Stop button. A typical "funny" moment? When one character slams a stranger's head into a concrete wall at a party and Stevo jumps on screen to yell at the camera "Punk rock! It's punk rock!" The best thing about Stevo is his UPS (United Pot Smokers) T-shirt, but for those "fighting the system" in this story, weed is just a way to combat boredom.

Slums of Beverly Hills (1998)

🌿🌿🌿🌿 It's 1976 and Murray Abromowitz (Alan Arkin), a single dad of three, is struggling to make do on little income and a nasty gambling habit. The dysfunctional family is moving for the third time in a year, always within Beverly Hills city limits (for the schools), slumming it and barely scraping by. Hardest hit is Vivian (Natasha Lyonne), a freshman in high school who's just coming into her own (or, as her father describes, "overnight, she got stacked like her mother") and battling two cruel brothers, stoner Ben (*Harold & Kumar*'s David Krumholtz), who buys a twenty-dollar bag from their neighbor Eliot (Kevin Corrigan) and rips from a three-foot bong, and little Rickey (Eli Marienthal), who all too willingly lights his bowl. Their luck seems to change when Rita (Marisa Tomei), Murray's niece, escapes a mental asylum and Mickey (Carl Reiner), his rich brother from back East, offers to pay the family to house her. But as much as Murray hopes Rita will be a positive influence on the hormonally challenged Viv (who suffers every female embarrassment imaginable, but sure knows her way with a vibrator), the pill-popping "fox" turns out to be more trouble than she's worth, especially when it comes to light that she and Uncle Murray have an extra-special relationship. Yes, this movie is dark, in the vein of *Welcome to the Dollhouse* or the truly twisted *Happiness*, a stark contrast to the sunny, palm tree–lined streets of Beverly Hills and with each character more pathetic than the next. But don't pity the Abromowitzes. They have each other, and there's always Sizzler.

Smiley Face (2007)

🌿🌿🌿🌿 If Kumar were a white girl, he'd be Jane F. (Anna Faris), an aspiring actress and full-time stoner whose sole purpose in life is to satiate whatever she's craving at that very moment. Usually, that involves food and pot—and not necessarily in that order. Her day starts with a monster bong-rip and, once the munchies kick in, she can't help but scarf down the mound of cupcakes in her fridge, which her creepy, uptight, sci-fi–obsessed roommate Steve (Danny Masterson), forbade her from touching. About forty minutes later, she realizes Steve isn't as uncool as she thought—the cupcakes were made with weed! The rest of her morning involves a string of misadventures as Jane scores more pot (an ounce, to be exact), ends up burning it while cooking it, tries to pawn off her high-grade stash of government weed to a casting agent, flushes it down the toilet, recruits Steve's geeky friend Brevin (John Krasinski) to help, steals a copy of *The Communist Manifesto*, and finally, after making a stop at a sausage factory, winds up on a Ferris wheel by the beach wondering how she got there.

Sound twisted? That's just the tip of the ice-bong-berg. If there were an Oscar for Best Pothead Performance, Faris would win it hands down. After all, Jane never breaks from being baked. It's not like she sleeps it off or has a morning moment of sobriety, we're talking hours upon hours of full-on space-cake high and slapstick physical comedy, which Faris pulls off almost effortlessly. Making this little-known indie flick all the more worthy of entry into the Reefer Movie Madness Hall of Fame is a stellar cast of bit players: Krasinski as the lovable Brevin, Adam Brody as Jane's white-boy-turned-Rasta dealer, Brian Posehn as the bus driver, John Cho as the sausage factory employee who gives Jane a ride (and fantasizes about letting her ride him), and Carrot Top—even Marion Ross, "Mrs. Cunningham," makes an appearance. But in the end, it's all about Jane, whose go-to excuse for every mishap—her chronic tardiness, money problems, and just generally being a klutz—goes something like this: "I'm really stoned, sorry."

WATCH YOUR STEP

Soul Plane (2004)

NWA Airlines' motto is "We fly. We party. We land." If only all of those promises were true. That's what we learn when the fleet's inaugural flight from L.A. to N.Y.C. doesn't exactly go as planned. Sure, the first-class lounge with its white leather couches and A-list service is pimpin', the stewardesses wearing revealing purple numbers are smokin', the upstairs nightclub is hoppin', while the downstairs business-class cabin, complete with strip club and gambling hall, is the place to be. But when Captain Mack (Snoop Dogg) overdoses on mushrooms and dies midflight (that's after blazing a blunt in the cockpit), it's up to entrepreneurial CEO Nashawn (Kevin Hart), who started the airline after winning a $100 million settlement, and his party-hard cousin Muggsey (Method Man) to land that plane. Like *Airplane!*, the plot is secondary to the details—or, in this case, the detailing: hydraulic lifts, neon purple accents, and spinning rims on the outside of the jet, subway-style ads and keep-your-key lockers in "low" class (a.k.a. coach), soul favorites like Roscoe's Chicken and a 99¢ store at NWA's Terminal X (as in Malcolm), to name a few. But it's the passengers, like fish-out-of-water white guy Mr. Hunkee (Tom Arnold) and the staff, especially security gals Shaniece (Loni Love) and Jamiqua (Mo'Nique), that push this already high-larious ride over the top. Captain Mack says it best: "I'm putting this bitch on autopilot so I can enjoy myself."

You might want to do the same.

> "Ladies and gentlemen, we have reached our cruising altitude of thirty-three thousand feet. Thirty-three thousand feet? Oh shit, man, we're fuckin' higher than Redman at the Source Awards."
>
> —Captain Mack

🌿 SNOOP DOGG'S STONER MOVIE TIPS 🌿

As one of Hollywood's most in-demand onscreen stoners, rapper-turned-actor Snoop Dogg brought the party to *Old School*, played lovable informant Huggy Bear in *Starsky & Hutch*, a cuckoo-for-chronic captain in *Soul Plane*, and an enterprising dealer in *The Wash*. Clearly high on casting directors' wish lists—and often in real life—the Doggfather offers his tips for stony movie-watching.

Reefer Movie Madness: It's late, you're stoned on the tour bus or at home, what's your go-to movie?

Snoop Dogg: A movie called *Which Way Is Up*. Richard Pryor plays three different characters, and it's the funniest movie of the seventies. It's something I grew up loving and I could never get it out of my system. I always laughed, and once I added some herb to the mix, it made it even funnier. It's one of the greatest movies ever. I watch it all the time.

RMM: What are some of your must-have movie-watching munchies?

SD: I gotta have pistachios, barbeque chips, Skittles, orange sodas, peanuts, Starbursts, and peanut M&Ms.

RMM: Of all the characters you've played, which movie was most fun for you?

SD: Probably *Starsky & Hutch*, because I was able to become Huggy Bear—a character I watched as a kid—and to add my own flavors. And to work with Ben Stiller, Owen Wilson, and Fred Williamson, it was the move.

Spanking the Monkey (1994)

🥄 🍸

🌿 🌿 🌿 A grunge-era Sundance winner directed and written by David O. Russell (*Flirting with Disaster*, *I ♥ Huckabees*), this is one those black comedies that's so dark, you're more likely to cry than laugh. In fact, the only slightly amusing thing about *Spanking the Monkey* is its title, which alludes to the main character's repeated masturbation attempts (interrupted every time). Yes, Ray (Jeremy Davies) is one horny-as-all-hell college student, returning home to New York on his summer break and then headed to Washington, D.C., for an internship with the surgeon general's office. But there's a change of plans when his mother, Susan (Alberta Watson), injures her leg and is bedridden for much of the summer. Ray stays behind to tend to her every need, which includes bathing and the occasional massage. That's where things get, er, sticky. Mom makes the move on her already confused son, throwing his sexual curiosity—and mental health—completely off track. With some very adult issues weighing heavily on his mind, Ray tries to push it aside and hang with his high school stoner buddies, Nicky (Matthew Pucket), Curtis (Zak Orth), and Joel (Josh Phillip Weinstein). Usually, he turns down the joint being passed around, but after Ray's Oedipal dalliance, he takes a toke, which prompts him to jump off a cliff (it must have been some seriously strong herb). He lives, but Ray's dramatic leap is the perfect way out of a truly twisted situation.

Spirit of '76, The (1990)

🥄 🍶 🔑

🌿 🌿 🌿 When a group of scientists from the year 2176 (led by chief "Minister of Knowledge" Chevron-17, played by Devo's Mark Mothersbaugh) send a delegation back in time to recover Earth documents lost in a magnetic storm (namely, the U.S. Constitution and the Declaration of Independence), the time machine mistakenly lands in 1976 instead of 1776. The futuristic crew of Adam-11 (seventies heartthrob David Cassidy), Chanel-6 (Olivia d'Abo), and Heinz-57 (Geoff Hoyle) arrive on Bicentennial Day and, after meeting stoners Chris and Tommy (Jeffrey and Steve McDonald of the seminal indie band Redd Kross), they try to blend in by donning bell-bottoms, glittered boots, and stars and stripes. But with the UFO-obsessed science nerd Rodney Snodgrass on their tail, and, soon after, the authorities, the group gets separated. Chanel hides in a head shop called Hokus Smokus, where she meets a pothead (played by Tommy Chong), who gives her a paraphernalia primer. And it's on a "bicentennial bong" that she first sees what the founding fathers look like. Heinz, meanwhile, ends up stuck at a self-improvement seminar by Dr. Von Mobile (Rob Reiner), while Adam works on fixing the time machine with Chris and Tommy's help (and a tankful of eye-drop liquid). After a quick disco dance-off with the studly Eddie Trojan (Leif Garrett), Chanel rejoins her time traveling buddies to put on an explosive show at the boys' high school science fair. *The Spirit of '76* is a Coppola family affair (Roman Coppola wrote the script with Lucas Reiner, son of Carl, and his sister Sofia—only seventeen during pre-production—was costume designer), that's hokey as hell, but redeems itself with the occasional burst of psychedelia and oddball seventies reference. File this time-travel flick in the half-baked idea pile.

Starsky & Hutch (2004)

🍸 🥄 🪒

🌿 🌿 🌿 🌿 In this comedic take on the seventies TV classic, Vince Vaughn plays funnyman coke dealer Reese Feldman, whose sunny criminal existence is put at risk when Bay City's finest policeman, David Starsky (Ben Stiller), and his new, easygoing partner Ken "Hutch" Hutchinson (Owen Wilson), find his card in a floater's wallet. It turns out Reese's right-hand man Kevin (Jason Bateman) has discovered a method to alter the cell structure of the coca plant and make it completely undetectable, thereby opening the floodgates to every scumbag looking to get his dirty hands on the clean streets of Bay City. Thanks to help from an informant, the sugar-sweet, smooth-as-butter Huggy Bear (Snoop Dogg), Starsky and Hutch are tipped off to a major coke deal

about to go down and the dragon-loving Big Earl (Will Ferrell), who's running the show. Meanwhile, the rest of the Bay City PD has yet to come across this new cocaine, and they write it off as artificial sweetener. Good thing Starsky is a heavy coffee drinker. When he runs out of sugar at home, guess what he uses as substitute? Determined to prove the powder is the real deal, Starsky and Hutch continue to trail Reese, going so far as to pose as mimes at his daughter's bat mitzvah, where they plan to make the bust, but screw it up and are suspended

from the force. Undeterred, they opt for the unofficial route and, with some clever disguises, Starsky's intuition, and Huggy's nine-iron, the guys take Reese down, but not before an awesome car chase which ends with Starsky's prized 1976 Gran Torino in the ocean.

Movies spun off from TV shows are often hit or miss (cough, cough, *Land of the Lost*), but director Todd Phillips (*Old School*) packs *Starsky & Hutch* with so many laughs and outrageous pop culture references that it's hard not to love.

Huggy Bear: "Look man, this grass is Alabama Creepin' Bend, as opposed to Georgia Creepin' Bend. It's lighter."

Still Smokin (1983)

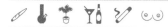

In more of a collection of skits than a plotted story, Cheech and Chong head to Amsterdam

---

for their fifth movie (directed by Chong). The dim-witted Dutch mistake them for Burt Reynolds and Dolly Parton, who were expected for a film festival. The tokey twosome arrive instead and head immediately to a café that serves marijuana food, not buds, though a big, (real) pot plant near the table signals the Netherlands' burgeoning transformation into a pothead haven. In dream sequences, Cheech and Chong reprise bits from their stand-up routines, such as Chong's blackface Blind Melon Chitlin and Marin's green-haired Ashley Roachclip. A highlight is "The Harder They Don't Come," with Marin playing a Rasta dealer, then breaking into a dead-on impression of Richard Pryor. In the final festival performance, Cheech (Ralph) and Chong (Herbie) end up on their knees sniffing each other's butts. Not up to the quality of their previous movies, this one was barely smokin.

> **"I'll have the cream of hash soup and the fresh buds—are they in season?"**
>
> **—Cheech**

Stir Crazy (1980)

🌿 🌿 🌿 In the second of four films they starred in together, Gene Wilder and Richard Pryor play Skip and Harry, best buds who both lose their jobs (Harry gets fired from a catering gig for bringing a jar of highly potent "'65 African Gunji" weed "from the motherland," which is mistaken for oregano at a dinner party) and decide to leave New York and head to Hollywood (where the women are "natural, robust, uninhibited, and healthy") to give show business a shot. But soon after arriving out West, they're swindled by two bank robbers and end up taking the punishment for a crime they didn't commit: a 125-year prison sentence. In jail, the warden (Barry Corbin of *WarGames* fame) discovers that Skip is a natural bull rider, and cuts a deal with him to compete in the inter-prison rodeo, which turns out to be the perfect escape opportunity. By then, the real robbers had been caught, and for the first time in their lives, Skip and Harry truly feel free. Directed by Sidney Poitier, *Stir Crazy* was among the highest-grossing films of 1980, alongside fellow RMM entry *Nine to Five*, which also features a singular pot scene. Harry's stash synopsis, however, is revealed within the first five minutes and features Pryor at his stoniest.

Harry: "My grass! Jesus, you cooked half my stash! My girlfriend, Caroline, just for a little bit of this, was not only gonna let me have her body and her mind but two of her girlfriends. One joint of this put southern California to sleep back in '65. Did you know there was a revolution in '65? We went to sleep and missed it, because of this."

Stoned Age, The (1994)

🌿 With the exception of its soundtrack (and an unexpected cameo by Frankie Avalon), there are few redeeming qualities to *The Stoned Age*, which by its title alone—and the fact that it came out a year after *Dazed and Confused* and centers on a group of stoners in the seventies—is designed to lure in unsuspecting potheads. But beware: This B movie is bunk. It's every clichéd stoner stereotype thrown together, starting with the main characters, Hubbs (Bradford Tatum) and Joe (Michael Kopelow), two tie-dye-wearing scraggly haired burnouts from the O.C. who spend their nights "driving around Torrance trying to get drunk, stoned, and laid." They're tipped off to a house party in Palos Verdes, and armed with some "skank weed" and peppermint schnapps, go in search of "chicks." Hubbs hooks up with the hot-to-trot Lanie (Renee Ammann), while Joe makes conversation and shares a can pipe toke with the hippie-minded Jill (China Kantner), but can't seem to "go for it." It's bad vibes all around in this pointless and juvenile flick—puke in the couch, piss in the ice tray, fights at every turn, complete disrespect for women, one creepy trip at a Blue Öyster Cult concert, and a harsh bust at the end, not to mention the seedy, twiggy ditch weed they're all smoking. Talk about a buzz kill.

Strange Wilderness (2008)

🌿🌿🌿 Picking up on the age-old stereotype that stoners love nature shows, here's a movie about a TV series made by potheads for potheads. Peter Gaulke's (Steve Zahn) father was a wildlife expert and lifelong friend of animals who starred in *Strange Wilderness*, but after his death, Peter took over as host and the show quickly devolved into uninformed antics produced by a group of imbeciles. There's Fred (Allen Covert) the sound guy, Milas (Ernest Borgnine) the cameraman, Cooker (Jonah Hill) the thong-wearing perpetual prankster, Whitaker (Kevin Heffernan) the mechanic-turned-animal-handler, and Milas's nephew, Junior (Justin Long), whose nonstop bong rips interrupt shooting on more than one occasion. When ratings plunge, the network decides to pull the plug on the graveyard shift program and replace it with one hosted by hotshot Sky Pierson (Harry Hamlin). Peter's Hail Mary for something "big" is answered when an old pal of his dad's discloses that he knows where Big Foot dwells. The motley crew hits its share of snags on the drive south of the border, not the least of which involves a turkey going deep throat on Peter's dick, but nothing can stop them from beating their rival Pierson to the location—not their tracker's betrayal, a full border search, or sexual acts in exchange for leniency. Once they do find Big Foot, the experience is short-lived and, naturally, they manage to screw it up. Looks like it's back to the aquarium water bong (goldfish included) for Peter.

Produced by Adam Sandler's Happy Madison Productions and featuring several members of the *Grandma's Boy* ensemble, *Strange Wilderness* has a similar crudeness, which doesn't always do a pothead proud. Long's portrayal of the perpetually baked Junior, however, is a hilarious high point that justifies at least one viewing.

> "This is fire season. Smokey the Bear says, put out the bong!"
>
> —Forest Patrol

Stripes (1981)

🌿🌿🌿🌿 Originally conceived as *Cheech & Chong Join the Army*, *Stripes*'s Bill Murray (John) and Harold Ramis (Russell) got the parts when the dopey duo was not available to play Ivan Reitman's sarcastic soldiers. Though there are no drugs in the original movie, almost any film starring Murray can be considered stony. Down on their luck, John and Russell enlist. John immediately locks horns with Drill Sergeant Hulka (Warren Oates) and becomes the company's cutup. After basic training, they're dispatched on a special mission that ends up in the former Czechoslovakia, where bumbling Russians are no match for John, Russell, and their MP girlfriends, Stella (P. J. Soles, who gets naked) and Louise (Sean Young). The movie's obvious stoner, Elmo (Judge Reinhold), has little screen time and, sadly, the one drug scene—a seven-minute segment where Russell doses on acid and smokes a huge Colombian joint—was deleted. Despite this gaffe, *Stripes* remains an indelible classic.

John: "Chicks dig me because I rarely wear underwear, and when I do, it's usually something unusual."

Superbad (2007)

Judd Apatow's revenge of the nerds continued in summer 2007, turning to his *Undeclared* collaborator Greg Mottola and writers Seth Rogen and Evan Goldberg for what essentially turned out to be a raunchy teenage prequel to the early-thirties slackers of *Knocked Up*. What *American Graffiti* was to the sixties, *Dazed and Confused* to the seventies, and *Fast Times at Ridgemont High* the eighties, *Superbad* is to their foul-mouthed, tits- and ass-obsessed, snot-nosed millennial successors, following a group of high schoolers on the eve of graduation and meanwhile grabbing the R-rated comic zeitgeist like a doctor administering a hernia test. Seth (Apatow protégé Jonah Hill) and Evan (*Arrested Development*'s fumbling Michael Cera) make a classic comedy duo, best buds for life, but on the verge of going in different directions. One is incorrigibly obnoxious but in reality vulnerable, the other painfully insecure and vulnerable, and both are virgins. Interspersing ruminations on Orson Welles peaking too soon with the merits of a porn site named "The Vag-tastic Voyage," the film is both up-to-the-minute pop culture savvy and crudely vulgar, but never less than exhilarating. Christopher Mintz-Plasse plays class geek McLovin like he just stepped from the halls of a San Fernando Valley high school, which he did, while *SNL*'s Bill Hader and Rogen himself appear as two Keystone Kops who make the kids look like models of civility. The film would be nothing more than a modern-day *Porky's* or *American Pie* if it weren't for the subtext of a sweetly sentimental bromance that completely nails the instant you change from boys to men, at once hilariously knowing and ironically anti-homophobic at the same time. And it's got a great funky seventies-style soundtrack, featuring everything from the Bar-Kays and Bootsy Collins to Van Halen's "Panama." This is not just another teen sex comedy, but a sex comedy that happens to star teens, offering some knowing pleasures for the perpetual adolescent still lurking inside all of us especially the guys.

STONER COPS

To protect, serve, and party! Now that's what we call the dream police.

Super Troopers: The opening scene is a classic, where the Spurbury, Vermont, highway cops totally mess with three stoners in a car, but never arrest them. Later, four troopers smoke a joint at the station house while watching a cartoon on TV.

Frank Serpico (*Serpico*): A pot-smoking, counterculture cop who exposes rampant corruption in the New York City police department? Now that's a stoner hero. Al Pacino brilliantly embraced the role of Frank Serpico in the 1973 film (based on a true story)—he famously smokes several times in his Greenwich Village apartment—and got his first Academy Award nomination for Best Actor.

Deputy Clementine Johnson (*Reno 911!: Miami*): On the TV show, Reno's big-bosomed trooper has a habit of stashing confiscated joints in her big hair. Facing impending death in the movie, Clemmy (Wendi McLendon-Covey) chooses "Legalize it" as her final words.

Sergeant Stedanko (*Up in Smoke*): The badass Keystone Kop of *Up in Smoke* has a conversion in *Nice Dreams*, and spends the entire movie getting high on the department's supply. "The only way to catch a doper is when you yourself become a smoker," Stedanko (Stacy Keach) says seriously. "The surest way to make them bleed is when you bust their ass and steal their weed."

Officers Slater and Michaels (*Superbad*): Bill Hader and Seth Rogen play police officers who'd rather join the party than bust it, which is exactly what happens when Slater and Michaels catch the underage McLovin (Christopher Mintz-Plasse) buying beer with a fake ID. Several six-packs and a totaled police cruiser later, the nerd comes out a hero and the cops score some cool cred.

Super Troopers (2001)

🖊️ 🍷 👀

🌿 🌿 🌿 🌿 Broken Lizard, the five-man comedy troupe headed by director Jay Chandrasekhar, is set loose in Vermont as state police nurse a grudge against the local cops. It's like Delta House versus Omega House in *Animal House*, but with police officers instead of frat boys. The pranks fly fast and furious, from chugging maple syrup to some man-on-bear action. Canadian weed is zooming across the Vermont border in tractor trailers, with support of the corrupt Spurbury doughnut eaters. The state police seize and sample the evidence. When Governor Jessman (Lynda Carter) stops by for a photo op and is told it's for a marijuana bust, she asks her assistant pointedly: "Then why are we here?" Best of all is the opening scene when three stoners are hassled by the highway cops, leading one (Geoffrey Arend) to scarf down two bags of chronic. Officer Thorny (Chandrasehkar) plays into their paranoia, asking: "Do you know why I pulled you over? For littering and littering, and littering, and littering and smokin' the reefer. To teach you a lesson we're going to stand here and watch you smoke the whole bag." Next scene, the stoners are in the backseat of the police car in hot pursuit of another vehicle. They never get busted, but do get their revenge (sort of) in the end.

🌿 DIRECTOR'S TAKE: JAY CHANDRASEKHAR 🌿

As an actor, director, and one-fifth of the comedy team Broken Lizard, Jay Chandrasekhar has played a key role in stoner movie history: He directed the kooky comedies *Super Troopers*, *Club Dread*, and *Beerfest* and bravely took on the big-screen version of *Dukes of Hazzard*. Chandrasekhar clued us in on some stony secrets from the set and what it's like to be a pothead player in Hollywood.

Reefer Movie Madness: *Super Troopers* is your definitive stoner movie. How did it come about?

Jay Chandrasekhar: We heard a story about a friend's bachelor party, where the plan was to go over the border from Vermont to Montreal, take mushrooms, and go to clubs. So they were in line to cross the border and saw that every car was getting pulled over and searched, and they weren't sure what to do. So one of the guys ate all the mushrooms that were intended for five people, the Canadian authorities searched the van, and they found half a joint. Nobody wanted to say whose it was, so they put them all in a cell while this poor guy was tripping out. That's sort of where we got the idea for the opening scene. As we were driving back to New York from this wedding, we saw a trooper who had pulled somebody over and we were laughing about that idea that suburban kids are always kind of tough about cops because they're trying to mimic gangster rappers, and when they get pulled over, they turn into these sniveling geeks. We thought it would be a fun dynamic for a movie. We were also heavily influenced by *Up in Smoke*.

RMM: It must have been a lot of fun making that movie.

JC: We did have a lot of fun. You don't have any sense that you're making a stoner movie. We were—and still are—stoners where we'd smoke almost every day. It's just what we did. Every single movie we saw, we'd go high; it was such a major part of our life. So we wrote that way, and anything we created would probably have some sort of stoner appeal.

RMM: What about the slasher-meets-stoner comedy *Club Dread*? Was it inspired by any of the great island flicks?

JC: We started with the goal of making an eighties slasher film, because the movies we grew up with and loved were the original *Halloween* and *Friday the 13th*. So the idea was there's a bunch of people on an island, everyone's getting killed, and they're trying to figure out who the murderer is. It was originally set at a mountain ski resort because I wanted to shoot in the snow, but budget-wise, it would've cost more. But the island setting was great because you can't get off it.

RMM: Where was it shot?

JC: On the west coast of Mexico—not Cancún, real Mexico—it was just beautiful. When it would get too dark to shoot, the entire crew tripped out and went swimming in the ocean. It was amazing. But we were very vigilant about making sure the script was solid before we got there, and that we didn't get blown away with this smoke-pot-in-the-sun mentality. It had to be a good film, because some of those island movies can be a little bit uneven. There are quite a few fans who dismiss that movie—people who saw *Super Troopers* and expected pure comedy, not blood, and were put off by that—but it has its fans, too.

RMM: You directed *Dukes of Hazzard*, which featured a short scene with Willie Nelson smoking a joint from an apple pipe. Was that in the original script?

JC: It might not have been, but we just knew we would shoot it. The funny thing is, before Willie came down to Louisiana, we had gotten into a phase of smoking out of an apple. We certainly didn't invent it; we just thought it was funny to pop a couple bowls in an apple, plus it was a healthier alternative to the tin can. I showed it to Willie and he just took to it. From then on, there would be, say, six or seven joints going around, and just as many apples. We would have a case of them in the bus—you'd grab one, smoke

it, inhale, and take a bite. So when we had this scene where he was supposed to be smoking a joint, he insisted on it being an apple. And I think he takes a bite of the apple, too. He improvised that part, and when I was shooting it, I was, like, I have to be in this scene. I can't let this go on and not be in it.

RMM: *Beerfest* seemed to resonate with stoners—is there a tangible connection between weed enthusiasts and beer lovers?

JC: We love beer as much as we love pot; it's not a mutually exclusive thing. But it's interesting: Our fanbase expanded dramatically in a more clean-cut Republican way after *Beerfest*. When people would ask us if we did anything else, and we'd say *Super Troopers*, they'd be, like, "That stoner comedy?" They were really different from our other fans.

RMM: The last scene in *Beerfest* hinted at a possible sequel called *Potfest*. Was that a joke or is there something in the works?

JC: It was a gag, but we've been asked about it so much that we've started to outline something. It's not a sequel about a pot-smoking competition; it's more of a quest movie where we play different characters. Basically, we're mulling over making a Broken Lizard pot movie. We also have pre-drafts done for a *Super Troopers* sequel that's shaping up very well.

RMM: What are some of your favorite movies to watch stoned?

JC: *Spinal Tap*, *Airplane!*, *Monty Python and the Holy Grail*, *48 Hours*. I also really like the Landis movies—*Animal House*, *Blues Brothers*, and *Trading Places*. There's one really obscure movie called *Billy Liar*, which we used to watch in college religiously. More recently, I absolutely loved *Pineapple Express*. I think it's one of the great great stoner comedies. It really captures the reality of smoking pot in the early scenes, and then gives stoners all that funny stony action that they want with a mindless, strung-together plot about the bad guys. Danny McBride is a gem in that movie and James Franco is just a great stoner.

Supergrass, The (1985)

🎭 ✂️ 💉 👀

🌿🌿🌿🌙 Dennis Carter (Adrian Edmondson) tries to impress a woman by telling her he's a drug smuggler (he's not) and is snagged by British police. He informs the cops about a shipment of heroin that's scheduled to arrive by boat in the seaside village of Hope Cove. Scotland Yard employs him as a "supergrass"—British slang for confidential informant or stool pigeon (not the popular rock band)—and he travels there with Harvey Duncan (director Peter Richardson) and Lesley Reynolds (Jennifer Saunders), an estranged cop couple. Two dealers (one in drag) are staying at the same hotel. No-nonsense detective Troy (Robbie Coltrane) arrives as well, equipped with a chain saw. Another dealer (Daniel Peacock), who blabbed about the drug boat to Dennis, sells Harvey a bag of scag for twenty quid in a club, then gets murdered in the hotel. The plot thickens as Harvey gets jealous of Dennis's dalliance with Lesley. When Troy chops up the wrong boat, the dealers get away with the white-powder stash and Dennis has a good larf. This lively caper pops with a jazzy score and the soulful theme song by P. P. Arnold.

Surfer, Dude (2008)

🖊️ 🍾 🎭 👀

🌿🌿🌿🌙 As world-renowned surfer Steve Addington, Matthew McConaughey reprises his Wooderson stoner character from *Dazed and Confused* and adds a touch of Spicoli to the mix. Steve refuses to sell out, despite efforts by his hippie manager Jack, played perfectly by Woody Harrelson ("we gotta, like, fertilize the money tree so it can keep growing"). A video-game company offers $50K to digitize Steve's image, but he smells a rat and declines the offer. Then the waves stop rolling in, which is a major bummer, man. Steve seeks weed and advice from Farmer Bob (Willie Nelson) and hooks up with Danni (Alexie Gilmore). Lots of joints are smoked and in one particularly outrageous scene, Steve's dad (Scott Glenn) breaks out a huge cola bud. Despite McConaughey's star power, the film

had a minimal theatrical release and went straight to DVD, but this sleeper is a stony keeper.

Jack: "You just harshed my morning mellow."

Tao of Steve, The (2000)

🖊️ 🍾 🎭 ✂️

🌿🌿🌿🌙 Donal Logue took a page out of fellow Canadian Bill Murray's comedy-actor's notebook for his lead role as Dex, an unrepentant womanizer who advises about how to pick up women to anyone who will listen. A part-time schoolteacher and self-professed Buddhist slacker, Dex has put on some weight over the years ("Now I'm fat Elvis"), but that hasn't slowed down his overactive libido. He wakes and bakes with bong hits, has a dog, and plays Frisbee with his stoner roommates. But he's not really happy until Syd (Greer Goodman), a woman he knew casually in college, comes back into his life. Their courtship is a philosophical and emotional tango. Syd's not convinced Dex is ready to settle down, and Dex has to put out some fires before he can move on with Syd. The "Steve" in the title is described by Dex as "the prototypical American male—Steve McGarrett, Steve Austin, Steve McQueen. Steve is a state of mind, it's a way of living. James Bond is a Steve. Spider-Man's a Steve."

Dex, however, begins to doubt his own dating rules—eliminate desire, do something excellent in the other person's presence (this demonstrates sexual worthiness), and then retreat. When Syd leaves Santa Fe for New York, Steve breaks from his theory of detachment and follows her there—though we're left to ponder how it all worked out. Directed by Jenniphr Goodman and her sister Greer, the film has just one star, Logue

> "Doing stuff is overrated. Hitler, he did a lot. But don't we all wish he would've just stayed home and gotten stoned."
>
> —Dex

(known best from the TV show *Growing Pains*), who carries it admirably with his standout performance.

Teen Wolf (1985)

🌿 🍷

🍁 🍁 🍁 In this offering of just-be-yourself pubescent fare and mindless fun, troubled teen Scott Howard (Michael J. Fox) takes his high school by storm upon discovering that he can change into a mystical wolf creature with more armpit hair than Cousin Itt. But, while Scott's special werewolf powers bring on incredible popularity, it's his friend Rupert "Stiles" Stilinsky (Jerry Levine) who should be getting all the attention. Dismissed by classmates for wearing novelty T-shirts ("What Are You Looking At, Dicknose?") and running his mouth,

Stiles always delivers the celebratory goods—either by acting as ringleader during a house party, scoring the keg, getting his portly friend Chubby (Mark Holton) to chow down an entire bowl of Jell-O inside a girl's blouse, or playing the devoted fan at every basketball game—the overlooked smartass's free-spirited attitude goes unnoticed. Though perhaps, in the end, Scott's the one who should get the praise. If it weren't for his wolf's mad sense of smell, Stiles would have never recovered that bag of shwag he lost in the garage.

Stiles: "If it's that intense, I'll need a solid buzz to think clearly."

🍁 HIGH FIVE: RICHARD LINKLATER FILMS 🍁

Over a long and stony career, Austin's No. 1 auteur balances heady philosophical dialogue with a lighthearted, irreverent tone.

Slacker (1991): In this peculiarly fascinating portrait of Austin, characters and storylines intersect, go off on tangents, and then disappear, never to be heard from again. No pot is smoked in Linklater's debut, but it sure feels like the director spiked the Kool-Aid.

Dazed and Confused (1993): Linklater ushered in the new wave of stoner movies with his tale of high-school life in 1976. Like *Fast Times at Ridgemont High*, *Dazed* introduced a stellar cast of young actors—Matthew McConaughey, Ben Affleck, Rory Cochrane, Parker Posey, Milla Jovovich, Joey Lauren Adams. It's hazing time for the frosh, and the seniors have big plans for them. Lots of pot smoking, a great stoner character (Slater), and the killer seventies soundtrack elevated the teen comedy to new heights.

School of Rock (2003): Lovable slacker Dewey Finn (Jack Black) is a hopeless wannabe rock star posing as a substitute teacher at a posh private school. On the curriculum: rock-and-roll. Dewey forms the greatest prepubescent band to ever hit the stage and finally discovers his own

sense of self-worth. Black reigns supreme as the hilarious head of the class in this kid-friendly comedy written by Mike White.

Fast Food Nation (2006): Eric Schlosser's exposé about the food industry comes to life in Linklater's expert hands. Mexicans are illegally imported to work at a slaughterhouse in Colorado, charges of meat tainted with manure are investigated, and students protest the dangerous conditions at the plant. Both dead serious and farcical, Linklater, a vegetarian, takes special relish in telling this story about corruption in the beef industry.

A Scanner Darkly (2006): As in *Waking Life* (2001), Linklater employs the unique rotoscoping animation technique for this amusing adaptation of Philip K. Dick's sci-fi novel about the government's evil plan to hook citizens on a drug called Substance D. Keanu Reeves plays narc Bob Arctor, who gets hooked on the stuff. His friends are a veritable cast of stoners, portrayed by Woody Harrelson, Robert Downey Jr., Rory Cochrane, and Winona Ryder.

Out-there fantasies and trippy hallucinations triggered by primo pot

Harold & Kumar Go to White Castle: To the tune of Heart's "Crazy On You," Kumar (Kal Penn) imagines life with a human-size bag of weed (a.k.a. Weedie)—from paddleboat rides to sex, marriage, and the inevitable domestic violence. Weedie also made an appearance in the sequel as part of a threesome.

Tenacious D in the Pick of Destiny: When JB (Jack Black) picks mushrooms at the side of the road and eats them, he goes off on an animated ride on the back of Sasquatch (John C. Reilly).

The Big Lebowski: After The Dude (Jeff Bridges) is drugged at porn king Jackie Treehorn's house, he has a psychedelic dream featuring Saddam Hussein as a bowling alley attendant, synchronized dancing by a bevy of long-legged beauties wearing bowling-pin bouffants, and himself floating between them.

The first edition's LSD-inspired song "Just Dropped In (To See What Condition My Condition Was In)" serves as soundtrack to the beloved scene known as "Gutterballs."

Nine to Five: After sharing a joint, the overworked, underappreciated ladies of Consolidated trade fantasies of how they'd off their jerk of a boss: Judy's (Jane Fonda) idea is execution by rifle, Doralee's (Dolly Parton) is humiliation and emasculation, and, from the twisted mind of Violet (Lily Tomlin), kill him with kindness, adorable Disney-like creatures, and a paralyzing mystery poison. Now that's what you call a triple threat.

High Times' Pot Luck: Mobster Frank (Frank Adonis) gets high for the first time and, his head spinning, dreams that he's in a fantasy with Beatles-style British voices speaking to him.

Tenacious D in the Pick of Destiny (2006)

🍷 🍄

🌿 🌿 🌿 🌿 Like Cheech & Chong before them, Tenacious D—Jack Black (JB) and Kyle Gass (KG)—worked their way up from live shows to the movie screen. Both duos share a love of comedy and music, though not even C & C were so audacious as to write a rock opera. Director Liam Lynch, who had a British hit with "United States of Whatever," adds to the musical equation.

This whimsical rock-and-roll fable is set in Venice Beach, California, where JB and KG meet and begin their beautiful relationship, sealed with bong hits. Just like in *Up in Smoke,* the goal is to win a band

contest. When they learn about the mythical pick—fashioned from the devil's tooth—and its magical powers (as told to them by Ben Stiller in a cameo as a Guitar Center specialist), JB and KG devise a plan to steal it from the Rock & Roll History Museum. Along the way, JB eats mushrooms and flies off with Sasquatch in an animated sequence. In the final showdown with Satan (Foo Fighters's Dave Grohl), they learn, like Dorothy in *The Wizard of Oz*, that they don't need any special powers to accomplish their goals. One of the devil's horns breaks off and, at the end, the victorious rockers smoke out of the Bong of Destiny, exhaling green pixie dust. Except for cuts by The Who and Ronnie James Dio (he makes a cameo, as does Meatloaf), the soundtrack is pure D, including highlights "Master Exploder" and "The Metal." On the DVD, don't miss Black and Gass's commentary: It's a stoner essential.

KG: "Go score me a dime bag."

JB: "A what?"

KG: "Ten dollars' worth of weed. Now listen: Go down to Wake & Bake Pizza, ask for Jojo. Tell him you want the Bob Marley Extra Crispy. He'll know what you're talkin' about."

JB: "All right, dude, roger that. One Extra Crispy comin' up!"

Thank God It's Friday (1978)

Hot damn, it's disco night in Los Angeles and time to boogie! That's the basic premise of this poor man's version of *Saturday Night Fever*, which tells interweaving stories of ten seemingly random people who find themselves at the same club on a Friday night. Fictional hot spot the Zoo (a more pedestrian version of Studio 54, complete with multiple levels, a game room, and even a jewelry store for big spenders), is hosting a dance contest and the Commodores are scheduled to perform, so the place is hopping. New-girl-in-town Jennifer (Debra Winger in her first major role) hits the bars in search of a decent guy (fat chance with pickup lines like this one: "Let's say we go back to my place and see God." Barf). High schoolers Frannie (Valerie Landsburg) and Jeannie (Terri Nunn) are determined to win the $200 prize so they can buy Kiss tickets. Kvetchy married couple Dave (Mark Lonow) and Sue (Andrea Howard) enter on a whim and soon consider casual sex with total strangers. Aspiring singer Nicole (Donna Summer) just wants to get her demo heard. And Latin lover Marv, a.k.a. Leatherman (Chick Vennera), is all about getting stoned and hitting the dance floor. Actually, Marv's post-toke parking lot routine could easily go up against Kevin Bacon's warehouse dance in *Footloose* as one of the best to ever hit the screen. And he's not the only one smoking. Two desperate bachelors Carl (Paul Jabara) and Ken (John Friedrich) light up a big spliff on their drive over, while drugged-out regular Jackie (Mews Small) sucks down a nitrous hit and swallows several mystery pills before the Commodores (dressed in full moonmen regalia with Lionel Richie sporting a monster 'fro) bust out "Too Hot to Trot." *Thank God It's Friday* won an Oscar (for "Last Dance" as best song) and as disco movies go, it holds up as a sweet relic that paints pot and people in a positive light. Good times, indeed.

Carl to Ken: "This is guaranteed to paralyze you. Here."

There's Something About Mary (1998)

🔖 🍸 🔪 💊

🌿 🌿 🌿 🌿 🌿 Only the Farrelly brothers (*Dumb and Dumber, Kingpin*) could come up with a love story as twisted, raunchy, and utterly brilliant as *There's Something About Mary*. It starts in the directors' hometown of Cumberland, Rhode Island, in 1985, where a brace-faced Ted (Ben Stiller) is so excited and nervous to take the gorgeous Mary (Cameron Diaz) to the prom, that he accidentally jams his "franks and beans" in his zipper. Ouch. Flash forward thirteen years and Ted wants to look up his unrequited high school love, and, on the advice of his friend Dom (Chris Elliott), hires shady would-be P.I. Pat Healy (Matt Dillon) to track her down in Miami. But after a few days of hardcore stalking, Healy falls for Mary and moves to Miami armed with an arsenal of guaranteed-to-work pickup lines (telling Ted, meanwhile, that Mary's a hefty wheelchaired mom of four and a mail-order bride). Ted also heads to Florida and is spotted almost immediately by Mary's mentally challenged brother, Warren (W. Earl Brown).

In time, Ted and Mary reconnect on an honest level, and even bond over a beachside joint (a nearly identical scene plays out with Ben Stiller and Michelle Monaghan in the Farrellys' *The Heartbreak Kid*), but he's got competition, not just from Healy, but Mary's friend Tucker (Lee Evans) and her ex, Woogie, all phonies to an extreme. Ted continues his series of unfortunate mishaps, not the least of which involves emptying his "loaded gun" (bad advice from Dom) before a date with Mary (which ends up in her hair), and is eventually found out as the one who stuck the sketchy Healy on Mary in the first place. Jeffrey Tambor and Sarah Silverman add to the hilarity in minor roles, indie god Jonathan Richman provides the soundtrack, and NFL star Brett Favre shows up for a cameo. It's a laugh-out-loud riot all the way.

🌿 FIVE MORE BY THE FARRELLY BROTHERS 🌿

Dumb and Dumber (1994): Heavy on bodily secretions (particularly in the painful seven-minute-long Turbo-Lax scene) and goofy physical comedy, Jim Carrey and Jeff Daniels play simpleton roommates who inadvertently foil a kidnapping plot by finding a briefcase full of cash.

Outside Providence (1999): The siblings from Rhode Island wrote and produced this pothead tale about a troublemaker who's sent off to prep school in the 1970s. It's their true stoner movie, with bong hits out of a fifty-five-gallon drum, a character named Drugs Delaney, and a very special use for dental clips.

Me, Myself & Irene (2000): Jim Carrey's second Farrelly project (costarring Renée Zellweger) is an absurd comedy caper that tackles multiple personalities, shameless adultery, and attempted murder. Zellweger as Irene has a funny line when she tells a cop, "So I smoked some pot, what is that, a crime?" Proceed with caution.

Shallow Hal (2001): Hal (Jack Black) only dates beautiful women, but once he is hypnotized by self-help guru Tony Robbins, he has visions that allow him to see the inner beauty of un-classically attractive girls. Not their best film, but there's some pleasure in seeing Gwyneth Paltrow in a fat suit.

The Heartbreak Kid (2007): In this remake of the 1972 Neil Simon comedy, Ben Stiller stars as the unlucky-in-love Eddie, who finds out that his newly betrothed dream girl is actually a nightmare. Malin Akerman, Michelle Monaghan, and Jerry Stiller costar, but it's Danny McBride who steals the show.

Things Are Tough All Over (1982)

Often overlooked, the fourth Cheech & Chong movie is one of their best. The duo plays dual roles—themselves and Arabs Mr. Slyman and Habib—as they drive a limo cross-country from Chicago to Las Vegas. They eventually trash the vehicle and end up in the Nevada desert tripping on peyote and singing "Me and My Old Lady." While it's fun to watch Cheech and Chong be their usual dopey selves—the laundromat scene with Cheech spinning inside a dryer is classic—their Middle Eastern doppelgängers steal the movie, with a switchblade-wielding Habib (Chong) disappearing into the role so effectively you have to squint real hard to make sure it's our loveable stoner.

Chong: "I don't do drugs anymore. I feel great. You got any?"

This Is Spiñal Tap (1984)

Though they currently reside in the "where are they now?" file, Spiñal Tap took the volume up to eleven as one of England's loudest bands during their heyday. This Is Spiñal Tap traces the hard-rocking group's history from its British Invasion beginnings and psychedelic roots through the seventies' metal years, all the way up to the controversial LP in 1982 and its fractious ac-

companying tour, replete with groupies, group infighting, disruptive girlfriends, declining popularity, malfunctioning stage props, and questionable set design.

If only they'd really existed. Oh, they did eventually, making a follow-up album and embarking on a couple of reunion tours. But Spiñal Tap were funniest when they were fictitious, a faux-rock band that spoofed the pretensions and excesses of seventies metal while mocking the dim-witted and egotistical rock star—with enough affection that they betrayed a lot of love for that kind of music. ("Not yours personally, just the whole genre of rock-and-roll.") Drawing on mystical stoner rock like Black Sabbath, Led Zeppelin, Blue Öyster Cult, and Deep Purple, the boys in Spiñal Tap endured critical disdain and the deaths of numerous drummers on the road to glory, which they finally achieved in an unusual setting.

The group—David St. Hubbins (Michael McKean), Derek Smalls (Harry Shearer), and Nigel Tufnel (Christopher Guest)—wrote and play ten original songs in the film, touching on creation myths, crude sex, Druidic fantasy, and the rock-and-roll experience, playing them wholly straight for maximum giggle effect. (There's also a memorable "jazz odyssey" that doesn't go over quite so well.) Cameos and bit parts from Billy Crystal, Anjelica Huston, Fran Drescher, Bruno Kirby, Paul Shaffer, and Ed Begley Jr., flesh out the story directed by Rob Reiner—and watch for a brief bit with a young Dana Carvey, years before he hit paydirt by partying in the basement with another metal-loving buddy.

Together (2000)

Set in Stockholm in 1975 in a communal house called the Together Collective, a group of friends and relatives grapple with the complex social issues of the day. Dialectical political arguing at the dinner table replaces TV, which is banned until Göran (Gustaf Hammarsten) brings one home for the kids to watch. There's a lot of sexual awakening and bed-swapping going on, but Göran draws his line at free love when Lena (Anja Lundkvist) starts sleeping with another housemate. The central story revolves around Göran's sister Elisabeth (Lisa Lundgren), who arrives with her two children after being punched by her alcoholic husband Rolf (Michael Nyqvist). More traditional than Göran, Elisabeth gradually warms up to her new surroundings and, by the end, when Rolf apologizes, declares she's become an armpit hair–growing Socialist. There's one reference to marijuana when Lasse (Ola Rapace) is accused of "growing cannabis on half the potato patch." To which he sheepishly replies, "It was only one plant."

Tommy Boy (1995)

🚬 🍸

🌿 🌿 🌿 As perpetual fuckup Tommy Boy, Chris Farley's first starring role in a feature film may be his finest. Fat, sloppy, and dumb as a stump, Tommy barely graduates college (where his favorite extracurricular activities are cow tipping

and upside-down bong hits), but as heir apparent of Callahan Auto Parts, the successful company that's been in his family for generations, his dad's unexpected death and its impact on that company becomes the most important test of his life. With snooty sidekick Richard (fellow *Saturday Night Live* alum David Spade) along for the ride, Tommy hits

---

🌿 STONY MOCKUMENTARIES 🌿

Faux docs that bring the funny

***This Is Spinal Tap* (1984):** Pioneering and unparalleled, the story of past-their-prime metal band Spinal Tap, told through a series of interviews with documentarian Marty DiBergi (Rob Reiner), was a first effort for the comedy trio of Michael McKean, Harry Shearer, and Christopher Guest, and undoubtedly their finest.

***Waiting for Guffman* (1996):** Though it preceded *Best in Show*, *A Mighty Wind*, and *For Your Consideration* by several years, in *Waiting for Guffman*, Christopher Guest had already perfected the mockumentary formula. The subjects: Blaine, Missouri, locals recruited for a community theater production by one kooky director named Corky (Guest) who has his own grandiose Broadway dreams.

***Drop Dead Gorgeous* (1999):** Kirsten Dunst takes center stage as one of a dozen Mount Rose, Minnesota, principals who are "interviewed" about the biggest thing ever to hit their town— the Sarah Rose Cosmetics American Teen Princess Pageant. You've got your Christ-loving frontrunner (Denise Richards), your bat-shit-crazy, win-at-all-costs mother (Kirstie Allie), and your questionable judges panel, consisting of the local pedophile, the guy who runs the hardware store, and his mentally challenged brother. Mockumentary gold.

***Best in Show* (2000):** Tapping into the notion that a stoner's perfect Saturday afternoon involves waking, baking, and watching Animal Planet, Michael McKean and Christopher Guest play proud dog owners who compete against a host of canine-crazed eccentrics at the prestigious Mayflower Kennel Club dog show. Eugene Levy, Parker Posey, Catherine O'Hara, and Jennifer Coolidge help take mockumentary hilarity to new heights.

***Trailer Park Boys: The Movie* (2006):** Canada's stoniest trio put their pathetic day-to-day lives on display documentary-style. Why would anyone care enough to tune in? Because as trailer trash poster boys go, Ricky, Julian, and Bubbles are as miserably funny as they come.

the road on a string of Midwest sales calls in a last-ditch attempt to save the company from the clutches of his dad's money-hungry widow (Bo Derek) and her alleged son (Rob Lowe). They hit snags at every stop on this highway to hell, but there are moments of tenderness, too—a passionate sing-along to the Carpenters in the car, late-night chats at roadside motels—and in the end, Tommy beats all expectations by hoodwinking rival parts maker Zalinsky (Dan Aykroyd) into placing a huge order just in the nick of time. Laugh-out-loud funny, thanks mostly to the late Farley's now-classic slapstick shtick, the movie proved his box-office might and opened the door to future lead turns in comedies like *Black Sheep* and *Beverly Hills Ninja*.

Totally Baked: A Pot-U-Mentary (2007)

🌿 🌿 The best intentions go awry in this slapdash production combining skits, fake interviews, and stand-up performances by the likes of Doug Benson (*Super High Me*), Tom Rhodes, and Jackie "The Joke Man" Martling. The main story line (narrated by producer/comic Craig Shoemaker) is about two medical-marijuana activists who take over a house of straights and turn them on to Bubbleberry and brownies. Hilarity ensues. Unfortunately, it's not very funny and, at times, embarrassingly bad. Exceptions include Marianne Curan's spot-on Martha Stewart spoof ("I'm a heroin junkie"), Stephen Tobolowsky's farmer Jesco Rollins, who grows fake pot, "one hundred percent legal and guaranteed not to get you high," and Rich Hardesty's heartfelt sing-along, "All My Friends Are Stoners."

Comic: "When in Rome, go to Amsterdam."

Trailer Park Boys: The Movie (2006)

🌿 🌿 🌿 🌿 Any pot smoker who hasn't caught wind of *The Trailer Park Boys* is missing out on what might be the funniest stoner team to hit

the screen since Cheech & Chong. The trio of Ricky (Robb Wells), Julian (John Paul Tremblay), and Bubbles (Mike Smith), residents of the white-trashiest trailer park in Nova Scotia, has had Canadian audiences in stitches since 2001, when the TV series first premiered on the Showcase network. It's since run through six additional seasons, which are aired in more than a dozen countries (unfortunately, the U.S. isn't one of them), and turned into a feature film with a sequel (*Countdown to Liquor Day*). And while the central characters are the driving force behind this farce, shot mockumentary-style, there's a whole assortment of wacky cohabitants (including Oscar winner Ellen Page, who got her pre-*Juno* break on *TPB*), each more absurdly oddball than the next, to keep you laughing at every possible moment.

You can see the whole sorry lot in *TPB*'s debut movie, which doesn't stray far from the sitcom's recurring script. Ricky and Julian are fresh out of jail and looking to score—girls, weed, cigarettes, liquor, pepperoni, cash, and other of life's basic necessities—but, as usual, Sunnyvale trailer park supervisor Mr. Lahey (John Dunsworth) and his shirtless "dirty onion ring bastard" (according to Bubbles) crony Randy (Patrick Roach) are conspiring to get them evicted. The boys decide that they'll rip off parking meters for change to raise money for their lot fees, then fixate on a giant coin ball at a local movie theater and come up with a plan to pull off the "Big Dirty." Meanwhile, Ricky's determined to get his girlfriend Lucy (Lucy Decoutere) back. She's working at a strip club and sleeping with the owner. One big shotgun hit does the trick. Ricky and Julian expend a lot of energy keeping hangers-on and perpetual idiots Trevor and Cory (Michael Jackson and Cory Bowles) in line, and also look out for their adorably dorky bespectacled buddy, Bubbles, who lives in a makeshift shack where he fixes supermarket carts for a living and cares for a couple dozen cats. They're all creatures of ridiculous habits—Julian, a man of few words, is never seen without his rum and Coke (even in jail and court), while Ricky is rarely without his permanent hand attachment: a joint—which is what makes repeated viewing of the series so enjoyable. The movie gives you a good taste of the *Trailer Park Boys* life—where toasting bread with a blowtorch and living out of a one-door car is de rigeur—but for a full-on experience, try watching a whole season on DVD in one day.

☘ Q & A: TRAILER PARK BOYS ☘

Canada's dumbest stoner trio is also its funniest. Over the span of seven TV seasons and two movies, Ricky (Robb Wells), Julian (John Paul Tremblay), and Bubbles (Mike Smith) have taken dopey antics to new lows, while surrounding themselves with a haggard group of misfits more pathetic than themselves. No wonder the Trailer Park Boys have gained a cult stoner following that only seems to grow with every rip of the bong. We caught up with the actors—and the characters—during a 2010 stop in Los Angeles and learned a lot about what makes these stony minds tick.

Interview with the Trailer Park Boys

Reefer Movie Madness: What are your favorite movies to watch stoned?

Julian: We went to see that *Avatar* 3-D movie baked, and it was really crazy. *Jacob's Ladder* is a good one to watch baked; it freaks you right out. *Silence of the Lambs* . . .

Ricky: Pretty much any movie's good if you're baked.

Bubbles: I like *The Wizard of Oz* with Pink Floyd playing behind it. That's one of my favorites.

RMM: You guys have a TV and DVD player to watch movies on?

Bubbles: I have a black-and-white TV that's high definition.

Ricky: I've got a VCR.

Bubbles: I've got a satellite J-Roc hooked up.

RMM: Did you guys go to the movies when you were kids?

Ricky: Yeah, we used to sneak into quite a few. *Star Wars* and stuff like that. Bubbles liked *Raiders of the Lost Ark*.

Bubbles: Yeah, I started dressing like Indiana Jones for about six months after that, jumping off buildings. I broke my leg. *Jaws* scared the nuts off me.

Ricky: I know Bubbles likes anything with Mel Gibson or Clint Eastwood.

RMM: Trailer Park Boys has two movies now. Where do you see yourself in the annals of stoner movie history?

Julian: Probably between *Up in Smoke* and *Fear & Loathing in Las Vegas*.

RMM: If someone were to play you in a movie version of your movie, who would it be?

Bubbles: Brad Pitt for me.

Ricky: Brad Pitt? That's an odd choice. Anthony Hopkins for me maybe.

Bubbles: He's a bit old, Ricky.

Julian: Michael Madsen maybe. He's tall like me.

Bubbles: Too bad Patrick Swayze passed on, because he would definitely play Julian.

Julian: You guys are fucked.

756873

Interview with Robb Wells, John Paul Tremblay, and Mike Smith

Reefer Movie Maddness: Was the idea for TPB born out of a session?

John Paul Tremblay: Yeah, we'd smoke a joint here and there, come up with some crazy ideas, and then shoot them.

RMM: When did you guys start smoking?

JPT: I started probably when I was fifteen or sixteen.

Robb Wells: I didn't start until my early twenties, believe it or not. I don't know why it was missing from my life before that.

RMM: It seems like Showcase, the network that aired the TPB TV show, let you get away with a lot in terms of pot use. Is Canada just more lax?

RW: They're not as restrictive on that sort of stuff up there. There's a little more freedom of speech, freedom to do what you want. But it wasn't so much about the pot. I don't think we ever tried to glorify it; that's just what Ricky did as a living. We never really had to tone it down. If anything, it was more about the swearing. We never did, but that was sort of what they were asking us to do.

RMM: Do you ever use real weed while shooting?

RW: While we're shooting? No. As soon as we're done shooting? Yes. There was one time where we were doing bottle hits. They were trying to get this fake stuff to burn like hash, and they couldn't find anything that worked, so I think they used real hash for that one.

RMM: What is the fake stuff you're smoking?

RW: We use a lot of rosemary, believe it or not. It's actually kinda smooth. I quit smoking cigarettes, but I was using that for the last couple seasons.

RMM: When did Bubbles come in as a character?

Mike Smith: On the original black-and-white movie, I was the soundman, but I was acting at the same time and doing this character every now and then. The glasses came from a flea market in Texas. Michael Adenberg saw me doing it, thought I'd be a good character, and wrote it in.

The Oscar-nominated Ellen Page got her start on *Trailer Park Boys* playing Mr. Lahey's exceptionally cool daughter.

RW: It's unbelievable. She's just such an incredible actor that it's freaky that she was ever on our show. Even at that age, she was just brilliant. It's like dealing with somebody three times her age.

RMM: Julian's permanently attached glass of rum and coke, can you tell us about it?

JPT: I think it was just one scene that we were shooting in the first season. I was just trying to look busy, so I decided to mix up a drink, and then Mike said, "Hey man, you should always have a drink." I was, like, "Yeah." So that's how it started. The story behind it is that my parents abandoned me and I was living underneath the trailer for a while, and there were a bunch of cases of rum under there from the old man, so I was drinking rum instead of juice.

RMM: Have you ever forgotten to include the drink?

JPT: Never. It's been in every single scene. It's a pain in the ass.

RW: He's basically a one-armed man.

JPT: I'm totally used to it now. I could lose this arm and have no problems functioning.

RMM: You've been working on these characters nonstop since 1995?

RW: Pretty much. We're always doing live appearances when we're not shooting. I've had sideburns now for ten years.

MS: Yeah, I've had the same haircut for fuckin' ten years.

Tropic Thunder (2008)

🔪 💉

🌿 🌿 🌿 🌿 Conceived and directed by Ben Stiller, this razor-sharp satire of an action flick has a killer ensemble cast, insane dialogue, big explosions, movies within movies, and cool fake trailers, and by virtue of its size and ambition, may just be Stiller's greatest achievement. After only five days of shooting Vietnam veteran John "Four-Leaf" Tayback's dramatic memoir *Tropic Thunder*, filming is already a month behind schedule. Desperate to complete the movie, director Damien Cockburn (Steve Coogan) inadvertently sends his group of spoiled actors into a drug-running region of the Golden Triangle. Once-popular action hero Tugg Speedman (Ben Stiller), Australian movie-star Kirk Lazarus (Robert Downey Jr.), drug-addict funnyman Jeff Portnoy (Jack Black), moneymaking rapper Alpa Chino (Brandon T. Jackson), and novice actor Kevin Sandusky (Jay Baruchel) are left to fight among themselves in the jungle before being thrown into a real wartime situation when Tugg is captured by the heroin-producing Flaming Dragon gang. As a blazingly funny indictment of the film industry parodying self-possessed actors and messing with some serious taboos, Downey stands out as method-acting Lazarus ("a dude playing a dude disguised as another dude"), whose skin-darkening operation and refusal to break character turns the concept of blackface inside out.

Actor Tugg Speedman's previous role as "Simple Jack" pushes the discussion of portraying mentally challenged people in film, and Tom Cruise's cameo as the bald-headed, big-butted, foul-mouthed Machiavellian Jewish studio executive Les Grossman is pure genius. The dramatic/comedic face-off between Stiller and Downey is priceless, as is Cruise's bizarre money-power-seduction dance with Matthew McConaughey (Speedman's agent Rick "Pecker" Peck) and Bill Hader (Grossman's ass-kissing assistant Rob Slolom).

Jeff Portnoy: "Doesn't matter what I do. I'll always be a screwup. No one will ever respect me."

Kevin Sandusky: "That is not true. You're not a screwup. You make so many people laugh."

Jeff Portnoy: "They only laugh at my farts."

Undercover Brother (2002)

✏️

🌿 🌿 🌿 This Bond-meets-blaxploitation spoof stars Eddie Griffin as the title character—a funky superhero secret agent who fights "The Man" on behalf of the B.R.O.T.H.E.R.H.O.O.D. The preening Mr. Feather (Chris Kattan) is his adversary. Undercover Brother infiltrates "M" (Multinational, a.k.a. The Man), doubling as a marketing whiz who proposes "The Fatty" as a replacement for the standard-sized cigarette. Dispatched to distract Undercover Brother, White She Devil (Denise Richards) changes sides, joining his team, which includes the weed-smoking Conspiracy Brother (Dave Chappelle); he gives a bag to uptight Lance (Neil Patrick Harris), telling him, "You need to lighten up." There are lots of fried-chicken-and-white-bread-sandwiches-with-mayonnaise jokes, and James Brown makes a cameo when Feather kidnaps him. Kudos to the solid soul soundtrack (including Snoop Dogg's "Undercova Funk"), the casting, and Griffin's stylized 'fro, colorful wardrobe, and gold Cadillac, but there's not much story here to get excited about.

Undercover Brother: "You mess with the 'fro, you got to go."

Up in Smoke (1978)

☘ ☘ ☘ ☘ ☘ The granddaddy of all stoner comedies "almost did not get released," Tommy Chong writes in his autobiography. From Harold & Kumar to Friday to Jay & Silent Bob, it has spawned a series of successors, though few reached the heights of this true original. When Pedro (Cheech) picks up the hitchhiking Man (Chong) on the Pacific Coast Highway, they forge an immediate friendship. Man turns Pedro on to a huge joint and the high jinks begin. The duo get deported to Mexico and drive a van made out of "fiberweed" back into the U.S. Sergeant Stedanko (Stacy Keach) heads up the Keystoned Kops who are constantly one step behind and hopelessly out of touch. Pedro and Man barely make it to Rock Fight of the Century—a battle of punk/New Wave bands at L.A.'s The Roxy where Man, stoned on 'ludes, knocks over the drum set and Pedro prances on stage in a pink tutu. But fumes from the smoking van outside revive Man and they go on to win the contest with a scorching rendition of "Earache My Eye." The movie was supposed to end there, but director Lou Adler tacked on what Chong calls the "this was a dream" ending. The compromise ending—what we see on film—has Pedro and Man back on Pacific Coast Highway, smoking hash as the "Up in Smoke" theme plays. The camera pulls back to a Malibu beach panorama and the credits roll, which is just fine with us.

> "Is that a joint, man? It looks like a quarter pounder! Is it heavy stuff? Will it blow me away?"
>
> —Pedro

Non-stoner comedies with a one-hit pot slip

10 (1979): "There's a joint in the ashtray," offers a sultry, fresh-out-of-the-shower Jenny (Bo Derek) to George (Dudley Moore), a muzak composer vacationing in Mexico. The two share that jay on a moonlit walk by the beach, and another later, back in her hotel room.

Trading Places (1983): This John Landis classic features Dan Aykroyd as Rasta Lionel Joseph. He has a rendezvous with Billy Ray (Eddie Murphy) and Ophelia (Jamie Lee Curtis) on the train, where Lionel lights a spliff. "Ba–boo–ya, ba–bow–ya, ba–boo–ya—hah!"

Desperately Seeking Susan (1985): In one of this film's more memorable moments, New Wave bad girl Susan (Madonna) gets comfy in a Jacuzzi tub, pulls a joint out of her ankle boot, and smokes out Gary (Mark Blum), her doppelgänger's husband.

Private Parts (1997): It was during Howard Stern's younger years—going as far back as high school—that the future shock jock started smoking joints in his bedroom, and having to hide that from his parents. In the movie based on his bestselling book, he explains the pot situation: "Because I had such a miniscule shlonger, I turned to drugs; unfortunately the drugs really made me paranoid."

Austin Powers in Goldmember (2002): Slimy Dutchman Johann van der Smut, a.k.a. Goldmember (Mike Myers), is nothing if not hospitable to his guests from the future. He offers super spies Austin (Myers) and Nigel Powers (Michael Caine): "A shmoke and a pancake? Pipe and a crepe? Bong and a blintz?"

Bringing Down the House (2003): When Peter's (Steve Martin) biggest law client, Mrs. Arness (Joan Plowright), is taken hostage in the 'hood by his new convict pal Charlene (Queen Latifah), the stodgy geezer throws up her hands and shares a joint with a couple of brothers. "I do believe I'm stoned," she later slurs. "Is there a twenty-four-hour diner around here? I'm dreadfully hungry."

Dukes of Hazzard (2005): Once order is restored to Hazzard County, Bo and Luke Duke's uncle Jesse (Willie Nelson) unwinds by smoking a joint out of an apple. In between hits of real weed, he relays an age-old saying to his nephews: "An apple a day."

Strangers With Candy (2005): When Monica (Elizabeth Harnois) offers forty-six-year-old high school student Jerri (Amy Sedaris) a joint, she initially refuses. "I shook that monkey off my back a long time ago and I won't go down that road again," Jerri insists, then says, "Let me see that." She takes one hit off the joint and completely loses it, breaking glasses, lamps, anything she can get her hands on. "It all came rushing back to me," Jerri explains as Monica screams, "Get out!"

Talladega Nights: The Ballad of Ricky Bobby (2006): When Ricky Bobby (Will Ferrell) makes a pizza delivery to Reese Bobby (Gary Cole), his daddy instructs, "Either close the door or come in—I've got weed in here, cowboy." Later, one of Ricky Bobby's sons, ten-year-old Cal (Austin Crim), asks Reese, "How much you selling that weed for, old man?"

The Heartbreak Kid (2007): In a scene that's nearly identical to one in the Farrelly brothers' *There's Something About Mary* (substitute Michelle Monaghan for Cameron Diaz), Eddie (Ben Stiller) shares a beachside joint with his dream girl, prompting her uptight cousin (Danny McBride) to observe: "I smell something weird out here. Somebody's been hittin' the devil's lettuce."

Van Wilder (2002)

🍁🍁🍁 In this National Lampoon film, Ryan Reynolds plays Van Wilder, a college student facing the ultimate dilemma: how to get through his seventh year of undergrad at Coolidge College without daddy paying for it? The enterprising cad hires Indian exchange student Taj (Kal Penn) to help him raise the tuition money, with fundraising schemes that include topless tutors and an event-planning company that hosts parties for everyone from dorky fraternities to the Hillel house. Meanwhile, Gwen (Tara Reid), an investigative reporter at the school, is assigned to interview Van Wilder. Her goal is to answer the campus's burning question: How does one dude maintain supreme alpha male status for seven consecutive years? Van unleashes a steady stream of gags as he tries to win Gwen's heart, while ruining her boyfriend's game—we're talking dog semen–filled pastries, farty strippers, flaming sex scenes, Jell-O shots being snorted, you get the gist—and in the end, he and Taj (who takes

over the lead role in the sequel *Van Wilder 2: The Rise of Taj*) come out on top. We can't say the same for their friend Huch (Teck Holmes of *Real World: Hawaii* fame), however—he rips a hit off a bong that turns out to be Taj's cock pump!

Very Bad Things (1998)

🍁🍁🍁🍁 Writer-director Peter Berg (*Hancock*) should have titled this twisted comedy "Very, Very Bad Things"—as in, borderline evil—but it's the absurdity of this dark tale about five friends and a Las Vegas bachelor party gone wrong that makes it so damn laughable. Jon Favreau is Kyle, the guest of honor at the coke-, booze-, and pot-fueled hotel room bash, whose wedding to bona fide bridezilla Laura (Cameron Diaz) is a week away. His party posse consists of brothers Mike (Jeremy Piven) and Adam (Daniel Stern), pipsqueak Charles (Leland Orser), and unofficial master of ceremonies Boyd (Christian Slater), who hires a sexy Asian prostitute to entertain them all. But when rough sex with Mike accidentally leads to her death, the guys agree to cover it up, and Boyd, in turn, insists on eliminating everyone who may have knowledge of their crime—a hotel security guard; Adam's wife, Lois (Jeanne Tripplehorn); and eventually Mike, too. Because something about Slater says "undiscriminating homicidal killer," Boyd feels like a continuation of his role in *Heathers*—an unflappable guy with complete disregard for human life who seems to thrive on danger and deception. But in *Very Bad Things*, he's not alone in that psychosis, as many of his cohorts are, by association, just as demented. It's one wacky trip to Sin City (predated *The Hangover* by eleven years) in its most literal sense, complete with a contradictory soundtrack that feels like it came straight out of *Swingers*. By the end, you'll be longing for the innocence of that Favreau Vegas trip.

> "You sound a little funny, honey. Did you do cocaine last night?"
>
> —Laura

Waiting... (2005)

🌿 🌿 🌿 🌿 Anyone with a weak (or very full) stomach might want to think twice before diving in to *Waiting...* which chronicles a typical work day at Shenaniganz, a Bennigan's knockoff serving mediocre food and every kitchen nightmare you ever dreaded. Spit, urine, snot, and pubic hair are common garnishes at this establishment, managed by the clueless Dan (David Koechner) and his staff of degenerate stoners. The studly Monty (Ryan Reynolds) is king of the waiters. He runs the pranks (namely, the ongoing surprise-someone-with-your-genitalia game), sleeps with high school girls, and trains the new guy, Mitch (*Freaks and Geeks'* John Francis Daley), all the while pining after his ex-girlfriend Serena (Anna Faris) and underage hostess Natasha (Vanessa Lengies). Dean (Justin Long) is the top server and all-around nice guy who's offered an assistant manager position but sees a lifetime of misery ahead. Raddimus (Luis Guzman) and Floyd (Dane Cook) man the kitchen, where the five-second rule can be pushed to ten, if the situation calls for it, while the "Bishop" (Chi McBride) doles out guru-like psychoanalysis from a corner near the sink. Busboys T-Dog (Max Kasch) and Nick (Andy Milonakis) are cornrowed wannabe gangstas often found slumped over in the walk-in fridge toking on a pipe or sucking on a whipped-cream canister. Salacious and obscene in the vein of *Superbad*, every character packs its own comedic punch, especially (and surprisingly) Cook as Floyd, who greets Mitch with one of his many belligerent zingers, "Welcome to Thunderdome, bitch." But really they're all a bunch of zany burnouts and drunks, as we find out when the staff reconvenes at Monty and Dean's house for their nightly post-shift rager. It's there that the movie starts, with an inhale on a joint, and ends with an exhale. Well played, stoners. Director Rob McKittrick followed with *Still Waiting...* in 2009.

Raddimus: "Shit, if it's gonna be that kind of a party, I'm gonna stick my dick in the mashed potatoes!"

🌿 ANDY MILONAKIS'S STONY MOVIE PICKS 🌿

The Stoned Age **(1994):** "I like bad comedies, and this is a really bad comedy, but I love it for that reason. The first time I watched it in high school, me and my friends shaved our heads afterward. We just felt crazy, we were, like, 'Fuck it. We're fucked up, we smoked weed, we shaved our heads,' so maybe it's a little nostalgic for me. It was like the first time I was officially becoming a fuck-up. But it's definitely a bad movie, the kind that you watch stoned and think, 'Wow, anybody can make a movie.'"

Cabin Boy **(1994):** "Chris Elliott is a fucking genius, and David Letterman loved him so much that he made his only cameo in what critics say is probably the worst movie ever made. It's a wacky comedy: Chris Elliott is a fancy lad with a white wig, and he's on a ship with all these old-school, clichéd pirates that basically treat him like a little bitch. And Letterman is selling, like, sock monkeys. Any movie that has a floating cupcake that's chewing tobacco and spitting it in people's faces, you can't get any more genius than that!"

Mac and Me **(1988):** "This is one of those horrible eighties comedies that are so fun to watch baked. It's basically a retarded rip-off of E.T. The alien looks so fake and cheesy, and there's a fully choreographed dance scene with the alien in a McDonald's—he's in a teddy-bear costume and steals kids' drinks! It's a perfect example of a horrible movie that never should have gotten made. It's almost like you're in the twilight zone when you see something like *Mac and Me*, but any movie with a dance scene involving Ronald McDonald deserves to be in this book. I'm making a case for that."

✹ Q & A: ANDY MILONAKIS ✹

The 2005 comedy *Waiting...* has everything you'd want in a stoner movie: It's set in a cheesy chain restaurant that offers frilly drinks and cheap munchies, it starts with a smoky blowout party and ends with a hazier one, and it features an all-star cast that includes Ryan Reynolds, Anna Faris, Justin Long, Dane Cook, Luis Guzmán, and Andy Milonakis, who sniffs nitrous in the fridge and hits the pipe out back. Call it a sleeper stoner flick, but it's one of our favorites. Reefer Movie Madness sat down with Milonakis, who also appears in the sequel *Still Waiting...* as white-boy wannabe-rapper Nick, to talk about the cult hit.

Reefer Movie Madness: It's made clear that pretty much everyone working at the restaurant smokes weed, but you're by far the biggest stoner. What did you think when the script was presented to you?

Andy Milonakis: I thought it was perfect. It was actually my first movie audition ever, way before my TV show or anything, but the casting director was ahead of the curve and saw some Internet videos of me rapping, and she sent me an e-mail. When I got the script, I was, like, a wannabe-black guy who smokes weed? Typecast.

RMM: What was the audition like?

AM: I had to do these crazy lines, and after I read, they were hinting at me to rap, so I did a rhyme for them: "I'll fuck you with a loaf of bread and make you cheat on Atkins." I thought I did pretty good, and the casting director had me come back in and offered me the part right there. Then they asked me to write a rap for the end credits. I was so psyched, it all worked out.

RMM: Did you smoke before or during filming?

AM: I wasn't a big stoner on the first *Waiting*.... I was just dabbling a little here and there, but it was the time when I started smoking a lot. On *Still Waiting...* I smoked every day in the trailer. I only had a few scenes so there was a lot of down time. I was, like, "Fuck, this is awesome, I have six hours until they call me; I can just chill out and smoke joints." It's so much better being high on a movie set and not having to wait there all sober.

RMM: Everyone can relate to having a degrading service job. Is that a big part of *Waiting...*'s appeal?

AM: I think so. I used to be a busboy when I was fifteen and I can definitely relate. I've experienced how shitty customers can be. I did customer service for a store that's like Kmart and had to handle the returns. I dealt with annoying people all day! So it was great to be in a movie that you're kind of getting back at those people. I would choose other methods than putting pubic hair in mashed potatoes or pissing in someone's food—that's not getting even, you're being the bigger bastard and I don't have it in me—but it's still kind of fun to watch.

RMM: Have you found that there's a big stoner following for *Waiting...*?

AM: When it came out in the theater, maybe two people mentioned it to me. When it was released on DVD, it all exploded. I think the movie made, like, ten times the amount on home video than it did in the theater, so it definitely has a big cult following. And with all those good actors in it and a funny script, I felt from the beginning that it was going to be a kind of cult stoner movie.

RMM: Think there will be a third *Waiting...*?

AM: Probably not, unless they do *Waiting on the Moon*. We all just bring a lot of weed up to the moon, start a restaurant, and serve aliens from *Mac and Me*. That would be sick.

Walk Hard: The Dewey Cox Story (2007)

 Spoofing some of the greatest music legends to have their life stories told on screen—Ray Charles, Bob Dylan, Jerry Lee Lewis, Jim Morrison, Brian Wilson, and Johnny Cash, to name a few—Judd Apatow turns the ever-popular biopic formula into hilarious vignettes of sheer absurdity. Dewey's journey starts with the prerequisite childhood trauma—he accidentally slices his brother in half with a machete. Dewey (John C. Reilly) turns into a supernatural talent (playing blues guitar) with a debilitating handicap (losing all sense of smell). He marries a minor (played by Kristen Wiig), has a subsequent baby, and eventually gets divorced. Darlene (Jenna Fischer) comes into Dewey's life as a duet partner, and like June Carter Cash, becomes wife number two, but Dewey's drug addiction is a constant battle (not pot, which is painted in a positive light for a change), and after an LSD trip in India with the dysfunctional Beatles takes a turn to the dark side (kudos to spot-on accents by Jack Black, Paul Rudd, Jason Schwartzman, and Justin Long as Paul, John, Ringo, and George, respectively), Dewey goes batshit crazy Brian Wilson–style and Darlene splits for good. Dewey's career then evolves from protest singer in the sixties to cheesy talk show host in the seventies to has-been in the eighties, until rapper Lil' Nutzzak samples "Walk Hard" in 1992 and saves Dewey from obscurity. Of course, there's redemption at the end of this road and Dewey finds it in the arms of his muse, Darlene, the music industry, and his twenty-two kids.

Reilly is capably multitasking guitar and vocal duties through multiple decades and disparate styles. Add to that a stellar supporting cast that includes Tim Meadows as his trusty drummer Sam, Harold Ramis as Hasidic record executive L'Chaim, and Jonah Hill as the ghost of his brother Nate, cameos by Jack White, Eddie Vedder, Ghostface Killah, and Fabolous, along with stars of The Office and 30 Rock, and a ridiculous soundtrack of hokey parodies, and you have all you need to rock out with your Cox out.

Dewey to Darlene: "Look, I know I've had my trouble with drugs in the past, but I'm addicted to coke, weed, booze, 'ludes and speed, not LSD. Nobody gets addicted to LSD. It was invented by a scientist, Ringo Starr just told me."

War on the War on Drugs, The (2002)

 Director Cevin D. Soling's cockeyed commentary about drug prohibition promotes thought and laughter. His inspired lunacy takes aim at the Partnership for a Drug Free America's commercials with about sixty of his own. But these aren't your grandfather's antidrug ads. Rather, we learn how to "Know Your Dealer," "What to Do If You Get Stopped by the Police," "Introducing Your Parents to Drugs," and "How to Beat a Drug Test" ("drink four glasses of water and take four aspirin"). In "Cooking with Carrie," stony chef Carrie Keranen makes brownies, explaining: "I prefer Afghani skunk weed, but Orange Crush or red-haired Purple Haze will also blend nicely." This subversive piece might not have you howling but it will tickle the funny bone.

Wash, The (2001)

 Twenty-five years after the original Car Wash, DJ Pooh (Friday, Next Friday, 3 Strikes) enlisted Dr. Dre (Sean) and Snoop Doog (Dee Loc) to star in the hip-hop update. Set in South Central Los Angeles, roommates Sean and Dee Loc both work at "The Wash." They have the usual money problems, which Dee offsets by selling weed ("six fo' a hundred"). Dee's connection is Tommy Chong, who gives him a large bag of fresh buds from Humboldt County plus a Chong Bong for $500. "I'm not selling weed, you dig?" Chong explains. "But I can sell you the bong. That way I'm not dealing." In other cameos, Paulie Shore shows up in a mobster's trunk and Shaquille O'Neal knocks one of the washers the fuck out. Even crazier is Chris (Eminem), a disgruntled former employee who makes threatening calls and shoots out the windows. When the boss, Mr. Washington (George Wallace), gets kidnapped by inept gangbangers, Dee Loc comes to the rescue, smoking blunts every step of the way. Loaded with Dr. Dre originals ("The Wash," "Bad Intentions"), the soundtrack adds to the overall quality of this very credible stony remake.

Wayne's World (1992)

Saturday Night Live's Mike Myers and Dana Carvey birthed Wayne Campbell and Garth Algar, two mullet-headed, heavy metal–loving slackers who broadcast a low-fi public access talk show out of Wayne's parents' Aurora, Illinois, basement. The characters quickly became among SNL's most popular, so a feature film (Myers's first) was a no-brainer at the time, and, as it turned out, it didn't suck (the same can't be said for its sequel, which upped the rock ante with the Waynestock festival). The story starts with an offer Wayne and Garth can't refuse: $5,000 each for the rights to the show. But when their slimy new producer, Benjamin (Rob Lowe), pressures the duo to sell out, and makes a move on Wayne's love interest, Cassandra (Tia Carrere), it's war between the burnouts and the yuppies, and you can guess who wins. Excellent! Chock-full of stony pop culture references (*Star Trek*, *Scooby-Doo*), juvenile commentary ("If she were a president, she'd be Baberaham Lincoln"), and, of course, Wayne and Garth's many mantras (most notably, "Party on!"), it's never really made clear whether they partake, but considering Wayne's fondness for Led Zeppelin, "Bohemian Rhapsody" (on cassette!), and hockey, and that Garth and most of their TV crew wear tie-dyes throughout, it's a safe bet, even if the PG-13 rating wouldn't let it out of the basement.

Weirdsville (2007)

Toeing the line between gritty *Requiem for a Dream*–level drug use and screwball comedy, *Weirdsville* is your typical tale of two idiots who owe a gangster money. Based in the fictional Canadian town of Weedsville, the movie focuses on the friendship between semi-smart Dexter (Scott Speedman) and his dumb but loyal pal Royce (Wes Bentley). The two are in debt to local bad guy Omar (Raoul Bhaneja) and agree to sell drugs for him to take care of their tab, but Royce's girl-friend Matilda (Taryn Manning) comes up with a different get-rich-quick scheme: looting the safe of a local Internet millionaire. Before they pull off the job, she ODs, and as Dexter and Royce attempt to bury her in the basement of the local drive-in, they run into a group of Satanists led by their school pal Abel (played by a fantastically straight-faced Greg Bryk). The goofball cult somehow manages to resuscitate Matilda, and the trio escapes, encountering a troupe of midget medieval knights while on the run. Plenty of weed gets smoked along the way, most notably when Royce knocks out the millionaire's nephew and then gets him high, so he'll forget it all.

> "You ever get the feeling that drugs are making you slow?"
> —Dexter

Encroaching on *Dumb and Dumber* territory (Royce's riff on "Sprayonaise," his million-dollar idea for sprayable mayo, for instance), the movie tries hard to segue between "I'm so high" jokes and "I'm too high" imagery. It's a bit heavy-handed at times; there are lots of slow motion peppered with quick cuts that occasionally walk the movie into music video land. But in the end, it's a positive conclusion: Royce offers his would-be millionaire victim the Sprayonaise idea as conciliation while bonding over hits from a gnome bong, or should we say, peace pipe.

Welcome to the Dollhouse (1995)

🌿 On the loser scale, it doesn't get more pathetic than Dawn "Wienerdog" Wiener (Heather Matarazzo)—the school outcast, ugly duckling, and nerd with zero fashion sense and an unfortunate last name all rolled into one. Seventh grade hasn't been easy on her, and neither has life so far. Dawn battles her tutu-wearing perfect younger sister, Missy (Daria Kalinina), and computer science–obsessed monotonous older brother, Mark (Matthew Faber), on a daily basis, then fends off taunts of "lesbo" from her classmates, and threats of rape from one snarly burnout, Brandon (Brendan Sexton III). Things get even more humiliating when Dawn develops a major crush on the high school hottie, Steve Rodgers (Eric Mabius), and take an unexpected turn as she and Brandon bond one afternoon (he smokes a joint, Dawn says she doesn't "feel like it"). Somewhere along the way, Missy gets kidnapped and their parents come close to a nervous breakdown—all of which is Dawn's fault. This is one twisted story, brilliantly told by writer-director Todd Solondz, who also brought the truly perverted *Happiness* to the world. Is there a payoff? Not really, but it will have you cringing for ninety minutes straight and likely feeling much better about your own junior high experience.

Dawn to Brandon: "I think marijuana should be legalized."

Wet Hot American Summer (2001)

🌿 A cult classic in every sense, the ensemble comedy *Wet Hot American Summer* (featuring many members of New York comedy troupe The State) totally tanked when it hit theaters, but has slowly become an endlessly quotable DVD hit in the years since. The key is in its simplicity: The whole movie takes place on the last day of summer camp in 1981, with various kids and counselors trying to get laid, get over an asshole ex, and prevent a piece of

Skylab from killing them all (don't ask). The cast's full of past and future stars—Paul Rudd is douchey jock Andy; Janeane Garofalo, camp director Beth; Bradley Cooper the closeted gay counselor, Ben; and SVU's Christopher Meloni plays Gene, the camp's Vietnam-vet chef, who dreams one day of being able to say out loud that he'd really like to hump a fridge (again, don't ask, just watch). Amy Poehler, David Hyde Pierce, Michael Ian Black, Molly Shannon, and Michael Showalter, who wrote the film, round out a virtual who's who of comedy. The group comes together for the movie's funniest scene, when Beth takes a truckload of counselors into town for an anything-goes excursion that starts with the crew sneaking a cigarette and quickly progresses to smoking a joint, robbing an old woman, sniffing lines, and inevitably detoxing from heroin, *Trainspotting*–style. The culmination? A counselor's take: "It's fun to get away from camp—even if it's just for an hour."

Gene: "Now finish up them 'taters; I'm going to go fondle my sweaters."

When Do We Eat? (2005)

🌿 As if we haven't all fantasized about dosing one (or both) of our parents at an all-important family dinner, wisenheimer Zeke Stuckman (Ben Feldman) actually goes through with the sinister plan by dropping a tab of Ecstasy into his father's antacid—during the holy and highly symbolic Passover seder, no less. The Stuckmans are your quintessential dysfunctional Jewish family. Ira (Michael Lerner) is a ballbuster who's constantly scrapping with his wife, Peggy (Lesley Ann Warren), and their four kids. Son Zeke is a pothead (he sports the same 420 T-shirt he wore to school for the festive meal) whom Ira insists on drug-testing, but always stays one step ahead of his dad. (During an earlier buy with the school dealer, Shaffer, played by Jeff D'Agostino, Zeke scores a bag of clean urine in addition to a forty-dollar tab of X and an eighth of weed. Son Ethan is a former man of finance who's decided to become an Orthodox Jew, if he can keep his lusty paws off his hot cousin. Daughter Nikki (Shiri Appleby) is a professional sex surrogate who helps

🌿 JOE TROHMAN'S STONY MOVIE PICKS 🌿

Fall Out Boy guitarist Joe Trohman considers himself a movie buff of the highest order, which is why he devoted hours of deep contemplation to coming up with just the right mix for his top five films to watch stoned. Like Joe's massive 'fro, this is some heady stuff.

The Secret of NIMH (1982): "Forget *Ratatouille* or *The Tale of Despereaux*. The ultimate rat-mouse relationship movie is *The Secret of NIMH*. First off, it's stony because it's a cartoon of a world with talking animals! But beyond that, it's basically about a mouse named Mrs. Brisby, who has a family and one of her youngest sons has pneumonia. These mice live on a farm, and there are these rats that live there, too. Anyway, she gets this medicine from a supersly, smart mouse, and gives it to her kid. He has to be in bed for three weeks, but it's almost moving time because the farmers are coming to plow. So she visits this great owl, who tells her to confer with the rats who are hyperintelligent. It's crazy. She gets help from the rats to move her house, so the kid lives. That's fuckin' deep."

Full Metal Jacket (1987): "I'm the type of guy that likes to look for comedy in movies that are downers, and what's amazing about *Full Metal Jacket* is how many incredible one-liners there are in that movie. And toward the end, when the platoon has gotten past the really brutal sniper scene where they shoot a woman in the head, they all start marching, singing the Mickey Mouse Club song. All that stuff is really trippy and weird. In general, Kubrick makes good stoner movies if you can handle something heavy. This is one of his more linear movies. It's not like *2001* at all, and it makes way more sense than *A Clockwork Orange*. Sometimes it's nice to understand what's going on, no matter how high you are."

Dead Alive (1992): "This is a premainstream Peter Jackson movie about a guy named Lionel [Timothy Balme] who lives with his terribly demanding mother. This crazy weird rat bites his mother, she suddenly dies but comes alive as a zombie and bites more people. Then these zombies in the basement have a baby zombie. Basically, it's a weird, really funny, supergory zombie flick. Peter Jackson mixes the comedy with the horror and there are a couple of hilarious moments: like when the zombie baby attacks Lionel and he pulls the baby by its leg, beats it silly, and throws it into a metal pole—brutal but comical. It's funny just thinking of two zombies having sex!"

Wet Hot American Summer (2001): "This is an insane movie for so many reasons, but it's more about the little things. Like when Ken Marino is running back to the camp and he does that super-slow-motion jump over the hay, or when the counselors decide to go into town and have fun, and they're, like, getting addicted to heroin within five minutes, then come back and everything's fine. It's perfect if you're stoned, because they tried to film it like it's an actual summer movie, but then threw in random things and insane lines that come from out of nowhere. Christopher Meloni, from *Law and Order: SVU*, is hilarious as the war-scarred camp cook who humps a refrigerator. That right there is out of control!"

Everything Is Illuminated (2005): "Being Jewish, you have a connection to Jewish films, like this one directed by Liev Schreiber and adapted from the Jonathan Safran Foer novel in which he goes to Ukraine and finds the village that his grandfather escaped from in World War II. It's shot really well with a lot of bright colors, like when Alex [Gogol Bordello's Eugene Hütz], the guy who's driving, pulls up to this old woman's house, you see these big sunflowers that are incredible looking! That's really intriguing when you're high; anything visual really gets you going. And the movie also has this really trippy wordage in it—Alex's misusage of English, how he talks about being close to a city by using the word 'proximal,' or he uses 'prime' meaning good, or sleep is 'repose.' It's awesome, and Eastern European is pretty much the only accent I can really do, so I throw out lines like nobody's business."

men get past their intimacy issues. And youngest son Lionel (Adam Lamberg) is an apparent idiot savant. Once everyone's seated for the seder—and asking the inevitable question "when do we eat?"—things fall apart fairly quickly. Long-festering animosities and disappointments are revealed (giving new meaning to the ritualistic "bitter herbs"), tension reaches an all-time high, and then the Ecstasy kicks in. Zeke 'fesses up and Ira is encouraged to go with it. Soon he sees the Haggadah come to life as psychedelic visions of a moving desert, lush flower gardens, waterfalls, and singing priests and starts to appreciate, not just where he came from, but where his kids are going. A luminescent Moses points the way from bad vibes to good and shows this family that, despite their heritage, they're not necessarily doomed to a life of misery. Offbeat and seldom seen, it's a little gem of a movie.

Where the Buffalo Roam (1980)

For his second film role (preceded by *Meatballs*), Bill Murray dove headfirst into the considerable legend of gonzo journalist Hunter S. Thompson. Eighteen years later Johnny Depp did the same in *Fear and Loathing in Las Vegas*. Murray's portrayal is, not surprisingly, the funnier of the two. It starts in a hospital as Thompson frolics with a nurse. His lawyer Lazlo (Peter Boyle) arrives and thus begins one of their many wild adventures. The first is a court proceeding during which Lazlo defends pot smokers busted for possession. When the merciless judge throws the book at them, Lazlo and Thompson deliver their own courtroom tantrums. As Thompson grows more famous from his articles in *Blast* (a fictional version of *Rolling Stone*), he becomes estranged from Lazlo, his political conscience. Thompson covers the Super Bowl and the 1972 presidential election (Nixon is a constant target), creating his unique brand of mayhem wherever he goes. What passed for humor then would probably be considered terrorism today. Ultimately, there's a sadness to the film—that the great era of Thompson's first-person, damn-the torpedoes writing style was coming to an end.

Whiteboyz (1999)

Taking a page from Martin Scorsese's *The King of Comedy* and Robert De Niro's wannabe stand-up comic Rupert Pupkin, Marc Levin (*Slum, Brooklyn Babylon*) sets Danny Hoch loose in the cornfields of Iowa to hilarious effect as Flip Dogg, a wannabe white rapper. As delusional as Pupkin, Flip tells anyone who will listen—his buds, parents, even his one African American friend (Eugene Byrd as Khalid): "I ain't white, I'm black—even though I live in Iowa, I still have the ghetto in my heart." It's a funny conceit that's played to the hilt, as Flip and his friends talk the talk and desperately try to walk the walk. But when they head to Chicago to buy coke, their small-town mentality almost gets them killed. Flip and his "shortie" Sara (Piper Perabo) make a cute couple in this hip-hop–friendly flick that includes a smokin' cameo and theme song by Snoop Dogg.

Withnail & I (1987)

Two unemployed actors (Richard E. Grant as one of cinema's greatest drunks, Withnail, and Paul McGann as the "I" in the title) go on a comedic misadventure in the English countryside. But before leaving from and after returning to their dingy 1969 London apartment, they are visited by pot and pill dealer Danny (Ralph Brown). He rolls the enormous spliff he claims to have invented (utilizing, he says, up to twelve rolling papers), which he calls the "Camberwell Carrot." Holding it aloft, Danny says in his mellow-meets-edgy fashion, "This will tend to make you very high." Brimming with memorably quotable lines, Bruce Robinson's film (co-produced by George Harrison) deservedly has as devoted a cult following in England as *The Big Lebowski* does in the U.S. The movie begins with King Curtis's version of "Whiter Shade of Pale" playing, and the Hendrix tracks "All Along the Watchtower" and "Voodoo Chile" bookend the actors' jangled drives to and from the country. Gonzo artist Ralph Steadman's graphics, and his photos of Grant and McGann rehearsing their characters, accompany the DVD.

Without a Paddle
(2004)

🌰 🍸 🔪

🍁 🍁 🍁 When a group of lifelong best buds loses one of its own, the three surviving friends—Tom (Dax Shepard), Dan (Seth Green), and Jerry (Matthew Lillard)—choose to fulfill the late Billy's childhood wish: to follow his map and track down D. B. Cooper's lost treasure purported to be somewhere deep in the Oregon forest. The trio canoes down a river, gets frighteningly close to a grizzly bear, and stumble upon a pot farm run by hotheaded, gun-toting rednecks Elwood and Dennis (Ethan Suplee and Abraham Benrubi)—the kind of dudes who name their attack dogs Lynyrd and Skynyrd. A chase ensues through the massive field of plants, but Elwood fires a flare for light that sets most of the bushes on fire and gets everybody (even the dogs) high. The gigglefest continues the next day when the guys meet two hippie girls living at one with nature in a palatial tree house (Tom remarks, "I think I might still be stoned"). Dan sees Flower (Rachel Blanchard) as "the kind, crazy hairy lady of my dreams," but their good vibes are short-lived once the bad guys return with guns. The dudes, now wearing only underwear, spend a rainy night huddled together for warmth (says Tom: "One minute you mock my sweaty ball sack, now you wanna cuddle with it?"), but a new day brings rejuvenation and hope as they're taken in by D.B.'s former partner, long-haired mountain man Del Knox (Burt Reynolds), who finally shows them the way back to civilization. Chock-full of stoner references—from

> "What's a camping trip without beer?"
>
> —Tom
>
> "It's still a camping trip, but less vomit."
>
> —Dan

Dan's Matrix-like bullet-dashing maneuvers to that decades-old pothead go-to, "Who you gonna call, Ghostbusters?"—and some truly funny lines (like when Tom is asked if he was ever a Boy Scout, and replies, "No, but I ate a Brownie once"), the film's huge, drool-worthy stash is unfortunately farmed by a couple of a-holes and ends up burning to the ground.

Young Doctors in Love (1982)

🖊 🌰 🍸 🔪 💊 👀

🍁 🍁 🍁 🍁 This zany hospital comedy feels a lot like Airplane! (right down to the white zone unloading joke) but with doctors and nurses instead of pilots and stewardesses, and thanks to some racy situations and plenty of gross-out gags involving pee ("Your attention, please: Due to a mix-up in urology, no apple juice will be served this morning"), it's equally ridiculous and laugh-out-loud funny. The story revolves around a group of interns getting their first hands-on experience as doctors. There's Simon (Michael McKean), the son of a world-class Beverly Hills surgeon; Stephanie (Sean Young), from Vermont, who plans to practice rural medicine back home; Phil the pill-popper from New York, who's holding two jobs and is constantly on the hunt for uppers; Bucky (Ted McGinley) the all-star; and, thrown in for good measure, Milton (Gary Friedkin), the midget. The doctors are another sorry bunch led by the stock market–obsessed Dr. Prang (Dabney Coleman) and alcoholic nutcase Dr. Ludwig (Harry Dean Stanton), with the uptight Nurse Sprockett (Pamela Reed) left to clean their messes. A hilarious side-story involves mob boss Sal (Titos Vandis), who ends up sharing a hospital room with his would-be assassin, played by a very young Michael Richards (of Seinfeld fame), while the Godfather's heir apparent, Angelo (Hector Elizondo), poses as a woman and unintentionally catches the eye of one of the male interns. Throw in oddball pop culture references to E.T., Jaws, Carrie, and Ms. Pac-Man, a couple of old ladies sharing a joint, pot plants marked "For Glaucoma Patients Only" and cameos by Christie Brinkley, Mr. T, Demi Moore, and a host of eighties soap opera stars. Kudos are in order for Garry Marshall (*Pretty Woman*) on his totally toke-worthy directorial debut.

Zapped! (1982)

 Scott Baio plays Barney, a brainy science buff who spends all his free time in the high school chemistry lab. It's there that he feeds miniscule amounts of whiskey to mice, grows pot under the cover of an orchid experiment, and accidentally causes a chemical explosion (which somehow involves cannabis extract) that gives him telekinetic powers. Once he has the ability to, say, pop open a girl's blouse just by looking at it, or make his model spaceship fly (resulting in one kooky fantasy sequence involving his dog and the Starship *Enterprise* crew), Barney and his buddy Peyton (Willie Aames) take on more pressing matters, like embarrassing the local douchebag, who's dating the hottest girl in school, and beating the rival baseball team. Things start to go bad when science and greed clash, and Barney's stash is discovered by English teacher Miss Burnhart (Sue Anne Langdon), forcing him to incinerate the plants. In one of the movie's zanier moments, baseball coach Dexter Jones (Scatman Crothers) gets a whiff of the weed in the boiler room, passes out and launches into a wacked-out dream sequence where he rides a bike with Albert Einstein through a meadow ("I'm feeling strange, someone's putting some shit on my mind"). Laughable video gimmicks (like rainbow-colored space trails) that are oh-so–*Mork & Mindy* keep the story moving, along with the requisite day at the amusement park (complete with stomach-dropping roller-coaster footage), but this teen relic, like many eighties classics, is all about gratuitous boob shots, and you'll certainly get your fill in assorted shapes and sizes.

Zoolander (2001)

 Derek Zoolander (Ben Stiller) is a dim-witted male model who's past his runway prime. His nemesis is up-and-comer Hansel (Owen Wilson), a hippie nomad–type who's just as likely to grace the cover of *High Times* as he is the side of a bus. But when Derek gets brainwashed to kill the prime minister of Malaysia, a sinister plot concocted by the fashion industry to keep children working in sweatshops—with one wacka-doodle poodle-haired designer named Mugatu (Will Ferrell) at the helm—he, Hansel, and *Time* magazine reporter Matilda (Christina Taylor) team up to foil the assassination attempt.

Idiotic premise? Without a doubt, but Stiller, who directed and co-wrote the movie, delivers a cast of characters so complete and so utterly ridiculous that it borders on genius. There are too many hilarious plot turns to list, but for starters: Derek's life dream to open the Derek Zoolander Center for Kids Who Can't Read Good and Wanna Learn to Do Other Stuff Good, Too. The Derek versus Hansel walk-off at the old Members Only Warehouse (refereed by David Bowie). Derek's dad (Jon Voight) and brothers (Vince Vaughn and Judah Friedlander) back in coal-mining country (Southern New Jersey). The mushroom tea–inspired orgy involving Matilda and untold numbers of midgets and sherpas ("No thanks for the freak-fest last night?"). And, of course, any scene involving Mugatu, his assistant, or his dog. There's no obvious drug use in *Zoolander*, outside of Hansel's mentions of various psychedelics, but considering his first line is lifted straight out of *Dazed and Confused* (Matthew McConaughey's "All right, all right, all riiiight"), it's fair to say Stiller and gang knew exactly the kind of audience they were going for with this far-fetched farce.

Hansel to Derek: "Me and my friends have been too busy bathing off the southern coast of St. Barts with spider monkeys for the past two weeks. Tripping on acid changed our whole perspective on shit."

DRAMAS

Acid House, The
(1998)

Adapted from a collection of short stories by Scottish novelist Irvine Welsh (*Trainspotting*), this bleak film tells three unconnected tales—each more demented than the last—in three acts. "The Granton Star Cause" follows the knobish Bob (Stephen McCole) through his worst day ever. After getting fired from his job, kicked out of his parents' house, and dumped by his girlfriend and football team, he meets God at a pub, fails to impress him, and is sentenced to life as a fly. Act two, "A Soft Touch," features wussy husband Johnny (Kevin McKidd), who is beaten down—mentally and physically—by his philandering wife and upstairs neighbor. Both acts exhibit their share of spliffs, pints, and fags, but the pièce de résistance is "The Acid House," during which another underachieving bloke, Colin "Coco" Bryce (Ewen Bremner), drops a tab and winds up switching places with a newborn. The concept of God is reprised in the form of LSD as sacrament, but what transpires is one bad trip. While it may be too raw and difficult to understand (literally, subtitles are a must) for some, fans of *Trainspotting* will undoubtedly appreciate its twisted, trippy core, and one stellar soundtrack.

Coco: "I just dropped a Super Mario in the toilet and it's starting to kick in really deep. It's all right though, I can handle my drugs."

All That Jazz (1979)

Broadway choreographer Joe Gideon (based on director Bob Fosse) is the ultimate narcissist. Played by Roy Scheider, Gideon wakes up every morning to a cigarette, several Dexedrines, and a shower. Then he goes to work, running his cast through their paces, often bringing dancers to tears. He's also cutting a film called *The Stand Up*, starring Davis Newman (Cliff Gorman doing his best Lenny Bruce impression). Joe regularly converses with Angelique (Jessica Lange)—she's the Angel of

Death—about his broken marriage and a life of philandering. Girlfriend Kate (Anne Reinking) nails him when she says, "I wish you weren't so generous with your cock." A scathing indictment of a Broadway system that fears innovation, Joe's inventive, highly erotic play never gets finished. Chain-smoking to the very end, Joe lies on his deathbed as his last musical production swirls around him. Painful to watch at times, *All That Jazz* was nominated for Best Picture, but lost to *Kramer vs. Kramer*.

Davis: "No more hard drugs. A little grass maybe, but that's it!"

Almost Famous (2000)

Rolling *Stone* writer–turned-director Cameron Crowe's portrait of the rock critic as a young man is arguably the best movie ever made about being a fan, as well as a loving look back at a time when the music really mattered. Fifteen-year-old William Miller (Patrick Fugit) serves as Crowe's precocious alter ego circa 1973, an aspiring music journalist growing up in San Diego who is turned on to the magic of rock-and-roll by his sister Anita (Zooey Deschanel) when she splits home to escape their overbearing single mom Elaine (Frances McDormand) and leaves William with her cherished collection of vinyl albums. William seeks the counsel of legendary rock critic Lester Bangs (Philip Seymour Hoffman) before meeting up with self-proclaimed "Band Aid"

Penny Lane (Kate Hudson) and joining her and rock band Stillwater on their tour bus, securing an assignment from *Rolling Stone* in the process. On the road, the cherubic, innocent William becomes infatuated with Penny, even though she's seeing the band's cocky lead guitarist Russell Hammond (Billy Crudup), who's immersed in a battle of ego with vocalist Jeff Bebe (Jason Lee) for control of the group. For a film about rock-and-roll, there isn't much sex and drugs (Elaine's admonition to William, "Don't take drugs," is a running gag), though Penny does overdose on Quaaludes and Bangs boasts of taking "speed and cough syrup" to write. The film's most famous scene involves William and Russell going to a post-show party at a fan's house in Topeka, where Russell takes acid, climbs on top of the roof, and declares, "I am a golden god!" Other memorable moments include the entire bus breaking out in song to Elton John's "Tiny Dancer" and an electric storm outside a chartered plane that scares everyone into confessing, including the band's drummer Ed Vallencourt (John Fedevich), who blurts out, "I'm gay!" Keep an eye out for Anna Paquin, *The Office*'s Rainn Wilson, Peter Frampton, the late comic Mitch Hedberg, Jimmy Fallon, and *Rolling Stone* founder Jann Wenner in a cab at the end.

William to party crowd about Russell: "Please don't give him any more acid. Thank you."

Alpha Dog (2006)

This harrowing tale, based on a true story, centers on an unconventional kidnapping gone horribly wrong. Small-time pot dealer Johnny Truelove (Emile Hirsch) is the kind of wannabe gangsta you don't want to mess with or owe money to. But when one of his customers, waste-oid Jake Mazursky (Ben Foster), does just that, Johnny abducts Jake's fifteen-year-old brother Zack (Anton Yelchin) in retaliation. Without a game plan, Zack is allowed to chill for a weekend in Palm Springs with Johnny's crew, who imbibe him with girls, joints, and alcohol. One associate in particular, Frankie (Justin Timberlake), takes to Zack like a big brother, and even puts him to work trimming a shed-full of dense pot plants. But when Johnny learns that

his actions could mean life in prison, he orders his ass-kissing crony Elvis (Shawn Hatosy) to eliminate the problem with a TEC-9 and a late-night trip out to the desert. You can't say Zack never had a chance, because plenty were offered to him, but he chose to hang out for the party. Like the real-life story (but with names altered: Johnny, for example, was really known as Jesse James Hollywood), it doesn't end there. Johnny goes on the lam south of the border, leaving his dad (Bruce Willis) and grandfather (Harry Dean Stanton) in the dark, while Zack's mom (Sharon Stone) simply goes crazy. Director Nick Cassavetes does a stellar job, considering that Hollywood had yet to be prosecuted and convicted by the time the film was released. He doesn't take sides and paints a rather dark portrait of a dealer gone bad.

Frankie: "Look at this shit right here. Daddy's pride and joy. Of course, that greedy bastard will smoke them all, but it's Frankie's job to take care of them."

Altered States (1980)

Magic mushrooms in an isolation tank? Harvard prof Eddie Jessup (William Hurt) is game. In fact, he truly wants to push the envelope, "to regress to some quasi-Simian creature." He starts with sensory deprivation, then ups the ante, traveling to Mexico, where he trips with Indians on Amanita muscaria, experiencing truly mind-blowing and even life-changing hallucinations. Eddie brings the strange brew back with him to the lab and that's when his body starts devolving into an ape, werewolf-style. One night he explodes out of the tank and ends up in the local zoo, gnawing on an antelope. It's pretty heady stuff, influenced by the work of psychonauts John C. Lilly and Timothy Leary. Despite her fears, his wife Emily (Blair Brown)—she smokes a joint at a party early in the film—comes along for Eddie's last ride, and they consummate their love on a completely cosmic plane. Full of special effects and boasting an Oscar-nominated score by John Corigliano, this is one of the great psychedelic movies, courtesy of Ken Russell. (P.S. Look for Drew Barrymore in her first-ever role as three-year-old Margaret.)

American Beauty
(1999)

🌿🌿🌿🌿🌿 Sam Mendes's brilliant Oscar-winning treatise on suburban dysfunction stars Kevin Spacey and Annette Bening as Lester and Carolyn Burnham, a couple whose marriage is on the rocks, and Thora Birch as their temperamental teenage daughter, Jane. Lester has spent much of his adult life going through the motions—holding down a 9-to-5 job, being a responsible parent—until one day he opens his eyes and sees the world differently. He likens this awakening to coming out of a coma, and with it, Lester starts rebelling by quitting his job, smoking with and buying pot (an outrageously expensive ounce of G-13 for $2,000) from next-door neighbor and part-time dealer Ricky (Wes Bentley), and fantasizing about one of Jane's classmates, Angela (Mena Suvari). When Carolyn jumps into an affair with Buddy (Peter Gallagher), the local real estate king, Angela's flirtations with Lester reach a fever pitch, and Ricky's super-strict Marine dad (Chris Cooper) gets the wrong idea, matters are complicated for all involved. Lester winds up with the short end of the stick—and one way overpriced bag of kind bud.

> "Well, I see you're smoking pot now. I think using psychotropic drugs is a very positive example to set for our daughter."
>
> **—Carolyn**

> "You're one to talk, you bloodless, money-grubbing freak."
>
> **—Lester**

American Graffiti
(1973)

🌿🌿🌿🌿🌿 An iconic soundtrack featuring the voice of Wolfman Jack binds this film together, which is set on the last night of summer 1962 and interweaves the stories of four teenagers in Modesto, California. Steve Bolander (Ron Howard) and Curt Henderson (Richard Dreyfuss) are scheduled to leave the next morning for a prestigious East Coast university. Bolander decides that, in order to determine if his relationship is solid, he and his

girlfriend Laurie (Cindy Williams) should see other people while he's away. The two of them spend the rest of the night alternating between earnest discussion and argument. Curt faces two dilemmas: He doesn't think he's ready to leave Modesto and a mysterious hot girl in a white Thunderbird winks at him. Meanwhile, their friends Terry "The Toad" Fields (Charlie Martin Smith) and John Milner (Paul Le Mat) have problems of their own. Fields, the dork of the group, has been entrusted with the care of Bolander's Chevy Impala. The hot rod gives him a sense of bravado, and he picks up wild rebel Debbie Dunham (Candy Clark). Unfortunately for Fields, his new status is only car-deep, and he has to scramble to keep up with her. Milner, the group's stud, plans on picking up a babe of his own, but ends up instead with foul-mouthed youngster Carol (Mackenzie Phillips) riding shotgun. To complicate maters more, the bigheaded Bob Falfa (Harrison Ford) challenges Milner's title as fastest drag racer on the strip.

The George Lucas–directed *Graffiti* paved the way for several future films, most notably the stoner classic *Dazed and Confused*. Dreyfuss, Ford, and Phillips (daughter of John Phillips, of sixties greats the Mamas and the Papas) both got their big break in the film, and it was the last time Ron Howard would be known as "Ronny."

Carol: "Hey, is this what they call copping a feel?"

Amongst Friends
(1993)

🌿 🌿 🌿 Before becoming a producer and writer of HBO's *Entourage*, Rob Weiss wrote and directed this feature film about three friends growing up and apart on New York's Long Island. Billy (Joseph Lindsey), Trevor (Patrick McGaw), and Andy (Steve Parlavecchio) become drug dealers, but each takes a different path to get there. Billy has the biggest aspiration: He wants to be a mobster. When Billy asks Andy to make a delivery, Trevor does it instead and gets popped. Billy is not only unapologetic about the bust, he steals Trevor's girlfriend Laura (Mira Sorvino) while Trevor's in jail. Trevor returns to the 'hood (Five Towns) and quickly wins Laura back. Jealous, Billy confronts Trevor. Later, Andy confronts Billy. As the body count rises, Andy heads out of town on his motorcycle, flashing back to the good old days when fights led to scrapes, not murders amongst friends. Unfortunately, Weiss and his cast don't have the chops to pull off this homage to Martin Scorsese's *Mean Streets*.

Eddie: "This is a fuckin' dream—he wants to get rid of a hundred pounds of hydroponic bud."

Vic: "Kindest bud you ever smoked, babe."

Anniversary Party,
The (2001)

🍸 🌿 😊 👀

🌿 🌿 🌿 To help celebrate the reconciliation of their marriage, Hollywood actress Sally (Jennifer Jason Leigh) and British novelist/director Joe (Alan Cumming, who also directs with Leigh), throw one hell of a memorable anniversary party, complete with their closest friends, family, and even a few enemies. From within the confines of a multimillion dollar Pacific Palisades house, Cal (Kevin Kline), Judy (Parker Posey), Mac (John C. Reilly), and other members of Hollywood's elite come together to honor the reunion and what is supposed to be a happy future for the couple in London. The entrance of Sally's mortal enemy, the young, lithe actress Skye (Gwyneth Paltrow) and the ever-complaining neighbors throw a wrench in the relative peace of the household. Tensions subside slightly, but later spiral out of control as the remaining revelers drop Ecstasy and begin traipsing around the backyard like stoned-out hippies. The night explodes into chaos when Sally and Joe's dog Otis escapes, Joe is caught making out with the neighbor, and an unexpected tragedy breaks up the party once and for all.

Talk, talk, and more talk rules the screen in this bona fide indie darling. Shot almost entirely within the house, the action consists of chatting over drinks and joints (courtesy of Cal), an impromptu charades sesh, various way-too-serious arguments, and a late-night skinny-dipping scene. While you may not laugh out loud, the dialogue is smart, funny, and self-deprecating, but perhaps a little too real, especially once the Ecstasy is consumed. Talk about a bad trip.

Another Day
in Paradise (1998)

🍸 💉 💊 💉 👀

🌿 🌿 🌿 James Woods's powerful performance as junkie/thief Mel overshadows those of addict girlfriend Sid (Melanie Griffith) and their teenaged disciples Bobbie (*Mad Men*'s Vincent Kartheiser) and Rosie (Natasha Gregson Wagner) in Larry Clark's grim *Drugstore Cowboy* clone. After ripping off a clinic, they peddle Black Beauties to Nazi bikers, leading to a *Scarface*-style motel shootout. Rosie ODs and Mel forces Bobbie to help him crack a safe. Sid protects Bobbie as Mel gets progressively crazier, screaming and threatening everyone. The thick-lipped Griffith shoots up in her thigh and neck, but she looks way too good for this low-life part.

Apocalypse Now (1979)

One of Hollywood's great epics, Francis Ford Coppola's Vietnam movie took years to make and caused one of its stars,

Martin Sheen, to have a heart attack on set in the Philippines. Sheen is Captain Willard, the main character in this story about a colonel operating outside military protocol and building a captive army of natives who worship him as a pagan idol. Willard's mission is to ride by boat up the Nung River from Vietnam into Cambodia, where he's supposed to "terminate" Colonel Kurtz (Marlon Brando) "with extreme prejudice." What a ride it is! Willard's boat crew includes Clean (a teenaged Laurence Fishburne), Chef (Frederic Forrest), Lance (Sam Bottoms), and Chief (Albert Hall). While Willard is dead serious about the mission, the crew just wants to smoke pot, listen to psychedelic rock, and survive as the boat snakes its way through enemy territory. First, they join Lieutenant Kilgore (Robert Duvall) as he leads an attack on a village while Wagner's "The Ride of the Valkyries" blares from helicopter speakers. "I love the smell of napalm in the morning," Kilgore infamously declares. "It smells like . . . victory." From there they stop at Han Phat, which is lit up like an amusement park for a USO gig featuring three Playboy bunnies and impresario Bill Graham, playing himself.

But danger lurks around every bend in the river, and soon Clean and Chief are each killed in guerrilla assaults. Lance doses on acid as they approach Kurtz's compound, which is littered with dead bodies. A babbling American photographer, played by Dennis Hopper in a major comeback role, greets them. When Willard finally meets his prey, Kurtz is visible only in shadows and cracks of light. Finally, he appears and declares menacingly, "You're an errand boy sent by grocery clerks to collect the bill." Rather than have Willard killed, Kurtz keeps him caged until the natives sacrifice a cow. As the animal is visciously hacked to death, Willard creeps up behind Kurtz and does the same. "The horror," Kurtz utters, "the horror . . . " Written by John Milius and Coppola (based on Joseph Conrad's novella *Heart of Darkness*) and filmed by Vittorio Storaro (he won the Oscar for cinematography), this is not only the greatest Vietnam movie ever made but also the most psychedelic, with multicolored flares and smoke achieving hallucinatory effects, and The Doors' organ-drenched contemplation, "The End," opening and closing the film. In 2001, *Apocalypse Now Redux* was released with forty-nine minutes tacked on to the original 2:33 running time. The two most significant additions are the exploitative Playmate scene, where the boat crew gets to hang with (and undress) the women inside their helicopter (Bill Graham is nowhere to be found) and the much more important French plantation scene, which occurs just before they arrive in Cambodia. After the French holdouts discuss the history of the conflict over dinner, Willard and Roxanne (Aurore Clement) repair to the bedroom for a lovely opium session.

Chef: "What's the matter with you—you're acting kind of weird."

Lance: "You know that last tab of acid I was saving? I dropped it."

Chef: "You dropped acid? Far out!"

☘ FIVE MORE VIETNAM MOVIES ☘

America's longest war is also among its most dramatized. From comedies like *Good Morning, Vietnam* to epics like *Apocalypse Now*, it takes a certain kind of director, writer, and actor to do it justice. Here, our picks for the five best 'Nam flicks.

The Deer Hunter (1978): The Oscar-winning epic follows three lifelong friends from the Pennsylvania steel mills to the Vietnamese jungle, where as POWs they're forced to play Russian roulette. Identities get lost in captivity, as does one's sanity upon escape. Starring Robert De Niro, Christopher Walken, and Meryl Streep in career-defining roles, and clocking in at just over three hours, it's director Michael Cimino's greatest work and a true classic of the Vietnam movie genre.

Platoon (1986): Real-life Vietnam vet Oliver Stone captures the brutality of the battlefield with this visceral view of war, which won four Oscars, including Best Picture. Charlie Sheen stars as newbie Chris Taylor, while Tom Berenger and Willem Dafoe play his superiors, but conflict within the platoon overshadows the fight against the Vietcong.

Good Morning, Vietnam (1987): Director Barry Levinson (*Diner*) allowed Robin Williams to liberally improvise as the unpredictable disc jockey GI who's transferred to the front lines of Vietnam. Williams's high-energy comedy actually doesn't subvert the more dramatic aspects of the film and it earned him an Oscar nomination for Best Actor.

Full Metal Jacket (1987): Stanley Kubrick's Vietnam treatise chronicles the Marine experience, with the first half of the film devoted to boot camp and the second to battles during and after the Tet Offensive. Matthew Modine takes the lead as Joker, a sergeant known for sporting a helmet that bears a peace sign alongside the words "Born to Kill"— conflicted to the core, like the war itself.

Casualties of War (1989): The moral ambiguity of wartime is put on full display in this Brian De Palma–directed drama that pits soldier against soldier in a battle of conscience. Michael J. Fox plays Private Eriksson, the only guy in his platoon to protest the rape of a suspected Vietcong, as encouraged by his superior Sergeant Meserve (Sean Penn, in one of his least sympathetic roles). John C. Reilly and John Leguizamo make their screen debuts in this difficult film.

Assisted Living (2003)

🌿🌿🌿 You wouldn't expect a movie about the machinations of a nursing home to be all that enticing, but this story of an unlikely bond between an orderly and a resident is stony as hell—mainly because shaggy-haired twentysomething Todd (Michael Bonsignore) sneaks a hit off a metal pipe at every possible opportunity. And who wouldn't in an environment so grim and seemingly hopeless? Director Elliot Greenebaum paints a realistic portrait, warts and all, but makes sure to inject just enough humanity into this docudrama. Central to that mission is the increasingly senile Mrs. Pearlman (Maggie Riley), who was once a dashing and dignified lady but is now confined to a wheelchair. She longs for the son who abandoned her, so Todd tries to take on that role. He fails miserably—and still finds the inclination to get high after her inevitable meltdown—but redeems himself later by making a break for it with Mrs. Pearlman in tow, à la *One Flew Over the Cuckoo's Nest*.

Todd's boss: "You come to work looking like you've got no sleep, that you've been out partying all night!"

Bad Lieutenant
(1992, 2009)

🌿🌿🌿🌿 Harvey Keitel plumbs the depths with his portrayal of LT, one of the dirtiest cops ever to appear on screen. In the first scene, he snorts coke in his car, tipping off viewers that this is not your ordinary New York police officer. In addition, LT smokes crack, shoots up, and drinks nonstop. He confiscates evidence and sells it back to dealers, and takes advantage of young women from New Jersey in town looking for a good time. While LT investigates the rape of a young, good-looking nun (Frankie Thorn), he gets deeper in debt gambling on baseball games—which ultimately leads to his downfall. While director Abel Ferrara skillfully depicted the dark side of police life in this original, Werner Herzog's 2009 update *Bad Lieutenant: Port of Call New Orleans* paints a more amusing portrait, with Nicolas Cage replacing Keitel as the drug-addled cop who stops at nothing to acquire drugs and abuses anyone who gets in his way. Cage typically overacts in contrast to Keitel's more nuanced performance. And unlike LT, Cage's Terence not only shakes his bookie, but he earns a promotion.

LT to women in car: "I know what it's like to get stoned a little bit, to get high a little bit. Got any grass there, coke?"

Basketball Diaries, The (1995)

🌿🌿🌿 Based on the cult classic memoir by Jim Carroll, which tells the author/rocker's tale of growing up way too fast on the streets of New York, the movie adaptation, directed by Scott Kalvert and starring a young Leonardo DiCaprio in a breakthrough role, is a harrowing story of addiction. The drugs fly fast and furious as Carroll makes a rapid descent from promising prep school basketball star to full-on junkie. The film is littered with emotionally grueling scenes, from Carroll and his cronies (including pal Mickey, played by Mark Wahlberg) robbing an elderly lady for money to score, to Carroll getting kicked off his basketball team after he's deemed too stoned to play, to his pièce de résistance blow-job hustle in a nasty Grand Central Station bathroom. But for pure acting chops, the scene where Carroll sits outside his mother's locked door screaming "I'm your son!" is the movie's emotional zenith and tip-off to the kind of actor DiCaprio would eventually become. His costar here is heroin, which is far from glamorized.

> "I felt dazed, like I just came out of a four-hour movie I didn't understand."
>
> **—Jim Carroll**

Beach, The (2000)

🌿 🍹 🥢 😶

🌿🌿🌿 Richard (Leonardo DiCaprio) is your typical Teva sandal–wearing American backpacker traveling through Southeast Asia in search of a radical departure from the life he knows. He finds that change—and a whole lot more—on a remote island in the Gulf of Thailand. It's a mythical spot, heralded to be a secret paradise and almost inaccessible from the mainland. But with a map handed down from fellow nomad Daffy (Robert Carlyle) in Bangkok,

Richard and his two French friends swim their way to shore, finding a giant pot field upon arrival—along with a slew of AK-47–toting Thai guards. The trio eventually arrive at "The Beach," where the three find a community of fellow travelers are living off the land in their own self-ruled mini-society. Of course, what looks idyllic—and idealistic—isn't always so, and when relationships within the commune and with their native neighbors sour, heaven on earth soon turns to hell. Directed by Danny Boyle (Trainspotting, Slumdog Millionaire), and adapted from Alex Garland's novel, with music by John Cale and Brian Eno and a soundtrack that features New Order, Blur, Underworld, and Moby, The Beach has all the visual stimuli of a far-out vacation, but with a sinister undercurrent that may be hard for stoners to handle. Despite being a bummer, anyone seeking a Lord of the Flies feel will nonetheless be satisfied.

Richard: "Mine is a generation that circles the globe and searches for something we haven't tried before. So never refuse an invitation, never resist the unfamiliar, never fail to be polite and never outstay the welcome. Just keep your mind open and suck in the experience. And if it hurts, you know what? It's probably worth it."

Beautiful Creatures (2000)

🌿 🥢 💉

🌿🌿🌿 An accidental murder turns into premeditated blackmail and a homicidal cover-up, not orchestrated by a crew of gangbangers or thugs, but rather by two dainty Scottish gals who happen to have horrific taste in men. Dorothy (Susan Lynch) and Petula (Rachel Weisz) meet by chance, but their chemistry is explosive from the get-go. After Petula's boyfriend roughs her up, the two knock him off and try to play it off as a kidnapping. The women set the ransom at a million pounds, planning to take the money and run, but when a cop gets wise and Dorothy's ex interferes, the plot is foiled—though not irreversibly. All of these men soon learn that nothing gets between these ladies and their freedom. Dorothy is painted as more responsible and not as prone to partying, even though she can shoot smack with the best of them. Petula, on the other hand, is the kind of girl who likes to roll a perfect cone-shaped spliff and smoke it to "calm down," which is ironic considering how dark and jumpy this comedy/thriller turns out to be. Dorothy and Petula are Thelma and Louise, only with male flings that look nothing like Brad Pitt.

Petula: "Do you have anything I could use as a roach?"

Dorothy: "Don't make yourself too comfy, flower, I didn't invite you back for a party."

Petula: "I'm sorry, I'm just still a bit shaky and it would help calm me down."

Dorothy: "OK, have a scrounge in my rucksack, there's bound to be something."

Beyond the Valley of the Dolls (1970)

🖋 🍾 🔪 💊 👁👁

🌿🌿🌿🌿 Directed by B-movie auteur and renowned breast man Russ Meyers, and written by future film critic Roger Ebert, this is not a sequel to *Valley of the Dolls*, the 1967 film about pill-popping actresses, but rather a freak flag–flying rock-and-roll fairy tale that crashes the Partridge Family bus through the gates of the Manson family compound. Kelly (Dolly Read), Pet (Marcia McBroom), and Casey (Cynthia Meyers) have a band called the Kelly Affair that lives the late-sixties dream of making it to the West Coast, only to find themselves wrecked on a road of sex, drugs, betrayal, and bad-acid-trip murders. Once in L.A., Kelly meets her long-lost aunt Susan (Phyllis Davis), a fashion designer who informs her that she's entitled to part of the family fortune, setting off fireworks with Aunt Susan's scheming lawyer Emerson Thorne (Harrison Page). Introduced to star-maker Ronnie "Z man" Barzell (John Lazar), the band is renamed the Carrie Nations and begins a rise to the top that will see loyalties shattered, genders bent, temptations indulged, and party after party of nude romping and drug use. Set to a soundtrack of Carrie Nation tunes that have decently stood the test of time, there's plenty of pre-MTV music video sequences and tons of T & A. There are also stylistic nods to a raunchier *Laugh In* and bits of psychedelic nonsense thrown in, all to excellent head-trip effect. When they're not smoking pot, they're talking about it, always with some square nearby to poo-poo it. In the end it's a cautionary tale with lives irreversibly changed, but who cares when it's so much fun being bad?

Kelly: "Hey, got any more grass, man?"

Pet: "I scored this afternoon . . . the cat swore up and down it was Acapulco Gold, so if we're lucky, maybe it's at least pot."

Kelly: "So we'll get an oregano high!"

Big Chill, The (1983)

🖋 🍾 🔪 💊 🔪

🌿🌿🌿🌿 Where *Dazed and Confused* represents stoners coming of age in the seventies and *Friday* feels so nineties, *The Big Chill* is unmistakably eighties. The story revolves around a group of University of Michigan grads reuniting for the first time in two decades after Alex, a mutual friend and part of the baby boomer crew, commits suicide. Problem is, after twenty years apart, they realize that outside of memories of their time together they have little in common. Enter one "rogue" mem-

ber, Nick Carlton (William Hurt), an erstwhile drug dealer who brings his stash of weed, coke, and other goodies to the funeral. The group, which includes TV star Sam Weber (Tom Berenger), doctor Sarah (Glenn Close), *People* magazine writer Michael (Jeff Goldblum), Alex's young girlfriend Chloe (Meg Tilly), business exec Harold (Kevin Kline), and desperate housewife Karen (JoBeth Williams), passes around a few joints, and before the first roach is extinguished their minds are back in Ann Arbor, contemplating love and loss, not to mention the meaning of life. Director Lawrence Kasdan shows deep affection both for his characters and the tool that enables them to rediscover their lost connection. The film (and accompanying soundtrack featuring early sixties rock and R & B classics) was so popular that it has generated some backlash over the years. Look no further than Jack Black's character Barry in 2000's *High Fidelity*, who notes that the Rolling Stones's "You Can't Always Get What You Want" gets an "immediate disqualification for its appearance in *The Big Chill*." But don't give way to the bad vibes. This is a fun character piece with great music and a loving view of weed—a welcome respite during the Reagan era.

Sam Weber: "Nothing's more important than sex!"

Michael: "Oh yeah, have you ever gone a week without a rationalization?"

Black Snake Moan
(2006)

Craig Brewer's somewhat disappointing follow-up to *Hustle and Flow* is infamous for its exploitative story line featuring Christina Ricci in chains. Ricci, who plays wild-child Rae in this Deep South drama, is literally chained to a radiator by her savior Lazarus (powerfully portrayed by Samuel L. Jackson) after he finds her beaten and lifeless near his backwoods home. Rae goes on a bender when her boyfriend Ronnie (Justin Timberlake) ships off to Iraq, popping a handful of pills and spreading her legs for just about anybody until one guy physically abuses her. Lazarus's rehabilitation of Rae is complete when Ronnie returns and they suddenly decide to get married. The terrific blues soundtrack includes cuts by North Mississippi Allstars, The Black Keys, and R. L. Burnside, plus Jackson sings the title track.

☘ MORE ONE-HIT WONDERS ☘

These dramas have two things in common: big-time star power and a little weed.

Mortal Thoughts (1991): Hot-tempered dirtbag husband James (Bruce Willis) rolls a joint with some E-Z Widers before putting the moves on his battered wife's best friend Cynthia (Demi Moore) in this murder mystery set in big-haired Bayonne, New Jersey.

The People vs. Larry Flynt (1996): Long before the *Hustler* founder developed an addiction to opiates, editorial meetings during the magazine's early days involved passing joints while brainstorming in Larry Flynt's tiny Cincinnati apartment. For the Oscar-nominated film's closing scene, Flynt (Woody Harrelson) watches a video of his late wife Althea (Courtney Love) prancing naked while puffing on a spliff.

Shattered Glass (2003): In a reenactment of one of journalist Stephen Glass's (Hayden Christensen) bogus *New Republic* articles, a group of Young Republicans party in a hotel suite during a convention. As a joint makes the rounds, the crew-cut conservatives lament the state of their party: "We're like this guy who has to pee, lost in the desert looking for a tree."

Imaginary Heroes (2004): Grieving over the death of her son, Sandy (Sigourney Weaver) finds a companion in marijuana. She smokes a blunt and then gets arrested for trying to cop weed at a head shop.

Into the Wild (2007): Along his road to self-discovery, Alexander Supertramp, née Christopher McCandless (Emile Hirsch), befriends hippie couple Jan (Catherine Keener) and Rainey (Brian Dierker), fellow nomads who travel the West Coast in a psychedelic RV and like to unwind with a joint. Curiously, the lit-obsessed protagonist doesn't partake in this Sean Penn–directed Oscar-nominated film.

Blow (2001)

Johnny Depp portrays George Jung, a real-life drug smuggler who gets rich importing marijuana and cocaine but can't stay out of jail. George moves Mexican *mota* across the border before getting popped holding 660 pounds. In prison, he meets Diego (Jordi Mollà), an associate of Colombian cocaine kingpin Pablo Escobar (Cliff Curtis). When George and his drug-dealing partner Derek (Paul Reubens) go into the coke business ("we invented the marketplace"), the movie suddenly resembles *Scarface*. George is repeatedly burned—by Diego, Derek, his second wife Mirtha (Penélope Cruz), long-time friend Dulli (Max Perlich), even his mother (Rachel Griffiths). It's a sad story of betrayal, and after his fourth bust, George accepts the fact that he's going to spend the rest of his life behind bars. While rich in period details, the film lacks a strong central figure: George is just a regular guy, not particularly smart or charismatic, and Depp struggles to bring him to life. Even sadder, director Ted Demme died of a cocaine overdose shortly after the movie's release.

George: "It's fuckin' 15 kilos—I piss 15 kilos!"

☘ DEALER DUDES ☘

Alternately funny and menacing, the characters that act out the roles of drug distributors leave their indelible mark on stoner cinema.

Slater in *Dazed and Confused*: "Ever look at a dollar bill, man? There's some spooky shit goin' on there," proclaims Rory Cochrane's Slater, who's the most lovable dealer, bong maker, and slacker philosopher that stoner cinema has ever seen.

Saul Silver in *Pineapple Express*: James Franco's dense Saul rarely leaves his living room, where he rocks two TVs and a stash of boutique strains. Among them: the film's titular favorite, which he cajoles Dale (Seth Rogen) into smoking via the extra powerful cross joint.

The Mr. Nice Guy crew in *Half Baked*: While buddy Kenny (Harland Williams) bides his time in jail, the trio of Thurgood (Dave Chappelle), Brian (Jim Breuer), and Scarface (Guillermo Díaz) turn a handsome profit running a delivery service out of their stoner pad. Among the Mr. Nice Guy clients: a scavenger smoker (Snoop Dogg), the you-should've-been-there smoker (Willie Nelson), and an enhancement smoker (Jon Stewart) who thinks "marijuana makes every activity that much better."

George Jung and Derek Foreal in *Blow*: What begins as an innocent beachside party turns into big business for wannabe supplier George (Johnny Depp) and his West Coast distributor Derek (Paul Reubens). The two dabble in weed at first, but quickly graduate to coke in massive quantities, courtesy of Pablo Escobar (Cliff Curtis).

Jay and Silent Bob in *Clerks, Clerks II, Jay and Silent Bob Strike Back, Mallrats, Dogma*: As card-carrying members of the "Jersey Brotherhood of Dealers," Jay (Jason Mewes) and Silent Bob (Kevin Smith) proudly—and loudly—sell their wares outside the Quick Stop convenience store in *Clerks*, eventually migrating to Mooby's fast food for the sequel. Ten years separate the two films, but the price of a nickel bag never changes. As Jay raps: "Fifteen bucks, little man, put that shit in my hand."

Dante in *Grandma's Boy*: Dante (Peter Dante) is nutty as a fruitcake. He sells weed strains named Frankenstein, the Green Monster, and Bling, rolls monster spliffs that would make Cheech and Chong jealous, and hangs out with an African, a martial artist, and a pot-smoking monkey.

Cisco Pike in *Cisco Pike*: Fresh out of jail, the movie's titular character, played by Kris Kristofferson in his first starring role, wants to stay clean, but dirty cop Leo Holland (Gene Hackman) won't let him. Holland lays 100 kilos of Mexican grass on Cisco and forces him to move it in seventy-two hours.

Lance in *Pulp Fiction*: When Mia (Uma Thurman) ODs on heroin, Vincent (John Travolta) calls Lance (Eric Stoltz), who reluctantly saves her life with a stiff jab of adrenaline to the heart.

Luke Shapiro in *The Wackness*: It doesn't get sweeter than a weed dealer who keeps his stash in an ice-cream cart. Josh Peck's Luke turns a tidy profit, almost enough to prevent his family from being evicted.

Ricky Fitts in *American Beauty*: Notable for his pricey pot, Wes Bentley's dealer-next-door sells ounces of G-13 for $2,000 dollars to neighbor Lester (Kevin Spacey), who marvels, "Jesus, things have changed since 1973."

Steve the Dealer in *Smiley Face*: "The profits I make trickle down through the economy in ways you can't even comprehend," Steve the Dealer (Adam Brody) declares, proving this white boy in Rasta dreads—who carries his goods in a suitcase—is definitely not your typical pot connection.

Todd Gaines in *Go*: When Ronna (Sarah Polley) doesn't pay Todd (Timothy Olyphant) for Ecstasy—"the real thing, pharmaceutical grade, not that crunchy herbal rave shit"—he seeks revenge but ends up making out with Ronna's friend Claire (Katie Holmes) instead.

Blow-Up (1966)

🌿 🌿 🌿 🌿 Just a year before the Summer of Love, Michelangelo Antonioni broke new ground with his first English-speaking feature. A fashion photographer (David Hemmings as Thomas) inadvertently shoots a murder at Greenwich Park in London. Jane (Vanessa Redgrave) wants the footage so much she'll take her clothes off and pose. When blow-ups mysteriously disappear from Thomas's studio, he searches in vain for Jane at a rock club where the Yardbirds (with Jimmy Page and Jeff Beck, who smashes his guitar) are playing, and at a party where joints are being rolled and passed. Thomas's nude frolic with two models, a band of raving mimes, and Herbie Hancock's jazz score add fun and depth to this enduring period piece.

Ron to Thomas: "Here, have a drag."

Blue Velvet (1986)

🌿 🌿 🌿 🌿 🌿

In the any-town American 'burb of Lumberton, teenager Jeffrey (Kyle MacLachlan) finds a severed ear in an abandoned lot, a discovery that plunges him into the darkness that lies beneath the surface of his idyllic neighborhood. Fueled by Jeffrey's overwhelming curiosity and his blossoming relationship with the wholesome Sandy (Laura Dern), the plot starts out like a *Hardy Boys* mystery and mutates into a whirlwind of kink. With Sandy's help, Jeffrey tracks down mysterious and troubled singer Dorothy Vallens (Isabella Rossellini) and becomes entangled with her sexually. Attracted to the innocent Sandy but tempted by the desperate and masochistic Dorothy, Jeffrey discovers that Dorothy is being tormented by drug dealer Frank (Dennis Hopper), a gas-mask–wearing, sadist who's kidnapped her husband and child and huffs an unidentified substance. In the inevitable confrontation, Frank takes Jeffrey on a hellish joyride of epic weirdness that he's lucky to survive. By the time a naked and bloodied Dorothy shows up at Sandy's house, there are dirty cops, bad disguises, and campy teenage monologues about life, and plenty of bad mojo S & M. Reasons are not given for much of the action, but that's part of the charm, like the femme Ben (Dean Stockwell) lip syncing into a utility lamp as Frank watches in tears. Hailed as director David Lynch's masterpiece, *Blue Velvet* delivers a commanding atmosphere where the familiar becomes alien and the dialogue cycles between folksy aphorisms and a straight-up Jungian head trip. In addition, the masterful score by Angelo Badelamenti, a well-placed Roy Orbison tune, and ominous sound design keep things on a razor's edge. Much more controversial upon release than it is today, *Blue Velvet* still packs a wallop.

Frank: "Let's drink up."

Ben: "Here's to your health."

Frank: "Ah shit, let's drink to something else . . . let's drink to fucking. You got to say, here's to your fuck, Frank."

Bobby (2006)

🍁🍁🍁🍁 Emilio Estevez followed up *Rated X* (2000) with this dazzling portrait of the last day of Robert F. Kennedy's life. Obsessed with RFK (he met him when he was five years old), Estevez assembled an incredible cast—all of whom converged on the Ambassador Hotel in Los Angeles on June 4, 1968, when Kennedy won the California primary. Next stop was the Democratic Convention in Chicago. But, of course, there would be no next stop for Kennedy, who was murdered by Sirhan Sirhan in the hotel kitchen late that night. Estevez focuses on a myriad of characters and storylines, all connected to the grand hotel—its employees, guests and RFK campaign workers. There's hotel manager Paul (William H. Macy), who's married to hairstylist Miriam (Sharon Stone) and banging phone-operator Angela (Heather Graham) on the side; drunken nightclub singer Virginia (Demi Moore) and her uptight manager husband Tim (Estevez); socialites Jack (Estevez's dad Martin Sheen) and his fragile wife Samantha (Helen Hunt); youngsters Diane (Lindsay Lohan) and William (Elijah Wood), who are getting married to keep William from being shipped off to Vietnam; campaign hotshots Wade (Joshua Jackson) and Dwayne (Nick Cannon); Mexican kitchen workers Miguel (Jacob Vargas) and Jose (Freddie Rodriguez); philosophical chef Edward (Laurence Fishburne) and his racially insensitive boss Daryl (Christian Slater); hotel old-timers John (Anthony Hopkins) and Nelson (Harry Belafonte); and best of all for the purposes of this book, canvassers Cooper (Shia LeBeouf) and Jimmy (Brian Geraghty), who blow off work that day to get stoned with house dealer Fisher (Ashton Kutcher). He turns them on to sugar cubes laced with lysergic acid diethylam-ide. "Are you ready to have a personal relationship with God?" the head-banded hippie asks. Coop and Jimmy's trip lasts the entire day—like any quality acid experience—leading them to wonder if it will ever end. The funniest scene finds them laughing hysterically during a game of stoner tennis. Foxy hotel waitress Susan (Mary Elizabeth Winstead) comes to their rescue ("your pupils look like saucers"). No one really plays Kennedy, who's seen in archival footage on the stump and from behind when he arrives at the hotel and then attempts to leave after his ballroom speech. Sirhan shoots the candidate and several of the characters (Samantha, Daryl, Coop, Jimmy, and William), creating chaos, sadness, grief, and fear for the state of the nation (just two months earlier Dr. Martin Luther King Jr. was gunned down as well). Despite some awkward moments and unnecessary speechifying, Estevez pulls it all off—something you'd never expect from the kid we first met in *The Breakfast Club*.

> "LSD was first discovered in 1938. She can be beautiful or she can be terrifying. The difference between a good trip and a bad trip is completely contingent on your willingness to let go and turn yourself over to her completely."
>
> **—Fisher**

Boogie Nights (1997)

🍁🍁🍁🍁 Hung like a horse, Dirk Diggler (Mark Wahlberg) is the porn industry's brightest hope circa 1977—that's when director Jack Horner (Burt Reynolds) discovers the seventeen-year-old busboy known as Eddie Adams, launches him to adult film superstardom, and invites him into the family. In no time, Dirk is having his way with the mothering Amber Waves (Julianne Moore) and the perpetually lost Rollergirl (Heather Graham) while establishing his thirteen-inch member as a bona fide star. Dirk and fellow stud Reed Rothchild (John C. Reilly) team up as action heroes Brock Landers and Chest Rockwell and their fame reaches new heights—even if their lives hit new lows. Increasingly dragged down by drugs (first coke, then meth with mentions of smack), insecurity, and narcissism, Dirk becomes a parody of himself, while Jack, who's battling an industry shift from film to videotape, starts to look like a relic. Philip Seymour Hoffman as boom operator (and Dirk's number one admirer) Scotty, William H. Macy as the tormented Assistant Director Little Bill, and Don Cheadle as the stereo-obsessed Buck round out a stellar cast, while a soundtrack of seventies and eighties hits is the perfect accompaniment to the film's use of long takes. Sunny skies and crystal-clear pools accent many scenes, but in the end, it's a grim outlook for one very dirty business. Still, seventies porn never looked this good.

Dirk: "It's fucking getting me fuckin' high, man."

Todd: "It's that carpet dope. The kind of dope they used to put carpet in. They would mix it up in the bathtub and while they were mixing it up in the bathtub, they'd drop in a hunk of carpet into it. It's a lot better than that pink shit, I tell you that. There's fish gills in that shit."

Born on the Fourth of July (1989)

🌿 🌿 🌿 🌿 Based on the bestselling autobiography of the same name, which both appalled and inspired director Oliver Stone, Tom Cruise stars as Ron Kovic, an impressionable Long Island teenager hell-bent on joining the Marines and serving his country in Vietnam. Wounded in battle during his second tour of duty and paralyzed from the chest down, Ron is sent to a decrepit Bronx VA hospital and then home in a wheelchair, where he quickly turns to alcohol to numb the pain. Ron soon becomes disillusioned with his country and the war, joining a growing number of veterans reconsidering their culpability. So he drops out for a stint, grows his hair long, and escapes to a seaside village in Mexico that caters to the paraplegic, where, after he's done indulging in whores and tequila, Ron starts coming to terms with his own war experience. Once he decides to officially side with the hippies he once mocked, he embraces activism with the same fury he once unleashed on the battlefield, becoming an outspoken advocate for veterans' rights and a critic of the VA system. Like Stone's *Platoon* (and featuring at least three of that movie's stars), this Oscar winner (Best Director and Best Film Editing) is graphic, weighty, and should not be entered into lightly.

Boys Don't Cry (1999)

🌿 🌿 🌿 🌿 In a career-making, Oscar-winning role based on a true story, Hilary Swank plays Brandon Teena, a kid from the wrong side of the tracks who suffers from a sexual identity disorder. Born Teena Brandon, a female, Brandon decided to live his adult life as a male, which often got him into trouble, forcing him to move around his home state of Nebraska. On one sojourn, Brandon winds up at a bar in Falls City, where he meets a foursome of friends: ex-cons John (Peter Sarsgaard) and Tom (Brendan Sexton III) and gal-pals Lana (Chloë Sevigny) and Candace (Alicia Goranson).

"Maybe you've had enough."
—Lana

"I ain't had any."
—Brandon

"No shit, man. People like you don't need drugs, you just hallucinate twenty-four hours a day."
—Tom

After several nights of hard-core partying (things to do in Fall City: bumper skiing, backseat bong hits, whip-its, and lots of behind-the-wheel beer), Brandon falls for Lana, and the two start dating. Brandon's physical charade involves wrapping his chest in tension badges to flatten his boobs and strapping socks to his crotch, but eventually, he lies to Lana and claims he's a hermaphrodite. When John and Tom find out, their jealousy and disgust culminates in a brutal rape scene that nearly got the film an NC-17 rating. There are only losers in the end as the hate crime escalates into a double homicide. Tragic and telling, intense and dark, this is the kind of movie you never forget—as much as you may want to.

Boyz N the Hood
(1991)

Not only did John Singleton make his directorial debut with this Los Angeles–based drama, it also introduced NWA rapper Ice Cube as an actor. We first meet Doughboy (Baha Jackson) as a ten-year-old in South Central, where gunshots ring out at all hours and dead bodies pile up in vacant lots. Seven years later, Doughboy (Cube) and his friends are high school students heading in different directions. A football star, Doughboy's brother Ricky (Morris Chestnut) is being

recruited by USC. His best friend Tre (Cuba Gooding Jr.) wants to marry Brandi (Nia Long). Doughboy sells drugs, but has no particular ambition. Tre's dad, Furious Styles (Laurence Fishburne)—he's divorced from Reva (Angela Bassett)—has devoted the last seven years to raising Tre and teaching him to not fight violence with more violence. Tre's tested when Ricky's gunned down by gangbangers over a petty dispute. Can Tre hold back his anger and desire for revenge or will he be just another fatality in the 'hood? *Boyz* would be the first of many movies set in South Central (*Menace II Society, Friday, Colors*)—and it's still the best.

Furious: "How you think the crack rock gets into the country? We don't own any planes. We don't own no ships. We are not the people that are flyin' and floatin' that shit in here . . . it wasn't a problem until it was in Iowa and showed up on Wall Street where there are hardly any black people."

Breakfast on Pluto
(2005)

In this Irish indie, directed by Neil Jordan (*The Crying Game*) and set in the seventies, Cillian Murphy stars as orphaned transvestite Patrick "Kitten" Braden. Known also as Patricia, Kitten hails from a tiny town on the Irish border where a conservative population—during the days of the Irish Republican Army—simply doesn't tolerate her kind. As a young adult, she narrowly escapes death when her glam-rock sugar daddy Billy (Gavin Friday) is discovered to be hiding guns for the IRA, so Kitten flees to London, where she hopes to track down her biological mother. As the androgynous sweetheart meets a sordid lot of characters, each acquaintance brings her one step closer to her goal, but two steps back in self-respect. Kitten turns tricks for a stint—she fends off a violent attack by a john (played by Roxy Music singer Bryan Ferry) with a spray of perfume—assists a magician, and works at a peep show, where her childhood pastor Father Liam (Liam Neeson) visits one day bearing news of her mother's whereabouts. Fans of *Hedwig and the Angry Inch* will appreciate Murphy's brilliant gender-bending turn as Kitten, the kind of gal who can share a spliff with a biker gang while they wax poetic about Druids and the space-time continuum—she's cool like that, and so is this surprisingly uplifting tale.

Brick (2005)

The high school experience gets the film noir treatment in Rian Johnson's convoluted Sundance winner. After discovering his ex-girlfriend's dead body in a sewer tunnel, loner Brendan (Joseph Gordon-Levitt) goes on a mission to find out who killed her and why. He channels Sherlock Holmes and follows leads that take him all over the social grounds of his high school, from the drama players to the jocks to the stoners. In one dizzying fight scene, Brendan takes a beating from football jock/school drug dealer Brad (Brian J. White). His search leads him to the drug kingpin of the "burgh," as they call it, a punch-happy stoner, Tugger (Noah Fleiss), who plays enforcer for the kingpin, aptly named The Pin (Lukas Haas). Ultimately, Brendan discovers that Tugger killed his beloved ex, Emily (Emilie de Ravin), partially because of her assumed role in the disappearance of a brick of The Pin's heroin. Using his best friend, The Brain (Matt O'Leary), and the school VP Trueman (Shaft's Richard Roundtree) as accomplices, Brendan exacts revenge on his fellow students.

Bright Lights, Big City (1988)

In the eighties, coke was considered as commonplace as pot and few movies reflected this shift in recreational drug use quite like James Bridges's adaptation of Jay McInerney's novel (McInerney wrote the script as well). Capturing the gritty essence of New York City circa 1988, the film centers on Jamie (Michael J. Fox), a fact-checker at a fictitious version of The New Yorker who holds his head under a reading lamp in a dreary literary office all day, then hangs with his coke buddy Tad (Kiefer Sutherland) into the wee hours of the night snot-poking in bathroom stalls. The feather-haired Jamie is a struggling writer who can't come to grips with his mother's death, and that his runway model wife (Phoebe Cates) just left him. Clichés aside, it's hilarious to watch a 145-pounder do such excessive amounts of booze and blow. If he's not tooting off his hand in the toilet, then he's pounding bottles of wine at the apartment of his sympathetic coworker Megan (Swoosie Kurtz). Jamie slurps down Stoli on the rocks like water and he has no problem with taking down his family antique wall mirror to use as a chopping block for his "Bolivian marching powder."

Jamie (looking at himself in the mirror): "You are way too high."

Brokedown Palace (1999)

Like Return to Paradise, released a year earlier, and the granddaddy of all smuggling movies, 1978's Midnight Express, Brokedown Palace—named for a Grateful Dead song—will scare you shitless. Two young American women, Alice (Clare Danes) and Darlene (Kate Beckinsale), jet off to Thailand on an impulsive vacation. In Bangkok, they squabble over suave traveler Nick (Daniel Lapaine), who invites them to fly with him to Hong Kong. They're searched at the airport and busted when heroin is found in their bags (clearly planted by

Nick). Dispatched to an antiquated women's prison, their secret trip is now officially a nightmare. They hire attorney Yankee Hank (Bill Pullman) to guide them through the Thai legal system, but the large quantity of dope and lack of a credible alibi (Nick is nowhere to be found) results in lengthy sentences (thirty-three years!). Ever the maverick, Alice smokes joints in jail to Darlene's consternation. After several appeals fail, and with Darlene increasingly losing it behind bars, Alice takes the rap. It's a bold but disingenuous resolution. Otherwise, Danes and Beckinsale are perfectly cast as naïve tourists who inadvertently get caught up in the international smuggling trade.

Alice to Darlene as she smokes a joint in jail: "If my brain wasn't on drugs I'd probably kill someone."

Brooklyn Babylon (2001)

🍁🍁🍁 Just as interborough tensions reach a boiling point in Brooklyn, an unlikely hookup between Rasta Solomon (The Roots' Tariq Trotter) and Orthodox Jew Sara (Karen Goberman) brings two distant worlds a little closer together. He's an artist, rapper, and proud member of The Lions; she's a good girl who's dating yarmulke-wearing hothead Judah (David Vadim) and when the two meet by way of a car accident, of all things, sparks fly—both literally and metaphorically. But neither his Jah brothers nor her insular family approve, which ignites several not-so-random acts of violence and forces the two to keep their dalliance secret. The culture clash escalates when a car gets torched and Jewish community leaders demand that the annual West Indian Day parade be canceled. It marches on and the couple takes a united stand atop a musical float. Call them Sheba and Solomon, Romeo and Juliet, or simply acknowledge that opposites attract, but outside of one great scene in which Sol introduces Sara to blunts on the beach in Coney Island, Mark Levin (Whiteboyz, Slam) directs a predictable love story that takes few chances. Still, The Lions's tunes, played by members of The Roots, are a high point.

Bully (2001)

🍁🍁🍁 Based on Jim Schutze's book about Florida teenagers who take revenge on a local bully, Larry Clark's third movie is probably his most controversial. After KIDS and Another Day in Paradise, Clark once again zeroed in on sexually active underaged drug abusers. Marty (Brad Renfro) and Bobby (Nick Stahl) are BFFs, but only because Bobby repeatedly punches and belittles him, forcing Marty to be his bitch. Marty asks his parent to move, but they ignore his requests, oblivious of the festering problem. Marty's new girlfriend Lisa (Rachel Minor) plants the initial seed about killing Bobby. She recruits her closest friends and relatives—the promiscuous Ali (Bijou Phillips), Donny (Michael Pitt), Heather (Kelli Garner), and cousin Derek (Danny Franzese)—slackers who regularly get baked and dose, perhaps not the best accomplices for a murder scheme. But they move ahead with the ill-fated plan, and after one false start, lure Bobby to the beach and stab him in a Lord of the Flies–style frenzy. From that point, it's a comedy of errors, with Lisa blabbing to friends about the killing and the body popping up out of the swamp. They're all arrested, sentenced, and jailed, some for life. What otherwise might have been an interesting story is marred by Clark's exploitative camera, which peers up Ali's shorts and down Donny's erect nipples. At times, Clark is as much a creep as Bobby—he's a bully with his own camera.

Lisa about Bobby: "He's even too weird for Ali and she's into everything."

Cash Crop (1998)

🍁🍁🍁 Stuart Burkin's only feature film (a.k.a. Harvest) focuses on family farmers in Pennsylvania who grow weed to prevent foreclosure. It's a topical story that would've benefited from a cameo by Willie Nelson. Instead, Evan Handler, who went on to star in Sex and the City and Californication, plays local pot dealer Ray. Actually, the cast is pretty solid, led by Dawson's Creek's James Van Der Beek as James, who wakes and bakes and listens to the Grateful Dead, and *Mad Men*'s John Slattery as sympathetic Sheriff Johnson. He protects the farmers when DEA Agent Becka Anslinger (note the familiar last name—played by Mary McCormack) arrives in fictional Oxford and starts snooping around. The farmers pull their crops and stash ten large bags of bud at a dilapidated drive-in. In an ironic twist, the antidrug son of one of the farmers torches the entire stash, which goes up in smoke in an aromatic final inferno—a major no-no in the wacky world of stoner movies.

Ray: "Those spineless cornhole motherfuck farmers really fucked me good. Smell that? That's some good fucking weed, bro."

Chappaqua (1966)

Eleven years after *The Man with the Golden Arm*, writer/director Conrad Rooks tackled a similar subject, but in a much more abstract, psychedelic fashion. An alcoholic and a heroin addict, Russel (Rooks) goes to France for a treatment administered by Dr. Benoit (Jean-Louis Barrault) at his sprawling estate. With Russel in a constant state of flashback, the movie plays out as a series of jarring cuts to vivid memories (often of a mysterious brown-haired woman) both in black-and-white and color. The opening scene in New York's Times Square at a rock club with LSD spelled out in sugar cubes, a woman crushing the cubes with her high heel and people licking it off the stage, is both sleazy and masterful. Russel literally runs into Allen Ginsberg Om-ing in Central Park and later William S. Burroughs (a.k.a. Opium Jones) in France. The terrific soundtrack features ragas by Ravi Shankar as well as the music of Phillip Glass. The Chappaqua of the title refers to Russel's hometown in upstate New York (where Bill and Hillary Clinton live), which he says, "was inhabited by the Indians. It means the sacred place of the running water. It's where all the tribes came to bury their dead. The Indians are all gone, dead, vanished, but they did dance there." Haunted by the past, Russel fights his way through the treatment and upon release is clearly warned by Dr. Benoit, "You must live without any drugs. This is for you a matter of life or death."

Chrystal (2004)

Limited theatrical release may have prevented buffs from catching Billy Bob Thornton (Joe) and Lisa Blount (Chrystal) work their peculiar magic in this Southern saga set in the Ozarks. Fresh out of jail, Joe crashes with Chrystal, who's damaged physically and emotionally from a car accident. A former marijuana farmer ("I have a green thumb"), Joe wants no part of the growing life. But he still smokes. The movie's one pot scene takes place in a car: After a shotgun hit, the joint is passed to Joe, who puffs as the two younger guys get the giggles. Director Ray McKinnon appears onscreen as Snake—Joe's nemesis—a snarling, unintelligible redneck. An ethnomusicology subplot involving two researchers and local folk-blues musicians—with stoner-movie stalwart Harry Dean Stanton on guitar and vocals—adds to the overall quality of the production.

Snake to Joe: "You can't grow no sticker bush without going through the Snake."

Cisco Pike (1972)

Bill L. Norton's counterculture classic introduced Kris Kristofferson as musician/drug dealer Cisco Pike. Twice busted, he's trying to stay clean, but along comes dirty cop Leo Holland (Gene Hackman), who entices him to sell 100 kilos of quality Mexican "grass" in exchange for prior charges against him being dropped. Despite his disapproving girlfriend Sue (Karen Black), Cisco hustles the weed for two hundred dollars a brick ("it's the best grass in L.A."). While Cisco runs around making deals, he meets Buffalo (Antonio Fargas), Rex (Doug Sahm), Merna (Viva), Reed (Hugh Romney, a.k.a. Wavy Gravy) and Jesse (Harry Dean Stanton), Cisco's former bandmate who ODs. A good chunk of the film consists of Cisco walking or driving as Kristofferson tunes like "The Pilgrim" ("He's a poet, he's a prophet, he's a pusher") play in the background. When the dragnet closes in, Holland is exposed, and Cisco manages to walk away with the cash and leftover dope.

Clockers (1995)

🍸 ✒️ 🧹

🌿🌿🌿 This Spike Lee joint, set in a Brooklyn housing project, focuses on two brothers—one's committed to a life of crime, while the other is a perpetual do-gooder. Strike (Mekhi Phifer) is a mid-level clocker (dealer) who's put to the test by longtime supplier Rodney Little (Delroy Lindo): kill or be killed. But when his brother Victor (Isaiah Washington) takes the fall for the murder, it's up to veteran detectives Rocco Klein (Harvey Keitel) and Larry Mazilli (John Turturro) to unravel the events of that fateful night. Based on Richard Price's novel and featuring Phifer in his first major role, this gritty look at growing up gangsta serves as the perfect predecessor to HBO's *The Wire*, which Price also worked on. But as weed-less Spike Lee joints go, its static setting pales in comparison to more colorful films like *Mo' Better Blues* and *Do the Right Thing*.

🌿 MORE SPIKE LEE JOINTS 🌿

Along with John Singleton, the iconoclastic Spike Lee defined a new African American sensibility in eighties and nineties cinema.

Do the Right Thing (1989): It's a hot summer in New York's Bedford-Stuyvesant 'hood and everyone is breathing down each other's necks in Lee's breakthrough film. Mookie (Lee) works at a pizzeria owned by longtime Italian-American merchant Sal (Danny Aiello). Mookie provokes Sal, asking why there are no photos of African American athletes on the walls. When the ribbing boils over into violence, Sal's shop goes up in smoke.

Mo' Better Blues (1990): Lee's jazz movie features music by Branford Marsalis and Terence Blanchard, and stars Denzel Washington as trumpeter Bleek, who has woman, band, and manager problems. He's juggling girlfriends, feuding with saxophonist Shadow (Wesley Snipes), and unable to rescue Giant (Lee), his manager, from a gambling debt. After a beatdown, Bleek and Giant give up the band. No one ever said the jazz life was easy.

Malcolm X (1992): Denzel Washington delivers an Oscar-worthy performance as the legendary African American leader in this epic biopic. While in jail, Malcolm X, a two-bit burglar and pot dealer with a taste for drugs and white women, discovered the Nation of Islam, an organization he would represent as a faithful disciple and public orator but which would eventually take him down.

Summer of Sam (1999): Conveying the sheer terror of living in New York City during the summer of 1977, Lee directs interweaving narratives of colorful outer-borough characters struggling to find their place in a harsh world, while serial killer David Berkowitz, a.k.a. "The Son of Sam," lurks in the shadows. Written by *The Sopranos*' Michael Imperioli and Victor Colicchio (*High Times' Pot Luck*), and starring John Leguizamo, Mira Sorvino, and Adrien Brody, *Summer of Sam* nails the clash of punk and disco cultures in the late seventies.

Clockwork Orange, A
(1971)

🔪 👓

🍁 🍁 🍁 🍁 🍁 Before tipping back their bowlers and setting out for an evening of mayhem and molestation, Alex (Malcolm McDowell) and his three Droogs—Pete (Michael Tarn), Georgie (James Marcus), and Dim (Warren Clarke)—pay a visit to the Korova Milk Bar. There, from the nipples of

cheesy nude statuary, they're served what Alex calls a "milk-plus," a concoction of "milk, plus vellocet or synthemesc or drencrom," which prepares them "for a bit of the old ultraviolence." The Droogs promptly visit a writer, whom they beat, and his wife, whom they gang-rape. A shocker for its time, the film initially received an X rating in the U.S. before director Stanley Kubrick trimmed some sexually explicit material. But amid all the controversy about content, critics remained oblivious to the highly moral message Anthony Burgess (the film is adapted from his novel) and Kubrick were imparting about free will, political oppression, and the definition of goodness. Is Alex, having undergone the Ludovico technique, rendering him incapable of further violence, *really* good just because he can't behave otherwise? Is a society in well-mannered lockstep really preferable to one in which individuals can make a choice? The fictional dosage with which Alex is injected before undergoing the grueling aversion therapy (which psychologically castrates him) is the more literal entry in a movie full of druglike elements. It's the ongoing aesthetic crime around him that has driven Alex to violence, and into the figurative arms of "Ludwig Van," as in Beethoven, whose "dreaded Ninth Symphony" provides much of the soundtrack to what is, if nothing else, an indictment of bad taste and an acknowledgment of what one sometimes has to do to get away from it. It's a moral that has not lost its bite.

Alex: "Naughty, naughty, naughty! You filthy old soomka!"

Colors (1988)

✏️ 🍸 🔪 🧹 👓

🍁 🍁 🍁 🍁 It's ironic that Dennis Hopper, who directed *Easy Rider* in 1969 and personified that era's embrace of outlaw culture, nearly twenty years later focused his camera on the police who were ostracized as "pigs" in the sixties and seventies. By the eighties, Los Angeles cops faced new enemies: the Crips and the Bloods. Hopper's fourth film effectively portrays street gang war through the eyes of two cops—Bob Hodges (Robert Duvall) and Danny McGavin (Sean Penn, six years after playing Spicoli in *Fast Times at Ridgemont High*—oh the irony!). Hodges has been on the beat for twenty years and McGavin is his cocky rookie partner. While Hodges finesses each potential confrontation, McGavin uses aggression and violence to get the upper hand. Numerous car and foot chases through narrow South Central alleyways lend authenticity to the location shooting by legendary cinematographer Haskell Wexler (*Coming Home, One Flew Over the Cuckoo's Nest*). McGavin woos Luisa (Maria Conchita Alonso), but loses her after assaulting her cousin. "You're sadistic," Luisa tells him. "You have a mean heart." It takes Luisa's words and Hodges's death for McGavin to see the error of his ways. Ice-T's gripping theme song about the continu-

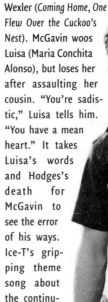

ing cycle of gang violence says it all: "We'll never die / Just multiply."

Hodges to T-Bone: "Y'all got any dope today?"

T-Bone: "Not us—we say no to drugs."

Coming Home (1978)

🖊 🍸 👓

🍁🍁🍁🍁 Jon Voight and Jane Fonda both won Oscars for their costarring turns in this Vietnam-era love story, directed by Hal Ashby (*Harold & Maude, Shampoo*)—he also received an Academy Award nomination—about the postwar trauma of the soldiers who return to the States and of their loved ones. Fonda plays Sally, a military wife with little going on in her life now that her Marine Corps officer husband Bob (Bruce Dern) has been deployed. She starts volunteering at the local VA hospital and meets the salty, wheelchair-bound Luke (Voight). They strike up a friendship, which soon turns into a full-on affair that's surprisingly uncomplicated. As paraplegic antiwar crusaders go, Luke is passionate and sharp if not a bit hot-tempered, but once Sally comes into his life, a calm takes over and things start looking up. That is, until an injury ships Bob home early. Featuring a superb sixties soundtrack, *Coming Home* is as much a time stamp as it is a scripted narrative, which makes the ending, featuring a supermarket sign that reads "Lucky OUT" and Tim Buckley's "Once I Was" all the more poignant: "Once I was a lover / And I searched behind your eyes for you / And soon there'll be another / To tell you I was just a lie."

Bob: "This whole fuckin' war is boring, but ladies, ol' Bob has gotta tell you one thing that is not boring: and that is a good old U.S. of A. martini, of which I am going to partake as much as I can, as quick as I can."

Cooley High (1975)

🖊 🍸 🔪

🍁🍁🍁🍁 Directed by Michael Schultz (*Car Wash*), and written by *Good Times* cocreator Eric Monte, this portrait of near-adulthood circa 1964 has been hailed as the black *American Graffiti*. High school seniors Leroy "Preach" Jackson (Glynn Turman) and Richard "Cochise" Morris (Lawrence Hilton-Jacobs) are best buds and classmates at Chicago's Cooley Vocational. They spend most days roaming their Chicago neighborhood, where their carefree lifestyle revolves around cards, cars, smoke, and hookups. When Preach and Cochise are actually in school, they're more likely to be found in the virtual den of sin that is the boys' bathroom—playing craps or smoking joints—than in a classroom. But as much as they seemingly try to be troublemakers (the proof is in the company they keep), they're actually smart kids. Preach is a voracious reader and poet while Cochise is dashing, well-spoken, and charming. Teacher Mr. Mason (Garrett Morris) notices and intervenes, trying to set the duo on the right path, but it all goes to hell when a thrill-seeking joyride leads to their arrest. *Cooley High* is said to have loosely inspired the sitcom *What's Happening*, but that couldn't have come from the last act, which crashes with a thud after more than an hour of cheer.

Preach's poem: "Basketball days and high nights. No tomorrows, unable to remember yesterday. We live for today."

Countryman (1982)

🖊 🥢 🍸 🔪 👓

🍁🍁🍁🍁 Ten years after Perry Henzell's *The Harder They Come* and a year following Bob Marley's death, Marley's former manager Dickie Jobson tapped the unknown Countryman to star in his engaging movie about a Jamaican fisherman with supernatural powers. After a plane crashes, Country rescues a couple and nurses the pilot, Bobby (Hiram Keller), who has broken his leg, back to health with a diet of fruits, vegetables, seafood, and spliffs. Meanwhile, the Jamaican government is in hot pursuit of Bobby, who they believe is a CIA agent. With the help of an "Obeah Man," Country fights off the police and delivers Bobby and his girlfriend Beau (Kristina St. Clair) to her father. As he smokes a huge cone-sized joint, Country declares: "I'm a stronger force. The wind, the sea, even the Earth defend I." The Island Records soundtrack is stocked with Marley classics ("Natural Mystic," "Three O'clock Roadblock," "Time Will Tell"). In 2005, Willie Nelson released a reggae album named for the movie, though the songs ("The Harder They Come," "Sitting in Limbo") are more of a tribute to Henzell's classic than Jobson's.

Cruel Intentions (1999)

This update of *Dangerous Liaisons* takes the original's Victorian sexual conniving and moves it to the wealthiest part of Manhattan, with mostly dated results. Ryan Phillippe and Sarah Michelle Gellar play Sebastian and Kathryn, a pair of extremely good-looking, privileged stepsiblings with a magnetic attraction to each other. The nose candy–dabbling Kathryn has been holding out on Sebastian, though, so she offers him a bet: If he bangs new-in-town virgin Annette (Reese Witherspoon) by the end of the summer, she'll offer herself up to him as well. Uncorrupted goodie-two-shoes Cecile (Selma Blair) locks lips with Kathryn in the film's much-parodied, still sexy lesbian make-out scene. Marred by overacting, *Cruel Intentions* offers plenty of pomp and not much circumstance.

> "This doesn't taste like an iced tea."
>
> —Cecile

> "It's from Long Island."
>
> —Sebastian

Dead Man (1995)

Johnny Depp stars as William Blake in Jim Jarmusch's contemplative Western set somewhere in the hills of Nevada. Blake arrives by train in Machine, a shit-hole mining town, circa mid-nineteenth century. Shot in black-and-white (with Jarmusch's familiar dissolves) and scored by Neil Young, we follow Blake on his adventure, which begins when he finds a job is not awaiting him as planned. John Dickinson (Robert Mitchum in one of his last roles), the owner of Dickinson Metalworks, sends Blake packing. When Blake shacks up with a woman who happened to be Dickinson's son's ex, he shoots his way out of town and into the mountains. A CPA from Cleveland, Blake is not very well equipped for the journey ahead. Native American outcast Nobody (Gary Farmer) befriends him, but Blake can barely understand his mystical ramblings, complaining: "I've had it up to here with your Indian malarkey." After Nobody shares peyote with him, Blake hallucinates and begins to connect with the natural environment. Followed by bounty hunters, Blake goes on a shooting spree, but he's hit as well. A city slicker named for the English poet, Blake proves to be no match for the Western wilderness.

Dealing: Or the Berkeley-to-Boston Forty-Brick Lost-Bag Blues (1972)

This lost gem, recently rediscovered and released as part of Warner Bros. Archive Collection, is based on the book by Michael Crichton and his brother Douglas under the nom de plume Michael Douglas (not to be confused with the actor of the same name) in 1971. John (John Lithgow in his first-ever role) and Peter (Robert F. Lyons) team up to smuggle a suitcase full of Michoacán marijuana from Berkeley to Boston. After Peter picks up the stash in California, the drug house gets busted, leaving him alone with Susan (Barbara Hershey). In the spirit of free love, they "get together" in a music studio where folkie Buzzy Linhart is rehearsing "You Got What It Takes." Peter and Susan fall hard for each other. He arranges for her to transport another forty bricks (a brick equals 1 kilo, or 2.2 pounds), but Susan's nabbed at Logan Airport. Watching the news on TV, John and Peter realize that only half of the haul was reported. They stake out Murphy (Charles Durning), the dirty cop who announced the collar, and not only recover the weed, but heroin-stuffed cigar tubes in the ripped-off suitcase as well. Peter deftly plays all parties as he orchestrates Susan's release, leaving the powder and a slew of dead bodies behind. Coke and pot mix here (Peter and Susan toot before they have sex), but junk's another story.

Departed, The (2006)

🌿 🌿 🌿 🌿 After six Best Director nominations, Martin Scorcese finally got his due with a mob movie that lacks the gleam of *GoodFellas* or the shine of *Casino* but brilliantly blurs the line between cop and criminal in Irish-run South Boston. Matt Damon plays Colin Sullivan, a high-ranking police officer tipping off local gangster Frank Costello (Jack Nicholson), who's been his longtime father figure. Billy Costigan (Leonardo DiCaprio) works undercover as one of Frank's thugs, only his job is constantly undermined by Colin. Staff Sergeant Dignam (Marc Wahlberg) and captains Queenan (Martin Sheen) and Ellerby (Alec Baldwin) try their best to control the puppet strings, but when it's revealed that Frank's a rat for the Feds and sexy shrink Madolyn (Vera Farmiga) is sleeping with Colin and Billy, bodies start piling up. Its genius plot twists, stellar soundtrack, and ridiculously quotable lines at every turn (Dignam's "I'm the guy who does his job; you must be the other guy," for example) makes *The Departed* a classic that only gets better with repeated viewings.

Frank Costello: "Want some coke? There it is. Don't move till you're numb."

Doors, The (1991)

🌿 🌿 🌿 🌿 This Oliver Stone–directed biopic could just as well have been named Jim since the rock band's story is secondary to the dramatic rise and fall of its singer. Val Kilmer takes center stage as Jim Morrison—a poet, free thinker, drinker, drug fiend, sex machine, and self-proclaimed "Lizard King." Deeply affected by a roadside accident he witnessed as a kid, Morrison looks to Native American culture for spirituality and inspiration, and many of the Doors's greatest hits reflect those themes.

Keyboardist Ray Manzarek (Kyle MacLachlan), a film-school buddy of Morrison's, recruits drummer John Densmore (*Entourage*'s Kevin Dillon) and guitarist Robbie Krieger (Frank Whaley) to form the band, and after bonding on a desert acid trip, where Morrison hallucinates dancing Indians (a scene that would be spoofed a year later in *Wayne's World 2*), the Doors are soon selling out Sunset Strip clubs and appearing on *The Ed Sullivan Show*. But with the peak of their popularity begins Morrison's decline, helped along by enabler girlfriends Pamela (Meg Ryan) and Patricia (Kathleen Quinlan), who indulge in everything from coke to heroin. In Stone's version, Morrison is a big-time boozer, though Manzarek has taken issue with the portrayal and, in fact, credits pot as the drug that sparked the band's creativity. There's the occasional joint in the movie, but far more common is a bottle of whiskey, particularly during long stretches of sloppy stage performances. Stone's depiction of Morrison is full of clichés—the rock star's spaced-out stare, unspoken daddy issues, and blatant disrespect for all thing female—but he still manages to capture the Dionysian world he inhabited. The singer's downfall was as much the fault of a society that feared his message of complete abandon and rebellion through music as was his refusal to conform, even when police were watching his every stage move and gyration. (He was arrested in Miami for allegedly exposing himself onstage.) Like Lenny Bruce, Morrison was way ahead of his time and would pay for his sins. Since the release of *The Doors*, it has been reported that Morrison died in a bathroom stall in Paris with a needle in his arm. However Morrison died, it was a great loss. At least we have the Doors's music and this powerful movie to remember them by.

Jim Morrison: "I believe in a long, prolonged derangement of the senses to attain the unknown."

Down in the Valley
(2005)

🌿 🌿 🌿 🌾 Free-spirited and rebellious Tobe, short for October (Evan Rachel Wood), meets Harlan (Edward Norton), a charming cowboy and gas station attendant, on a sticky summer day in L.A.'s San Fernando Valley. Sparks fly when Tobe invites Harlan to the beach, which he "ain't never seen," and their fiery affair starts with a first date that involves taking Ecstasy and listening to the fuzzy sounds of Mazzy Star. Soon it becomes obvious that Harlan has a screw loose, but as Tobe decides it might be wise to take a break from her new boyfriend, he just gets crazier and crazier until everyone's worst nightmare is realized and a shot is (accidentally) fired. Harlan convinces his friend Lonnie (Rory Culkin) to leave town with him and the two hide out in an old Western town, not realizing they're on a film set, which further adds to Harlan's psychopathic delusions. A serenading soundtrack of sunny and lazy guitar riffs fits well with the humid and golden images of the valley, providing the perfect backdrop to one screwed-up love story, and a sleeper indie flick worth watching.

Dreamers, The (2003)

🌿 🌿 🌿 🌿 Bernardo Bertolucci's final film is reminiscent of his sexually explicit Last Tango in Paris. Made three decades earlier, Last Tango starred Marlon Brando and Maria Schneider as strangers who have a steamy affair. For The Dreamers, Bertolucci uses the Paris student uprising of 1968 as the backdrop for this sociopolitical story about film buffs who become lovers. When American Matthew (Michael Pitt) meets French twins Isabelle (future Bond girl Eva Green) and Theo (Louis Garrel), they become fast friends. Though Isabelle and Theo are too close for Matthew's comfort, he agrees to have sex with Isabelle while Theo impassively watches. Sexy Isabelle wears little as she flounces about the apartment smoking joints and drinking wine. The trio plays psychological games, acting out scenes from classic movies. Theo joins the radicals, throwing a Molotov cocktail against Matthew's protestations as Hendrix's "Third Stone from the Sun" (one of the many great classic rock songs on the soundtrack) rumbles ominously, and the police charge. Matthew is literally and metaphorically separated from the twins, who clearly intend to remain together, no matter who else enters their lives.

Matthew: "Clapton plugs in a guitar, he plugs in an electric guitar and he plays it like an acoustic guitar. Hendrix plugs in an electric guitar, he plays it with his teeth. There are soldiers in the Vietnam War right now. Who are they listening to? Clapton? No, they're listening to Hendrix, the guy who tells the truth."

Drugstore Cowboy
(1989)

🌿 🌿 🌿 🌿 🌾 In Gus Van Sant's electric second film, Matt Dillon stars as Bob, ringleader of a junkie hit squad that rips off pharmacies for precious scripts. Bob, Diane (Kelly Lynch), Rick (James LeGros), and Nadine (a nineteen-year-old Heather Graham) shoot up and slack off in Portland until Nadine succumbs to a particularly powerful poke. Deciding to clean up his act, Bob enrolls in a methadone program, where he meets Father Tom, played perfectly by one of the dopest addicts of all time— Naked Lunch author William S. Burroughs—who predicts that "in the near future right wingers will use the drug hysteria as a pretext to set up an international police apparatus." (How right he was!) Despite his good intentions, bad karma catches up to Bob when rival dealer Dave (Max Perlich) settles an old score. Years before his Hollywood hits (Good Will Hunting, Milk), Van Sant scored major indie points with this scathing look at hard-drug culture, which is now considered a stoner cinema classic.

> "I was once a shameless full-time dope fiend."
>
> —Bob

DOPE HARD-DRUG MOVIES

Heroin, coke, and meth dominate these ten druggy dramas.

Killing Zoe (1993): A heroin-fueled bank heist goes down in Paris on Bastille Day led by American safecracker Zed (Eric Stoltz) and his longtime friend Eric (Jean-Hugues Anglade). Julie Delpy is Zoe, a prostitute and kindred spirit whose Parisian swagger perfectly complements the film's jazzy soundtrack and smoky vibe.

Basquiat (1996): Andy Warhol protégé Jean-Michel Basquiat (Jeffrey Wright) garnered praise in the New York art world for his graffiti-inspired paintings, but as AIDS ripped through the downtown scene, Basquiat's promising career was derailed by a predilection for speedballs and high-risk behavior. David Bowie (Warhol), Dennis Hopper, Parker Posey, and Christopher Walken have roles in this Julian Schnabel film.

Permanent Midnight (1998): In a rare dramatic role, based on Jerry Stahl's book, Ben Stiller plays Stahl, a successful TV writer and barely functioning heroin addict driven to extremes in order to support a six-thousand-dollar-a-week habit. Owen Wilson is drug buddy Nicky, Elizabeth Hurley his in-denial wife Sandra, and Janeane Garofalo his tough-as-nails agent Jana. Harsh and unforgiving, it's hard to forget the image of Stahl trying to jump out a window but crashing into the pane glass instead.

High Art (1998): A lesbian love triangle forms when ambitious and bicurious young editor Sydney (Radha Mitchell) gets involved with semi-retired photographer Lucy (Ally Sheedy) and her girlfriend Greta (Patricia Clarkson). Unfortunately for all involved, Lucy's affections go beyond the female form to the "white lady," a.k.a. cocaine.

Bobby G. Can't Swim (1999): John-Luke Montias directs, writes, and stars in this bleak New York–set drama about a junkie who sets up a heroin deal but can't deliver the goods. Similar to Al Pacino's kinetic performance in *The Panic in Needle Park*, Montias plumbs the depths of druggy despair.

The Salton Sea (2002): Val Kilmer is a mohawked tweaker-turned-informant who orchestrates a massive meth deal to push forward his own agenda. Adam Goldberg and Peter Saarsgard play his hopelessly addicted friends living in "the land of the perpetual night party." This heavy film veers off the chronology course, jumping between moments of sobriety and days on end of gacked-out indulgence, but at the heart of this story is a guy looking to settle some personal scores—at any cost.

Spun (2002): Three sleepless days in the life of a speed freak are chronicled in Jonas Åkerlund's dizzying drama. Jason Schwartzman and Brittany Murphy costar as crystal meth addicts; John Leguizamo, Patrick Fugit, and Eric Roberts play dealers; and Mickey Rourke is unforgettable as "The Cook," a hardened meth maker in constant need of a "ride."

Party Monster (2003): Early nineties excess in New York City's club scene is the focus of this tragic—and true—tale of outcast-turned-promoter Michael Alig (Macaulay Culkin), whose flair for outrageous costumes and drug-fueled all-night dance parties makes him a hero to club kids coast-to-coast. An insatiable appetite for coke, heroin, and crack drags Alig and his cohorts (played by Seth Green, Wilmer Valderrama, Chloë Sevigny, and Natasha Lyonne) down to a murderous act of desperation.

Candy (2006): Heath Ledger and Abbie Cornish costar as Australian couple Dan and Candy, torn over their love for each other and for heroin. What starts as careless fun—doing smack while sitting through a car wash—turns into a devastating addiction as the two lie, cheat, and steal to get their next fix.

Half Nelson (2006): Ryan Gosling plays crack-addicted schoolteacher Dan Dunne, whose life intertwines with his students' in this provocative flick.

Easy Rider (1969)

🌿🌿🌿🌿🌿 With his turn as biker gang leader Heavenly Blues in Roger Corman's *The Wild Angels* in 1966, Peter Fonda was among the first actors (along with Marlon Brando in *The Wild One* in 1953) to identify with this new breed of rebel outsider. A year later, Jack Nicholson joined the movement as a biker wannabe in Richard Rush's *Hell's Angels on Wheels*. Both films had all the biker-flick hallmarks: cool language, antisocial behavior, sadism, drugs, and detestable treatment of women. In 1969, Fonda, Dennis Hopper, and Terry Southern shook up the biker-movie formula when they got together to write *Easy Rider* (Hopper directed). It begins with Wyatt, a.k.a. Captain America (Fonda), and Billy (Hopper) making a coke deal with "The Connection" (Phil Spector, who arrives in a Rolls-Royce). Flush with cash, they "head out on the highway looking for adventure" on their Harleys as Steppenwolf's "Born to Be Wild" roars over the opening credits and Lazlo Kovacs's camera pans the Western landscape. Their road trip makes several significant stops en route to New Orleans. A hitchhiker (Luke Askew) brings them to a commune where they skinny dip and leave with a gift of LSD. Locked up for "parading without a permit" after cruising a small-town Main Street festivity, they meet George Hanson (Nicholson) in jail. George joins the duo, hopping aboard Wyatt's chopper for a short-lived joyride wearing a football helmet. This leads to the famous campfire smoke-out during which Wyatt rolls joints and passes one to George. "I can't afford to get hooked," George says nervously as he inspects and smells the joint. "All right then. How do you do it?" After his first toke, Wyatt instructs, "Hold it in your lungs longer, George." During a hilarious discussion about UFOs with Billy, Wyatt tells George to save the rest of the joint for the morning: "It gives you a whole new way of looking at the day." As they cross into Louisiana, tensions arise at a redneck-filled café. They hightail it out of town, but are followed and that night George is beaten to death. Wyatt and Billy continue on, and once in New Orleans head to a brothel George had recommended. Along with hookers Karen (Karen Black) and Mary (Toni Basil, who sang "Mickey" in 1982), they all dose on acid at a cemetery. This is the original psychedelic scene in a major movie. During the trip, Wyatt has a premonition, and later that night tells a confused Billy, "We blew it." The next day, while heading back west across the Mississippi River, a redneck in a pickup truck blows them both away with a shotgun as Bob Dylan's, "It's Alright Ma (I'm Only Bleeding)" plays wistfully ("darkness at the break of noon"). No other film has so clearly depicted the divisions in American society during this extremely charged period. The stoic Fonda and frazzled Hopper nailed their characters, becoming Hollywood's first stoner buds. And the brilliant soundtrack—including songs by Steppenwolf ("The Pusher"), the Byrds ("The Weight"), Jimi Hendrix ("If Six Were Nine"), Fraternity of Man ("Don't Bogart Me"), and Dylan—was the first to marry movies with rock-and-roll.

Wyatt: "You're stoned out of your mind, man."

8 Mile (2002)

🌿🌿🌿 Loosely based on Eminem's real-life ascent from poverty in Detroit, *8 Mile* tells the story of aspiring rapper Jimmy "B-Rabbit" Smith, who tries to gain some cred at a local freestyle battle but chokes horribly. After breaking up with his girlfriend, Janeane (Taryn Manning), Rabbit has nowhere to go but back to his alcoholic mother (Kim Basinger), who lives in a run-down trailer park. No car, no future, a dead-end job at an auto steel plant, and few friends who truly understand him, Rabbit hits rock bottom and contemplates abandoning his dream of getting a record deal, deciding instead to live in the now and simply accept the future he's destined for. Struggling to maintain his sanity amidst a dysfunctional living situation, the lyrical genius manages to pull it together. He shows off his skills at the freestyle battle, where Eminem rhymes to the bitter end, sending his opponents, the Free World crew, back to 8 Mile with their heads down. Aside from proving Eminem can act, the Curtis Hanson–directed movie that inspired every kid in America to learn to rap is surprisingly solid, and boasts an impressive cast, including Brittany Murphy as Rabbit's latest fling and Mekhi Phifer as battle commander "Future." It also won an Oscar for Eminem's inspirational anthem, "Lose Yourself," just one of many worthwhile joints on the soundtrack that may prompt you to pull out those old Mobb Deep and Biggie albums.

B-Rabbit: "As a matter of fact, dawg, here's a pencil. Go home, write some shit, make it suspenseful, and don't come back till somethin' dope hits you. Fuck it, you can take the mic home wit' you."

Even Cowgirls Get the Blues (1994)

🌿🌿 Gus Van Sant's adaptation of the popular Tom Robbins novel is all about Sissy (Uma Thurman), the girl with enormous thumbs. Not content to see her double digits as a disability, Sissy becomes a wanderer, a powerful hitchhiker with thumbs that eventually bring her to New York City and to her benefactor, the Russian Countess stuck in a Southern white man's body (and played to the hilt by John Hurt). When an opportunity arises for Sissy at the Rubber Rose Ranch, the Countess sends her there and into the waiting arms of the Cowgirls, a group of women with more than roping on their minds.

It's one of Van Sant's weirdest, most inaccessible films aided by generous helpings of pot and peyote—which is doled out mostly by the Cowgirls, Bonanza Jellybean (Rain Phoenix) and Delores Del Ruby (Lorraine Bracco) among them. Keep your eyes peeled for appearances by counterculture luminaries William S. Burroughs and Ken Kesey, whose presence lends the film artsy, stoner cred.

Event, The (2003)

🌿🌿🌿🌿 In this heavy film, rather than whither away from AIDS, Matt (Don McKellar) decides to orchestrate his own death with one big assisted-suicide party. Matt's gay friends and his family—his mother, Lila (Olympia Dukakis), and younger sister, Dana (Sarah Polley)—all participate in the invite-only "event." Lila bakes cookies for Matt. "I made them with pot," she says with glee. "I read about it. There's a nice woman in San Francisco named Brownie Mary. Isn't that cute?" (Brownie Mary Rathbun died in 1999.) Nick (Parker Posey) from the D.A.'s office investigates and ultimately arrests six people who participated in the party. Thom Fitzgerald's wistful film not only pays tribute to a generation of gay men who succumbed to the dreaded HIV virus, but to the fallen Twin Towers—the film is set in New York in 2000 and 2001, with flags and a frame of the 9/11 lights.

"Where did you get pot?"

—Matt

"Cousin Stevie. I think he sells it. I got a pound very cheap."

—Lila

Eyes Wide Shut (1999)

🚬 🍷 💉 👁

🌿 🌿 🌿 From the outside, Dr. Bill Harford (Tom Cruise) and his wife, Alice (Nicole Kidman), seem to be living the perfect life. They have a giant apartment in Manhattan, attend high-society parties, are parents to a beautiful young daughter, and both have successful and highly lucrative careers. But their equilibrium is thrown off when Alice (high

on pot) admits to having fantasies about other men. Faced with the burden of examining the realities of his own sexuality, Bill gains access to an exclusive masked orgy party where he quickly learns that he's in way over his head. Now his newly surfaced sexual urges endanger both him and his family and he must find a way out before he hurts those closest to him. Directed by Stanley Kubrick, it's a mind-fuck. That said, *Eyes Wide Shut* is probably his sexiest film, especially with then-married Tom Cruise and Nicole Kidman's palpable on-screen chemistry, and the missus butt naked and stoned out of her mind.

Alice Harford: "I do love you and you know there is something very important we need to do as soon as possible."

Dr. Bill Harford: "What's that?"

Alice: "Fuck."

Factory Girl (2006)

🚬 🍷 💉 💊 ⚗ 💉 👁

🌿 🌿 🌿 This is the true story of Edie Sedgwick (Sienna Miller), a trust-fund kid and art-school dropout who falls into the Andy Warhol (Guy Pearce) "Factory" crowd in the late sixties and quickly becomes his number one "It" girl. Sedgwick's ascent in the downtown New York City scene starts innocently enough, by appearing in Warhol's films and supporting his artwork, but as she gains in status and popularity, so does her drug use. Over time, Sedgwick gets involved with brooding musician Billy Quinn (Hayden Christiansen), who bears a striking resemblance to Bob Dylan. When Quinn visits the Factory, he's dismissive of Warhol's art and offers him a joint. Jealous and angry about her defection, Warhol unceremoniously closes Edie out of the inner circle, driving her deeper into addiction. Methamphetamine is her drug of choice—

> "I would sure like to work with her. I've never seen a girl with so many problems."
>
> **—Andy Warhol**

often injected by needle in the derriere—but nights at the Factory regularly run the drug gamut from pot to pills to smack. This sensationalistic and shallow look at a life of nonstop partying features a slew of sordid, sycophantic, unsympathetic characters—chief among them, Sedgwick herself.

Falcon and the Snowman, The (1985)

🍸🥃 ⚗️ 💉 👯

🌿🌿🌿🌿🌿 Two budding Hollywood stars of the eighties, Sean Penn and Timothy

Hutton, built their careers partly on the strength of John Schlesinger's trenchant drugs-and-espionage caper, based on a true story written by Robert Lindsey. Daulton (Penn) and Chris (Hutton) are altar boys who go different directions as young adults. While Daulton racks up drug arrest after drug arrest, Chris leaves the seminary and accepts a job at a top-secret government agency, RTX, thanks to his FBI dad (Pat Hingle). When Chris spies misrouted CIA cables about covert activity in Australia and after Daulton's latest coke bust, they conspire to sell information to the Soviet Union. Disconnected from his right-wing father and influenced by Nixon's impeachment, Chris quietly steals communiqués and takes photos of documents, which are delivered to the Soviet Embassy in Mexico City by the increasingly jittery, erratic, and paranoid Daulton. Penn peaks in this early role, his voice squealing and speech halted as he shoves coke and brown heroin up his nose. The Soviets dismiss Daulton and want to deal with Chris instead. Not to be cut out, Daulton repeatedly returns to the Mexican capital until he's framed as a cop killer, tortured, and deported to the U.S., where a police dragnet awaits him. While the "Snowman" moniker is self-explanatory, "Falcon" refers to Chris's love of birds of prey. Ultimately, they became the prey, charged as traitors and jailed for life (Daulton) and forty years (Chris).

Daulton: "I work for them and I'm a dead man. I'm not an informer. It's against my principles and I'm not going to prison. Get me out on bail tonight."

Fame (1980)

✏️ 🍸🥃 👯

🌿🌿🌿🌿 Part gritty New York City drama, part pop-rock opera, *Fame* was 1980's little movie that could, winning two Academy Awards, spawning a TV show, merchandise, and, over the years, commanding a loyal cult following. Indeed, it's a special, slow-moving film that covers, in four parts (freshman to senior year), the lives of a dozen students at New York's run-down yet prestigious School of Performing Arts. Central characters include Leroy Johnson (Gene Anthony Ray), a talented but undisciplined dancer, and Ralph Garci (Barry Miller), an aspiring comedian living in poverty. Well ahead of the game are keyboardist Bruno Martelli (Lee Curreri) and singer Coco Hernandez (Irene Cara), while wannabe actors Montgomery McNeil (Paul McCrane) and Doris Finsecker (Maureen Teefy) are still trying to find themselves. In fact, it's the timid Doris who provides one of the movie's most memorable and revelatory moments: At a midnight showing of *The Rocky Horror Picture Show*, she smokes a joint for the first time and is inspired to rip off her shirt and join the trannies on stage. Before the Internet, beepers, or even touch-tone telephones, *Fame* captured a time and place that was both harsh and romantic, a paradox made all the more potent by weighty issues like abortion, homosexuality, and adult predators. But in the end, it's also about the music, which, as the song goes, lives forever.

Doris Finsecker: "I'm about as flamboyant as a bagel."

Fear and Loathing in Las Vegas (1998)

Hero worship is on display as Johnny Depp plays Raoul Duke—Hunter S. Thompson's *Rolling Stone* alter ego—and Benicio Del Toro, his demented lawyer Dr. Gonzo, in Terry Gilliam's literal adaptation of Thompson's 1972 drug-lit classic. The movie opens like *Up in Smoke*, two buds on the road. But the drugs are harder: In the trunk, there's "two bags of weed, seventy-five pellets of mescaline, some high-powered blotter acid, a salt shaker half-filled with cocaine, a whole galaxy of multicolored uppers, downers, screamers, laughers—also a quart of tequila, a quart of rum, a case of beer, a pint of ether, two dozen amyls . . . " In Gilliam's heavy hands, Vegas proves to be the ultimate bad trip. The dopey duo destroy two hotel rooms while Duke covers a dirt-bike rally and a sheriff's convention. Unlike Art Linson's more playful *Where the Buffalo Roam*, Gilliam focuses on the macabre—the colors are varying shades of red, faces distort, and lizard tails appear. But when Gilliam (*Brazil*) clears his way out of the ether, so to speak, and truly contemplates the countercultural crossroads Thompson so poignantly chronicled, the movie soars. Look for lots of great cameos—Tobey Maguire as a hitchhiker, Ellen Barkin as a waitress, Gary Busey as a cop, Christina Ricci as a runaway, Cameron Diaz as a reporter, and stoner-movie staple Harry Dean Stanton as a judge.

> **"We were somewhere around Barstow on the edge of the desert when the drugs began to take hold."**
>
> **—Raoul Duke**

☘ FIVE MORE BY TERRY GILLIAM ☘

Former Monty Python troupe member and animator Terry Gilliam has had a pretty brilliant solo career as a director. Here are a few more faves.

Time Bandits (1981): Gilliam disguised this dark fantasy as a family film and ended up with a stoner's alternative to *The Wizard of Oz*. As young Kevin (Craig Warnock) and six amusing dwarves journey across time for fun and ill-gained profit, they encounter characters like Robin Hood (John Cleese) and Napoléon (Ian Holm) before landing on the sinking *Titanic*. Gilliam's low-budget flair adds to the chaotic story line concerning trust, disillusionment, and good versus evil—a surreal harbinger of his films to come.

Brazil (1985): Forget 1984. Gilliam's *Brazil* supplanted the classic Orwellian nightmare with his own futuristic dystopia—one littered with bizarre props and quaint special effects. Thanks to a bureaucratic case of mistaken identity, paranoia prevails when harmless Sam Lowry (Jonathan Pryce) breaks the constraints of his lowly government job for the sake of love. Sam's flights of heroic fancy get him branded as a suspected terrorist, and even Robert De Niro's kooky Tuttle can't save him—except in his mind.

The Adventures of Baron Munchausen (1988): Perennially under-budgeted, Gilliam embraced the story of the world's greatest liar with mixed results. After a serendipitous introduction to an audience of townspeople in late eighteenth-century Europe, Baron Munchausen (John Neville) takes his newfound listeners on a wild, nonstop ride—including flying on a cannonball, ballooning to the moon, and being swallowed by a sea monster, Jonah-style. His amazing allies on these journeys include the greatest sharpshooter, the fastest runner, and a super-strongman.

The Fisher King (1991): Jeff Bridges is a radio shock jock whose on-air antics provoke a nightclub massacre. He embarks on an unlikely friendship with an eccentric homeless man (Robin William) widowed by the shooting spree, and tries to help him find the Holy Grail. Sound unlikely? Somehow it works.

Twelve Monkeys (1995): More Gilliam madness, future-shock paranoia, and time travel when prisoner James Cole (Bruce Willis) is sent back to the nineties to prevent a man-made plague. Institutionalized in a psychiatric hospital, Cole meets sexy scientist Dr. Kathryn Railly (Madeleine Stowe) and ranting, batshit crazy animal lover Jeffrey Goines (Brad Pitt). Reality becomes anyone's guess since Cole is haunted by voices and other monkey business as he desperately traces an assumed conspiracy before the predicted annihilation unfolds.

Feel the Noise (2007)

🖊 🍾 ✂

🌿🌿 In this forgettable vehicle for real-life R & B star Omarion, he plays Rob Vega, an aspiring rapper from Harlem who, after ripping off the wrong pair of hubcaps, gets shot at by a local thug nicknamed Electric (Pras). To avoid further violence, Rob's mother ships him off to live with his estranged father in Puerto Rico. Initially, Rob is none too thrilled, but when his stepbrother, Javi (Victor Rasuk), pulls out a joint within minutes of their first meeting (followed by a snow-cone munchiefest), his attitude picks up. Javi introduces Rob to reggaeton music and the San Juan club scene (co-producer Jennifer Lopez makes a cameo), and in no time, the two start collaborating musically and grab the ears of a New York record executive. All is looking up for the duo until the shady scout shows not just an interest in their tunes, but also in Rob's would-be girlfriend, C.C. (Zulay Henao). Things fall apart when the threesome end up in New York, where Electric follows through on Rob's belated beat-down, and the Vega brothers walk away from their potential recording deal. Lessons learned? Know whose cap you're jacking, stay true to your sound, and family comes first.

Javi: "You smoke?"

Rob: "Smoke what?"

Five Easy Pieces (1970)

🍾 ✂ ◉◉

🌿🌿🌿🌿 Jack Nicholson followed up his breakout supporting role in *Easy Rider* as hard-partying oil-field worker and former piano-playing prodigy Bobby Dupea. Directed and cowritten by Bob Rafelson (with Carole Eastman) and shot by László Kovács (*Easy Rider, Psych-Out*), the movie begins in Texas, where Bobby lives with needy, ditzy girlfriend Rayette (Karen Black) and hangs with coworker Elton (Billy Green Bush). When Bobby and Elton spend the night with Betty (a young Sally Struthers—Gloria on *All in the Family*) and Stoney (Fannie Flagg), Ray cries and pouts. After some arguing, Bobby and Ray go on a road trip to visit his family in Washington State. Along the way they pick up Palm (Helena Kallianiotes) and Terry (Toni Basil, who, along with Black, also appears in *Easy Rider*), a proto-lesbian couple who participate in the film's famous chicken salad diner scene, which helped create Nicholson's rep as an acerbic badass. "You want me to hold the chicken?" the waitress asks Bobby, incredulously. "I want you to hold it between your knees!" he sneers, then clears the table with one sweep of his arm. The last act, at Bobby's family house, where his invalid father is being cared for by his sister and brother, is almost a completely different movie. While Ray is holed up in a nearby motel, Bobby pursues his brother's wife, Catherine (Susan Anspach). "I move around a lot," Bobby tells his mute father. "Not because I'm looking for anything, really, because I'm getting away from things that get bad if I stay." Unsatisfied with Ray's insecurity and constant nagging, Bobby moves on again, hitching a ride in a logging truck. It's an impulsive, and inevitable, resolution for this desultory seventies film.

Bobby: "Keep telling me about the good life, Elton, because it makes me puke."

Fresh Cut Grass (2004)

🖊 🍸 🍾 ✂ 🍄

🌿🌿🌿 This grainy indie feels a little like a low-budget *Garden State*, but set in Long Island, New York, instead of New Jersey. Deep thinker Zac Peace (David Wike) is still coming to terms with the recent death of his father, and returns home from college to work a landscaping job with a few of his dopey friends. The boss, Sam (James McCaffrey), is a former publishing executive who traded in the corporate world long ago for a life of leisure near the ocean, where he can read without obligation and smoke pot freely. He acts as a mentor to Zac and gifts him with a bag of mushrooms, hoping the trip will sort out some of his issues. Does it ever. After traipsing around in the woods, Zac ends up at the ocean, where he meets his father. The two grab a stool at a makeshift beachside bar and talk things through. As it turns out, Zac's summer of mowing lawns becomes a pivotal point in his life when he falls in love with Eastern (Katy Hansz), the kind of girl who notes a difference between going on a hike and taking a walk. Zac delves deep into self-reflection by sharing letters he wrote to his late father, and ends up reconciling with his mother, whom he had started to alienate. Along the way, he and his buds indulge in their fair share of joints, bong hits, and drunken nights. More than once, Zac has to ask himself, "Why are all my friends so vulgar?" Unlike *Garden State*'s ragtag crew, these guys are far less nuanced and come off as idiot douche bags, which makes you question why someone as smart as Zac would even hang out with them. Oh yeah, the weed.

Garden Party (2008)

🌿 🌿 🌿 The seedy side of Los Angeles is on full display in this indie flick about runaways and transplants trying to get by and the people who take advantage of them. New to Hollywood is baby-faced April (Willa Holland) and emo poster boy Sammy (Erik Smith), each crashing on couches or floors while exchanging sexual favors for money and pot. The sexy Sally St. Claire (Vinessa Shaw) doubles as a weed dealer and a real estate agent. Together with her pervy client Todd (Richard Gunn), they conspire to bring down a network of nudie photo purveyors—among them her longtime listing rival Davey Diamond (Christopher Allport). Sally's sexually conflicted assistant Nathan (Alexander Cendese) is also responsible for her pot garden. Always at the right place at the right time, Sammy elevates his game by hooking up with girls, guys, and bands, eventually landing a record deal. April, meanwhile, cavorts with a couple of lesbians before stealing Nathan's job. But everything really revolves around Sally, the kind of woman who demands perfection, never takes no for an answer, and always makes sure her Audi's ashtray is packed with pre-rolled joints. That and her massive grow-op are just about the only bright spots in this dark, twisted tale.

Sally: "Do you get high?"

Todd: "Not in years."

Sally: "Mind if I fire up?"

Todd: "It won't affect your driving?"

Sally: "Nah, not really, I probably drive better stoned."

Gene Krupa Story, The (1959)

🌿 🌿 🌿 🌿 Busted in 1943 for marijuana, or "reefers," jazzman Gene Krupa earned his own biopic primarily due to his madcap drumming style. In fact, Krupa was the first true drum soloist—playing with the likes of Benny Goodman, Tommy Dorsey, and Anita O'Day. We're introduced to Krupa (portrayed by Sal Mineo) in 1927, living at home in Chicago with his Polish parents who want him to be a priest—but Gene has other ideas. After a year at the seminary, he joins a band and plays in Prohibition-era speakeasies. Gene moves to New York with Eddie (James Darren), his best friend and a trumpet player, where they quickly find work in the swinging big-band scene. Gene develops a reputation for stealing the show with his madcap solos, but it's singer Dorissa Dinell (Susan Oliver) who turns him on to his first reefer. "Don't diddle it, go on," she says. "Put your miseries out to pasture." Living the high life in his penthouse, Gene plays and parties until backstage one day, two vice cops cuff him for possessing two joints. After spending three months in jail, the blackballed drummer plays dives and burlesque joints before Dorsey gives him his comeback break. What's seriously lacking in this movie is Krupa's role in Goodman's integrated quartet that famously headlined Carnegie Hall in 1938. (Incredibly, Krupa never even takes his signature "Sing, Sing, Sing" solo.) Krupa and Goodman had a falling out, which probably explains why there's no Goodman music in the movie. It's a major glitch in the telling of Krupa's life story.

Go (1999)

🌿 🌿 🌿 🌿 Before he moved into the big-budget bracket with *The Bourne Identity* and *Mr. & Mrs. Smith*, Doug Liman made offbeat L.A. films like *Swingers* and his superlative stoner flick, *Go*. Three stories overlap, connecting a group of friends who get into all kinds of trouble, mostly due to an Ecstasy deal that goes bad, sort of. Ronna (Sarah Polley)

needs rent money or she's going to be evicted. Gay couple Zack (Jay Mohr) and Adam (Scott Wolf) set Ronna up in order to clean their own record. She buys twenty hits of Ecstasy from Todd (Timothy Olyphant), but flushes them when Zack tips her off to the impending bust. Now doubly desperate to make up the rent money *and* pay Todd back, Ronna sells over-the-counter drugs as Ecstasy at a local rave. In the film's stoniest scene, Ronna and Claire (Katie Holmes) hustle a van full of tweakers. "You know what makes it better?" Ronna suggests. "If you take a lot of pot with it. I mean, like a *lot* of pot." But karma bites Ronna back when she's accidentally hit by a car driven by none other than Adam. Meanwhile, Todd's bud Simon (Desmond Askew) and three friends create several scenes in Las Vegas, one of which involves a gun in a strip club. They hightail it back to L.A., followed by angry mobsters. The third story focuses on Zack and Adam's weird dinner with narc Burke (William Fichtner) and his wife, Irene (Jane Krakowski). Ronna survives the crash and pays her rent, Claire makes out with Todd, and Simon takes a bullet in the arm as this rollicking roller-coaster ride swerves around the last turn and gently grinds to a halt. Olyphant's menacing dealer is one of the genre's best ever, and Nathan Bexton, who plays Ronna and Claire's friend Mannie, spends half the movie stoned out of his gourd on Ecstasy that Todd warns is "the real thing, pharmaceutical grade, not that crunchy herbal rave shit. Don't let anybody double dose. You'll be frying eggs off them in the emergency room. One hit per headbanger." Mannie, of course, takes two.

Parking Lot Stoner: "It's like a wave or like a zoom. It's like floating. It's like, hey man, how's the ground down there?"

Good Girl, The (2002)

🪴 🍸 🖌️

🌿 🌿 🌿 🌿 Seeing Jennifer Aniston's and John C. Reilly's names in the credits to *The Good Girl*, you might think: comedy. And while some may view this twisted story of two discount-store clerks who find fleeting love to be somewhat cynical, you'd be hard-pressed to locate many laughs in this depressing tale. Justine (Aniston) is married to Phil (Reilly), a beer-swigging, pot-smoking house painter who's

almost always found vegging on the couch smoking a joint with his buddy, Bubba (Tim Blake Nelson). Justine works a dead-end job at the Wal-Mart–like Retail Rodeo, where she meets the brooding loner Holden (Jake Gyllenhaal), a college dropout and aspiring writer who lives with his parents. The two start an affair, which soon turns into a quasi-obsession for Holden, and once they're spotted at a motel, everything goes downhill. Blackmail, a pregnancy, the all-telling credit card bill, and Justine ends up juggling three different guys and many lies. But when Holden (who named himself after *Catcher in the Rye*'s Holden Caulfield) has a major meltdown, a happy ending is an impossibility. Just about the only bright spot is when Justine finally stops harshing on Phil's pot use. Zooey Deschanel and Mike White add to the colorful array of Retail Rodeo characters, but the overall tone of this film is undeniably dark.

Justine: "Gwen says smoking marijuana lowers your sperm."

Phil: "Lowers it to where?"

GoodFellas (1990)

🍸 🖌️ 🔨

🌿 🌿 🌿 🌿 🌿 Martin Scorsese's rock-and-roll gangster epic stole from *The Godfather* and inspired *The Sopranos*. Real-life mob insider Henry Hill (Ray Liotta) turns on his wiseguy pals after being busted for coke. Along with Tommy (Joe Pesci) and Jimmy (Robert De Niro), they lived the high life, killing anyone who got in their way. But mistakes land Henry and Tommy in jail, and Jimmy pays for his sadistic streak. The first half is reminiscent of *The Godfather*, but when Henry decides to go into the coke business, it's all Scorsese. Sweating and thoroughly paranoid, as the soundtrack pulses with Rolling Stones cuts ("Gimme Shelter," "Monkey Man"), Henry ultimately falls into the police's lap. Among the many great scenes, Pesci's stand out, especially when he teases Henry ("I amuse you? How am I funny? What's so fuckin' funny about me?"). That Scorsese didn't receive an Academy Award for *GoodFellas* (or *Raging Bull*, for that matter) and had to wait sixteen years to finally snag the Best Picture Oscar (for the relatively inferior *The Departed*) is a Hollywood crime of the highest order.

Henry: "I had paper bags filled with jewelry stashed in the kitchen. I had a sugar bowl full of coke next to the bed . . . "

☘ RAUL MALO'S STONY MOVIE PICKS ☘

As a former member of Grammy-winning band the Mavericks and now a solo act, country singer Raul Malo has spent the better part of twenty years on the road. Among the many ways to kill time on the bus: watching movies. Here, a few of his stony faves.

***Apocalypse Now* (1979):** "This is a really heavy movie. As the story develops, the jungle gets more and more crazy. Willard [Martin Sheen] starts to really get into the Colonel's mind and how he operates. He starts to read his letters and his correspondence, and by the time it gets to the confrontation, you're just so enveloped in the story that it makes for a great time. The whole thing when they get off the boat and get attacked by a tiger—'Never get off the boat, man, never get off the boat!' That pretty much applies to a touring musician—'Never get off the bus, man, never get off the bus!' We say that all the time, because you never know what's waiting outside."

***GoodFellas* (1990):** "It's one of the most genius films ever and another favorite on the bus, especially the first hour and that whole early period. There's the nightclub scene where it's one long, continuous shot—Henry [Ray Liotta] gets there with Karen [Lorraine Bracco], they walk in the back door, through the kitchen, all the way to the table right up at the front, no questions asked. As a fan of good films, you've got to appreciate the work that went into *GoodFellas*."

***No Country for Old Men* (2007):** "This is a really intense movie—in a good way. The scene where Javier Bardem [Anton] walks into that little convenience store and starts grilling the old man, you just go, 'Oh my god, he's gonna kill him.' You've seen all the horrific things he just finished doing, he's going across the state looking for the money, and he walks into a store and that poor old fucker is behind the counter. It's so brilliantly done; how the old guy is being a good ol' country boy, like very courteous, but there's a point where he starts to get a little suspicious, and it's just so intense! I remember crawling out of my skin watching it, but it was really great, especially enhanced by the 420 experience."

Elvis Presley movies: "You want to get stoned and see some weird shit? Watch an old Elvis Presley movie. Especially the stuff in the sixties like *Blue Hawaii* [1961] and *Girls! Girls! Girls!* [1962]. Those are bizarre and the scripts were just terrible. I watched a marathon on television one day, and talk about sitting there in wonderment and amazement. Like, 'My God, somebody financed this? They got a major star in this? Elvis Presley is doing this crap?' But one thing I realized after watching, especially in that state, is how brilliantly diabolical those movies were. There was nothing artistic, creative, or redeeming about it—they were created just to make Elvis stand up there singing a ridiculous song next to some pretty girl. It was all for the sole purpose of making women fall in love with him. And they were all box-office hits! Certainly Elvis was the king of rock-and-roll, but something happens when you're on the silver screen. These movies really propelled him to that larger-than-life status."

Graduate, The (1967)

Mike Nichols won an Oscar for his film about a disenchanted college grad (Dustin Hoffman's Benjamin) who has an affair with an older woman (Anne Bancroft's Mrs. Robinson). The smart screenplay (co-written by Buck Henry) and savvy soundtrack, which features Simon & Garfunkel's genre-defining hits ("Sounds of Silence," "Scarborough Fair," and, of course, "Mrs. Robinson"), set an appropriate tone for Benjamin's forlorn state. The cinematography clearly had the stoner in mind—quick cuts that visualize Benjamin's every subliminal thought (with eyes shifting accordingly), long breaths that drown out the noise of his parents, seamless transitions between images of a mundane home life and his salacious nighttime activities, long, dialogue-free scenes in the pool. His secret affair with Mrs. Robinson starts quirkily enough, but when Benjamin gets reacquainted with her daughter Elaine (Katharine Ross), things turn tense. On a mission to win Elaine's heart, he indulges his rebellious side and takes off for Berkeley, then crashes her wedding (a scene reenacted some thirty years later in *Wayne's World 2*). In the movie, which was released the winter after the Summer of Love, Benjamin limits his smoking to cigarettes, while Mrs. Robinson is an admitted alcoholic. A little pot would have equaled perfection.

Mr. Braddock: "Ben, this whole idea sounds pretty half-baked."

Benjamin: "Oh, it's not. It's completely baked."

Gridlock'd (1997)

Tupac Shakur plays functioning junkie Spoon, a cokehead and jazz musician who may well be the luckiest lawbreaker in Detroit. On the day he and his heroin-addicted buddy and bandmate Stretch (Tim Roth) decide to get clean, the two happen by a dealer's murder and take off with the stash. As they outrun the gangsters responsible for the crime and continually con the cops so as not to become suspects themselves, Spoon and Stretch decide detox and rehab are their only viable options. Now if only they could cut through the bureaucratic red tape when they most desperately need it. With little gloss added to this gritty tale—the opening scene shows Spoon's girlfriend Cookie (Thandie Newton) overdosing on smack after trying it for the first time—and smoky interludes to set the tone (one scene involves the three of them sharing a spliff), this film is undoubtedly dark, but, at the same time, oddly hopeful. Released only months after Shakur's death, it also offers a glimpse of an actor with boundless talent and promise. After all, not every rapper can pull off the movie's closing "Life is a traffic jam" scat.

Spoon: "Don't you just love people that smoke three packs a day talking about, 'I'm a vegetarian.' Fuck that. You talk to me about health when you stop smoking, OK?"

Cookie: "Oh yeah? Well, you talk to me about smoking when you stop doing blow, asshole. I win."

Groove (2000)

🌿🌿🌿🌿 Savvy urban guerrillas convert a San Francisco warehouse into a techno wonderland in Greg Harrison's rave movie. While the dedicated anarchists decorate the building with video screens, art, and flashing lights, numerous locals make plans for the big night. Colin (Denny Kirkwood), Harmony (Mackenzie Firgens), and David (Hamish Linklater) arrive and immediately take acid. Newbie David meets Leyla (Lola Glaudini), who guides him through his maiden psychedelic voyage. As ecstatic dancers ride the sound waves, cathartic memories rise to the surface. Colin and Harmony deal with a sexual flirtation, and David tries to connect with the laid-back Leyla. Police finally raid the warehouse, but after a brief scare and the late arrival of master mixer John Digweed, the party revives for one last blast at 4 A.M. Dealer Cliff (Ari Gold) has some of the best lines, especially when he informs an LSD customer that he's won "an all-expense-paid trip to your cerebral cortex." For anyone who's tripped the night fantastic, this flick will feel like a veritable flashback.

> "If you're going to be a successful drug user, you've got to be well informed."
>
> —Cliff

Harder They Come, The (1972)

🌿🌿🌿🌿🌿 The first feature film ever to come out of Jamaica starred Jimmy Cliff in a career-making role as musician/weed dealer Ivan Martin. Perry Henzell cuts back and forth between the lush countryside and Kingston's busy streets and wretched slums in this gritty and super-realistic film. Ivan records the title track, but is forced to accept a mere twenty dollars for what would become a huge hit. This pushes him into the corrupt ganja trade. Unhappy with his cut, the stylish and cocky Ivan challenges Jose (Carl Bradshaw), who snitches on him to the police. Only Rasta Pedro (Ras Daniel Hartman) backs Ivan as he hides from the authorities. When Ivan just misses his chance to escape to Cuba on a boat, he's outnumbered on the beach and goes out in a hail of bullets, the true antihero for the starving masses. In addition to "The Harder They Come," the soundtrack includes such reggae classics as Cliff's "You Can Get It If You Really Want" and "Sitting in Limbo," and the Maytals's "Pressure Drop." Sadly, Henzell directed only one other film, *No Place Like Home*, before passing away in 2006.

Harvard Man (2001)

🌿🌿🌿 James Toback's cautionary tale of campus drug use—specifically 15,000 micrograms of LSD—rings false even though it's based on his own experience. Alan (*Entourage*'s Adrian Grenier) is a philosophy student who also plays for Harvard's basketball team. When his parents' Kansas home is wrecked by a tornado, Alan figures out a way to raise $100K fast with the help of his girlfriend Cindy (Sarah Michelle Gellar), whose dad (Gianni Russo) is a mobster. Alan shaves points so Harvard doesn't cover the spread against Dartmouth. While on the plane returning from Kansas, he takes three doses of "pure, exact LSD-25" provided by campus chemist Sandy (Chantal Cousineau). Tailed by FBI agents Teddy (Eric Stoltz) and Kelly (Rebecca Gayheart), Alan has a really bad trip. Faces distort and voices repeat in his head to the point that he thinks he's losing his mind. Alan's professor Chesney Cort (Joey Lauren Adams) comes to his rescue, directing him to a doctor (John Neville) who shoots him up with an antidote. "You will never take another drug of any kind ever," Dr. Reese instructs. "Your drug-taking career has come to an absolute conclusion." This may have happened to Toback, but it's not believable. Alan experiences a flashback at the end, further reinforcing Toback's antidrug message.

Sandy: "You want to open the door, don't you? This will do the trick. This will let you see what's inside. It's transcendent. It makes regular acid seem like Diet Sprite."

Haven (2004)

🌿 🍸 ✒️

🌿🌿🌿🌿 Frank E. Flowers's overly ambitious Caribbean drama set on the Grand Cayman Islands tells two entirely separate stories that might have made two fairly decent movies. Story One is about businessman Carl Ridley (Bill Paxton), who's been stashing his money in the friendly Cayman banks, but the Feds are on to him. He leaves his home in Florida in a hurry and drags daughter Pippa (Agnes Bruckner) along with him. Pippa immediately gets into trouble with local hustler Fritz (Victor Rasuk), who takes her to a party where she prefers a joint to a bump. "Do you have any pot?" Pippa asks a group of coke fiends. "It really helps me focus." Story Two features an interracial love affair between Shy (Orlando Bloom) and Andrea (Zoe Saldana). Andrea's father (Robert Wisdom) and brother Hammer (Anthony Mackie) don't approve, and Hammer splashes Shy with acid, disfiguring his face. The two stories never really intersect, and there are long breaks between the two, making you wonder what's happening to the other characters. Carl gets busted and Shy takes off on a boat, leaving the lovely Pippa, Andrea, and Carl's girlfriend Sheila (Joy Bryant) behind.

Havoc (2005)

🌿 🍸 ✒️ 👀

🌿🌿 A group of teens from Pacific Palisades, a ritzy L.A. neighborhood like Beverly Hills, learn the hard way that rich kids plus boredom equals big trouble when the barrio is a mere freeway ride away. Anne Hathaway plays Allison, a B-girl and shameless slut who's dating the school tool, wannabe gangsta Toby (Mike Vogel), while fending off advances by her best friend Emily (Bijou Phillips). One night, the posse heads east, where they buy weed from Hector (Freddy Rodríguez), a member of the Latino Sixteenth Street gang. The transaction ends with a gun pointed at Toby's head, but that doesn't prevent Allison and Emily from coming back for more the next day. The girls befriend Hector and his band of real-life gangsters and drug dealers by flirting gingerly and talking smack, which though

entertaining at first, turns ugly soon enough. Back home, the two try smoking crack and quickly disassociate from their sheltered high school life; but downtown is no place for the upper crust, as they discover at a boozy, smoky motel room party where shots, dice, and blunts lead to a brutal gang bang. In a bid to shed her good girl image, Hathaway takes this post–*Princess Diaries* role to an extreme with multiple boob shots and pitiful white girl attempts at rapping (no wonder it went straight to DVD). You could say the same of Rodríguez, coming off *Six Feet Under*, but where a movie like *Thirteen* succeeds in communicating teenage angst, *Havoc* just offends.

> "Whitney was right— crack is whack!"
> —Allison

Heart Beat (1980)

✒️ 🌱 🍸 🍾 💉 💊

🌿🌿🌿🌿 In Hollywood's only dramatic stab at telling the Jack Kerouac story, John Heard stars as the brooding, disconsolate author of *On the Road* who, to many, was the face and voice of the Beat Generation. Kerouac's life changes forever when Ira (Ray Sharkey as a thinly veiled Allen Ginsberg) introduces him to Neal Cassady (Nick Nolte). A ladies' man and car thief, Cassady is everything Kerouac's not, and becomes his muse. They drive cross-country from New York to San Francisco, where they meet and are both smitten with Carolyn (Sissy Spacek). Thus begins the movie's central relationship. The threesome hang out at jazz clubs and flirt with one other, but it's Neal whom Carolyn ultimately chooses, knowing Jack is married to his writing. During this heady period, Kerouac churns out *On the Road* in Benzedrine-fueled sessions. He pops a few "bennies" and hits the typewriter keys "like Charlie Parker." Famously written on a long scroll, the manuscript is roundly rejected by the New York publishing establishment. Kerouac travels and works odd jobs as he pounds out more novels and finally returns to California to find the Cassadys unhappily married with three kids, living in the suburbs. He moves in and they live unorthodoxly together for a while, planting pot in the front yard and smoking the homegrown right in front of the kids. Carolyn Cassady, whose memoir the movie is based on, relishes the rare opportunity to love both men while she has the chance. Kerouac finally sells *On the Road* and, as his star rises, he drifts away from Neal and Carolyn again. After Cassady is busted for pot, the movie fast-forwards to the mid-sixties, with him now divorced, behind the wheel of Ken Kesey's Furthur bus, rolling down the hippie highway. It's a fun scene, but Cassady appears lost without Carolyn and Jack. John Byrum's wistful film, along with *The Subterraneans* (1960), remains among the few that have attempted to document this important and pivotal era.

Jack: "They've got free tea growing in the goddamned fields [in Mexico]."

Neal: "So then we'll just get high driving around with the windows open."

Higher Learning (1995)

Leave it to John Singleton to over-dramatize racial tensions at a California college campus. While white students are allowed to party with immunity, the radical black contingent—led by Fudge (Ice Cube), who spews Black Panther rhetoric like Huey Newton—is subject to harsh treatment at the hands of campus security and local police. Malik (Omar Epps) and Remy (Michael Rapaport) are roommates, but not for long. Malik's on an athletic scholarship for track and field and hits it off with fellow runner Deja (Tyra Banks). A loner from Idaho, the disaffected Remy is recruited by white supremacists. While students try to clear the air with Peace Fest, Remy climbs to the roof of a school building and starts shooting. Nothing good can come out of such an event, but Singleton finds the silver lining when Professor Phipps (Laurence Fishburne) reminds Malik, "Without struggle, there is no progress." Yeah, right.

Davis: "Who's the genius who matches roommates, man? They moved me in with a psycho dickhead. It's like the Bates Hotel at my place."

High School Confidential (1958)

Part *Reefer Madness*, part *Rebel Without a Cause*, Jack Arnold's black-and-white flick set in small-town America opens with Jerry Lee Lewis singing the title song on a flatbed truck. There's a new kid in town: The jive-talking Tony Baker (Russ Tamblyn), who's living with his floozy aunt Gwen (platinum-coiffed Mamie Van Doren). What the kids don't know is Tony's a narc. He starts out buying "reefers" for "a buck a stick" from J.I. (Drew Barrymore's dad, John) and works his way up to Mr. A (Jackie Coogan), who pushes "the hard stuff" (heroin). The loud and clear message here is marijuana leads to harder drugs. One junkie character writhes in agony in several scenes, and even self-professed "weedhead" Joan (Diane Jergens) gets the shakes when she can't cop a joint ("I'm dying to blast"). The preachy voice-over ending about "this insidious menace" (drugs in schools) is laughable, sending the film over the top into blatant propaganda. But the period dialogue and Tamblyn's turn as a faux hipster (predating Riff in *West Side Story* by three years) make this a must-see.

Jack to a classmate named Mary Jane: "You pulverize me. Mary Jane's a crazy name. It just makes me cry. I get my kicks saying your name, Mary Jane."

Holy Land, The (2003)

This Israeli film tells the story of a young Orthodox Jew facing an identity crisis. Mendy (Oren Rehany) is the son of a rabbi who's been raised in a strict religious home his entire life. Torn between staying true to his faith and exploring what the rest of the world has to offer (he slips a copy of Herman Hesse's *Siddhartha* into his prayer book), Mendy's Torah studies suffer when his hormones get the best of him. The rabbinical solution? Go see a prostitute in Tel Aviv to "get it out of your system." Only in this unconventional love story, the Hasid falls for the hooker, a Russian transplant named Sasha (Tchelet Semel), and his regimented life starts to come apart. Mendy moves in with Mike (Saul Stein), a Jerusalem bar owner, and, along with a motley crew of random friends, including an Arab real estate agent and a trigger-happy Israeli elder, they smoke out of a hookah, take a drive through the desert, and get shit-faced drunk on a nightly basis. But Sasha, a dead ringer for Natasha Lyonne, has serious baggage, and the relationship turns out to be anything but reciprocal. Once she gets wind of Mendy's American citizenship, her intentions become even foggier. Anyone who's ever visited Israel will instantly sense an authenticity to this film— the ominous cloud of political unrest hangs over the story with occasional bursts of sunlight, and the dialogue (mostly in English) and accents are spot-on. The Holy Land also exposes the feeling of displacement that many Russian immigrants to Israel grapple with in their new homeland, and it does so honestly. With more than one Dylan reference, a pack of blue Rizla's on the coffee table, and stoners waxing existential about "where God lives," it's all you need to get your biblical buzz on, though it does take a dark turn toward the end.

Mike: "You think the party stops when the sun comes up? No, no, no . . . I'm gonna take you guys on a little adventure, back in space and time, back into another dimension, back into the land of the Bible."

Holy Smoke (1999)

Kate Winslet and Harvey Keitel go mano a mano in the Australian outback in Jane Campion's off-the-wall drama. Ruth (Winslet) is on a spiritual quest in India when she's rudely whisked back to Sydney by her mum (Julie Hamilton) and thrust into a weird intervention led by professional "cult exiter" PJ Waters (Keitel). Despite her frazzled state, Ruth ultimately gets the upper hand by seducing PJ. After several days of hot sex, PJ is reduced to a slobbering, pathetic letch. In the one pot scene, Ruth's friends smoke a spliff in a car en route to a club, but PJ tosses it out the window just as Ruth takes a drag (ouch!). Winslet bares all in this daring role and even kisses a girl. As for Keitel, he's a force of nature. PJ, made up with lipstick, a dress, and cowboy boots, has a breakdown that is staggering, yet somehow Ruth comes back to him. It's a pretty touching story after all.

Home at the End of the World, A (2004)

Michael Mayer's compelling adaptation of Michael Cunningham's 1990 novel is a gay stoner movie, one of the very few cataloged in this book (along with The Event). Bobby and Jonathan meet in high school in the mid-seventies. The free-spirited Bobby (Erik Smith) turns Jonathan (Harris Allan) on to marijuana in a wonderful scene where Jonathan's mother Alice (Sissy Spacek) also smokes for the first time. "What will it do exactly?" Alice asks as Laura Nyro sings "It's Gonna Take a Miracle" in the background. "What should I prepare myself for?" Alice asks. Bobby assures her not to worry, that "it's all goodness." That night, the boys do some sexual experimenting. Fast-forward to 1982: Jonathan (Dallas Roberts) is living in New York with East Village hipster Clare (Robin Wright), who he has a close platonic relationship with while cruising the city's gay scene. Bobby (Colin Farrell) arrives from Cleveland and moves in with them, eventually falling for Clare. While Jonathan's a classic drama queen, Bobby spouts platitudes like a hippie savant. It's a little unclear what everyone sees in him (Clare calls Bobby a "strange and mysterious creature"). Bobby's perma-glow likely has something to do with the traumatic death of his brother Carlton (Ryan Donowho) when Bobby was nine and they both tripped on LSD. Sadly, Jonathan becomes afflicted with HIV. When Clare splits, Bobby calmly focuses his attention on his dying lover and best friend. It's a necessary resolution to their complicated triangle.

Bobby: "Mrs. Glover, you've been so nice to me, I was wondering—do you want a hit?"

Homegrown (1998)

Northern California's hippie-dippie marijuana growers take a stand against mob infiltration in Stephen Gyllenhaal's pot-fueled drama, co-written with sixties radical Jonah Raskin. A trio of growers tends a large outdoor plantation. Jack (Billy Bob Thornton) masterminds while Carter (Hank Azaria) and Harlan (Ryan Phillippe) vie for Lucy (Kelly Lynch), who provides the stash house. When their boss Malcom (John Lithgow) turns up dead, Jack arranges to sell 1,500 pounds to Danny (Jon Bon Jovi). All parties converge at the local Harvest Party, where Sierra (Jamie Lee Curtis) exhorts the crowd to "get ripped." But ultimately the deal falls apart, the police confiscate the weed, and it all goes up in smoke, bonfire-style (stoner movie no-no!). Gyllenhaal mines the local flavor but veers off course into violence with the warmed-over gun-pointing *Reservoir Dogs* scene towards the end. Guns and buds? Not a great combination.

Malcolm's twin brother, Robert: "This is not Fantasy Island. You are not winning the marijuana lottery here. You are giving the Mary Jane as promised to Gianni the Wop."

Humboldt County
(2008)

🌿 🌿 🌿 🌿 Set in the lush Redwood forests of California's weed-growing Mecca, codirectors and writers Darren Grodsky and Danny Jacobs tell the story of a straitlaced UCLA medical student who winds up in the company of cannabis cultivators, pretty much against his will. After a one-night stand, jazz singer Bogart (Fairuza Balk) and Peter (Jeremy Strong) drive north to visit her extended Humboldt family. But when Bogart splits, Peter's left on his own in the hippie house with patriarch Jack (Brad Dourif), his wacky wife, Rosie (Frances Conroy), and their risk-taking son, Max (Chris Messina). Despite DEA and local cops clamping down on pot farms, Chris enlists Peter to help him irrigate his plants. Jack doesn't approve, warning, "It's a foolish man who underestimates his enemies. It's a stupid man who underestimates the Feds." Jack recommends a twenty-plant plot to stay within county medical-marijuana regulations. "Upon this land we farm pot," he says sagely, "but I live a life without greed. If we allow greed to enter into our lives, then we've destroyed the very thing we came here for." Peter puffs for the first time with Max, and with that he decides to stick around and help out. But when the Feds do show up and pull Max's plants, that sends him literally over the edge. Peter's dad (Peter Bogdanovich) shows up to take Peter home, but Peter's a changed man and decides to forgo his education and not return to L.A. with his unsupportive father. Strong's flat, fish-out-of-water performance is the weak link in this otherwise topical drama.

Jack: "This herb has been a part of human civilization before we were civilized. Hemp fibers have been found in archaeological digs in China dating back to 4000 B.C. Taoists monks in the fifth century thought it could tell the future. But it is currently illegal."

Hurlyburly (1998)

🌿 🌿 🌿 Lots of bloated theatrical babble fills the reel time in Anthony Drazan's screen adaptation of David Rabe's cynical Hollywood play, but there's so much seriously luscious partying going on, it's hard not to be enamored by the film. Showbiz moguls Mickey (Kevin Spacey) and Eddie (Sean Penn) share a cushy pad in the Hills where every night the door is open to their industry brethren Artie (Garry Shandling) and Phil (Chazz Palminteri), along with trusting floozy Bonnie (Meg Ryan), for friendly sit-downs that consist of relentless amounts of alcohol, weed, coke, and yapping. Everyone's miserable and going through his or her own midlife crisis, but it all seems surprisingly fun—the cocktail glasses gleam, cigarettes give off a delicious hiss, and the yayo is as gorgeous as fresh Aspen snow. This is one of the few druggy flicks that make turning blow pro look somewhat attractive.

Hustle & Flow (2005)

🖊 🍸 🔪 🧹

🍁🍁🍁🍁 Terrence Howard, in his breakthrough role, plays DJay—a pimp to braided streetwalker Nola (Taryn Manning) and a low-level weed dealer with a heart of gold and rhymes on his mind. Making the most of his meager resources, DJay charms and schemes everyone he needs to in order to get his demo tape finished. He's obviously a man of integrity, but we're never sure how much of his talk is hustle. Single-mindedly focusing on recording in his makeshift home studio with the help of sound mixers Key (Anthony Anderson) and Shelby (DJ Qualls), the scenes of his vocal takes verge on the overly heartwarming but have real spirit. Seeing no real hope in his dream, his "family" of ladies begins to fragment around him and he places all hope on his one shot at getting the tape in the hands of Skinny Black (Ludacris), the successful MC who made it out of the neighborhood. Bearing the gift of his finest bud to Skinny's annual homecoming party, DJay bonds with Skinny, smoking and drinking him under the table. But even with old-school love abounding, DJay discovers his demo tape dumped in the toilet and, in a heartsick rage, beats Skinny senseless. His subsequent arrest actually bonds the family together, and with the demo tape making its way to radio, even the guards in jail line up to audition for DJay. All ends well, leaving your buzz intact.

DJay: "I'm here trying to squeeze a dollar out of a dime, and I ain't even got a cent, man."

🍁 Q & A: TARYN MANNING 🍁

From strictly PG-rated fare like *Crazy/Beautiful* to R-rated hits like *Hustle & Flow* and *8 Mile*, Taryn Manning has played more than her share of outsiders. She's often cast as troubled, rebellious, and exceptionally strong women. The actress and Boomkat singer, who appears in no less than four RMM picks, explains why.

Reefer Movie Madness: Not to typecast, Taryn, but you're so good at playing stoners and nonconformists; where does that come from?

Taryn Manning: I grew up with an interesting background—my father was a musician and I saw a lot, hanging around him. When my parents split up, I was going back and forth between them and there was a lot of drama, so I was forced to be independent. I can't really explain how I play these roles so well. I can make believe and pretend—like, growing up, I pretended that my life wasn't what it appeared

to be—but people literally thought that [*Hustle & Flow* director] Craig Brewer plucked a real hooker off the street. Part of that is a compliment, and then it's like, "I guess I look like a trash bag." It's really about the attitude. [With Nola] I just went in and gave it all I had. That was one of the first times I got a character arc—starting in one place and ending up somewhere else. That's the best, when your character gets transformed.

RMM: Is your character Nola the "hustle" in *Hustle & Flow*?

TM: I've never thought about it like that, but it is accurate—DJay [Terrence Howard] hustles his demo, but gets in trouble, and in the end, [Nola's] in charge. They wanted to explore that more, and they actually have a *Hustle & Flow* 2 written. I don't know if it will ever become a reality, but I would love it to.

RMM: In *Weirdsville*, you play Matilda, a heroin addict who overdoses. That too must have been a stretch . . .

TM: Obviously I'm not a junkie. I'm just a people watcher and I've been around a couple of heroin addicts. One time I was shooting in Vancouver and, just for fun, I went down to that area where all the kids run amok on the streets. To see children so strung out, I cried when I left. But I'm fascinated by it. Even as a kid, my mom told me that the only way she could get me to go to sleep was to take me for a drive, and I wanted to go downtown so I could look at the bums, hookers, and weirdos walking the streets and try to make sense of it. She couldn't believe it.

RMM: You've also done a lot of hip-hop movies. Are you a fan of the genre personally?

TM: I love hip-hop. My brother is a huge hip-hop head and breakdancer. He listened to a lot of A Tribe Called Quest and Cypress Hill. I've always loved Eminem and I knew about him a long time ago. I think I end up in these films because I'm a musician, and I feel lucky to get films that resonate with me. And maybe I resonate with certain directors, because of that side of me. I know for *8 Mile* [she played Janeane], Eminem had a big part in picking the actors. For *Crazy/Beautiful*, there were five of us who went in to read with Kirsten Dunst—there were Asian girls, black girls, and I was the only blond girl. I looked a lot like Kirsten, but the director [John Stockwell] was pretty innovative: He thought, best friends start to look alike, which is totally true, so he picked me.

RMM: Female stoner characters are few and far between. Is there a role that sticks out in your mind where you were really impressed with a fellow actress?

TM: Erika Christensen in *Traffic*. We went to acting school together and I was very impressed. I never saw that side of her. I was so blown away and pleasantly surprised in how she's so cute and classy, but was kind of prissy. She did that role and I was like, "Damn!"

RMM: Wes Bentley played one of the coolest weed dealers ever as the poker-faced Ricky in *American Beauty*, but in *Weirdsville*, he takes on more of a kooky pothead role.

TM: Wes Bentley is definitely one of the best actors of his generation, and it was so cool to be able to act with him and watch him do his thing. The best part about Wes is he loves *Weirdsville*, probably because he could play a goof for once. And he is a goof, but he always plays these really intense characters. Wes is also a musician, and that brings out another amazing layer. And *Weirdsville*, as weird as it is, it's one of the best movies ever. I don't really know how it did out there, but I think it's gaining a cult following.

RMM: It's sometimes hard to translate the sensation of being high to the screen, but *Weirdsville* does it pretty well, wouldn't you agree?

TM: I agree that they achieved that feeling. There's a lot of imagery and great cinematography. The actors were part of it, but the way the director [Allan Moyle] brought the audience in and made them feel high through the lighting and cinematography, that's also a big part of filmmaking. Like *Requiem for a Dream*. That movie made me feel crazy. I was just blown away by the acting. Ellen Burstyn was on another level to me.

RMM: Are you a fan of any classic stoner movies?

TM: *Dazed and Confused* totally rules. I love Cheech & Chong. Would you consider *Boogie Nights* a stoner movie? That's one I love.

Ice Storm, The (1997)

🌿🌿🌿🌿🌿 A prep schooler who likes to rip from a three-foot bong and then contemplate the virtues of the Fantastic Four, Paul (Tobey Maguire) is perhaps the only member of his family who understands how suburban life can seem like a pointless exercise. Ang Lee's melancholic movie, based on the book by Rick Moody, centers around a fierce northeast freeze that touched down on Thanksgiving weekend in 1973 and paralyzed public transportation in and out of New York City, downed power lines, and made any kind of travel, by car or foot, treacherous. It's against this grim backdrop that we meet two hopelessly dysfunctional Connecticut families, each possessing a cheating spouse and at least one hyper-sexually-curious child: fourteen-year-old Wendy (Christina Ricci) and the awkward Mikey (Elijah Wood) get it on in the basement while her father Benjamin (Kevin Kline) and Mikey's mom Janey (Sigourney Weaver) carry on an illicit affair upstairs. Things get more twisted later that night when both sets of parents wind up at a swinging "key party" and are forced to face their infidelities. Paul, meanwhile, heads to New York City with his private school pals Francis (David Krumholtz) and Libbets (Katie Holmes), where they smoke joints and pop pills. On an emotional level, the characters struggle with everything from kleptomania and adultery to alcoholism and chronic depression. It's not a pretty picture, and sadly it doesn't end well.

🌿 MOVIE STRAINS 🌿

Boutique buds have had starring roles in many a stoner movie. Here are five unforgettable film strains.

G-13 (American Beauty): Looking to replicate the previous night's high, Lester (Kevin Spacey) buys a bag of G-13 from his dark and brooding neighbor Ricky (Wes Bentley). "This shit is top of the line," says the teenage dealer. "It's genetically engineered by the U.S. government. It's extremely potent but a completely mellow high. No paranoia."

Labrador (Up in Smoke): In one of the stoner classic's most famous scenes, Pedro (Cheech) and Man (Chong) share a massive joint made up of mostly Maui Wowie with a hint of Labrador, courtesy of Man's dog, who ate his stash. "Gets ya high, don't it?" says Man. Pedro's response: "I wonder what Great Dane tastes like."

Pineapple Express (Pineapple Express): Dopey dealer Saul's (James Franco) specialty strain is the rare Pineapple Express, pot so good, "it's almost a shame to smoke it—it's like killing a unicorn." Stoner Dale (Seth Rogen) wants in on the bud described as "God's vagina," but after Dale witnesses a murder and drops the roach, the strain's unique DNA is easily traced back to Saul by the criminals.

Strawberry Cough (Children of Men): In the chaotic, childless world of 2027, reluctant activist-turned-renegade Theo (Clive Owen) hides the pregnant Kee (Clare-Hope Ashitey) in the secluded UK home of hippie Jaspar (Michael Caine), who grows his own pot, which he sells to a nearby internment camp. Jaspar's favorite strain: Strawberry Cough.

Thai Stick (The Big Lebowski, The Ice Storm, Cheech & Chong's Next Movie, and Up in Smoke): The Big Lebowski's Dude (Jeff Bridges) brags that, in addition to bowling and occupying various administra-tion buildings, his college years were spent "smoking a lot of Thai Stick." Likewise, The Ice Storm's Paul Hood (Tobey Maguire) takes a bong hit of the "precious" pot with his private school roommate Francis (David Krumholtz). In Cheech & Chong's Next Movie, Chong bribes Cheech with some Thai Stick, but in Up in Smoke, Cheech, trying to impress Chong, mispronounces the popular seventies strain as "tied stick—you know, stuff that's tied to a stick."

Indian Runner, The (1991)

🖊 🍸 🎷 👀

🍁 🍁 🍁 🍁 Sean Penn's brooding and unsentimental directorial debut is a sibling story—one brother's a cop, the other keeps running afoul of the law. Frank (Viggo Mortensen) returns from Vietnam and quickly ends up in jail. Older brother Officer Joe (David Morse) invites Frank and his girlfriend Dorothy (Patricia Arquette) to stay with him and his wife, Maria (Valerie Golino), at their home in Nebraska. Frank gets a job, and while the brothers are away during the day the women bond with the help of marijuana. (Everyone else in this movie smokes cigarettes practically nonstop.) All is going well, but you know it won't last. Frank's demons prevent him from loving anyone and, after several violent incidents (he hits a bartender, played by Dennis Hopper, over the head with a chair), Frank speeds away like the mysterious character Penn named his movie for.

Frank: "What can I say? I fucked up. I get in a violent way. I look around the room and I want to bust it all to hell."

In Too Deep (1999)

🖊 🍸 🎷 🥄

🍁 🍁 🍁 You have to be one serious badass to carry the nickname "God," and Cincinnati's notorious drug kingpin Dwight Gittens (LL Cool J) certainly looks the part. As the target of an undercover sting, he's priority number one for local police and the DEA, who are looking to bust his operation and put him away for life ("We figure he's hooked into about eighty percent of the crack in the city," notes one lawman). But this isn't your ordinary bad guy. God's the kind of brother who takes care of his community, his baby, and his boys—so long as you don't step to the leader. When a young, confident cop named Jeff Cole (Omar Epps) is enlisted to penetrate the gang's inner circle, he bonds with God over boxing. In no time, J. Reid, as he's known to the crew, is out on drive-bys and in on major drug deals, coming dangerously close to crossing the criminal line on more than one occasion. *Jackie Brown*'s Pam Grier, *Weeds*'s Guillermo Diaz, and music producer Jermaine Dupri take on bit roles in this crime drama, which feels like an early stab at *The Wire* but isn't as convincing.

Jacob's Ladder (1990)

🖊 🍸 👀

🍁 🍁 🍁 🍁 Adrian Lynne's mind-bending thriller begins with soldiers passing a joint in Vietnam; a gun battle breaks out and soon Jacob is stabbed with a bayonet. Back home in New York, Jacob (Tim Robbins) works as a postman and lives with the vivacious Jezzie (Elizabeth Pena). But something's not quite right with Jacob. He has visions of demons with whirling heads and hears voices. Everything becomes a hallucination. And he's being followed. What the hell's going on? Well, it takes most of the movie to find out that he and his fellow soldiers were guinea pigs in an army drug experiment to increase aggression and turn them into absolute killing machines and that the government would go to any length to prevent Jacob and the other survivors from his platoon from blowing the whistle. Hippie chemist Michael Newman (Matt Craven) tracks Jacob down and reveals the dirty secret, which resulted in two hundred deaths during that battle, but even worse, the drug caused the soldiers to fight each other, hence Jacob's stabbing. The ladder, Newman explains, is "a fast trip right to the primal fear, right to the base anger." The CIA indeed conducted experiments using LSD on soldiers, known

as the MK-Ultra program, but those experiments took place in hospitals, not on the battlefield. *Jacob's Ladder* plays like a horror movie, with all kinds of cool special effects, especially the devil having his way with Jezzie to the tune of James Brown's "My Thang." Lynne's New York is gritty and scary—a true representation of the city in the early seventies. Best of all, Lynne never gives the central premise away—whether Jacob is a dead man walking or if he is as alive as he boasts to anyone who wonders (several do). Robbins is terrific as the harried, paranoid, and perhaps delusional vet; and look for an uncredited Macauley Culkin as his ten-year-old son, Gabe.

Rod: "You're all fuckin' paranoid. It was bad grass, it's all it was. There's no such thing as fuckin' demons, come on!"

Jesus' Son (1999)

🌿🌿🌿🌿 Billy Crudup plays one of Hollywood's most sympathetic junkies in Alison Maclean's adaptation of Denis Johnson's book of short stories. FH (Crudup) lives in Iowa, where he falls in love with mainliner Michelle (Samantha Morton). Their relationship is at the core of this movie, which careens wildly from one subplot to the next. Through nine titled episodes (including "Stan," "Work," and "Emergency"), we follow FH and Michelle as they break up and make up over and over again. FH stands for "fuck head," his nickname due to his penchant for making bad decisions. But he's a lovable loser with a heart of gold. FH gets emotional when hospital worker Georgie (Jack Black) runs over a rabbit, has a soft spot for a local Mennonite couple, and, against his better judgment (such as it is), trashes a house with fellow user Wayne (Denis Leary) for scrap metal. The body count is high (Michelle, Wayne), but FH manages to survive. He goes to rehab (Dennis Hopper makes a cameo there as Bill), works at a *Cuckoo's Nest*–style retirement home, and eventually finds another woman, Mira (Holly Hunter), who's damaged like him. Black is particularly funny in his brief role as the pill-popping orderly who grooves to "Cowgirl in the Sand" and carries a large stash. "The blue ones will make you nod out, the yellows will keep you going for the

duration," he tells FH, who asks, "Which one do you want?" "I'll take both," says Georgie, which pretty much sums up the peripatetic *Jesus' Son.*

Michelle to FH: "You ever seen anyone shoot up before?"

Joe (1970)

🌿🌿🌿🌿 Just like Dennis Hopper did in 1969 with *Easy Rider*, John G. Avildsen explores the deep chasm in American society between straights and the drug culture with *Joe*. Melissa (Susan Sarandon in her first-ever role) lives with junkie dealer Frank (Patrick McDermott) in an East Village pad. Frank's not the nicest guy, and one day he talks Melissa into taking too much speed, which lands her in the hospital. Melissa's father, Bill (Dennis Patrick), flies into a rage and kills Frank. But when Joe (Peter Boyle) overhears Bill confess to the crime at a nearby bar, the story takes an unusual turn. Joe's a blowhard racist and hippie hater of the worst kind and he applauds Bill's choice of victim. Joe doesn't exactly blackmail Bill, but he makes his life a living hell. The pivotal scene involves Joe, Bill, a group of hippies, and a stash of pot, coke, hash, speed, and mushrooms. When they all smoke out of a hookah and Joe's instructed, "Suck it in and hold it in until it hurts," he knowingly retorts, "I see it on TV all the time." As a psychedelic guitar jams in the background, the couples pair off and have sex. After the hippies steal Joe's wallet, Joe and Bill go on a deadly shooting spree. Avildsen, who would later direct *Save the Tiger* and *Rocky*, offers no solutions, just a stark dose of early seventies reality.

Frank to Bill: "When I met Melissa she was balling her way up the aisle at the Fillmore."

Juice (1992)

🌿🌿🌿 A naïve inner-city crew gets in too deep when one of its wannabes finds the thug life a little too enticing. It all starts innocently enough—lifelong friends Q (Omar Epps), Bishop (Tupac Shakur), Raheem (Khalil Kain), and Steel (Jermaine

Hopkins) are your typical early nineties Harlem teenagers, running around hassling the neighborhood girls, stealing LPs, and scrapping with the local Spanish gang. But when Bishop convinces his buddies to rob a bodega and then shoots the owner, the bonds of this brotherhood are broken for good. In a bid for supremacy—or "juice"—Bishop starts offing anyone who gets in his way, eventually pointing the gun at his own crew: An aspiring DJ who impresses at a local Mixxmaster Massacre contest (featuring cameos by Fab Five Freddy, EPMD, Ed Lover, and Doctor Dre, and a bit part by Queen Latifah), Q struggles most with issues of loyalty and morality while trying to keep the blood off his hands. As gangster movies go, *Juice* is a pretty lightweight joint—there's little action and not a lot of weed—but there's no denying Tupac's talent in his menacing portrayal of Bishop. Even Samuel L. Jackson, who was cast as local pool hall manager Trip, must have been impressed.

Bishop: "All we do is fucking run. I feel like I'm on the goddamn track team!"

Keys to Tulsa (1997)

In another of his many stoner film roles, Eric Stoltz plays the privileged Richter, son of Oklahoma socialite Cynthia Boudreau (Mary Tyler Moore) and a movie reviewer by trade. He lives a life of leisure on mom's dime, fraternizing with all kinds of shady folks, like heroin-addicted stripper Cherry (Joanna Going), his ex-girlfriend Vicky (Deborah Kara Unger), and her gun-toting psychopath brother, Keith (Michael Rooker), and drug-dealer husband, Ronnie (James Spader). In a tangled web that involves a prominent local businessman murdering a prostitute, the joint-smoking, coke-snorting Richter becomes involved in a blackmail scheme that sends him running to the newsroom, only it's too late—his boss fires him for being "on narcotics." Complicating matters even more, Richter jumps into an affair with Vicky and Ronnie finds out about it. A boozy confrontation between all parties ends in gunshots and ultimately seals Richter's perfectly tolerable fate. Dark, dense, and at times convoluted, *Keys of Tulsa* isn't Stoltz's most memorable turn, but Spader as a tracksuit-wearing hairy-chested pusher is a sight to behold.

Kids (1995)

Larry Clark's directorial debut follows a group of New York City teens on an average day—one filled with unprotected sex, drugs, and innocence lost too young and too fast. For its honest depiction of Generation Y running wild in the streets, the film was handed an NC-17 rating and deemed borderline pornographic. Some would say rightly so: Watching the main character, seventeen-year-old Telly (Leo Fitzpatrick) swear to a naïve thirteen-year-old girl that he really cares about her before brashly taking her virginity, is about as uncomfortable as movie viewing gets, and can leave you feeling confused, curious, and guilty all at once. And that's not the worst of it. We follow Jennie (Chloë Sevigny) as she tests positive for HIV, then tries to find Telly, who deflowered her the previous summer, to tell him that he's carrying the deadly disease. Then there's Telly, who believes he can avoid STDs by only having sex with virgins and embarks on his quest to hookup with two in the same day. The sweaty story line takes us in and out of different social cliques, intercutting guys and girls, and eavesdropping on conversations. Case in point: waiting for Casper (Justin Pierce) to pass that blunt, chilling in Washington Square Park and figuring out where the night's party is at. As a purely observational and unobtrusive look at a culture, *Kids* is as rough and raw as the city itself: unapologetic, eye-opening, jaw-dropping, and incredibly intense.

Kush (2007)

The spoils and stresses of life as a high-end pot dealer are put on full display in this *Alpha Dog* knock-off. Dusty (Bret Roberts) has been selling weed since his teens. Under the tutelage of King (William Atherton), he graduates from part-time bagman to full-time pusher supervising a team of dealers, one of which includes King's screwup son, Christian (Mike Erwin). Dusty's one rule, both in life and business? Don't mess with cocaine. So once one of his customers demands he score the white powder, and Christian starts messing with bumps here and there, Dusty senses that things are about to get ugly. Indeed, when Christian fronts the crack-addicted Todd (Alex Feldman) $30K worth of Kush and fails to collect, he ends up kidnapping the dude's fifteen-year-old brother and holding him as collateral. At first, it's all chill—Christian and his buds smoke the kid out and stash him at a friend's house with a bunch of hot, coked-out girls—but when they can't get ahold of Todd . . . Well, you can figure out how this one ends. And that's the problem with *Kush*: It feels like a rehash, only with a second-rate cast. But what it does have going for it is the movement of pounds upon pounds of primo pot. Its grow rooms are impressive too, even if some of the presumably fake plants look too perfect to be true.

Dusty: "Nowadays, the weed you buy represents your social status or your fuckability. You might get laid more if you get the Diesel or the White Russian, or you might be a more sophisticated pothead if you're holding some organic boutique shit with a cute label on it. But the point is, people with money will pay more for the boutique, only this shit doesn't grow accidentally in your backyard or your roommate's closet. This is the Kush."

La Bamba (1987)

🌿🌿🌿🌿 This biopic of Latino rock and roller Ritchie Valens's short but prolific music career has its ups and downs—for every wide-eyed happy moment that looks ahead to a bright future,

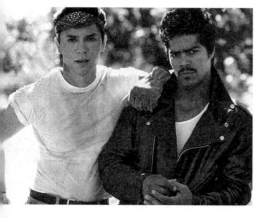

there's the nagging flashback of a horrific two-plane collision that took place in the skies above his elementary school. Lou Diamond Phillips stars as Valens, who deals with his bad boy, pot-smuggling, alcoholic older brother, Bob (Esai Morales), the rampant racism of the fifties, and his search for love. The women in Valens's life—his mother, Connie (Rosanna DeSoto); girlfriend, Donna (Danielle von Zerneck); and sister-in-law, Rosie (Elizabeth Pena)—play a major role in his development as a person, but it's the tunes that take him out of the barrio and onto the radio dial. Making it to *American Bandstand*, however, requires Valens to get over his fear of flying, which he does. Sadly, Valens, Buddy Holly, and J. P. Richardson (a.k.a. The Big Bopper) died in rock's most famous plane crash—known as "The Day the Music Died"—on February 3, 1959.

Bob to Rosie: "Come on, take a hit, man! Put a little *mota* in our love life!"

L.A. Confidential (1997)

🌿🌿🌿🌿 One clean cop challenges an entire force of corrupt ones in Curtis Hanson's captivating film noir homage starring Kevin Spacey (Jack), Guy Pearce (Ed), and Russell Crowe (Bud). It's 1953, and pot's just starting to catch on in Hollywood—in fact, Jack's credited with busting Robert Mitchum several years earlier. Craven tabloid editor Sid Hudgens (Danny DeVito) pays Jack to set up cannabis collars for his mag *Hush-Hush* ("scourge of grasshoppers and dope fiends everywhere"). But this is pretty tame stuff compared to what's to follow: As Captain Smith (Dudley Cromwell) methodically attempts to take control of organized crime in Los Angeles after the death of kingpin Mickey Cohen, Ed finds evidence of a cover up. At stake are twenty-five pounds of heroin. Kim Basinger won an Oscar for her supporting role as Veronica Lake look-alike call girl/moll Lynn Bracken, and Hanson received a justified nomination as well.

Sid: "It's Christmas Eve in the City of Angels and while decent citizens sleep the sleep of the righteous, hopheads prowl for marijuana . . . "

Last Days (2005)

🖉

🌿 🌿 🌿 🌿 "Inspired" by the death of Kurt Cobain in 1994, Gus Van Sant re-creates the scene at a fictional rock-and-roller's sprawling home and property somewhere in the Pacific Northwest. Blake (Michael Pitt) sure looks like Cobain, and in several scenes even wears his trademark red-striped sweater and round white-framed sunglasses. Blake barely speaks throughout the entire film; rather, he mumbles like Popeye. Not much happens. Slacker friends come and go, but they mostly ignore Blake as he stumbles around the house and in the woods. In one scene, he nods out, only to have a friend prop him back up. No one seems to be too concerned about Blake's frail psychological condition, except for a record exec played by Kim Gordon of Sonic Youth, who pays a visit, calls him a "rock-and-roll cliché," and splits. There are several references to Blake's wife or girlfriend (obviously Courtney Love), who's away while the stoners play. Though Blake sings "Death to Birth" in a cracked voice, strumming an acoustic guitar at one point, the soundtrack mostly repeats the Velvet Underground's "Venus in Furs." A detective (Ricky Jay) sniffs around the property, but Blake sneaks away. Then, without the sound of a gunshot, he's found dead, leaving viewers to wonder what actually happened. Was it suicide? Clearly, that is Van Sant's conclusion, though some have suggested a conspiracy behind Cobain's death. The only conspiracy here is among Blake's friends, who condone his self-destructive behavior by not confronting him before it is too late. Yet another of Van Sant's daring movies, Last Days fits right in with his increasingly odd oeuvre.

🌿 FIVE MORE BY GUS VAN SANT 🌿

Equally adept at delivering big-budget fare like Good Will Hunting and Milk or druggy dramas like Drugstore Cowboy, Gus Van Sant walks the fine line between indie and commercial filmmaking.

Mala Noche (1985): Van Sant's first feature is a tale of unrequited love between a white, gay convenience store clerk and a handsome Mexican drifter. The edgy cinematography is black-and-white, but the emotions aren't.

Drugstore Cowboy (1989): Small-time thieves rip off pharmacies and party until they need more. Matt Dillon (Bob) and Kelly Lynch (Dianne) star as a couple who loves drugs more than they do each other. Bob goes into rehab, where he meets Tom the Priest (played by William S. Burroughs), but Diane leaves him. Sober boyfriends just don't turn her on.

Even Cowgirls Get the Blues (1993): Van Sant's adaptation of Tom Robbins's 1976 novel is as phantasmagorical as the book. Sissy (Uma Thurman) has oversized thumbs, which she uses to hitchhike around the country with great success. The large cast includes Van Sant stalwarts Keanu Reeves, William S. Burroughs, and Heather Graham, along with an uncredited River Phoenix and his sister Rain as Bonanza Jellybean.

To Die For (1995): Nicole Kidman gives an Oscar-worthy performance as Suzanne Stone, an aspiring news anchor who crosses the line by befriending the subjects of her self-produced "documentary." She sleeps with stoner Jimmy (Joaquin Phoenix), then recruits him and his burnout buddy Russell (Casey Affleck) to murder her husband (Matt Dillon). It's a twisted tale replete with teenage angst and awkwardness that's eternally captivating.

Paranoid Park (2007): Another view of Portland—the setting for Drugstore Cowboy and My Own Private Idaho—from the perspective of skate punks who inhabit a slab of cement near the train yards. Teens Alex (Gabe Nevins) and Jennifer (Gossip Girl's Taylor Momsen) try to unravel the death of a security guard who patrolled Paranoid Park.

🌿 GANJA GIRLS 🌿

While most stoner movies focus on slapstick male bonding, here we pay tribute to cinema's distaff danksters.

Jennifer Aniston (*Friends with Money, Office Space***):** In *Friends with Money*, depressed, single, and lonely Olivia is a full-time slacker and part-time maid who finds a friend in weed—a reversal for Aniston, who played the staunchly antipot Justine in *The Good Girl*. But her role as the only female in *Office Space* will forever endear her to the stoner crowd.

Claire Danes (*Brokedown Palace, Igby Goes Down***):** Busted for heroin in Thailand, Danes's Alice smokes pot in prison in *Brokedown Palace*. In *Igby*, her Sookie claims, "I roll perfect joints," to which Igby (Kiernan Culkin) snickers, "It's incredible that a human being can make such neat, little joints."

Anna Faris (*Smiley Face, Waiting..., Scary Movie 1, 2, 3, and 4***):** She plays party-hard waitress Serena in *Waiting...* and repeat screamer Cindy in the stoner-centric *Scary Movie* series, but it's as cupcake-scarfing perpetual pothead Jane in *Smiley Face* that Faris reached a new career high.

Bridget Fonda (*Jackie Brown***):** Like father like daughter, Bridget emulates dad Peter, who taught Jack Nicholson how to puff in *Easy Rider*. Here, as couch potato Melanie, she instructs Robert De Niro's ex-con Louis how to properly inhale a bong hit. "Coughing's good," Melanie coaxes. "It gets you higher."

Danneel Harris (*Harold & Kumar Escape from Guantanamo Bay***):** Kumar's sexy ex-girlfriend Vanessa seals his stoner fate when she gets the brainiac high for the first time—by shotgunning a hit while hiding between the library stacks. Flash-forward to her wedding day, and she's sneaking a toke before taking the plunge—ultimately choosing weed over her Republican, "date-rape-faced" groom-to-be.

Kate Hudson (*Almost Famous***):** As queen groupie in Cameron Crowe's rock-and-roll classic, Hudson's Penny Lane charms in every scene—even when her stomach's being pumped to the tune of Stevie Wonder's "My Cherie Amour."

Milla Jovovich (*Dazed and Confused***):** As guitar-playing, lighter-wielding stoner beauties go, few compare to *Dazed and Confused*'s Michelle, even if she doesn't say much. Ditto for Milla's turn in *Zoolander* as Katinka, only here her spark has much more bite.

Frances McDormand (*Laurel Canyon***):** Keeping the sex, drugs, and rock-and-roll spirit alive long after the music died in the Hollywood Hills, producer Jane (McDormand) relies on a steady supply of joints (and booze and bong hits) to get her creative juices flowing.

Amy Smart (*Outside Providence, Road Trip***):** As the brainy Brown-bound Jane in *Outside Providence*, Smart's a real catch for dopey Tim (Shawn Hatosy), who gives her dental roach clips for her birthday. Smart is in *Road Trip* as Beth, who's quick to undress for Josh's video camera.

Kristen Stewart (*Adventureland, Into the Wild***):** When it comes to a stony summer fling, the mellow Em is every guy's fantasy. Infinitely cool—even while patrolling the arcade wearing a ratty staff T-shirt—Stewart delivers not your average teen character in *Adventureland*, while in *Into the Wild*, she inhabits a wanderer's soul as Emile Hirsch's unrequited love, Tracy.

Laurel Canyon (2002)

🚬 🍾 🔑 🍸 💉 👁👁

🍁 🍁 🍁 The Los Angeles neighborhood that was home to some of the greatest musical voices of the sixties and seventies serves as the setting for this modern-day drama about a rock producer who's looking to connect with her straitlaced son. Jane (Frances McDormand) and Sam (Christian Bale) live on opposite coasts and worlds apart—she's the kind of gal who does a bong hit in the morning, he's a recent medical school graduate who takes everything too seriously. When a hospital job brings Sam back home, Mom offers to house him and his fiancée Alex (Kate Beckinsale) for an extended stay—so long as they don't mind the band that's recording on the property. To the contrary, brainy Alex takes a strong liking to Ian (Allessandro Nivola), the British singer and Chris Martin look-alike who's seeing Jane. In due time, the three start sharing joints, late-night hangs, and one boozy turn in the pool where things get a little steamy. Sam, meanwhile, is entertaining lustful thoughts of fellow resident Sara (Natascha McElhone) and beginning to question his own relationship. Fidelity (or lack thereof) is the central theme here, along with the highly relatable condition of fearing adulthood. But even though McDormand impresses, these characters are entirely paint-by-numbers. Director Lisa Cholodenko (*High Art*) certainly had good intentions in romanticizing the Canyon, but not even a racy lesbian scene can save it from feeling clichéd.

Lenny (1974)

🚬 🍸 💉 💊 👁👁

🍁 🍁 🍁 🍁 It's pretty amazing to think that Lenny Bruce was arrested for saying "cocksucker" on stage in 1961, and busted again and again on obscenity and drug charges until he died of a morphine overdose at the age of forty. Clearly, the American legal system drove Bruce to his premature death. Bob Fosse's gripping black-and-white biopic cuts back and forth between live stand-up and dramatic scenes of Bruce (Dustin Hoffman) and his stripper wife, Honey (Valerie Perrine). Arrested

for pot in Hawaii during the fifties, Honey spent two years in jail. An early scene in the movie depicts pot smokers in a jazzy setting with Miles Davis on the soundtrack. Later, the couple turns to heroin and pills. Understandably obsessed with his legal troubles, Bruce loses his comic edge and his adoring audience. Every single "dirty" comic who has come along since Lenny Bruce owes this true American trailblazer a huge debt.

Lenny: "The thing that I'm trying to tell you is it's harassment, it's repression, it's club owners being called up in the middle of the night and being told not to hire me or they're going to lose their liquor licenses, it's Vietnam, it's atrocities here and there."

Less Than Zero (1987)

🍸 💉 🚬

🌿🌿🌿🌿 One of the classic eighties coke flicks, based on the popular Bret Easton Ellis novel, *Less Than Zero* takes an exceedingly cool look at the Beverly Hills drug scene in a time of excess and eternal youth. As a group of friends' post–high school relationships become strained, your typical prep-school rich-kid culture meets some very adult problems. Julian (Robert Downey Jr.) turns to stealing and prostitution to feed his coke habit, while beautiful model Blair (Jami Gertz) and friend Clay (Andrew McCarthy), home for his first Christmas since moving East for college, try their hardest to take care of their addicted pal. Raw, sexy, and unfiltered, the movie transitions from house party to nightclub to a swanky hotel suite in Palm Springs, each setting knocking Julian down a notch closer to the bottom. In the end, it winds up being a cautionary tale against overindulgence and, at the same time, an argument for not using any drugs other than pot.

Clay to Blair: "Well, you're fucked up, you look like shit, but hey, no problem, all you need is a better cut of cocaine."

Looking for Mr. Goodbar (1977)

✏️ 🍸 💉 🚬 👀

🌿🌿🌿🌿 The same year Diane Keaton dazzled audiences in the title role of pot-smoking *Annie Hall* (she won the Academy Award for her performance opposite Woody Allen), the actress took an even more daring step as the sexually promiscuous femme fatale in Richard Brooks's devastating disco-era drama. Theresa, a recent college grad who moves from Boston to New York, likes to meet men in bars. This was before AIDS, so she protects herself with birth control and hopes for the best. Her choices are questionable, such as hophead Tony (Richard Gere in an early, memorable role), who breaks into Theresa's apartment, beats her, and snitches her out to the police (they bust her for coke). Theresa's older sister, Katherine (Tuesday Weld), likes to party, too. She and her friends smoke pot, watch "home movies" (porn), and have orgies. Theresa prefers anonymous sex and one-night stands, but Gary (Tom Berenger, also in an early role) sadly becomes her last. The black-lit finale is a shocking reminder of the dangers of being a single, liberated woman in a big city.

> "Snow baby! Dime-bag white lady! You got a coke kick? Well, I say Co-Caine! Where'd you get this stuff? It makes America beautiful."
>
> —Tony to Theresa

Lost in Translation
(2003)

🍸 ✏️

🌿🌿🌿🌿 Perfectly capturing that dreamlike jet lag when you're not quite awake or asleep, the bulk of Sofia Coppola's film takes place in the hotel where fellow travelers Bob Harris (Bill Murray) and Charlotte (Scarlett Johansson) meet. Both are wandering through their lives and, recognizing each other's aimlessness, form a brief but intense platonic relationship. Bob's an aging actor who's in Tokyo filming an ad campaign, while Charlotte is a young woman unsure of herself or her direction. Basically abandoned for days at a time by her distracted, clueless photographer husband, John (Giovanni Ribisi), Charlotte finds Bob the caring companion she longs for and the movie manages to make the arc of their short time together feel real and engaging. Coppola's subtle approach is oftentimes not about the dialogue or the scenery; more is communicated by a halfway glance, a semi-embarrassed shrug, or a well-placed song. The pace is gentle and calming as the pair float through the unfamiliar trappings of Japan, adrift in both language and body clock. Always striking just the right emotional notes, Murray plays the right amount of funny and sad, making the weight of years read on his face like the map of a lifetime. There's no weed here, just a clock that reads 4:20 A.M. in Bob's hotel room on his first jet-lagged night in Japan, but stoner queen Anna Faris makes a couple of fantastically funny appearances as the ditzy blond actress Kelly in Tokyo to promote her action movie and My Bloody Valentine's Kevin Shields contributes several songs to the near-perfect soundtrack. A movie for romantics who don't like their love sappy, Lost in Translation is a perfect ambient backdrop for the most sleepless of nights.

🌿 420 REFERENCES 🌿

Six more movies that slip the stoner code, whether accidentally or intentionally.

Network (1976): In this broadcast news satire, anchor Howard Beale (Peter Finch) delivers his famous line, "I'm as mad as hell and I'm not gonna take this anymore!" while seated in front of a clock set to 4:20 P.M. in Los Angeles.

Fast Times at Ridgemont High (1982): After a Mustang belonging to football star Charles Jefferson (Forest Whitaker) shows up on the Ridgemont campus seemingly trashed by rival team Lincoln High, that team gets its ass handed to them by the burly giant at the big game. Final score displayed on the board: Ridgemont: 42, Lincoln: 0.

Pulp Fiction (1994): In "The Gold Watch" chapter of the Quentin Tarantino classic, after Butch the boxer (Bruce Willis) escapes the clutches of a couple of pawnshop redneck rapists, he grabs a samurai sword and quietly slinks his way down the stairs to retaliate, passing a clock set to 4:20.

Evil Bong (2006): Eebee the wicked bong seduces and then kills stoners after they take a hit from her hookah-like tubes. She claims her first victim, surfer dude Bachman (Mitch Eakins), at exactly 4:20 P.M.

Harold & Kumar Escape from Guantanamo Bay (2008): If it wasn't obvious from the movie's title, the trailer for the Harold & Kumar sequel baited stoners with this line: "Flight 420 to Amsterdam now boarding..." "It's gonna be exactly like *Euro Trip*," Kumar (Kal Penn) promises, "only it's not gonna suck."

Garden Party (2008): Looking to impress emo drifter Sammy (Erik Smith), the sexually ambiguous Nathan (Alexander Cendese) opens a door to a massive grow-op. The secret code to the lock? 0-4-2-0.

Love and a .45 (1994)

🌿 🌿 🌿 The grunge era Bonnie and Clyde is Texas twosome Watty (Gil Bellows) and Starlene (Renée Zellweger). Caught up in a robbery gone wrong, the couple flees south to Mexico with the cops and their speed freak friend Billy (Rory Cochrane) hot on their tail. They make a few pit stops: one to get married and another to visit Starlene's hippie parents (played by Peter Fonda and Ann Wedgeworth), who gift the newlyweds a vial of highly potent liquid acid. As Watty and Starlene continue down a bloody, twisted path, their reputation precedes them and, in no time, they're tabloid TV stars. But this is a couple riddled with contradictions—like Watty's constant assertion that he's "not a violent man"—and also hyperaware of the fact that luck eventually runs out. The question is, can karma hold out until they've crossed the border? Like *Natural Born Killers* and *True Romance*, this is a passion-fueled ultraviolent love story, but where those films introduce truly complex characters, Watty and Star come up short.

Man with the Golden Arm, The (1955)

🌿 🌿 🌿 🌿 Frank Sinatra stars in Hollywood's first-ever serious drug movie as Frankie Machine, a.k.a. "Dealer." Frankie deals poker, hence the "Golden Arm" moniker, which is also a metaphor for mainlining heroin. Fresh out of jail, he falls back into old habits, shooting dope and running late-night card games. Frankie wants to play the drums and joins the musicians union, but suffers the shakes and fails his audition. Married to his allegedly crippled wife, Zosch (Eleanore Parker), Frankie pines for supportive, curvy cocktail waitress Molly (Kim Novak), who helps him kick his habit in one of the Hollywood's sexiest "cold turkey" scenes. In Nelson Algren's novel, Frankie commits suicide, but in Otto Preminger's gripping film he wakes up to a brand-new day, free of the "forty-pound monkey" on his back. Elmer Bernstein's big-band score charts Frankie's high and lows—when he shoots up, the brass figuratively penetrates Frankie's skin. Darren McGavin's pusher man Louie is a smooth-talking archetype, the first of many such sleazy characters to come.

Maryjane (1968)

🌿 🌿 🌿 From *Reefer Madness* (1936) to *High School Confidential* (1958) to Maury Dexter's B-movie rarity, the story remains the same: Kids love to get high on pot. This exploitation flick is set in Oakdale High School, where marijuana's the new big thing and the authorities are trying to put a stop to all the fun and games. Typical of American International's biker flicks, there's a gang of sorts who are part pranksters and part legitimate troublemakers, all led by tough-guy Jordan (Kevin Couglin), who provides pot at a buck a joint. Mostly, the kids are content to puff and make out at the town lake. Art teacher Phil Blake (fifties and sixties teen idol Fabian) gets drawn into the controversy when police come to Oakdale and ask the teachers to squeal on the students. "I've read about marijuana," Blake protests. "It does less damage than cigarettes or alcohol. The worst thing I know about it is that it's illegal." But once Blake admits he'd smoked marijuana in college, the cops target him as well. Next thing, Blake's in jail on a pot possession charge (the scene's a freak show with a junkie writhing through cold turkey) and out of a job. No longer sympathetic to the cause, Blake intercepts a shipment of Acapulco Gold stashed in an ice-cream truck (thirteen years before *Nice Dreams*) that's intended for Jordan and dumps it in the toilet. The locals who prepaid for the Mexi high-grade ("we don't dig that crabgrass, we're waiting for the Gold") aren't happy and pound Jordan and his emissary Jerry (Michael Margotta) as the movie comes to a sudden halt. The faded and choppy reproduction available on DVD is packaged with an additional DVD of Mike Curb's jazz-rock soundtrack music.

McCabe & Mrs. Miller
(1971)

🗝 🍸 💉 👀

🌿 🌿 🌿 🌿 🌿 An admitted lifelong stoner, director Robert Altman spent much of his career crafting either idiosyncratic epics (*Nashville*, *The Player*) or offbeat cult hits (*The Long Goodbye*, *3 Women*), but he was at his headiest best early on, as this Western proves. Warren Beatty is John McCabe, a lapsed gunfighter who wanders into a nascent Washington town called Presbyterian Church, which is just as the first of three alluring and recurring Leonard Cohen songs describes it—like "some Joseph looking for a manger." It's the start of the twentieth century, and mumbling "Pudgy" McCabe aims to take over this muddy one-saloon mining town by opening a bathhouse and brothel. Yet he's stubbornly small-time, fleecing the same men he pays to work in the mines by plying them with whores, "so you'll have something to do at night besides go home and play with Mary Five Fingers." Constance Miller (Julie Christie), a strict but kindly English madam, shows McCabe how to send profits soaring. She occasionally drifts off into what all the girls call "quiet times," when she disappears into her own private opium den. No sooner do they succeed as business partners—lovers is another matter—than McCabe and Mrs. Miller's endeavor starts to crumble. The wealthier Harrison Shaughnessy company wants to buy up their holdings—and they're not known for being refused. When McCabe plays hardball, the company turns ruthless, and three henchman are dispatched to hunt McCabe down in a snowy cat-and-mouse climax that is the icing on two hours of breathtaking visuals. Altman's patented overlapping dialogue, enhanced by a large, improvising coterie of the director's regulars (Shelley Duvall, Keith Carradine, Michael Murphy), only adds to the realism. But it's Beatty and Christie, real-life lovers at the time, who leap off the screen—as ambitious but doomed antiheroes, they remain indelible icons for the turned-on mind.

🌿 MORE OPIUM SCENES 🌿

The poppy produces many derivatives, the first and most natural of which is opium. Here are six scenes illustrating how it's been depicted on the silver screen.

The Wizard of Oz **(1939):** En route to Oz, Dorothy, the Scarecow, the Tin Man, and the Cowardly Lion fall asleep after the Wicked Witch of the West casts a spell of poppies, but Glinda makes it snow and saves the day.

Confessions of an Opium Eater **(1962):** Based on *Confessions of an English Opium-Eater*, Thomas De Quincey's 1821 first-person account of his addiction to laudanum (an early opiate combined with alcohol), the screen adaptation stars Vincent Price and is set in San Francisco, where De Quincey frequents opium dens and fights tong wars in Chinatown.

Once Upon a Time in America **(1984):** Sergio Leone's nearly four-hour gangster epic begins with Noodles (Robert De Niro) in an opium den. He inhales mightily from a long pipe, then barely escapes as police arrive. Flashing back to the twenties and ahead to the sixties, Noodles is a survivor of the mob wars.

Pandaemonium **(2000):** Suffering from a toothache, nineteenth-century British poet Samuel Taylor Coleridge (Linus Roache) discovers the healing powers of laudanum, then goes on to write his most famous works, "The Rime of the Ancient Mariner" and "Kubla Khan."

From Hell **(2001):** Johnny Depp stars as Inspector Abberline in this Hughes Brothers production. While he attempts to solve the Jack the Ripper crime spree that has late nineteenth-century London in a panic, he resorts to opium and absinthe in order to enhance his unusual psychic powers.

Apocalypse Now Redux **(2001):** Deleted from the original film, Willard (Martin Sheen) shares an opium pipe and bed with Roxanne (Aurora Clément) at the French plantation.

Menace II Society (1993)

🌿 🌿 🌿 ◡ Two years after John Singleton's ground-breaking *Boyz N the Hood*, Albert and Allen Hughes offered a similar story line about gangsta life in Los Angeles's hard-scrabble neighborhoods. The Hughes brothers provide more historical context than Singleton, starting with black-and-white footage of the 1965 Watts riots. Over a decade later, drugs flow freely at a house party where Tat (Samuel L. Jackson) smokes a joint and his wife Karen (Khandi Alexander) shoots up in front of five-year-old Caine. "My father sold dope and my mother was a heroin addict," he explains in a voice-over. The Hughes take a cue from *GoodFellas* when Tat shoots a fellow card player for no particular reason. Cut to 1993 and now Caine (Tyrin Turner) has grown up to be a cold-hearted drug dealer like his dad. He pals around with fun-loving pot-head O-Dog (Larenz Tate), but Caine has a major chip on his shoulder. Another one of his friends, Pernell (Glenn Plummer), is doing time, and he looks after Pernell's wife, Ronnie (Jada Pinkett Smith), and son. Eventually they get involved and Ronnie asks Caine to go away with them to Atlanta. It's a familiar plot device: the good woman trying to change the hardened criminal. But Caine's not ready to leave his business, such as it is, or his friends behind. And after one too many drive-bys, shoot-outs, and fistfights, Caine's enemies finally catch up with him. Despite Turner's wooden performance, this is a raw and powerful film about the mean streets of Compton.

> "I learned how to make drugs when I was little—heroin, cocaine, all of it. My dad taught me. That was the only thing he taught me before he was killed."
>
> **—Caine**

Me Without You (2001)

🌿 🌿 🌿 ◡ It's 1970s London, and polar opposite preteens Holly (Michelle Williams) and Marina (Anna Friel) have decided to be best friends for life. Bookish Holly comes from a protective and nurturing Jewish family while free-spirited Marina is from a broken home with a pill-popping mother and an absent father. An alcohol and drug-fueled night sparks a connection between Holly and Marina's older brother Nat (Oliver Milburn), and as the years go by, the girls experience the pains and pleasures of growing up: drugs, booze, sex, rock-and-roll, college, heartbreak, and loss. When their lives finally go in different directions, they both have to learn how to let go of the past and grow up. Holly and Marina experiment and make the usual teenage mistakes while decked out in seventies and eighties duds. Anyone who's ever had a best friend will relate to the ups and downs of their tumultuous relationship.

Marina: "You should dye your hair, Holly, you look like a virgin."

Holly: "I am a virgin."

Marina: "But you don't need to broadcast it."

Midnight Cowboy (1969)

🌿 🌿 🌿 🌿 Originally rated X, John Schlesinger's gritty New York film won Best Picture and Director Oscars. Dim-witted Texan Joe Buck (Jon Voight) moves to New York in hopes of becoming a high-end stud for hire. Hopelessly out of his element, he meets crippled and disheveled street hustler Ratso Rizzo (Dustin Hoffman), who, after delivering his famous "I'm walkin' here!" line, easily cons him out of twenty dollars. Despite this unsettling start, Joe moves into Ratso's squat, where they pool their resources and become partners in crime. Ratso is in pretty bad shape—he's barely able to walk and coughs constantly—and the last thing bicurious

Joe expects is to care so deeply. Hailed as a cinéma vérité masterpiece, Schlesinger's movie expertly projects the grime of New York City and all of its lost souls. Whether you've only visited, or lived there forever, it's like seeing Manhattan with fresh eyes— much like Joe and Ratso's psychedelic experience at a Factory-like party-cum-orgy (featuring cameos by real-life Andy Warhol disciples) where Joe gets high for the first time, then downs a mysterious pill and proceeds to trip his face off.

Joe Buck: "I only get carsick on boats."

Midnight Express (1978)

🍸🍷 ✂️ 💉 👀

🌿🌿🌿🌿🌿 The harrowing saga of Billy Hayes and the book and movie about his experience spending five years in a Turkish prison for smuggling two kilos of hash is significant on a number of levels: It was the first movie to deal with drug smuggling—many have followed, such as *Brokedown Palace* and *Return to Paradise*—and it introduced Oliver Stone, who wrote the screenplay based on Hayes's book. Hayes (Brad Davis) gets busted at Istanbul's Atatürk Airport in 1970 and the nightmare begins. Virtually the entire film is set in a large, run-down prison housing hundreds of men. Hayes is beaten and quickly befriended by fellow American Jimmy (Randy Quaid), Englishman Max (John Hurt),

and Swede Erich (Norbert Weisser). At first Hayes is given a four-year sentence, but that's overruled and another twenty-five years are tacked on. "I know you kids smoke that stuff and we drink booze," Billy's dad says during a painful visit to the jail, "but taking it across the border, that's stupid." After Erich is released, the three amigos plan an escape. They're caught and punished, but by 1975 Hayes ultimately figures another way out. Alan Parker's direction and Stone's script go beyond prison movie clichés (though there is one tender almost-gay scene between Billy and Erich). While Davis, whose resemblance to Brad Pitt is uncanny, would never have another major lead role, the guitar-playing Quaid ("got the ol' Istanbul blues") and quivering junkie Hurt would star in many movies to come.

Max: "The best thing to do is get your ass out of here. Catch the Midnight Express. It's a prison word for escape, but it doesn't stop around here."

Milk (2008)

✏️ 🍸🍷 ✂️

🌿🌿🌿🌿 Sean Penn's masterful performance as Harvey Milk in Gus Van Sant's unsentimental biopic earned him a much-deserved Oscar. Milk, the first "out of the closet" politician elected to office in America in the seventies, epitomized the San Francisco scene, which embraced gay rights, marijuana reform, and other liberal causes. The film fleetingly depicts cannabis activist Dennis Peron (Ted Jan Roberts), the pot dealer friend of Milk's who, in real life, would spearhead San Francisco and California's medical-marijuana laws in the nineties. Milk smokes with lover Scott (James Franco), but as his political aspirations grow, he chops off his ponytail and instructs Scott, "Worry about gun control, not marijuana control." Milk's a charismatic leader and speaker, whose opening line is "My name is Harvey Milk and I'm here to recruit you!" After winning a seat on the Board of Supervisors, Milk meets his true adversary, fellow Supervisor Dan White (Josh Brolin), who's extremely uptight and has some screws loose. White ultimately assassinates Milk and Mayor George Moscone (Victor Garber) in one of the worst moments in American political history. Nevertheless, Milk's spirit lives on in the ongoing campaign to secure gay rights and in this important film.

Scott to Harvey: "I bought an ounce of pot."

Moneytree, The (1992)

The Dienstag brothers will never be confused with the Coen brothers, but they are somewhat known for their little marijuana movie that could. Alan Dienstag directs and Christopher Dienstag plays the lead, David, a Northern California pot grower who's in the middle of cultivating a crop. His girlfriend, Erica (Monica Caldwell), doesn't approve and another friend, Pasquel (Carlos Deloche), tries to draw him into a coke deal that turns deadly. While the acting, script, and production are amateurish, the buds are top notch and David's paranoia is very real. When a cop stops his pickup truck packing thirty pounds of freshly dried cannabis flowers under the tarp, but then lets him go, you'll breathe a sigh of relief.

> "You know why marijuana's illegal? Because they can't control it and they can't get their cut."
>
> **—David**

My Own Private Idaho (1991)

Director Gus Van Sant has made his share of strange movies (Last Days, Gerry), but this is his strangest. Two years prior to his death, River Phoenix starred as a narcoleptic male prostitute, Mike, who is troubled by his mysterious Idaho upbringing. The movie begins with Mike lying in the middle of a road in Big Sky Country, asleep. We next find him giving a hand job to an older john in Seattle.

Most of the action takes place in Portland, where Mike and Scott (Keanu Reeves) hustle gay men and hang out with their guru Bob (William Rickert), an overweight blowhard who surrounds himself with teenaged acolytes (including Budd, played by Red Hot Chili Peppers' Flea). Besides constantly passing out, Mike is an ill-defined character, vacant and devoid of personality. He visits his brother Richard (James Russo), who may actually be his father. When Mike and Scott fly to Italy to find Mike's mom, she's not there, and Scott dumps Mike for Carmella (Chiara Caselli), who returns with him to the States. Scott's family is rich and he decides to stop slumming when he turns twenty-one. This bums out Mike and Bob ("the great psychedelic Popeye"); Bob, in fact, dies upon learning of Scott's conversion and is ceremoniously remembered by his kids at the local cemetery. Back on the road in Idaho, Mike hits the pavement once again, forever dazed and confused. Seventeen years later, Van Sant, who is gay, made an infinitely better movie about homosexuality—Milk.

Scott to Bob: "I don't know you, old man, please leave me alone . . . There was a time when I had the need to learn from you, my former and psychedelic teacher."

Naked Lunch (1991)

🍸 💉 🥄 ⚗️ 💉

🍁 🍁 🍁 Bizzare and surreal, David Cronenberg's adaptation of William S. Burroughs's counterculture classic tells the story of an exterminator (Peter Weller) who accidentally kills his wife (Judy Davis), and then becomes wrapped up in international, noir-ish intrigue when his typewriter turns into a bug and starts giving him instructions about how to deal with a criminal plot that may or may not just be drug-induced hallucinations. The plot's secondary, though, to the weirdness: Depending on how you look at it, the movie's about addiction, homosexuality, writer's block, or some combination of the above. Cronenberg creates a foggy dreamscape, with actors occasionally drifting in and out of roles and grotesque creatures who speak (and spit) out of every orifice. Watching this movie on acid is not recommended.

Bill Lee: "Did I ever tell you about the man who taught his asshole to talk?"

New Jack City (1991)

🍸 💉 🥄

🍁 🍁 🍁 🍁 Mario Van Peebles's most passionate directorial effort wasn't just a maddening fictionalization of the Reagan era crack epidemic in New York. It opened the door for a new wave of blaxploitation that, for a large part of the nineties, took over the big screen and created awareness about downtrodden ghetto life. But among all those titles during that period (notably Boyz N the Hood, Menace II Society, and Juice), the ruthless edge of the city slums was depicted best in the New York–set New Jack City. Ruthless dope lord Nino Brown (Wesley Snipes) may epitomize urban villainy, but the movie is really about Pookie (Chris Rock)—a junkie who tries to clean his act up and redeem himself by stool-pigeoning for the cops, but whose love for the glass pipe brings him down in the end.

Pookie: "They call it the Enterprise Room, man, because it's for people who wanna be beamed up to Scotty."

North Dallas Forty (1979)

✒️ 🍸 💉 💊 👀

🍁 🍁 🍁 🍁 Phil Elliot (Nick Nolte) has great hands. He catches footballs by day and parties hard at night. When Phil runs afoul of the strict team rules, he's the target of an internal league investigation. But that doesn't stop North Dallas (based on the Cowboys) from shooting him up with cortisone and B-12 to make the daily pains of playing football go away. Phil grunts and groans his way though the film, and smokes a lot of joints to help numb his aching legs. But mostly he takes pills, lots of them, chased with beer and cigarettes. Despite making a key touchdown catch in the championship game (though North Dallas loses), the team suspends Phil for using illegal drugs. "For smoking grass?" he asks incredulously. "If you nailed all the ballplayers who smoke grass you wouldn't even be able to field a punt-return team." Based on Pete Gent's novel, directed by Ted Kotchkoff (The Apprenticeship of Duddy Kravitz), and costarring Mac Davis as pot-smoking quarterback Seth Maxwell, this is arguably the best football movie ever made.

Phil: "If you last long enough, you realize the only way to survive is the pills and the shot."

Notorious (2009)

✒️ 🍸 🥄

🍁 🍁 🍁 🍁 Based on the true-life story of rapper Christopher Wallace, a.k.a. Notorious B.I.G., beginning in Brooklyn circa 1983, young Christopher (Wallace's actual son, Christopher Jordan Wallace) experiences his first taste of heartbreak and hustle, two common themes of his music. He smokes blunts and deals crack, but eventually gets caught. Behind bars, he begins to rap and write, filling journals and his walls with lyrics, waiting to unleash them on the world as soon as he's free. With new focus and a will to succeed, Biggie meets hip-hop entrepreneur Sean "Puffy" Combs (Derek Luke), who takes his career to the next level. As Biggie blows up, beefs develop and the media game of East vs. West starts to drag him down. In addition, he's also dealing with his two girlfriends: Lil' Kim (Naturi Naughton) and Faith Evans (Antonique Smith). The rise of this hip-hop icon is portrayed masterfully by newcomer Jamal Woolard and the film is full of amazing live performances. After he's gunned down at the Peterson Automotive Museum in Los Angeles, what resonates is the actual footage of B.I.G.'s funeral procession driving through Brooklyn and people partying in the streets to his anthem, "Big Poppa."

Outsiders, The (1983)

Adapted from the 1967 novel of the same name, directed by Francis Ford Coppola and starring an A-list ensemble cast that boasts Matt Dillon, Patrick Swayze, Rob Lowe, Tom Cruise, and Diane Lane, this classic teenage tale pitting the haves against the have-nots remains undeniably timeless. C. Thomas Howell plays Ponyboy Curtis, the exceptionally bright youngest brother of orphaned greasers Darryl (Swayze) and Sodapop (Lowe). His best friend Johnny (Ralph Macchio) also comes from a dysfunctional family, and relies on his greaser mentor Dallas (Dillon) to look out for him. In their jeans and ratty T-shirts, and with slicked-back hair, they're perpetually feuding with the Socs (pronounced so-shez), rich kids who drive Mustangs and wear fancy clothes. When a fight turns fatal, Ponyboy and Johnny, with Dallas's guidance, go into hiding, and, in the process, face adulthood on their own. Beautifully shot in vivid shades of blue and gold and faithful to the book in conveying the emotion and essence of these rich characters, this was Rebel Without a Cause for a new generation.

Over the Edge (1979)

Notable for featuring Matt Dillon in his first major movie role (as Richie), this B-grade disaffected suburban youth exploitation flick centers on a group of kids and their rec center in a wasteland of half-finished condos. With nowhere to go and nothing to do, they get high, vandalize whatever's around them, and taunt the police. It all leads to a night of rioting where the kids form a mob and padlock the doors of the middle school while their parents and the police are having a meeting about "youth discipline." The kids set fire to most of the parking lot, leading to the final shot of a girl waving to a boy as he's hauled away in a school bus full of juvies.

Between tracks by Cheap Trick, the Ramones, and Jimi Hendrix, the kids wander aimlessly through the flatlands looking for kicks. Plenty of joints are smoked, and pot leaves are drawn on school blackboards and proudly displayed on belt buckles and T-shirts. Kids take acid in art class, continually fighting boredom by getting stoned. But in the end, this film isn't about the dangers of drugs. It's the out-of-touch parents and the cops who are the villains here.

Richie: "I only got one law—that's any kid that tells on another kid is a dead kid."

Panic in Needle Park, The (1971)

Just a year before he electrified audiences as reluctant gangster Michael Corleone in The Godfather, Al Pacino portrayed a New York junkie in this breakout screen role. Bobby is the king of Needle Park, a slice of upper Manhattan where dealers and dope fiends congregate. He meets Helen (Kitty Winn), an out-of-towner from Indiana without a habit. It doesn't take long for her to get hooked and start turning tricks. Bobby's a world-class street hustler—he'll steal anything that's not nailed down, and brags, "I've been in jail eight times." Narc Hotch (Alan Vint) is on to Bobby and Helen and squeezes Helen to snitch Bobby out. Director Jerry Schatzberg—working with a script by Joan Didion and John Gregory Dunne (based on James Mills's book)—

"I'm a dope addict. I'm a sex-crazed dope fiend."

—Bobby

captures character-filled New York at its seediest. While Pacino would go on to a brilliant career, Winn, who holds her own as a sensitive woman trying to cope in the concrete jungle, appeared in both *Exorcist* movies before falling off the movie map.

Performance (1970)

The Rolling Stones's Mick Jagger made his acting debut in this psychedelic flick shot at the glorious end of London's swinging sixties. Playing a pop-star-turned-artist, the heavily painted, lipstick-wearing Turner is all about sex, drugs, and rock-and-roll. But while living the ultimate bohemian lifestyle in a basement apartment he shares with two female lovers, Pherber (Anita Pallenberg) and Lucy (Michèle Breton), Turner's world of love and peace is shattered when Chas (James Fox), the muscle man (or "performer") for a local gang, comes to crash. The two don't mesh at first, but when drugs enter the picture—in the form of magic mushrooms that grow in the yard—Chas is exposed to a world of brilliant textures, sounds, and threesomes (a common occurrence for Turner and the ladies). At one point, Turner brandishes a fluorescent tube light saber-style, and just as his trip is peaking, he experiments with a brand-new high-tech gadget called the synthesizer. Regarded as a classic of British cinema, the years have been kind to *Performance*, which is often hailed for its innovations in directing (Donald Cammell and Nicolas Roeg) and credited as an influence on the MTV style and directors like Quentin Tarantino and Guy Ritchie. And while some may find the first half hard to follow, there's no denying the hotness of the ménage á trois in the opening scene. That sex is on fire.

Chas: "I need a bohemian atmosphere."

Platoon (1986)

Oliver Stone's "sequel" to *Apocalypse Now* finds Charlie Sheen (Chris) in Vietnam just as his father, Martin (as Captain Willard), was in Francis Ford Coppola's war epic seven years earlier. It even features similar voice-overs and ominous orchestral music. But where Coppola's crew journeys upriver and only occasionally encounters enemy fire, Stone's platoon is mired in the rain and muck of the jungle, fighting Vietcong at every turn. Upon Chris's arrival, he's immediately initiated with a shotgun hit of Southeast Asian weed. "Put your mouth on this," Sergeant Elias (Willem Dafoe) orders, as he hits a joint and blows the smoke through the rifle chamber to Chris at the other end. This platoon sure knows how to party, but soon they split ranks when Elias and fellow sergeant Barnes (Tom Berenger) come to blows over how to extract information from the enemy. An anything-goes sadist, Barnes kills for the sake of killing, while the pot-smoking Elias is the platoon's conscience. Chris sides with Elias and ultimately avenges his death after an all-night battle that claims hundreds of soldiers on both sides. Look for Kevin Dillon, John C. McGinley, Keith David, and Johnny Depp in early roles (Depp's is a super-brief cameo). Stone, who served in Vietnam, drops you right into the foxhole. The cacophony of grenades, bombs, and syncopated rifle fire is extremely realistic, as are the blood, limbs, and lives the soldiers sacrifice in a losing effort. *Platoon* deservedly received eight Oscar nominations, winning four (for Best Picture, Director, Film Editing, and Sound).

Barnes: "Y'all know about killin'? Well, I'd like to hear about it, potheads. You smoke this shit to escape from reality. I don't need this shit. I am reality."

🎸 FAR-OUT ACID FLICKS 🎸

LSD took underground cinema by storm in the sixties. Tune in, turn on, and drop out while watching these trippy mind-benders.

Hallucination Generation (1966): Director Edward Mann put all the bad acid film clichés in one basket. There's a beatnik love shack run by a weird older dude (George Montgomery), a hot German chick, and a trust fund San Francisco hipster expatriate (the movie's set in Spain); violence; domestic abuse; homophobia; sex; drug use; and the requisite LSD trip-out scene. Though much of the script is delivered in the pidgin English of the hot German and assorted Spanish extras, Montgomery gets the line of a lifetime at the film's finale when he utters sadly, "This universe is a jawbreaker, a sourball, lemon-flavored, round and hard." Suck on that, stoners!

The Trip (1967): B-movie maestro Roger Corman saw dollar signs in the burgeoning youth freak-out of the late sixties and acted accordingly. Enlisting a cast and crew of Hollywood weirdos who would eventually evolve into the new generation's warped version of the Rat Pack, *The Trip* is cheap, silly, and totally of the era. In the film, written by Jack Nicholson, Peter Fonda plays Paul Groves, an uptight ad exec set (somewhat) free by his first LSD experience. Bruce Dern (John) guides him along, and Dennis Hopper (Max) runs the hippie house where the slow-paced action takes place.

Psych-Out (1968): Much of the same stony crew that populates *The Trip* reappears here, including Susan Strasberg as deaf runaway Jenny. Searching for her long-lost brother (Bruce Dern as the freaked-out, monosyllabic Seeker) in San Francisco's Haight-Ashbury, Jenny's taken under the wing of Jack Nicholson's Stoney, who sports a ponytail, smokes pot, and plays guitar in a band called Mumblin' Jim.

Head (1968): Co-written by Jack Nicholson, helmed by Bob Rafelson (*Five Easy Pieces*), and starring the Monkees (by then eager to shed their G-rated image), this is one of the best of the American-made acid movies. With cameos from a slew of the era's movers and shakers including (the late) Dennis Hopper, Teri Garr, and Frank Zappa, *Head* is a truthful but abstract take on the opening of the doors of perception.

Alice in Acidland (1968): Lewis Carroll's already tripped-out childhood classic slips down a rabbit hole that leads to sex, drugs, and rock-and-roll. Alice (Colleen Murphy) is not a wee Victorian girl, but rather a super hot sixties coed who smokes her first spliff and magically enters a wonderland of casual lesbian encounters, frequent orgiastic gatherings, and finally, behind the last door, a wild LSD journey, when the film transforms from black-and-white into utterly whacked-out animated color. Look out for the only "super giant dancing boobies" scene in the history of cinema.

The Acid Eaters (1968): This film takes the acid/stoner genre and dials it up to eleven. The loosely coherent narrative follows a bunch of office nerds who throw off their white collars after work on Fridays and metamorphose into a gang of insane bohemians (but just for the weekend). Part biker flick, part soft-core sexploitation romp, *The Acid Eaters* combines crime, death, and high-speed motorcycle antics with casual marijuana use and body painting. The weirdness includes a subplot about Satan and a twenty-foot-high pyramid of acid-dosed sugar cubes, as well as a quicksand death and zombielike resurrection courtesy of Native American magic.

The Grasshopper (1970): Apparently Women's Lib once meant that if you lost interest in your boring bank job and beau, you could head to Vegas, take a bunch of mescaline, and eventually become a high-priced hooker. Jacqueline Bisset (as Christine) is at the peak of her hotness here, and for some that might be enough to make this pseudofeminist classic (directed by Jerry Paris of *The Dick Van Dyke Show*) worth the watch. Bisset exudes both naïveté and badassness as her character embarks on a journey that includes prostitution, drug abuse, and a marriage to Tommy Marcott, a former football star played by Jim Brown.

The Last Movie (1971): Dennis Hopper's follow-up to *Easy Rider* is either masterful or masturbatory, depending on whom you ask. Hopper co-writes, directs, and stars as stuntman Kansas working a low-budget Western in Peru. When the crew leaves, Kansas remains, and he watches as Hollywood's violent residue eats away at the purity of the local Indians. Hopper's brilliance borders on madness, and you can't deny the power of the film's imagery, symbolism, and soundtrack. Joined by Kris Kristofferson, Peter Fonda, and Hopper's then-girlfriend Michelle Phillips, the film was considered a fiasco and grounded Hopper's career until his comeback in *Apocalypse Now*.

Zachariah (1971): After killing a man in a saloon, hippie gunfighter Zachariah (John Rubenstein) becomes an outlaw. Joined by Country Joe & the Fish (dubbed the Crackers) and a selection of the Firesign Theatre comedians, this cosmic Western was inspired by Hermann Hesse's *Siddhartha*. The film follows the band of Merry Pranksters as they try their best to preach love and peace. The excellent soundtrack features Country Joe, the James Gang (they appear as Job Cain's Band), and Cajun fiddler Doug Kershaw.

The Holy Mountain (1973): Hot on the heels of his psychedelic Western *El Topo*, Alejandro Jodorowsky found himself under the warm wing of none other than John Lennon. A huge fan of the Chilean filmmaker's work, Lennon and his manager Allen Klein funded this surrealistic epic. A visually stunning kaleidoscope of color, costumes, and highly stylized set pieces, Jodorowsky re-creates a kind of divine LSD-induced journey.

Poetic Justice (1993)

🍁 🍁 It's South Central L.A. in 1993 and poet/hairstylist Justice (Janet Jackson) watches as her boyfriend gets killed at the drive-in movie theater. Lucky (Tupac Shakur), her seemingly polar opposite, is fed up with the routine and tired of dead-end games. After Lesha (Regina King) invites Justice on a road trip/blind date, Justice goes out on a limb and tries something new. That blind date is Lucky. After the two stubborn poets start to get along, they make their way to Oakland so Lucky can meet his cousin to discuss getting his recording career in gear. But by the time they get there, Lucky's cousin has been shot to death. Lucky and Justice make out, fight . . . and make up. Director John Singleton (*Boyz N The Hood*) is not at his best here and Jackson deservedly earned a Razzie Award for her laughable performance. But it's worth watching for Tupac.

Postcards from the Edge (1990)

🍁 🍁 Suzanne Vale (Meryl Streep) is the 1990 equivalent of Lindsay Lohan—an actress who's having a hard time getting insured to work on movie sets. After a night of heavy partying and pill-popping lands her in the hospital, she's forced to go to rehab and then to live with her overbearing mother, famous entertainer (and alcoholic) Doris Mann (Shirley MacLaine). Estrogen-fueled quarrels ensue, and Suzanne's fling with pot-smoker Jack (Dennis Quaid) ends badly, but it's all part of her struggle for sobriety. With a screenplay written by Carrie Fisher (her-

> "How are you doing on the drugs?
>
> —Doctor Frankenthal
>
> "Oh, I wanna do them all the time."
>
> —Suzanne

self a recovering addict and the daughter of Debbie Reynolds), the story screams semi-autobiographical, however unlikely it might be that someone's life is so ridiculously sappy. But what is realistic about *Postcards* is its behind-the-scenes look at the magic (and often misery) of moviemaking, featuring some familiar faces: Rob Reiner, Annette Bening, and Gene Hackman among them. Without all that talent, the film would surely be relegated to after-school special status.

Psych-Out (1968)

🍁 🍁 🍁 With the hippie movement in full flower, Richard Rush (*Hells Angels on Wheels*) left the biker scene behind for this psychedelic flick

set in San Francisco's Haight-Ashbury, starring Jack Nicholson, Bruce Dern, Dean Stockwell, and Susan Strasberg. Stoney (Nicholson) plays guitar in Mumblin' Jim, a blues-rock band on the rise. He lives in a huge Victorian house/crash pad decorated with every imaginable black-light poster. Deaf runaway Jenny (Strasberg) arrives in town looking for her brother, Steve (a.k.a. The Seeker, played by Dern in a long wig and beard). Though Stoney's into free love, he digs Jenny, who gets a little too stoned on STP (described knowingly as LSD, coke, and meth) at one point. The archetypal Nicholson character begins to take shape here—he's curt and insensitive but at the same time caring. In his next films, Nicholson would play jovial alcoholic George in *Easy Rider* and moody drifter Bob in *Five Easy Pieces*. It's fun to watch him here jamming like Hendrix and smoking joints with carefree abandon. Live performances by the Strawberry Alarm Clock ("Incense and Peppermints") and the Seeds add authenticity, and the visuals in this Dick Clark–produced period piece are positively groovy, baby.

Stoney: "Hey man, it's not money, it's life . . . don't need acid to see that. All you gotta do is know where your head is at."

Pusher Trilogy (1996, 2004, 2005)

🌿 🌿 🌿 🌿 Denmark's answer to Quentin Tarantino, Nicholas Winding Refn leaves no stoner unturned in his vivid look at Copenhagen's druggy underground. The three movies each focus on one major deal and the violent repercussions when the deals go bad. In the first film, *Pusher*, Frank (Kim Bodnia) dumps seven ounces of heroin in a lake rather than get busted, and spends the rest of the movie hustling and fighting his way out of imminent danger. But it's his girlfriend Vic (Laura Drasbæk) who makes the biggest score. In *Pusher II*, Frank's friend Tonny (Mads Mikkelsen) is just out of jail and looking for trouble. He joins a car-stealing ring, regularly snorts coke, and has to deal with Charlotte (Anne Sørensen), who claims to have had his child while he was in the pen. Charlotte and her best friend Gry (Maria Erwolter) snort lines and smoke large spliffs while berating Tonny, whose bud "Kurt the Cunt" (Kurt Nielsen) gets into the same sort of jam as Frank when he unnecessarily flushes a large stash of dope that doesn't belong to him. (Clearly, Refn's characters are not too smart.) Tonny takes his anger out on his father in a brutal act of patricide. In *Pusher III*, Milo (Zlatko Buric)—the dealer who bullied Frank in Part 1—returns nine years later and still has a heroin habit the size of his large frame and ego. Threatened by younger dealers, Milo sells Ecstasy ("new generation, new market") instead of dope and it costs him when the pills he receives are fake. The bloodletting in this episode pays homage to *Pulp Fiction*, with Radovan (Slavko Labovic) doing his best Harvey Keitel imitation. Refn's vérité-style direction brings you deep inside his characters' lives, and even if there is very little

to redeem them, you marvel at their abilities to survive the most untenable situations.

Charlotte to Tonny: "First you try to kill me and then you ruin our high."

Ray (2004)

🌿 🌿 🌿 🌙 Jamie Foxx won an Oscar for his portrayal of the legendary soul man, released within months of Ray Charles's death, and chronicling Charles's rags-to-riches story from childhood to the top of the charts. The film delves into Ray's drug use, which begins innocently enough with a joint of "gage" to ease his pre-show nerves— "Hold it in, it'll calm you down," instructs Oberon (*Harry Potter*'s Warwick Davis)—but evolves into a full-blown heroin addiction. His best work happens to come during those drug-addled years, when Charles, who went blind at the age of seven, gets his first taste of independence and success. His brand of gospel married with rock-and-roll goes on to sell millions of records and win countless awards, while his home life also flourishes. But being married to the churchgoing Bea (Kerry Washington) and father to their two sons does little to curb Charles's penchant for cheating (he chooses his hookups with a feel of the wrist). Only after a drug bust, the threat of divorce, and a rehab stint is he able to clean up his act and reflect on a life of accomplishment—not the least of which involved speaking out against the Jim Crow laws of a segregated South, an act of defiance that resulted in Georgia's banning him from performing in the state. But where the script is weak at points, the music more than makes up for it—and you can thank the real Ray for that.

Oberon: "Here, smoke some of this."

Ray: "This ain't no tobacco, man!"

Reefer Madness (1936)

Reefer Madness's release—a year before marijuana was prohibited—is clear enough evidence that the film was part and parcel of the federal government's campaign to ban cannabis in America. Its ludicrous premise—that marijuana leads to "acts of shocking violence ending in incurable insanity"—remains the basis for laws that are still on the books more than seven decades later.

Directed by Louis J. Gasnier and also named "Teach Your Children," Reefer Madness became an immediate cult classic and midnight-movie favorite when New Line Cinema rescued it from the Library of Congress and released it in the early seventies (see "The True Story of Reefer Madness" on the next page). Due to its grainy visuals, campy language, and risqué content, audiences howled with "sudden, violent uncontrollable laughter," just as the narrator Dr. Alfred Carroll (Josef Forte) warns is a consequence of this "unspeakable scourge" and "ghastly menace" in the prologue.

The film begins documentary-style with cool footage of pot plants growing in a vacant lot in Brooklyn. We learn that the "dried leaves and berries are ground up and made into cigarettes by a simple hand machine." This may be the first real representation of marijuana in the movies. The main story is about a group of clean-cut high school students who get drawn into smoking marijuana by adults who prey on them. At the malt shop, Hot Fingers Pirelli plays stride piano, then sneaks into a closet and lights up a "reefer"—also an on-screen first. Some of the kids head over to a tea pad run by Mae (Thelma White) and Jack (Carleton Young). Bill (Kenneth Craig) and Jimmy (Warren McCollum) are quickly seduced by the party atmosphere and smoke joints offered to them. While Bill gets cozy with an older woman, Blanche (Lillian Miles), Jimmy drives Jack to his supplier. Hopped up on pot ("I'm red hot!"), Jimmy speeds and runs over an elderly pedestrian on the drive back. This is the first truly absurd moment in the film (besides the prologue). Hooked on reefers, Bill falls for Blanche, dumps his girl Mary (Dorothy Short), and starts messing up in school. When Mary finds him at Mae's, raging pothead Ralph (Dave O'Brian) gets Mary stoned and makes his move on her. Bill rescues Mary, but Jack attacks him with his gun butt and in the struggle the gun goes off, hitting Mary. Next thing the cops bust up the tea pad and arrest Bill (he was set up by Jack), who stands trial and is found guilty. Distraught, Blanche and Ralph smoke joints as she plays the piano—"faster, faster, play faster," the increasingly deranged Ralph implores. Finally, Blanche spills the beans, takes the rap for the murder (even though it was Jack who accidentally shot Mary) and rather than go to jail, jumps out a window to her death. Well, that'll show you how marijuana leads to nothing but death and degradation. Reefer Madness is so funny we forgot to laugh.

Mae to Bill: "If you want a good smoke, try one of these."

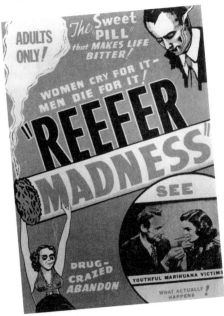

☘ THE TRUE STORY OF REEFER MADNESS ☘

By Keith Stroup

In the seventy-plus years since its release, *Reefer Madness* went from anti-pot propaganda to hilarious campus classic, thanks in part to the man who lifted the film out of obscurity, NORML founder Keith Stroup. Here, he explains his discovery.

Wikipedia's claim that I was the individual responsible for discovering and disseminating the 1936 movie *Reefer Madness* to the world in the 1970s is a bit of a stretch. I did use the film as part of my college lecture program through most of that decade, but it was actually discovered in the archives of the Library of Congress by some unnamed person at a lecture bureau I had begun to use back then.

It was in NORML's very early years, in 1971 and 1972, when I began to get a few inquiries from college lecture bureaus asking if we were interested in speaking to their students about NORML and what we were trying to achieve. Some of those calls came from New Line Productions, then a small lecture agency based in New York that was focusing on the campus market and looking for what might be called "fringe" speakers—those whose messages may have been a bit out of the mainstream and thus appealing to many college audiences.

I accepted a few of these early gigs, and I quickly realized that while my principal motivation was to inform the students, it was far more important that I develop a standard stump speech designed to entertain a college crowd. That meant keeping my presentation under an hour, which was about the upper end of their attention span.

At one of these early bookings, New Line marketed my lecture as part of an evening that also included a showing of the old anti-marijuana propaganda film *Reefer Madness*. The movie presented the ultimate stereotype: an overwrought, hysterical story line in which the principal character smokes a marijuana cigarette and immediately goes crazy, raping and killing anyone within reach. It was not a good movie by any standards, but the absurdity of it all touched a nerve with the students, and it made the program campy and undeniably entertaining. But the original version was far too long at nearly an hour and a half, and it became boring after about thirty minutes. What's more, the combination of my lecture and a few questions, followed by the movie, made for just too long a night to keep the audience's attention.

I asked New Line about the movie, and they advised me that they had obtained a copy of it from the Library of Congress, as the copyright had been allowed to lapse and thus *Reefer Madness* was in the public domain and available to anyone who bothered to look for it.

I promptly obtained a copy from the Library of Congress, sent it to my old friend Terry Ingram, a filmmaker and commercial producer living in Texas, and he edited the movie down to about forty minutes. For the next several years, New Line marketed my NORML lecture with this abbreviated version of *Reefer Madness* to scores of colleges across the country, and it became a wonderful way for us both to raise some significant funding for the organization and to get the word out about NORML and our efforts to legalize marijuana in America.

So while I accept some credit for recognizing the value of the film to NORML, and for popularizing the movie as a campy college phenomenon during the seventies, I was not the one who actually discovered it. Sorry, Wikipedia.

Keith Stroup founded NORML in 1970.

Hollywood's treatment of marijuana in the thirties, forties, and fifties was both loathsome and hilarious. Intended as propaganda, the antipot films of the era certainly contributed to the prohibition of the plant in 1937. While *Reefer Madness* is the most famous "marihuana" exploitation film, there were, alas, several others.

Marihuana (1936): Sleazy dealers prey on youngsters, selling them pot, then H (heroin) and C (cocaine)—pure gateway theory propaganda. Burma (Harley Wood) is a good girl until she starts smoking reefers—then it's dancing and laughing, high on "giggle weed." During a risqué nude romp in the ocean, one of the girls drowns. Burma heads downhill fast, shooting up as the cops close in on the dealers. Beware: The current DVD version of this film has many skips and cuts.

Assassin of Youth (1937): As ridiculous as *Reefer Madness*, here a group of friends enjoy smoking pot and dancing. Two cousins battle over an inheritance. Linda (Fay McKenzie) sells joints and tries to set up Joan (Luana Walters) so that Linda will be awarded the money in a court hearing. Meanwhile, a reporter goes undercover and ultimately helps Joan bust the crime ring. Just in case you're not sure which side this film is on, look for the mini-film within the film, *The Marijuana Menace*.

Wild Weed (1949): Sam Newfield's tale of the descent of naïve chorus girl Anne Lester (Lila Leeds) into the seedy world of marijuana is ludicrous by all standards. Turned on by dealer Markey (Alan Baxter), Anne's quickly hooked and soon fired from her job. She begins selling "sticks" (three for five dollars), gets busted, and serves fifty days in jail. The lurid plot includes the suicide of Anne's brother when he learns of her new occupation and a freak-show tour of destitute junkies (what Anne will surely turn into if she keeps smoking pot). Anne becomes an informant and sets up Markey. In an ironic twist of fate, the year before the film's release, Leeds was arrested with actor Robert Mitchum for marijuana possession and spent two months in jail.

High School Confidential! (1958): Tough-guy Tony Baker (Russ Tamblyn) shows up at Santa Bellow High School bent on infiltrating the drug scene, but what no one seems to be able to figure out is he's a narc. Tony hangs with the stoner crowd, but doesn't smoke the stuff—he just wants to sell it. With its preachy antidrug message and hep-cat dialogue, this is *Reefer Madness* meets *Rebel Without a Cause*.

Requiem for a Dream
(2000)

A woman past her prime, Sara Goldfarb (Ellen Burstyn) is addicted to a rainbow-colored collection of diet pills, and dreams of hitting it big on a TV game show. Her son Harry (Jared Leto) and his girlfriend Marion (Jennifer Connelly) have their own drug problems with heroin, which is slowly destroying their relationship and bodies. Harry's dealer-friend Tyrone (Marlon Wayans) finds himself backed into a corner from which he can't escape. They all yearn for better lives, but won't find it at the end of a syringe or the bottom of a pill bottle. Director Darren Aronofsky takes the romance and the allure out of recreational drug use and turns it into a real-life hell for the four main characters. These aren't your everyday stoners or weekend warriors, but victims of the iron clamp of addiction. Burstyn's performance is reason enough to give this difficult-to-watch film a whirl. But beware the brutal climactic scene with Marion and a double dildo.

Return to Paradise (1998)

🖊️ 🔨 🍸 💉 👓

🌿🌿🌿 "We know you Westerners don't understand our attitude toward drugs, but we don't understand yours!" With these words and the pound of a gavel, a Malaysian judge orders American Lewis McBride (Joaquin Phoenix) to be executed by hanging. His crime? Carrying a brick of hash while his two vacation pals, Sheriff (Vince Vaughn) and Tony (David Conrad), headed back to New York blissfully unaware. Fast forward two years and the guys are Lewis's only hope of avoiding the death penalty: They need to take equal responsibility for the hash, which the court dictates is a quantity large enough to be prosecuted for trafficking. Complicating an already delicate situation is one persistent lawyer (Anne Heche) and a nosy reporter (Jada Pinkett Smith) with opposing agendas, but the crux of this story lies in the conflicted mind of Sheriff, who had taunted Lewis for being a "long-haired, Greenpeace, tree-hugger guy," but beneath the surface, admired his buddy's capacity for caring—the irony being that Lewis stuck around to work with animals, only to end up caged like one. Like *Midnight Express* before it, and *Brokedown Palace* after, it's an all-too-common tale that rarely has a happy ending. To that end, Phoenix delivers a gritty, powerful performance, while the posse's carefree days of soaking in the sun and hitting the bamboo bong are short-lived in this big-time bummer.

Sheriff: "The plan was to party till we ran out of cash in Malaysia—it was a paradise of rum, girls, and cheap hash."

River's Edge (1986)

🖊️ 🍸 💉 👓

🌿🌿🌿 Devastatingly dark and bleak, this movie is no John Hughes picnic. When high school student "Samson" John Tollet (Daniel Roebuck) kills his girlfriend Jamie (Danyi Deats) by the banks of the river "for talking shit," he brings his friends to the scene of the crime to show them her body. These kids are so lost, bored, and numb

that their reactions to the murder have to filter up through layers of disbelief and amorality before they act at all. Turning to the cops or parents doesn't seem to be an option for most of them. Speed freak Layne (Crispin Glover at his Slayer-listening, steering wheel–drumming best) seems to view the whole situation as if it's an adventure movie come to life and a test of loyalty. Layne tries his best to bring this little band of friends together to cover up the murder, but he's too wired to make it work. Local weed dealer Feck (Dennis Hopper) hides John from the eventual police heat. Another of Hopper's classic characters, Feck has a fake leg, dates a blow-up doll, killed his real girlfriend years ago, and answers the door with a gun in his hand. Needless to say, Feck and John make lousy roommates. John spirals out of control, and Feck gets caught up in John's death wish. The movie's conscience is stoner Matt (Keanu Reeves), who manages to link enough brain cells together to navigate his broken home life and go to the police, who naturally threaten and berate him. He finds kinship and comfort in Clarissa (Ione Skye) and manages to wait out the carnage in a park, their predawn, post-sex sleeping bag rapture shattered by the sounds of gunshots by the river.

Rockers (1978)

🖊️ 🥄

🌿🌿🌿🌿🌿 The most authentic movie about Jamaica's Rastafarian culture is also Theodorus Bafaloukos's only feature. Leroy "Horsemouth" Wallace plays himself—a reggae drummer who declares war on the local Mafia when his motorcycle is stolen. "Horsey" travels back and forth from Kingston to the nearby countryside, recruiting supporters for his scheme—to rip off two mob-owned homes and a warehouse—and ultimately give the goods back to the people. He's a regular Rasta Robin Hood. Performances by Jacob

Miller and Gregory Isaacs, plenty of spliff and chalice smoking, huge dreads, and patois so thick that subtitles are required make this a must-see for anyone who ever nodded their head to a reggae beat.

Rose, The (1979)

☘ ☘ ☘ From the opening scene in which hungover singer Rose (Bette Midler) emerges from her private plane blinded by sunlight and proceeds to drop her bottle of booze on the tarmac, you know this is going to be one gritty rock-and-roll tale. Rose is like a late seventies version of Janis Joplin: Her voice has got undeniable soul and, despite being labeled a hippie, she has managed to break through to the mainstream and sell millions of albums. But to keep the money train rolling, her tough-love British manager Rudge (Alan Bates) books a demanding tour, and she relies on liquor and drugs to keep going. "People wanna know how I keep this tired, battered old body in shape," Rose says from the stage in one of the early live scenes, "the same way we're goin' to get the whole goddamn world into shape: drugs, sex, and rock-and-roll!" And Rose means it. She parties hard and loves harder, as slow-talking chauffeur Houston Dyer (Frederic Forrest) soon learns. The cowboy hat-wearing Texan joins Rose on the road, where, outside of anything-goes New York City, the two get into a heap of trouble—none worse than in her hometown, where skeletons are buried at every street corner. Rose hopes to make a triumphant return with a sold-out show, but after scoring some "reds" off an old buddy, who also gifts her a bag of heroin, she's a goner. But a svelte Bette singing her ass off in the film's many concert scenes is a sight to see. Warts and all, you've got to love her tour-de-force performance.

> "We don't serve hippies."
>
> —Restaurant Manager

> "That's OK because we don't eat 'em."
>
> —Rose

Rules of Attraction, The (2002)

☘ ☘ ☘ Featuring romantic entanglements of Shakespearean proportions, this movie, directed by Roger Avery and based on Bret Eatson Ellis's novel, focuses on a group of college students who love nothing more than getting trashed every weekend at absurdly named parties (the Pre–Saturday Party Party), then going home with the person of the moment, since no one can be with the one they want. The college pick-up line with the highest success rate seems to be: "I have some (insert drug of choice here) in my dorm room. Want some?" Lauren (Shannyn Sossamon) is saving herself for Victor (Kip Pardue), who has been off slutting it up in Europe. She also dated Paul (Ian Somerhalder), who now spends most nights unsuccessfully trying to pick up closeted males. Paul falls in love with drug-dealer Sean (James Van Der Beek of *Dawson's Creek* fame), who owes his supplier $3,000 and can't seem to get his rich student customers to pay up. This love pentagon is completed when Sean, who is indifferent to Paul's adoration, falls for the virginal and pure Lauren. The feeling is momentarily mutual, but Sean messes that up when he screws her ultra-slutty roommate, Lara (Jessica Biel). Sean's the anti-Dawson: He has sex with passed out girls, slices a man's arm with a chainsaw, punches a girl in the face, and tries to kill himself before faking suicide.

Paul to friends: "He's not ODing. He's a freshman. Freshmen don't OD."

Running on Empty (1988)

☘ ☘ ☘ ☘ This Sidney Lumet–directed drama follows a family that's spent nearly two decades on the run from the Feds. Their crime? An act of political defiance gone wrong. Arthur (Judd Hirsch) and Annie Pope (Christine Lahti) were college radicals opposed to the Vietnam War when, in the early 1970s, they bombed a napalm laboratory and severely injured a janitor working inside what was supposed to be an empty building. Along with their two kids, Danny (River Phoenix) and Harry (Jonas Abry), they've been a fugitive fam on the lam ever since. The clan lands in New Jersey just as Danny is halfway through his senior year of high school, and unlike with most of their pit stops, Danny grows attached to the town, his school, and a music teacher's daughter, Lorna (Martha Plimpton)—the kind of girl who proudly hangs a Bob Marley poster on her bedroom wall. The two fall in love, an old underground pal comes back into the Popes' lives, and things start to unravel. Not the least of their problems is Danny's desire to attend Juilliard. When it's time to leave, Arthur and Annie face the second-biggest moral quandary of their lives—whether to let Danny go and risk never seeing him again. Despite its hippie trappings, there's no pot in *Running on Empty* (which is loosely based on members of real-life radicals the Weather Underground), but the movie makes up for this oversight with a feel-good, grab-your-partner sing-along of James Taylor's "Fire and Rain." The late River Phoenix (brother of Joaquin), who was seventeen at the time and looking ahead to a long, thriving career, received an Academy Award nomination for his supporting role—and well deserved: He could cry like nobody's business.

Running with Scissors (2006)

Yô ✂ 💊

🌿🌿🌿🌿 Colorful, bizarre, and utterly depressing, this wacky flick produced by Brad Pitt's production company and based on Augusten Burroughs's bestselling memoir takes the Oedipus complex to new levels of derangement. Annette Bening plays mom Deirdre, an aspiring poet longing for recognition who, despite being deluged by rejection letters, is absolutely worshipped by her son Augusten (Joseph Cross). After she and her al-coholic husband, Norman (Alec Baldwin), divorce, Deirdre impulsively decides to ship her kid off to live with her therapist Dr. Finch (Brian Cox) and his kooky family—hoarder wife Agnes (Jill Clayburgh) and daughters Natalie (Evan Rachel Wood) and Hope (Gwyneth Paltrow)—in their dilapidated house. While Augusten bonds with Natalie over disco, Hope kills her cat, Agnes suffers silently, and Deirdre's instability worsens. The same can be said for the pill-happy Dr. Finch, who seems to do more harm than good for his patients, which include Augusten's much-older boyfriend Bookman (Joseph Fiennes). The Finch brood has no boundaries when it comes to dinner conversation or bathroom etiquette (the doctor claims he can read hidden messages in his poop), but somehow Augusten manages to make it to the other side, albeit seriously damaged. Pills and cigarettes are the go-to vices here, but this dysfunctional family's world, which brings to mind the freakish *Royal Tenenbaums*, is as stony as it gets, and oh so messy.

Agnes Finch: "What are you all doing in here? You better not be engaging in pot or other activities."

Rush (1991)

✒ Yô ✂ 💊 🔪 💉

🌿🌿🌿🌿 Gregg Allman doesn't say much as club owner Gaines in Lili Fini Zanuck's only feature film, adapted from Kim Wozencraft's book. He's the target of a drug investigation by two narcs—Jim (Jason Patric) and Kristen (Jennifer Jason Leigh). Jim's a hard-core doper, while Kristen's a newbie who wants to prove she can hang with the big boys. Both get high on their own supply, shooting up and snorting lines (Kristen also rolls and smokes a joint). En route to setting up Gaines, they befriend Walker (Max Perlich), who reluctantly agrees to inform on his druggy cohorts. As the film descends into paranoia and violence, Kristen makes a courageous decision that ultimately frees Gaines. While this may have been Patric's best-ever performance, it was one of many daring early roles that established Leigh (*Last Exit to Brooklyn*, *Miami Blues*) as a star on the rise.

Willie Red: "Red gets the best. You kinda feel like you're floating on a cloud of titties."

Salvador (1986)

Former Vietnam War correspondent Richard Boyle (James Woods) and his disc jockey friend Doctor Rock (James Belushi) head south of the border on a reefer-fueled road trip circa 1980–1981. Miserable failures in San Francisco, Rock thinks that he and his fellow sleaze are bound for sun and "great dope" in Guatemala. However, unbeknownst to Rock, the slippery Boyle points them even farther south: into civil war–torn El Salvador, where he can find journalism work. There, Boyle and Rock encounter death squad victims at a mass dumping ground, right-wing paramilitaries, Marxist guerrillas, and Reagan-administration interventionists who purposely overlook human rights violations by the El Salvadoran power elites (including the rape and murder of American aid-worker nuns) in order to advance their Cold War agenda. The daredevil duo smoke "Guatemala Gold" and drink Tic Tack (a fiery Salvadoran 72-proof cane vodka), and Rock spikes an uptight American newscaster's drink with acid. Despite wild fluctuations in tone, the film is comical, melodramatic, and haunting, with Woods (nominated for an Academy Award) at his hyperactive best. It was released the same year as *Platoon*, which would turn director Oliver Stone into a household name.

☙ FIVE MORE BY OLIVER STONE ☙

Beyond Oscar-winning portrayals of Vietnam jungle tokes and stateside cloaks, Oliver Stone delivers political conspiracy like no other (*Nixon*, *W*, *JFK*), not to mention insanity (*Natural Born Killers*), rock debauchery (*The Doors*), and good old-fashioned greed (*Wall Street* and its forthcoming sequel). A self-declared pot smoker, no other director has more counterculture credibility than Stone. Here are five more of his stoniest films.

Midnight Express **(1978):** Stone won a Best Writing Oscar for his screen adaptation of this harrowing true story. American student Billy Hayes gets busted in a Turkish airport with several bricks of hash taped to his body—two kilos in total. He's sentenced to thirty years in prison, serves five (during which Hayes is routinely tortured and violated), and manages to escape. It's among Stone's earliest works and also his darkest.

Scarface **(1983):** Written by Stone and starring Al Pacino as Cuban drug kingpin Tony Montana, Brian De Palma's cocaine opus—based on the 1932 film of the same name—is an ultra-violent, pathological thriller that took eighties excess to new extremes. Greed is the main motivator for this Miami street thug looking to make a name for himself—that and the mound of blow Tony dips his face into.

Platoon **(1986):** The first of Stone's three Vietnam War movies won the Oscar for Best Picture. Internal problems within a platoon splits the group in half, with some siding with stoner Sergeant Elias (Willem Dafoe), who initiates new recruits with shotgun hits, and others backing hard-nosed, take-no-prisoners Sergeant Barnes (Tom Berenger). As it all plays out on the battlefield, it's clear that the enemy is truly within.

The Doors **(1991):** Peyote, acid, coke, pills, smack, and booze—Stone's dramatization of Jim Morrison's life with The Doors is a drug-fueled roller-coaster ride that ends as hazily as it starts. Val Kilmer perfects Morrison's bleary-eyed sway, Kyle MacLachlan means business as keyboardist Ray Manzarek, and Meg Ryan forgoes her good-girl image playing Morrison's sweetheart, Pamela.

Natural Born Killers **(1994):** Casting a psychedelic glow on celebrity serial killers and the tabloid media that sensationalize them, Stone's tripped-out, ultra-violent take on *Bonnie and Clyde* stars Woody Harrelson and Juliette Lewis as indiscriminate murderers Mickey and Mallory, and Robert Downey Jr. as Australian TV host Wayne Gale. It's raw, provocative, and controversial.

Serpico (1973)

🔪 🍽 ✂ 👀

🍁🍁🍁🍁 Sidney Lumet's Oscar-nominated film is based on the true-life account of detective Frank "Paco" Serpico's growing disgust with corruption in the New York City police department. Confronted with lies, shady dealings, and roadblocks at every turn, Serpico (Al Pacino) becomes more and more alienated, forcing him to go outside of the force to get the answers he wants. A free spirit, Serpico lives with his girlfriend Laurie (Barbara Eda-Young) and Saint Bernard in New York's Greenwich Village, where they smoke pot together. Even better is the scene where officers are instructed how to recognize marijuana and narcotic suspects. Serpico laughs knowingly when they're given the actual herb to inspect and roll. The further Serpico goes to prove his point, the more isolated he gets, which is perilous when you're working undercover. Featuring a great performance by Pacino right on the heels of *The Godfather*, *Serpico* also revolutionized the cop movie, paving the way for future police department corruption films like L.A. *Confidential* and *Training Day*.

Instructor: "Among users of the drug, a marijuana cigarette is referred to as a reefer, stick, roach, joint. The drug itself is referred to as pot, tea, boo, stuff, grass."

Seven-Per-Cent Solution, The (1976)

✂ 🔪 💉

🍁🍁🍁🍁 Sherlock Holmes had an addiction, and it wasn't to what he pinched into his pipe. Ever so discreetly, he would load up a needle with what he called a "seven percent solution" of cocaine and regularly pop it into his veins. Only his closest ally and friend Dr. Watson knew about it. Herbert Ross's clever adaptation of Nicholas Meyers's 1974 novel starts with Holmes (Nicol Williamson) in the throes of addiction: In the opening scene, he raves like a madman, nervously fidgeting and pacing, obsessed about his longtime nemesis Professor Moriarty (Laurence Olivier). For those not familiar with Arthur Conan Doyle's Holmes series, Moriarty is like Lex Luther to Superman—the only person who can outpoint Holmes's amazing powers of deduction. Watson (Robert Duvall) and Holmes's brother Mycroft (Charles Gray) cook up a scheme to get Holmes to Vienna, where none other than the esteemed psychologist Sigmund Freud is prepared to unravel Holmes's curious addiction. Of course, the only way Holmes will leave London is if he's in pursuit of Moriarty. Since Holmes is not aware of the plan, this plays out as a sort of intervention. "For as long as I've known him he used it," Watson confides. "He began taking it during cases to relieve the ennui, the boredom." Freud (Alan Arkin) admits, "I've taken cocaine, and I'm free from its power. It will take time and it will not be pleasant." Once Freud hypnotizes Holmes, deep truths pour out. He goes through agonizing cold turkey (complete with hallucinations) and finally flashes back to the death of his mother at the hands of his father, who caught her in bed with—who else?—Moriarty! Oh, the irony! Rather than return to London with Watson and their trusty bloodhound Toby, Holmes goes on a boat excursion where he meets Lola (Vanessa Redgrave), who will clearly make him forget about Moriarty—at least until his next riveting case.

Short Cuts (1993)

✐ 🍸 ⚗ ◡◡

🌿🌿🌿🌿🌿 Before Paul Thomas Anderson's *Magnolia*, Robert Altman's *Short Cuts* perfected the art of interlocking story lines, taking a seemingly disconnected group of Los Angeles nobodies and demonstrating how one person's actions can have lasting effects on the strangers he or she comes in contact with. It's one of the legendary director's darker films, revealing the often unspoken tension that comes with suburban frustration and constant attempts at overstimulation. In telling their stories, the characters (twenty-two in total!) manage to squash many of the basic principles by which most people live their lives. Thou shall not commit adultery? Salty L.A. cop Gene (Tim Robbins) takes guilt-free infidelity to another level. As for coveting thy neighbor's wife, he's got that in the bag, too, as does Bill (Robert Downey Jr.) and his pool-man buddy Jerry (Chris Penn), all desperate to escape the monotony of monogamy. It gets more tragic still with Lily Tomlin's character, Doreen, who's married to an alcoholic (played brilliantly by Tom Waits), lives in a trailer park, works as a waitress, and has the unfortunate mishap of hitting an eight-year-old boy with her car. That kid, the son of a helicopter mom (Andie MacDowell), ends up in the hospital, which sparks an unending barrage of harassing phone calls by a crusty baker (Lyle Lovett). And just when you think it can't get any grimmer, there's a murder (though not perpetuated by any of the main characters), a suicide, and a natural disaster. Just about the only bright spot is Jennifer Jason Leigh's character, Lois, who operates a phone-sex line from her house, and likes to unwind from a day of talking dirty and caring for the kids with a joint. Julianne Moore (who famously stomps around panty-less in one key scene), Matthew Modine, Anne Archer, and Fred Ward round out a truly amazing ensemble cast, along with smaller roles by Huey Lewis, Jack Lemmon, Lori Singer, and Buck Henry. But at nearly three hours long and with so many interwoven plots to keep track of, *Short Cuts* is a major investment in time and brainpower. Make sure to be in the right head space before taking on the commitment.

Shrink (2009)

✐ 🍸 ⚗

🌿 🌿 Henry Carter (Kevin Spacey) is a psychiatrist with a bestselling book, but he's the one in need of help. His wife just committed suicide and during his downward spiral, Henry prefers smoking pot to seeing patients. When friends stage an intervention (for weed?), Henry storms out, declaring, "I'm not some drug addict on Wilshire Boulevard. I'm going to my car and I'm gonna take a big hit from a self-medicating joint and then I'm gonna go to Kentucky Fried Chicken, because it's finger lickin' good." It's a smartly written line, but you just know that Henry will eventually deliver the film's antidrug message. Each of Henry's patients has their own story line: comedian Jack (an uncredited Robin Williams), uber-agent Patrick (Dallas Roberts), wannabe screenwriter Jeremy (Mark Webber), high school student Jemma (Keke Palmer), aging actress Kate (Saffron Burrows), and partying actor Shamus (Jack Huston). The interconnecting Hollywood stories tip the movie in the direction of *Entourage*, *The Player*, and *Crash*. In a pivotal scene, Henry's dealer Jesus (Jesse Plemons) sells him a special strain called "Christmas in Vietnam" that lands them both in the hospital (the joints are laced with embalming fluid). Though this is not at all believable, it is Henry's rock bottom. Back home, he flushes his buds down the toilet (nooooo!). Mournfully, Henry tells Jemma, "I used to smoke a lot of weed. Not anymore." Blaming Henry's problems on marijuana is a cheap shot. Director Jonas Pate and writer Thomas Moffett take the low road and their movie suffers for it.

Sid & Nancy (1986)

🍸 🍾 ⚗ 🔪 💉

🌿 🌿 🌿 Like a Shakespearean play, this love story for the ages ends in tragedy as punk rock's first couple succumbs to a life of miserable heroin addiction. Or maybe it was doomed from the start. Sid Vicious (Gary Oldman), barely proficient bassist for Britain's the Sex Pistols, and Nancy Spungen (Chloe Webb), an American groupie toiling around London, fall in love at first spike. Sid is a lanky habitual self-mutilator, while Nancy wears a constant snarl and is covered in bruises—but they have a lot in common: a destructive streak, issues with their parents, animosity toward the mainstream, and an insatiable hunger for drugs. But where few expect Sid to amount to much of anything, Nancy has faith in his rock star potential and, as misguided as her devotion seems to be, she turns out to be right— that is, when the two manage to get out of bed. They spend much of the film's second half holed up in a dingy room at New York's Chelsea Hotel—until Nancy sets it on fire. Countless bags of smack later, this is where she meets her end. Director Alex Cox (*Repo Man*) keeps the mood, like the subject matter, grim, gray, and loud. But there are occasional moments of quiet exultation, like when Sid and Nancy casually stumble away from a police bust following the Pistols's famed sail down the Thames. Another highlight: seeing a pudgy pre-Cobain Courtney Love in her show biz debut as Nancy's pal Gretchen. And there's the music, which never gets old. But audiences are split on this biopic's legacy—some contend it glorifies heroin use, others complain it doesn't give the Sex Pistols their due. Real-life Sex Pistols singer Johnny Rotten called it a "fucking fantasy." And a sad one, at that.

Nancy: "Sid, we had a deal! We said we weren't gonna do any more smack until after the gig, you asshole!"

Silkwood (1983)

🌿 🌿 🌿 🌿 Before Julia Roberts embodied Erin Brockovich, a mulleted Meryl Streep gave an Oscar-worthy performance as real-life whistle blower Karen Silkwood, the fast-talking, hard-living employee of an Oklahoma plutonium plant who accidentally "gets cooked" (exposed to radiation) on the job. On the surface, she's anything but your typical union organizer or activist—Karen likes to puff and drive, she lives with her boyfriend Drew (Kurt Russell) and a lesbian roommate Dolly (Cher) who sifts pot at the kitchen table—but Silkwood is also one deceptively smart cookie, and it's her shrewd undercover work that eventually exposes a host of potentially life-threatening safety violations, making her a prime target for the powers-that-be. Directed by Mike Nichols (*The Graduate*) and released during the apex of nuclear anxiety in the early eighties, it's a bold indictment of greed and negligence, with little reprieve from a highly toxic environment.

Station Agent, The (2003)

🌿 🌿 🌿 🌿 When train enthusiast and little person Fin (Peter Dinklage) inherits and moves into an old trackside depot in the rural town of Newfoundland, New Jersey, he forms an unlikely friendship with a few of its townspeople, including Joe (Bobby Cannavale), a good-natured greaser running his sick father's coffee truck, and Olivia (Patricia Clarkson), a soon-to-be-divorcée still struggling with the death of her young son. The three spend their afternoons going on long walks, where Fin indulges his love of locomotive history, and their evenings sharing beers, joints, and all manner of stony conversation—from the mundane to the heart-gripping. Eventually the company wears on Fin, and emotions reach a boiling point when Joe overstays his welcome and Olivia has a meltdown. This nuanced indie won many awards, and deservedly so; it's sweet but sad, sensitive yet cruel, and it's that constant paradox that draws these characters to each other. The film also subtly blurs the line of time. Fin doesn't have a computer, phone, or car (even a shower is questionable in the station house he calls home), yet cell phones are going off non-stop, as the old world meets the new in a remote corner of the densest state in the union. Look for minor roles by Michelle Williams, *Mad Men*'s John Slattery, and *Reno: 911!*'s Joe Lo Truglio, but keep in mind the movie's unspoken motto: don't judge.

Stealing Beauty (1996)

Liv Tyler plays Lucy, a virginal nineteen-year-old American who travels to Italy in search of answers. Revisiting a communal Tuscan villa where her recently deceased mother had spent years as a resident poet, Lucy bonds with an eccentric crew of characters—all artists with a taste for wine, weed, sex, and gossip—while trying to figure out who her real father might be. She becomes especially close to Brit Alex Parrish (Jeremy Irons), who's dying of cancer with only months to live. When they first meet, the two share a joint (Lucy smokes with fist-clenched chillum-style whenever passing is involved) and within minutes, she reveals her naïveté of all things sex. Lucy's company, Alex later says, is like having his "own personal walking IV." As the summer rolls along, Lucy starts to let loose—she shows a little skin, hooks up with a couple of guys, and finally decides to lose her virginity (to a local boy who is all too happy to oblige), while learning she's not alone in her quest for self-discovery. As the other women in the house eventually lay bare, not everybody is happy, which begs the question: What's wrong with these people? How is it possible to not be completely overjoyed at a life of art and leisure high atop an Italian hillside? It's a major flaw in a slow-moving

"You wouldn't happen to have any more of that exotic brand of cigarette I can smell, would you?"

—Alex

script, but Tyler is so convincing in this breakout role that it's worth seeing. If you're Euro-craving, pair it with a spliff and a nice bottle of red.

Stepmom (1998)

Julia Roberts and Susan Sarandon costar in this tearjerker about a family coping with divorce and cancer. Luke Harrison (Ed Harris) has a new live-in girlfriend, Isabel (Roberts). His ex-wife Jackie (Sarandon) is a mom with a serious martyr complex. Stuck in the middle of this estrogen-fueled tug-of-war are their kids, Anna (Jena Malone) and Ben (Liam Aiken). From minute one, the tension is palpable, with Isabel struggling to gain the children's respect and Jackie holding on while keeping her terminal disease a secret, but all that bravado subsides when a series of treatments fail. And maybe the joint Jackie smokes helps a bit, too. Once she drops her guard, the two women come together, the kids bond with their future stepmother, and it all makes for one sweet and sad holiday portrait.

Jackie: "Life's a tradeoff. It's finally legal to smoke dope, but you got to have cancer."

Suburbia (1984)

Los Angeles in the eighties is a huge drag for poor Evan Johnson (Bill Coyne), a teen from the 'burbs who just wants to read his comic books in peace. Filled to the brim with teenage angst and aching to escape his alcoholic mother, Evan puts his stuff in a trash bag and heads to Hollywood to escape his personal hell. After wandering the streets and into a rowdy punk show, Evan ends up sleeping in his own puke until Jack (Chris Pedersen), a kindly gutter punk, scoops him up. They end up at the abandoned tract home he shares with a gaggle of runaways, including a baby-faced, crazy-eyed Flea (of Red Hot Chili Peppers fame), a trio of messed-up girls, and a handful of leather jacket–clad dudes. Newly indoctrinated into the punk gang T.R. (The Rejected), Evan cuts off his shaggy 'do and quickly assimilates into the lifestyle of robbery, drugs, alcohol, and fighting off douchebags, cops, and squares. Tragedy strikes and kills the buzz more than once, but smartassed one-liners spouted by each character keep the movie's edge. Though the acting is rough (director Penelope Spheeris cast mostly nonprofessional actors), the low-budget shots of L.A.'s eighties punk scene and cameos from legends T.S.O.L, the Vandals, and D.I. are enough to spark a hint of nostalgia for the Reagan years.

Jack to the gang: "My old man's gonna be back soon and if we're still here he's gonna shit Twinkies."

Sweet Bird of Youth (1962)

Four years after appearing as Brick in *Cat on a Hot Tin Roof*, Paul Newman returned to the Tennessee Williams playbook, starring as Chance—a small-town Louisiana guy with big Hollywood dreams—in Richard Brooks's riveting big-screen adaptation. The pill-popping Chance arrives home with washed-up actress Alexandra Del Lago (Geraldine Page)—a drunk who treats him poorly, but Chance doesn't seem to mind. In the movie's most controversial scene, they smoke marijuana together—a first for a mainstream Hollywood movie. "Where is the stuff?" she asks. Chance has it hidden between the mattress and the box spring in the hotel room where they're staying. "This is pretty high-class pot—where'd you get it?" Chance asks. He rolls a joint and they smoke. "One thing that will help you forget oblivion is this stuff," she sighs. "Princess, just smoke," advises Chance, who has old business with the daughter of local political hack Boss Finley (Ed Begley). Despite all of his efforts to see Heavenly (Shirley Knight), her father and brother Tom (Rip Torn) do everything in their power to prevent him, including roughing him up. It turns out Heavenly had aborted Chance's baby. When the scandal goes public, Heavenly races off with Chance, leaving St. Cloud and the princess behind.

Chance: "Don't forget you're the one who introduced me to this fine old Moroccan hash."

Alexandra: "Chance Wayne—you're stoned!"

Sweet Sixteen (2002)

Scottish teenager Liam (Martin Compston) wants a piece of the older drug dealers' action in Ken Loach's compelling drama. He sells "tenners" of "gear" (heroin) on a moped along with pizza delivery orders. But Liam's friends Pinball (William Ruane) and Chantelle (Annmarie Fulton) don't approve of his new business venture. Liam's goal is to make enough money to get a new apartment for his mother (Michelle Coulter), who's in jail on a drug-possession charge, when she's released. Liam loathes her pusher boyfriend Stan (Gary McCormack), who set his mother up, and after a violent confrontation with the much-larger Stan, Liam decides to go on the lam.

Liam to Pinball: "They want reliable dealers, no fucking junkies that are using more than they're selling."

Taking Woodstock (2009)

Re-creating Woodstock is no small feat. Tony Goldwyn gave it a try in 1999's *A Walk on the Moon*, which focused on a New York family's summer vacation near the site of the Woodstock festival and the transformation they go through there. Ang Lee's *Taking Woodstock* is the true story of another traditional family caught in the eye of the Woodstock storm. Elliot Tiber (Demetri Martin) and his parents run El Monaco Motel in the Catskill Mountains. When Elliot (the movie is based on his book) learns that the festival has been booted out of Woodstock (twenty miles away), he calls organizer Michael Lang (Jonathan Groff) and offers his property as a substitute site. With neighboring farmer Max Yasgur (Eugene Levy) on board, the festival is back on. A straight shooter, Elliot gradually comes around as the hippies move in and take over El Monaco and the surrounding farmland. His awakening begins when he leaves the hotel and immediately finds himself inside a trippy VW van, dosing on LSD, but Elliot is just too ambivalent and uptight to truly enjoy himself during the defining moment of the sixties. Adding depth and pathos, Lee's cast of colorful characters includes embittered Vietnam War vet Billy (Emile Hirsch), drag queen Vilma (Liev Schreiber, who also played the dad in *A Walk on the Moon*), and Devon (Dan Fogler), leader of the often-nude Earthlight Players guerrilla theater troupe. While the soundtrack includes era classics like "Wooden Ships," "Freedom," and "Volunteers," there are no live performances. Lee (*Brokeback Mountain*; *Crouching Tiger, Hidden Dragon*) is a great director, but he's a little out of his element here. Despite all the pot smoking and LSD gobbling, you can leave *Taking Woodstock*.

Thelma & Louise
(1991)

Thelma (Geena Davis) and Louise (Susan Sarandon) plan a weekend away from their respective man problems—Thelma has a verbally abusive husband, Louise an unreliable boyfriend—but it all goes awry when an encounter with an aggressive dude at a roadside bar ends in blood. The resulting road movie is a classic of proto-feminism wrapped in some wry, dark humor, and succeeds thanks to its leads and a few good men—Jimmy (Michael Madsen), Louise's inept, loving boyfriend, and a detective (the awesome Harvey Keitel) who tries to pull them back from the edge. Once unleashed, however, the browbeaten Thelma discovers she has a penchant for bad deeds, and she cultivates a Wild Turkey habit to match. A series of crimes and bad dudes (Brad Pitt has a supporting role as sexy drifter J.D.) lead Thelma and Louise to

discover that they (and their friendship) are worth more than they've been given credit for. There's one funny, stony scene: a police officer is manhandled by Thelma and Louise and locked in his car's trunk (with some bullet holes to breathe through). When a dreadlocked cyclist rides by, he calmly takes a drag on a huge spliff and exhales into one of the trunk's bullet holes. It's a moment of levity the movie desperately needs.

Louise: "Thelma, what are you doin'?"

Thelma: "I'm smoking. 'Hey, I'm Louise.'"

Louise: "You seem like you're crazy, or on drugs."

Thelma: "I'm not on drugs, but I might be crazy!"

Thirteen (2003)

From the opening scene, in which seventh graders Tracy (Evan Rachel Wood) and Evie (Nikki Reed) huff a can of duster (compressed air) and proceed to violently beat each other up just for fun, you know this teen drama is no after-school special. Directed by Catherine Hardwick (*Lords of Dogtown*, *Twilight*) who co-wrote the script with a then–fourteen-year-old Reed, it's a common tale, though rarely shown quite so raw: good girl meets bad girl, gets a bunch of piercings, grades start to drop, and mom is left scratching her head as two thirteen-year-olds engage in some seriously high-risk behavior like stealing, drug use, self-mutilation, and promiscuity. Hooking up with random boys they meet on the street, Tracy and Evie attempt a threesome with the one person who believes in a higher moral ground, Tracy's twentysomething neighbor Luke (Kip Pardue). Secondary to their intense friendship, which involves some predictable girl-on-girl experimentation, is Tracy's relationship with her recovering addict mother, Melanie (Holly Hunter), which starts deteriorating the minute Evie enters the picture. Melanie's live-in boyfriend, Brady (Jeremy Sisto), also a former cokehead, only complicates an already contentious situation. In the big picture, it doesn't take all that long for Tracy to go from playing with Barbie dolls to popping pills to giving head in the back of a tattoo parlor, or for Melanie to graduate from gullible pushover to proper parent, but it sure is a rough ride.

Touch of Evil (1958)

 Orson Welles's last great movie is set in a fictional Mexican border town where an American police captain (Welles as Hank Quinlin) and a Mexican narcotics officer (Charlton Heston as Mike Vargas) investigate a car bombing. Vargas plays the good cop and Quinlin the vile protagonist who'll do anything to make a collar. To scare off Vargas, Quinlin hires hoods who drug Vargas's wife, Susie (Janet Leigh), and plant reefer "stubs" and needles in her hotel room. "You know what marijuana is, don't you?" one asks. "You know what Mary Jane is?" Though no one is seen smoking *mota*, it's one of the first references to pot in a mainstream movie. Welles's script is sharp and his camera angles expansive, with lots of long shots and his trademark shadows (the film was shot in black-and-white). While Quinlin gets progressively drunker, Vargas keeps his cool despite racial taunts from Quinlin and his men. The last scene, with Vargas following Quinlin and a wired Sergeant Menzies (Joseph Calleia), builds to a chilling climax, as good ultimately overcomes evil.

Quinlin: "I don't speak Mexican. Let's keep it in English, Vargas."

Vargas: "That's all right with me. I'm sure he's just as unpleasant in any language."

Traffic (2000)

Steven Soderbergh's drug-war treatise, adapted from Alastair Reed's 1989 six-part British miniseries *Traffik*, skips back and forth between three story lines. In Mexico, a corrupt general (Tomas Milion as Salazar) teams up with the Tijuana drug cartel while one good cop, Javier (Benicio Del Toro), refuses countless opportunities to look the other way. In Washington, Judge Robert Wakefield (Michael Douglas) has been of-

fered the drug czar position by the White House, while back home in Cincinnati his straight-A daughter Caroline (Erika Christensen) is experimenting with various illegal drugs. And in San Diego, the DEA nabs coke smuggler Carlos Ayala (Steven Bauer) and his connection, Eduardo Ruiz (Miguel Ferrer). The feared Obregón brothers put a hit out on Ruiz, who's guarded by comical agents Montel (Don Cheadle) and Ray (Luis Guzmán). Without skipping a beat, Ayala's wife, Helena (Catherine Zeta-Jones), takes

over her husband's business. Back in Ohio, Caroline repeatedly disappears with her druggy boyfriend Seth (Topher Grace), and Wakefield finally finds her doped up in a sleazy downtown hotel. When it comes time for him to accept the White House position and issue a strong antidrug message, Wakefield chokes up. "I can't do this," he tells the startled audience. "If there is a war on drugs, then many of our family members are the enemy. And I don't know how you wage war on your family." Caroline ends up in rehab, as if twelve-step programs are the solution. But clearly, Soderbergh takes sides, aiming at the U.S. government, which, as Ruiz says, "surrendered this war a long fucking time ago." Shot in gauzy yellows (Mexico) and steely blues (Washington), this two-and-a-half hour opus unfortunately lost the Best Picture Oscar to *Gladiator*, though Soderbergh (director) and Del Toro (supporting actor) each took home well-deserved Academy Awards.

Helena: "I want our debt forgiven, I want to be the exclusive distributor of Obregón brothers cocaine in the United States and I want the principle witness against my husband, Eduardo Ruiz, killed."

Trainspotting (1996)

🍸 ✂️ 💉 👀

🍁🍁🍁🍁 Twelve years before his Oscar-winning *Slumdog Millionaire*, Danny Boyle directed one of the best hard-drug movies ever, adapted from Irvine Welsh's novel and set primarily in Scotland. Renton (Ewan McGregor) and his mates—Spud (Ewen Bremner), Sick Boy (Jonny Lee Miller), Tommy (Kevin McKidd), and Allison (Susan Vidler)—live for their next heroin fix, which Renton describes in one of the film's many voice-overs: "Take the best orgasm you ever had, multiply that by a thousand and you're still nowhere near it." Renton is a true addict, starting and stopping over and over again. His first attempt at cold turkey is a classic: He dives headfirst into a toilet in search of dope-filled suppositories. The second is more hallucinatory, with a dead baby crawling on the ceiling. When Renton moves to London, Spud, Sick Boy, and their one non–drug using friend, the hyperviolent Begbie (Robert Carlyle), follow. They deal two kilos of skag for £16K, but Begbie's vicious behavior and bullying proves to be too much for Renton, who decides to scoot with the loot. On the lighter side, Renton's one-night stand, Diane (Kelly Macdonald), turns out to be a high school student who threatens to expose him if he stops seeing her. McGregor, Macdonald, and Carlyle head a stellar young cast that would go on to bigger and perhaps better things, as would director Boyle.

Renton: "No matter how much you stash or how much you steal, you never have enough."

True Believer (1989)

✂️

🍁🍁🍁🍂 Public defender Eddie Dodd (James Woods) is a sixties throwback who's lost his way and purpose in life. The ponytailed hippie holdover has an office in New York's Greenwich Village, where he likes to kick back and smoke joints. When green law clerk Roger Baron (a very good, very young Robert Downey Jr.) joins Dodd's firm, he challenges him to get off his ass and start caring about his profession again. Roger even dares to question Eddie's considerable pot consumption. In this above-average legal thriller, Dodd takes a case that revitalizes him. But thankfully he keeps smoking. That's the sixties spirit!

Eddie Dodd: "No . . . Coke dealers pay cash—they subsidize the pot possession cases. They're free."

Valley of the Dolls (1967)

🍸 ✂️ 💊 👀

🍁🍁🍁🍂 Veteran Hollywood director Mark Robson (*The Harder They Fall*, *Von Ryan's Express*, *Peyton Place*) made a sharp left turn with this melodramatic adaptation of Jacqueline Susann's steamy novel about three women trying to find their way in the liberated sixties. The dolls in the title refer to pills—specifically barbiturates—that pop singer Neely (Patti Duke) abuses and soft-core porn actress Jennifer (Sharon Tate) overdoses on. Before pot and psychedelic drugs became popular in the sixties, 'scripts and booze were the drugs of choice. And despite the cool pop art décor and snazzy fashions, this movie and book were slightly behind the times. Still, the soap-opera story lines are fun to follow. Neely rises from Broadway rookie to movie star and recording artist, moves to Los Angeles, and quickly becomes jaded and depressed (hence the "dolls"). Who knew child-actress Patti Duke could sing? She can also emote, especially when she's shipped off to the sanitarium (sixties speak for rehab): "I'm not nutty, I'm just hooked on dolls. I need a doll.

Get me a doll. Just one!" Her overacting is reminiscent of Frank Sinatra's in *The Man with the Golden Arm*, when Frankie Machine craves a fix. Tate, who was murdered two years later by Charles Manson, plays the vapid Jennifer, whose impressive chest is her best attribute ("I know, all I have is my body"). The third female character, Anne (Barbara Parkins), is the most grounded; she overcomes her boyfriend's infidelity and decides to pursue a single life. Even racier than the drug talk and a few side-boob camera shots are the numerous scatological references to gay character Ted Casablanca.

Velvet Goldmine (1998)

Loosely based on real-life glam rocker David Bowie, Jonathan Rhys Meyers plays Brian Slade, bisexual superstar and idol to thousands of British teens, among them future journalist Arthur Stuart (Christian Bale). Glitter, platforms, and guyliner ruled the early seventies London scene, which was birthed from "sexual liberation of the flower power set." But whether a mod or a rocker, nothing compares to the scandal-prone Brian, who famously declares, "Rock-and-roll is a prostitute: it should be tarted up and performed." Through a series of flashbacks, Arthur recounts the legend of Brian Slade, who faked his own death ten years earlier and was subsequently written off for the hoax. Brian's first wife Mandy (Toni Collette) explains his rocky relationship with the Iggy Pop–like Curt Wild (Ewan McGregor), a provocative heroin-addicted punk rocker who lives up to his surname. As it turns out, Arthur and Curt had their own one night hookup many moons ago, and now he's been assigned to write about his former fling's great love. Confused? Blame it on the film's habit of jumping back and forth between past and present. Executive-produced by R.E.M. singer Michael Stipe (who wrote music for the film), *Velvet Goldmine* also features glam-era tracks by the likes of Brian Eno, Roxy Music, and T-Rex (plus a guest vocal by Radiohead's Thom Yorke). The music and fashions far outshine the story, but McGregor, who goes full frontal during one onstage scene, is a standout.

Brian Slade: "How can we help you? You must tell us: what do you need?"

Curt Wild: "Everything. See, heroin was my main man, but now I'm on the methadone and getting my act together, and you come here and say you wanna help and I say, far out. You can be my main man."

Virgin Suicides, The (1999)

Sofia Coppola's first film is about the life and death of the Lisbon girls—five sisters who commit suicide before they ever get a chance to fall in love, finish high school, or experience sex (all, that is, except the misguided Lux, played hypnotically by Kirsten Dunst). But deeper down it's also about love, loss, memory, and the difficult business of growing up, as seen through the eyes of a group of boys who adored the Lisbon girls. Coppola's film, based on the novel by Jeffrey Eugenides, is a pretty one, with sun-dappled seventies suburbia playing a starring role. But its true power is in the nuanced performances by James Woods and Kathleen Turner as the girls' struggling parents, and the loping, pot-loving Trip Fontaine (Josh Hartnett), who glides around like a sexier, dreamier Shaggy (minus Scooby-Doo) with a glint of masculine mischief in his eyes.

> "As was his custom, he went out to his car to smoke the marijuana he took as regularly as Peter Petrovich, the diabetic kid, took his insulin."
>
> **—Narrator**

Wackness, The (2008)

Wacky, not wack, Jonathan Levine's smart and tender New York City flick, set in 1994, pairs two generations of stoners—

eighteen-year-old wigger Luke (Josh Peck) and fiftysomething shrink Dr. Jeffrey Squires (Sir Ben Kingsley). Luke trades weed for therapy sessions ("This is a short one, I'll only charge you a dime bag") and sells to Squires's stepdaughter Stephanie (Olivia Thirlby) from an ice cream cart (à la *Nice Dreams*). As Luke raises money to help prevent his family from being evicted, Squires contemplates divorcing his bored, chain-smoking wife, Kristin (Famke Janssen), and, worse, suicide. Josh's summer fling with the sexually experienced Stephanie proves to be a bummer as well. Highlights include meaty cameos by Method Man (Jamaican ganja dealer Percy) and Mary-Kate Olsen (hippie chick Union—she kisses Kingsley!), the Notorious B.I.G.–dominated soundtrack, and Kingsley kicking it with a large glass bong.

Squires: "Never trust anyone who doesn't smoke pot or listen to Bob Dylan."

Walk on the Moon, A (1999)

🌿 🌿 🌿 🌿 Director Tony Goldwyn portrays a traditional Jewish family coming apart at the seams during the epochal 1969 summer of Woodstock and the Apollo moon landing. The Kantrowitzs—Pearl (Diane Lane) and Marty (Liev Schreiber)—head to Pine Glen Cottages for their annual Catskills getaway with the kids, fourteen-year-old Alison (Anna Paquin) and precocious six-year-old Daniel (Bobby Borielli), plus Marty's yenta mom (Tovah Feldshuh). But when Marty returns to work at his TV repair shop in the city, Pearl's eye wanders in the direction of hippie-dippie blouse salesman Walker (Viggo Mortensen), who shows up regularly in his cool bus selling *schmatas* to the ladies. Pearl's burgeoning relationship with Walker parallels Alison's maiden romance with Ross (Joseph Perrino). Everything comes to a head when Pearl and Alison separately sneak off to the nearby festival in White Lake with their respective boyfriends. Jugs of wine spiked with acid and joints are passed around as Richie Havens sings "Freedom." Pearl and Walker, faces painted Day-Glo colors, trip hard. Walker offers to take Pearl cross-country, but ultimately she returns to Marty, who realizes he better start smoking pot and listening to Jimi Hendrix lest he lose Pearl for real. The solid soundtrack includes a couple of Grateful Dead songs ("Ripple," "Uncle John's Band"), Jefferson Airplane's "Today," Joni Mitchell's "Cactus Tree," and, if you wait through the credits, Morcheeba's cover of "Crystal Blue Persuasion." Though released with little fanfare, *A Walk on the Moon* more effectively captures the spirit of the era than Ang Lee's bigger-budget *Taking Woodstock*.

Marty to Pearl about Woodstock: "Was it groovy, far out, out of sight?"

Walk the Line (2005)

🌿 🌿 🌿 In this part biopic, part love story, Joaquin Phoenix and Reese Witherspoon take center stage as Johnny Cash and June Carter, country music's golden couple. Beginning in childhood and spanning two decades, the film chronicles Johnny's rise to the top of the charts, failed first marriage, strained relationship with his father,

and unwavering determination to win June's heart. It also delves into his pill addiction, which started while on tour in the fifties. When he's assured, "Elvis takes 'em," Johnny jumps on the speed bandwagon. Fast-forward a few years, and Johnny's being arrested at the airport after replenishing his stash in Mexico. After the bust, he shares a run-down apartment with outlaw pal Waylon Jennings (played by Waylon's real-life son Shooter Jennings), before buying a property outside of Nashville. June shepherds Johnny through withdrawal and, within months, his career is resuscitated via the now legendary concert at Folsom Prison, which the "Man in Black" kicks off with a song about cocaine and murder. This is a paint-by-numbers rock-doc, but Witherspoon, who won a Best Actress Oscar, and Phoenix deliver performances in the truest sense of the word—they actually sing every note!

Jerry Lee Lewis: "God gave us a great big apple, see, and he said don't touch it. He didn't say touch it once in a while; he didn't say take a nibble when you're hungry; he said don't touch it! Don't think about touchin' it, don't sing about touchin' it, don't think about singin' about touchin' it!"

Whose Life Is It Anyway? (1981)

You'd think this film would be the biggest downer ever. For one thing, it's about a sculptor left paralyzed from the neck down after a tragic car accident. As if that wasn't depressing enough, he's so incapacitated and reliant on machines that he's basically been sentenced to life in a hospital bed with no chance of leaving. But thanks to a skillful performance by Richard Dreyfuss as Ken Harrison, the most good-natured shut-in that doctors Michael Emerson (John Cassavetes) and Clare Scott (Christine Latti) ever did meet, there are laughs—the loudest being Ken's post-spliff giggle fit in the hospital basement, where Jamaican orderly John (Thomas Carter) sets up a secret private concert-for-one starring his own stony band. Of course, there are deep issues to consider here: euthanasia, suicide, psychiatric commitment, and a doctor's

obligation to prolong life. Ken keeps it focused by only taking his discharge fight to a judge and sums it all up in one concise thought: "All's well that ends." Heavy.

Wild in the Streets (1968)

If you took only one movie that depicted the youthful energy, idealism, and eccentricity of the sixties counterculture and put it in a time capsule, this might be it. Released by American International—home to many of the era's most offbeat movies—Barry Shear's film is so audacious it ultimately comes off as a comedy, or better yet, a farce. Rock star Max Frost (Christopher Jones) leads a band (including Richard Pryor as drummer Stanley X) of beatniks and proto-bikers dressed up in hippie clothes. Their garage-style music—written by Brill Building vets Barry Mann and Cynthia Weil—is pretty good, especially the oft-repeated theme song, "The Shape of Things to Come." When Frost throws his support behind a progressive senatorial candidate and Johnny Fergus (Hal Holbrook) wins, Frost realizes the power he wields among the under-thirty crowd and fashions a campaign to reduce the voting age to fourteen ("Fourteen or Fight"). First, Frost calls for a huge demonstration on Los Angeles's Sunset Strip. Next, he and his Merry Pranksters spike Washington's water supply with LSD, precipitating a near-mass freak-out on Capitol Hill. Finally, Frost is elected president by his teenage and twentysomething followers. But power indeed goes to Frost's head as he interns "old people" (such as his mother, Daphne, played by Shelley Winters, who goes through a transformation during the movie, smoking pot and donning hippie duds) in rehabilitation camps. "Citizens will report to them after five years, at the age of thirty-five," he explains, "and there, in groovy surroundings, we're going to psych them out on LSD, babies!" But Frost, who is twenty-four by the end of the movie, realizes that his reign only has five years to go before he's cast off as he's done to others.

Max: "I want the hippies, I want the heads, I want all of you!"

Y Tu Mamá También
(2001)

Alfonso Cuarón's Mexican road movie is a complicated trip. Two oversexed, pot-smoking teenage amigos, Julio (Gael García Bernal) and Tenoch (Diego Luna), invite Tenoch's cousin by marriage, Luisa (Maribel Verdú), to join them on a beach vacation. When Luisa learns that her husband has been cheating on her, she takes them up on their offer. It's a colorful, authentic tour from Mexico City to the Pacific Coast. Along the way, Luisa has sex with both guys, setting off fiery arguments and candid revelations that only heightens the tension. Luisa has a secret of her own which explains her flirty behavior. They all get raging drunk their last night together and during a menagé à trois, the guys kiss and end up sleeping together, to their great embarrassment the morning after. While Luisa stays behind, Julio and Tenoch drive home, their friendship irrevocably fractured. What starts off as a lively, fun romp turns some surprising corners and has a sad resolution, but the poignant story and vivid scenery are well worth the ride.

Saba: "Once we're stoned we'll drop a little E . . . [About the weed] Just some dog shit. Total Cheech and Chong."

☆ MORE FOREIGN STONER FILMS ☆

No matter the language, drugs find their way into every country's cinema.

Christiane F. (1981): David Bowie is ever present in this druggy German flick in which a fourteen-year-old girl takes to the harsh streets of West Berlin for a crash course in adulthood. All-night acid trips at the local disco lead to a flirtation with heroin and then a full-on addiction as the beautiful Christiane (Natja Brunckhorst) descends into a life of prostitution and despair.

Pusher (1996): Beginning in 1996, Danish director Nicolas Winding Refn issued the first of three dark films about Copenhagen's druggy underground. The saga continued with the sequels *Pusher II* (2004) and *Pusher 3* (2005). Only one character, dealer Milo (Zlatko Buric), appears in all three. Whether he's being ripped off in *Pusher* and exacts payback or is challenged by would-be successors in *Pusher 3*, Milo manages to survive, which is about the only optimistic aspect of these daring dramas.

Scarlet Diva (2000): Directed by Asia Argento, daughter of Italian horror-film auteur Dario, *Scarlet Diva* introduced American audiences to her unusual talents as both an actress and writer. Asia plays Anna in what would appear to be an autobiographical story about an actress who travels to Paris, Los Angeles, and Amsterdam and has a series of bizarre, drug-fueled encounters. In 2004 she followed with *The Heart Is Deceitful Above All Things*.

City of God / Cidade de Deus (2002): Boys grow up to be men in Fernando Meirelles's kaleidoscopic epic about life in Rio de Janeiro's slums. While some are content to smoke pot and be hippies, others want a piece of the cocaine action. Shootouts and gang warfare play out like a Brazilian *Scarface* in this colorful, action-packed stunner.

The Dreamers (2003): Bernardo Bertolucci's meditation on the Paris riots of 1968 stars Michael Pitt as American cinephile Matthew, who meets film buffs Isabel (Eva Green) and Theo (Louis Garrel) and starts an intense friendship with the twins. Isabel smokes spliffs and is quick to disrobe as she seduces Matthew. But Isabel and Theo are just too close for Matthew's comfort.

You Can Count on Me (2000)

🍃 🍃 🍃 This tug-at-your-heartstrings story has all the makings of a sappy romance novel, only it's about a brother and sister reconnecting after a long absence. Sammy (Laura Linney) is a single mom to eight-year-old Rudy (Rory Culkin), and has been living in the same northeastern town her entire life. She toils away at a dead-end job, avoids meaningful relationships, and dotes on her son obsessively. When Sammy's troublemaker brother Terry (Mark Ruffalo) comes for a visit, at first she's relieved to have extra help. Besides sneaking the occasional joint, Terry takes Rudy to a bar in an attempt to teach him how to hustle a game of pool, and even confronts his nephew's deadbeat biological dad, all of which infuriates Sammy. But she's no saint, either: Sammy is having an affair with her uptight bank manager boss Brian (Matthew Broderick). In the end, Terry learns about responsibility, Sammy reclaims a touch of rebelliousness, and Rudy is better prepared for adolescence, even if the town he's stuck in offers little hope of escape.

Zabriskie Point (1970)

🍃 🍃 🍃 🍃 Michelangelo Antonioni's movie, set in Southern California in the sixties, opens at a counterculture politico meeting with the usual partisan bickering that tended to diffuse spontaneous action during those times. The film's antihero, Mark (Mark Frechette), says he's willing to die, just not of boredom. Strapped with guns, Mark and a friend go to a campus demonstration, where a nervous cop shoots a black student for no apparent reason. Mark shoots the cop and becomes a fugitive. He steals a small plane and takes off, flying east into the desert. At the same time, Daria (Daria Halprin), a college student and part-time assistant to a low-life developer, is driving to meet her boss near Phoenix, with a stop in a nearby ghost town where she's taunted by a group of preadolescent boys, but gets away, only to be buzzed by Mark in his small plane, which is low on fuel and lands. Mark and Daria head to an overlook called Zabriskie Point and make love in the sand. During the love scene Daria has flashbacks to some sort of stylized orgy that seems to have taken place in the same spot in the recent past. An old resident helps Mark get fuel and they all paint the plane together in psychedelic colors. Daria tries to talk Mark into driving with her to Phoenix, but he declines and they go their separate ways. Inexplicably, the police know he's returning to the airport and take him down in a hail of bullets. While Frechette and Halprin give solid performances, the rest of the cast is uneven and the script's a bit spotty. Music by the Grateful Dead, Pink Floyd, and the Rolling Stones provides the perfect soundtrack for this impressionistic film.

Zachariah (1971)

🍃 🍃 🍃 A wayward cowboy rides through the sun-soaked desert, but soon it's clear that this is no standard Western as a giant electric guitar and amp glisten in the distance. Instead of the sappy twang of a banjo, a raucous rock-and-roll theme sets the tone for this campy hippie-esque sendup of the Old West. Zachariah, played by a Jew-fro'd John Rubenstein, is the youthful cowboy in search of something meaningful in his life. What he finds is a gun, which he takes to his buddy Matthew (a ponytailed Don Johnson—yes, *that* Don Johnson). Together, they set out to become gunslingers and find a "band" of outlaws named The Crackers (Country Joe & the Fish) who are failures as banditos ("they play better than they rob") and love to set up their drums and guitars and rock out at every bar they come to. The anachronistic blend of the Old West and rock-and-roll is made all the more apparent as Matthew tells Zach how "far-out" his new gun is, topless go-go dancers shimmy in the border town called Casino, and the boys wonder if they are on the same "trip." Elvin Jones, as top gun Joe Cain, provides the most exhilarating moment of the movie when, after killing his latest victim, he hits the drums for a classic, sweat-inducing five-minute solo. Zach eventually comes upon "Old Man" (Edward Challee), who has a persistent smile on his face and trite words of wisdom. This hippie Western written by Firesign Theatre could have been much funnier, although its attempt at profundity makes for a good laugh.

Adventures of Buckaroo Banzai Across the 8th Dimension, The (1984)

꤭ ꤖ

🌿 🌿 🌿 Existing in a universe entirely its own, this fast-talking takeoff on the adventure reels of the thirties and forties has a convoluted backstory that it spends no time explaining. Instead, it drops you into the middle of a would-be sci-fi series. Buckaroo Banzai (Peter Weller) is a particle physicist, neurosurgeon, and rock-star comic-book hero who manages to drive his jet car through solid matter and into the eighth dimension. Banzai's amazing feat—traveling straight through a mountain—and technological innovation, the "oscillation overthruster," gets the attention of the Red Lectroids, a group of suited bad guy aliens who came to Earth during the radio broadcast of War of the Worlds. The Red Lectroids want Banzai's overthruster to get back to Planet 10 and take over. With help from the Black Lectroids, Rasta aliens, also from Planet 10, and The Hong Kong Cavaliers, a rock band–turned–gang–turned–think tank, Banzai attempts to thwart the Red Lectroids' goals of conquest. If Banzai and his mouthy team can't stop the Red Lectroids from opening the door to the eighth dimension, the Black Lectroids will fake a U.S. attack on Russia and start a thermonuclear war. Got it? The all-star cast features John Lithgow as Dr. Emilio Lizardo, a (literally) high-voltage Italian scientist possessed by the Red Lectroids' leader; Jeff Goldblum as New Jersey, a fellow neurosurgeon in a red cowboy suit; Christopher Lloyd as John Bigboote, a nefarious Black Lectroid; and Ellen Barkin as Penny Priddy, Banzai's love interest, who may or may not be the twin sister of his dead wife. Short on effects and heavy on rapid techie exposition, the film will have you feeling like a genius if you can follow the action and keep up with the discussions of astrophysics. For a movie about reptilian aliens and rock-star scientists that looks like an episode of Quincy most of the time, Buckaroo Banzai's deadpan tone keeps its potent mix of conceptual density, half-mumbled scientific pontifications, and "Let's go, team!" silliness focused. A potent blend of Thomas Pynchon, Terry Southern, and Back to the Future zaniness, and turned it into a cult film of epic late-night VHS proportions, it's no wonder spouting quotes from Buckaroo Banzai has become uber-nerd chic.

Alien (1978)

ꤖ

🌿 🌿 🌿 🌿 🌿 Set in a gritty realistic future that has become the gold standard for sci-fi noir, Alien is the source of nightmarish Jungian archetypes—the face hugger, the chest-splitting birth scene, and the countdown to self-destruction sequence: a formula oft repeated, but rarely equaled. Director Ridley Scott's masterpiece was so far ahead of its time that it looks fantastic even today. Building on the elegance of Stanley Kubrick's 2001: A Space Odyssey, Alien takes that version of the future and films it from the perspective of the workers' dirty trenches. The crew of the Nostromo, a deep-space mining ship, has been awakened from hypersleep by Mother, the ship's computer. An unknown signal from the unexplored planet LV-426 has been encountered, and the crew's contracts with their employer, the Company, require that they check out anything that might lead to the discovery of intelligent life. They find out too late that the signal is a warning. On the planet, crewmember Kane (John Hurt) is attacked; he returns to the ship with a smothering organism attached to his face. This organism represents just one stage of the alien's life cycle. It soon spawns a larger beast that threatens the entire crew. Taking them out one by one, the bio-mechanoid creature, whose design was inspired by H. R. Geiger, is truly one of cinema's most horrific visions come to life. Beautifully paced and at its core an exercise in dread, Alien focuses on a pair of nuanced characters that elevate the movie far above normal sci-fi-horror tropes: tough-as-nails heroine Ellen Ripley (Sigourney Weaver in one of her most memorable roles) and her undercover robot nemesis, the double-crossing science officer Ash (Ian Holm). Ash, a Company spy who wants to bring the organism back for weapons research, manages to be as evil as the unknowable alien. The crew is thus seen as expendable from both an industrial and an existential angle—they are truly marooned in space. A long, slow turn of the screw, Alien's atmosphere fluctuates between technological purity, everyday oil rig grittiness, and night terror liquidity as elements of gender and domination play themselves out in what is really a simple story of man versus monster.

Barbarella (1968)

🌿🌿🌿🌗 This sixties sci-fi classic stars Jane Fonda as the title character, the sexiest adventurer ever to ride off into space (at least until Sigourney Weaver did a striptease in *Alien* ten years later). The opening scene is a doozy, with Barbarella writhing out of her suit and boots to reveal her entirely naked body as the soundtrack coos, "Barbarella's psychedela . . . get me up high, teach me to fly, electrify." Representing Earth, she's sent on a mission to find and disarm Durand-Durand (Milo O'Shea), keeper of the dreaded Positronic Ray. Her voyage is fantastic: Barbarella bangs her way through the galaxy, from ice man Mark Hand (Ugo Tognazzi) to blind angel Pygar (John Phillip Law) to revolutionary Dildano (David Hemmings, star of *Blow-Up*). She ends up confronting Durand-Durand on SoGo, which is run by the Great Tyrant (Anita Pallenberg), a.k.a. the lesbian Black Queen. It's all pretty ridiculous but fun to watch. The special effects are a cross between early *Star Trek* and bad Japanese sci-fi. At one point, Barbarella, whose wardrobe is stunning, finds herself in the Palace of Pleasure, where everyone is lying around stoned, smoking out of a huge hookah (it's so big a man swims around in the glass chamber). "What is it?" Barbarella asks. "Essence of man," a woman says, handing her the green hose. Barbarella inhales, then is whisked away by

Durand-Durand and placed in the Excessive Machine. Failing to kill her with pleasure, Durand-Durand directs the Positronic Ray at his enemies, but it backfires. Vanquished, he declares, "You win, Barbarella, but the world has lost its last great dictator." Fonda plays it tongue-in-cheek, like Sean Connery in the Bond movies. Asked by Dildano if she's a "typical Earth woman," Barbarella replies, "I'm just average." Hardly.

Blade Runner (1982)

🌿🌿🌿🌿🌿 Its somewhat glacial pace, unending rain, and overwrought art design makes Ridley Scott's *Blade Runner* a stony delight from the very first moment. Add in killer clone androids, Han Solo doing his best Raymond Chandler gumshoe imitation, a synthesizer masterpiece of a score by Vangelis, and you have a film so heavy, it's practically a narcotic. Based on a story by head-fuck sci-fi mastermind Philip K. Dick, *Blade Runner*'s noir detective narrative asks questions about what it means to be an "authentic" human, even as it seems that everyone gets shot at on sight. Deckard (Harrison Ford) is a police officer who has been brought in from the cold to track down four rogue replicants (artificial humans) who have returned to earth illegally. Facing an accelerated life span of only four years, the psychotically violent soldier replicant Roy Batty (Rutger Hauer) and the others are desperate to extend their lives. Set in a future Los Angeles that's almost always in darkness, there is a sadness to the action here: Roy's final rooftop soliloquy (supposedly improvised) is nearly Shakespearean in dimension, the world is gloomy and in decline, and floating platforms constantly hawk the promise of a better life "offworld." Playing on themes of memory and technological augmentation, the fact that the loner Deckard becomes romantically linked to a woman (Sean Young as Rachael) who has just recently discovered that she is a replicant adds weight to the cyberpunk melancholy. Released in several different versions, the director's cut jettisons the meddlesome studio's happy ending and leaves you wondering if Deckard is himself a replicant. And score extra credit by looking for scenes that share the same sets as the director's other stoner fantasy film, *Legend*.

Brother from Another Planet, The (1984)

*This early eighties fish-out-of-water comedy is hardly laugh-out-loud funny. Directed by John Sayles (Eight Men Out), the film begins with its own big bang—an alien pod headed for a collision course with Earth. Inside is an escaped extraterrestrial slave, who looks like your everyday black man circa 1984, but with three-toed chicken feet. Roaming the streets of New York City, the mute Brother (Joe Morton) learns the ropes quickly. He picks up language and human mannerisms at a dodgy bar, discovers women through advertising and, after a quick study of arcade video games, uses his machine healing power to land a job. He also dabbles in drugs while hanging with the homeless crowd in abandoned Harlem courtyards—the Brother samples a spliff when a Rasta takes a liking to him, and tries heroin when he finds a needle sticking out of a dead addict's arm—and gets to experience his first hangover. Taking absurdity to the next level, two men in black (one played by Sayles) are hounding the Brother, looking to extradite him back to their home planet. Only now the Brother's got his own brothers looking out for him, like bartender Odell (Steve James) and patron Fly (Daryl Edwards)—and with solidarity comes confidence and a new understanding of race in modern times. Any movie where an alien has sex with a human and does a bunch of drugs is a major score, but the vividly realistic depiction of the city's sights and sounds drives home a strong message: that you don't have to be an alien to feel like one in New York.

Cabin Fever (2002)

*Writer-director Eli Roth has garnered plenty of street cred via his gruesome Hostel series as well as his turn as the Bear Jew in Quentin Tarantino's Inglourious Basterds, but let's not forget his crafty directorial debut about a group of college kids who meet their doom one weekend in the woods. These five coeds contract a skin-eating virus, fend off sadistic rednecks, and wind up turning on one another. Roth doesn't hold back on the torture, but at least his characters get to party first. The movie begins with a wicked bonfire, replete with cases of brew and one fat-ass sack of ganja provided by a random camper named Grim (played by Roth). "That's a positive bonfire—got room for one more?" he says to the group. "Actually, man, we were kind of having a private conversation," Jeff (Joey Kern) says, trying to blow him off. Grim pulls out the stinky Ziploc: "Oh, so I guess I gotta smoke all this weed by myself?" On second thought, Jeff decides, "It's not that private of a conversation." It's perhaps the kindest moment Roth has ever bestowed upon his characters.

Charlie and the Chocolate Factory (2005)

*Remaking a classic is challenging enough, but how about remaking two at once? That's the nutty proposition proposed by director Tim Burton in this totally tripped-out reimagining of Mel Stuart's Willy Wonka & the Chocolate Factory (1971), starring Gene Wilder, and Roald Dahl's beloved book, whose original title Burton uses. The story is much the same: a humble young boy named Charlie Bucket (Freddie Highmore) lives in a destitute shack with his family, but is engrossed with the chocolates that come from the mysterious Wonka factory, where his grandfather used to work. One day, the factory's owner, Willy Wonka (Johnny Depp), announces a promotion: a few golden tickets will be hidden among his Wonka bars, and each lucky kid who finds one will win a tour of the factory. Of course, Bucket wins and what follows is a bizarre fantasy involving rooms made of chocolate, girls who chew way too much gum, and an earnest youngster who covets his family above all else. What's most incredible is that Burton finds freshness in an already overtold story; much of that is thanks to Depp, who plays Wonka like a weirdo cross between Michael Jackson and your college Ecstasy dealer, weaving strange detachment and childlike innocence together for a bizarro character that jibes perfectly with Burton's consistently acid-trippy vision.

Christmas on Mars
(2008)

🌿 🌿 🌿 🌿 A project of the Flaming Lips, *Christmas on Mars* is a good-hearted rambling sci-fi miniature that's sweet and weird, just like the Lips themselves. Filmed mainly in black-and-white (several abstract sequences are in color) with obvious stylistic debts to *Eraserhead*, *Holy Mountain*, and *2001: A Space Odyssey*, it's the story of a mute green-skinned alien (frontman Wayne Coyne) who shows up outside of a decaying Mars colony around the holidays. One of the colonists, Major Syrtis (Steven Drozd), is trying to put on a Christmas pageant, but his Santa Claus has just committed suicide. Naturally, Coyne's mysterious Martian is going to have to step in. Featuring a surreal techno-pregnancy and a sometimes brutally noisy score, *Christmas on Mars* manages to transcend its duct tape–and-spit editing, plot holes, and occasional blank-stare acting to become something lovely. Perfect for a long, slow comedown, this movie, which features small roles by Fred Armisen and Adam Goldberg, does a lot with a little, pulling off the trick that the Lips are so good at: making the magic feel real and not manufactured.

Noachis: "He's having what they call a third stage of a psychotic episode. He's staring at something and it's not even really there. Doctor Scott told me about it this morning. He says that it's caused by a confrontation with the cosmic reality."

🌿 Q & A: WAYNE COYNE 🌿

He's not the first rock star to sit in the director's chair (Rob Zombie, Fred Durst, and RZA all have Hollywood credits), but Flaming Lips singer Wayne Coyne may be the zaniest. The creative mastermind explains *Christmas on Mars*'s stoniest scenes.

Reefer Movie Madness: Were you on something when you first thought of *Christmas on Mars*?

Wayne Coyne: I've been wrongly pegged as a person who has a lot of drug damage. I mean, I've been around drugs my whole life, my brothers always did drugs, people know I sold pot when I was sixteen, but I never really indulged in drugs. I saw John Lennon taking acid and writing songs, but every time I got profoundly stoned, I would go into a long panic attack. And the times I did acid, I never liked it. There were moments I thought were interesting, but I wished it were over a lot quicker. I liked the idea of the drug experience more than the actual experience.

RMM: Fair enough, but is *Christmas on Mars* meant to be watched stoned?

WC: Well, yeah. When we put it out in summer 2008, we took it to a lot of music festivals and the feeling was, if we played the movie at midnight or one in the morning, anybody in there would already be on some sort of drug already—whether it was acid, or mushrooms, or X, we made it for people who would be up all night. We also wanted viewers to be actively involved—to get the laughs and scream and say hooray at the movie screen—the same way if the Flaming Lips were in front of you. Part of it is your state of mind, but it can be whatever you want it to be, pay attention to what you want, make it your own trip. I wish Stanley Kubrick came out and told me that about *2001: A Space Odyssey*.

RMM: Why do you say that?

WC: Because there's something about intense art where you kind of second-guess yourself and think, "Am I understanding it the way they intended me to?" With *Christmas on Mars*, however you understand it, that's the way I want you to understand it. I won't dispute whatever you get out of it.

RMM: What's the backstory with *Christmas on Mars*—a crew of stoner astronauts celebrate the holidays?

WC: It's their idea of, "Let's get stoned outside and put up this Christmas tree." It's a dumb, stoner thing to do. In my mind, these characters go out [of the spaceship] to smoke pot in their space suits, and all the smoke stays inside their suit, so not only are they stoned, they can't see out of their helmets and they can't plug in their light. Part of the idea is, even though they're on Mars and they're supposed to be these serious technicians, they're just getting stoned. When their Santa Claus character runs past them, they have to go in and tell the captain and they don't know what to say—he's already a belligerent asshole and they have to go in there so stoned. I don't really know if *Christmas on Mars* is set in the future or sometime in the past. I think that's kind of the beauty of it. The fact that it's about Christmas makes it even funnier—that and me with a marching band with giant genitals on their heads. Christmas is about birth, and birth involves vaginal things—what can I tell ya?

RMM: What's space weed like?

WC: It would be like the worst mega-make-you-paranoid weed there is. It wouldn't be some shitty homegrown stuff your sister had. They knew they were going to Mars and they had a special stash they were going to smoke on Christmas Eve—something utterly exotic, like the seed got shit out by some panther in the mountains of Peru or something.

RMM: For a low-budget film, the sets are awesome. Did your limitations actually become creative assets?

WC: I don't think it necessarily looked cheap. I actually wished they'd look a little cheaper, so people believe that we did it in my backyard. I mean, literally—some of it is in my backyard. There's a scene where Fred Armisen is in a strange little room; that's a shack behind my house. Even when I watch *Star Wars*, none of that is real, it's just people making it. We have a scene with a pool of guts; that's really just some pig uterus that I bought down at the grocery store. I live in Oklahoma City and for seventy-five cents, you can get a bucket of them. And, man, those things smell a lot worse than you would think.

RMM: How did Fred Armisen and Adam Goldberg come to be involved?

WC: Mostly just being fans of the band. They would come to shows and I told them I was going to make a movie, and, "Hey, you're actors, why don't we do this thing?" Sheepishly, they're, like, "OK." As strange little characters, they're great. They're truly people you look at and think they might be interesting.

RMM: The movie is exceptionally loud. Why did you do that?

WC: We go to the movies a lot, and sometimes we're disappointed by the power of the sound-track. Since we weren't restricted in any way, we said, "Let's fuckin' go for it," and it is loud. But in one scene, I made it so you purposely can't hear what anyone's saying because there's a machine that's too loud. I would just go with whatever made the scene better.

RMM: Is there a message you were trying to convey with the movie?

WC: There are a lot of messages and there's a story and an idea in mind. It's about believing in the power of some form of humanistic magic. We don't wait for God or some magical power to show up, we just think about creating the magic ourselves. I think that's basically the message to all the things we do: it is magic because we created it.

Clash of the Titans
(1981)

(⊙‿⊙)

🌿🌿🌿🌿 Despite the cheesy-by-to-day's-standards special effects, *Clash of the Titans* was the *Troy* of its time, and one of the top-grossing films of 1981. For those with the attention span to follow it, the plot is a tad convoluted, based on a Greek myth with elements of various other mythologies thrown in. By the decree of the bitter goddess Thetis (Maggie Smith), Perseus (Harry Hamlin) must defeat a monster known as the Kraken in order to save his city, Joppa, and the hide of his betrothed, Andromeda (Judi Bowker). On Perseus and Andromeda's wedding day, Thetis, bitter over the death of her son, Calibos, Andromeda's previous fiancé, and irked by an offhand comparison of Andromeda's beauty to her own made by the mother of the bride, interrupts the nuptials with payback on her mind. She demands that Andromeda be presented as a virgin sacrifice to the Kraken in thirty days, or the Kraken will destroy Joppa.

It's up to Perseus to find a way to defeat the Kraken before the deadline. His weapon of choice: the head of Medusa the Gorgon. Anyone who looks directly at Medusa's hideous snake-coiffed mug immediately turns to stone. So Perseus is faced with the unenviable task of killing Medusa, obtaining her head (without gazing at it directly), and using it to turn the Kraken to stone. How will he fare against Medusa? And will he make it back from her lair on the Isle of the Dead, across the River Styx at the edge of the underworld, in time to conquer the Kraken? It's a nail-biter, for sure. Just don't sneak a peek at Medusa's scary noggin or you're toast.

Princess Andromeda: "In my mind's eye, I see three circles joined in priceless, graceful harmony. Two full as the moon, one hollow as a crown. Two from the sea, five fathoms down. One from the earth, deep under the ground. The whole, a mark of high renown. Tell me, what can it be?"

Class of Nuke 'Em High (1986)

✏️ 🌴 🥜 🚬 (⊙‿⊙)

🌿🌿🌿 This mid-eighties nugget of B-movie insanity is brought to you by the pros in el cheapo entertainment, Troma. And in true Troma form, there are teenage girls in bikinis, mutant zombies, lesbians, rock bands, bikers, grade-Z gore, and plenty of weed. A nuclear accident at the local reactor has contaminated the town of Tromaville, and strange things are happening. The high school honor society has become a gang of freaks called the Cretins who are selling irradiated ganja to kids at the inflated price of twenty bucks a joint. The kids love the atomic weed and when teen lovers Chrissy (Janelle Brady) and Warren (Gilbert Brenton) finally smoke and get it on, their monster baby is born in the girls' room a day later. The weird, spermlike creature makes its way to a barrel of radioactive waste, gains strength, and starts offing everyone it encounters. Warren becomes a pulsating, shambling mess that attacks the Cretins. He mutates back to his good-guy self the next day, which is a shame because he made a great killer zombie. The second and third acts slow down even though the Cretins get all Mad Max on everyone, guys in biohazard suits with Geiger counters swarm all over the school, and the monster racks up kills. But what would a teen movie be if you didn't blow up the school? Extra points for the hallucination sequence where the reactor tower and pot plants are superimposed over Warren's rapidly mutating penis and the deliciously horrible "Nuke 'Em High" theme song that sounds like a demented Hall & Oates B side.

Chrissy: "I want that joint! I want that joint!"

Warren: "You had a joint a long time ago. I put that out."

Chrissy (hands on Warren's crotch): "Not that joint."

Close Encounters of the Third Kind (1977)

As a team of scientists discovers clues that suggest an extraterrestrial intelligence may be attempting to communicate with humanity, lost ships and airplanes are found in the desert, and residents of rural Indiana are visited by a plethora of psychedelic UFOs in Steven Spielberg's follow-up to Jaws. Roy (Richard Dreyfuss) is a lineman whose encounter with a swarm of flying lights leaves him obsessed with a strange mountainous shape. As his behavior becomes increasingly bizarre, his wife, Ronnie (Teri Garr), takes the kids and leaves. Roy finds kinship with Gillian (Melinda Dillon), who is plagued with similar visions after her son, Barry (Cary Guffey), is abducted by aliens in a terrifying attack.

The government and scientists have some idea of what's going on: They prepare for the alien arrival, arrange for experts to debunk the increased UFO activity, and fake a disaster to clear the countryside around the landing area. The bogus train wreck that supposedly involves dangerous gas has an unintended side effect as television coverage of the disaster shows that the distinctive mountain that Roy and Gillian have been envisioning is actually Devil's Tower in Wyoming. Roy and Gillian make their way on foot to the site, where they find that they are not the only ones to make the trip.

It takes a while to get there, but the mothership landing sequence is well worth the wait and the light show is spectacular, with that now-famous melody ("da da da da da") bridging the gap between species. Kind of corny and awesome at the same time,

the ship looks like a cross between Emerald City in *The Wizard of Oz*, the gold standard in fantasy film, and a football stadium, where all things American come true. Roy makes it to the landing site and is prepped by the scientists to board the mothership. After abductees from the near and distant past, including Barry, emerge from the vessel, Roy is picked by the little aliens to leave with them. (Some versions of the film have final sequences showing the inside of the mothership, something supposedly done to get a commitment from the studio for a director's cut. Though trippy, they feel tacked on and unnecessary.) *Close Encounters* has all the usual touches of a Spielberg movie: cute kids, amazing cinematography, plenty of small human moments even as the action builds, and commanding moments of shock and horror. The visual effects, groundbreaking at the time, still look great in this CGI age, and even Spielberg's use of light and shadow is worth noting. A bit dour at times, there's a big payoff at the end—if you haven't dozed off by then.

Scientist (after interviewing a local in the desert): "He says the sun came out last night. He says it sang to him."

Conan the Barbarian
(1982)

Based on the classic comic book, written by Oliver Stone, directed by John Milus (*Apocalypse Now*), and starring body builder and former pothead (and later, governor of California) Arnold Schwarzenegger, *Conan the Barbarian* begins in a small, snowbound village where Conan's parents are killed in front of him by death cult leader Thulsa Doom (James Earl Jones). The first ten minutes are superintense, scored to epic opera music. Conan is sold into slavery, trained to become a pit fighter, and earns his freedom by destroying all of his opponents. The over-the-top violence is cartoonish. Under the influence of black lotus, a fictional hallucinogen, Conan punches a camel for no apparent reason. He seeks revenge for his father and goes after the death cult.

The movie's plot technically comes from Stone's original script, but the character himself has solid roots in the Marvel Comics canon. The big-screen Conan features warlords and monsters as well as barely decipherable lines about swords and sorcery recited by tanned beefcake Arnold Schwarzenegger. He plays the titular orphaned gladiator out for revenge, who, while lumbering in his delivery, is most compelling kicking ass in a loincloth. The special collector's edition DVD has a commentary track featuring Schwarzenegger's awesomely awkward anecdotes. During a sex scene with a witch, Arnold boasts, "I do get laid a lot in dis movie."

> Mongol general: "Conan, what is best in life?"
>
> Conan: "To crush your enemies, to see them driven before you, and to hear the lamentations of their women."

MORE STONY COMIC BOOK ADAPTATIONS

Howard the Duck (1986): Here we have a live-action film, based on the comics character, about a macho duck (voiced by Chip Zien) from another world that shacks up with—and comes alarmingly close to doing the horizontal tango with—a Midwestern rock chick (Lea Thompson). Needless to say, despite being panned by critics, the movie went on to become a cult favorite.

Mystery Men (1999): The comics series about bumbling superhero crime fighters inspired this comedy. Among its sprawling cast: Ben Stiller as a dude whose power is to get really angry (less the requisite muscle power) and Paul Reubens as a gypsy-cursed man endowed with extreme flatulence. Improbably, Tom Waits makes an appearance as a scientist who spends his time creating peaceful weaponry and hitting on geriatric ladies at nursing homes.

Ghost World (2001): Daniel Clowes's graphic novel made for a wry, witty movie about Enid and Rebecca, two just-out-of-high-school teens (played by Thora Birch and Scarlett Johansson, respectively) who attempt to allay suburban ennui by prank-calling and then following a sad-sack fast-food worker (Steve Buscemi). His appeal? Notes Enid, "In a way, he's such a clueless dork, he's almost kind of cool."

Iron Man (2008): An absurdly rich, cutthroat industrialist finds his soul after being abducted by terrorists and building a Robocopish suit of tricks. What transpires in the superhero's quest for justice are a host of explosions and rapid-fire lines rattled off by lead man Robert Downey Jr., a world-class deadpanner whose delivery is matched only by Sideshow Bob . . . or Liz Lemon.

Dark Crystal, The
(1982)

🌿🌿🌿 Fueled by the success of the Muppet franchise, Jim Henson's magnum opus *The Dark Crystal* is a somber affair, inhabiting some freakish netherworld between kids' movie, uber-geek Dungeons & Dragons worship, and creepazoid LSD passion play. Visually groundbreaking at the time, it's a superserious bummer of a puppet movie, with an elaborate mythology and a Tolkien-like attention to detail that bottoms out in a staid plot and inane dialogue. You'll either be on board with the idiosyncratic puppeteering or be thanking your lucky stars you live in an age of CGI. The archetypes are all here: last-of-his-kind Jen, the innocent Gelfling orphan—watched over since birth by the urRu, a race of gentle, Jedi-like mystic lizards—learns that he is prophesied to save his world from the evil empire of the Skeksis, vulturelike creatures who tend to a massive broken crystal that gives them their power. The imminent thousand-year alignment of the three suns will determine who rules the next age, so Jen is sent out into a world he barely understands to heal the crystal with a shard that's been sitting around since the last alignment. Along the way he battles crab soldiers, struggles through swamps, finds a female Gelfling who is way more badass than him, meets her adoptive hippie family of Podlings, enters the evil castle through the sewers, and saves the day—healing the crystal at the exact moment of alignment as the universe shifts to another frequency. A cult favorite among hippies and goths alike, it's a love-it-or-hate-it affair. Powered by a heady dose of Henson come-on with an admirable desire to etch its detailed world and characters into the fantasy canon, *The Dark Crystal* is a gray and enveloping Sunday afternoon comedown with flashes of WTF that's best for those who dig scratchy wool blankets and other such discomforting pleasures.

> "What in the world? This place is weird."
>
> —Jen

Dark Star (1974)

🖋️

🌿🌿🌿🌿 He would later direct *Halloween*, *Escape from New York*, and *Christine*, but John Carpenter's debut is a kooky sci-fi comedy. Billed as "The Spaced Out Odyssey," *Dark Star* tells of a time in the not-so-distant-future (the twenty-second century, to be exact) when armed space stations travel the universe looking to take out any "unstable planets" that might get in the way of colonization plans. Of course, what the future looked like in 1974 is right around real-life 1986 for those of us who lived through it, meaning that computers feel about as antiquated as an Atari video game console and an alien is nothing more than a beach ball with claws. That said, the prevailing tone here is interstellar stony. Manning this ship, along with a cryogenically frozen commander, is a crew of four glassy-eyed, long-haired, bearded underlings—Lt. Doolittle (Brian Narelle), Boiler (Cal Kuniholm), Sgt. Pinback (Dan O'Bannon), and Talby (Dre Pahich)—all bored silly by the monotony of space life. A steady diet of comic books, artificial food, the occasional cigar, and unauthorized target practice keeps them occupied, until a malfunction sets their computer to self-detonate and things really perk up. It's now up to the humans to try to reason with the machine and convince it to abort its mission. Their method: a calm, philosophical discussion about existence between Doolittle, a former surfer, and the bomb, which is ridiculous, hilarious, and somewhat genius—sort of like the primitive graphics, flashes of psychedelic colors, cartoonish asteroids, and a hokey theme song that could've been played between sets at Woodstock. It's all endearing in its own way. As with 2001: A Space Odyssey, which came out six years earlier, you're never sure where this story is going but you know it's probably a dead end. Still, what a gnarly ride getting there.

Doolittle: "I used to be a great surfer. The waves at Malibu and Zuma are so fantastic in the spring, Talby. I can remember running down to the beach those early spring mornings with my surfboard and my wet suit. The waves would really be peaking—high—get that one! Before you know it, you're coming down off one of those walls you just ride and it's perfect. You know, I guess I miss the waves and my board more than anything."

Donnie Darko (2001)

🍸 🗡️

🍁 🍁 🍁 🍁 A confused suburbanite with a superhero name, Donnie Darko (Jake Gyllenhaal) may be just that: a wonder who can transcend space and time with a superb destiny in a fuzzy and confused wormhole. The movie follows the title character and his visions of a large bunny rabbit named Frank, who clues Donnie in on the date of Armageddon. When a jet engine inexplicably falls through Donnie's room while he's out with Frank, his seemingly schizophrenic philosophies and loneliness increase. Eventually, a sleepwalking Donnie busts a water main with an ax, flooding his school. Dark comedy meets eighties high-school movie as

Donnie meets the new girl, Gretchen (Jena Malone), and discovers that the two have a predetermined bond, which pokes destiny on Halloween night. A motivational speaker named Jim Cunningham (Patrick Swayze) swings into the picture spewing vocal vomit and propaganda, but Donnie sees through the bullshit, uncovering Cunningham's kiddie porn dungeon and showing everyone that things are not always what they seem. You could say the same of the entire film. The story then swirls through the time and space continuum like a blizzard, demonstrating that our wildest dreams may be just a step away, either in the future or the past. Donnie meets a girl he loves: He must die without her ever knowing him, or he indirectly causes her death. (You may need to ponder that one, stoner!) Also starring Drew Barrymore and Maggie Gyllenhaal, Donnie Darko is a revelation, binding teen angst with phantasmagorical theories. Set in 1988 and rocking an awesome soundtrack complete with Echo and the Bunnymen, Joy Division, and Duran Duran, the film had a dismal opening when it was released not long after 9/11. It engendered a cult following after its DVD release, which led to special midnight screenings in New York City and a whole new appreciation for this mind-bending, time-warped classic. Deservedly so.

Gretchen: "What if you could go back in time and take all those hours of pain and darkness, and replace them with something better?"

Dr. Jekyll and Mr. Hyde (1920, 1931, 1941)

🍸 🗡️

🍁 🍁 🍁 🍁, 🍁 🍁 🍁, 🍁 🍁 🍁 Robert Louis Stevenson's literary classic, written in 1885, has been adapted countless times, but the earliest ones are the best. The 1920 silent version stars John Barrymore (Drew's grandfather) as Dr. Jekyll, who concocts a potion that alters his body and personality into that of the psychotic Hyde. Once Jekyll makes his discovery, he moves out of his house and creates a separate life for himself as Hyde. Unfortunately, Jekyll can't control the experiment and after several doses he slips

and tortures Ivy while bewildering Beatrix, her father, and his colleagues with his constant, er, mood swings. This 1941 version has the cleverest ending of the three, involving Jekyll's use of a poison ring to put an end to the madness and mayhem he's caused.

Dune (1984)

Based on the first of a series of beloved sci-fi novels by Frank Herbert, director David Lynch's *Dune* has been hailed as both oddball camp masterpiece and disastrous folly. A mix of nerdtastic detail and hippie mysticism, Lynch's usual deadeye aim for the golden heart of the eternal space void is a bit off here, but his essential weirdness keeps the transitions nice and psychedelic. The story is of Paul, a.k.a. Muad'Dib (Kyle MacLachlan), from the House Atreides. His family has been banished from their home planet by Emperor Padishah Shaddam IV (José Ferrer) and forced to oversee the grim, desert world Arrakis. The planet is the source of the "spice," a psychoactive drug that fuels the abilities of the Spacing Guild to travel throughout the galactic empire. Paul and his mother survive the family's decimation by the opposing House Harkonnen and ally with the Fremen, the native desert warriors. Paul assumes the name Muad'Dib and starts a guerrilla war that eventually disrupts spice production. He also takes the psychedelic "water of life," developing psychic superpowers and leading his armies atop giant sandworms to triumph over his enemies.

If you can get past the lengthy voice-over and convoluted backstory—explained in mind-numbing detail and accompanied by paintings that look like they were stolen from the Motel 6 at the galactic core—this overbearing quasi-religious acid trip of a movie gets just weird enough to make it worth the dive into the deep end. Still, it's a low point for Lynch, who makes a cameo as the radio operator on a spice harvester before it's eaten by a worm. The 189-minute extended edition accords directorial credit to "Alan Smithee" (Hollywood's traditional bailout name—Lynch was not involved with the recut) and is the way to go if you want to get *Dune* in all its misshapen and blue-eyed lumpy glory. There's so much fat in this version that characters literally repeat lines over and over again as if time had folded in on itself. Milking every bit of overacted footage for all it's got, it's the *Showgirls* of sci-fi.

back and forth between both personalities at the least opportune moments. The brown interiors and blue exteriors, exquisite dialogue cards, and piano accompaniment give this version its quirky charm. Frederic March's Jekyll in Rouben Mamoulian's opulent 1931 version may have won him an Oscar for Best Actor, but he's the corniest Jekyll of the three, and his Hyde is more of a grunting, primitive monkey man. There's a clue about the potion when Jekyll writes a note asking for the "phials" with the initials A, H, S, T, R, and M. He basically mixes up chemicals (usually four at a time) that produce a smoking reaction and he drinks it. The transformation is immediate; all his facial features contort, fingers extend, hair grows long—pretty much like a werewolf or William Hurt in *Altered States*. So we never do find out what's in the cocktail he's dosing himself with. The World War II–era rendition, directed by Victor Fleming (*The Wizard of Oz*, *Gone with the Wind*) features a great cast, starting with Spencer Tracy as a more spirited and likable Jekyll. He's engaged to Beatrix (Lana Turner) and bewitched by barmaid Ivy (a luminous Ingrid Bergman). Her father puts off the wedding, indirectly prompting Jekyll to proceed with his split-personality experiment. By having to "wait" for Beatrix (remember, this is the late nineteenth century), he succumbs to temptation by kissing Ivy. But as Hyde, he's a creep who torments

Empire Strikes Back, The (1980)

🌿🌿🌿🌿🌿 One of *Star Wars*'s darkest chapters is also its most beloved. Part two of George Lucas's original trilogy picks up three years after the Death Star is destroyed. The rebels have taken cover on the icy planet Hoth and are organizing another offensive against the evil Empire, but Darth Vader and Co. get wise to their plans. The romantic tension never lets up between Han Solo (Harrison Ford at his finest) and Princess Leia (Carrie Fisher) as they flirt endlessly while attempting to escape the clutches of the Imperial forces, a bounty hunter hot on the *Millennium Falcon*'s trail, and friend-turned-traitor Lando Calrissian (Billy Dee Williams). Meanwhile, Luke Skywalker (Mark Hamill) has heeded Obi-Wan Kenobi's advice to study with master Jedi Yoda on the swampy world of Dagobah. There, he learns how to mellow out, use the Force to levitate large objects, and face his greatest fears, but Luke cuts his studies short to rush to his friends' side and right into Vader's trap. Heavy on themes of loyalty, love, and family, they all come to a head in the tremendously trippy Cloud City where Lando betrays Han and Vader delivers the saga's most famous line, later to be mocked by Seth Rogen's character in *Knocked Up* while hitting a gas-mask bong: "Luke, I am your stoner."

> **"Afraid I was gonna leave without giving you a good-bye kiss?"**
> —Han Solo
>
> **"I'd just as soon kiss a Wookie."**
> —Princess Leia
>
> **"I can arrange that."**
> —Han Solo

🌿 TRIPPY SPACESHIPS 🌿

***2001: A Space Odyssey* (1968):** Stanley Kubrick's scenes of life onboard the spaceship *Discovery One* move at a glacial pace, but odd angles and near-silence make even mundane tasks extraordinary. Of course, the most psychedelic of visuals don't compare to the menacing HAL, a self-aware computer with an iconic calming voice who has his own agenda. Talk about a bad trip.

***Star Wars* (1978):** The appearance of the Imperial Star Destroyer in the opening scene of the very first *Star Wars* lets you know that, when it comes to spaceships, this film means business. At first, you only see the vessel's tip, then it keeps going, and going, and going, until it fills the entire screen. Space travel had never boasted this size and grandeur. This scene, establishing the Empire as a force to be reckoned with, became one of the most famous in sci-fi history.

***Alien* (1979):** The derelict horseshoe-shaped ship is as creepy as they come. Designed by psychedelic artist H. R. Geiger, its entrances are oddly vaginal while the interior is a Jungian hellhole of phallic imagery and biomorphic construction. The discovery of alien eggs in the belly of the ship foreshadows the future freakiness of this terrifying series.

***Battle Beyond the Stars* (1980):** A Roger Corman camp classic, *Battle* is a *Star Wars* rip-off featuring a space vessel that looks like a pair of flying metal breasts attached to a fallopian tube. Blame James Cameron, who worked on the effects scenes, but at least he came up with a way to work some boobs into a PG-rated space opera.

***The Hitchhiker's Guide to the Galaxy* (2005):** The orblike *Heart of Gold* is arguably one of the sillier spaceships. Powered by the Infinite Improbability Drive, it can go anywhere in the universe and turn an incoming missile into a whale and a bowl of petunias. The fact that it belongs to the dim-witted, two-headed president of the galaxy only makes this whole thing more ridiculous.

Evil Bong (2006)

 In this campy horror comedy, a nerd moves in with three stoners who all die after taking a potent hit off a bong that's believed to be possessed. Surfer dude Bachman (Mitch Eakins) is the first to go (at exactly 4:20 P.M.), followed by rich kid Larnell (John Patrick Jordan) and jock Brett (Brian Lloyd), until only dorky Alister (David Weidoff) is left to solve the mystery. Turns out that a rip-off Eebee the Bong (voiced by Michele Mais) opens the door to a stoner fantasy world complete with topless strippers whose sole purpose is to fulfill your every desire— then mangle you with sharklike ferocity. *I Dream of Jeannie* she's not: Eebee cackles like Mo'Nique, has the looks of a blowfish in drag, and, oh yeah, she's evil! Enter Jimbo (Tommy Chong), Eebee's true owner, who explains her seductive curse. In a bid to save his crush, who got sucked into the bong's lair, Alister takes a hit, dives in, and saves the day, sacrificing Jimbo in the process. But fret not; the stoner elder lives on in Bong World, where half-naked girls pleasure him with Hot Wheels cars. Silly, bloody, and so bad it's worth watching once. Enter at your own risk.

> **"It killed all my friends, man. And it almost got me.**
>
> **Well, it got all my brain cells, but that's OK because I wasn't using them anyway."**
>
> **—Jimbo**

Faculty, The (1998)

 Director Robert Rodriguez teamed up with Kevin Williamson, writer of *Scream* and *Dawson's Creek*, to create this sci-fi flick about teachers that turn into aliens, starring a veritable who's who of late-nineties newcomers, including Jordana Brewster and Josh Hartnett. After Mr. Furlong (Jon Stewart) and his science class discover an unknown mutating parasite, teach decides to go in for a closer look and gets bitten by the mysterious fishlike creature. In an instant, he's infected with an alien disease (the alien in your body is the disease), which

spreads like wildfire through the school. Things go from bad to worse for Herrington High when the mind-controlled staff and students slowly turn the building into a zombie land, with only a few brave pupils—among them, the curious clique of perpetual loner Zeke (Hartnett), new girl Marybeth (Laura Harris), proud lesbian Stokely (Clea DuVall), Gabe (R & B star Usher), and Casey (Elijah Wood)—willing and able to fight back. As it turns out, Zeke's own cocainelike creation is the only antidote for the alien infection, which enters the body through the ear. It's best administered in a pen with a stab to the eye, as Mr. Furlong soon learns. Ouch! Sending the unexpected message that experimenting with the makeup of psychotropic drugs is sometimes a good thing, *The Faculty* is, for the most part, your average horror movie, with good shock value in a high school setting. What sets it apart is the sheer Rodriguezness of it all.

Stokely: "I'm not putting that hack drug up my nose, it's so eighties!"

Zeke: "Aliens are taking over the earth. Weigh it!"

Flash Gordon (1980)

🌿 🌿 🌿 🌿 Based on the Golden Age comics and serials of the 1930s, nice guy hero Flash Gordon (Sam J. Jones) faces off against uber-villain Emperor Ming the Merciless (Max von Sydow) in this camp classic. Flash and plucky girlfriend Dale (Melody Anderson), along with mad supergenius professor Dr. Hans Zarkov (Chaim Topol), travel to planet Mongo to save Earth from certain destruction and are captured by Ming and his slow-moving minions.

After an unintentionally silly battle between Flash and Ming's henchmen at Ming's royal court, Flash is sentenced to death. Saved at the last minute by Ming's scheming daughter, Princess Aura (Omelia Muti), to be her plaything, Flash escapes to foster rebellion among the many races of the Imperial planets. No-nonsense Dale finds herself among the royal concubines as Ming has decided to marry the Earth girl! All seems lost as Professor Zarkov is forced to get cozy with a mind-erasing ray gun. Bonus points go to the chief of Ming's secret police, the glam, chrome-faced, Darth Vader-esque Klytus (Peter Wyngarde). The plot is all episodic twists and turns, daring escapes, spaceship battles, and swamps on far-off planets, but who cares when the trip to get there is mainly by rocket cycle? Over-the-top doesn't begin to describe the art direction. With visual shades of *Barbarella*, *The Abominable Dr. Phibes*, and early-seventies British glam rock (hence the soundtrack by Queen), *Flash Gordon*, though named for its American hero, is a Euro-disco-and-spandex fever dream of eye-popping metallic costumes, crazy future-shock sets, and stupefyingly cheezoid visual effects. Like gorging on cotton candy, by the time you realize you should stop eating, the sugar coma has set in.

Galaxy Quest (1999)

🍸

🌿 🌿 🌿 🌿 Talk about a head-trip. When the cast members of *Galaxy Quest*, a *Star Trek*–like hit TV show from the eighties, are thrown into a real-life intergalactic war, they risk the extinction of a group of extraterrestrials who have been mimicking their space adventure moves for years. Actor Jason Nesmith (Tim Allen), the egomaniacal commander Taggart of the NSEA *Protector*, figures this out after he's recruited by Mathesar (Enrico Colantoni) and his Thermian crew (one of whom is played by *The Office*'s Rainn Wilson) to negotiate with Sarris (Robin Sachs), a lizardly foe who's hell-bent on destruction. Based on the *Galaxy Quest* "historical documents" (a.k.a. episodes), the Thermians have surmised that the *Protector* command, which includes the Spock-esque Dr. Lazarus (Alan Rickman); sexy computer operator Tawny Madison, née Gwen DeMarco (Sigourney Weaver); and hilariously stony Tech Sergeant Chen, né Fred Kwan (Tony Shaloub), is their only hope for survival. Of course, it's all fun and games until someone suffocates from oxygen deprivation. Once the Thermians understand that *Galaxy Quest* is a work of fiction, their faith seems irrevocably shattered. Leave it to a nerdtastic teenage fan, played brilliantly by a young Justin Long, to save the day. This sci-fi sleeper, featuring creatures and makeup designed by Stan Winston, has gained a massive following thanks to repeat airings on cable. You could even say it was ahead of its time. After all, its premise gives new meaning to reality television.

> "Hi, guys. Listen, they're telling me the generators won't take it; the ship is breaking apart and all that . . . Just FYI."
>
> —**Fred Kwan**

Ganjasaurus Rex
(1987)

🌿 🌱 🍸

🍁 🍁 This Humboldt County classic (available only on VHS) was a lo-fi favorite of the *High Times* crowd in the eighties. Set on the Lost Coast of California, where growers have been cultivating the kindest of buds since the beginning of time, the latest strain comes from the coconut-sized Cannabis sequoia seed, produced by Honey (Rosie Jones) and her husband, Moss (Howard Phun). Brothers Frank (Paul Bassis) and Cloud (Dave Fresh) plan to grow the "tree-sized" plants and, after meditating on a rock with heavy vibes, Cloud picks the perfect spot. Little do they all know that, in the process, a long dormant dinosaur would be awakened to feast on their crop. At the same time, cops and the Republican Just Say No–spewing a-holes known as C.A.M.P. (Campaign Against Marijuana Planting) are plotting a massive raid on any grow-ops they can find, only Ganjasaurus Rex beats them to the punch by snatching bundles of weed out of the helicopter's

---

🍁 AUSTIN WINKLER'S STONY MOVIE PICKS 🍁

Hinder frontman Austin Winkler, who sang "Get Stoned" on the band's double-platinum debut album, *Extreme Behavior*, certainly takes his movie-watching seriously. Here are his five favorite flicks to smoke to.

The Dark Knight (2008): "I thought it was a very intriguing movie, and I was obsessed with the fact that Heath Ledger was the Joker, so I watched it over and over again. Every scene that he's in, I'm thinking he's got to be losing it to go to that place. It's insane! I think he blew [Jack] Nicholson out of the water. He took the Joker up over the top and created this whole new very, very dark side of villains. Every time I get baked [on the tour bus], I go in my bunk, put on *The Dark Knight*, and just wait for his scenes."

The Strangers (2008): "I'm obsessed with horror, but *The Strangers* is so scary because it doesn't have the jumps and there's hardly any music in the whole thing. It's an unsolved mystery that's based on real events and set in a house in the middle of nowhere, but they created this really eerie story around it. Watching it stoned, you just focus on nothing else but the TV. It's fucking awesome."

1408 (2007): "A John Cusack movie I love is *1408*. It's based on a Stephen King story about an author [Mike Enslin] who's writing a book on haunted places and he hears about room 1408 at this hotel in New York City. He wants to rent this room, but they don't rent it out to anybody because it's evil. So he finds a way to go in there and really trippy shit starts to happen. The eeriest part is when he looks across the street and sees himself. He stands up, starts to wave. At one point, he opens the window and tries to climb out. He was planning on going over to the next room, and he goes out on a ledge, and he keeps going and going. There's only one window in this huge building! It's all crazy and fucking sick."

28 Days Later (2002): "This guy wakes up in the middle of London, and there's nothing around except for this disease that turns people into zombies. There's some really scary shit in that movie—the scene where they've escaped the city and they come across this abandoned gas station and find a little kid zombie; Cillian Murphy's character Jim knocks him out with a baseball bat. There's a real sense of horror in the movie, and Murphy does a great job at coming to terms with the fact that the world he knew is gone."

High Fidelity (2000): "I love the whole concept of *High Fidelity*, where everything is in Top Five lists. Jack Black is great, the music is unbelievable, and the way it's autobiographical—how John Cusack's character, Rob, kind of looks at the camera and talks so slow—I think for the whole movie, he's a little bit baked. Or maybe that's because whenever I watch it, I'm stoned."

clutches. Attracted by the smell of pot, the giant green monster soon makes his way into town and the residents panic. Naturally, it's up to the stony band of brothers and one kooky professor to trick the creature out to sea. A B movie of the highest order—and with its primitive camcorder trickery, poor sound quality, subpar acting, and a plot that's barely there—G-Rex is so bad it's almost good.

Frank to Rex: "This bud's for you."

Island of Dr. Moreau, The (1996)

The third film adaptation of H. G. Wells's 1896 novel—following 1933's *The Island of Lost Souls*, starring Bela Lugosi, and the 1977 version with Burt Lancaster—is the least compelling, but it does feature Val Kilmer repeatedly smoking a spliff as he slowly loses his mind. As the story goes, the year is 2010 and Dr. Moreau (Marlon Brando) has taken to playing God on a remote island where he experiments in crossbreeding humans and animals. The resulting man-beasts' animalistic behaviors are then suppressed using drugs. If they get out of line, a little shock therapy goes a long way—Dr. Moreau can zap them back into submission with the touch of a button. But when one of the deformed freaks figures out how to neutralize Moreau's weapon and goes after the self-proclaimed father, all hell breaks loose as the inmates take over the asylum and regress to a lawless, primitive society within hours. Moreau's dope-smoking number two, Dr. Montgomery (Kilmer), tries to fill the big man's shoes, but is quickly taken out of commission, leaving only UN negotiator Edward Douglas (David Thewlis), who'd survived a plane crash and was brought ashore, and Moreau's daughter, Aissa (Fairuza Balk), to come up with a way to stave off the natives and escape. It's not nearly as

> "There's so much you don't understand. Why don't you smoke this? Maybe you'll start."
>
> —Dr. Montgomery

dark and foreboding as the earlier treatments, and any suspense that does manage to make its way on screen is quickly diffused by some cheesy humanimals. Where's CGI when you need it?

Jason and the Argonauts (1963)

If you're in the mood for *Clash of the Titans* but looking to kick it old-school and see where the cinematic archetypical fantasy tropes originated, famed stop-motion animator Ray

Harryhausen's effects-laden masterpiece is an excellent choice. Based on the Greek mythological tale of Jason and the Golden Fleece, this film stumbles through exposition performed by a wooden but charming cast to deliver the goods when it finally gets down to battle-time with lovingly rendered monsters that emote in ways CGI has yet to match. The plot, however, is a little thin. Evil Pelias (Douglas Wilmer) kills King Aristo of Thessaly (never seen) and is cursed by the gods to be killed one day by Aristo's son Jason (Todd Armstrong). When a chance meeting brings them together, Pelias sends Jason on a quest to the end of the world to find a magical Golden Fleece. Through games of strength and skill, Jason puts together ship and crew, which includes even the mighty Hercules (a fantastically preening Nigel Green). He is watched over by the wife of Zeus (Niall MacGinnis), the scheming goddess Hera (Honor Blackman), who seems to have the hots for Jason, even taking up residence in the figurehead of his ship, the *Argo*. The quest is really just a way to link one stop-motion sequence to another; along the way, Jason slays multiheaded dragons, topples a giant bronze colossus, and clashes with sword-wielding skeletons. The pacing is brisk, Jason's love interest Medea (Nancy Kovack) is a stone-faced belly-dancing hottie, and there are plenty of fog-laden scenes of the gods on Mount Olympus mirthfully playing with the lives of humans. Harryhausen's monsters still look like nothing else before or since as they shimmy and shake, and *Jason and the Argonauts* remains a slice of even-keeled psychedelia that will stick in your brain for hours.

J-Men Forever (1979)

This black-and-white hodgepodge of amateur sci-fi trickery (the kind where you can practically see the string holding the flying saucer) stars the J-Men, unsung superheroes who, through a series of unfortunate events, battle the Lightning Bug, an ever-evolving villain intent on destroying Earth with a combination of rock-and-roll and drugs (mainly hash gas). Using a combination of old-time public domain serials from the thirties and forties and creative overdubbing, the gang plays out a series of scenarios that include encounters with all kinds of characters: a black widow here, Nazi there, Arabian sheiks peddling hash oil everywhere. The fight reaches radio airwaves, too, where, in cahoots with the F.C.C. (Federal Culture Control), the J-Men counter the Lightning Bug's awesome rock music (the soundtrack features killer tunes by The Tubes, Budgie, and Badazz, along with R & B keyboardist Billy Preston) with schmaltzy Muzak (created by M.U.S.A.C., the Military Underground Sugared Airwaves Command). But the Bug strikes back with a hash missile which he uses to bomb Los Angeles. Things just get kookier from there—the plot is as fuzzy as the late-night session that probably prompted it. Written by Philip Proctor and Peter Bergman of the Firesign Theatre, the troupe that brought stoner favorite *Zachariah* to the screen, *J-Men Forever* was a late-night staple in the eighties, thanks to repeat airings on USA Network's *Night Flight*. Since its release on DVD, the movie's cult status has grown exponentially, prompting a new appreciation for its inventiveness and zany dialogue (just one of the many ridiculous lines: "I love what hash gas does to earthlings, especially girls"). If only the original *Reefer Madness* was this much fun to watch.

Lightning Bug: "It's time for my other secret weapon: drugs. Yes, the buds and the drugs. My boys have got the weed we need, and soon the world will go to pot!"

Krull (1983)

Like a more acid-drenched version of *Clash of the Titans* crossed with *Lord of the Rings* and *Star Wars*, Krull pits young Prince Colwyn (Ken Marshall) against the Beast (Trevor Martin), an evil demon lord who has captured his virginal girlfriend-princess on their wedding day and trapped her in the constantly teleporting Black Fortress. Set on the distant planet Krull, the film offers constant eye candy: psychedelic sets; Colwyn's flying, spinning blade weapon; Rell (Bernard Bresslaw), a cyclops with a weird toylike eye; horses with hooves that make bridges of fire through the sky; the truly evil-looking space-suited minions of the Beast; and a detailed stop-motion glass spider. The movie's predictable story line drags this motley crew of heroes though dry ice swamps and giant spiderwebs to the final battle at the Black Fortress. The odd pairing of laser weapons and swords makes for some awkward battle sequences, but there's always a weird animated flash of light to let you know special powers are at work, attempting to make up for the stilted pacing.

Colwyn: "The Glaive is just an ancient symbol; it doesn't exist."

Ynyr the Old One: "It exists . . . in a cave up on the highest peak . . . "

Labyrinth (1986)

🌿 🌿 🌿 The last film from famed Muppet master Jim Henson finds David Bowie looking like a hair metal Jersey housewife. This typical fantasy story is about a young girl, Sarah (a teenage Jennifer Connelly), who wishes out loud that goblins would come and take away her crying baby brother, Toby (Toby Froud). Unaware that Jareth the Goblin King (Bowie) is near, her wish comes true and her brother disappears. Jareth appears to Sarah and tells her that she must solve his magical maze, the Labyrinth, if she wishes to save her brother. Transported to a magical land, she meets funny animals and creatures who help her navigate the twists and turns of the treacherous Labyrinth. Sir Didymus (voiced by David Shaughnessy), a fox riding a sheepdog, and Ludo (Ron Mueck), the inevitable furry gentle giant, become Sarah's closest friends and allies on her quest, rollicking around like a shaggy C3PO and hulking Chewbacca. Jareth is a cruel ruler over the creatures of the Labyrinth, but none are truly that scary or vicious. In fact, most seem like they're ready to punch out and leave the posturing to Bowie, who's always lurking in one corner or another making evil villain faces. The final showdown in Jareth's topsy-turvy castle has Bowie in full sneer as he spends most of his time walking on the ceiling, occasionally lapsing into singing the type of middling synthy ballads that sank his career. Connelly is her usual charming self as a young woman determined to avoid damsel-in-distress status. Even though the handsome Jareth does his best to seduce her, she still remembers the magic phrases that send her home to her cozy bedroom, safe and sound. Less ponderous than Henson's cosmic opus *The Dark Crystal*, not quite as endearing as *The NeverEnding Story*, and

---

🌿 ADRIANNE CURRY'S STONY MOVIE PICKS 🌿

Reality TV star Adrianne Curry was the first winner of *America's Next Top Model*, a former *Surreal Life* cast member, and the star of VH1's *My Fair Brady*, alongside her husband, Christopher Knight. She's also a loud and proud pot smoker and, when it comes to movies, a lover of all things fantastical. Here, her five favorite fantasy films.

***The NeverEnding Story* (1984):** "Back in the eighties, there were these weird, trippy kids' movies. You have to wonder: why on earth did they make this for children? It's scary, and strange, and I dig that. I think it helped make me the weirdo I am today. *The NeverEnding Story* is one of those movies and it rules because it's got all kinds of talking animals: there's flying magical lockdragons (that's a big dog) with names like Gmork, the bad guy is a talking wolf, there's a big talking turtle and a racing snail . . . It's so fun to smoke and watch the cheesy eighties effects. I think I even tripped to it a few times."

***Legend* (1985):** "This is one of Tom Cruise's first movies, back when he was really cute. He plays a guy who falls in love with a pretty girl named Princess Lily and is friends with little leprechauns and fairies in these mystical woods. There are these unicorns that symbolized God or life. They're supposed to remain untouched but this girl touches them, and, according to legend, something bad happens. So the unicorn is captured and its horn gets chopped up, which takes away all the light and brings in eternal darkness. The rest of the movie is about this guy and girl trying to save this unicorn. But Lily gets sucked in. Satan [Tim Curry] tries to seduce her, and dresses her in these goth clothes. She's dancing with this faceless thing; it's pretty dope. Happy ending: She ends up not fucking Satan, and releases the unicorn at the last second, just before Jack [Cruise] has to kill her with a bow and arrow. They put the horn back on the dead unicorn, it comes back to life, God is reborn, and they live happily ever after. Mystical things, hot people, Tom Cruise making out with a chick where he really seems to mean it, hokey eighties effects—beginning to end, this movie is great to get stoned to."

less visually psychedelic than *Legend*, *Labyrinth* nevertheless has its girlish charms. But it's all a bit lightweight here—no hidden fangs are ever really bared, and the battles between goblins and heroes have the gravitas of middle school recess. Working its way to a happy ending from the very start, *Labyrinth* is a sweet confection that wears off rapidly.

Jareth to Sarah: "I have reordered time, I have turned the world upside down and I have done it all for you. I'm exhausted living up to your expectations."

Return to Oz (1985): "This is like the bizarro *Wizard of Oz*. Fairuza Balk, who was in *The Craft* and *American History X*, plays Dorothy back in Kansas. Her parents think she's psychotic because she keeps talking about Oz, so they send her to a mental hospital to get electroshock therapy. She and this little girl try to escape the hospital right before her ass is about to be zapped. There's a storm, the power goes off and they're like, 'Let's get the fuck out of here!' They try to swim through this river and get swept away, and all of a sudden, Dorothy finds herself back in Oz, but it's been overrun by a witch and the Cowardly Lion, has been turned to stone. It's a dreary Oz—run-down, the yellow brick road is all messed up, the Munchkins aren't there, it's awful. Oh yeah, this movie is dark and twisted in the beginning, but everything turns out good in the end."

Labyrinth (1986): "I saw *Labyrinth* long before I started getting stoned, and it's another one of those movies where you wonder why kids were ever allowed to watch it. David Bowie's nutsack is on full display in these little spandex, and he's trying to fuck Jennifer Connelly who's, like, thirteen. That's how I fell in love with Bowie. I loved his hair and the music. But there are lots of stony characters,

like Pluto, this big hairy beast who reminds me of a stoner. He's all like, 'Meeeeeee hungryyyyy.' And the labyrinth itself is pretty awesome. It's Jim Henson, so cheesy but so great."

The Fountain (2006): "Talk about a head-trip, *The Fountain* is like a romantic *Donnie Darko* that takes place in three different times. It starts in the medieval days, where this guy Thomas [Hugh Jackman] is a conquistador, and a Queen Elizabeth–like chick, played by Rachel Weisz, orders him to find the tree of life, which they think is in an ancient Mayan temple. All of a sudden, it skips to modern times where she's dying of cancer and he's trying to save her. Then it skips forward to the future where she dies, and he's found the tree of life. He's in a spaceship going up to this dying star and it's insanely beautiful as he goes through all these layers. At the very end, he sacrifices himself to rebirth the tree because there's this old Mayan saying that the first father sacrificed himself to have the world grow. It's heavy, trippy Buddhist shit, and it's also really sad—it's about loving someone, letting them go, and allowing fate to run its course. You can watch it again and again and find different meanings."

Laserblast (1978)

🍁 🍁 🍁 🍁 As low-budget as sci-fi films get, *Laserblast* begins with a tripped-out, green-faced creature who's packing a laser gun and combing the desert, only to be startled by a flying spacecraft clearly being held by a string over a painted background. The spacecraft opens its doors for freaky-looking Claymation aliens also armed with lasers. A massive laser battle ensues, leaving behind a memento. Back in reality, we wake up with Billy (Kim Milford), a golden-haired, shirtless beach boy whose mother ditches him for Acapulco. The very definition of a stoner, he's always driving his van around aimlessly and dreaming he's an alien. Billy's wish comes true when he happens upon a laser gun. He becomes drunk from its laser beam, and blasts every cactus he can find as well as his archnemesis's blue Caddy. The more Billy uses the laser gun, the more he craves it and the creature it turns him into. He goes on a few more rampages, even blowing up a *Star Wars* billboard, but things start turning sour for Billy when a "dude from Washington" shows up asking all sorts of questions. Because he pissed off the aliens, Billy eventually meets his end, but only after several awesome scenes of cars exploding. A tripped-out experiment that succeeded, it doesn't get more stoner-friendly than cops getting high, which happens in *Laserblast* when deputies hit a joint they confiscated while staking out speeders.

Deputy Pete Ungar (Dennis Burkley): "The kid's nuts; he's seen *Star Wars* five times."

Legend (1986)

🍁 🍁 🍁 Set in a fairy-tale forest that's more scary than magical, this dreamlike movie is your basic good-versus-evil story with Tim Curry turning in a stellar performance as Darkness, the evil horned king who manages to blend true cruelty with childlike innocence. He far outshines bland hero Jack (Tom Cruise), the forest boy who struggles to save his pretty girlfriend, Lily (Mia Sara, Ferris Bueller's squeeze), and a unicorn from being sacrificed at the altar of Curry's interdimensional outer-space gate. With lots of elves and funny leprechauns, slow-motion shots of leaves in the wind, demon kitchen cooks, and magic everywhere, it's a long wait for the unicorn payoff, but worth it in the end. Tangerine Dream provides the essential space-rock drone soundtrack and most of *Legend* feels like it's running at half-speed. While you're waiting for screwball Billy Barty's dwarf character to climb up the chimney and place the mirror that will bring true sunlight into the hall of the evil lord, you find that time has begun to run really, really slowly.

Lily: "You are nothing but an animal."

Darkness: "We are all animals, milady."

Little Shop of Horrors (1960, 1986)

🍁 🍁 🍁, 🍁 🍁 🍁 🍁 Now a staple of the high school musical circuit, this fantastical tale of a flower shop employee and his blood-sucking plant was first introduced to theater audiences as a 1960 B movie directed by Roger Corman (*The Trip*, *The Wild Angels*). Shot in just two days, the black-and-white picture stars Jonathan Haze as dopey botanist Seymour Krelboyne and features a twenty-three-year-old Jack Nicholson as pain-loving dental patient Wilbur Force. Watch it now and it's hard not to chuckle at the frequent mentions

Halloween **(1978):** Headed to babysitting gigs, Laurie (Jamie Lee Curtis) and her friend Annie (Nancy Kyes) smoke a joint in the car while listening to Blue Öyster Cult's "Don't Fear the Reaper." An unexpected run-in with Annie's cop dad is a close call, but nothing compared to the killer on their tail. Remarks Laurie: "I think he knew. He could smell it."

Poltergeist **(1982):** One violently stormy night, parents Steve (Craig T. Nelson) and Diane (JoBeth Williams) casually share a joint and the giggles in bed. When spooked son Robbie (Oliver Robins) interrupts the fun, it's Dad's duty to explain the wisdom of scary old trees. As for the TV that's talking to daughter Carol Anne (Heather O'Rourke)? That leaves the doting parents baffled.

Cape Fear **(1991):** In one of the film's best known and most provocative scenes, young Danielle (Juliette Lewis) encounters ex-con Max Cady (Robert De Niro) smoking grass in a Candyland-like house on a darkened school theater stage. Posing as the drama teacher, he offers Danielle the joint, gets her high, then seduces her, famously sticking his thumb in her mouth.

Friday the 13th **(2009):** After what's ostensibly a flashback from the original, fast-forward thirty years and five kids go camping at Crystal Lake and try to locate "the crop." They get lost in the woods, but find the weed by accidentally pissing on the plants. Eventually, they all get killed. Six weeks later, another blissfully unaware group arrives with bong in tow, and you can guess how that trip turns out.

of buds and the second-rate Jewish humor, not to mention the plant's hokey hypnotic powers. Some two decades later, the musical version debuted on Broadway, followed by a 1986 film adapted from the stage show, directed by Frank Oz (of *Muppet Show* fame), and starring Rick Moranis as Seymour, Steve Martin as the sadistic dentist and Elvis look-alike who gets high on his own nitrous supply, and Bill Murray as his masochistic patient. Meanwhile the plant, named Audrey II rather than the passé Audrey Jr., is a soul brother voiced by Levi Stubbs of the Four Tops and a self-declared "mean green mother from outer space" hell-bent on being bad. Catchy tunes, the brilliant pairing of Martin and Murray, and an ever-so-slight subversive undertone thanks to the twisted premise (which earned it a PG-13 rating) all make for a good time. And, in both incarnations, can you really go wrong with a giant bud that looks like a vagina?

[1960 version] Audrey: "Seymour, what do you wanna be?"

Seymour: "I wanna grow things. If I had a lot of money I'd go to the South Seas where they grow the most fabulous plants in the world."

Lord of the Rings: The Fellowship of the Ring (2001)

Lord of the Rings: The Two Towers (2002)

Lord of the Rings: The Return of the King (2003)

🔑 ⚥◊ 🍄

🌿🌿🌿, 🌿🌿🌿🌿, 🌿🌿🌿🌿🌿, Visually stunning and epic in scope, the Lord of the Rings trilogy is a worthy translation of the eternally popular J. R. R. Tolkien books that seemed impossible to bring to the big screen. Director Peter Jackson's series, easy to watch and follow even for the swords-and-sorcery neophyte, is packed to the brim with the kind of geeky detail that brings life to every microscopic character and backstory myth that populates this fully realized world. The eventful narrative, which concerns the denizens of Middle Earth, features an impressive range of races—some rather humanlike, some less so—who band together to fight Sauron the Dark Lord who threatens to bring eternal evil to their lands. A blend of emotional character development and massive battlefield CGI set pieces will rattle your speakers and the inside of your skull, so you'll want to watch this on the biggest screen possible.

Now, stoners everywhere, raise your bongs high to the smallest pipe-hitting creatures of all—the furry-footed hobbits Merry (Dominic Monaghan) and Pippin (Billy Boyd). These two lunkheads and unlikely heros, Middle Earth's Cheech and Chong, spend most of their time looking for a good snack (mushrooms, yum!) and bemoaning that their "pipe weed" is running out. And what are they smoking anyhow? They get very, very hungry afterward. Then there's the great wizard Gandalf (Sir Ian McKellen); he sure has his pipe skills together, as he blows a smoke ring that takes the form of a ship. Trippy. Yet, the stoniest substance by far is The Ring made of gold—or what a freaky bald, alien-looking fella named Gollum (Andy Serkis) calls "my precious." Hobbit Frodo Baggins (Elijah Woods) is saddled with the task of having to leave his happy Shire village to travel far and dangerous distances in order to destroy the deviously addictive ring. Doing so will bring down its evil maker, Sauron, whose war machine is gearing up to enslave everyone in Middle Earth.

Whether you watch all three movies in succession, or just one at a time, you'll find something new in each viewing. The world that Jackson created is so vast and its species so numerous (elves and orcs and talking trees, oh my!) that it's easy to get lost in it—and it's all the more dizzying when experienced in an altered state. Over three successive years, the films picked up seventeen Oscars out of thirty nominations, including a Best Picture win for The Return of the King in 2003.

Merry (taking a drag from his pipe and chewing on a bun): "It's good . . . definitely from the Shire. Long Bottom leaf . . . hmm?"

Pippin (toking from his own pipe): "Mmmm! I feel I'm back at the Green Dragon, a mug of ale in my hand, putting my feet up on a settee after a hard day's work."

Merry: "Only . . . you've never done a hard day's work!"

Man with the X-Ray Eyes, The (1963)

🍸 ✂

🌿 🌿 🌿 🌿 In this early psychedelic classic, Roger Corman directs Ray Milland as Dr. James Xavier, a mad scientist of sorts who invents an eye fluid that allows him to see virtually everything. At first, it's fun—at a party where all the kids do the twist, the dancers are naked (you see a lot of curvy backs and legs). But his real power is to heal, and after being drummed out of the hospital as a quack, he winds up in a sideshow at a carnival where Don Rickles plays an opportunistic barker (he's terrific as the sleazy Crane). Xavier's rescued by Dr. Fairbanks (Diana Van de Vlis), his quasi–love interest, but he's too far gone by then. Wearing thick shades to hide his now-metallic eyes, he can see only images that are blurred as if viewed through a prism, with streaks of flashing colors. The opening purple swirl sets the strange tone and Les Baxter's jazzy score keeps toes tapping. You'll need a sense of humor for the film's shocking tent revival finale.

Xavier: "Soon I'll be able to see what no man has ever seen."

Matrix, The (1999)

🍸 💊

🌿 🌿 🌿 🌿 🌿 Toward the beginning of the Wachowski brothers' classic sci-fi action extravaganza The Matrix, Neo (a perfectly innocent Keanu Reeves) is asked by Morpheus (Laurence Fishburne) to choose between a red and blue pill, one of which will allow him to continue the life he's always led (which, we learn, is actually a computer-generated hallucination), and the other, which will open his eyes to a nightmarish future world, full of human farms run by machines hell-bent on using our race as living batteries. It's the only direct drug reference in the movie, but, man, is this film heady: using theories of life from a slew of philosophers, The Matrix manages to be both thoughtful and exciting. Even more surprisingly, it stands up over a decade later as a richly conceived, envelope-pushing thriller, thanks both to a story that still feels fresh (Morpheus decides Neo is "the One," the only person who can free the entire human race) and the special effects, which find Reeves and Fishburne dodging gunfire in super-slo-mo "bullet time." Rarely has an alternate universe's mythology been more intensely thought through—which is why the tossed-togetherness of both 2003 sequels, The Matrix Revolutions and The Matrix Reloaded, thoroughly disappoints. The original, though, is a shoot-'em-up with a heart and a purpose, grounded enough to seem almost real, but crazy enough to definitely inspire a heartfelt "Whoa!"

Monster High (1989)

✏ 🪴

🌿 🌿 🌿 Like any eighties sci-fi comedy worth its salt, Monster High starts with a warning: some of the material may be considered objectionable by sensitive viewers, dead people, and farm animals. Swiftly, the story moves just a couple of blocks past the farthest imaginable point in the universe, with the godlike Monster in Charge noticing that the destruction of Earth has been postponed. After receiving an in-depth report from a topless secretary, the Monster in Charge realizes his archnemesis, Mr. Armageddon (David Marriott), has been captured by two clumsy, freestyle-rapping aliens, Dume (Robert Lind) and Glume (Sean Haines). After a hasty escape, Dume and Glume accidentally transport themselves to Earth, dropping out of the sky with their stolen goods and landing atop a chihuahua right in front of Montgomery Sterling High School. When the two idiotic aliens open the box marked "Doomsday Device," they find a basketball containing the deadliest weapon known to man. It explodes to reveal a very angry Armageddon, who starts the doomsday party off right by transforming a statue into a horny rubber monster. Mind you this is all before the opening credits even take place. As it turns out, Montgomery Sterling is a big basketball school, which pleases Mr. Armageddon and convinces him to stick around for a while, killing video game nerds with their own computers and inspiring a stoner's crop to come to life in form of a gigantic plant that wanders the hallways eating students. Hokey, ridiculous, and oddly fun, file this low-rent monster movie concept under B for "baked."

Plan 9 from Outer Space (1959)

Director Ed Wood's magnum opus teeters on the edge of cohesion, surfing a wave of weirdness that's more about just getting it on film than mundane things such as plot, character development, and continuity. It's a flying saucer movie where you can see the wires, everyone moves really, really, really slowly, and cheapo soundstage shots are butted up against even cheaper location footage like you're switching channels. Characters wander in and out of scenes as if they're caught in the time flow of a parallel universe, occasionally rattling off some kind of exposition that's often oddly self-contradictory and has to be explained via voice-over to keep the whole thing from running off the rails. This grade-Z graveyard is the final resting place of Bela Lugosi, who died before shooting could be completed and was replaced mid-movie. The insane solution to his sad unavailability: another actor who is always shown with a caped arm in front of his face and still manages to look nothing like the horror film legend. It sort of doesn't matter, as Lugosi just floats in and out of the film anyhow, with a thin shred of logic connecting him to the plot, which involves an alien invasion force resurrecting the newly dead from a graveyard in the San Fernando Valley. Suffice it to say that alien grave robbers, zombies, and goth princess Vampira wandering around in a fog (literally and figuratively) may get you in the door, but you won't stay for the story. More force of will than movie, *Plan 9* is a heavy, stupefying high that glues you to your seat like the gravity of a thousand suns. Too bizarre to live, too weird to die, it will probably be the only movie left at the end of time, leaving people to wonder what the big deal was about these "humans" and their "cinemas."

Pot Zombies (2005)

A low-budget, shot-on-video gorefest running on zero plot, this series of unconnected setups never changes: lame dialogue, someone smokes some weed, turns into a green zombie, and kills everyone around them. Puff, puff, pass, repeat. The radioactive "nevas cannibus setiva" [*sic*] is treated with some kind of dastardly material that gets no explanation, and the punk rock soundtrack does little to dismiss the sneaking feeling that, at its heart, this is more about just getting it on film antiweed film than a horror goof. And that's aside from the disclosure in the beginning that the makers "do not condone the use of marijuana" and the graphics that come up stating that the weed isn't real and that you "shouldn't try this at home." To top off the stereotype, every stoner is a fumbling, loser dumb-ass who can barely compose an intelligible sentence and starts freaking out from the pot even before they transition into a zombie. With humor that sinks way below the level of a horny juvenile and gore that's subpar, *Pot Zombies* fails to succeed even on the level of so-bad-it's-good. The "demonic chronic" is phony, remember?

Predator 2 (1990)

Rival drug gangs—Columbian and Jamaican, in all their politically incorrect splendor (we see them fueling up on cocaine and supersize spliffs, respectively)—take it to the streets, obliterating each other in tireless machine-gun fights. Clearly an opportunist, the Predator (Kevin Peter Hall) joins in, leaving both narcotics peddlers, and the officers trying to catch them, in various states of disembowelment. The Predator manages to relocate from the backwoods of Guatemala to the concrete jungle of L.A. with nothing but a wing, a prayer, the power of heat vision, and an insatiable desire to gut homo sapiens. Gruff, seasoned cop Lt. Mike Harrigan (Danny Glover) and his crew—including Gary Busey, Bill Paxton, and Ruben Blades—follow a trail that leads to the bloodthirsty Predator itself, who they learn has a soft spot for pregnant ladies. Awww, he has feelings; too bad the tagline to this sequel reads "Hunting season opens again." Without the Arnold Schwarzenegger/Carl Weathers/Jesse Ventura trifecta of macho from the original *Predator* (1987), this here story lacks muscle. But let's not be hasty! Consider *Predator 2*, instead, a college drinking game abounding in eighties big-budget movie clichés.

Princess Bride, The
(1987)

🍸🧴 💊

🌿🌿🌿🌿 In all its sweetness, this enchanting kids' flick may seem sappy, but it's also smart and surprisingly stony, what with far-out Bosch-esque locales like the Cliffs of Insanity and the Pit of Despair, and mythical creatures like shrieking eels and the Fire Swamp's gnarly ROUSes, or "rodents of unusual size." But first and foremost, it's a love story about Buttercup (Robin Wright), a would-be princess, and former farm boy Westley (Cary Elwes), who is rumored to be dead but lives on as the Dread Pirate Roberts. She's about to marry evil Prince Humperdink (Chris Sarandon), and it's up to her true love to get her back. With the help of friendly orge Fezzik (Andre the Giant), Spanish swordsman Inigo Montoya (Mandy Patinkin), and a pill courtesy of Mr. and Mrs. Miracle Max (Carol Kane and Billy Crystal), Westley is revived and re-united with Buttercup, while Humperdink and his sinister number two, Count Rugen (Christopher Guest), are put out of commission. Dire Straits's Mark Knopfler handles the score to this quirky flick, which, for once, lives up to the "fun for the whole family" promise.

Inigo Montoya: "That's a miracle pill?"

Mrs. Max: "The chocolate coating makes it go down easier, but you have to wait fifteen minutes before potency and shouldn't go swimming for at least, what?"

Miracle Max: "An hour. A good hour."

🌿 UNICORNS AND OTHER STONY CREATURES 🌿

Fantasy is best served with hind legs. Here, some stony big screen scenes that feature a host of trippy mythical animals.

Legend (1985): Director Ridley Scott keeps his unicorns—with manes that part like clouds in the morning sky—in slow motion with rose petals fluttering around them. But the pure heart of Legend's universe all goes dark when one loses its horn to the evil goblins. The reunion of horn and horse in the final act is cheesy but awesome with plenty of jubilant rearing and jumping. Consider it unicorn porn at its cinematic height.

Lord of the Rings: The Two Towers (2002): As guardians of the forest, the shaggy, moss-covered talking trees known as the Ents think slow and talk slower but unleash a major can of whoop ass on Saruman's army, making for the Two Towers' best battle scenes.

Anchorman: The Legend of Ron Burgundy (2004): Riding matching pink-and-blue unicorns through the cartoon Pleasure Town, Ron Burgundy (Will Ferrell) and Veronica Corningstone (Christina Applegate) consummate their love on "the most glorious rainbow ever," then slide down its cloudlike rays back to reality.

Napoleon Dynamite (2004): Eternally dorky Napoleon Dynamite (Jon Heder) wears his unicorn obsession proudly (who can forget his "Pegasus Xing" door sign), but takes it a step further by constantly perfecting sketches of his favorite animal, the Liger. "It's like a lion and a tiger mixed," he tells Deb (Tina Majorino) at school. "Bred for its skills in magic."

Harold & Kumar Escape from Guantanamo Bay (2008): In one of Guantanamo Bay's stand-out moments, Neil Patrick Harris scarfs a bag of mushrooms, then rides off into the psychedelic Milky Way on his twinkling pink-horned unicorn, beckoning to his tripping NPH self, "If you want to know the secret of being, you will come with us."

Pumpkinhead II: Blood Wings (1994)

🗡 🍸

🌿🌿 This ridiculous horror flick starts with a flashback: it's the 1950s and a deformed kid named Tommy, who lives in the woods, is constantly being teased by some good ol' boys from the local high school. One day, the mocking goes a little too far and they end up slashing Tommy with their greaser switchblades and leaving him for dead. Fast-forward to the 1990s and meet Danny Dixon (J. Trevor Edmond), a smooth dude who likes to smoke weed and hit on chicks. He meets the new girl, Jenny (Amy Dolenz), on her first day of school and offers a joint and a ride. The two play hooky and head into the woods to light up and drink some beer. Turns out Jenny is the new sheriff's daughter, and when they get caught for ditching school, he makes her promise not to hang with the badasses anymore. The partying teens accidentally run over a sketchy-looking witch lurking about in the woods, and the plot goes all I Know What You Did Last Summer. Naturally, these dumb kids head to the witch's cabin, where they discover a spell to raise the dead. They dig up Tommy's pentagram-shaped grave and it erupts into a giant alien monster that wants revenge on all who had to do with his death. By now, of course, we've all figured out that Tommy is Pumpkinhead and that Danny's dad was the head of the bullies way back when. With new conviction, Pumpkinhead viciously murders Danny, his friends, and, as promised, all who had a hand in his death, leaving you almost satisfied that everyone got what they deserved.

Return of the Jedi (1983)

🔥 🔑 🍸

🌿🌿🌿🌿 The Star Wars franchise's final showdown starts in the desert and ends in the forest as the Rebel Alliance sets out to destroy a partially rebuilt Death Star. But first, there's the matter of Han Solo (Harrison Ford) frozen in carbonite. Han was captured by bounty hunter Boba Fett at the end of Empire Strikes Back, and handed off to Jabba the Hutt. The slimy crime lord rules his sordid lair from a throne fit for a blob, drinking space booze and puffing on a hookahlike waterpipe with a hot lady shackled to his side. But he's no match for the Force, and the feather-haired Luke Skywalker (Mark Hamill) is out to prove himself yet again. With an assist from Princess Leia (Carrie Fisher) in the slinky metal bikini, Lando Calrissian (Billy Dee Williams), Chewbacca, and droids C3PO and R2D2, Han is thawed and all live to fight another day on the planet Endor. That's where furry little creatures called Ewoks—only slightly less annoying predecessors to Phantom Menace's Jar Jar Binks—dwell and wait for their golden god. But the mini-bears, whose forest parties involve pipe smoking and drum circles, aren't completely useless—they help the rebels shut down the empire's energy field. Luke, meanwhile, faces his familial fate by confronting Darth Vader, now confirmed to be his father. Fighting the emperor and the power of the dark side takes all his might, but after a dramatic light-saber duel, good triumphs over evil and the book is officially closed. As hotly anticipated as its predecessor, Jedi's big revelation was the half-human under Vader's machine mask. To that end, Anakin Skywalker, bearing little resemblance to Hayden Christensen, who would play him in the future, er, past, may seem a bit anticlimactic. But compared to the CGI overindulgence to come, consider it a fond reminder of the end of an era.

Scanner Darkly, A (2006)

🗡 🍸 ✒ 🥄 👀

🌿🌿🌿🌿 Five years after their groundbreaking first animated flick, Waking Life, Dazed and Confused director Richard Linklater and CGI whiz Bob Sabiston fixed their psychedelic, rotoscoping eyes on an actual story: an adaptation of Philip K. Dick's cautionary tale of an undercover narcotics agent hooked on the very drug he's supposed to stamp out. In a near-future dystopia set in Disneyland's hometown, where most of the non-neocons have turned into junkies, Bob Arctor (a fascinatingly stiff Keanu Reeves) works as a narc codenamed "Fred," who's assigned to observe shady characters inside his own home through video surveillance. His goal: deduce the high-level dealer of Substance D—red psycho-active pills that sever the brain's cognitive powers, inducing paranoia and hallucinations of giant bugs straight out of *Naked Lunch*. It's a heavy trip: "There are no weekend warriors on the D," says Arctor's drug buddy James Barris (a twitchy Robert Downey Jr., channeling Hunter S. Thompson). "You're either on it, or you haven't tried it."

Arctor attempts to draw out the source by buying from (and wooing) cokehead Donna Hawthorne (a sometimes naked Winona Ryder) while averting the attention of his two tweaked housemates, highly suspicious Barris and perma-doper Ernie Luckman (a loopy Woody Harrelson in beach-bum gear). But instead of posing as a user, Arctor digs in and gets addicted. Eventually, he loses touch with reality and is unable to discern friend from foe. A stinging sci-fi indictment of Nixon/Bush–style governmental control drenched in dark comedy, *Scanner* teems with memorable dialogue ("I'm gonna knock your 'nads up into your nostrils!") and wicked visuals, none more mind-bending than Arctor's "scramble suit," a constantly morphing identity shield that can leave viewers feeling like they're looking at a hundred people at once.

☘ STONY SCI-FI COMEDIES ☘

Is there anything stonier than creatures from out of this world? Besides the beloved *Buckaroo Banzai* and the incomparable *Galaxy Quest*, here are five more sci-fi flicks guaranteed to give you the giggles.

Ghostbusters (1984): Goblins and ghosts go hog wild on New York City, inhabiting a grand Central Park apartment building along with the bodies of several of its tenants. It's up to kooky parapsychologists the Ghostbusters—the perfect comedic trifecta of Bill Murray, Harold Ramis, and Dan Aykroyd—to restore order by trapping the green and gooey nuisances, but not before all hell breaks loose and a giant, sinister Stay-Puft Marshmallow Man descends on the city's streets Godzilla-style. Who you gonna call?

Real Genius (1985): This comedy, which helped launch Val Kilmer's career, centers on student Chris Knight (Kilmer), who's both an overachiever and a hopeless slacker. Thanks to his brilliance, party animal Chris is sailing through his senior year until his professor asks him to build a secret weapon. Nifty student gadgetry abounds, along with girls and a government agenda. Throw in *Top Secret* for a stony Kilmer double feature.

Earth Girls Are Easy (1988): Aliens crash-land in a pool outside of Los Angeles and a couple of Valley girls turn them into eighties studs? Geena Davis stars in this musical as manicurist Valerie Gail, who, along with gal pal Candy Pink (Julie Brown) shows Mac (Jeff Goldblum), Wiploc (Jim Carrey), and Zeebo (Damon Wayans) the ropes. They, in turn, spark rainbow-colored trails with the touch of the hand. Also flying high? Michael McKean as stoner surfer Woody and the spaceship's final destination: a giant donut in the sky.

Mars Attacks! (1996): Earth's worst nightmare comes true when its major cities are incinerated by nasty little deceptive Martians in Tim Burton's version of the alien apocalypse. Nothing seems to faze these buggers, who can suck down the thrust of a nuclear missile like it was a bong hit. Jack Nicholson as the president heads an all-star cast that includes Glenn Close, Annette Bening, Pierce Brosnan, and Sarah Jessica Parker, but it's the kids (Natalie Portman and Lukas Haas) who save the day.

Men in Black (1997): Agents K (Tommy Lee Jones) and J (Will Smith) are on a mission to find a miniature galaxy hidden by an alien on a cat's collar. If that's not a zany enough premise for you, how about animatronic alien bugs; a groovy sixties-inspired Men in Black headquarters; and one no-nonsense wreck of a car with an all-powerful red button. For these space protectors, the future's so bright, they gotta wear shades.

Shrooms (2007)

 When a group of American college buds head to Ireland in search of a magical mushroom trip, they get a deadly dose of their own medicine, starting with some indigenous people armed with axes who come close to hacking up the travelers for running over the goat they were hunting. Once the Americans set up camp, the group embarks on their 'shrooms hunt, with a guide leading the way and helping distinguish the mushrooms they can consume from black nipple cap, also known as death head's fungi, which explodes your heart and fries your kidneys. Too bad for Tara (Lindsey Haun), who missed that part of the tour. She munches down a black cap, and suffers a seizurelike meltdown. Once their guide spits out the local ghost stories, the paranoid shit hits the fan. Tara starts having visions of the future, and predicts the murder of their friend Bluto (Robert Hoffman), who drinks too much mushroom tea and stumbles into the forest, losing his mind and, eventually, his penis at the hands of a grim reaper–like monster. Confused between reality and the scary psychedelic hell world Tara is stuck in, the group follows suit and the story disintegrates just as fast. Despite the lame script, the crisp cinematography and location save the film. And while the psychedelic visuals are a little lackluster for a movie called *Shrooms*, it's trippy nonetheless.

> "I overdosed on the heroin of 'shrooms!"
>
> —Tara

Silent Running (1972)

 From its opening montage of nature in bloom, with Bruce Dern sauntering through a floating forest wearing the 1972 version of a Snuggie, you know this is no ordinary sci-fi flick. Indeed, you could say *Silent Running* was way ahead of its time in predicting environmental catastrophe. The story begins in an unspecified year when all plant life on Earth has become extinct. A replica of a terrestrial forest, with several indigenous creatures, is being meticulously maintained in space in hopes that the planet can one day be reforested. The bio-domed greenhouse in endless orbit looks like a giant snow globe glistening in the sun, albeit a sad and lonely one—much like chief botanist Freeman Lowell (Dern), who's stationed alone on the massive space freighter after killing off his crewmates for trying to detonate the forest. For company, he reprograms three robots that, like the future R2D2, exhibit human emotions and essentially become his friends. Lowell takes the ship off course through the psychedelic rings of Jupiter and is essentially written off by his superiors back on Earth. It's exactly what this loner and rebel wants—conservation on his terms (complete with accompaniment by sixties folkie Joan Baez). It's no coincidence that the slow crawl of massive machinery has that 2001: *A Space Odyssey* feel—this film was directed by Douglas Trumbull, who worked on the special effects for 2001. Only this time around, the computer is far less sophisticated and the human is very much in control.

Sin City (2005)

 Processed into a gleaming black-and-white eternal night, Sin City is a stunning tour de force that occasionally explodes with shockingly bold colors. Co-directors Robert Rodriguez and Frank Miller bring Miller's gritty urban noir graphic novels to life, staying incredibly true to the original in both visual form and dialogue. A careening hell ride that is stunning to look at, it exists in a moral realm of its own, where violence is justified and even required to restore order and balance. Focusing on three vignettes from Miller's saga, each features a stoic male lead who seems to eat bullets and deal death at all turns, all in the service of some dame that's stolen his heart. Mickey Rourke turns in a sledgehammer performance as Marv, a gonzo strongman on a rampage to avenge the death of a hooker who was kind to him for a single night. With machinelike single-mindedness, he blazes a trail of blood that leads him to cannibalistic murderer Kevin (Elijah Wood) and ultimately to the electric chair, laughing as they throw the switch. Clive Owen follows as Dwight, a hard-nosed hustler who tries to protect the hookers of Old Town from the lecherous advances of crooked cop Jackie Boy (Benicio Del Toro). Jackie Boy winds up dead at the hands of pixie ninja Miho (Devon Aoki in an involved but nonspeaking role). As a gang turf war threatens to break out, Dwight struggles to rescue his ex-girlfriend Gale (geek goddess Rosario Dawson) from the clutches of the mob. All looks lost, until the girls show up with submachine guns raining hellfire on the doomed gangsters. Bookending both stories is Bruce Willis as Hartigan, a hero cop with one foot perpetually in the grave. He saves a little girl, Nancy (Makenzie Vega), from psychotic pedophile Roarke Jr. (Nick Stahl). Leaving his adversary mortally wounded, Hartigan is betrayed and takes the fall for the crime. Years pass and Hartigan unknowingly leads the mutated Roarke Jr. (now the Yellow Bastard) back to Nancy (Jessica Alba). She's kidnapped by the Yellow Bastard for a second time and a bullet-ridden Hartigan staves off his heart attack long enough to rescue her—this time free and safe forever.

With a body count like an advanced calculus class, Sin City has been described as a "translation" of Miller's original work in which every frame looks and feels like his graphic novel. The film is beautiful, a cathedral of shadows and stolen cars, the violence a symphony of carnage and revenge, final blows most likely delivered by the swing of an ax, the twist of a knife, or a good old fashioned beating. Brutes they may all be, but the dialogue, quick and short, bursts like gunfire filled with the kind of gritty one-liners that stick with you for days. A tale of modern primitives surviving in the Darwinian urban chaos, it's twenty-first-century noir with the contrast on eleven.

Star Trek: The Motion Picture (1979)

A bit like hanging with your grandparents (if they were dosed on some kind of hallucinogenic), this 1979 reboot, the first major installment in the Star Trek canon after the original TV series was canceled, moves at its own stately pace and is a little cranky at times. The story finds the old gang back together on the Enterprise, the only starship in range to confront a cloud of massive energy headed toward Earth and destroying all in its path. Easily wiping out a trio of Klingon warships with lightninglike disintegrator pulses, you know this cloud means business. Captain James T. Kirk (William Shatner in all his scene-chewing, smirking glory) has assumed command of the recently rebuilt Enterprise. With the help of Spock (Leonard Nimoy), Doctor McCoy (DeForest Kelley), and first officer Willard Decker (Stephen Collins), he discovers that the massive cloud actually houses a giant living machine called V'ger. The being attacks the Enterprise, killing its navigator Ilia (Persis Khambatta) and replacing her with a robotic clone that acts as V'ger's herald. The crew finds the ancient U.S. space probe Voyager 6 at the sentient machine's core—V'ger has come looking for its "creator." Decker and the robot Ilia are absorbed by V'ger, which promptly vanishes into thin air. Sublimely trippy in parts, and owing a huge debt to 2001: A Space Odyssey, Star Trek: The Motion Picture is a stew of kaleidoscopic visuals and serious Trekkie nerdiness. The 2009 update, while not explicitly stony, may be a better option if you're looking for a Star Trek fix. And you can't go wrong with The Voyage Home, 1986's fish-out-of-water treatment of the crew's return to Earth, or The Wrath of Khan.

Star Wars (1977)

🔥 🍸

🌿 🌿 🌿 🌿 In the very first *Star Wars*, later retitled with the addendum *Episode IV: A New Hope*, many questions are presented about the origins of the Rebellion, and also some answers. We learn that a young Luke Skywalker (Mark Hamill) is destined for the life of a Jedi, that Obi-Wan Kenobi (Alec Guiness) will serve as mentor and martyr, that a galactic senate has been dismantled, that the Death Star is operational, that Princess Leia (Carrie Fisher) is one badass babe, and that Darth Vader is scary as hell and can make atrocious things happen with the pinch of a finger. We're also introduced to key ancillary characters like Han Solo (Harrison Ford) and his first mate Chewbacca (Peter Mayhew) and sidekicks droids R2D2 and C3PO. It's a small, young group with a mystical Force on its side going up against an evil empire one hundred times its size. Talk about an underdog story. The beauty of George Lucas's *Star Wars* is its simplicity—the plot, the sets, the space battles—and while some may say the film looks amateurish, since it long predates modern special effects (it was deemed revolutionary at the time), the

---

🌿 STAR WARS FOR STONERS 🌿

By Margaret Cho

Comedian Margaret Cho saw the very first *Star Wars* movie on the big screen back in 1977, and remembers, "People were passing joints in the theater, which is incredible to think of now. Of course, I didn't realize until years later that it was pot I was smelling." But by the time *Return of the Jedi* came around, Cho had unleashed her inner stoner and developed a whole new appreciation for the trilogy and every film, book, and cartoon that's come since. This die-hard fan offers her thoughts to keep in mind next time you smoke out to *Star Wars*.

Tatooine = grower's paradise; Death Star = stoner doom: "If you're a stoner, Tatooine seems like the ideal place to live. They have grow rooms in those mud huts and good light. It's the perfect place to hydroponically grow your own pot. And you could take that cruiser that hovers above the ground to pick up all your growing supplies. As opposed to the Death Star, where you could never have a grow room go undetected. You can't even puff there—there'd be smoke detectors everywhere and you'd be superparanoid. Plus, you know the Empire would drug-test all the time."

Chewbacca's secret stash and Jabba's bong: "I love Chewbacca more than anything, but I've always wanted to know: what's in his weird little messenger bag? I think there's a bowcaster that he carries around, but you know he's got a one-hitter in there, too. And then there's Jabba the Hutt, who smokes a hookah. It's like a modified waterless bong, which is the bomb!"

Yoda as stoner guru: "Yoda is very intuitive and has this old stoner wisdom about him—even in the new films, I still love him as this trippy character. Plus, he's green!"

Laser light–saber show: "I love the light sabers in the old films. They're very potent, exciting, and they have trails. They're somewhat akin to a laser light show, which was a big stoner activity in the seventies and eighties—where planetariums would put on a light show based on Pink Floyd's *The Wall* or, in my time, an album by Oingo Boingo. Of course, they're nothing compared to what we see now in CGI, but back then, it was a big deal."

The Force as the "stoner ideal": "When you think about it, the Force is kind of Buddhist—the more you try, the less you achieve. It's about *not* trying and trusting your inner strength, which is kind of a stoner ideal. Like, trust in your inner stoner."

original is all about imagination. *Star Wars*, the 1977 version (sadly, the DVD version includes significant revisionism and subpar digital enhancements), is a trip back to simpler times—when ass-faced monsters drank weird space booze at the portside bar, aliens puffed vapor from a hookahlike tube, and a light-saber duel was a fair fight involving only two opponents.

> "The Force is what gives a Jedi his power. It's an energy field created by all living things. It surrounds us and penetrates us. It binds the galaxy together."
>
> **—Obi-Wan**

Star Wars Episode I: The Phantom Menace (1999)

Star Wars Episode II: Attack of the Clones (2002)

Star Wars Episode III: Revenge of the Sith (2005)

✏ 🍸🕯

🍁 🍁, 🍁 🍁 🍁, 🍁 🍁 🍁 Comedian Patton Oswald has a bit where he wants to create a time machine for the sole purpose of offing George Lucas before he could release the *Star Wars* prequels. He may have a point—after all, Ewoks or not, the first three movies are bona fide stoner classics, with heady philosophy, before-their-time special FX, and the first glimpse of Yoda. The prequels are a mess of bad acting, lopsided story lines, and the first glimpse of Jar Jar Binks.

That being said, all three movies do address a lot of long-unanswered questions, while raising plenty of new ones. The films also get better in succession as the characters mature, though some would argue that the acting declines. And that's the thing about the *Star Wars* prequels—they're like one big compromise and a whole lot of give and take. To please the pre-teen crowd, Lucas injected kid-friendly creatures. To sew up the Luke and Leia story, he took his time with the budding romance of Queen Padmé Amidala (Natalie Portman) and Anakin Skywalker (Jake Lloyd, then Hayden Christensen) in the first two films, then rushed it to a conclusion in Episode III. As for the visual effects, the films score big points for imagination, but often fail in execution and feel like a never-ending series of spaceships landing and taking off. But the most common complaint? Sensory overload (in the form of a million lasers, light sabers, and sundry artillery all going off at once) and thinly veiled racism (look no further than *Phantom Menace*'s Binks).

Still, there are positives. Ewan McGregor playing Obi-Wan Kenobi is simply meant to be. Same goes for Liam Neeson as Jedi master Qui-Gon Jinn. There's an unexpected quasi–weed reference in *Attack of the Clones*, when a disheveled slacker tries to offer Obi-Wan a couple of "death sticks" at a bar. And the exotic locales (a desert planet here, a snow moon there, a lava field everywhere) will often make you forget about the disjointed plot, which, by *Revenge of the Sith*, finds Anakin knocking up Queen Amidala, then betraying her as he's led to the dark side of the Force, eventually becoming the baddest bad guy of them all, Darth Vader.

As entertainment, each movie stands on its own merits, but as a whole, the prequels suffer from being all pomp and no circumstance—a beautiful piece of CGI wizardry that, even seen through a stony haze, doesn't hold a candle to its simpler, classic predecessors.

Obi-Wan (using a Jedi mind trick): "You don't want to sell me death sticks . . . You want to go home and rethink your life."

Sunshine (2007)

🍁 🍁 🍁 🍁 Danny Boyle's first science fiction film is full of stunningly beautiful moments and frightening freak occurrences as crewmembers of the *Icarus 2* are sent to outer space to reignite the sun in hopes of saving all civilization. Among the most awesome spaceships to ever grace the screen, the *Icarus 2* has an observation deck for stargazing and planet watching, a fully functional garden that creates the ship's air supply, and a psychiatric center equipped with a virtual reality room where you can relive happy moments on Earth with friends and loved ones. But it also has a solemn duty: to travel into the heart of the sun and detonate a bomb as a desperate attempt to reboot. See, the sun is dying. But now the *Icarus 2* team hears a distress signal from their predecessors, a ship thought to be lost over seven years ago. They dangerously alter their plotted course and when they reach the ship, there is a creepy final transmission from the sun-blistered Captain Pinbacker (Mark Strong), prophesizing that mankind has no choice if the sun wants to die: "At the end of time, a moment will come when just one man remains. Then, the moment will pass. Man will be gone. There will be nothing to show that we were ever here . . . but stardust." With amazing visuals and breathtakingly beautiful depictions of space, *Sunshine* will, quite simply, blow your mind.

Capa: "If you wake up one morning, and it's a particularly beautiful day, you'll know we made it. I'll see you in a couple years."

THX 1138 (1971)

🍁 🍁 🍁 🍁 A bummer *Logan's Run*, this dystopian look at the future by *Star Wars* mastermind George Lucas traces the journey of worker THX 1138 (Robert Duvall) off his meds and out of a state-enforced utopia. After ditching the happy pills that everyone is obliged to take, THX experiences feelings for the first time and is jailed in a featureless white prison for having unauthorized sex with his hot roommate. The extended escape sequence is punctuated by shots of a display totting up the escalating costs for the police apparatus to chase THX. He escapes in the end only because his white-masked robot pursuers run out of money. Looking alternately cheesy and cool, the future world of THX is oddly disturbing, almost as if everything everywhere was decorated by Ikea's office furniture department. And building on that featureless dread, special mention needs to be made of the film's near-total lack of a score. The best scene in the film, which relies on little dialogue, is the one in which THX's bathroom medicine cabinet encourages him to self-medicate, like a Wal-Mart version of *2001: A Space Odyssey*'s HAL computer.

> "If you feel you are not properly sedated, call 348-844 immediately. Failure to do so may result in prosecution for criminal drug evasion."
>
> —Medicine cabinet (female voice)

Tingler, The (1959)

🍁 🍁 🍁 Vincent Price as Dr. Warren Chapin took the first LSD trip in film history in William Castle's campy thriller. Chapin is researching his theory that the tingling you feel during extreme fear involves a lobsterlike creature dubbed the Tingler that attaches itself to one's spine and can only be fought off by screaming madly. Since nothing scares Chapin, he decides to try LSD provided by his assistant David (Darryl Hickman) ("It can produce some pretty weird effects"). First, he reads a manual, *Fright Effects Induced by Injection of Lysergic Acid—LSD-25*, then shoots himself a 100-milligram dose. The walls close in on Chapin, his vision gets blurry, and finally he screams with fear (clearly, a bad trip). Next, the doc doses a mute woman who, of course, can't scream; she also has a bad trip and dies. The rest of the movie follows the actual Tingler as it escapes and crawls up the aisle of a theater showing a silent movie. Following Chapin's instruction, the captive audience "screams for their lives," ultimately warding off the creepy crawler. Shot in black-and-white, the film begins with an intro from Castle à la Hitchcock, and Price is, well, Vincent Price—thin mustache, cultured elocution, and weird as hell.

Chapin: "The Tingler exists in every human being and it's extremely powerful."

Tripper, The (2007)

🌿 🌿 🌿 Your prototypical horror movie plot gets the hippie treatment in this David Arquette vehicle (he wrote, directed, and stars). We start in northern California circa 1967, as an Irishman lumberjack snaps on some tree huggers, shredding a hippie's torso with a chain saw, then we fast-forward to current times. A bus carrying a group of young, pot-smoking concertgoers (Jaime King, Lukas Haas, and Jason Mewes) is on its way to the Free Love Festival in the Redwoods. Naturally, people start to disappear almost immediately. Sure, the locals have set up traps in the forest to protect their marijuana crops, but that's

> **"I thought you Deadheads believed believed in flower power and shit."**
>
> **—Redneck**

not the only reason kids are vanishing—there's a nutcase dressed as Ronald Reagan running through the forest with an ax! Acid-fueled twists and turns keep pupils dilated as the festival turns into a free-for-all murder spree with some unpleasant bad trip scenes and plenty of gross-out shock value.

Tron (1982)

🌿 🌿 🌿 🌿 A watershed moment in computer animation, this Disney film is about the Users and their respective programs inside of the mainframe computer at a corporation called ENCOM still looks amazingly futuristic. While the acting is wooden, the effects are fantastic, with battles between hulking hunter killer robots, cybernetic tanks, light cycles, and warrior programs in skin-tight suits of glowing circuitry wielding killer Frisbees. A mix of *Star Wars*, early eighties arcade video games, and full-on neon Euro-disco fallout, *Tron* is all about falling through the looking glass to the other side of the screen. It's primarily the story of a frustrated programmer, Flynn (Jeff Bridges), who's hacking into ENCOM seeking credit for video games stolen by evil CEO Ed Dillenger (David Warner). Aided by geeky scientist couple Alan Bradley (Bruce Boxleitner) and Lora (Cindy Morgan), Flynn manages to get to a terminal inside the ENCOM R & D facility and piss off the sentient Master Control Program, lord of the ENCOM mainframe. Transferred into the computer, Flynn is forced to compete in the video games that he wrote. What could be just childish play is given an air of menace as the MCP is bent on torturing Flynn, now just another program, and killing him off as part of its plan for world domination. Escaping the games through the help of an independent security program named Tron (played by Boxleitner), Flynn and Tron travel the canyons of data, getting drunk on pure power streams, and fly some funky dat*ships. Brain-damaging kids for years to come, *Tron*'s light cycle sequence has been ripped off again and again (we're looking at you, George Lucas), but a 2010 update, *The Tron Legacy*, with a digitally recreated young Jeff Bridges, promises a whole other level of stoniness. Bring it on, 2010 *Tron*!

Sark to Tron: "Your User can't help you now, my little program."

2001: A Space Odyssey (1968)

🍁🍁🍁🍁🍁 Before *Star Wars* and *Close Encounters*, there was *2001*, Stanley Kubrick's breathtaking journey to Jupiter and the Moon. The thread that holds the abstract story together is the existence of a black monolith dating back four million years, first encountered by African apes. The film begins with the iconic musical theme, Richard Strauss's *Also sprach Zarathustra*, set to a black screen. The sun rises over Africa as wildlife graze. A fight between rival primate groups turns deadly when bones are used as weapons. After a conquest, an ape throws a bone triumphantly in the air. From "The Dawn of Man," Kubrick leaps millions of years into the future. Dr. Floyd (William Sylvester) is being ferried to Space Station 5 and Clavius Base on the moon. At zero gravity, the station and base are perfect for walking on the walls and the ceilings. Eighteen months later, the *Discovery One* spaceship takes off for Jupiter, helmed by Dr. Bowman (Keir Dullea), Dr. Poole (Gary Lockwood), and a preco-cious computer named HAL. At first HAL's a team player, but when the mainframe jeopardizes the mission, Bowman has no choice but to deactivate HAL despite its insistent pleadings. Put on your seat belt for the next segment, "Jupiter: Beyond the Infinite," during which Bowman rides through the harrowing Star Gate lit up with psychedelic imagery like that seen years later in video games such as *Tempest*. It's a long ride, so just settle in with a spliff and enjoy the virtual reality. Much of the movie is glacially paced; in fact, there's less than an hour of dialogue in the 140-minute film. The special effects, groundbreaking at the time, pale by today's standards, but the music is for the ages, especially Johann Strauss's "The Blue Danube," played in its entirely through the credits, which adds ten minutes to the running time. Kubrick directed very few films: he's noted for *Lolita*, *Dr. Strangelove*, *Full Metal Jacket*, and, of course, *The Shining*. But *2001: A Space Odyssey* remains his crowning achievement.

HAL: "Look, Dave. I can see you're really upset about this. I honestly think you ought to sit down calmly, take a stress pill, and think things over."

☘ 2001: A STONER ODYSSEY ☘

By P-Nut of 311

As the bassist for road warriors 311, P-Nut has nearly twenty years of knee-buckling, head-banging rock under his belt—and many, many hours cooped up in a bus bunk watching movies. Which makes his stony pick, Stanley Kubrick's slow-moving epic *2001: A Space Odyssey*, all the more fitting.

I've seen 2001 well over twenty times and I was definitely high the first time. I was a teenager in Omaha, maybe sixteen or so, just exploring film and the psychoactive effects of THC at the same time. Like, nothing better to do but screw around and watch movies. But I had always heard about 2001—that it was unlike anything I'd ever seen or probably ever will. And now having watched and studied it, it really was made for the kind of insightful thinking that goes along with being high while watching a movie. It's a 140-minute movie, with less than an hour of dialogue, so it really relies on the visuals and using the viewer's imagination, as well. That said, it's definitely not what people expect the first time around.

What Stanley Kubrick did best was test the limits of ideas and preconceived notions, especially in the first contact kind of story. Nothing can really be expected, the future is unknown, there's more out there then we could ever possibly believe, the universe is infinite . . . I think he captured that perfectly. 2001 is also about understanding man's struggle with technology. It was the first time since *Metropolis*, which was a pre-talkie 1920s black-and-white film, that the idea of a machine gone mad wasn't dorky. And 2001 really brought it down to a personal degree—like, this machine is going to kill us because it's got a higher purpose in mind, and if we humans get in the way, then the machine will strike us down. And that's exactly what happens.

Kubrick was way ahead of his time. There were no pictures of inter-solar system travel yet. Nothing like that existed, it was all kind of conceptual, but it looks as real as anything now. The way they filmed the spaceship and built the centrifuge, it was a very expensive set that Kubrick thought was a very necessary part of the film—where gravity was tripped out and he was able to film the main actors running through the centrifuge, seemingly upside down while the camera tracks behind them or to the side of them. And having the longest jump cut in any film, going from Neanderthals to the space age—the caveman throwing a bone in the air to the satellite going around the moon . . . It's just so cool, endlessly imaginative, and ballsy—just as Kubrick was ready to shake things up in that way. It's a visual masterpiece that has yet to be equaled and probably never will be because of the time when it was made and Kubrick's eye for precision.

Kubrick was also the ultimate taskmaster. He employed the best people to do the job. The tripped-out psychedelic dimension travel beam at the end of the movie? That was something the artist came up with on his own. Kubrick was asked, "What should I do for this scene?" And his answer was basically, "You know what to do, I don't need to tell you how, just make it great and we'll both know when we see it." And I think that's a cool way of doing things—kind of a hands-off approach to art history that really allows the artist to be as creative as possible, and not be limited by the director or the writer's point of view. That totally adds to the stoner mentality as well. We need to let our imagination be as free as possible, and that's what 2001 is about.

If you put too many words on it, you're going to squander the experience. It's more like, let your imagination do the talking, make all that mindless chatter up in your head go away, and you'll be more open-minded to the possibilities out there in the universe.

☘ FILM SCHOOL 101 ☘

By Ray Manzarek of the Doors

Before he became the keyboardist for the Doors, Ray Manzarek was just a wide-eyed film student at UCLA. In fact, it was there that he first met Jim Morrison. In honor of that fateful meeting, RMM asked Manzarek for five key moments in film history that any self-respecting stoner cinephile should know.

El Topo (1970) and Un Chien Andalou (1929): "*El Topo* (1970) by Alejandro Jodorowsky, that's one wacky, psychedelic, and very trippy film. Mexican surrealism in good intense color, it takes the great Spanish film director Luis Buñuel to the next level. He's another director to look into, going all the way back to 1929's *Un Chien Andalou* (An Andalusian dog), which he made with Salvador Dalí as an experimental silent movie."

Shanghai Express (1932): "Directed by Josef von Sternberg, *Shanghai Express* stars Marlene Dietrich and Anna May Wong as two extremely elegant prostitutes working the coast between Shanghai and Beijing. In the movie, they're called coasters. Dietrich is the infamous Shanghai Lily, and her ex-lover, Captain Harvey, is on the train. He says to her, 'So you're Shanghai Lily?' That's a great line. Wouldn't you like to find a couple prostitutes like that? That would be expensive."

The Battleship Potemkin (1925) and October: Ten Days That Shook the World (1927): "Note kids: it's today's editing style from the silent era. Sergei Eisenstein was the first to do repetitious cutting, bam-bam-bam cutting. It was so insane and revolutionary, people didn't know what to make of him. Plus his composition, where he put the camera and how he found the Russian constructivist angles, it's just so dynamic. *The Battleship Potemkin* is about a mutiny that takes place at the beginning of the revolution around 1905. The protest against the sailors was the beginning of the downfall of the czar, culminating with the revolution in October. So you can watch *Potemkin* and then *October* and see the result of where it all went."

Citizen Kane (1941): "The man who was influenced by the angles of Eisenstein: Orson Welles and *Citizen Kane*, a film that keeps being named one of the best of all time. It's about a newspaper magnate named Charles Foster Kane and, of course, a right-wing manipulator. Welles directed and starred—a total fluke—and was only twenty-five years old at the time, holy shit!"

The Killing (1956) and 2001: A Space Odyssey (1968): "*The Killing* is a small Stanley Kubrick film about the robbery of a racetrack. He tells the story like a chess match—the pacing is so taut, the black-and-white photography, how he keeps jumping back in time as we watch different criminals preparing for and executing their task, then collecting the money, running away, and then finally all coming together. The shit hits the fan, and there's a nasty conclusion, but wait till you see what happens to Sterling Hayden, who has the money—holy cow, the irony!

Talk about trippy, trippy, trippy: *2001: A Space Odyssey*. When it came out, somebody got the Doors tickets to the Los Angeles premiere. We rehearsed in the afternoon, smoked a joint before we left, and went over to the movie theater in Hollywood, which had a Cinemascope screen. The place is packed, and the only seats left are in the front row. Of course, that's the last place you want to sit to watch a movie because everything's out of proportion, but we said what the hell, we're stoned, we'll just sit down and watch the movie. Turned out, they were the best seats in the house. Sitting in front of that screen with nothing in front of you but outer space, first those apes and the sunrise, the opening with that music . . . it was absolutely overwhelming. We sat there with our mouths agape. Morrison stood up after the first two minutes when it went black with that sequence right before the apes, and said, 'Well, that's the best movie I've ever seen, we can go now.' Jim, sit down, you comedian."

Willy Wonka & the Chocolate Factory
(1971)

🍷🍸

🍁🍁🍁🍁 A kids' movie in the same way "Puff the Magic Dragon" is a children's folk tune, the original *Willy Wonka*, starring Gene Wilder as the reclusive candy kingpin who opens his chocolate factory to a group of five contest winners and their plus ones, is an engaging, charming masterpiece that offers such a visual and auditory feast for the senses it might be the greatest acid trip ever put on celluloid. Wilder chews up the screen with a combination of creepiness, wisdom, and subtext that bursts forth like a Keith Moon drum solo. Then there's the fictional candy—three-course meals in a small piece of gum,

> "Candy is dandy, but liquor is quicker!"
> —**Willy Wonka**

chocolate rivers, candy mushrooms you can dip your hand into, soda that makes you fly. This colorful, food-filled world will seriously test your craving for sweet munchies. And, lest we forget, the musical numbers, the most famous of which has to be the Oompa Loompa theme song, performed by freaky little orange people who sing and dance while handling the candy factory's odd jobs. If eerie midgets, a psychedelic boat ride, and little girls turning into giant blueberries or bad eggs isn't your idea of a good trip, then you need to look elsewhere, like Johnny Depp's Michael Jackson–esque imitation in the 2005 remake, *Charlie and the Chocolate Factory*.

Wizard of Oz, The
(1939)

🍁🍁🍁🍁 "Toto, I've a feeling we're not in Kansas anymore." And so begins the long, strange trip of twelve-year-old Dorothy and her dog, Toto. When a tornado rips through her black-and-white Kansas town, Dorothy (Judy Garland, seventeen at the time) is knocked unconscious and wakes up in a Technicolor nightmare. Location: Munchkinland. Population: diminutive. At the start of her quest to get out of Munchkinland and find her way back home to Aunt Em (Clara Blandick) and Uncle Henry (Charles Grapewin), she befriends a live Scarecrow (Ray Bolger), a Tin Man (Jack Haley), and a Cowardly Lion (Bert Lahr). She also encounters assorted Munchkins (not of the Dunkin Donuts variety), flying monkeys, and various witches, good and bad. The quartet (quintet, if you count Toto) follows the yellow brick road, tiptoeing through a field of poisonous poppies to somewhere over the rainbow, cheating death and committing a felony or two (actually, two, both manslaughter) along the way. They're off to see the wizard, the wonderful wizard of Oz in Emerald City. The Wizard (Frank Morgan) is Dorothy's only hope—or so she thinks—the guy who just might have the power to send her home, give the Scarecrow a brain, the Tin Man a heart, and the Cowardly Lion courage. It's a tall order, and first, per the Wizard's instructions, Dorothy and her travel companions must bring him the broomstick of the Wicked Witch

☙ THE WIZARD AND ME ❧

By Wayne Coyne of The Flaming Lips

The Wizard of Oz has sort of been conflated with Pink Floyd's Dark Side of the Moon, because then it takes on mega-stoner status. I think for me, putting those together, unlike a Reese's Peanut Butter Cup, which combines chocolate and peanut butter and they come out better in the end, I don't think either one of those do. I think Dark Side is utterly stellar, great music that you could listen to in any state of mind. And I think The Wizard of Oz without Dark Side is much more sad and powerful. It's a movie—it's the mood, the music, the themes, and all that, and the idea that it's kind of a drug movie, but an optimistic one, it's just full of endless imagination.

Everywhere you turn on it, it's unexpected and cool, but heartfelt. The trippiest part would have to be that tornado. I mean, it's not trippy in that it's colorful and musical, but there's a sense of, "My God, this looks better than a real tornado!" And that's coming from a guy who's from Oklahoma. To me, it's really kind of scary and horrific, and strange in that way.

I think my life parallels some of the things in Wizard of Oz. That part when the Good Witch descends in the bubble? That's something I've carried with me since I was three years old, that I watched with my brothers when they were taking acid. And here I am, almost fifty, and I'm known for descending on crowds in a bubble. There are elements where my life has, in some ways, become The Wizard of Oz. And when people bring their kids over to my house, they tell them they're visiting the Wizard, and I'm, like, "Yeah!" That's the greatest thing that could ever be said about me, that I could be in some way like the Wizard of Oz. What I like best about him is not that he has all these gadgets, but when they pull the curtain on him, he essentially tells you, "Yeah, all this stuff I do is fake, and it is fantastical, but there are real things about humans that are utterly magic, that will never go away." When he talks about the virtues of being a good human, to me, that's what makes it meaningful. Not the fire and the giant green floating head—those things are great, but the insight really makes it all worthwhile.

of the West (Margaret Hamilton), who, incidentally, wants Dorothy dead for killing her sister, the Wicked Witch of the East, when Dorothy's house fell on her. There's also the matter of Dorothy's magical ruby-red shoes, which belonged to the Wicked Witch of the East but were given to Dorothy by Glinda, the Good Witch of the North (Billie Burke). The Wicked Witch of the West wants those shoes, and she'll do whatever's necessary to get them. Bad dream or bong-induced journey? Well, this is a children's story, so the answer should be obvious. Then again, the mind-bending synergy when playing the movie along with Pink Floyd's Dark Side of the Moon would make anyone think otherwise. Bottom line: If toking could take you to such fascinating, off-the-wall places, we'd all be booking our trips down the yellow brick road to Emerald City.

> "You crazy brat! Look what you've done! I'm melting! Melting! Oh, my world, my world. Who would have thought a good little girl like you could have destroyed my beautiful wickedness?"
>
> **—The Wicked Witch of the West to Dorothy**

ACTION & SPORTS

Bull Durham (1988)

🌿 🍸 🗡

🌿🌿🌿🌿 Pot is generally nonexistent in baseball movies, but director Ron Shelton broke the barrier with his look at the minor-league Durham Bulls. While rookie flamethrower Nuke LaLoosh (Tim Robbins) has major-league dreams, veteran catcher Crash Davis (Kevin Costner) is at the end of his career, and bohemian uber-fan Annie Savoy (Susan Sarandon) comforts both. She contemplates the season with a joint, and later recovers a roach after an intense night of sex with Crash. Though her eccentricity is not defined by marijuana, it may explain why she sees so much poetry in baseball. During a fertile period for movies about the national pastime that also yielded *Eight Men Out*, *Field of Dreams*, and *The Natural*, this film humanizes players whether behind-the-scenes or on the diamond. It's simply one of the best baseball films ever.

Annie: "When you know how to make love, you'll know how to pitch."

Cell, The (2000)

🌿 🗡

🌿🌿🌿 By far the oddest choice of her film career, *The Cell* finds Jennifer Lopez, pop star extraordinaire with the perfect derriere, in the lead role of Catherine Deane, a child psychologist who travels into the brains of troubled children. Lying suspended in a plastic rubber suit with a magic hankie adorned with circuitry covering her face, she enters their minds to help them confront their deepest fears. Her job is out there, all right, which might explain why upon getting home from work, she lights up a fattie with considerable aplomb and muses over solving the complexities of her bizarre line of work. Then she goes to sleep watching *Fantastic Planet*. The next day, Catherine's asked by FBI agent Peter Novak (Vince Vaughn) to plumb the mental depths of serial killer Carl Stargher, played by a mumbling Vincent D'Onofrio. Prone to seizures, Stargher has fallen into a coma after kidnapping a girl and placing her in a glass cage that will fill with water and kill her in a few hours. Entering his head space, Catherine winds up in a phantasmagorical world reminiscent of a Nine Inch Nails or Marilyn Manson music video. There's some truly psychedelic weirdness, but it's all kind of dull. And of course, being in his mind proves deadly, but J Lo perseveres and saves the day.

Catherine to Novak: "Don't you feel there are different sides to every personality? Maybe even the worst of us is capable of one decent act. We're all human."

Children of Men (2006)

🌿 🪴 🍸 🗡 👀

🌿🌿🌿🌿 Set in Britain in the year 2027, when humans are no longer able to procreate and the youngest living being, an eighteen-year-old, has just been assassinated, this fully realized dystopian future is as heavy as it gets. Civilization has basically fallen apart, and Britain has taken in all of the world's refugees (or 'fugees) and gathered them in concentration camps—terrifying, Gaza-like ghettos with shades of Abu Ghraib and Auschwitz. In the middle of all that terror, one young black teenager is pregnant, and it's up to former activist Theo Faron (Clive Owen) to shepherd her to safety outside UK borders—no small feat considering much of the so-called police state is a lawless free-for-all for vigilantes of all stripes and political persuasions. Theo's only respite from this horrible world

is a stint at the home of his friend Jasper (Michael Caine), a hippie who lives off the grid and grows pot (his specialty strain: Strawberry Cough) that he sells to nearby Bexhill refugee camp. Jasper's wife Janice (Philippa Urquhart) is catatonic and very clearly scarred by the world she's come into. Her story is told beautifully with one long pan of various memorabilia and news clippings—as if to say, she can't speak, so the camera speaks for her. This small sequence conveys the extraordinary detail that comes with every scene in Alfonso Cuarón's film. There are single camera shots that travel through entire war zones, spinning 360 degrees in the process, with audio so realistic and scary that it could trigger flashbacks in veterans. Visually speaking, *Children of Men* is, quite simply, a masterpiece. But the true impact of this movie is more on an emotional level, and an uneasy one at that. The story is so incredibly sad, and even though is has what Hollywood would call a happy ending, it's really just a relief from all the bleakness.

Jasper: "Dirty government hands out suicide kits and antidepressants in the rations, but ganja is still illegal. Most of my weed goes to Bexhill now. This bloke buys it from me and smuggles it in."

City of God (Cidade de Deus) (2002)

🌿 🌿 🌿 🌿 🌿 Among the greatest drug movies ever made, Fernando Meirelles and

Kátia Lund's pungent picaresque about Rio de Janiero's underworld (adapted from Pablo Lins's novel) is right up there with *GoodFellas*, *Scarface*, and *Traffic*. Told over two decades ("The Sixties," "The Seventies"), we first meet the fledgling gangsters of City of God, a dusty suburban tract outside of Rio, where youngsters learn the trades of robbery and killing with the hopes of surviving and moving to the big city one day. The older hoods—Shaggy (Jonathan Haagensen), Clipper (Jefechander Suplino), and Goose (Renato de Souza)—beget a new generation, whose story is the focus of the seventies section; it takes up two-thirds of the movie, and is told through the eyes of Goose's young brother, Rocket (Alexandre Rodrigues). Unlike most of the boys, Rocket has no aspiration to be a gangster, and ultimately his photographs of the street warfare will land him a real job. Another of the City of God kids, Li'l Zé (Leandro Firmino), aims to take over the local drug business and will kill anyone who get in his way. He's a seriously dangerous sociopath armed to the teeth with machine guns and supported by a murderous gang that includes the "runts," the youngest of the neighborhood's litter. Zé challenges Carrot (Matheus Nachtergaele) for supremacy, leading to several shoot-outs. But behind the scenes, Zé's second-in-command, Benny (Phellipe Haagensen), preaches peace and love, smokes lots of pot with his girlfriend, Angelica (Alice Braga, Sonia Braga's niece), and plans to escape the slums and violence for a quiet life outside Rio. As is usually the case in mobster movies, the good guys don't fare well, and when Benny is killed, all hell breaks loose. Knockout Ned (singer Seu Jorge) joins Carrot in his war with Zé. Armed only with a camera, Rocket documents the mayhem and sells the photos to a newspaper. When the kids turn on Zé *Lord-of-the-Flies*-style, Rocket's there to capture the local legend's last breath. This exhilarating film, which takes you deep inside Brazil's *favelas* like never before, was nominated for four Academy Awards (but incredibly not for Best Foreign Language Picture). Meirelles and Lund spun the film off into the Brazilian TV series *City of Men*, which aired from 2002 to 2005.

Rocket voice-over: "The city teemed with addicts and Li'l Zé grew rich. If dealing were legal, Li'l Zé would have been Man of the Year."

Cleopatra Jones (1973)

🔧

🌿🌿🌿 In this blaxploitation classic directed by biker film vet Jack Starrett, Tamara Dobson is a one-woman wrecking crew as Cleopatra Jones— the sexy drug agent who takes down a heroin ring headed by none other than Shelly Winters (as Mommy). Cleo drives a Corvette, has a car phone, and delivers a swift kick; she's doesn't do guns, ya dig? The hip language, loud fashions, and horn-heavy soundtrack are undeniable trademarks of the genre, as is the B-movie story of competing drug gangs. Cleo sides with the black dealers, of course, but not before shaking down Snake (Christopher Joy), who claims to be selling "light stuff . . . grass, pills, and uppers." Undeterred, Cleo forces Snake to flush the white powder. The junkyard showdown between Cleo and Mommy and their respective soldiers is both tongue-in-cheek and brutal. A black-power salute sends Cleo off to another assignment. Dobson starred in the 1975 sequel, *Cleopatra Jones and the Casino of Gold.*

Cleo to Snake: "I want to ask you about your business, pusher man."

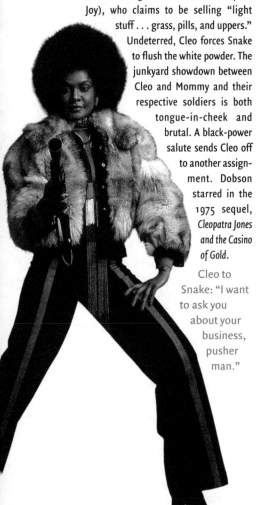

Coffy (1973)

🍸🍾 🔧 👓

🌿🌿🌿🌿 Pam Grier busts out all over in this blaxploitation thriller. Her nurse/avenger Coffy targets the "dope pushers," both black and white, who turned her little sister onto heroin. Cops, drug thugs, and a dirty local politician are no match for Coffy; she entices with her ample body, then blows her victims away. Cult movie vet Jack Hill (*Foxy Brown*) lays the violence on thick. In one particularly disturbing scene, white hit men whack pimp-daddy Big George (George DoQui) by tying a noose around his neck and dragging him. Roy Ayers provides the funky score and Dee Dee Bridgewater sings over the credits, "You're a shining symbol of black pride." Right on!

> "This is the end of your rotten life, you motherfucking dope pusher!"
>
> —Coffy

Cool Runnings (1993)

🍸🍾 🩹

🌿🌿🌿 Loosely based on a true story, this endearing Disney flick dramatizes the Jamaican bobsled team's surprise showing at the 1988 Olympics in Calgary. Determined to qualify for the games, local track star Derice Bannock (Leon Robinson) teams up with an American living in the Caribbean island, shamed former bobsledder-turned-bookie Irv Blitzer (John Candy), who theorizes that "sprinters make the best bobsledders." With his friend and expert pushcart racer Sanka Coffie (Doug E. Doug) by his side, Derice recruits muscleman Yul Brenner (Malik Yoba) and rich kid Junior Bevil (Rawle D. Lewis) to round out the team. They practice in a clunky wooden box, but make it to Calgary, where the team is met with snickers and the constant threat of disqualification. Making their Olympic run all the more challenging is Alberta's bitter cold, which Sanka just can't hang with. "I'm freezing my royal Rastafarian nay-nays off!" says the tie-dye-wearing wingman, providing comic relief. Predictably, their race time is impressive, and while they don't win a medal, the team does earn respect from their peers, parents, countrymen, and coach. But in the end, it's their Rasta Rocket motto "Cool Runnings," or "Peace be the journey," that truly prevails.

Derice Bannock: "Sanka, mon, whatcha smoking?"

Sanka Coffie: "I'm not smoking, I'm breathing!"

Dead Presidents (1995)

Following the success of *Menace II Society*, the Hughes brothers directorial duo took on the Vietnam era to tell the story of Anthony Curtis (Larenz Tate) from his early high school years through two tours of duty and back to the sad reality of life as a shell-shocked veteran with barely any government help. It all begins in 1968 as Anthony is just about to graduate and the future is looking bright for him and his best friends, Skip (Chris Tucker) and José (Freddy Rodriguez). Three years later, all three are fighting in the jungle halfway around the world, but instead of heroism, Anthony finds the same rampant racism that plagued him at home. Case in point: a note left behind that reads "Black men go home, this isn't your war." He also witnesses mind-bending destruction, abhorrent acts of torture—fellow soldier D'ambrosio (Michael Imperioli) is castrated alive—and death. When he's sent home in 1973, he finds a very different Bronx than the one he left. Skip is all hopped up on heroin, José lost his hand in the war and is a full-blown pyro, his little sister Delilah (N'Bushe Wright) is a Black Panther, and a sketchy pimp named Cutty (Clifton Powell) is sleeping with his girl. Confused, broke, and headed deeper into alcoholism, Anthony turns to armed robbery until the law catches up with him. With five times the budget of *Menace II Society*, the Hughes Brothers spared no expense in this coming-of-age movie, and while it was Tucker's only dramatic role, several scenes have gone on to be brilliantly spoofed in comedies (like *Half Baked*), forever cementing its legacy in film history.

Delilah: "It's not your fault you've been brainwashed by America."

☘ ISLAND ACTION ☘

A fair number of films set in the Caribbean—especially Jamaica—share a lot with blaxploitation movies: they're druggy, raw, and violent. Here are five faves.

***The Harder They Come* (1973):** The first film to come out of Jamaica turned Jimmy Cliff—playing reggae musician Ivan—into a star. He takes on record producers, ganja dealers, and ultimately the police in Perry Henzell's powerful thriller.

***Dancehall Queen* (1997):** The only movie on this list with a female lead stars Audrey Reid as Marcia, a Kingston street vendor who dreams of becoming the titular Dancehall Queen. There are lots of gyrating bodies and risqué outfits, but no drugs.

***Third World Cop* (1999):** Shot in digital, this inferior-looking production set in Kingston stars Paul Campbell as Capone, who shuts down a gun-running operation, and Carl Bradshaw (*The Harder They Come, Countryman*) as One Hand. He literally smokes spliffs with a claw!

***Shottas* (2002):** Cess Silvera's superviolent movie is about boyhood friends who grow up to be gangsters. Ky-Mani Marley stars as Biggs, leader of a small pack of wanton killers who extort Miami drug dealers.

***Haven* (2004):** The one non-Jamaican movie on this list takes place on Grand Cayman Island, where Carl (Bill Paxton) stashes his money, his daughter Pipa (Agnes Bruckner) gets arrested, and Shy (Orlando Bloom) and Andrea (Zoe Saldana) are forbidden lovers. And yes, they smoke ganja on the Caymans too.

Deep Cover (1992)

🍸 🍾 ✂ 🥢 👀

🍁🍁🍁 Having witnessed his junkie father's murder, John Hull (Laurence Fishburne) vows for a different life and joins the police force. After a stint in uniform, he's recruited by the DEA to bring down the Latin American drug lords supplying much of the West Coast's crack and cocaine. Partnering up with businessman David Jason (Jeff Goldblum), John slowly infiltrates a complex network of suppliers, dealers, and money launderers, eventually meeting a chemist who's cooked up a new designer drug that "increases attention, energy [and] cognitive powers, yet with a smooth opiatelike emotional surface," and also happens to be legal. John has never tried a drug or killed anybody, but in his work as an undercover, he crosses the line on both fronts. Complicating matters further are his superior's political ambitions, David's own insecurities, and John's long festering hang-ups. In the end, victory for the good guys is unclear—is supplying thousands of addicts with poison worth John's barely appreciated police work? Because of the realness of that dilemma, Deep Cover stands a cut above your average cop action movie. Adding to its street cred: a theme song written and produced by Dr. Dre featuring then-newcomer Snoop Doggy Dogg.

John Hull: "The money doesn't know where it comes from, but I do. If I keep it, I'm a criminal. If I give it to the government, I'm a fool. If I try and do some good with it, maybe it just makes things worse."

Desperado (1995)

🍸 🍾 🥢 👀

🍁🍁🍁🍁 In director Robert Rodriguez's follow-up to El Mariachi—his festival-rocking, $7,000 feature debut released three years earlier—the musician El Mariachi (played by a then-testosterone-oozing Antonio Banderas) is a tacit, itinerant dude who dresses in Johnny Cash black and, with Clint Eastwood cool, unfurls a hailstorm of whoop ass on any evildoer who so much as looks at his lady. Salma Hayek is the object of his gaze. Mexico's answer to Sophia Loren, Hayek stars as bookstore owner Caroline who stops traffic just by crossing the street. Unfortunately, she can also count the local drug lord among her fervent admirers, so El Mariachi, already in town to search and destroy the man who killed his previous girl-

friend (pistols in guitar case and all), vows to defend his new lover's honor. Set in a dusty Mexican town populated by an unrelenting body count—and yet plenty of cerveza on tap (Cheech Marin plays Short Bartender)—Desperado wears its spaghetti Western homage well. True, you'll be hard-pressed to take seriously any movie that distills the term Mexican standoff to its violent extreme, there's no arguing the voyeuristic satisfaction in the way Desperado contrasts this carnage with its two protagonists' explosive chemistry.

Donnie Brasco (1997)

🍸 🍾 🥢 👀

🍁🍁🍁🍁 Johnny Depp (Joe Pistone, a.k.a. Donnie Brasco) and Al Pacino (Lefty) are terrifically paired as wiseguys who work for a New York organized crime boss in Mike Newell's stellar mob movie. But Brasco is actually an FBI mole who wins Lefty's confidence and works his way inside the operation. The suspense builds as Brasco's cover is nearly blown on several occasions. When fellow wiseguy Nicky (Bruno Kirby) keeps one for himself, he gets whacked. "Man held out," Lefty says. "He held out on a coke deal." One of Depp's first significant lead roles is marked by a thick New Yawk accent and the actor's keen ability to underplay his roles. In another great performance, Pacino's Lefty pays the price for being too trusting.

Formula 51 (2001)

🌿 🌿 🌿 With a pharmacology degree, a sack of weed riding shotgun, and a joint in his hand, the first stop in the drug-making career of chemist Elmo McElroy (Samuel L. Jackson) is an unfortunate one: He gets pulled over by California Highway Patrol. The cop, in an ultimate show of authority, teases the recent grad by hitting the joint, then stomping it out. "The sixties are over, man," he harshes. Flash-forward three decades to 2001 and Elmo has perfected the ultimate high, a pill "fifty-one times stronger than cocaine, fifty-one times more hallucinogenic than acid, and fifty-one times more explosive than Ecstasy . . . It's like getting a personal visit . . . from God." After bailing on the Lizard (Meat Loaf), a hefty drug kingpin, Elmo relocates to the United Kingdom, shilling the POS 51 formula for some $20 million to football-obsessed Liverpudlian Iki (Rhys Ifans).

> "Football and drugs: a perfect Saturday afternoon."
>
> —Iki

An attempt to test the drug at a local rave fails when the club is raided by police, and in due time, it's revealed that the "power for suggestion" is as strong as complex chemical compounds. Jackson carries this otherwise choppy British indie flick, which is also known as The 51st State, even if he is wearing a kilt for two-thirds of the time (it's never explained why). But if it's explosions, shoot-outs, and gut-splitting body breakdowns you're seeking, Elmo and his minions go way beyond the call of duty.

Foxy Brown (1974)

🌿 🌿 🌿 🌿 Pam Grier teamed up again with B-movie director Jack Hill for this follow-up to Coffy.

Essentially, Grier plays the same role: the sexy anti-drug avenger. When Foxy's brother, Link (Antonio Fargas), doesn't pay his bill to a gang of drug dealers, they send a couple of hit men who ultimately murder him and Foxy's narc boyfriend, Michael (Terry Carter). Foxy infiltrates the drug gang, which doubles as a call girl service, and enlists the local Black Panther-style revolutionaries to help her take them down. The requisite funky soundtrack, anchored by Willie Hutch's theme song, keeps the pace lively, and the language is raw with mentions of "spook," "jigaboo," and the n-word.

French Connection, The (1971)

🌿 🌿 🌿 🌿 🌿 When this film came out in 1971, it redefined the police drama genre. Based on a true story and a book by Robin Cook, the irreverent tone is immediately set by director William Friedkin: We're introduced to Detective Popeye Doyle (Gene Hackman) and his partner, Buddy Russo (Roy Scheider), while they go about their daily routines. To meet with an informant, they stage a raid on a bar where all the patrons are holding a variety of illicit materials. The smorgasbord of pills, coke, pot, smack, and weapons drops to the floor as Doyle zeroes in on one of the customers. He takes the informant into the bathroom where it's revealed that a major drug shipment will be arriving from France. To cover his back, Doyle leaves the snitch with a black eye—definitely not your average undercover cop. Indeed, it's his relentless pursuit of the smugglers and the arriving shipment that bookmarks the film's many classic scenes: the sequence in which Doyle tails Alain Charnier (Fernando Rey), the Frenchman spearheading the operation, on a Times Square subway shuttle is a masterful chess game of wits between equally matched counterparts, as is the infamous car chase through the streets of Brooklyn that leaves you breathless. Then there's the heroin-testing scene, which quickly qualifies the batch as the purest stuff New York had ever seen. A classic in every sense of the word, it's no wonder this genre-defining flick won Best Picture and four more Academy Awards. In 1975, Hackman returned as Doyle in John Frankenheimer's sequel, French Connection 2.

Jackie Brown (1997)

Quentin Tarantino's dizzying homage to the blaxploitation era stars Pam Grier as the titular character—a flight attendant who takes on cold-blooded Ordell (Samuel L. Jackson) and the ATF. After she's busted for smuggling drugs (coke) and money ($50K) into LAX, Jackie hatches a scheme that will buy her freedom and make her rich. She does it with the help of mild-mannered bail bondsman Max (Robert Forster). Pot smokers don't fair well in this film. Ordell shoots Beaumont (Chris Tucker) after he puffs a joint, and bong hitters Melanie (Bridget Fonda) and Louis (Robert De Niro) are murdered when the money exchange goes wrong. A terrific R & B soundtrack and the director's long takes and attention to detail make this one of Tarantino's best.

Melanie: "Coughing's good. It opens up the capillaries. When you cough you're pulling air, in this case smoke, in the parts of the lungs that don't normally get used. So coughing's good—it gets you higher."

🌿 JESSE HUGHES'S STONY MOVIE PICKS 🌿

He's one-half of stoner rock stalwarts Eagles of Death Metal and an unabashed gun-toting Republican, but when it comes to movies, Jesse Hughes started out like the rest of us: with a heavy dose of *Dazed and Confused*. "It was life-changing," he says. The always outspoken and insightful guitarist offers four more of his stony classics . . .

The Outlaw Josey Wales (1976): "This is my number one go-to movie. It came out in 1976 and it's an El Paso picture directed by and starring Clint Eastwood that depicts the tyranny of the Union troops towards the end of the Civil War. Josey Wales is a farmer and his family gets killed by Union soldiers called the Redlegs. Remember, in the seventies it was hip to be a rebel, so he spends the movie going after them and kicking ass. It's great to watch when you're stoned because every delivery of every line is almost like the TV is talking to you. And sometimes, it will really get your attention by saying things like, 'Worm's gotta eat, same as birds.' This movie rules. And my uncle is in it! He plays one of the Redlegs with the long peacock."

Wedding Crashers (2005): "You would think it's just another romantic comedy, but when you're stoned, *Wedding Crashers* is a very subtle and passive celebration of machismo and classic stereotypical chauvinism. Because at no time do they ever really condemn what they did as wedding crashers . . . You can analyze it to no end, but the final scene when they're in the car figuring out how they're going to go crash a wedding, which plays to the sounds of 'Stay With Me' by Faces, is the final corruption taking its place. There are so many rad lines in this movie, it's unbelievable. 'You shut your mouth when you're talking to me!' You almost shit yourself laughing. It's one of my absolute new favorites."

River's Edge (1986): "It's known for being Keanu Reeves's first movie, but *River's Edge* has Crispin Glover's amazing performance of Layne. It's the true story of a dude who strangled his girlfriend by the river, and his friends tried to help him cover it up. Layne is a speed freak and his lines are unbelievable. Like he's playing a video game, loses, and he goes, 'That's fucked up, the people who own this place fixed it, because they know if I put another quarter in this machine, I'll take over the fuckin' universe.' I know dudes like that. I love that shit, it makes me laugh."

Repo Man (1984): "*Repo Man* back-to-back with *River's Edge*, holy shit! They're filled with the most quotable lines: 'John Wayne was a fag,' and 'He will kill you boys.' Anything about a alien space car being trapped by black hack government agents with a punker somehow ruthlessly getting involved listening to Black Flag . . . These are movies that were really the 'Rebels Without a Cause' for that punk generation."

Jezebels, The (1975)

🔪 🍸 💊 👀

🌿🌿🌿 Quentin Tarantino loves Jack Hill's exploitation chick flick so much that Miramax rereleased it (renamed *Switchblade Sisters*) as part of his Rolling Thunder Pictures series in 2000. Fans of *Kill Bill* will see the resemblance. The Dagger Debs (and their brother gang, the Silver Daggers) don't take shit from anyone—whether it's feisty new recruit Maggie (Joanne Neil) or rival gang the Crabs. Queen bee Lace (Robbie Lee) hearts hunky Dominic (Asher Brauna), but he has eyes for Maggie and rapes her while Lace is in jail. The prison scene is a hoot, with the Debs (the chubby one, Donut, is played by Lenny Bruce's daughter Kitty) ganging up on "dyke" guard Mom Smackley (Kate Murtagh). As Lace and Maggie vie for Dom's attention, the guys smoke pot and goof off. After Dom's shot by the Crabs, Maggie hooks up with a Maoist black revolutionary group. Under a hail of machine-gun fire and Molotov cocktails, the Crabs are no match for the newly rechristened Jezebels and their radical friends. A nasty knife fight between Maggie and Lace concludes this rather ludicrous exercise.

Lace to Maggie: "These are the Silver Daggers and we're the Dagger Debs. What gang you with? Everybody's gotta be in a gang—just ain't healthy to lone it."

Killer Bud (2001)

🔪 🌿 🍸 ✂

🌿🌿🌿 This semi-amusing stoner slacker story is like a cross between *Clerks* and *Harold & Kumar* with Jewish gangsters thrown into the mix. After best buds Waylon (Corin Nemec) and Buzz (David Faustino) get fired from the latest in a string of jobs, they head to a bar to drown their sorrows and dream of one day moving to Amsterdam. There, they meet two women willing to go home with them, but only if they can score some weed. Four stops later, they finally cop some "crazy Peruvian butt pot" off of biology teacher-turned-drug dealer Fievel Tenenbaum (Maurice Chasse), but Barbie (Danielle Harris) and Kristi (Caroline Keenan) get the munch-ies and only a particular junk food will do. So in the name of hooking up, Waylon and Buzz, who's now seeing cartoons thanks to the superpotent strain, break into a convenience store and then can't get out. Of course, one can think of worst places to be stuck all night. This is especially true of Sam's snack bar, which, as it turns out, has a basement that doubles as a grow room. Toking on some fresh buds straight off the plant, Buzz and Waylon set off the sprinkler system, which alerts the cops and one trigger-happy CIA agent named Gooch (Robert Stack). By the time they manage an escape, the girls are long gone, the fuzz is hot on their trail, and the bags seal their fate. But all hope of a future in Holland is not lost as Gooch arrives to save the day, guns a-blazing.

> "If we're going to jail, we might as well go down stoned."
> —Buzz

King of New York (1990)

🔪 🍸 🗡 💊 ⚔ 👀

🌿🌿🌿 Christopher Walken plays New York drug lord Frank White, a longtime gangster just released from prison who jumps right back into crime. Setting up headquarters at the posh Plaza Hotel, Frank and his cronies, including muscleman Jimmy Jump (Laurence—then credited as Larry—Fishburne) and expert chemist Test Tube (Steve Buscemi), plan a full-scale assault on the city's rival gangs, hitting drug traffickers from the Bronx to Little Italy and Chinatown. With his insatiable taste for coke, girls, and guns, Frank's ultraviolent streak has the cops working overtime, while his indiscriminate murder run claims lives in the double digits. "I never killed anyone who didn't deserve it," he says, delivering the film's most famous line. Officers Gilley (David Caruso), Bishop (Victor Argo), and Flanigan (Wesley Snipes) do their best to curb his rampage, and in the end, Frank's taste of freedom is short-lived. The Abel Ferrara film didn't make tremendous waves when it was first released, but has since gained major cred in the hip-hop world thanks to a stellar soundtrack featuring Schoolly D and several references by rappers who came after (The Notorious B.I.G. declared himself the black Frank White on his 1994 album, *Ready to Die*). As dope-pushing OGs go, White is your usual walking paradox: a wannabe Robin Hood who wreaks havoc on his own 'hood. To that end, Walken's skillful portrayal is spot-on, but Frank White is no Frank Lucas.

Frank White: "From here on, nothing goes down unless I'm involved. No blackjack, no dope deals, nothing. A nickel bag gets sold in the park, I want in."

Last of the Finest, The (1990)

This standard-issue policer pits LAPD versus a drug operation that's tied to running guns to Central America. Set in the eighties, when the U.S. exchanged arms for drugs on the Nicaragua end of the Iran-Contra scandal, Brian Dennehy leads a decent cast (Bill Paxton, Joe Pantoliano) in John Mackenzie's shoot-'em-up that's full of gratuitous pyrotechnics.

Pantoliano: "There's enough coke in there to build a ski slope."

Lock, Stock and Two Smoking Barrels (1998)

Guy Ritchie's breakout film is a mix of slapstick comedy and small-time hood drama with plenty of blood and head-butts to go around. Four mates enter a rigged poker game and wind up big losers. They decide to rip off a heist team that cleans out a marijuana operation. The peaceful growers Winston (Steven Mackintosh) and J (Nicholas Rowe) never really have a chance. Influenced mightily by Quentin Tarantino's *Reservoir Dogs* and *Pulp Fiction*, the stylish action and clever camera angles keep you riveted, but the high body count and one particularly nasty torture scene repulse. Among a cast of relative unknowns is Sting, who plays the father of one of the mates. Joints are toked and the funky soundtrack (James Brown, Stone Roses) is, well, smokin'.

Winston: "We grow copious amounts of ganja here . . . You're carrying a wasted girl and a bag of fertilizer. You don't look like the average horticulturist."

Lords of Dogtown (2005)

This biographical account of skateboarding's formative years has that pale blue overlay and icy tone that director Catherine Hardwicke (*Thirteen*, *Twilight*) is known for, which is ironic considering this story takes place under the sunny skies of Southern California. It's also a fitting treatment for the meager beginnings of an antiestablishment sport, born of neglected Venice Beach docks and waterless pools emptied during the drought of 1977. Dogtown's stars include legendary skaters Tony Alva (Victor Rasuk), Jay Adams (Emile Hirsch), and Stacy Peralta (John Robinson), who wrote the script, with sick pal Sid (Michael Angarano) and Tony's semislutty sister Kathy (Nikki Reed) on the sidelines. Their erstwhile leader is seemingly hopeless wastoid Skip, played brilliantly by Heath Ledger, who owns a ratty surf shop, has the foresight to start the Zephyr team, and, in turn, changes the course of skateboarding. It's a rags-to-riches story, but goes way deeper than your prototypical kid-from-the-wrong-side-of-the-tracks-hits-it-big narrative. To varying degrees, these guys are all dealing with issues of abandonment, abuse, and jealousy—not to mention hormones in overdrive—and there's plenty of booze and bud to go around. The exhilarating pool and party scenes demonstrate how these trailblazers with their never-before-seen tricks revolutionized an industry. Stricken with AIDS, fellow skateboarded Sid (Michael Angarano) requires medical marijuana in the film's sad ending. Look for cameos and bit roles by the real-life Z-Boys, Tony Hawk as an astronaut, the late Mitch Hedberg, and Johnny Knoxville as the slicked out Tugger Brooks.

Marked for Death
(1990)

🌿 🌿 Chock full of shoot-outs, martial arts combat, and chase scenes, this antidrug Steven Seagal vehicle pits his retired DEA agent John Hatcher against a viscous Jamaican crack gang led by psycho-Rasta Screwface (Basil Wallace). After they

---

🌿 STONY SPORTS FLICKS 🌿

Classic underdog stories with a subversive twist, here are five of our favorite sports-themed comedies.

Slap Shot **(1977):** This black-eyed brawler of a hockey movie features the long-haired Hanson brothers—the Ramones of sports films—who take ultraviolent idiot tendencies to new heights. Paul Newman plays the Charlestown Chiefs' sly charmer coach in a movie that borders on the surreal and feels like the haze that comes after a hockey puck hit to the head.

Caddyshack **(1980):** The original golf goof set the bar high for all sports-themed comedies that followed. You can thank Bill Murray for that. As groundskeeper Carl Spackler, he played the dopey pothead to perfection and made us all long for a course grown out of Kentucky Bluegrass crossed with Northern California Sensimilla.

Dodgeball: A True Underdog Story **(2004):** As the legend goes: The sport of dodgeball was invented in the fifteenth century by opium-addicted Chinamen, only using heads instead of the ADAA-approved balls of today. Jump forward five hundred years and a ragtag team of misfits takes on a bunch of muscle-obsessed 'roid ragers in a battle of the balls. Vince Vaughn plays slacker gym owner Peter LaFleur, captain of the Average Joes, who must defeat his archnemesis, Globo-Gym's White Goodman (Ben Stiller), in order to save his business.

Talladega Nights: The Ballad of Ricky Bobby **(2006):** It takes a pot-dealing, peyote-loving burnout dad (Billy Bob Thornton) to make a NASCAR star, and Ricky Bobby (Will Ferrell) was the best the sport had ever seen—until a formidable foe, gay Frenchman Jean Girard (Sacha Baron Cohen), challenges his supremacy. Nothing that Ricky and longtime pal and pardner Cal (John C. Reilly) can't overcome with some good old American shake 'n' bake!

Blades of Glory **(2007):** Former figure skating champion and showman Chazz Michael Michaels (Will Ferrell) is a burned out, sex-addicted drunk relegated to the "Grublets on Ice" circuit. His only hope for career redemption is pairing up with longtime rival Jimmy McElroy (Jon Heder), the goofy man-child who got him kicked out of the sport in the first place.

Semi-Pro **(2008):** Will Ferrell sports a massive 1976 'fro as basketballer Jackie Moon, a former singer who used the royalties from his one hit song, "Love Me Sexy," to purchase Michigan's Flint Tropics. With the team teetering on extinction, it's up to him and coach Ed Monix (Woody Harrelson) to save the franchise. Among Jackie's kooky marketing tactics: a contest awarding $10K to the audience member who makes a basket from the opposite side of the court. The winner? Stoner hippie Dukes, who sparks this comment from the peanut gallery: "Look at this guy, he's so hopped up on goofballs and grass, he's got no idea what's going on."

kill his niece and threaten his sister, Hatch recruits phys-ed teacher Max (Keith David) and Jamaican narc Charles (Tom Wright) for a revenge mission in Kingston. Screwface's special powers apparently include duplicating himself, since Hatch has to kill him twice. What Seagal lacks in charisma, he makes up for with swift kicks, deadly aim, and the uncanny ability to literally break bones. No James Bond, Hatch does have the last laugh when he walks away triumphantly after finishing off Screwface a second time and quips, "I hope they weren't triplets."

Miami Vice (2006)

The movie version of the popular eighties TV show is all about hard drugs and fast cars with lots of slow-motion kills and sexy scenes of Jamie Foxx in the shower. Colin Farrell plays super-suave, Ferrari-driving Miami undercover cop Sonny Crockett, who, along with his partner, Rico Tubbs (Foxx), poses as a speedboat racer to bust a Cuban coke dealer using South Florida neo-Nazis to move his product. Directed by Michael Mann and shot mostly on HD by Dion Beebe, also Mann's cinematographer on Collateral, the film has an interesting look, but plotwise, it's totally lacking, especially the ending, which feels like a rushed compromise resulting from tons of rewrites. Cocaine Cowboys it's not, but if mindless action is what you're looking for, Miami Vice is an enjoyable enough ride.

Sonny Crockett: "I'm a fiend for mojitos."

Murphy's Law (1986)

Charles Bronson is Jack Murphy, a badass cop who hits the sauce a bit too often. After stepping on the wrong criminal's toes, an ex-con he helped put away sets him up by killing his stripper ex-wife and her new boyfriend. Nobody, not even his peers on the force, believes he was framed, so Murphy gets thrown in the slammer, but prison walls can't contain this determined detective from clearing his name and finding the real killer—you can bet the farm, he takes no prisoners when it comes to a manhunt. He breaks out of jail and steals a police chopper, which he lands safely on a barn before it collapses, revealing a weed-growing biker gang. When the biker dudes try to rape his new sidekick, Arabella (Kathleen Wilhoite), Murphy steals their guns and blows their operation to bits. Chock-full of ridiculous dialogue, sometimes nonsensical explosions, and a prototypical eighties soundtrack, Murphy's Law is a slow game of cat and mouse played by a stone-faced Bronson with a little action, lots of melodrama, and plenty of cheese.

Murphy: "The only law I know is 'Jack Murphy's law.' It's very simple. Don't fuck with Jack Murphy. You remember that."

Natural Born Killers (1994)

Conceived by one genius (Quentin Tarantino, who came up with the story) and constructed by another (director Oliver Stone), Natural Born Killers is the rare collaboration that's at least as good as the sum of its parts. Thanks to top-notch acting from a first-rate cast, this is the kind of trippily edited marathon of destruction that's more likely to sober you up than help your high. Relentless serial killers Mickey and Mallory Knox (Woody Harrelson and Juliette Lewis, respectively) go on a murder spree spurred by boredom and majorly abusive childhoods, and are reverently followed by Australian tabloid news reporter Wayne Gale (Robert Downey Jr., never better) and sadistic detective Jack Scagnetti (Tom Sizemore). Along the way, Mickey and Mallory take a nasty mushroom trip in the desert, which ends with the murdering of a Native American elder. They become media darlings, all amid rapid-fire editing, crazy camera trickery, and a prison-break scene as intense as anything ever put on film. Controversial upon release for all the right reasons (and some not-so-right ones: a slew of actual murders were blamed on copycats), Natural Born Killers wasn't just a document of its time, but a look forward at what's become, in many ways, an equally bleak future.

Mallory: "You make every day feel like kindergarten."

Next Day Air (2009)

🖊️ ✂️ 🥄 👀

🌿🌿🌿🍃 Benny Boom's action comedy has a lot in common with *Pineapple Express*. In both films, the lead character is a pot smoker who stumbles upon a crime. Like Dale (Seth Rogen) in *Pineapple*, Leo (*Scrubs*'s Donald Faison) in *Next Day Air* likes to light up on the job. Leo's so stoned one day that he mistakenly delivers a large box containing 10 kilos of cocaine shipped from Los Angeles to Philadelphia to the wrong apartment. Instead of it going to Jesus (Cisco Reyes) in Apartment 302, Leo (he works for NDA) drops the Bolivian booty off with the hustlers next door. To them, it's manna from heaven and they immediately try to sell the stash. But Brody (*Next Friday*'s Mike Epps) and Guch (Wood Harris) are bumbling drug dealers at best. While Brody calls his cousin Shavoo (Omari Hardwicke), Jesus is being pressured by kingpin Bodega Diablo (Emilio Rivera) to find the coke. They look for Leo, who's busy getting high with Eric (Mos Def). All parties converge on Brody and Guch's apartment, guns a-blazing. It's a particularly brutal shoot-out, with stabbings and slit throats. Leo walks away with the loot and Jesus grabs the coke before the police show up. Combining the humor of *Friday* with the cold-blooded violence of a blaxploitation film, *Next Day Air*—like *Pineapple Express*—is one of those rare action movies that will make you laugh.

Leo: "All I really need is weed."

Phase IV (2001)

🌿🍃 This muddled mess pits Big Pharma against patients in an experimental drug program and a doctor who knows too much. The drug in question—Phase II—fights the HIV virus. However, Phase III eliminates positive effects from the previous stage, forcing patients to seek treatment, which the firm Stroyker Pierson provides. And Phase IV? "It's the status quo," crooked Senator Karnes (Nigel Bennett) tells journalist student-turned-crime fighter Simon (Dean Cain). Several chase scenes with a green Charger in hot pursuit is as good as this bad movie gets.

Pulp Fiction (1994)

🔧 🍸 ✂️ 🌿 💉 👀

🌿🌿🌿🌿🌿 A collection of vignettes featuring a nonlinear narrative structure that's since become de rigueur, Quentin Tarantino's low-life ensemble is the epitome of nineties cool. With several plot lines interweaving backward and forward in time, what could be a cinematic mess is a complete masterpiece with knife-sharp dialogue and points off the scale for style. Hit men, drug dealers, boxers, petty thieves, gun molls, sodomizing hillbilly leather boys, and gangster dons all chatter on like cultural theorists, their banter normalizing the casually intense violence at the heart of this film. Like the dime-store novels that inspired the movie's name, it's a trip through an imagined Los Angeles underworld of Kerouacian talkiness and chop-socky enthusiasm. And like the wallet that belongs to sermonizing hit man Jules Winnfield (Samuel L. Jackson), *Pulp Fiction* is the one that says "Bad Motherfucker" on it.

In just one small thread through the intricately braided plot, Vincent Vega (John Travolta in his comeback role), a hip dude and assassin-for-hire, has just returned home to Los Angeles after years of mellowing out in Amsterdam. But Vincent's not into hash—he digs cheeseburgers and heroin. After scoring at the home of his dealer, Lance (Eric Stoltz), Vincent heads out for a night of chaperoning Mia Wallace (Uma Thurman), the boss man's wife. After stressing in the bathroom about sleeping with Mia, Vincent emerges to find her OD-ing, having mistaken his heroin for cocaine. A frantic car ride takes them to the emergency cure: a shot of adrenaline administered on Lance's floor directly into her heart. After all the insanity, Jody (Rosanna Arquette), Lance's wife, just pronounces with a wide-eyed purr that the whole scene is, in a word, "trippy."

A movie one step away from a gunshot at all times, it's a roller-coaster ride of beatings, shootings, hard-core drug use, and biblical theorizing wrapped up in hilarious back-and-forth dialogue about everything from foot massages to pancakes to coffee. Occasionally, it will make your head spin, but you'll never feel this good watching people act so bad.

☘ UNKNOWN PLEASURES ☘

Movie drugs come in different shapes, sizes, colors, and names but all have one thing in common: They get you off. Here are our favorite fictional narcotics.

The pill (*Barbarella*): It seems that in the forty-first century, nobody has physical sex anymore, they just take the pill, or "exhaltation transference pellet," which causes two people to "be joined in psychosexual union." That's not good enough for the dude who reacquaints Barbarella (Jane Fonda) with the act of primitive love—and she digs it.

Moloko (*A Clockwork Orange*): A potpourri of designer drugs are available in the dystopian world of *A Clockwork Orange*. Chief among them: moloko, a milk spiced with various psychoactive agents (synthemesc, drencrom) that Alex and his droog cronies drink at the popular Korova Milkbar before heading out for a night of "the old ultraviolence."

The Orb (*Sleeper*): In Woody Allen's sole sci-fi flick, he introduces a silver sphere known as the Orb, which, when touched by humans, gives off a wave of immense pleasure. A gigglefest ensues at one party when the Orb is passed around from guest to guest. Sound familiar? Later, Miles (Allen) turns down a hit off the Orb. "I'm cool," he says.

Polydichloric euthimal (*Outland*): Working the titanium ore mines on a distant moon off Jupiter for months on end can get tedious, which is why some of Con Am 27's manual laborers have taken to injecting a synthetic amphetamine that allows you to "do fourteen hours of work in six." But eleven months later, its users turn psychotic as the drug literally fries their brains. Sean Connery stars in this tense sci-fi Western.

The Spice (*Dune*): In *Dune*, he who controls the spice controls the universe. The coveted element (also known as melange), produced by sandworms and found on planet Arrakis, gives you psychic powers, heightened awareness, trippy blue eyes, and prolonged life. Used by the navigators of the Spacing Guild, it allows them to fold space so that starships can travel safely between star systems. Talk about mind-bending.

Mystery inhalant (*Blue Velvet*): In the David Lynch film's darkest moment, teenage wannabe detective Jeffrey (Kyle MacLachlan) finds his way into the apartment of Dorothy Vallens (Isabella Rossellini) and gets more than he bargained for when he watches sociopath Frank Booth (Dennis Hopper) violently have his way with her while taking hits off of an unspecified inhalant.

The briefcase (*Pulp Fiction*): They never do say what's in the briefcase that everybody's trying to get their hands on—drugs, money, guns, gold?—but its luminescent glow brings to mind something ecstatic.

Ghost orchid (*Adaptation*): The story of this rare orchid's extract—a green powder, which, when snorted, produces Ecstasy-like results and makes everything "fascinating"— is secondary to the Spike Jonze–directed, Oscar-winning tale of screenwriting twins Charlie and Donald Kaufman (both played by Nicolas Cage), one of whom (Charlie, writer of *Being John Malkovich*) actually exists. Susan Orlean (Meryl Streep), whose book the movie is, um, adapted from, and John Laroche (Chris Cooper, who won for Best Supporting Role) do the snorting.

POS 51 (*Formula 51*): It looks like a bright blue M&M, but pop this rave-friendly treat in your mouth, and you'll feel a high "fifty-one times stronger than cocaine, fifty-one times more hallucinogenic than acid, and fifty-one times more explosive than ecstasy." Pharmacology wiz Elmo (Samuel L. Jackson) shills his product all over England, and takes his British buyers for a ride.

Neuroin (*Minority Report*): In Phillip K. Dick's futuristic Precrime caper, John Anderton (Tom Cruise) is among the many U.S. residents hooked on Neuroin in the year 2054. He uses a plastic inhaler to take a hit of the heroin-like gas while watching old videos of his missing son.

Death sticks (*Star Wars Episode II: Attack of the Clones*): In a blink-and-you'll-miss-it bar exchange, Obi-Wan Kenobi (Ewan McGregor) is offered a jointlike "death stick," a potent hallucinogen made from mushroom spores, while waiting for a shot of blue space booze. Using the Jedi mind trick, he reasons with the slacker known as Elan Sleazebaggano, telling the lad: "You don't want to sell me death sticks . . . You want to go home and rethink your life."

Substance D (*A Scanner Darkly*): The powderlike Substance D is as much a star of this Richard Linklater–directed adaptation of Phillip K. Dick's novel as Keanu Reeves or Woody Harrelson. Said to trigger a dream state of intoxication replete with bizarre hallucinations, undercover cop Bob Arctor (Reeves) gets hooked and damages his brain permanently.

Quiet Cool (1986)

A biker gang terrorizes a California community. Sound familiar? That's pretty much the stock plot for most biker movies. This one has a little twist, though: The bikers are also pot growers who guard their crops with booby traps and machine guns. New York cop Joe (James Remar) flies out at the request of former girlfriend Katy (Daphne Ashbrook) whose brother has disappeared. Joe challenges the bikers, especially Valence (a young Nick Cassavetes), and eventually takes them down in a blazing inferno. Along the way a few joints are smoked, but in true sadistic biker movie style, one character, Toke (Joe Sagal), has a lit cigarette placed in his ear. Ouch!

🌿 BADASS BIKER FLICKS 🌿

Part beatnik, rebel, greaser, juvenile delinquent, and common criminal, bikers roared onto the American landscape in the fifties like cowboys on steroids. Hollywood's B-movie directors and film companies took notice, launching a new genre—the "biker movie"—that began with *The Wild One* in 1953, starring Marlon Brando in a breakout role as the leather-clad leader of the Black Rebel Motorcycle Club, and peaked with *Easy Rider* in 1969. Here are six other biker-movie classics.

The Wild Angels (1966): Directed by B-movie icon Roger Corman, it stars Peter Fonda in his first biker role as gang leader Heavenly Blues and Bruce Dern as Loser, who's shot by the police. After he dies, the gang stages a wild wake in a church that includes the rape of Loser's girlfriend. Nancy Sinatra as Blues's babe, Monkey, is surprisingly good in this sadistic caper.

Hells Angels on Wheels (1967): Jack Nicholson (Poet) joins the Angels, but he never really fits in. He and the jefe, played by Adam Roarke, come to blows over a girl, but it's Roarke who suffers a fiery death. A young László Kovács provides the lush cinematography.

The Born Losers (1967): This first of four *Billy Jack* movies is the best, with director Tom Laughlin also starring as half-breed Vietnam vet Billy Jack. The Born Losers biker gang bait Billy with racist taunts, and rape and traumatize local girls. After Billy falls for Vicky (Elizabeth James, who also wrote the script), an extremely naïve, bikini-clad biker-chick, he avenges her rough treatment by the Losers in a shoot-out finale.

The Cycle Savages (1969): Bruce Dern takes the helm as Keeg, a paranoid, cool creep who stabs a local artist simply for drawing portraits of him and his disciples. The slim story line includes a particularly vicious gang rape and a prostitution ring led by Keeg's brother (Casey Kasem!). Predictably, Keeg gets what's coming to him in the end.

Angels Unchained (1970): American International Pictures's follow-up to *Easy Rider* pitted bikers versus hippies versus rancher/townies in the Arizona desert. Tyne Daly costars as Merilee, a hippie chick who invites outcast biker Angel (Don Stroud) to stay at the commune. When locals threaten the hippies, the Exile & Nomads gang shows up and the usual mayhem ensues.

Electra Glide in Blue (1973): The only film ever directed by James William Guercio (he produced the bands Chicago and Blood, Sweat & Tears) introduced Robert Blake as good-guy motorcycle cop John Wintergreen, who frowns on his colleagues' bad behavior, which includes falsely pinning a local's death on a biker. Ironically, hippies who Blake had helped eventually do him in. Set in the high Arizona desert, the film would be among the last in a genre that has since earned cult status.

Romancing the Stone (1984)

🌱 🍸 🔪

🍁 🍁 🍁 🍁 If there was any doubt whether Michael Douglas could hold his own as a leading man, this early-eighties romantic comedy with an action-adventure twist put that to rest for good. Douglas plays Jack Colton, a free-spirited opportunist collecting birds in the Colombian jungle, who meets stranded American Joan Wilder (Kathleen Turner), a romance novelist attempting to free her captured sister, Elaine (Mary Ellen Trainor). The ransom: an old treasure map mailed to Joan just before her brother-in-law's death. But Elaine's captors, who include repeat bungler Ralph (Danny DeVito), aren't the only ones trying to get their hands on El Corazón, the giant emerald waiting where X marks the spot. The map hunt puts Joan—and by association, Jack—in danger and keeps them both on the run. In one of the movie's most memorable moments, the two happen upon a plane that had crashed deep in the jungle, where all that remains is a skeleton wearing a Grateful Dead shirt, an old copy of *Rolling Stone*, and many kilos of pot. Jack uses the bricks to make a bonfire, taking long, deep breaths until Joan announces that she's "getting dizzy." Amazingly, though there's not a single cell phone or GPS system to be found, nothing about *Romancing the Stone* feels dated—a feat few films of its time can claim.

Joan: "What is all this?"

Jack: "All this? About five to life in the States, a couple of centuries down here."

Joan: "Oh, marijuana."

Jack: "Oh, you smoke it?"

Joan: "I went to college."

Scarface (1932)

🍸 🔪

🍁 🍁 🍁 🍁 Banned because of its depiction of wanton gang violence, the original *Scarface*, directed by Howard Hawks, was among the wave of crime movies that came out during Prohibition in the early 1930s. Italian immigrant Tony Camonte (Paul Muni) strong-arms Chicago saloon keepers, forcing them to buy barrels of illicit beer at high prices. But when he barges into the Irish-run North Side, a full-scale gang war breaks out. Much of the violence is tame, with no blood spilled because of censorship codes. Plus, moralistic messages ("This movie is an indictment of gang rule in America") were tacked on to make the movie more palatable. A reshot ending has Tony standing trial and receiving the death penalty rather than dying at the hands of overzealous cops. Oliver Stone ripped off some of the dialogue for the 1983 remake, but what he failed to copy was the humorous banter between Tony and his male secretary, Angelo (Vincent Barnett), who can't read or write.

Tony: "Beer isn't a nickel game anymore, it's a business. There are three thousand saloons on the South Side, a half a million customers. Figure it out . . . "

Scarface (1983)

🍸 🔪 🔪 👀

🍁 🍁 🍁 🍁 🍁 Brian De Palma's update of the 1932 Prohibition-era gangster saga stars Al Pacino as Tony Montana in one of Hollywood's

most enduring and imitated roles. Pacino's tour de force performance picks up where Michael Corleone left off in the *Godfather* movies, but with renewed vigor. Among the former Cuban prisoners who fled en masse to the U.S. in 1980 as part of the Mariel boatlift, Tony quickly climbs to the top of a cocaine distribution operation in Miami that's buying directly from Bolivia. With a brilliant script by Oliver Stone and De Palma at the helm, the pace is fast and furious, the action brutally violent. The chain-saw shower scene is a classic, as is the finale with Tony proclaiming, "Say hello to my little friend!"—machine-gun fire explodes and he dies in a hail of bullets. Though it may appear to be antidrug, Stone was sure to add a subtle message about "legalizing and taxing" drugs to "drive out the organized crime element." The excellent supporting cast includes Michelle Pfeiffer as Tony's sexy trophy wife, Elvira; Steven Bauer as his number two, Manny; Mary Elizabeth Mastrantonio as his little sister, Gina; Robert Loggia as his mentor-turned-betrayer Frank; F. Murray Abraham as Omar; and Paul Shenar as the Escobar-like Sosa. But it's Tony who eats up the scenery whether he's slaying his rivals, romancing Elvira, obsessing about his sister, or shoveling obscene amounts of coke ("yayo") up his nose.

Tony: "Is this what's it's all about, Manny? Eating, drinking, fucking, sucking, snorting—then what?"

Set It Off (1996)

Beat down by the everyday struggle of life in the projects, toiling away at a cleaning lady's job, four longtime girlfriends—nicknamed Stony (Jada Pinkett Smith), Frankie (Vivica A. Fox), Cleo (Queen Latifah), and T.T. (Kimberly Elise)—decide to rob banks as a way to escape their harsh reality. Wearing wigs and sunglasses, with guns and lowriders as their tools, these badass babes start mopping up cash in no time, until the cops get wind of their scheme and your classic shoot-out/car chase ensues. By far the hardest of this girl gang is the corn-rowed Cleo, who's not only gay (she and her lover share an awesome little scene on top of Cleo's 1962 Chevy Impala), but can handle an Uzi like nobody's business. And while *Set It Off* has its share of sappy melodrama, it also features women hitting a rooftop blunt to the tune of Bone Thugs-n-Harmony's "Days of Our Livez." An appearance by Dr. Dre also helps set this film apart, but all in all, it's about the ladies going for broke. Now that's girl power.

Speed Racer (2008)

It took almost fifty years for the Japanese anime series, a favorite Saturday morning cartoon in the U.S., to get a film adaptation, but it was well worth the wait. And while the Wachowski brothers (*The Matrix*, *V for Vendetta*) ultimately gave *Speed Racer* the kids' treatment, the psychedelic, kaleidescopic ocean of colors are fit for a stoner. Even as the opening credits are rolling, every inch of the screen is already awash in a rainbow of vapor trails as a young Speed Racer (Emile Hirsch) daydreams of the track where his big brother Rex (Scott Porter) made his name—then tarnished the family's. Jump forward to when a teenage Speed is the great hope of Mom and Pops Racer (Susan Sarandon and John Goodman), not to mention a prime target for every corporate power-monger in this neon-infested postmodern milieu. Chief among his suitors: E. P. Arnold Royalton (Roger Allam), head of Royalton Industries, a smarmy billionaire who's determined to sign Speed and fix future races, like the harrowing Casa Cristo Classic 5000. Speed turns Royalton down and a bounty is put on his head, but with Racer X (Matthew Fox) in his corner and girlfriend Trixie (Christina Ricci) on the lookout in her hot pink 'copter, he races on as an independent, defying the odds and determined to redeem his family name. G-rated story aside (even a tongueless kiss between Speed and Trixie is preempted with a cooties warning), this fantastical world, where roads feel like a cross between a skateboarding ramp and a roller coaster, flowers can bloom three times in multiple colors, people zip around on Segways, and a pet chimp barely registers a second glance, is on par with the best of trippy visuals.

Trixie: "Oh my god, was that a ninja?"

Pops Racer: "More like a 'non'-ja. Terrible what passes for a ninja these days."

Super Fly (1972)

🪶 🐌 ⚱ 👓

🌿 🌿 🌿 🌿 Made in the same early seventies verité style as *The French Connection* and *The Panic in Needle Park* and also set in New York, this blaxploitation classic pits cocaine dealer Priest (Ron O'Neal) against rival pushers, dirty cops, and even his own partner. Priest dresses loudly, drives a fierce black El Dorado, and wears a coke spoon around his neck.

He doesn't think twice about getting high on his own supply, repeatedly snorting (one spoon per nostril per session). But he wants out of the game, and plots a final score—30 kilos worth $1 million on the street. Acquiring that much coke gets the attention of the police, who bust Priest's cohort Freddie (Charles MacGregor). Unlike Priest, Freddie smokes weed. In a nightclub scene, he tells a dealer (Nate Adams), "Give me one of those joints," then instructs his wife (Yvonne Delaine), "Light that." Freddie inhales and asks, "Where'd you get this from, Cuba?" "Hey, man," the dealer replies. "That's seventy-five dollars an ounce. It's good!" Unfortunately, Freddie is run over after escaping from police custody, hence the Curtis Mayfield soundtrack gem, "Freddie's Dead." Priest gets the last laugh, scaring off Deputy Police Commissioner Riordan (Mike Richards) with a barrage of insults and threats. O'Neal's sensitive performance and Mayfield's powerful songs (the title track and "Pusherman," which he plays live) and score make up for the B-movie production and racy language (lots of n- and f-bombs). The DVD is chock-full of "Fly Features." Oh yeah, we dig.

Priest: "Nothing—NOTHING—better happen to one hair on my gorgeous head, can you dig?"

Tequila Sunrise (1988)

🪶 🍸 🐌 ⚱

🌿 🌿 🌿 In this convoluted drug caper, Mel Gibson plays Dale "Mac" McKussic, a former dealer trying to go straight. Kurt Russell is Nick Frescia, Mac's old friend who's determined to keep him on the right path, but also a detective looking for a lead to Mexican drug kingpin Carlos (the late Raul Julia). In Mac's new life, temptation lurks at every turn, not just for drugs, but for love in the form of Jo Ann Vallenari (Michelle Pfeiffer), a sexy restaurant owner with an icy disposition (their steamy hot tub scene has become an eighties pop culture benchmark). A love triangle takes shape and both Nick and Mac undergo a test of loyalty while Carlos asserts his own dominance—with millions in cocaine profits on the line, he's not about to let anybody get in the way. Nick tries to bend the investigation so that his friend is out of the line of fire, but when Mac gives in to a toke off a joint (Carlos: "Come on buddy, when was the last time we smoked some really good shit, eh? Life is serious enough")—and presumably a snort, since a pile of coke sits nearby—a shoot-out puts all in danger, and Carlos winds up on the wrong end of the stick. Directed by Robert Towne (he wrote *Chinatown*), the film was a commercial success, even if the complex story made little sense to audiences then—or now, for that matter. Its saving grace is the suave Julia, whose character has the foresight to predict pot's popularity in the nineties. "I got

> **"I've seen it coming for some time. Cocaine is no goddamn good for anybody. The future is grass."**
>
> **—Carlos**

sixty ton of Thai Stick coming in," says Carlos in his final scene, imagining what could have been.

True Romance (1993)

🔥 🍸 🎋 ✂️

🌿 🌿 🌿 🌿 🌿 Quentin Tarantino's project (he wrote it) between *Reservoir Dogs* and *Pulp Fiction* is *GoodFellas* meets *Bonnie and Clyde*. Elvis-obsessed Clarence (Christian Slater) and Alabama (Patricia Arquette in a breakout role) steal 20 kilos of cocaine from the mob in Detroit and try to move it before a team of hit men find them. An early, drawn-out, violent scene in which Vincenzo (Christopher Walken) beats and kills Clarence's father (stoner favorite Dennis

> "Do you guys want to smoke a bowl?"
>
> —Floyd to hit men

Hopper) sets the tone. Later, Alabama overcomes Virgil (James Gandolfini), torching and then blowing him away. It's a singular moment for strong women in a male-dominated genre. In pure Tarantino fashion, the climax pitches three sets of adversaries against each other in one room—but not before pothead couch potato Floyd (Brad Pitt) demonstrates the use of a honey bear bong (a first in stoner cinema). Clarence and Alabama (barely) survive the shoot-out, (definitely) wind up with the loot, and (presumably) live happily ever after on a beach in Mexico.

The Warriors (1979)

✏️ 🍸 🎋

🌿 🌿 🌿 Set in a not-so-distant future based on the graffiti strewn urban rot of late-seventies New York City, this campy action flick follows the trials of a street gang called the Warriors who are unjustly accused of killing Cyrus (Roger Hill), the de facto head of all gangs in the city. Targeted for reprisal, the Warriors must make their way home from the Bronx to Coney Island, hopping subway trains and navigating parks and dark alleys. Warrior war chief Swan (Michael Beck) leads his troop of misfits into battle against a slew of ridiculously costumed gangs. Fantastically fashion-forward, they all coordinate their look so you can tell them apart. There are the Punks, who wear overalls; the Baseball Furies, in baseball uniforms; the bald-headed Turnbull AC's; leatherboys the Rogues; and Cyrus's gang, the Gramercy Riffs, who match karate to a Black Panther vibe. If Cyrus's opening speech to the assembled rival gangs about banding together seems familiar, that's because his "cannn youuu diggg itt" mantra has become a dance music sample favorite. Cyrus's true killer, Luther (David Patrick Kelly), clinks bottles together on his fingers, presaging Freddy Krueger's talon scrapes whining "Warriors . . . come out and play" in one of the movie's creepiest scenes. There's a bad girl love interest, Mercy (Deborah Van Valkenberg), and a few exciting chase sequences, but it's all about the meathead acting and one-liners. Props to the female gang, the Lizzies, for being the only ones with the sense to spark one up in their dive bar seduction scene, before they try to blow the Warriors away.

Alice in Wonderland (1951)

🌿🌿🌿🌿 This Walt Disney classic has all the makings of a psychedelic head-trip: a world of wonder where proportions don't apply, flowers sing, tea kettles dance, rabbits run, and butterflies morph into a loaf of bread. Adapted from Lewis Carroll's children's books *Alice's Adventures in Wonderland* and *Through the Looking Glass*, it introduces iconic characters like the Mad Hatter, the Red Queen, the Cheshire Cat, Tweedledee and Tweedledum, the Dormouse, and stoniest of all: a bleary-eyed blue Caterpillar who smokes from a hookah and instructs Alice to nibble on a mushroom in order to shrink or expand. Indeed, it's mainly because of this snooty insect, who blows colored smoke rings while lounging atop a giant 'shroom, that *Alice in Wonderland* gained its stoner cred, but it's not the only reason. For one, Alice runs into the Caterpillar after she's ejected from the garden of flowers for being a "weed." A couple of scenes earlier, the White Rabbit and a pipe-smoking Dodo, upon discovering a giant Alice bulging out of a tiny house, chant, "We'll smoke the monster out!" And, simply put, Carroll's imagination is just out there, especially considering the book came out in 1865. Still, whether intentional or not, the 1951 film could have easily been named "Acid Adventures in Wonderland."

"Just as I suspected! She's nothing but a common mobile vulgaris!"

—Snapdragon

"Oh no!"

—Flowers

"A common what?"

—Alice

"To put it bluntly: a weed!"

—Snapdragon

American Pop (1981)

🌿🌿🌿🌿 In one of animation pioneer Ralph Bakshi's most heralded feature films, the history of American pop music is chronicled through parallel stories of four generations of aspiring entertainers. From the start, Zalmie, the son of a rabbi killed in an 1895 Russian pogrom, squeaks by with a singing job at a burlesque club where he gets tangled up with the mob, and his offspring, Benny, a soldier and skilled piano player, meets his end by the gun of a German soldier. Things pick up once Tony, armed only with a thick New York accent and his father Benny's harmonica, comes into the picture. Tony steals a car and heads west to California, where he falls in with a bunch of longhairs playing in a band. To the tunes of Bob Dylan and Jefferson Airplane, they graduate from club gigs to ballrooms, and Tony is exposed to everything from joints to pills to acid, while silky-voiced front woman Frankie descends into alcoholism and heroin use. Archival footage of the Vietnam War and the Kent State shootings interspersed with psychedelic colors and kaleidoscopic patterns set the uneven tone, as the music of Janis Joplin and Jimi Hendrix take the mayhem to new levels and make way for the Velvet Underground and the razor-sharp punk rock movement. Pete, a bright little orphaned boy Tony ostensibly fosters, is the last segment's star. Drug dealing becomes Pete's main source of income, and also leads him into a New York recording studio where he impresses with some high-quality cocaine and his own (though technically, Bob Seger's) "Night Moves." Soon after, he's rocking an arena stage looking like a postmodern Elvis Presley complete with laser light show that climaxes with Heart's "Crazy on You." Visually speaking, vivid city details accent nearly every frame of *American Pop*, and where the plot could be riddled with clichés, this crash course in drug culture and music from Prohibition to the eighties is anything but, thanks to Bakshi's stonercentric vision.

Musician: "You got the coke, daddy-o?"

Pete: "What do I look like, man? A soda fountain?"

Aqua Teen Hunger Force Colon Movie Film for Theaters
(2007)

Incongruous, surreal, and nearly unwatchable, this extension of the cult-classic *Adult Swim* show starts promisingly enough, with a spoof of those "Let's go out to the movies" prescreening cartoons that becomes a frighteningly hilarious apocalyptic metal tune. Unfortunately, that's the best part of the movie. Even if you've been stone-cold sober, good luck making heads or tails out of the plot, which finds Frylock (Carey Means), Meatwad (Dave Willis), and Master Shake (Dana Snyder) attempting to bulk up on an exercise machine to score chicks. Somehow along the way, they get involved with an intergalactic conspiracy that involves Abe Lincoln and a talking piece of watermelon. Taken in snippets, it's almost enjoyable, but trying to make sense of the film as a whole will drive you absolutely bonkers.

WHEN FOOD COMES TO LIFE

Talking, dancing, singing, running . . . when the purpose of food goes beyond eating, there's a stoner in mind.

Dancing mushrooms (*Fantasia*): In one of the Walt Disney classic's most beloved and well-known acts (set to the tune of Tchaikovsky's *Nutcracker* Suite), a ridiculously cute cluster of mushrooms does the "Chinese Dance," an appropriate preamble to the psychedelic imagery that lies ahead.

Giant banana, celery, strawberry (*Sleeper*): Woody Allen's sci-fi caper was way ahead of its time if you equate the gigantic fruit he envisioned in the early seventies with what we now call organic food. Okay, maybe a twenty-second-century banana "the size of a canoe" has yet to emerge, but even in the future, the slip-on-the-peel joke never gets old, and neither does watching Allen grab onto a towering celery stalk and pummel a dude with a mammoth strawberry.

Stay-Puft Marshmallow Man (*Ghostbusters*): Both adorable and menacing, the building-sized doughboy that Dr. Ray Stantz (Dan Aykroyd) imagines when instructed to clear his mind has but one purpose: to offer the Ghostbusters as sacrifice to the pagan god Gozer. "We used to roast Stay-Puft marshmallows at Camp Waconda," Stantz recalls. Says Venkman (Bill Murray): "Great! The marshmallows are about to get their revenge."

The Van Halen burger (*Better Off Dead*): Bored to death toiling away as a line cook at Pig Burger, perpetual loser Lane Meyer (John Cusack) fantasizes that he's Dr. Frankenstein giving life to a burger who shreds on Van Halen's "Everybody Wants Some." The Claymation rock star has friends, too: sexy little French fries skinny-dipping in a pool of hot oil.

Land of Burgers (*Harold & Kumar Go to White Castle*): After getting thrown from the cheetah, the love-struck Harold (John Cho) passes out and dreams of a Land of Burgers, where the sky twinkles with pot leaf stars and he leads a charge of giggly two-bunned critters through fries-and-soda-lined streets to his beloved Maria waiting beyond the bong gates. Just like heaven.

Beavis and Butt-Head Do America (1996)

🍸 🌿

🌿🌿 A classic road movie, a classic buddy movie, and perhaps the dumbest thing you'll ever watch, *Beavis and Butt-Head Do America* follows two high school losers (and MTV icons) who sit around on the couch all day watching videos on TV and not doing much of anything else. The movie begins with a tragedy: Their television gets stolen, which leads to a series of high jinks. In order to find it, the duo travel to the Hoover Dam (Beavis asks: "Is this a god dam?"), trip out on peyote in the middle of the desert, and end up taking a meeting with President Clinton in the White House—not that it matters to these burnouts, or that they even know who he is. Celebrity voices abound (Bruce Willis and Demi Moore play a pair of career criminals who pull Beavis and Butt-Head into their master plan), but the cameo that makes the greatest impact in retrospect is that of animated character Tom Anderson, who's a beer-chugging, trailer-owning precursor to director Mike Judge's other great stoner icon, syndicated-into-eternity white-trash hero Hank Hill.

Tom Anderson: "Boy, I never seen two kids do so much damn whacking!"

Beavis: "I need T.P. for my bunghole!"

Cool World (1992)

🍸 🌿 👀

🌿 Combining live action with animation, Ralph Bakshi's final film effort is his least compelling. Brad Pitt plays Frank Harris, a soldier just home from World War II who gets drafted into an alternate cartoon world after a car accident kills his mother. There, he becomes a cop determined to keep the doodles in line. Meanwhile, in a parallel universe, cartoonist Jack Deebs (Gabriel Byrne), the man behind the popular comic book series *Cool World*, is fresh out of prison and interacting with characters he created. When he has sex with femme fatale Holli Would (Kim Basinger), a Marilyn Monroe–like seductress who's determined to cross over to the real world, the metaphorical walls separating the doodles and the "noids" (humans) come tumbling down. The animated portions of *Cool World* have their moments—the city's fun house vibe with bendy buildings shaped like faces and roller coaster–like roads, warped perspectives that trigger kaleidoscopic patterns—but when it comes to the acting and sets, the film feels like an amateurish *Roger Rabbit* clone (Pitt himself described it as "*Roger Rabbit* on acid"). Basinger in particular plays the human Holli so unconvincingly, it's hard to believe she's the same sultry character. Stick with Bakshi's earlier works for a true understanding of why he's considered the godfather of adult animation.

Fantasia (1940)

🍸 🍄 👀

🌿🌿🌿🌿🌿 The Walt Disney classic (only the third feature film the legendary studio produced) is an explosion of color, top-notch animation, and the world's greatest classical music, which was hailed as a "Technicolor triumph" when it premiered in 1940, but ended up a box-office dud. That was until the movie's undeniable psychedelic gleam was rediscovered in the sixties. Mushrooms dancing to the *Nutcracker Suite*, tie-dyed light trails at the hands of the Sorcerer and his lazy Apprentice, armies of marching brooms, alligators courting hippos, a rainbow-colored mythical world of unicorns, cupids, and topless centaurs . . . Is it any wonder stoners and acidheads embraced *Fantasia* with open arms and minds? Rereleased in 1969—and touting stereophonic sound on its newly psychedelic poster—*Fantasia* has since become a stoner must-see that's unparalleled in the world of animated film, whether under the influence or not. Look no further than the dazzling *Rite of Spring* sequence for proof. The story of Earth's birth is so gloriously illustrated, from the big bang to a volcanic tsunami, oceanic rebirth, and the age of dinosaurs, only Stanley Kubrick's *2001: A Space Odyssey* comes close to adequately visualizing such an epic undertaking. And while the orchestral program led by musical director Leopold Stokowski may seem boring to some, if you put the visuals aside for a minute, close your eyes and listen, it's a whole other *Fantasia* experience.

Fantastic Mr. Fox
(2009)

🍸🍾 🔪 💊

🌿🌿🌿🌿 Wes Anderson transformed Roald Dahl's wonderfully imaginative novel into an instant classic with this groundbreaking work of stop-motion animation. Mr. Fox (voiced by George Clooney) promises his wife Felicity (Meryl Streep) that he will give up chicken hunting forever, and with the birth of son Ash (Jason Schwartzman) and a new career as a newspaper columnist, it's time for him to settle down and buy a house. But he's still feeling unfulfilled, so Mr. Fox seeks adventure and finds it right next door at a massive facility run by farmers Boggis, Bunce, and Bean. An elaborate plot by Mr. Fox and his opos-sum landlord, Kylie (Wallace Wolodarsky), to steal chickens, turkeys, and alcoholic cider is hatched, which includes drugging the guard dogs with blue-berry sedatives. They pull it off, but it's not long before the farmers catch wind of the clever duo and band together to assassinate Mr. Fox at his den. After being shot, nearly blown up, and drowned, Mr. Fox sets up a mock surrender, where, with a little help from his furry friends, he strikes with all the fox power known to man, sending fiery pinecone grenades that devastate the area but also land a few of his pals in the sewers. Anderson fans will delight in the dry humor and quirky soundtrack that has become the direc-tor's trademark, but visually speaking, *Fox* offers a fantastical display in every frame that's downright stupefying.

Mr. Fox: "Why a fox? Why not a horse, or a beetle, or a bald eagle? I'm saying this more as like, existentialism, you know? Who am I? And how can a fox ever be happy without, you'll forgive the expression, a chicken in its teeth?"

Kylie: "I don't know what you're talking about, but it sounds illegal."

Fritz the Cat (1972)

🔪 🔑 🍸🍾 💊 💉 👀

🌿🌿🌿 The first-ever "X-rated and ani-mated" feature film—directed by cartoon auteur Ralph Bakshi and based on the character created by underground comic book icon Robert Crumb—stars the shit-talking, pot-smoking, womanizing Fritz, a jaded college type who's constantly mocking the state of intellectualism. He's got only one thing on his mind: booty, which in the free-lovin' sixties can mean a threesome of pussycats in the bath-tub on one night, and a crow in the alley on an-other. No ordinary bird, mind you—this brown sugar drug dealer named Bertha stashes a handful of spliffs in her hoochie, then lights them all in Fritz's mouth sparking waves of tie-dye-colored clouds and trippy trails. For these animals, feeling the high is called being "there," but weed, as it turns out, also has a debilitating effect—it makes them so horny that it practically blinds them to all else. New York City is the backdrop for most of this raunchy romp (a highlight: the psychedelic rabbis praying) until Fritz and his foxy girlfriend hit the road and head for San Francisco. Along the way, things take a dramatic turn when revolutionaries recruit Fritz to help them blow up a power station. Talk about a bad trip.

> "Fritz, you ever been high on pot?"
> —Crow

> "Are you kidding, man, grass? Who doesn't, you know? What do you think, I'm some kind of a hick?"
> —Fritz

Heavy Metal (1981)

🔪 🍸🍾 🔪 🥄 👀

🌿🌿🌿 Take comic books, rock-and-roll, hot naked women, aliens, science fiction, and horror, mix them all together, and you've got the ultimate adolescent fantasy movie for every stoner who ever skipped school. A series of vignettes tied together by a green orb called the Loc-Nar, which doubles as evil incarnate, *Heavy Metal* starts with the Loc-

Nar killing the astronaut who brings it home and terrorizing his daughter. Among the six tales: "Harry Canyon," is about a cynical New York cabbie who gets entangled with a woman being pursued by the Loc-Nar's killer goons; In "Den," a nerd is transformed into a muscleman and is overwhelmed with beautiful women; "So Beautiful, So Dangerous," features the buxom Gloria, who while in possession of the Loc-Nar is sucked into a spaceship, where she has robot sex while burnout aliens Edsel and Zeke snort cocainelike plutonian nyborg and crash-land their ship; and in "Taarna," a lone heroine must save Earth from the Loc-Nar, which is turning people into murderous barbarians. The rocking soundtrack includes Black Sabbath, Sammy Hagar, Blue Öyster Cult, and Cheap Trick.

> "You okay to land
> this thing?"
>
> —Edsel
>
> "No problem, man."
>
> —Zeke
>
> "I think you're going
> a little high, man."
>
> —Edsel
>
> "It's okay, man, if there's one
> thing I know, it's how to drive
> when I'm stoned. It's like, you
> know your perspective's
> fucked, see? You just have to let
> your hands work the controls
> as if you're straight."
>
> —Zeke

Paprika (2006)

🍸 🔪 ⊙⊙

🌿 🌿 🌿 🌿 🌿 Anime is an inherently psychedelic genre—kaleidoscopic colors, weird creatures, outsider fantasies made manifest in hyperanimation—but even in anime terms, Paprika is crazy trippy. Based on a bestselling novel of the same name, this recent Japanese classic is set in a near future where the invention of the DC Mini allows people to view their own dreams. The title character, a young, attractive female psychoanalyst, uses the DC Mini to cure a gruff detective's trauma. Following the basic plotline of a great forties noir, the device, of course, falls into the wrong hands. From this point on the narrative steers into sometimes sublime, sometimes creepy, always wonderful chaos. Paprika is weird in the way only Japanese anime masterpieces are, a journey into the deep subconscious involving clowns, fairies, and clarinet-playing frogs. The visuals are nothing less than extraordinary. This isn't kids' stuff—there's a heady metaphysical subtext here (something about accepting your true nature) and the dream imagery is stunning and surreal.

Paprika: "Don't you think dreams and the Internet are similar? They are both areas where the repressed conscious mind vents."

Simpsons Movie, The (2007)

🍶 🍸 🔪 ⊙⊙

🌿 🌿 🌿 The wait for a Simpsons movie goes back almost as far as the series itself, and with free reign to curse, expose a boob (or penis), and smoke some weed, expectations were high, to say the least. Which is why the slightly saccharine and message-heavy Simpsons Movie may have been a disappointment to the stoner crowd (though there is a brief, gratuitous shot of Otto hitting a bong). After all, it's the drunks and potheads that can best relate to Homer Simpson's blatant disregard for adult responsibilities and his overall dopiness. Still, the movie has its moments, starting with a performance

by Green Day kicking off a far-fetched plot: Homer adopts a pet pig and unknowingly pollutes the entire town of Springfield. The damage turns out to be so bad that the EPA and President Schwarzenegger order a glass dome to quarantine the infestation, turning the community against Homer, Marge, Bart, and Lisa and forcing the family to flee to Alaska. Only after a visit from a mysterious shaman does Homer see the light—that in order to save the town from being demolished to make way for a new Grand Canyon, he must also save himself . . . from himself.

South Park: Bigger, Longer & Uncut (1999)

🚬

🌿 🌿 🌿 🌿 Prior to Pixar's computer-animated hegemony, the mawkish Alan Menken musicals of the Walt Disney Renaissance dominated the 1990s. But by the decade's close, the formulaic misfires of Hercules and Mulan exemplified how ripe the subgenre was for parody. Enter Trey Parker and Matt Stone, the comedic geniuses behind hit Comedy Central show South Park, who take savage, smart, and scatological potshots at everything from U.S. jingoism to Tipper Gore–era censorship to Brian Boitano. The absurdity begins after Kyle, Kenny, Stan, and Cartman sneak into the new Terrance and

Phillip movie, Asses of Fire, and learn a litany of new curse words—including a song, "Uncle Fucker." Drama ensues when the boys direct their filthy vernacular toward their teacher, Mr. Garrison, earning a trip to the principal's office and phone calls home to their mothers. Aghast at the filth emanating from Terrance and Phillip's Canadian homeland, Kyle's mom, Sheila Broflovski, scapegoats her neighbors to the north for corrupting America's youth (and for Bryan Adams), and ultimately imprisons the gaseous comedy duo. In retaliation, the Canadian government bombs the Baldwin brothers' residence, leading to all-out war. Simultaneously, Satan and his gay lover, Saddam Hussein, plot to take over the world, a scheme that briefly comes to fruition once the blood of the Canucks spills on American soil. Along the way, there are jabs at Les Misérables, Windows 98, and Gandhi (who apparently lives in hell). Regularly ranked among the funniest animated films of all time, the South Park movie not only received an Academy Award nomination for Best Original Song ("Blame Canada"), it managed to set the Guinness World Records mark for Most Swear Words in an Animated Film: 399—about as many bong rips as you'll want to take while watching.

Billy Baldwin: "Hey Alec, you know what sucks about being a Baldwin?"

Alec Baldwin: "No, what?"

Billy Baldwin: "Nothing!"

SpongeBob SquarePants Movie, The (2004)

🍸🎵

🌿🌿🌿🌿 An offshoot of the totally wacky cartoon hit, this mostly animated movie follows the tribulations of SpongeBob SquarePants (the voice of Tom Kenny) and his buddy Patrick (Bill Fagerbakke), whose life in the underwater town of Bikini Bottom is interrupted by Plankton (Doug Lawrence), an interloper who steals King Neptune's crown and blames it on the owner of Krusty Krab, a fast-food franchise whose recipe he wants to reproduce to achieve fame and fortune. There are pirates, a bounty hunter, SpongeBob's ice cream hangover, even David Hasselhoff. It's all for the better, though—with this movie's next-level, absurdist humor, weed is an abetment, rather than a necessity.

> "I'm a goofy goober /
> you're a goofy goober."
>
> **—Multiple Characters**

🌿 ARE THEY OR AREN'T THEY STONERS? 🌿

Popeye: Consider this sailor man's stoner credentials: He always has a pipe hanging out of his mouth and he gets his superhuman strength from a green leaf. He also talks funny, giggles a lot, mumbles to himself, and has a decent amount of ink on his sleeve. Robin Williams portrayed the comic book icon brilliantly in the 1980 live-action film directed by Robert Altman.

Blue Caterpillar in *Alice in Wonderland*: The Jefferson Airplane spelled it out in 1967 in "White Rabbit": "One pill makes you larger and one pill makes you small." In the numerous versions of *Alice in Wonderland*, Alice comes upon the hookah-smoking Blue Cater-pillar who clues her in to the ways of Wonderland and encourages her to eat a mushroom. "And your mind is moving slow . . . "

Scooby-Doo and Shaggy: The coed cartoon gang was born in 1969, when CBS first aired *Scooby-Doo*, the Saturday morning series about a group of mystery-solving teenagers and their kooky dog, Scooby, whose insatiable appetite for Scooby Snacks means having the munchies all the time. You could say the same for Scooby's BFF. In the 2002 live-action movie, Shaggy (Matthew Lillard), a vegetarian who lives out of his surf van, always wears a green shirt, and says "dude" a lot, and falls for a girl named Mary Jane (Isla Fisher) whom he first spots while eating a sandwich.

Pee-wee Herman: Considering one of his first appearances is in *Cheech & Chong's Next Movie*, it would stand to reason that if Paul Reubens's Pee-wee doesn't partake, he at least approves of pot. How else can you explain the giggly man-child's toy- and gadget-filled playhouse (where appliances and furniture talk), his obsession with a shiny red bike, and his utter cluelessness when it comes to the advances of girls like Dottie and Miss Yvonne? Whether it's the Saturday morning series or the much beloved movie *Pee-wee's Big Adventure*, few kid-friendly characters are as stony.

SpongeBob SquarePants: Most of the time, he's a good-natured, fun-loving sea sponge who sees the bright side to everything—even his own dead-end job as a fry cook at the Krusty Krab restaurant. But between those moments of eternal optimism and clueless bliss is the occasional unshakeable sense of pure paranoia. Bikini bottom line: SpongeBob is happiest when chilling in the comfort of his own pineapple-shaped home.

Garfield: For this facetious feline, the two most important things in life are the most basic: food and sleep (you can never have enough of both). It's no wonder Garfield is believed to be of the stoner persuasion—he's fat, always craving lasagna, and often dreams of junk food.

Waking Life (2001)

🍸 🔫 💉

🌿 🌿 🌿 🌿 In the opening moments of this hazy, ever-morphing animated mindscape, Wiley Wiggins, the stringy-haired, butt-paddled freshman from Richard Linklater's *Dazed and Confused*, steps off a train and into a boat driven like a car. Soon after, his fellow passenger (the director, who reappears in the film's final sequence playing pinball and quoting Philip K. Dick) tells the boat-car's captain a specific spot to cast Wiley ashore. Minutes later, Wiley reaches down to pick up a note in the middle of the street: "Look to your right." He does—and a car nails him square in the face. The screen loses color for an instant . . . and Wiley appears to awaken from a dream. But did he really? "I keep waking up," he realizes later on, "but I'm just waking up into another dream." Will he remain stuck in a lucid limbo? Is he en route to eternity? Or is life just one long daydream, all of us forever trapped in time? Those are the underlying questions for the next ninety minutes, as Wiley floats *Slacker*-style through a hypnotizing parade of faces "sleepwalking through their waking state or wakewalking through their dreams." Each person he encounters—at college lectures and coffeehouses, in bed or in jail—grapples with similar existential conundrums, perpetually pondering the interconnectedness of all things.

It's a rather serene acid trip, with talking heads mostly unknown to anyone but philosophy majors, although Ethan Hawke and Julie Delpy briefly revive their chatty *Before Sunrise* roles and comedians Adam Goldberg and Lewis Black zip by in surly cameos. The seasick dazzle of it all, however, compensates for low star power. Casual tokers and overly analytic stoners alike will find them-

> **"There's only one instant, and it's right now. And it's eternity."**
>
> **—Pinball Playing Man**

selves sinking fast into Linklater's roiling ocean of rotoscoped images, drowning in a labyrinth of riddling questions.

Wall-E (2008)

🌿 🌿 🌿 🌿 🌱 In this beloved and foreboding statement on consumerism, beaten-up, boggle-eyed, boxy little waste-collecting robot Wall-E trundles around the barren surface of post-apocalyptic Earth collecting scraps and doodads. An old flickering VHS copy of *Hello, Dolly!* warms his battery-driven heart with a longing for romance, which is finally fulfilled when oval-shaped, Apple-designed laser-blasting surveillance love interest EVE drops out of the sky. Wall-E hitches a ride on her spaceship which is packed with the bloated, sentient, junk-guzzling remains of what was once the human race, then sets forth to restore Earth, one seed at a time. Damn you, Pixar, for being this accomplished! Who else could deliver a heart-melting love story that also serves as a disgusted slap in the face to the burger-chomping, Coke-swilling, corporate lackeys who make up its audience? "Get off your fat asses and save this planet," they warn us. "Oh, and don't forget to buy plush Wall-E's from our retail store!" Our hat's off.

EVE: "Wall-E."

Watership Down (1978)

🌿 🌿 🌱 This dark and somewhat disturbing British animated feature delivers rabbit mythology in vivid watercolors as a crew of tripped-out bunnies scramble to escape their soon-to-be-destroyed homes. In a vision, a young runt named Fiver (John Hurt) sees a storm looming just beyond the horizon, forcing the warren to find new shelter. After failing to convince their leader of the coming danger, some of the more paranoid, red-eyed rabbits heed Fiver's psychic advice and seek new lodging in the village of Watership Down. But their journey proves to be quite difficult, teeming with bloodied rabbits, new enemies, predators that shred their rivals into pieces, and that pesky creature named man. It should come as no surprise that this cartoon is far from kid-friendly. Hell, there are adults that still suffer nightmares from having seen it in their teenage years, so tread carefully. That said, these humanistic cottontails are one hell of a trip.

Who Framed Roger Rabbit (1988)

🍸 ✒️

🌿 🌿 🌿 It wasn't the first time a movie had combined animation with live action (the technology goes at least as far back as 1964's *Mary Poppins*), but the Robert Zemeckis–directed, Steven Spielberg–produced, 'toon-themed film noir is certainly among the most heralded. Set in an alternate L.A. during the 1940s, private investigator and drunk Eddie Valiant (Bob Hoskins) is probing the sexy Jessica Rabbit, who's believed to be cheating on her husband, Roger Rabbit, by quite literally playing patty-cake with Acme Corporation's Marvin Acme. At the same time, Judge Doom (Christopher Lloyd) and his 'toon henchmen, a posse of smoking gangster dogs, is using the Dip, a substance powerful enough to kill even cartoons, as a weapon against anyone who stands in the way of their *Chinatown*-esque domination of the local transportation system. This all goes down in and around the totally trippy Toontown, the kind of place where toddlers smoke cigarettes and foul-mouthed animated babies puff on cigars, but a complex web of subplots and conspiracies muddle an already difficult-to-follow, boozy movie. Still, when it comes to humans interacting with cartoons, *Roger Rabbit* exhibits some groundbreaking work, not to mention cameos by A-list animated stars like Daffy Duck, Betty Boop, Mickey Mouse, Tweety Bird, and the Tasmanian Devil.

> "Who needs a car in L.A.? We have the best public transportation system in the world."
>
> —**Eddie Valiant**

Wizards (1977)

🔑 🍸 🍼 👀

🌿 🌿 🌿 🌿 Set in a future Earth destroyed by terrorists' atomic warfare, acclaimed animator Ralph Bakshi's 1977 "family" movie is a fairy tale with Nazi footage and tits. A story about two brother wizards, good Avatar (Bob Holt, sounding very much like a perpetually stoned Peter Falk) and evil Blackwolf (Steve Gravers), representing the twin, opposing forces of magic and technology, *Wizards* is a mixture of Saturday morning cartoon cuteness, cosmic funk doobiness, and horrific, bad-trip violence. Years ago, Avatar—who looks like a cross between a Smurf, the Fabulous Furry Freak Brothers, and cartoonist Vaughn Bodé's Cheech Wizard—cast a defeated Blackwolf out of the idyllic land of Montagar and into the radiated badlands of Scorch. Digging up ancient technology and building a mutant army, Blackwolf and his secret weapon, a "dream projector" filled with ancient Nazi propaganda reels, begin a war to conquer the world, terrorizing the elfin defenders and bringing destruction down upon the land. Avatar, along with his hoochie fairy-in-training girlfriend, Elinore (Jesse Welles), and rehabilitated robot assassin Peace (David Proval), travels to Scorch for the inevitable showdown with Blackwolf, during which Avatar proves that even magic has to rely on technology to win a fight sometimes.

Like a super-psychedelic *Scooby-Doo* episode, albeit one with tank battles and sexy fairies in see-through clothing, *Wizards* switches animation styles repeatedly, making use of violent war footage through rotoscoping and live motion backgrounds. It gets really dark and heavy with images of swastikas, Hitler, and the Nazi blitzkrieg, making for an odd juxtaposition with the goofy fairies and Hanna-Barbera-esque "good guy" characters. There's a bit of elfin smoking in the trenches and one would have to imagine that Avatar has a bong stashed somewhere up his cape, but it's the synthesized score that occasionally starts to fry your brainpan with its odd twists and turns. Changing tack at every scene, Andrew Belling's music is oddly disjointed, like someone desperately spinning a radio dial looking for the appropriate accompaniment. In an interview

in the extras portion of the *Wizards* DVD, Bakshi repeatedly claims this is a kids' movie that doesn't talk down to kids, but it's more like Bakshi is just doing his Bakshi thing with less cartoon nudity and profanity, not caring that kids are in the room.

Avatar: "I'm too old for this sort of thing. Just wake me up when the planet's destroyed."

Yellow Submarine
(1968)

This psychedelic animated masterpiece, a Homeric journey stuffed with phantasmagorical creatures, existential quandaries, and absurd one-liners wouldn't mean a thing without the film's protagonists, who just happen to be the greatest rock band of the twentieth century. Surprisingly, The Beatles' involvement in the movie was minimal: Aside from the songs, hired actors were brought in to voice the characters and the band appears only briefly, in the epilogue.

The tension at the heart of *Yellow Submarine* revolves around the music-hating Blue Meanies who overrun the idyllic burg of Pepperland, turning its inhabitants to stone and stilling all music. Old Fred, the lone escapee, flees in a Yellow Submarine atop an exploding pyramid and recruits The Beatles—à la Kurosawa's *Seven Samurai*—to aid in liberating Pepperland. The Fab Four must navigate a treacherous oceanic obstacle course through the Sea of Green, the Sea of Time, the Sea of Science, the Sea of Holes, and the Sea of Monsters before facing off with their rotund indigo occupiers. Highlights, among so very many, include two original George Harrison compositions, "Only a Northern Song" and "It's All Too Much"; the lysergic Foothills of the Headlands scene complete with a blinking brain-field and "Lucy in the Sky with Diamonds"; and the mind-bending Sea of Holes with "Nowhere Man" Jeremy Hillary Boob.

Much credit is due to Heinz Edelmann, the Czech-German art director who oversaw up to two hundred artists and nearly went blind after a sleepless year spent working on the film. The incredible tripped-out Technicolor animation is steeped in surrealism, Dadaism, and pop art and evokes the likes of Peter Max, Andy Warhol, Salvador Dalí, and René Magritte—on acid. As you might want to be on, too.

George: "It's all in the mind."

Across the Universe
(2007)

This daring and often dazzling Beatles tribute, which received decidedly mixed reviews, is a film you either embrace or reject from the outset, but its reimagining of the Fab Four's music and how it defined the sixties is no *Sgt. Pepper's Lonely Hearts Club Band*. The film's main character, Jude (all the characters take their names from Beatles songs), kicks things off with the plaintive opening lines from *Rubber Soul*'s "Girl": "Is there anybody going to listen to my story / All about the girl that came to stay?"

Jude (Jim Burgess) is a young Londoner, a dockworker who heads to the U.S. to find the American father (Robert Chohessy) who deserted him and his mother (Angela Mounsey) before he was born. Landing in New York, Jude befriends the shaggy-haired Max (Joe Anderson) and his younger sister, Lucy (Evan Rachel Wood), a privileged and protected high school student about to send her boyfriend (Spencer Liff) off to war. Jude and Max share a Lower East Side crash pad with a variety of characters, including Joplin-esque singer Sadie (Dana Fuchs), her Hendrix-like guitarist Jo-Jo (Martin Luther), and free-spirited lesbian Prudence (T. V. Carpio), embarking on a series of countercultural adventures. The narrative, spoken-word scenes in between the stunning set pieces can be a bit clichéd, as are the sometimes too-literal interpretations of the lyrics— but the kaleidoscopic effect of squeezing a decade into two hours gives the movie its trippy high. There are some way-cool rock references, including a climactic re-creation of the rooftop *Let It Be* concert and spirited cameos by Joe Cocker (as a bum, a pimp, and a street hippie), Bono (as Timothy Leary–styled LSD guru Dr. Robert), Eddie Izzard (as the sardonic Mr. Kite), and Salma Hayek (as a nurse putting "Happiness" into the "Warm Gun" ode to heroin). It's a fond dream of the sixties, filtered through The Beatles' songs and lyrics—part *Hair*, part *Tommy*, but all *Lion King* auteur Julie Taymor, both for those who were there and those who just wish they were.

Mr. Kite to Jude: "Just tune in, turn off, drop out, drop in, switch off, switch on, and explode."

Bird (1988)

Clint Eastwood produced and directed this well-intentioned biopic devoted to brilliant bebop saxophonist Charlie Parker, who lived the tortured life of a junkie alcoholic until his death at the young age of thirty-four. Over two and half hours long, it's something of an endurance test despite brave, earnest performances by Forest Whitaker as the supremely talented but self-destructive "Bird" and Diane Venora as Charlie's wife, Chan. Eastwood is a huge jazz fanatic, and the numerous scenes devoted to Bird playing on the bandstand or in the studio are realistic and lengthy—requiring some sincere appreciation of the genre. Eastwood made the film with the cooperation of the real Chan Parker, and much of Bird's music heard in the film comes from her private collection of Parker recordings. Samuel E. Wright is fairly convincing as Dizzy Gillespie, who quickly wearies of Bird's erratic behavior, and Michael Zelniker plays the young white and idealistic trumpeter Red Rodney, who looks up to Charlie. There's a lot of time spent with Charlie and/or Chan crying (sometimes together, sometimes separately), as well as several scenes where it's raining. In between moments making fantastic music, Charlie gets institutionalized, tries to commit suicide after the death of their young daughter, tries to kick heroin, fails to kick, degenerates both physically and emotionally, and finally dies in the plush apartment of Baroness Pannonica "Nica" de Koenigswarter. Bummer.

Bittersweet Motel
(2000)

🔑 🍸 💉 👓

🌿🌿🌿🌿 Even the brilliant minds behind twentieth-century fads like Clear Pepsi, *Batman Forever*, and the creepy Furby couldn't have predicted the massive success of a band called Phish. *Bittersweet Motel*, directed with aim and precision by acclaimed filmmaker Todd Phillips (*The Hangover*, *Old School*, *Road Trip*), aims to capture the mania of the Phish scene in all its tie-dyed glory, but the rockumentary also happens upon four guys who had reached a crossroads of sorts—a creative peak as a group, where the next step remained unclear. Given full access to the band on their summer and fall 1997 tours, Phillips provides an in-depth look at the inner workings of the Phish machine, cracks and all, but also ventures into the parking lots to document the life of phans who follow the band from coast to coast. Strolling the festival-like grounds, the cameras expose your typical search for kind bud, as concertgoers describe the difference between schwag and hydro and suck down hits of nitrous as the sun rises. Fun and titillating time for longtime Phish phans and newcomers alike, the only thing bittersweet about this movie is thinking where has the time gone.

Phan: "Kind bud gets you wasted . . . if that's what you're looking for."

Trey Anastasio: "I'm a child of the seventies."

Carter, The (2009)

✏️ 🖋️

🌿🌿🌿🌿 There's no shortage of blunts or cough syrup in *The Carter*, a documentary that follows rapper Lil Wayne in his life onstage and off, but it's not always a pretty picture. So much so that the controversial hip-hop great tried (in vain) to have the movie banned shortly after it premiered at the 2009 Sundance Film Festival, where it received stellar reviews. So what's the beef? The scenes that show his drug use, meaning just about every few minutes. Wayne's poison is a cocktail of choice called sizzurp or drank—cough syrup mixed with soda and occasionally, Jolly Ranchers, which he's constantly sucking on. And if it's not the drank, it's the weed that had Wayne worried he was being portrayed in a negative light. Indeed, the film does have moments that show a gifted and motivated twenty-seven-year-old struggling with his rapid success and excessive consumption, so much so that his manager can't stand speaking to him when he's high. Behind the scenes, Wayne is up and down, quiet and loud all at the same time, with his brain moving so quickly, you can almost see it in action. There's no denying the rhymes these substances often trigger, perfected after ten years of practice, during which he composed over seven hundred songs and released dozens of mixtapes. Curiously, when describing his rapping style, Wayne says that, though he never writes his rhymes down, he doesn't consider it freestyling. Rather, it's some freaky photographic memory, which is just another reason why this film, like the man himself, is both intriguing and complicated.

Concert for Bangladesh, The
(1972)

💉

🌿🌿🌿 Featuring a who's who of long-haired and bearded early-seventies music luminaries, George Harrison leads the rock god pack in organizing this 1971 benefit concert to raise money for relief efforts in war- and cyclone-ravaged Bangladesh. The former Beatle chose the best performances from the two-day stint at New York City's Madison Square Garden—all under the direction of Phil Spector, music producer for the recordings and subsequent film. Harrison offers a beautiful rendition of "My Sweet Lord" right up front, before stepping aside for his peers and a string of killer jams. With a front row view of the action, you can see and truly appreciate the musicianship of these iconic figures—the simple strut of Ringo Starr's drumming; how Eric Clapton's guitar playing is so effortless, he almost looks bored (more likely the result of a crippling heroin addiction he was battling at the time); and the otherworldly stage presence of a young, acoustic Bob Dylan. Deafening applause accompanies epic numbers like Harrison's "While My Guitar Gently Weeps" and "Here Comes the Sun," which showcase a sea of six-strings in glorious union. Dylan delivers his classics "A Hard Rain's A-Gonna Fall," "Blowin' in the Wind," and "Just Like a Woman"; Leon Russell kills on the bluesy "Young Blood"; and Ravi Shankar offers a taste of the East to kick things off. Light on pomp and circumstance, this is as bare-bones as all-star shows go, but so very special. The DVD's bonus disc featuring behind-the-scenes snippets of the days leading up to the concert is also a can't-miss. Even cooler: that sales of the album and DVD continue to benefit UNICEF.

Control (2007)

An enduring post-punk icon, Ian Curtis, lead singer of seminal British band Joy Division, committed suicide at the young age of twenty-three on the eve of the band's first American tour. With the slow iceberg inevitability of the *Titanic*, this 2007 biopic sets off with a teenage Curtis (Sam Riley) meeting and wooing his wife Deborah (Samantha Morton). Marrying young and having a child, their problems take shape even before the

---

☘ WILLIE NELSON'S STONIEST ROLES ☘

He's a stoner legend, a country music icon, an activist, a veteran actor, and, sometimes, all of the above—like on this list of onscreen appearances, which range from earnest dramatic depictions to comic relief with a twist.

Barbarosa (1982): Set south of the border in Mexico, Willie plays the title character, an outlaw with many enemies who is married to a Mexican woman and ends up on the run. Farmboy Karl (Gary Busey) lends a hand, but meets a tragic end. With phenomenal cinematography, rugged scenery, and a stark setting (it was filmed in Big Bend National Park), it's a true Willie Nelson Western—horses and all.

Wag the Dog (1997): In this twisted Barry Levinson political comedy, Nelson plays songwriter-for-hire Johnny Dean, who's commissioned to write the theme song for a fake war. Not entirely inspired to pen "Good Ol' Shoe," a ballad of loss and redemption, Dean quips, "I was just on my way to get drunk."

Half Baked (1998): As one of several note-worthy cameos in the Dave Chappelle classic (others include Jon Stewart and Snoop Dogg), Willie plays the you-should've-been-there smoker during the pot dealing montage that details who the Mr. Nice Guys sell their stolen stash to. Shocked by the high price of a bag (sixty bucks), the character known as "historian smoker" comments, "I remember when a dime bag cost a dime."

Beerfest (2006): Nelson shows up at the very end of this Broken Lizard tribute to brews. As the victorious American beer drinking team wanders the streets of Amsterdam, they run into the country legend, playing himself and smoking a joint, 'natch, in a dark alley. Stranded at a pot smoking competition after Cheech and Chong bailed on him, Nelson invites the brew crew to be his new teammates. Talk about saving the best for last.

The Dukes of Hazzard (2007): In this remake of the seventies TV classic, Nelson plays Uncle Jesse to Jessica Simpson's Daisy Duke. In what's essentially a mainstream family comedy, Jay Chandrasekhar manages to sneak in a key smoking scene towards the end, during which Uncle Jesse hits an apple pipe packed with real weed.

Surfer, Dude (2008): Nelson plays Farmer Bob in this underrated stoner comedy starring Matthew McConaughey and Woody Harrelson. A grower in the truest sense, Bob gifts surf legend Steve Addington (McConaughey) a paper bag of buds and praises the plants by saying, "Bless the flower," to which Steve responds, "Bless the weed." *Alright, alright, alright . . .*

band does. Then, as Joy Division navigates the burgeoning Mancunian punk scene, begins to tour, and wins recognition, Ian meets gorgeous Belgian rock journalist Annik Honoré (Alexandra Maria Lara) and falls in love all over again. Like all classic love triangles, he's stuck between the woman who loved him for what he was and the woman who loves him for the rock star he's become. Adding to the distress are the epileptic seizures that plague Curtis, frequently becoming part of the stage spectacle. *Control* is as much a love story as a rock-and-roll fable—Deborah can't hold onto a young lover's dream, Annik can't save her lover from himself, and Ian, unable to break the chains of his parochial past and trapped in a body that's betraying him, can no longer see love as enough reason to hold on.

Already majestic and gloomy, the band's music becomes especially poignant in a sequence of recording sessions that frames Ian's vocal performance as a haunting lament. Shot in luscious black-and-white and directed by Anton Corbijn, the photographer responsible for some of Joy Division's iconic imagery, each frame is like a painting, with the city of Manchester just as much a character as Curtis himself. Joy Division's development is seen through a series of live performances: The actors did all their own singing and playing—not only are they on point, but the resemblance is truly uncanny. Likely to be overlooked in the musical biopic canon, *Control* nonetheless sets a new standard for life-changing music movies, so prepare to have your mind blown.

> "Side effects include: drowsiness, apathy, and blurred vision . . . I'm taking two."
>
> —Ian Curtis

Dave Chappelle's Block Party (2005)

Anyone who's ever seen *Chappelle's Show* knows the comedian Dave Chappelle is a huge hip-hop fan—he cherry-picked the top groups to appear each week on his Comedy Central series that ran from 2003 to 2006. For Michel Gondry's film, Chappelle went one step further and called on his rapper friends to perform at an outdoor show in Brooklyn's rough Bedford-Stuyvesant neighborhood. Gondry tells the story leading up to the event, but rather than save the music for later, he segues from setup to performances in a jumble of cuts. But it's not all about hip-hop and Brooklyn. Chappelle, who lives in Ohio, invites his neighbors and the Central State University marching band to attend, chartering buses for the long drive. Dressed in maroon-and-gold uniforms, the Marching Marauders kick off the show, stomping in and joining Kanye West on "Get 'Em High." Chappelle's lineup is the crème of New York's conscious hip-hop crop, including The Roots, Mos Def, Talib Kweli, Common, and Dead Prez. Singers Jill Scott and Erykah Badu provide some needed female energy. The highlight is a reunion set by the Fugees, with Lauryn Hill reshaping her hit cover of "Killing Me Softly." But it's ultimately Chappelle's show, and the comedian doesn't disappoint. Whether he's barking commands via megaphone, singing blues with the house band, or playing piano, he's in top form, always quick to joke or mug for the camera. "Hey, I smell reefer," Chappelle says during the show. "I'm calling the police." Not!

DiG! (2004)

Director Ondi Timoner (*Behind Those Eyes*, *Join Us*) provides a shockingly candid account of seven years on the road with indie rock darlings The Dandy Warhols and The Brian Jonestown Massacre. Through drug busts, breakups, and all-out brawls, this rockumentary follows the bands as they rattle and hum through the nineties, signing major label deals, filming six-figure music videos, and doing lots and lots of drugs. The two groups start out in similar indie territory but take very different paths to success, and the friendship that had once started a music scene turns into an interband rivalry. Much of this is due to BJM lead singer Anton Newcombe's many personal issues. A lyrical genius, the hippiefied multi-instrumentalist can't seem to keep his band—or himself—together, firing members onstage, inciting riots, and threatening to kill Warhols lead singer Courtney Taylor-Taylor. *DiG!* won the Grand Jury Prize at the 2004 Sundance Film Festival and deservedly so. Sort of like watching a car crash, this is a film that will make you cringe, but it's hard to turn away.

Don't Look Back
(1967)

D. A. Pennebaker followed Bob Dylan around with a handheld black-and-white camera during his 1965 British tour. The resulting film became the standard for all music docs to come. (Pennebaker also directed *Monterey Pop*.) The oft-copied opening "music video" features Dylan singing "Subterranean Homesick Blues" while flashing cue cards (look for an Allen Ginsberg cameo). Dylan fields stupid questions from straight-press panderers and smokes an unhealthy amount of cigarettes. After fallaciously telling an outdated *Time* magazine reporter "there's no great message" in his sermonizing sociopolitical songs, the confrontational Dylan half-jokingly insists he "hits notes just as good as Caruso." There's also his childish outburst concerning someone breaking glass in the street, where the accusatory Woody Guthrie protégé tells an antagonistic guy to "either be groovy or leave." Backstage guests include then-girlfriend Joan Baez, curmudgeonly manager Albert Grossman, ex–Animals keyboardist Alan Price, and still-green Dylan disciple Donovan. Though Dylan had already "turned on" with The Beatles in 1964 and would soon have a hit single with "Rainy Day Women #12 & 35" (with its commanding "Everybody must get stoned" chorus), no weed or other mind-altering substances were apparently consumed during this ultimate backstage diary.

Bob Dylan: "Keep a good head and always carry a light bulb."

Festival Express (2003)

What do you get when you put four of the biggest rock bands together on a freight train? Discord, harmony, and a rocking documentary about the "Festival Express." This account of the now infamous tour combines classic live footage with interviews from promoters, musicians, and attendees of the 1970 trek. A success in the eyes of the musicians (Janis Joplin, The Band, The Flying Burrito Brothers, Grateful Dead, and Buddy Guy, among others), the tour was somewhat of a financial disaster, albeit well intentioned. Taking an alternate route from the usual festival setup, the traveling rock show crisscrossed Canada with the idea of creating a comfortable environment for the musicians that would inspire all-night jam sessions and lead to new friendships. And did it ever. Among the alcohol- and acid-fueled highlights is a late night performance of The Band's "The Weight," the Dead's acoustic "Don't Ease Me In," and Janis Joplin's incomparable "Cry Baby." As musician Kenny Gradney comments, "It was better than Woodstock, as great as Woodstock was." Ironically, the tour's problems resulted from overly zealous, ultraidealistic music fans who protested that it be free and showed up refusing to pay the fourteen-dollar admission.

> "It was a train full of insane people careening across the countryside."
>
> **—Phil Lesh**

Gimme Shelter (1970)

🍁 🍁 🍁 🍁 🍁 A dramatic snapshot of all the sixties confusion and turbulence, Albert and David Maysles's film countered the hippie utopia of Michael Wadleigh's *Woodstock* with virulent biker squalor, slamming the door on the most fertile musical period in history. Three hundred thousand people gathered near San Francisco at Altamont Speedway for a free concert featuring The Rolling Stones, Grateful Dead, Jefferson Airplane, and The Flying Burrito Brothers. Showing how little control rock bands had over a volatile organization such as the Hell's Angels, who were hired to provide security, four deaths occurred but the show went on. The worst act of the violence—the murder of Meredith Hunter in front of the stage by drunken Angels—is captured by the Maysleses, and played over and over as if it's the Zapruder film. The Stones, who took the stage three hours late, accepted no responsibility. Jefferson Airplane had already dealt with unruliness when guitarist Marty Balin got smashed in the head onstage. Mick Jagger's feeble "either these cats cool it or we don't play" threat went unheeded. The Stones wanted "Sympathy for the Devil," but got hatred from the Angels instead. Two years after the Summer of Love and just four months after Woodstock, Altamont signaled the end of the peace and love era (so did the Manson murders). Jerry Garcia summed the event up perfectly: "An afternoon in hell."

LET'S SPEND THE NIGHT TOGETHER: THE ROLLING STONES ON FILM

In addition to Albert and David Maysles (see *Gimme Shelter* at left), directors love The Rolling Stones. Martin Scorsese, Robert Frank, and Jean-Luc Godard have all made films about them. Here are our faves:

Sympathy for the Devil (1968): For his first English-speaking film, French auteur Jean-Luc Godard went inside the Rolling Stones's studio for a unique look at the band rehearsing their most famous song. At first, "Sympathy for the Devil" is slow and unstructured, but gradually it speeds up and finally solidifies into the fierce, driving magnum opus of the Stones's most fruitful period. Godard doesn't bother to interview anyone. His camera slowly pans the room, never in a hurry, the antitheses of what years later would be known as MTV-style fast cutting. Actors posing as Marxists and Black Power revolutionaries eat up a lot of the screen time, but just as you're ready to press the Fast-Forward button, Godard smartly heads back to the studio.

The Rolling Stones Rock and Roll Circus (1968): Recorded in 1968, but not released until eight years later, the Stones hosted this carnival-style event with the help of some of their musician friends. The Who and Jethro Tull each have one song, and a supergroup known as the Dirty Mac (John Lennon, Eric Clapton, Keith Richards, and Mitch Mitchell) perform The Beatles's "Yer Blues." (Yoko One joins them for her usual shriek session.) These openers as well as a trapeze act and fire-eater set the stage for a short but incendiary Stones set that includes "Sympathy for the Devil," "You Can't Always Get What You Want," and the rare blues "Parachute Woman."

Cocksucker Blues (1972): A supposedly fictional account captured in grainy bootleg quality by renowned filmmaker/photographer Robert Frank, this may be the most indulgently rewarding cinema verité rock-u-drama ever made. Though never officially released, the oft-bootlegged documentary finds The Rolling Stones meandering through the U.S. behind The Exile on Main Street tour in 1972—three years after the Altamont debacle. Though lacking in thematic cohesion, its raw insider perspective brings airplane debauchery, backstage images, hotel shots, and recreational narcotics into focus like never before and maybe since. Mick Jagger passes a joint on a countryside ride, snorts coke backstage, and leers at his Glimmer Twin, strung-out Keith Richards. Cluttered scenes, poor audio, and way-too-brief performances ("Brown Sugar" and "Happy" are highlights) downgrade this lasciviously provocative period piece.

Shine a Light (2006): Filmed at New York's Beacon Theater during the Stones's A Bigger Bang Tour, Scorsese's concert doc begins with the director frantically trying to find out what the show's set list is going to be. Quick cuts and extreme close-ups capture Jagger awkwardly shimmying about the stage and catwalk, and Richards joyfully leading the thirteen-piece band (including backup singers and horns). Special guest Jack White nervously duets with Jagger on "Loving Cup," Buddy Guy brings genuine blues ferocity to Muddy Waters's "Champagne & Reefer," and Christina Aguilera climbs octaves on "Live With Me." Scorsese intersperses archival interview footage between songs. Toward the end of the eighteen-song set, the Stones's signature centerpiece "Sympathy for the Devil" oddly falls flat. But "Brown Sugar" proves to be a rousing finale. It's the nature of their game.

Grateful Dead Movie, The (1977)

During the height of the Grateful Dead's popularity, but before the band started selling out arenas, Jerry Garcia's pet project was this concert movie, a two-hour-plus time capsule about Deadhead culture. Like a Dead show itself—or an acid trip (the two are somewhat interchangeable)—the movie ebbs and flows, reaching several musical highs, but also exploring the sights, sounds and fashions surrounding the band's 1974 five-night stand at San Francisco's Winterland Ballroom. That means dudes smoking openly on the sidewalk (a joint out of a can bong, no less) and popping 'shrooms like "they're Chiclets" while lining up to secure a good spot up front, braless beauties—hairy pits and all—twirling their way to ecstasy, and hippies sucking down hits from a nitrous tank backstage. Equally fascinating are the behind-the-scenes workings of the tour: transporting gear in multiple trucks, constructing the towering wall of sound, tweaking the instruments, monitoring the stage—the cameras follow every step of the Dead experience, all the way to the taking of the ticket. Bookending these segments, which include bassist Phil Lesh brilliantly demonstrating the bounce of sound in the "Phil Zone," are psychedelic animations by Gary Gutierrez that feature the Dead's many characters and icons along with kaleidoscopic patterns, tripped-out pinball plays, and wall scribbles with messages like "See you on the other side." Indeed, it's a veritable potpourri of stoniness from beginning to end, complete with an intermission and the obligatory random-dude-in-the-crowd-tripping-his-balls-off, but when it comes to the Dead, nothing matters more than the music. And the sampling offered here—signature songs like "Goin' Down the Road Feelin' Bad," "Truckin'," "Casey Jones," and "Sugar Magnolia," along with a glorious "Morning Dew"—doesn't disappoint. As one fan explains when prompted by the interviewer to "say something intelligent": "Bottom line of the whole scene is very simply stated—there is nothing like a Grateful Dead concert. Never will be. Period."

Jerry Garcia: "There's no relationship that I've ever been able to hear on tapes between the way I feel and the way it went down."

Hair (1979)

Four years after the fall of Saigon, the Broadway musical *Hair*, which first ran in 1968, got its film makeover. Directed by Miloš Forman (*One Flew Over the Cuckoo's Nest*, *The People vs. Larry Flynt*), the pressure was on to match the emotional

intensity of the stage version, along with songs and dances that had become beloved, without devolving into a hokey piece of hippie nostalgia. Did it succeed? For the most part, yes. Though it's slightly altered from the original story, Oklahoman Claude Bukowski (John Savage) travels to New York City to join the Army and fight in the Vietnam War when he happens upon a posse of hippies in Central Park. Led by long-haired ne'er-do-well George Berger (Treat Williams), the group introduces the straight-edge Claude to pot, LSD, the concept of free love, and bohemian living. And wouldn't you know it, he digs it. Claude also fancies a blonde debutante named Sheila (Beverly D'Angelo, the future Mrs. Griswold), who is converted almost as quickly into a card-carrying "Good Morning Starshine"-singing flower child. In the days these unlikely cohorts spend together, Claude trips on a sugar cube of acid and imagines a church buzzing with electric groove, Berger gyrates atop the table at an upper-crust dinner, and who can forget the hippies' horselike dance celebrating the dawning of Aquarius—spoofed to hilarious effect at the very end of *The 40-Year-Old Virgin*. They sing of everything from hashish to Hare Krishnas, war to, yes, hair, until it's time for Claude to head to boot camp. Berger looks for one last hurrah with his buddy, but one of them never comes back from 'Nam. The beauty of this wartime story? That these pot-smoking, peace-loving idealists never judge Claude, but welcome him with open arms. The irony? That Berger looks so much better with his hair short.

Hairspray (1988, 2007)

✏ 🍸 🖊

🌿 🌿 🌿 🌿, 🌿 🌿 🌿 The original John Waters version of *Hairspray*, which didn't have anything resembling an A-list cast or a big budget, kicks the update's ass. That's because the story has heart and its setting offers authenticity, a winning combination for a true indie classic, while the musical version offers a twist on the Broadway play, and is thus an adaptation of an adaptation. Still, the sweet and fantastical tale of pleasantly plump hair hopper Tracy Turnblad doesn't vary much between the two. Ricki Lake stars in the earlier film opposite Michael St. Gerard, who plays Link, the sexy star

of a local Baltimore dance show circa 1962. Thanks to scorned popular girl Amber Von Tussle (Colleen Fitzpatrick), whose racist, money-hungry parents (played by Sonny Bono and Blondie's Debbie Harry) are hell-bent on keeping public spaces like amusement parks and television segregated, Tracy and her bestie, Penny Pingleton (Leslie Ann Powers), are motivated to cross the color line and get their black friends on *The Corny Collins Show*. Run-ins with parents, teachers, the police, and a couple of pot-smoking bohos (brilliantly played by The Cars' Ric Ocasek and eighties star Pia Zadora, credited as Beatnik Cat and Chick) open Tracy's eyes and flatten her hair, until she emerges a hometown hero and Amber is exposed as the true brat that she is.

In the 2007 version, Nikki Blonsky (Tracy), Zac Efron (Link), John Travolta (Edna Turnblad), Michelle Pfeiffer (Velma Von Tussle), Queen Latifah ("Motormouth" Maybelle), and Christopher Walken (Wilbur Turnblad) all take part in the song and dance that was a key element of the stage production. In the 1988 movie, the stars capture the choreography, while the songs, somewhat obscure local hits from the era, are left to the original artists. That's not to say the later version is all that bad. Efron is perfectly cast as the slick and unaffected Link while Amanda Bynes dazzles as the ditzy Penny. As for Travolta wearing a fat suit and a dress? It's a long way from *Pulp Fiction*, but even with the added pounds, he's still got the moves.

> "Let's do some reefer. We'll get high and I'll iron the chick's hair."
> —Beatnik Chick

I'm Not There (2007)

✏ 🍸 🖊

🌿 🌿 🌿 🌿 Todd Haynes's ambitious foray into cinematic Dylanology is an impressionistic music film that provides plenty of biographical content in sometimes subversive fashion. Haynes flips the script by using six different actors to portray various aspects of Bob Dylan's checkered life story, with a method that's haphazardly linear, often symbolic, and chock-full of Dylan secret handshakes. Talented actors like Christian Bale, Richard Gere, and Heath Ledger give life to their Dylan-inspired characters, but it's Jude, Cate Blanchett's spot-on evocation of the folk-rock star in debauched mid-sixties bloom, that impresses most. (Comedian David Cross also makes a great Allen Ginsberg.) Those unfamiliar with the many signposts of Dylan's career may not enjoy this as much as his hard-core fans, but the movie is lovingly crafted and illuminates Dylan's kaleidoscopic career, from his infamous motorcycle accident and affair with Edie Sedgwick to the respective influences of Woody Guthrie and Billy the Kid and his born-again phase to classic confrontations with the press and a failed marriage. It's a Dylan primer—far-out fables, fractured facts, and all.

Jude: "Sleep's for dreamers. I haven't slept in thirty days, man. Takes a lot of medicine to keep up this pace."

Imagine: John Lennon (1988)

🍸 🥃

🌿 🌿 🌿 🌿 This intimate portrait of John Lennon, told via home movies, TV appearances, and portions of interviews with the late Beatle as well as his family members and friends, comes closest to revealing the real man behind the music. From the loss of his mother to the band's early days in Hamburg, covering The Beatles's greatest professional highs and personal lows and then transitioning to life as a solo

> "Surrealism had a great effect on me because then I realized that my imagery in my mind wasn't insanity. Psychedelic vision is reality to me."
>
> —John Lennon

artist, husband, and new dad, a swath of emotions are put on display, warts and all. We see Lennon when he's angry, hopeful, bitter, reflective, reclusive, generous, and at times simply befuddled, like when a determined fan (who'd now likely be considered a stalker) camps out at his estate hoping for some face time. He gets it, along with tea and a little nosh. Yoko Ono explains that Lennon somehow felt responsible for his devotees, who read into every line he ever wrote. In fact, it was one such confused follower (Mark David Chapman) that would shoot Lennon down in the darkness of night after asking for an autograph. Expectedly, there's a sadness throughout this tribute, especially during sit-downs with Sean Lennon and Yoko, who was involved in the production and doesn't sugarcoat moments like her husband's "lost weekend" in the seventies. In the end, no one appreciates more than Yoko that the loss is truly all of ours.

Kids Are Alright, The (1979)

🍸 🥃

🌿 🌿 🌿 🌿 🌿 This 1979 rock doc and perennial midnight movie about The Who is a baker's delight of odds and sods (and mods) from this mercurial band's then-fifteen-year-old career. Stuffed with 149 minutes worth of nonlinear classic live footage, interviews, silly interstitials, TV appearances, and instrument smashing, Kids thankfully eschews Behind the Music narration, allowing the amazing footage to speak for itself. The film opens rather symbolically with an awkward 1967 appearance on The Smothers Brothers Comedy Hour. Tommy Smothers, replete in uber-square blue blazer, tie, and crew cut, issues a line that could be the movie's alternate title: "You guys are really too much." Next, an unexpected explosion during the band's equipment-destroying coda to their stuttering angst rock anthem "My Generation" damages singer Roger Daltrey's and guitarist Pete Townshend's hearing (the latter's hair catches fire, as well) and causes Bette Davis to collapse backstage. The best moments include Keith Moon's hilarious hard-core S & M send-up, Townsend falling asleep during a German interviewer's ten-part existential question, bassist John Entwistle skeet-shooting gold records, and the inebriated interviews with Ringo Starr and Moon. However, there's a bit too much self-indulgent Woodstock footage and focus on Daltry's collection of chest-baring, fringed suede jackets. Rob Reiner might have swiped some of *Kids'* now classic rock doc tropes for *This Is Spinal Tap*, including the spontaneously combusting drummer, off-key four-part harmony (The Who's painful version of "Barbara Ann"), and bad sixties hair and hippie clothing. Windmill on your air guitar for the "Substitute"/"Pictures of Lily"/"Magic Bus" medley, "A Quick One While He's Away" from *The Rolling Stones Rock and Roll Circus*, and the "Won't Get Fooled Again" finale. Sadly, *Kids* is also something of an elegy to Moon, who fatally OD'd shortly before the film's release.

Ringo Starr: "Well, I'm sure most of [Keith Moon's] friends have been on here . . . and they've told you about all the mad things he's done in life. Such as, breaking up rooms . . . driving his car into swimming pools . . . and driving his car into foyers. Well, I'm not gonna tell you about any of that."

✹ MORE STONY MUSIC BIOPICS ✹

From *La Bamba* to *Sid & Nancy*, *Ray* to *Walk the Line*, musicians make good movie subjects, which is one reason why studios consistently churn out biopics. Here are five more druggy biographies worth seeking out.

***Lady Sings the Blues* (1972):** This Oscar contender stars Diana Ross as Billie Holiday, the legendary jazz singer who made it to the top but battled a crippling heroin addiction much of the way. It's a weighty drama and her unbelievable triumph has all the makings of your typical rags-to-riches story with a stellar soundtrack to boot.

***Coal Miner's Daughter* (1980):** Nobody does country quite like Sissy Spacek in this Oscar-winning role as singer Loretta Lynn. Meager beginnings and old-timey bluegrass songs in the Kentucky mountains (The Band's Levon Helm plays Loretta's coal miner dad) bring out the sweet little voice that would go on to sell millions. A boozy husband—played brilliantly by Tommy Lee Jones—pills, and a seemingly endless stream of children only make this first lady of country music stronger.

***Great Balls of Fire* (1989):** This fun-loving feature about piano man Jerry Lee Lewis stars Dennis Quaid in a high-energy performance and paints a rich portrait of Memphis's Sun Records scene that was home to Elvis Presley, Roy Orbison, and other great rockers. Famously known for marrying his twelve-year-old cousin, Myra (Winona Ryder), that story is played out heavily in the movie with the scandal eventually sidelining his career.

***Backbeat* (1994):** Original Beatles bassist Stuart Sutcliffe (Stephen Dorff) is the star in this dramatization of the band's speed-fueled early days in Hamburg, Germany. It's there that Sutcliffe, a painter and best mate of John Lennon (Ian Hart), falls for photographer Astrid Kirchherr (Sheryl Lee), who introduces him to cool clothes, the underground art scene, and the mop top. While the story has holes, the tunes, performed by a who's who of nineties rockers (Dave Grohl, Sonic Youth's Thurston Moore, R.E.M.'s Mike Mills), never sounded better.

***Stoned* (2005):** Rock-and-roll takes a back-seat to sex, drugs, and S & M in this disturbing portrait of Rolling Stones guitarist and founder Brian Jones (Leo Gregory). It's told through the eyes of assistant-cum-handyman Frank (Paddy Considine), who supplied Jones with a steady stream of pills and booze and, according to the film, later drowned him in his backyard pool. Violent and egomaniacal, Jones is at first revered and just as quickly reviled after the band's ill-fated trip to Marrakech. His best pot-smoking, acid-taking days are sadly put behind him.

Last Waltz, The (1978)

🌿 🌿 🌿 🌿 🌿 The archetypal concert film of the seventies was crafted by an ambitious, drug-fueled Martin Scorsese and featured The Band's onstage farewell with an amazing cast of guest superstars paying their respects. Filmed on Thanksgiving 1976 at Bill Graham's Winterland Ballroom in San Francisco, this fabled documentary ignores internal and backstage conflicts and highlights top-notch performances by all. Besides playing their greatest hits and showcasing three great singers in Richard Manuel, Levon Helm, and Rick Danko, The Band serves as a killer backing group during prime appearances from the likes of Neil Young, Joni Mitchell, Eric Clapton, Van Morrison, Dr. John, and Bob Dylan. There's also a pair of marvelous soundstage performances by The Band accompanied by Emmylou Harris and The Staple Singers. Scorsese wisely intersperses bittersweet interviews with all five members of the group but is mostly focused on charismatic guitarist/songwriter Robbie Robertson. Everybody's high and looks it—too bad, he edited out the cocaine hanging from Neil Young's nose.

Led Zeppelin: The Song Remains the Same (1976)

🌿 🌿 🌿 🌿 Although Led Zeppelin is arguably the greatest rock band of all time (or at least the only band that can rival The Beatles for the title), as far as stoner acts go, they never had the reputation of fellow Brits Pink Floyd. But that does not diminish in any way, shape, or form the majesty or value per bong hit of *The Song Remains the Same*, a cinematic look at the mighty Zep in concert and a seventies midnight movie staple. On their own and devoid of a gimmicky light show, the live versions of classics such as "Stairway to Heaven," "Since I've Been Loving You," and "Dazed and Confused" are rock-and-roll bliss. The interwoven fantasy sequences like the extended opening scene with manager Peter Grant as a mob hit man, singer Robert Plant's turn as a knight on horseback rescuing a maiden complete with sword fights, and guitarist Jimmy Page's mythological quest for the Hermit from the tarot deck amp up the buzz factor immensely. But perhaps most enlightening are Grant's backstage antics on this momentous night at New York's Madison Square Garden. *The Song Remains the Same* is simply one of rock's greatest concert films and a hell of a trip.

☘ MORE ROCKIN' CONCERT FILMS ☘

The Last Waltz, Woodstock, Stop Making Sense, The Song Remains the Same . . . all made ordinary concert footage seem extraordinary and set the gold standard for every concert film that followed. Here are five more spectacular shows-turned-movies that hold a special place in our hearts.

Neil Young & Crazy Horse: Rust Never Sleeps (1979): Neil Young lets the music tell a story in this straightforward and directly shot self-directed concert film. Documenting one momentous show at San Francisco's Cow Palace in October 1978, a youthful, energized Young runs through sixteen of his most cherished songs, including a ten-minute-plus "Like a Hurricane," "Hey Hey, My My," and "After the Gold Rush," in which he reminisces, "There was a band playing in my head, and I felt like getting high."

Willie Nelson's 4th of July Celebration (1979): If you want to experience what a Willie Nelson party was like in the seventies, seek out this hard-to-find DVD. Filmed in 1974 at Nelson's annual Texas barbecue, the barely edited film is part drunken hootenanny, part all-star jam and tribute (fellow outlaw Waylon Jennings takes the stage for a few songs, including his serenade "Willie the Wandering Gypsy"), and never a dull moment.

Simon & Garfunkel: The Concert in Central Park (1982): A decade after their acrimonious split, folk-rock's greatest duo reunited for one free concert in New York's Central Park that drew more than 500,000 people to its vast Great Lawn. During the stellar set list, there are moments when you can sense tension between the two. There are also Simon's bad jokes and Garfunkel's barely

there acknowledgment of the line in "Late in the Evening" about smoking "a jay." Clearly, these guys had grown apart.

Ziggy Stardust and the Spiders from Mars: The Motion Picture (1983): David Bowie declared his androgynous spaceman character the "be all, end all of rock-and-roll stars," and in 1973 when director D. A. Pennebaker (*Don't Look Back*, *Monterey Pop*) shot this two-night stand at London's Hammersmith Odeon, he lived up to the reputation and then some. Mounds of makeup and multiple wardrobe changes—everything from knit leotards to short satin skirts—brings Ziggy to life as beloved classics like "Moonage Daydream," "Changes," and "Suffragette City" prove timeless. Pennebaker provides performance footage and the occasional peek backstage, but don't expect any flying saucers during "Space Oddity," just the twinkle of the disco ball and the star power of Bowie in all his glam glory.

Awesome; I Fuckin' Shot That! (2006): Always thinking outside the box, the Beastie Boys challenged fifty fans to shoot their own concert footage, with camcorders provided by the band. The result is a visual cacophony that covers every angle of the Beasties experience, bringing Madison Square Garden to the viewer. Or, as one review noted, making "you feel as if you had been there . . . on acid."

Medicine Ball Caravan (1971)

🍁🍁🍁 A year after Woodstock, Warner Bros. seized the moment, releasing the *Woodstock* movie and organizing the Medicine Ball Caravan—a Lollapalooza for its time. Five buses leave San Francisco heading east on the three-week tour. The hippie crew stays in teepees and paints the buses psychedelic colors. The bands on tour are no match for Woodstock: Alice Cooper, B. B. King, Doug Kershaw, and Brainstorm. Everything goes relatively smoothly until the caravan hits Antioch College in Ohio, where political protesters call the tour a corporate rip-off—"Woodstock for the elite," says future *High Times* founder Tom Forcade, who along with sidekick David Peel, provide French director

---

🍁 JASON MRAZ'S STONY MOVIE PICKS 🍁

An affinity for pop catapulted singer Jason Mraz to the top of the music charts, while his affection for pot kept him firmly planted to the couch. The singer-songwriter whose reggae-tinged "I'm Yours" spent a record seventy-six weeks on the *Billboard* Hot 100, lists his five favorite mind-blowing films.

***Powers of Ten* (1977):** "This short film by Charles and Ray Eames about the relative size of the universe will freak you (or inspire you) unlike anything you've ever experienced. Travel billions of light years out into the vastness of space, and then fall from space into a human body, going the same distance within. The payoff is seeing how deep space and deep soul are one and the same. The film is the perfect companion for subatomic stoner physicists and free-loving philosophizers."

***Microcosmos* (1996):** "Dinosaurs still exist and they live in your backyard. This amazing film is all about that parallel universe dwelling in the dirt just below the fresh cut clippings of the grass. Radical macro photography gives you a front seat to a ladybug sex show as well as the hottest make-out sequence you've ever seen involving two snails. This film is loaded with trippy creatures and classical music, perfect for the seeker of a blown mind."

***R. Kelly's Trapped in the Closet, Chapters 1–12* (2005):** "It doesn't matter which music genre you think you're into, everyone loves *Trapped in the Closet*. Chapters 1–12 total a thirty-five-minute R & B musical soap opera written and sung entirely by capital R himself, though it's performed by an all-star cast mouthing along to his words. It's full of surprises and bizarre sex scandals, perfect for group viewing. Though, heed my warning that a song that long takes weeks to get out of your head. I still wake up singing, 'Oh my god, a rubber, rubber, rubber!'"

***Baraka* (1992):** "This might be the ultimate stoner flick. Why? Because there is no dialogue, no story, no point. It's like the best screen saver you'd ever hoped to be locked into. Music from all over the world is mashed together in a cacophonous symphony, blasting over strange beauty, bizarre rituals, a monkey in a steam bath, and time-lapsed photography so intoxicating that it's perfect for all you visually stimulated trail seekers. It took filmmakers seven years and thirty-something laps around the planet to get the images for this film. All it takes for you to get completely awed is less than two hours on a comfy couch with some Bubba Kush (cat on lap is optional)."

***What the #$*! Do We Know!?* (2004):** "If you never went to college or church, but consider yourself a knowledgeable and spiritual person, then this film will give you plenty to talk about when you go off on one of your superstoned rants about life, theology, and how nothing really matters because nothing really exists. Owning it supports your pursuit of slack and gives just cause to your just sitting there."

François Reichenbach with a compelling side story. Except for this departure and largely due to the weak lineup, *Medicine Ball Caravan* is pretty much a snooze.

Monterey Pop (1968)

🌿

🌿🌿🌿🌿 There's no doubt Monterey Pop set the stage for Woodstock and every other multiday rock fests that followed. Held in June 1967 just as the Summer of Love was picking up steam, flower children from all over the Bay Area and beyond were treated to a stellar line-up of the day's hottest acts—Janis Joplin, Jefferson Airplane, The Who, Jimi Hendrix, Simon & Garfunkel, the Grateful Dead, The Byrds, and Otis Redding, among others. Credit organizers Lou Adler, producer of movies like *Up in Smoke* and *The Rocky Horror Picture Show*, and singer John Phillips of The Mamas & The Papas for a job well done, but sadly, not all the artists made it to this documentary directed by D. A. Pennebaker (*Don't Look Back*). Even so, the snippets of performances that did are some of the concert's finest: The Who delivering "My Generation," then trashing the stage; Janis Joplin fronting Big Brother and the Holding Company on the spine-chilling "Ball and Chain"; and Jimi Hendrix setting his guitar on fire to the tune of "Wild Thing." Light on backstage antics and crowd color, it doesn't showcase the prevailing drug culture like the Woodstock movie did; it's an element that feels like it's missing from this hippie time capsule. Still, you can't deny the groundbreaking music (another highlight: the closing number by Indian sitar legend Ravi Shankar), outta-sight fashions, psychedelic imagery, and the innocence of youth just as the counterculture was about to flower.

Murder at the Vanities (1934)

🍸 🌿

🌿🌿🌿🌿 One of the last movies released before the Hollywood Production Code went into effect in 1934, this reefer-jazz-era classic directed by Mitchell Leisen from the play by Earl Carroll and Rufus King is noted for its risqué choreography—the chorus girls are scantily clad throughout—and Gertrude Mitchell's Mexican-style performance of "Sweet Marijuana." All hell breaks loose backstage at the *Vanities*, an opulent production starring Ann Ware (Kitty Carlisle) and Eric Lander (Carl Brissom). Rita Ross (Mitchell) is jealous of Ann and Eric's relationship, and it appears she'll do anything to prevent them from getting married. The plot twists and turns, but never slows down the show, which of course must go on. The highlight is indeed "Sweet Marijuana," as Rita sings, "Soothe me with your caress, help me with my distress, Sweet Marijuana." Written by Arthur Johnson and Sam Coslow, the songs are sublime, culminating in the "Cocktails for Two" finale. Duke Ellington and his amazing big band also deliver a swinging rendition of "Ebony Rhapsody." Except for a few brief blackouts, the restored film does justice to the original black-and-white photography.

Pink Floyd: Live at Pompeii (1972)

🍸 🌿

🌿🌿🌿🌿 Pink Floyd's preamble to *The Wall* is a private concert without a crowd. Set up in an ancient Roman amphitheater in Pompeii, Italy, the band plays several songs in their entirety, from "Echoes" and "One of These Days" off the album *Meddle* to the instrumental "A Saucerful of Secrets." These live numbers alternate with studio footage of tracks coming together for the seminal *Dark Side of the Moon* album ("Us and Them," "Brain Damage") and the occasional interview. Roman ruins and artwork accent the film along with scenes of nature, volcanic ash, and space, but most astounding is the quartet of ridiculously talented guitarist David Gilmour, bassist Roger Waters, drummer Nick Mason, and keyboardist Richard Wright. Dive into the director's cut, released on DVD in 2003, for the full ninety-minute-plus experience.

> "Most people think of us as a very drug-orientated group. Of course we're not. You can trust us."
>
> —David Gilmour

Pink Floyd The Wall
(1982)

🍸 🍶 ✂️ 💊 💉 👀

🌿🌿🌿🌿 Almost anything related to prog-rock deity Pink Floyd functions as a pothead's playground, but even the headiest fans may find this convoluted visualization of the band's 1979 magnum opus about insanity and rock star alienation a serious downer. The sickly and stone-faced Pink (Bob Geldof), traumatized by the loss of his father in World War II and seemingly incapable of relating to women (his protective mother, his soon-to-stray wife, any number of celebrity-sucking groupies), isolates himself in one luxury hotel room after another. Vacantly channel surfing and lost in a permanent haze, the pale, lanky superstar muses on how his world got so walled in via flashbacks to the heartbreak of his childhood, his dehumanizing school days, and the sullen obligation and disintegration of his marriage. He's a shell of his former self and far removed from reality. (Geldof, by the way, speaks only one line that isn't a lyric, screaming "Next time, fuckers!" after hurling a television out a window.)

Darkly stylized visuals that sear the imagination make Pink's torment a trip worth taking. Essentially one very long music video, this collaboration of director Alan Parker (*Midnight Express*) and Floyd mastermind and primary architect Roger Waters is greatly heightened by fantastical animation from Gerald Scarfe, who draws demonic symbolism into "Goodbye Blue Sky," makes hammers march like the Gestapo during "Waiting for the Worms," and vividly brings the album sleeve's grotesqueries to wild life during "The Trial." At its most intoxicatingly sour, the flick skillfully combines tunes and toons to enhance Parker's growing horror show, as when Pink is chased around an empty room by a serpentine shadow; or goes over the brink, floating in a blood-red pool and scratching at himself; or is bloodily transformed into a freaky, eyebrow-free neo-Nazi rocker once madness fully sets in. "If you want to find out what's behind these cold eyes," Pink sings, "you'll just have to claw your way through this disguise." No need: the film literally tears through the façade for us, as we wallow in Pink's violent despair until he's finally "Comfortably Numb," completely reborn as a fascist caricature and found guilty in a court of his own mind.

🌿 TRIPPY ROCK OPERAS 🌿

Whether born out of a stage production or a seminal album, these five films feature scores that goes way beyond background music—the songs actually inform the plot, while outlandish costuming and sets keep things nice and stony . . .

Jesus Christ Superstar (1973): Norman Jewison directed this Andrew Lloyd Webber–Tim Rice stage show just after he made the film version of *Fiddler on the Roof*. It's an outrageously colorful take on Christ's final weeks before the crucifixion, complete with singing and dancing disciples drenched in satin, glitter, and fringe. Even with the campy tunes, Ted Neeley's portrayal of Jesus remains one of the most enduring in film history, certainly outshining the likes of Mel Gibson.

The Rocky Horror Picture Show (1975): Originally a flop, this stage adaptation was later reintroduced to the public as a midnight movie, causing a sensation and inspiring people to dress up as the characters, yell lines of dialogue, and pull out props on cue. While it helped launch the careers of Tim Curry, Susan Sarandon, Barry Bostwick, and Meat Loaf, even for those who can't get down with the film's thin plot and transsexual costumes, the tunes still rule.

Tommy (1975): The Who's great rock opera gets the Ken Russell camp treatment in this landmark music film featuring over-the-top performances by an all-star cast, including exceptional turns by Ann-Margret and Tina Turner. However, the odd plot about an abused deaf, dumb, and blind boy who becomes a messiah figure remains confounding. Still, there's no denying the acid trip vibe of this film, with all the bells and whistles of the best pinball game.

Pink Floyd The Wall (1982): In the movie version of the Pink Floyd album that came out three years earlier, Bob Geldof plays Pink, a jaded, isolated rock star who goes insane. His fragile mental state is linked to Nazism, grammar school, and memories of World War II, all nightmarishly animated by Gerald Scarfe. It's long been a high school favorite for the "We don't need no education" crowd.

Hedwig and the Angry Inch (2001): Part *Velvet Goldmine*, part *Rocky Horror Picture Show* with a hip transgender twist, John Cameron Mitchell plays East German glam rocker Hedwig, whose string of failed relationships leads to many inspired pop songs and the creation of the perfect rock star. The styles and sounds of David Bowie, Iggy Pop, and Lou Reed are conjured up in this adaptation of Mitchell's off-Broadway musical, which has since inspired hundreds of productions all over the world.

Quadrophenia (1979)

🍸 🔬 💊 ◉◉

🌿🌿🌿🌙 In this dramatic interpretation of The Who's 1973 rock opera, the mods are pitted against the rockers in a battle of working-class cool. Jimmy Cooper (Phil Daniels) is the kind of bloke who rides a Vespa, is acutely aware of fashion, leans toward soul and ska music, and pops speed pills like they're Tic Tacs. It's your typical London mod, circa 1964. Fed up with a dead-end office job and generally disenchanted with his life, Jimmy takes to fighting, parties, girls, beer, and drugs to cure his boredom—sometimes all in one weekend. The rockers, who also enjoy a good rumble, are more like a biker gang, clad in leather and rough around the edges. To Jimmy, they represent the pack mentality, but his aversion to the rockers becomes less clear when his childhood friend Kevin (Ray Winstone) reveals he is one. The rivalry comes to a head in the seaside town of Brighton where a full-on riot ensues, and Jimmy escapes mid-battle to shag a girl in an alley. He comes to terms with his identity crisis upon spotting mod poster boy Ace Face, played by a baby-faced Sting, doubling as a hotel bellboy. Stocked with a stellar soundtrack of classics by The Who ("Love, Reign o'er Me," "The Real Me") along with sixties girl group greats like the Chiffons and Ronettes, the film moves with the music, but it's during the final scenes where, like The Who's most epic numbers, it all comes to a glorious climax.

Reefer Madness: The Movie Musical (2005)

🚬 🍶 🪴

🌿🌿🌿🌿🌙 The lunacy of Andy Fickman's adaptation of the classic thirties marijuana exploitation flick is absolutely inspired. What began as a theater production in Los Angeles became a "movie musical" when Showtime put up the money and Fickman began recruiting stars like Alan Cumming, Neve Campbell, and Kristen Bell. It's the same old story—naïve boy (Jimmy, played by Neve's brother Christian) gets hooked on "giggle sticks" when dealer Jack (Steven Weber) invites him over to the tea pad for a smoke. His girl, Mary Lane (Bell), is too busy singing and dancing "Down at the Ol' Five and Dime," one of the film's better numbers, to notice. Cumming is the leering "lecturer" who relates the gory story of "dope slaves" hooked on loco weed. Perhaps campy to a fault (there's lots of faux blood, zombies, and ghouls, plus Jesus and the Devil make cameos), the sharp script and even better songs propel the story to its frenetic finale. Little known then, Bell's a revelation; she positively shines on "Mary Jane, Mary Lane," her duet with Campbell. Watch the DVD or, better yet, catch the traveling stage production. This hilarious retelling of *Reefer Madness* never gets old.

Mae to Ralph: "You better cool off on the muggles."

Rock 'n' Roll High School (1979)

🚬 🔬 🍸 🎷 ◉◉

🌿🌿🌿🌿🌙 B-movie king Roger Corman produced this low-budget update of the "wild teen" rock-and-roll movies of the fifties and sixties. Director Allan Arkush cast the Ramones, New York's leather-jacketed punk pioneers, even though you would have been hard-pressed to find an entire high school full of Ramones freaks in the late seventies. P. J. Soles stars as Riff Randell, the Ramones's self-proclaimed number-one fan, who has a joint-fueled fantasy sequence that puts Joey Ramone in the beyond-awkward position of sex symbol. When Vince Lombardi High's new principal, the fantastically fascist Miss Togar (Mary Woronov), bans the group's records and tries to prevent Randell from going to a Ramones concert, the ensuing teen rebellion leads to wanton rule breaking, loud rock music, crazed dancing, school destruction and, um, smoking the peace pipe with a giant white mouse. "Things sure have changed since we got kicked out of high school," deadpans Johnny Ramone. It's one of rock's silliest, best-ever films, courtesy of the schlock genius behind *Teenage Caveman* and *Attack of the Giant Leeches*.

Rocky Horror Picture Show, The (1975)

🍸 ✂ ◡◡

🌿🌿🌿🌿 The film with the longest continuous theatrical run in cinematic history (thirty-four years and counting) is technically a comedy, but while *The Rocky Horror Picture Show* is no doubt amusing in its inherent wackiness—the far-fetched story, the tranny costumes, the nonsensical dialogue—it's really all about the music. Most of the songs come from the original 1973 London stage production of the show, but amazingly, the soundtrack (which includes alltime classic "The Time Warp") still holds up today. And since there are so few spoken lines in *Rocky Horror*, that's a big plus considering the songs push the plot along. As for the story, straitlaced couple Brad (Barry Bostwick) and Janet (Susan Sarandon) get a flat tire on a rainy night and take shelter in a spooky mansion, where they meet Dr. Frank-N-Furter (Tim Curry), a proud "sweet transvestite from Transylvania" (sporting heavy glamrock-era makeup, a corset, and fishnet stockings) and his group of weird devotees. The doctor invites Brad and Janet into his lab, where he's created the perfect specimen of man—the blond and buff Rocky, who immediately drives a wedge between him and his disciples. Before the whole motley crew can be beamed up to space, Eddie the biker (Meat Loaf) is stabbed with an ice pick, a mutiny goes down, and . . . oh hell, we have no idea what happens at the end. But the fun is in getting there (especially for the first forty minutes) and singing along. Full audience participation with shadow casts and cues, which still happen at midnight screenings nationwide, is a treat every freak, stoner, and outcast should experience at least once. If your town doesn't have an awesome art house, you can also find line-by-line instructions on the Web and play (and smoke) along at home with friends.

> "I would like, if I may, to take you on a strange journey."
> —The Criminologist

Sgt. Pepper's Lonely Hearts Club Band
(1978)

🌿🌿 Looking to cash in on the massive success of *Saturday Night Fever* and *Grease*, music impresario and film producer Robert Sitgwood thought he had a surefire hit with this musical based on The Beatles's seminal album, starring pop megastars the Bee Gees and Peter Frampton. He couldn't have been more wrong. Adapted from an off-Broadway play, which tried to construct a story out of characters like Mr. Kite and Mean Mr. Mustard, the Gibb brothers (Barry, Robin, and Maurice) play the good-natured Hendersons, who, along with their buddy Billy Shears (Frampton) form a band in hopes of making it big outside of their hometown of Heartland. After catching the eye of music biz hotshot B.D. (Donald Pleasence), the boys head to Hollywood where they're wined, dined, and sixty-nined into signing a contract with the evil record company, which arranges to get them high, then drains their bank account and self-respect. Meanwhile, back in Heartland, a doe-eyed Strawberry Fields (Sandy Farina) takes a bus to the big city in search of her missing boyfriend, Billy, and finds him in the clutches of Lucy and her Diamond sisters, but eventually wins him back, just in time for the guys to save Heartland from becoming another neglected ghetto, but too late for her own survival. Truthfully, the story barely matters. In fact, what made the movie a momentary stoner hit in the eighties was watching it with the sound off, but there's no denying some kooky cameos: Steve Martin as Dr. Maxwell, whose silver hammer turns out-of-shape old people into young, nubile teenagers, a precursor to his role in *The Little Shop of Horrors*; George Burns as the kind Mr. Kite; Aerosmith (credited as Villain Band) doing "Come Together"; Earth, Wind & Fire funking up "Got to Get You into My Life"; and Alice Cooper as the Sun King singing a creepy "Because." Even *Old School*'s Blue (Patrick Cranshaw) turns up as a Western Union man. But the piéce de résistance is the grand finale, a chorus line reprise of the title track featuring a who's who of stars, including Tina Turner, Carol Channing, Robert Palmer, Frankie Valli, and Sha Na Na. The only thing missing are some muppets. Camp? You betcha. So bad, it's good? Debatable.

> "Because the wind is high it blows my mind."
>
> —The Sun King

☘ BAKED WITH THE BEATLES ☘

Their music may have had very few missteps, but some of their films . . . well, that's another story. We break down The Beatles's movies from the bakey best to the nonsensical mess.

A *Hard Day's Night* (1964): As Beatlemania swept the globe, the next logical step for the band was its first feature film. Richard Lester's *A Hard Day's Night* is a sharp, beautifully shot (in black-and-white) romp through the hysteria and mayhem that enveloped The Beatles's daily lives, with pacing and wit that make you feel like you're part of the inner circle. The fanaticism that surrounded the band was real, and its portrayed on film in a rare mix of staging and verité that provides a clever, behind-the-scenes peek at pop stardom. And if that doesn't interest you, certainly the charisma and vigor that John Lennon, Paul McCartney, George Harrison, and Ringo Starr project will easily pull you in. Considered a British cinema classic, it continues to influence modern video production and editing and its sense of mass hysteria has yet to be replicated with as much intensity.

Help! (1965): The Beatles's second feature film was a valuable vehicle for the band to promote itself, its songs, and its ever-evolving place at the center of youth drug culture and burgeoning hippiedom. As such, they didn't veer much from the *Hard Day's Night* formula, though this time the Keystone Kops–styled shenanigans fit into a slightly more cohesive "Keep Ringo's ring from the bad guys" plot line. Infused with a healthy dose of witty Beatles charm and, of course, some of the greatest pop music ever created, it makes for light, well-paced viewing. Scenes saturated in primary colors weave in and out of what are essentially videos for "Help," "You've Got to Hide Your Love Away," and other classics. FYI: Paul McCartney and Ringo Starr reportedly smoke a joint while filming the curling scene.

Magical Mystery Tour (1967): Widely regarded as The Beatles's first flop, this film features iconic clips of legendary songs—"I Am the Walrus," "Fool on the Hill," "Your Mother Should Know"—interspersed with annoying vignettes full of rambling dialogue and dull visuals. It apparently originated with McCartney, whose concept was to simply shoot random peoples' comings and goings. But despite the rest of the Fab Four appearing quite visibly "elsewhere," never before has a psychedelic film felt or looked so gruelingly unpsychedelic. Add to that the amateur acting, poor production, lack of direction, and bargain-basement art design, and *Magical Mystery* becomes a deeply aggravating view. No wonder it confounded critics and fans alike.

Yellow Submarine (1968): A colorful cornucopia of kaleidoscopic proportion, *Yellow Submarine* would be considered a masterful work of motion picture pop art even without The Beatles's involvement. As it turned out, the band's participation was minimal, but vivid psychedelic imagery and cheeky witticisms coupled with some of their druggiest tunes ("Lucy in the Sky with Diamonds," "With a Little Help from My Friends," and the eternally stony "A Day in the Life") come together to create perhaps the best and brightest Beatles film to get lost in.

Let It Be (1970): Having exhilarated their fans and exhausted their chops through intense studio sessions for *Sgt. Pepper's* and the White Album, The Beatles were intent to get back to their roots. They attempted to hatch a project that would culminate in their first live show since 1966. The result is a verité account of their rehearsals at Twickenham Studios, run-throughs and final live performance as a band on the roof of the Apple building. Despite demonstrating some of their best, most straightforward rockers in early 1969, The Beatles were not a happy bunch. Sparks of genius are captured on film as are heated words, meandering rehearsals, and one too many McCartney piano ballad. It's an awkward film to watch, but also a compelling one.

⚜ BEST STONER SOUNDTRACKS ⚜

A soundtrack, like the movie it accompanies, is also a work of art requiring just the right mix of songs and sentiment. Here are our ten favorite collections where the music is as stony as the film itself.

Easy Rider (1969): The first rock soundtrack album revs its motorcycle engines from the opening notes of Steppenwolf's "Born to Be Wild," to Jimi Hendrix ("If 6 Was 9") to The Band's "The Weight." Stoner favs "The Pusher" (also by Steppenwolf) and Fraternity Man's "Don't Bogart Me" ("Don't bogart that joint, pass it over to me") are highlights, as is Roger McGuinn's cover of Bob Dylan's "It's Alright, Ma, I'm Only Bleeding," which plays over the movie's brief credits.

Super Fly (1972): Maybe America wasn't ready to embrace the blaxploitation genre in the early seventies, but it certainly had no qualms with its music. As such, Super Fly is one of those rare soundtracks whose sales outgrossed the film, thanks entirely to Curtis Mayfield, who lays down some timeless soul-funk, killer keyboard licks, and chilled-out grooves. Nearly four decades later, songs like "Freddie's Dead" and "Pusherman" still sound ahead of their time.

The Harder They Come (1972): Like the movie it came from, The Harder They Come soundtrack is a revered reggae touchstone and one of the few bestselling genre anthologies not to have Bob Marley on it. Only four songs on the album were written especially for the film,

but all are undeniable classics, especially Jimmy Cliff's iconic title track and "You Can Get It If You Really Want," both of which have become cover-song staples for any band looking to get in touch with its Rastafarian roots.

Dazed and Confused (1993): It's only fitting that one of the quintessential movies about coming of age in the seventies would have a soundtrack this worthy of Camaro cruising. Highlights include Foghat's "Slow Ride," Alice Cooper's "School's Out," and Aerosmith's "Sweet Emotion." The album was so popular, it spawned a sequel.

Pulp Fiction (1994): From Dick Dale's surf-rock anthem "Miserlou" to Urge Overkill's moody cover of Neil Diamond's "Girl, You'll Be

a Woman Soon" to Dusty Springfield's carnal "Son of a Preacher Man," each piece of music in *Pulp Fiction* is as integral to the near-perfection of this groundbreaking Quentin Tarantino film as John Travolta and Samuel L. Jackson discussing a Royale with Cheese. Indeed, the music direction was so captivating that the soundtrack went on to sell over three million copies.

Friday (1995): It's no surprise that perhaps the best hip-hop stoner movie of all time would have an equally stony soundtrack. After all, it was *Friday* that truly transformed Ice Cube from rapper to movie star. Naturally, he contributes the title track. Other highlights include Cypress Hill's "Roll It Up, Light It Up, Smoke It Up," Rick James's "Mary Jane," and War's Compton classic, "Low Rider."

The Big Lebowski (1998): With dream sequences set to stoned-out classics by Bob Dylan ("The Man In Me") and Kenny Rogers ("Just Dropped in (To See What Condition My Condition Was In)") and plot points that involve the seminal (and fictional) German group Autobahn, as well as The Eagles and Creedence Clearwater Revival, it's fair to mark this as another great stoner movie made even better by its music.

Velvet Goldmine (1998): Todd Haynes's film is arguably a fictionalized biography of David Bowie, but since the Thin White Duke wouldn't sign using his music, the director put together a pair of supergroups to tell the hedonistic rock tale. Contributors include members of Radiohead (Thom Yorke and Jonny Greenwood) and Sonic Youth (Thurston Moore and Steve Shelly) covering the New York Dolls and T-Rex and conjuring up a cultural moment defined by music . . . and massive amounts of drugs.

High Fidelity (2000): If you were to ask characters Rob (John Cusack) and Barry (Jack Black) for their ultimate stoner soundtrack, it might sound a lot like this album full of hipster musts, includings tracks by The Velvet Underground, John Wesley Harding, and The Beta Band. Indeed, music snobbery hasn't sounded this good since Beethoven and Mozart.

Garden State (2004): "You gotta hear this one song. It'll change your life, I swear." This is what dream girl Sam (Natalie Portman) tells nebbishy, neurotic Andrew (Zach Braff) minutes after meeting him, and just before pressing play on The Shins' wistful "New Slang." It's a throwaway moment that triggered a nerd revolution and an indie rock explosion. Iron & Wine cover The Postal Service's "Such Great Heights" and Coldplay woefully pine about living in a beautiful world in "Don't Panic." Hipsters everywhere realized that sensitivity is a virtue, especially when experienced while in a dutiful haze.

Shotguns and Accordions: Music of the Marijuana Growing Regions of Colombia (1983)

🌱

🍁 🍁 🍁 🍁 Once home to Colombia's thriving marijuana trade, the Sierra Nevada de Santa Marta also produces some of country's most engaging music. As part of his Channel 4 series *Beats of the Heart*, Jeremy Marre takes us deep into the mountains where the local cumbia music is led by accordion players, some of whom "praise the marijuana men who have become part of local lore" in song. The lively musical segments are field recordings of the highest quality. Between accordions, horns, flutes, drums, and guitars, it's a full and sometimes raucous sound, reminiscent of New Orleans second-line and zydeco. Even more interesting is the marijuana story: By the early eighties, the industry, which began with the "Colombian gold rush" of the sixties and seventies, had collapsed due to inferior quality yerba, resulting in poverty for many throughout the region. Police burn down one packing site filled with huge bails of gold buds. This is contrasted with a rigged music competition where Nafer Duran is deprived of a prize. As he sings plaintively, the stash goes up in smoke. "Typically Colombian," Duran sighs.

Stop Making Sense (1984)

🍁 🍁 🍁 🍁 It's obvious from the first moment of this stunning concert film starring David Byrne and the rest of Talking Heads, directed by future Academy Award winner Jonathan Demme (*The Silence of the Lambs*) at Hollywood's famed Pantages Theater, that *Stop Making Sense* isn't your run-of-the-mill multicamera shoot of an ordinary rock show. Armed only with a boom box and acoustic guitar, Byrne walks out onto a curtainless stage and launches into the band's classic "Psycho Killer," culminating in a spastic dance. From that point on, Byrne builds his backing band member by member, transforming a sparse stage into a virtual circus of backup dancers, guitarists, and even P-Funk keyboardist Bernie Worrell, with each song more hyperactively celebratory than the last. For his final trick, Byrne wears a massively shoulder-padded suit while hilariously writhing to "Crosseyed and Painless." Filmed more than twenty-five years ago, it still feels ahead of its time today.

Tommy (1975)

🌱 🍸 🍾 💉 👅

🍁 🍁 🍁 Director Ken Russell's movie version of The Who's rock opera is the story of Tommy, a young boy who witnesses his war hero father's brutal murder by his mother's lover, and how he transforms into a godlike figure both worshipped and exploited by the masses. From the time his mother (Ann-Margret) and her lover (Oliver Reed) tell Tommy that "he didn't see it, he didn't hear it, and he won't say nothing about it," he becomes so traumatized that he becomes deaf, dumb, and blind and retreats into a private world. As someone who is "different," Tommy is subjected to all kinds of physical and mental abuse in post–World War II London. His guilt-ridden mother takes him to a variety of specialists, none of whom are able to find a cure. Things change drastically as the teenage Tommy (Roger Daltrey) finds a bridge to the real world when he discovers pinball and becomes a phenomenon. As news of his ability grows, Tommy attains messiah-like status, even as he continues to be exploited by his mother and stepfather. Seeing him as their ticket to financial success, they launch a promotional blitz of licensed Tommy products that feeds the hungry public. It all comes crashing down when Tommy, through finally reliving his father's murder, gets all his senses

back and, along with the now cynical public, rejects it all and is reborn.

Russell treats the viewer to his signature kaleidoscopic colors and visuals in telling his interpretation of this well-known story. From a casting perspective, in addition to the Oscar-nominated performance of Ann-Margret, Russell stacks the deck with some interesting choices: Elton John is the Pinball Wizard, Eric Clapton plays the Preacher, Tina Turner brings to life the Acid Queen, Keith Moon appears as your Wicked Uncle Ernie (a part he was born to play), and Jack Nicholson drops in as the Specialist.

24 Hour Party People (2002)

Manchester's fertile music era from the late seventies to the mid-nineties was born of a single 1976 Sex Pistols concert—only 42 people attended, but all of them would "go out and perform wondrous deeds." This embellished moment comes early in Michael Winterbottom's heavily dramatized, colorfully styled feature about the scene that would spawn, among many others, Joy Division, New Order, Happy Mondays, and Ecstasy-fueled rave culture. Steve Coogan portrays quixotic TV presenter/Factory Records boss Tony Wilson, who signs Joy Division in his own blood only to have front man Ian Curtis hang himself and the band reborn as chart-toppers New Order. The film literally turns Technicolor after Wilson discovers drug-gobbling hedonists Happy Mondays, who end up bankrupting the label after recording in Barbados an expensive new album and returning with tossed-off instrumentals and raging crack habits. The era also saw Wilson and Factory launch the legendary Hacienda nightclub, where acid house was the dominant sound. The abundant Ecstasy that coursed through the sweaty crowds made loads of money for dealers but none for the club, which would close in the late nineties. On its final night, Wilson wanders up to the Hacienda's roof, smokes a "brilliant" joint, and sees God, who promptly chastises him for not signing The Smiths. "Most of all," says Wilson, "I love Manchester. The crumbling warehouses, the railway arches, the cheap abundant drugs . . . that is my heroic flaw, my excess of civic pride."

Tony Wilson: "I am not a lump of hash. I'm in charge of Factory Records. I think."

Wattstax (1973)

What Woodstock lacked in diversity, Wattstax made up for big time. Commemorating the seven-year anniversary of the Watts riots in Los Angeles, the producers brought together acts from the Memphis record label Stax for an all-day event at the Los Angeles Coliseum. Mel Stuart (*Willy Wonka & the Chocolate Factory*) focuses as much on the music as he does on local characters who rap about everything from black power to male-female relationships. Numerous vignettes feature Richard Pryor doing routines that would become nationally known by the end of the decade. Isaac Hayes (introduced by Jesse

Jackson), The Staple Singers, Bar-Kays, Rufus and Carla Thomas, Luther Ingram, and Albert King are the stars of the show. The most riveting performance comes from Rufus "Funky Chicken" Thomas, who at first instructs people to hop the fences and dance on the field during his set, then spends quite a bit of time sending then right back, with no help from the police or security whatsoever. Though integration had changed the social politics of America, nary a white face can be seen among the afros and colorful clothes on this day of "black awareness."

Isaac Hayes (singing "Soulville"): "Some like to smoke and some like to blow / And some are even strung out on a $50 jones."

Wiz, The (1978)

The Motown version of the age-old classic got panned upon release, but as movie musicals go, there are far worse offenders. In Sidney Lumet's ultravivid, soultastic version of *The Wizard of Oz*, Diana Ross plays Dorothy, Michael Jackson is the Scarecrow, Richard Pryor portrays the Wiz, and the city of Oz is very obviously played by Manhattan (the Twin Towers can be seen in all their former glory).

Life in Harlem has been especially harsh to Dorothy, who winds up in a fantasy world of abandoned amusement parks, dancing crows, flying monkeys, and a yellow brick road that runs through subway stations and across the Brooklyn Bridge. Colorful at every turn, the visuals get downright trippy as the foursome inches closer to the Wiz's lair. At the Poppy Love perfume company-turned-nightclub, fumes make Dorothy light-headed, and after Evillene (Mabel King) is defeated, a chorus line of scantily clad sweatshop workers shimmy and shake in glitter and gold. The sets and costumes may be over-the-top (look no further than Lena Horne as Glinda, the Good Witch of the South), but the tunes are solid and hold up surprisingly well more than thirty years later. Ease on down that road. You never know where it might take you.

Woodstock (1970)

 The greatest rock festival of all time was the subject of the greatest music doc of all time, courtesy of Michael Wadleigh and his incredible camera crew that included Martin Scorsese. The twenty-fifth anniversary director's cut added forty-five minutes to the original three-hour length, and it's worth watching every last minute. Wadleigh's scope is broad, following the setup, the crowd's arrival, and their almost eerie disappearance by the end as Jimi Hendrix serenades the remaining few with a lengthy improv on "Purple Haze." Fifteen bands and solo acts perform a total of thirty-one songs. Many of the musical highlights are contained on the second disc: Sly & the Family Stone's incendiary "I Wanna Take You Higher," Santana's percussion-heavy "Soul Sacrifice," and

Hendrix, whose set is expanded considerably in the long version. The Who, Jefferson Airplane, Ten Years After, Richie Havens, Joan Baez, Arlo Guthrie, John Sebastian, Canned Heat, and Crosby, Stills & Nash all chip in memorable performances and get Wadleigh's then-innovative split-screen treatment. Only Janis Joplin's overwrought "Work Me Lord" (also an addition) is a disappointment. Almost as entertaining as the music are the interviews with attendees, locals, producers, and even a Port-o-San cleaner. There's plenty of pot smoking, skinny-dipping, rain, mud, nudity, and campy stage announcements ("The brown acid is not specifically too good—it's suggested that you do stay away from that, but it's your trip"). On stage, it's all about the afros, fringed jackets, tie-dyes, sideburns, and groovy language (Guthrie: "I was rappin' to the fuzz—the New York's Thruway's closed—it's far out"). While Wadleigh's sprawling film was a stunning achievement as a musical documentary, it also proved to be a clarion call to a generation that was just beginning to realize its vast potential.

Xanadu (1980)

Maligned and campy, to put it gently, the eternally eighties *Xanadu* stars a post-*Warriors* Michael Beck trading in his baseball bat and leather jacket for wheels when he falls in love with roller skating muse Kira (Olivia Newton-John). She's been sent by the gods to free Sonny Malone (Beck) from his unfulfilling job (re-creating album covers for billboards and posters), and to complete her mission, she teams him with aging clarinetist Danny McGuire (Gene Kelly) to start a nightclub called Xanadu. But complications arise when Kira falls for Sonny, leading to a standout, super-stony scene where Sonny skates through a mural of Kira and her seven sisters to confront Zeus, enters another dimension of black and neon lights and responds to the booming voice of the Greek god with a simple admission: "I've fallen for your daughter." Absurd? Absolutely, but it's also deceptively likeable on so many levels, especially the superb tunes by ELO. A glorious testament to neon, disco, the roller skating craze, and the drop-dead gorgeousness of Newton-John post-*Grease*, this is one deserved cult favorite.

DOCUMEN-TARIES

a/k/a Tommy Chong
(2005)

Director Josh Gilbert follows Tommy Chong as he prepares to go to jail in 2003 for selling drug paraphernalia across state lines. Until his arrest, Chong was best known as half of the Cheech & Chong comedy duo. When he started a glass bong company with his son Paris, the Feds took notice, making him the feature bust in their Operation Pipe Dreams campaign and sentencing him to nine months in prison. Gilbert focuses on the political nature of the dragnet that snared the comedian, interviews supporters like Bill Maher and Jay Leno, and digs back into Chong's early years as a Motown musician and bawdy comic. The whole experience clearly changed Chong, who says, "I made a living for thirty years talking about a culture and now finally I'm going to have to stand up and be counted."

> "They asked me
> if I had any narcotics
> in the house.
> I said, 'Of course,
> I'm Tommy Chong.'"
>
> —Chong

Acapulco Gold (1973)

The first marijuana documentary from the stoner's perspective takes us from the hemp fields of the Midwest to the doc's namesake in the mountains of Mexico. Director Bob Grosvenor is on a search for what he calls "superweed." He starts in Missouri, where locals known as the Kaw Valley Hemp Pickers Association harvest tall stalks of leafy ditchweed, but ultimately ditches that weed in favor of some Kentucky homegrown which isn't much better (we do learn about the state's fascinating hemp history, though). Finally, Grosvenor decides to go south of the border (to the tune of Rainy Daze's psychedelic pop classic, "Acapulco Gold," and wonderfully animated by Artie Wong). The Mexican footage is raw and exciting. Our intrepid smuggler buys 100 kilos for thirty-six dollars per, presses it into bricks, and leaves it to a swimmer, the last member of the relay team responsible for getting the cannabis contraband into the States. It's a fun ride, but Grosvenor omits the best part: the actual smoking of marijuana. Rather than ending with the smuggler's arrival, they all should have kicked back with some celebratory joints. What's lacking in marijuana quality in the original is made up for somewhat with "The Secret Garden" extra on the 2000 DVD, featuring WAMM's luscious medical-marijuana grow-op.

Rainy Daze (singing "Acapulco Gold"): "We're goin' south / Where the streets are lined with Acapulco Gold."

A Decade Under the Influence (2003)

🖊 🍸 ⚗ 💉 👀

🌿🌿🌿🌿 Chronicling the evolution—and revolution—of modern cinema during its most electrifying period, from the late sixties through the seventies, the late Ted Demme (*Blow*) issued an unabashed love letter to the filmmakers, actors, and writers who influenced his generation and those before and after. Through interviews with many of its key players, including Dennis Hopper, Robert Altman, Martin Scorsese, Francis Ford Coppola, Peter Bogdanavich, Ellen Burstyn, Bruce Dern, and Jon Voight, this three-part IFC doc starts by

> "The filmmakers who influenced me the most, I don't know their names. Because I would go see a film, hate it, and say 'I've got to remember never to do anything like that again!'"
>
> —**Robert Altman**

explaining how the counterculture stepped in as the studio system was falling apart, then, with their unconventional views of sex, drugs, race, war, and politics, managed to attract critical acclaim and a mass mainstream audience while completely redefining film as an art form. Their own influences (Antonioni, Fellini, Bergman, Cassavetes), many of them foreign, are explored, as are polar-opposite box-office juggernauts like *Star Wars*, which would come later in the seventies and ostensibly close the chapter on this free-wheeling era. Smart, exhilarating, and respectful, a sadness creeps in over the latter half of this doc, bookended by the untimely passing of its director from a cocaine overdose three months before its premiere. But the movies live on. For more on this subject, see *Easy Riders, Raging Bulls*, which also came out in 2003.

American Drug War: The Last Great White Hope (2007)

🖊 🔪 🍄 🔧 ⚗ 💉 👀

🌿🌿🌿🌿🌿 Kevin Booth (*How Weed Won the West, Bill Hicks: Sane Man*) takes the War on Drugs personally. Several family members had drug problems and Booth confesses to his own addiction to painkillers. The director's main focus is Ricky Ross and the Iran-Contra scandal that flooded cocaine into Los Angeles in the eighties. A chief beneficiary of the CIA's covert drug operation, Ross ultimately was busted and speaks to Booth via phone calls from prison. "Cocaine came along and gave me a new horizon," he explains. Booth clearly sides with the radical fringe: Gary Webb's *Dark Alliance*, and conspiracy theorists Mike Ruppert, Joe Rogan, and Joe Pietri are all components in this compelling agitprop doc. Most entertaining is the debate Booth sparks between former New Mexico governor Gary Johnson, who favors legalizing drugs, and Arizona sheriff Joe Arpaio, who oversees the sprawling Maricopa County Jail. Booth also visits Tommy Chong in prison, where the comedian spent nine months for selling bongs in 2003. Eventually, Booth steers in the direction of medical marijuana. But the story ends with Ross, who describes the drug war as "the last great white hope," hence the title.

An Inconvenient Truth (2006)

 This documentary follows former U.S. vice-president Al Gore on his heroic and often thankless quest to thwart global warming, one lecture at a time. Delivering a much-needed wake-up call, the film exposes the ways that we have all contributed to the ills of our planet, ills that may become terminal if they continue to be ignored. Presenting the most convincing argument yet that global warming is real, glaciers are melting, and animals are losing their habitats, the film mainly follows a jaw-dropping presentation by Gore—explosive facts layered with visual proof that we are in trouble—and also travels with the politician-turned-crusader back home, where we learn about his upbringing and education. Fascinating and tragic, chilling and inspiring, it's an eye-opener and (hopefully) a kick in the butt that will spark a fact-based debate and not just controversy. It's no wonder it took home the Academy Award for Best Documentary in 2006, as well as Best Original Song by Melissa Etheridge, who, after seeing Gore's presentation, was inspired to write "I Need to Wake Up."

> "I'm Al Gore, I used to be the next president of the United States of America."
>
> —**Al Gore**

MELISSA ETHERIDGE'S STONY DOCUMENTARY PICKS

Rocker and activist Melissa Etheridge, who won an Academy Award for "I Need to Wake Up," the theme song to *An Inconvenient Truth*, says about the eco-doc, "It's very heavy. You will seriously get bummed. A doc is like going on a journey—you really want to learn something." Here are five of Etheridge's favorite journeys.

Hands on a Hard Body (1997): "When you're under the influence of cannabis, it's easier to see and understand human nature, so the documentary to start with is this one about a Texas town where, every year, they have an endurance competition at a car dealership to give a pickup truck away. The last person standing with their hand on the truck gets the truck. It goes into the actual science of what happens to a body when they don't have sleep, and then the determination of each of the contestants—why they need the truck, how this is the only way they can get the truck, the will to be the last one standing—and you just see people crack. It's a study in human nature that will blow your mind."

Grey Gardens (1975): "I often think of documentaries, especially American ones, as representing our own society trying to understand and get out from the oppression of capitalism. *Grey Gardens* follows a family—a mother and daughter who are related to Jackie Kennedy Onassis—that has a lot of money, yet they're literally out of their minds. They were part of that whole East Hampton culture, and you see the decay of their minds, their bodies, and their homes. That's something else cannabis will do—it can sort of balance out the left-brain patriotic agenda that we have built for ourselves. But I would recommend watching the documentary first before seeing the 2009 HBO movie with Drew Barrymore to get a true understanding of what family dynamics do to us, and money, and perception."

Loose Change (2005, 2006, 2007, 2009): "If you dare to step over to the conspiracy side, there are documentaries that will unwrap every preconceived notion you have about our

Hurricane Katrina
August 29, 2005

Photo: NOAA

country, our world, our government, and what's really going on. I find most people start with the mother of all conspiracies, 9/11. What really happened? Michael Moore's *Fahrenheit 9/11* is like conspiracy light, but once you start looking at stone-cold facts that are presented in documentaries like *Loose Change*, which they keep updating with different versions, it's even harder facts, and harder to understand the story that we have been told—it just doesn't fit."

Grass (1999): "Watching the documentary *Grass*, narrated by Woody Harrelson, you start to understand our government, who's been in charge, and what their agendas are. Everything starts to unravel when it comes to America's war on drugs. There's so much history, since the beginning of time, when man first smoked cannabis. And there's a reason they call it weed, because you can grow it anywhere! It's a very special plant. *Grass* starts with prohibition in the twenties and thirties, it exposes Harry Anslinger, a superstrict Christian who wanted no one to have any fun at all. He campaigned against alcohol and cannabis, but he didn't succeed with alcohol. *Grass* doesn't even get into the pharmaceutical industry trying to keep cannabis illegal, the doctors and patients behind bars and all that stuff. There needs to be a part two."

Zeitgeist, the Movie (2007): "So now that you're really ready to go down the rabbit hole—and I mean, totally, like, you're gonna take the blue pill or the red pill and go down—this is a documentary you won't find on Netflix or iTunes, you have to go searching for it (Google Video usually has it, or you can get it in pieces on YouTube). If you follow the conspiracies far enough, you come out the other end, like, wait a minute, our government is screwed up, our whole world is screwed up. And once you think it's all too much, you start getting to know these physicists and scientists, and then you end up on the spiritual side. *Zeitgeist* will just blow the top of your head off."

Better Living Through Circuitry
(1999)

🌿🌿🌿 This rave primer dives headfirst into the electronic scene of the late nineties. Starting at the 1997 Winter Music Conference, a week-long dance music festival in Miami that has offered a platform for the world's most promising DJs since 1985, the film features interviews with artists like The Crystal Method, BT, Roni Size, and DJ Spooky, mixed in with veteran ravegoers and scene promoters. The passion of this devoted group of pioneers is put on full display, as an emerging scene colors itself like the Wild West on acid. Shot entirely on an early digital camera (the Sony VX1000) smuggled in with a backpack, its cool visuals, informative tips (like what you need to bring to a rave), and a behind-the-scenes look at what goes into throwing one of these massive, Ecstasy-fueled parties are like a VIP pass into a hedonistic underground world. But most importantly, director Jonathan Reiss lets the scenesters speak for themselves. As one partier says, "When you're inside the rave, it's like nothing else matters."

Chicago 10 (2008)

🌿🌿🌿🌿🌿 Of all the traumatic events of the sixties, the riots at the 1968 Democratic National Convention in Chicago rank pretty high. Except for Haskell Wexler's *Medium Cool* (1969), which used the riots as a backdrop for a fairly conventional narrative, that story had gone untold cinematically until Brett Morgen got a hold of the Chicago 8 court transcripts and decided to make a documentary about the four days in August that changed the world. In a lot of ways, Chicago was America's Tiananmen Square, with peaceful protesters pitted against heavily armed troops just itching for a fight—and they got one. Morgen's inspired treatment blends archival footage with animated reenactments from the trial, which Abbie Hoffman (voiced by Hank Azaria)—one of the defendants charged with conspiracy to riot—described as "unbelievable theater, a great show."

Inside the courtroom, it's Hoffman and the others—including lawyers William Kunstler (Liev Schreiber) and Leonard Weinglass (himself), the ninth and tenth members of the "Chicago 10"—versus Judge Julius Hoffman (Roy Scheider), whose contempt for the long-haired hippie defendants is hardly disguised. Outside, protesters mass by the day. The rhetoric and chants are fiery: "By any means necessary," "LBJ, Fuck You!" and the more tame "Peace Now!" By the fourth day, August 28, all the pent-up rage on both sides explodes into a fierce pitched battle, though only one side has weapons. As Bobby Seale is bound and gagged in the courtroom, batons and bayonets rain down on the angry protesters outside. Despite what was perhaps one of the worst moments in American protest history, Morgen finds levity, thanks largely to Abbie Hoffman's comic flair. Hoffman shines, and so does this terrific and important doc.

> "It will be a coming together of pot and politics. We'll radicalize every hippie in the country, man."
>
> —**Abbie Hoffman**

Cocaine Cowboys
(2006)

Cocaine Cowboys 2
(2008)

🌿🌿🌿, 🌿🌿🌿 The true-life *Scarface* era is chronicled in the first of these docs, a two-hour narration-free montage of life in Miami from the mid-seventies through the eighties. It was then that cocaine cartels from Cuba and Colombia practically took over the city, making horrific violence an everyday reality. Told through interviews with key players on both sides of the drug war—the DEA, local police, and government officials, as well as dealers, transporters, financiers, and gangsters of every persuasion—along with groovy archival footage, director Billy Corben paints a bloody portrait of greed and ego as small-time pushers like smuggler Mickey Munday graduate from handling kilos to moving tons. The stakes become downright deadly for all involved once "cocaine queen" Griselda Blanco makes her presence known. The self-declared Godmother was as ruthless as they come, a so-called black widow whose husbands all died mysteriously, a mentor to legendary Colombian drug lord Pablo Escobar, and a cold-blooded killer, but also a shrewd businesswoman and mother. She made millions off of Miami's "weekend warriors," rich folks who head to South Beach for three-day, powder-fueled parties, thereby contributing to the downfall of the city, dubbed "Paradise Lost" in a famous *Time* magazine cover story. The criminals were winning, all right, and would continue to claim victory over addicts for many years to come. Part two covers the Godmother's migration to California and eventual imprisonment, during which time she made contact with aspiring gangster Charles Crosby, a pioneer of sorts in the crack trade. Told almost entirely through his own detailed recollections, it lacks the cosmopolitan feel of its predecessor, but on a certain level is equally fascinating.

Dreadheads: Portrait of a Subculture (2006)

Dreadlocked and Caucasian is the central theme to this documentary, which attempts to understand the attraction of young suburbanites to the age-old symbol of Rastafarianism: dreaded hair. Speaking with tie-dyed and bleary-eyed followers of the Grateful Dead, Phish, and Widespread Panic, filmmakers Steven Hurlburt and J. Flournoy Holmes get a variety of answers: from letting go of vanity to being rebellious to "chicks dig 'em, man!" Needless to say, some of these natty nomads are as far out as heads get. Whether it's explaining bad karma dreads, or how one isn't homeless, but rather "homemore" (everywhere is your home), they have their own language ("antentacles," anyone?), fashions, and mannerisms that, whether intentional or not, come off as high-larious. Even interview subjects like The Dead's Bob Weir, Widespread's John Bell, and Woodstock emcee Wavy Gravy struggle to explain the movement. Nonnarrated segments take

the viewer through tales of "Bad hair daze," "What my parents thought," police entanglement, and what it's like to "make love with dreadlocks," while a detailed account of the many critters that can end up making a home in your hair borders on nauseating. Lice aside, this insightful look at a flourishing subculture, complete with pot-laced brownies, elaborate glass pipes, psychedelic art, high potency acid, and the constant hiss of the nitrous balloons, is a jovial one. Join the hair party.

Easy Riders, Raging Bulls: How the Sex, Drugs and Rock 'N' Roll Generation Saved Hollywood (2003)

Based on Peter Biskind's book, which was in part the inspiration for *Reefer Movie Madness*, Kenneth Bowser dives into the fertile history of Hollywood's stoner years, when directors were kings and the infidels stormed the studios' gates. This made-for-TV doc covers about a decade, from *Bonnie and Clyde* (1967) to *Star Wars* (1977), and features a veritable who's who of outsider auteurs who would eventually become the industry's biggest stars. Steven Spielberg may not have been a druggie, but he hung out in Malibu during those heady years with the likes of George Lucas, Martin Scorsese, Francis Ford Coppola, Warren Beatty, Roman Polanski, and Peter Bogdanovich. It was one big party, complete with piles of coke, lots of joints, and an ocean of booze. *Easy Rider* takes center stage, hailed as one of the movies that broke though to the burgeoning youth audience. Dennis Hopper makes a great point when he explains, "We'd gone through the sixties and nobody had ever seen drugs being smoked without going out and committing some kind of murder or atrocity." Clearly, the *Reefer Madness* mentality that had permeated Hollywood since the thirties was out. But the cocaine boom also had its casualties, as described in the film's assessment of Sam Peckinpah's death. Bowser (and Biskind) contends that seventies excess ultimately destroyed the sixties revolution, but it sure was fun while it lasted.

Emperor of Hemp
(1999)

🌿🌿🌿🌿 Jeff Jones's pointed portrait of marijuana activist Jack Herer provides a solid hour of hemp history. The author of *The Emperor Wears No Clothes* (1985), which exposed the conspiracy behind the U.S.'s prohibition of cannabis in 1937, has earned hero status among tokers for his daring book and dynamic rally speeches. Herer, who was born in 1939 in Brooklyn, New York, didn't smoke pot until 1967. Caught up in California's hippie revolution, he bought a head shop and began focusing on changing the state's marijuana laws. In 1989, four years after the book was published, Herer discovered *Hemp for Victory*, a fifteen-minute World War II–era government film, in the Library of Congress, which proved his point about hemp's utilitarian place in American history. In addition to Herer, talking heads include NORML founder Keith Stroup, marijuana historian Michael Aldrich, and Herer's smoking buddy, *Ocean's 11* author George Clayton Johnson.

Herer: "I don't know if hemp is going to save the world, but I'll tell you this—it's the only thing that can."

Flipping Out (2008)

🌿🌿🌿🌿 Many Israeli soldiers hottail it to India after they're discharged, losing themselves in the country's druggy culture, from high in the mountains to the beaches of Goa. Some are well adjusted, while others "flip out," experiencing psychotic episodes that require intervention. Enter troubleshooters Danny and Hilk. They travel to remote locations brimming with confidence that they can get their fellow Israelis on firm footing, whether it's reconnecting them with their religious roots or literally shipping them back to Israel, or both. Two particular outcasts meet this fate as others kick back with chillums, happy Jewish hippies in a strange land.

Danny: "The Jew's soul is always searching for something. If he doesn't find it, he will take drugs or climb mountains."

F.U.B.A.R. (2002)

🌿🌿🌿 The true meaning of Michael Dowse's F.U.B.A.R.—fucked up beyond all recognition—pretty much sums up "hockey-haired" best pals Dean (Paul Spence) and Terry (Dave Lawrence), who grew up together in Alberta, Canada, eventually graduating from shot-gunning beers to examining the true depths of friendship. Dean has been crashing at Terry's house for some time, and with all the drinking and girlfriend problems, their kooky life is prime material for a young documentary filmmaker, Farrel (Gordon Skilling), who decides to shoot their every move, mockumentary-style. Only it's revealed soon enough that Dean has testicular cancer, and, while he doesn't seem to be too bothered by it, his girlfriend, Trixie (Tracey Lawrence), insists he seek treatment. So for Dean's last weekend before surgery, he and Terry embark on a camping trip, taking the film crew with them. Supplies: beer and candy. Goal: getting "right wrecked." The party is too much for Farrel, who blacks out face-first in the dirt after trying to fight Dean and Terry, who seemingly don't fully understand his motives for the film. In one of the film's most infamous scenes, Farrel—hung over and sick of being tortured—dives into the lake, breaks his neck, and supposedly dies, which plays out beautifully when Dean and Terry crash the memorial and tell a few racist jokes. As mockumentaries go, F.U.B.A.R., which uses the f-word no less than 274 times, is a party in itself.

Ganja Queen (2007)

🌿🌿🌿 A real-life *Brokedown Place*, Janine Hosking's HBO doc examines the story of Schapelle Corby, an Australian woman sentenced to twenty years in a Bali prison after she was found guilty of smuggling more than nine pounds of pot into the country. Despite the court's decision, this is a whodunit, with Corby claiming innocence. A large package of marijuana was found inside her boogie board bag upon arrival in Bali in 2004. Did a baggage handler in a smuggling chain at Sydney Airport place the pot in Corby's bag? During the course of the trial, it's disclosed that her father had been arrested for drugs in the seventies. A supporter suggests the Bail government is looking for a bribe. That Corby and her family members can barely control their volatile emotions doesn't help her case either. It all adds up to one woman rotting in jail for marijuana, whether it was hers or not, which is sad.

Go Further (2003)

🔑 🎺

🌿 🌿 🌿 🌙 *Grass* narrator Woody Harrelson is the subject of Ron Mann's engaging follow-up to that fine doc. Known for both acting and hemp activism, Harrelson embarks on a 1,300-mile bike trip, from Seattle to Santa Barbara. The tour, dubbed SOL for Simple Organic Living, makes stops at colleges, where enthusiastic students warm to Harrelson's message of sustainable living by eating raw foods, practicing yoga, wearing and using hemp, and pumping biodiesel made from hemp seeds into the tour's bus. The highlight is a visit to Ken Kesey's farm in Oregon, home of the original Furthur/Merry Pranksters bus, where the elder Prankster regales them with stories about his own bus trips in the sixties. Mann recruits Dave Matthews, Bob Weir, Natalie Merchant, Michael Franti, String Cheese Incident, and Medeski Martin & Wood to perform songs in unusual settings (Weir sings "The Other One" at a bus stop). By the end, Harrelson is back to business in Hollywood, but his points have been well taken.

Gonzo: The Life and Work of Dr. Hunter S. Thompson (2008)

✏️ 🍸 🍾 🎺 💊 👅 ⚰️ 👀

🌿 🌿 🌿 🌿 🌙 For his follow-up to the Oscar-winning *Taxi to the Dark Side*, Alex Gibney decided to go "gonzo." His sharp and extremely well researched doc about outsider journalist Hunter S. Thompson, who committed suicide in 2005, is a fun ride through sixties and seventies counterculture and political history. Johnny Depp, who played

Thompson in *Fear and Loathing in Las Vegas*, periodically reads from Thompson's seminal books as Gibney intersperses Thompson footage and talking-head interviews (Tom Wolfe, Jimmy Buffett, George McGovern, and Pat Buchanan, along with Thompson's widow, Anita, and former wife Sandy). Gibney rightly focuses on *Hell's Angels*, *Fear and Loathing in Las Vegas*, *Fear and Loathing on the Campaign Trail*, and Thompson's later *Rolling Stone* and ESPN articles and columns. An unabashed drug user, Thompson smokes pot in several clips and says, while running for sheriff of Colorado's Pitkin County in 1970, "Marijuana laws are one of the reasons that's engendered this lack of respect that cops complain about all the time in this country. . . . Even the police know it's a silly law." He lost, but that didn't stop him from being the life of a million parties—a bottle of Wild Turkey in one hand and a cigarette (always in a holder) in the other. Several people speculate that Thompson became a victim of his own myth, and he even jokes, "I'm not only no longer necessary, I'm in the way." Depressed by George W. Bush's reelection in 2004, Thompson acted on the promise he'd made to his family and closest friends that when the time came he would end his own life with a self-inflicted shot from one of the guns in his large collection. But Thompson wasn't quite done yet: he orchestrates the funeral via his will. With a crowd assembled on his Owl Farm property, his ashes are fired into the distant mountains, one final bolt of gonzo genius from the late and great Hunter S. Thompson.

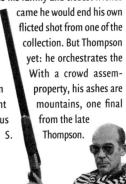

Grass (1999)

For his eighth documentary, Canadian filmmaker Ron Mann zeroed in on marijuana prohibition. The story begins in 1929 with a scene from *High on the Range*, a silent featuring cowboys getting stoned. Mann tosses clips from exploitation classics like *Reefer Madness* and *Marihuana* into his cinematic blender, and mixes them up to comical effect. One of the funniest is a cop trying to explain addiction while puffing on a cigarette. Animation and visual effects by Paul Mavrides (*Fabulous Furry Freak Brothers*) break up the clip parade. After a long prologue set in the jazz era, Mann moves briskly through the following decades, stopping long enough to acknowledge the hippie revolution of the sixties, the decriminalization movement of the seventies, and the Just Say No revisionism of the eighties. What's surprising is Mann's omission of the medical-marijuana explosion of the nineties. And there's nary a mention of Bill Clinton and his infamous inability to inhale.

> "Marijuana smoking, experts point out, can make a helpless addict out of its victim within weeks, causing physical and moral ruin and death. Should you ever be confronted with the temptation of even taking that first puff of a marijuana cigarette, don't do it."
>
> —**Narrator of vintage P.S.A.**

🌿 FOUR MORE BY RON MANN 🌿

Since the eighties, Canadian filmmaker Ron Mann has zeroed in on a number of historical topics (marijuana, comics, hotrods, jazz) and stony subjects (marijuana, mushrooms, Woody Harrelson). Here are four more favs, in addition to *Grass*:

Comic Book Confidential (1988): Mann's first relative hit set the tone for many of his docs to come. Here he traces the history of American comic book art from the thirties on, with plenty of attention paid to DC and Marvel's stables of superheroes (Superman, Batman, Spider-Man). R. Crumb discusses moving to San Francisco and taking acid in a stony section featuring the Grateful Dead's "Truckin'" and "Dark Star."

Go Further (2003): Four years after narrating *Grass*, Harrelson became Mann's subject as he biked down the West Coast, making college-speaking stops along the way. Raw food, yoga, hemp fuel, and even a little weed are all part of Harrelson's mission to change the world.

Tales of the Rat Fink (2006): Mann's liveliest doc is all about graphic artist Ed "Big Daddy" Roth (voiced by John Goodman), whose wild custom car painting was all the rage in the fifties and sixties. He also created the Rat Fink character, which appears in numerous animated montages. Even more fun are the talking segments, featuring Jay Leno (Flamethrower) and Ann-Margret (Heartbreaker), and The Sadies's garage-rock soundtrack.

Know Your Mushrooms (2008): Diving deep into the world of funghiphiles, Mann covers the intricate science of picking wild mushrooms—and, yes, the magic kind—by shadowing the eccentric Larry Evans, a.k.a. "the Indiana Jones of mushroom hunters," and others who make their way to the annual Telluride Mushroom Festival. Using animation, time-lapse photography, and music by The Flaming Lips, Mann once again expertly blends sound with vision.

Grateful Dawg (2000)

During the last five years of his life, Jerry Garcia reunited with mandolinist David Grisman, and the duo recorded a series of bluegrass-style albums. Already busy touring with the Grateful Dead and working with his own Jerry Garcia Band, the guitarist found the time to stretch his acoustic chops, thanks to Grisman's guidance. This doc's a family affair, with daughter Gillian Grisman directing and David's wife, Pam, and their sons Monroe and Sam offering commentary. Overweight and chain smoking, Garcia nevertheless is in great voice, effortlessly singing leads on "Friend of the Devil," "Sitting Here in Limbo," and "The Thrill Is Gone," and matching musical wits with Grisman on "Arabia" and "Dawg's Waltz." Told over nine chapters, director Grisman has a lot of footage to work with—live performances at the Warfield and Sweetwater's, and a "home movie" of the duo rehearsing in the Grismans' living room. "We're kinda trying all kinds of things and it all feels good," Garcia says. Sounds good, too.

Heavy Metal Parking Lot (1986)

Who knew that sixteen minutes of amateur video taken at a Judas Priest concert would become a pivotal pop culture moment? That's exactly what happened when the VHS version of Heavy Metal Parking Lot started making the rounds shortly after its release. Offering no narration, background, or even names to these whacked-out characters—big-haired eighties groupie types; beer guzzling burnouts with mullets; headbangers of all shapes, sizes, and creeds—tailgating outside Maryland's Capital Center, it simply captures a moment in time, punctuated by acid, a little weed, Jack Daniel's straight from the bottle, and lots and lots of beer. Really, this short can all be summed up in one key moment: Taking the antiquated wired microphone from the producer, a female Priest fan mock-interviews her friend and asks, "What's your philosophy on life?" His response: "It sucks shit." She says, "Heavy metal rules!"

> "What's your name?"
> —Producer
>
> "Graham, man. Like gram of dope and shit.
> —Fan

Hemp Revolution, The (1995)

Before Grass, Super High Me, American Drug War, and The Union, Australian director Anthony Clarke made the case for ending the prohibition of marijuana and its precursor, hemp. He starts in Nepal, where hemp has been produced for paper and fiber for centuries. Clarke skips back and forth between his native Australia and the United States to tell the story of the efforts to restore hemp as a legal crop. First and foremost, hemp could replace the need to clear-cut forests for paper pulp. "Hemp is seventy-seven percent cellulose," one expert says. "It's ideal for papermaking." Another quality of the plant is that it requires no pesticides (unlike cotton). Like Jack Herer did in The Emperor Wears No Clothes, Clarke traces hemp prohibition to a conspiracy involving DuPont and the Hearst newspapers, which helped stir up the Reefer Madness hysteria of the thirties with lurid stories about how hemp (renamed marijuana) caused insanity and deviant behavior. He explores medicinal use with federal pot patient Elvy Musikka (she has glaucoma), author Andrew Weil ("it's so nontoxic"), and Harvard professor Lester Grinspoon. Clarke saves his best interview—Terence McKenna—for nearly last. "More money has been spent trying to find something wrong with cannabis than any other vegetable material in history," says the late Food of the Gods author/psychonaut, "and what they've come up with is so pathetically thin that I'm confident it amounts to a clean bill of health for this stuff." Besides a few animated interludes, Clarke presents his case with few bells and whistles, but all of his salient points about pot are well taken.

High: The True Tale of American Marijuana (2008)

🪴 💊

🌿🌿🌿 A fascinating look at the reasons behind cannabis prohibition or a polemic about pain? John Holowach's retelling of marijuana history is accurate, but offers little new information. Perhaps that's why he eventually focuses on more graphic subjects like addiction, rehab, prison brutality, and one doctor's fight against the DEA. (He prescribes opiates, not marijuana.) Before this departure, Holowach (he also narrates) interviews NORML founder Keith Stroup, researcher Dr. Lyle Craker, and It Takes a Plant author Ricardo Cortes. The animated "Drug War in a Nut Shell" segment is a highlight in this otherwise muddled effort.

In Pot We Trust (2007)

🌿🔧💊

🌿🌿🌿🌿 In this made-for-Showtime doc, Star Price focuses on four medical-marijuana patients, a pot lobbyist, and a narc. Each patient has a compelling story: Irvin Rosenfeld is one of a handful of federal patients who receive three hundred joints (as much as ten years old and freeze-dried) per month from the government; Rhonda O'Donnell has MS and decides to start smoking pot again after Rhode Island legalized medical marijuana in 2006; Tom McMullen counters posttraumatic stress with marijuana ("my nightmares were gone"); and cerebral palsy sufferer Jacqueline Patterson struggles to speak without a steady supply of pot. At the opposite ends of the spectrum are Aaron Houston and Steve Reed: one's on a mission to get a bill passed in Congress that would shield legal users of medical marijuana under state laws from federal prosecution; the other wants to eradicate as much marijuana as possible. As it turns out, Houston

fails (the Hinchey-Rohrabacher Medical Marijuana Amendment loses by a 259–163 House vote) and Reed succeeds, eradicating seventeen thousand plants during a forest raid. Bummer. Price really gets the pot debate going: Legalizer Ethan Nadlesmann takes on antidrug heavies Robert DuPont and Joseph Califano. DuPont: "It is not possible that any disease would ever be treated with smoked marijuana." Nadelmann: "Smoking your medicine may be an unusual way of taking your medicine, but it works, and the reason so many people do it is because it works." Touché!

Kerouac (1985)

🌿 🍸 ⚗️ 💊

🌿🌿🌿🌿 Many of the key Beat Generation players—Allen Ginsberg, William S. Burroughs, Herbert Huncke—contribute to John Antonelli's incisive doc about Jack Kerouac. Talking-head interviews and reenacts of Kerouac's life as told through his many novels are carefully woven together. We follow Kerouac (Jack Coulter) from Lowell, Massachusetts, to New York to San Francisco, where he meets Neal Cassady (David Andrews), otherwise known as Dean Moriarty from On the Road, which when it's published several years later makes Kerouac famous overnight . Edie Kerouac Parker, his first wife, reveals it was jazz great Lester Young who first turned Jack on to marijuana, and Ginsberg talks about Benzedrine inhalers being used as a writer's aid. Kerouac became an alcoholic and he died of a brain hemorrhage in 1968. (Walter Cronkite eulogizes him as the "bridge between older bohemian movements and today's hippies.") Coulter's perfunctory acting is no match for Kerouac, seen reading passionately as Steve Allen plays piano in the 1959 clip that opens and closes the film.

Kerouac: "The idea that I had—the Beat Generation was a generation of beatitude, pleasure in life and tenderness."

Koyaanisqatsi (1982)

🌿🌿🌿🌿 The spellbinding visual style of Godfrey Reggio, combined with Philip Glass's hypnotic score, is an acquired taste. Lacking narration and dialogue, the eclectic montages and daring musical compositions leave much to the imagination in this unusual film. Aside from the recurring theme chant, the soundtrack is dominated by grand arpeggios and swirling crescendos. Reggio begins by soaring slo-mo over the desert mountain landscapes of Monument Valley. From sand sculptures and cloud formations to waterfalls and ocean waves, he contrasts natural beauty with urban sprawl and industrial decay. Reggio speeds up the camera, creating psychedelic streaks of red and white car lights, like traffic on LSD. In fact, this film is probably best experienced under that influence while watching on a projection screen with surround sound. Reggio didn't stop there. He followed with the grim *Powaqqatsi* in 1998, but rebounded in 2002 with *Naqoyqatsi*, this time using powerful digital effects to create his hallucinatory montages.

☙ STONY ROCKUMENTARIES ☙

It goes without saying that *This Is Spiñal Tap* is the best rock mockumentary of all time, but when it comes to the real thing, the choices are endless. Here are five of our faves.

Meeting People Is Easy (1998):
Documentary cameras shadow Radiohead as the seminal British band promotes its groundbreaking 1997 album, *OK Computer*, and tours the world several times over. Revealing interviews, often capturing a terse Thom Yorke, combined with light-show heavy live footage and ultratrippy travel interstitials keep the film moving at a brisk pace, but it's the music that will truly blow you away.

The Filth and the Fury (2000):
Julien Temple's second film about the rise and fall of the Sex Pistols from the band's point of view and gives some historical context. From meager beginnings in rough-and-tumble London to massive success on their home turf and far beyond, archival footage coupled with recent interviews reveal the punk pioneers' true mission and its greatest loss. Says singer John Lydon (a.k.a. Johnny Rotten) of bassist Sid Vicious, who died of an overdose in 1979: "I could take on England, but I couldn't take on one heroin addict."

I Am Trying to Break Your Heart: A Film About Wilco (2002):
Painful and exhilarating at the same time, the inner struggles of one of rock's most respected and revered bands are on full display in this tense black-and-white doc directed by Sam Jones. Intended to chronicle the making of Wilco's fourth album, *Yankee Hotel Foxtrot*, the film also exposes the backroom dealings of the music business, where, sadly, sales usually trumps cultural significance. It may be a tough road getting there, but like all that's good and pure, Wilco winds up on top.

The Devil and Daniel Johnston (2006):
Among Austin's greatest creative forces is the bipolar Daniel Johnston, whose affinity for prose, art, and melodies cemented his place in indie rock history from the mid-eighties on. In this award-winning documentary, filmmaker Jeff Feuerzeig delves deep into the mind of a brilliant but mentally unstable artist (allegedly, his condition was spurred by a bad acid trip) whose influence reached far beyond Texas. Look no further than the late Kurt Cobain, who often wore a T-shirt adorned with the kooky frog that served as the cover image to Johnston's classic album *Hi, How Are You*.

Soul Power (2008):
Five years after Woodstock, a few of America's greatest R & B stars converged on Zaire for a three-day concert the likes of which the African nation (now the Democratic Republic of the Congo) had never seen. In Jeffrey Levy-Hinte's doc, the sights and sounds of James Brown, B. B. King, The Spinners, and other soul luminaries (much of the footage was unreleased for thirty years) are captured in such mind-blowing, high-def detail. Every shake of the tambourine is pristine, every blow of the horn squawks momentous, and every bead of sweat on James Brown's hefty chest glistens with purpose.

Lenny Bruce
Without Tears (1972)

🍸🥃 💉 💊 👀

🌿🌿🌿🌿🌿 Both this doc and Bob Fosse's *Lenny* (1974), starring Dustin Hoffman, are pretty much all you need to see in order to understand the sheer audacity of Lenny Bruce, the most arrested comedian of all time. Bruce burst on the club scene in the fifties like a Jew out of hell. Steeped in the Borsht Belt comedy tradition, Bruce embraced the burgeoning hipster culture, speaking in jive jargon ("dig?") and taking drugs. Though marijuana was not his personal favorite (Bruce preferred speed and, later, heroin), he supported (and predicted) its eventual legalization. Bruce's 1961 obscenity arrest in San Francisco was the first of many, culminating with his bust three years later at New York's Café Au Go Go that resulted in a four-month jail sentence. While appealing the conviction, Bruce died of an overdose in 1966. So we're left with two Lenny Bruces: the incredibly inventive and irreverent comic visionary and the beaten-down victim of government censorship. A brilliant parodist, master of voices and accents, and student of the movies, Bruce blazed the trail for Richard Pryor, Robin Williams, and other "sick" and "offensive" comics to come. John Magnuson's black-and-white film depicts Bruce, warts and all, but mostly he just stands back, watches and listens. It's pure genius.

> "It's chic to arrest me. I'm the Louis Pasteur of junkiedom."
>
> —**Lenny Bruce**

🌿 MUST-SEE STONY STAND-UP MOVIES 🌿

These stand-up comedians with a rebellious bent will have you rolling . . . with laughter.

Richard Pryor: Live on the Sunset Strip **(1982):** In 1980, Richard Pryor caught fire while smoking freebase cocaine. He spent six weeks in the hospital and started performing again in 1982. This concert movie is known best for Pryor's famous twenty-minute routine/explanation about the freebase incident: "Ten million motherfuckers freebase, I gotta burn up." Pryor voices the pipe: "You let me get a little low yesterday. I don't like that. Keep me full at all times." Even dealers stopped selling him coke: "I never heard of a dope dealer doing that. You'd sooner get a free meal at a Chinese restaurant." The preceding hundred minutes are peak Pryor, with great bits about Africa, jail, and lawyers, and what he said was the last time he'll ever break out his alcoholic Mudbone character (not true).

Eddie Murphy Raw **(1987):** Among Eddie Murphy's many career highs is this oft-quoted concert movie (the sequel to 1983's *Delirious*), which grossed more than fifty million dollars and holds the decade's record for most uses of the word "fuck" on the big screen. From his classic "What have you done for me lately?" rant to his hilarious take on divorce ("Half!") and very un-PC admission that he'd like to find an African "bush bitch" clueless to the ways of the Western world, clearly, Murphy was having women problems at the time, and his bitterness shows through. Issues aside, he never was funnier, taking down Italians, Bill Cosby, and Michael Jackson (who was no doubt an inspiration for Murphy's purple leather ensemble) and living up to the movie's name one crude but brilliant bit at a time.

Bill Hicks: Sane Man (1989): Like the better-known Sam Kinison, who also died in his thirties, Bill Hicks had a flair for the outrageous. Thanks in part to searing performances like the one Kevin Booth (*American Drug War*) captured in 1989 at an Austin comedy club, it's Hicks who now has a larger cult following. The Texas-born Hicks tolerated no fools. His bristling humor targeted Republicans and pop stars alike (Hicks hated George Bush and Ronald Reagan as much as he did George Michael and Debbie Gibson) and his drug riffs are unparalleled. "I've had some killer times on drugs," he says before launching into several hysterical acid flashbacks. Even better is this zinger: "Not only do I think pot should be legalized, I think it should be mandatory." Nuff said!

Sex, Drugs, Rock & Roll (1991): As a monologist, Eric Bogosian's characters bristle with comic energy. The drugs equation of his one-man play adapted for the screen by John McNaughton (*Wild Things*) is best represented in his rock star, who hilariously recalls: "I used to get up every morning and before I'd brush my teeth, I'd smoke a joint. While I was smoking a joint, I'd pop a beer. While I was sipping up the beer, pick up a spoon of heroin, cocaine, or whatever's lying around the house, stick it right in my arm. Get totally wasted."

Sarah Silverman: Jesus Is Magic (2005): She's hot, Jewish, endlessly sassy, and has no qualms offending everyone from Holocaust victims to Asians, the handicapped to the homeless. If that doesn't make you instantly fall in love with Sarah Silverman, then the massive bong she straddles in the opening scene to this concert film certainly will. Gigantic bong hits aside, Silverman covers a lot of ground from her stand-up act, and director Liam Lynch incorporates a series of hilarious music videos and bits costarring pals like Brian Posehn, Bob Odenkirk, and Steve Agee along with her sister Laura. Crass, shocking, brilliant—how you judge her makes no difference to Silverman, who declares matter-of-factly, "I don't care if you think I'm racist. I just want you to think I'm thin."

Katt Williams: The Pimp Chronicles Pt. 1 (2006): Katt Williams's mandate, to embody the comedic spirit of greats like Richard Pryor and Redd Foxx, is put on full display in this HBO special. It starts offstage, with a *Casino*-like meeting in the back of a Cadillac between Williams and the Doggfather himself, Snoop Dogg, then Williams launches into an hour-long tirade that bites into everything from cars to women to weed. "Enjoy your life," he declares. "Smoke weed!"

Pumping Iron (1977)

🍶 ⛏️

🌿🌿🌿🌙 Before *The Terminator* and the Governor, Arnold Schwarzenegger starred in the little documentary that could. One of the greatest bodybuilders of all time, Schwarzenegger was nearing the end of his weight-training career when George Butler and Robert Fiore aimed their cameras at the "Austrian Oaf." Just twenty-eight years old and 240 pounds of sculpted muscle, Schwarzenegger proved a game subject. The main story line is his pursuit of the Mr. Olympia title at a competition in South Africa in 1975 against a field of musclemen that includes Lou Ferrigno, a twenty-four-year-old, 275-pound upstart from Brooklyn who would go on to play the Incredible Hulk on TV. While Schwarzenegger works out in Gold's Gym in Venice Beach just yards from the Pacific Ocean, Ferrigno does reps in his family's basement a few subway stops from Coney Island. Loose, gregarious, and charismatic, Schwarzenegger offers a sharp contrast to Ferrigno, who has a speech impediment and is deaf in one ear. The filmmakers handle what would appear to be a freak show of hairless torsoed men rippling their pecs and shoulders for delirious crowds both sensitively and seriously. After Arnold aces the contest, he retires from professional bodybuilding. And the first thing he does is light up a joint. Take a long hit and exhale deeply. In 2002, Cinemax celebrated the film's twenty-fifth anniversary with "Raw Iron: The Making of *Pumping Iron*," which appears on the DVD.

Arnold Schwarzenegger: "Milk are for babies. When you get older you drink beer."

Running Down a Dream: Tom Petty and the Heartbreakers (2007)

✒️

🌿🌿🌿 Unless you're a diehard Tom Petty fan, you may have to be high to get through this four-hour documentary about the Florida-born rocker and his longtime band, The Heartbreakers. Peter Bogdanovich (*The Last Picture Show*) hauls out the star power with enthusiastic talking heads like Eddie Vedder, Stevie Nicks, Dave Grohl, Rick Rubin, Johnny Depp, and the late George Harrison. Portrayed as the consummate songwriter and bandleader who won't ever back down, Petty's formative years are the most interesting. There are some long-haired hippie home movie clips and frank discussions about the band's pot and drug use, but after breaking down their personnel and their amazing ascent past adversity to the peaks of rock royalty, the movie just keeps on going. Surviving the decades with minimal changes to their lineup, The Heartbreakers rival Bruce Springsteen's E Street Band for longevity and consistency. Credit Bogdanovich for not cutting classic performances short, but this flick could have been edited down without sacrificing Petty's history or his legend.

Tom Petty: "'God, I love you / God I need you / This time I've got both feet on the ground . . .' I could smoke a joint and come up with three better lines than that."

The Source (1999)

🍶 💉

🌿🌿🌿🌿🌙 For a comprehensive history of the Beats, you need not look any further than this impressive doc by Chuck Workman. It starts with Jack Kerouac, Allen Ginsberg, and William S. Burroughs meeting at Columbia University in 1944. Workman quickly zeroes in on their most important works—*On the Road* (Kerouac), *Howl* (Ginsberg), and *Naked Lunch* (Burroughs)—employing actors to read, contrasted with footage of the actual writers doing the same. While Johnny Depp and John Turturro gingerly portray Kerouac and Ginsberg, Dennis Hopper stunningly nails Burroughs, from the fedora hat and thin tie to his pitched Midwestern accent. It was Burroughs who described the Beats as "the source" for future generations of outlaws and renegades. Ed Sanders points to the Be-In in San Francisco in 1965, organized by Ginsberg and Timothy Leary (he gets his section in the film as well), when the term "hippie" replaced "beatnik," which came from being "beat" (tired, put down, a drag) or "beatitude" (happiness) and also derived from Sputnik, the Russian satellite that was launched in 1957. Workman shines the spotlight on many other Beat luminaries, including Neal Cassady, Lawrence Ferlinghetti, Gregory Corso, Michael McClure, Gary Snyder, and David Amram (he co-wrote the film's score). The shortage of women is explained simply. Many of the Beats were gay, such as Burroughs, who offers his wisdom about a lifetime of drug use: "What might be a negative experience for someone else can be a very positive experience for a writer." Future generations of poets pay tribute to these hallowed giants, but it's evident their shoes will never quite be filled.

Stepping Razor: Red X (1992)

🌿 🌿 🌿 🌿 🌿 Politically provocative and immensely entertaining, Nicholas Campbell's portrait of Peter Tosh focuses on the reggae martyr's musical life and mysterious death. An original member of the Wailers with Bob Marley and Bunny Livingston, Tosh was extremely critical of the Jamaican government (what he called the "shit-stem") and its prejudicial treatment of Rastafarians. Tosh wrote "Legalize It," and he's seldom seen in footage without a spliff in hand ("Jah created it for the motivation of the mind of man"). After Marley's death in 1981, he grew increasingly paranoid, and often rambled about duppies and other evil forces on cassette tapes heard throughout the film. Though one man was charged with Tosh's murder, it remains unclear to this day if it was a botched robbery or an assassination due to his fiery rhetoric and music. The live performance clips ("Equal Rights," "Stepping Razor"), talking-head interviews, and grainy look add to overall quality of this powerful doc.

Super High Me (2008)

🌿 🌿 🌿 🌿 When comedian Doug Benson saw Morgan Spurlock's award-winning documentary *Super Size Me*, he got the munchies—and the inspiration for his own film, the aptly titled *Super High Me*, in which he goes thirty days without pot (and alcohol) and another thirty blazing 24/7. What transpires is a fascinating study on the physical and mental impact of being stoned versus sober, during which Benson undergoes a series of scientific tests: he has his lung capacity monitored and tests his psychic ability (which, not surprisingly, is significantly increased while high), sperm count, intelligence, and memory skills. Interspersed throughout the experimental portion of the movie are bits of Benson's stand-up routine, which show the full-time comedian traveling tirelessly from city to city, encountering the occasional generous pothead who gifts him a bud or a joint. On the serious side of things, director Michael Blieden (*The Comedians of Comedy*) also focuses on the Bush-era conflict between federal and state law, the medical benefits of marijuana, the proliferation of dispensaries all over Los Angeles, the success of Oaksterdam, and Johnny Q. Law, who's intent on shutting the whole thing down. Many of Benson's funny famous friends make cameos in favor of the cause, including Sarah Silverman (who hits a vaporizer like an old pro), Patton Oswalt, Greg Proops, Zach Galifianakis, and Bob Odenkirk, who doesn't dig the weed like everyone else in the film. In the end, the results speak for themselves: stoned or sober, medically, Benson's pretty much the same. One notable difference: He did gain eight pounds during the second thirty days. Informative and clever, with an insane amount of smoking going on in the second half of the film, Benson more than earns his place in pot culture with this high-larious historical document.

> "So it's been six days and I'm doing OK. I don't think it's as addictive as some people think. Like, I only think about smoking pot constantly."
>
> **—Doug Benson**

☘ Q & A: DOUG BENSON ☘

Comedian Doug Benson claimed his place in the Stoner Hall of Fame back in 2004, when he and buddies Arj Barker and Tony Camin came up with The Marijuana-Logues, an off-Broadway play and book that hilariously deconstructs the stoner lifestyle. But his reputation for all things pot reached new heights with the release of 2008's *Super High Me*, a documentary that chronicles Doug's weed experiments (thirty days clean, followed by thirty days of nonstop blazing) and gives an inside look at L.A.'s dispensary culture. As the name of his podcast suggests (I Love Movies with Doug Benson), Doug Benson loves movies, and we love his. Here, a chat with the tireless stand-up stoner.

Reefer Movie Madness: How did the idea for *Super High Me* evolve from a bit to a movie?

Doug Benson: Originally, it was a silly joke about how, if Morgan Sperlock could make *Super Size Me*, a movie where he eats McDonald's for thirty days, and people paid money to watch it, why can't I make a movie where I smoke pot for thirty days and call it *Super High Me*? Or *Business as Usual*? That was the joke onstage. Then I was at Patton Oswalt's wedding where I saw Michael Blieden, who had directed the movie *The Comedians of Comedy*, which I enjoyed, and I'd also smoked pot with him a few times, so I told him the joke and asked, "Do you think that's a movie?" And he said, "Yeah!" He was fired up and got very excited about the notion of doing the experiment.

RMM: So the experiment was thirty days without pot or alcohol, then another thirty of blazing constantly?

DB: Yes. I was very determined to do thirty days without smoking first. A lot of people would say, "What difference does that make?" Well, because I've been smoking for years, to quit now would be hard; I wouldn't suffer any sort of physical withdrawal, but it wouldn't be pleasant. If I quit after thirty days of smoking constantly, at least for the beginning, it might just be a break from all the smoking. As it turns out, after thirty days without I was very excited about smoking, but not so anxious that it was making my life bad. And then after thirty days of smoking constantly I was more than happy to light up on day thirty-one, and I've maintained ever since. I smoke everyday, I just don't smoke constantly.

RMM: In the month you weren't smoking, what was the most noticeable difference to you?

DB: I did everything I normally do, and maybe I was a little more anxious, things were a little less fun, and it was easier not to gain weight. The harder part for me was not drinking alcohol, and I did that for the entire sixty days because it would be so easy to not smoke pot if I could drink—you're in a comedy club every night, people are offering you free cocktails, you've got time to kill, and you're inside and not smoking weed. So I got through the whole sixty days without a single drop of alcohol, and that was my biggest accomplishment in the movie.

RMM: And in the thirty days that you were partaking constantly, what did that entail?

DB: On average, I'd start at about eight or nine in the morning and go until around midnight or 1 A.M. I'd sleep about seven hours every night, sometimes a nap in the afternoon, but other than that, I just smoked the whole time I was awake.

RMM: In the movie, we see you smoking joints, using a vaporizer, hitting the bowl. What's your preferred method of puffing?

DB: The change-up was more to suit the production. We would use a vaporizer while I was in my apartment; joints, pipes, and blunts when I was out and about; and I'd have to do edibles in public or if traveling was going to be involved. Sometimes it would be a mix of all those things, or on many days, I just had Cocoa Krispies for breakfast that were full of pot—the edibles keep you high for many hours. So that on top of continually smoking, I was pretty high the whole time.

RMM: There's a scene in the movie where you're in the backseat of your friend's car, and he specifically asked you not to smoke, but you did anyway. Are you still friends with him?

DB: Yeah, we're still good friends. He loves to talk about it to this day. Pot smoke doesn't linger in the car. And he doesn't mind it anyway; he's playing up how mad he is about it. But I never say to a taxi driver, like in *The Big Lebowski*, "Mind if I smoke a J?" Some of my friends are more brazen than I am. I still don't feel like it's something you can get away with, but that scene in the movie is more about me fucking with my friend.

RMM: People must offer you weed all the time, especially since the movie came out . . .

DB: I already had enough of a snowballing reputation as a stoner to get marijuana at shows, but the problem is people want to smoke with me, and they often want to do it in their setting—their car, their parking lot, their house, whatever . . . And after a show, with the number of offers I get, I can't go smoke with each one.

I can't say, "Hey everyone, let's all just do it in the greenroom or behind the club," because there's too many people. So I end up having to politely say no to most people, and sneak off with a friend. A lot of folks just want to give me weed, and I love that because I can smoke it back at the hotel, but I want people to understand that as much as I appreciate it, I can't act on every case, and I'm not singling anyone out or being rude. But donations are always welcome.

RMM: Who were you trying to reach with the movie?

DB: I didn't really set out to reach anyone specific, I just wanted to make a funny movie that people would enjoy—the more the merrier! It's nice when a person who's not a stoner sees it and appreciates that just because somebody really likes pot, doesn't make him a waste of space. I do worry that there's gonna be more conservative members of the audience, more so than your average comedy club, but I seem to not be offending anybody with the pot material. That's really good. It shows that pot is not something people are angry about. They just need to learn that your average AIDS patient is not likely to interfere with their lives in any way because they're smoking pot.

RMM: Will you do another movie?

DB: Yes. It's not going to be another stunt movie, but I am interested in doing something about my ongoing experiences with life and marijuana, whether it's fictional or not. Pot has to be involved, because I made my bed, I have to lie in it, but it doesn't necessarily have to be just about pot. Part of why *Super High Me* came to be is because I love movies so much, so I want to do it again.

Tie-Died: Rock 'n' Roll's Most Deadicated Fans (1995)

🌿 🌿 🌿 🌿 The darkness was about to give on a Grateful Dead tour in 1994, which Andrew Behar decided to follow with his video camera. A year later, Jerry Garcia died, putting an end to the traveling circus of Deadheads that had followed the group since the seventies. This is a mostly cheerful doc—lots of drumming, spinning, and hippie chit-chat outside several summer tour stops. But around the edges lurks the specter of problems on the scene: excessive drug use, arrests and police infiltration, homelessness and wanton behavior. "Don't deal on tour," former *Relix* publisher Toni Brown advises, but unfortunately it's too late for the hundreds, even thousands of Deadheads who'd been busted for possessing or selling drugs while on tour. The interview quality is so good, you really don't need to be inside the venue or hear one speck of Grateful Dead music. It's implied and it works. Stick around for Peter Shapiro's brief "Conversation with Ken Kesey" that follows the credits.

directed by O. B. Babbs and A. J. Catoline. Babbs's father, Ken, was one of the Merry Pranksters who visited Millbrook in 1964 as part of their cross-country bus trip. That visit didn't go so well (Leary said he was sick at the time), but years later Leary and head Prankster Ken Kesey became friends. It's truly a meeting of great stoner minds. Leary died on May 12, 1996, just three weeks after Babbs and Catoline finished filming.

> "Many of us feel that the current marijuana laws are not only unconstitutional, but extremely severe and these laws are going to be tested in my appeal to the high court."
> **—Leary**

Timothy Leary's Dead (1996)

🌿 🌿 🌿 Named after the opening line of the Moody Blues song "Legend of a Mind," Paul Davids's doc about LSD guru Timothy Leary means well, but suffers from poor production quality and jagged editing. We follow the intrepid psychonaut from Harvard (where he was fired) to the famous Millbrook estate in New York to his marijuana busts in 1965 and 1968 to his daring 1970 prison escape to his underground adventures in Africa and Afghanistan to his later years as a lecturer and cyber-geek. The controversy surrounding the film regards the ending, during which Leary's head is removed and frozen cryogenically. This never happened, but if you're not a student of psychedelic history you might get confused. Less complicated and more engaging is *Timothy Leary's Last Trip* (1997), an hour-long film

20 to Life: The Life and Times of John Sinclair (2007)

🌿 🌿 🌿 🌿 Activist/poet John Sinclair was arrested for selling two joints to a narc in 1969. He spent a couple of years in jail before being suddenly released after a high-profile benefit concert featuring John Lennon, Yoko Ono, Stevie Wonder, Bob Seger, and other Michigan music luminaries (he was busted in Ann Arbor). Sinclair founded Translove Energies and the White Panther Party, and managed the MC5, coining "Rock-and-roll, dope, and fucking in the streets" as the scene's motto. Lennon briefly performs "John Sinclair" at the 1971 concert and wryly comments, "So flower power didn't work. We start again." Sinclair eventually moved to New Orleans and Amsterdam, where he performs his gruff spoken-word polemics with jazz bands. Juxtaposing the past and present, Steve Gebhardt's doc captures the essence of this aging political activist.

Sinclair (discussing jail): "I came out of that pretty much determined to try to permanently alter the marijuana laws. I was a confirmed lifelong smoker of marijuana."

Union: The Business Behind Getting High, The (2008)

🌿🌿🌿 This broadside about marijuana prohibition from Canadian filmmaker Brett Harvey assembles a strong cast of talking heads (including one of this book's coauthors) and terrific archival footage, all in the hopes of unraveling the code that has kept pot illegal in the U.S. since 1937. Adam Scorgie writes and narrates, taking viewers on a tour of Vancouver and parts of British Columbia, the home of BC Bud. Pretty much every base is covered—from marijuana myths (cancer, brain damage, laziness) to medicinal use to industrial hemp to prison privatization. An incredulous Tommy Chong discusses his 2001 paraphernalia bust: "I didn't ship anything to anybody. I was just the face on the bong." Other quality interviewees include LEAP's Jack Cole, former Vancouver mayor Larry Campbell, ex-Seattle police chief Norm Stamper, the late Dr. Tod Mikuriya, and Harvard professors Lester Grinspoon and Jeff Miron. Harvey's kitchen-sink approach fills every available screen moment with a colorful or nostalgic snippet. At times you wonder how a particular momentary clip fits the narrative, but then realize it's all part of the director's whimsical visual style. Will pot prohibition ever end? Grinspoon opines sagely, "You can't sustain a lie like that forever."

Waiting to Inhale (2005)

🌿🌿🌿 Picking up where Ron Mann's *Grass* left off, Jed Riffe targets the medical-marijuana explosion of the late nineties and early twenty-first century. His chief concern is WAMM—the Wo/Men's Alliance for Medical Marijuana in Santa Cruz, California, whose grow operation was raided during the making of the film. The history of medical marijuana in American is illustrated clearly—from nineteenth-century usage to the U.S. government's own program that has been quietly providing marijuana to a handful of patients since 1975 to the modern medipot movement and its states' rights objectives (as of this writing, fourteen states have legalized the medical use of marijuana). Talking heads include Representative Barney Frank, Harvard professor Lester Grinspoon, federal patient Irv Rosenfeld, cannabis researcher Dr. Donald I. Abrams, WAMM's Valerie and Mike Corral, and Mae "Grandma Marijuana" Nutt. While Riffe allows the DEA a platform to call "medical marijuana a fraud," this is pure agitprop with just the right amount of journalistic integrity.

Wetlands Preserved: The Story of an Activist Nightclub (2008)

🌿🌿🌿 Home to New York's emerging jam-band scene from 1989 to 2001, Wetlands Preserve was more than just a rock club: Money raised from shows went to environmental causes and funded demonstrations and actions. Over seventy interviews pack Dean Budnick's doc (including one of the authors of this book) like the club's tiny dance floor. It all started with the singular vision of Larry Bloch, who wanted to merge music and eco-politics in an urban club setting. Wetlands performers included Phish, Dave Matthews Band, Blues Traveler, Spin Doctors, Widespread Panic, Gov't Mule, Sublime, The Roots, Ben Harper, Spearhead, and more. Rather than use live music clips, Budnick cleverly creates band montages with photos and visual razzle-dazzle. Sadly, twelve years after opening shop, Wetlands lost its lease and had to close a week earlier than planned due to the 9/11 tragedy (Wetlands was just blocks away from the World Trade Center).

Dave Matthews: "I remember being so stoned once that I started a song and then couldn't remember how it went. It was just in an endless loop. The same chord with absolutely no idea of how to get out of it."

Photography Credits

P. 15: *Alice's Restaurant* (United Artists / Courtesy Neal Peters Collection); P. 17: *Animal House* (Universal Pictures / Courtesy Neal Peters Collection); P. 18: *The Banger Sisters* (Fox Searchlight Pictures / Courtesy Neal Peters Collection); P. 21: Jeff "The Dude" Dowd / Bob Berg P. 23: *Bill & Ted's Excellent Adventure* (MGM / Courtesy Neal Peters Collection); P. 24: *Blazing Saddles* (Warner Bros. Pictures / Photo12/ Polaris); P. 26: *Borat* (20th Century Fox Film Corp. / Courtesy Neal Peters Collection); P. 28: *Caddyshack* (Warner Bros. Pictures / Courtesy Neal Peters Collection); P. 29: *Up in Smoke* (Paramount Pictures / Photo12/Polaris) P. 30–31: *Nice Dreams* (Columbia Pictures / Courtesy Neal Peters Collection); P. 34: *Dazed and Confused* (Universal Pictures / Courtesy Neal Peters Collection); P. 35: (top) *Three Amigos!* (MGM / Courtesy Neal Peters Collection); P. 35: (bottom) Nathan Followill (Dean Chalkley) P. 38: *Dick* (Columbia Pictures / Courtesy Neal Peters Collection); P. 39: *Dogma* (Lionsgate Films / Courtesy Neal Peters Collection); P. 41: *Dude, Where's My Car?* (20th Century Fox Film Corp. / Photo12/Polaris); P. 42: *Everything's Gone Green* (First Independent Pictures / Courtesy Neal Peters Collection); P. 44: *Fast Times at Ridgemont High* (Universal Pictures / Courtesy Neal Peters Collection); P. 45: *Feeling Minnesota* (New Line Cinema / Courtesy Neal Peters Collection); P. 46: *Ferris Bueller's Day Off* (Paramount Pictures / Photo12/ Polaris); P. 48: *The 40-Year-Old Virgin* (Universal Pictures / Courtesy Neal Peters Collection); P. 51: *Garden State* (Fox Searchlight Pictures / Courtesy Neal Peters Collection); P. 54: *Harold & Kumar Go to White Castle* (New Line Cinema / Courtesy Neal Peters Collection); P. 57: *Harold & Kumar Escape from Guatanamo Bay* (United Artists / Photo12/Polaris) P. 59: *How High* (Universal Pictures / Courtesy Neal Peters Collection); P. 60: *Igby Goes Down* (United Artists / Photo12/ Polaris); P. 63: *Kingpin* (MGM / Courtesy Neal Peters Collection); P. 68: *M.A.S.H.* (20th Century Fox Film Corp. / Courtesy Neal Peters Collection); P. 69: *Meet the Parents* (Universal Pictures / Courtesy Neal Peters Collection); P. 72: *National Lampoon's Vacation* (Warner Bros. Pictures / Photo12/Polaris); P. 74: *Nine to Five* (20th Century Fox Film Corp. / Courtesy Neal Peters Collection); P. 75: *Office Space* (20th Century Fox Film Corp. / Courtesy Neal Peters Collection); P. 76: *Outside Providence* (Miramax Films / Courtesy Neal Peters Collection); P. 77: *Parenthood* (Universal Pictures / Photo12/Polaris); P. 79: *Pee-wee's Big Adventure* (Warner Bros. Pictures / Photo12/Polaris); P. 80: B-Real (Sony Music Entertainment Inc.) P. 81: *Pick-Up Summer* (Film Ventures International / Courtesy Neal Peters Collection); P. 82: *Pineapple Express* (Columbia Pictures / Photo12/Polaris); P. 84: *Pretty in Pink* (Paramount Pictures / Courtesy Neal Peters Collection); P. 87: *Reality Bites* (Universal Pictures / Courtesy Neal Peters Collection); P. 88: *Reno 911!: Miami* (20th Century Fox Film Corp. / Photo12/ Polaris); P. 89: *Risky Business* (Warner Bros. Pictures / Photo12/Polaris); P. 90: *Road Trip* (DreamWorks / Photo12/ Polaris); P. 94: *Scary Movie* (Dimension Films / Photo12/ Polaris); P. 95: *Shampoo* (Columbia Pictures / Photo12/ Polaris); P. 97: *Smiley Face* (First Look International / Photo12/Polaris); P. 98: Snoop Dogg (Photo12/Polaris); P. 100: *Starsky & Hutch* (Warner Bros. Pictures / Courtesy Neal Peters Collection); P. 102: *Stripes* (Columbia Pictures / Courtesy Neal Peters Collection); P. 104: *Super Troopers* (Fox Searchlight Pictures / Courtesy Neal Peters Collection); P. 107: *Teen Wolf* (Atlantic Releasing Corp. / Photo12/Polaris); P. 108: *Tenacious D in the Pick of Destiny* (New Line Cinema / Photo12/Polaris); P. 109: *Thank God It's Friday* (Columbia Pictures / Courtesy Neal Peters Collection); P. 110: *There's Something About Mary* (20th Century Fox Film Corp. / Photo12/Polaris); P. 111: *This Is Spiñal Tap* (Embassy Pictures Corp. / Photo12/Polaris); P. 112: *Tommy Boy* (Paramount Pictures / Courtesy Neal Peters Collection); P. 114: *Trailer Park Boys* (CAVU Releasing / Courtesy Neal Peters Collection); P. 116: *Tropic Thunder* (Paramount Pictures / Photo12/Polaris); P. 117: *Up in Smoke* (Paramount Pictures / Photo12/Polaris); P. 118: *Austin Powers in Goldmember* (New Line Cinema / Courtesy Neal Peters Collection); P. 119: *Van Wilder* (Lionsgate Films / Courtesy Neal Peters Collection); P. 123: *Wayne's World* (Paramount Pictures / Photo12/Polaris); P. 128: *Zoolander* (Paramount Pictures / Photo12/Polaris); P. 130: *Almost Famous* (DreamWorks / Courtesy Neal Peters Collection); P. 132: *American Graffiti* (Universal Pictures / Courtesy Neal Peters Collection); P. 134: *Apocalypse Now* (United Artists / Courtesy Neal Peters Collection); P. 135: *Full Metal Jacket* (Warner Bros. Pictures / Photo12/Polaris); P. 137: *The Beach* (20th Century Fox Film Corp. / Photo12/ Polaris); P. 138: *The Big Chill* (Columbia Pictures / Courtesy Neal Peters Collection); P. 140: *Blow* (New Line Cinema / Photo12/Polaris); P. 141: *The Wackness* (Sony Pictures Classics / Photo12/Polaris); P. 142: *Blow-Up* (Premier Productions / Courtesy Neal Peters Collection); P. 145: *Boyz N the Hood* (Columbia Pictures / Courtesy Neal Peters Collection); P. 146: *Brokedown Palace* (20th Century Fox Film Corp. / Photo12/Polaris); P. 149: *Clockers* (Universal Pictures / Photo12/Polaris); P. 150: (L) *A Clockwork Orange* (Warner Bros. Pictures / Courtesy Neal Peters Collection); P. 150: (R) *Colors* (MGM / Courtesy Neal Peters Collection); P. 153: *The Doors* (TriStar Pictures / Photo12/Polaris); P. 156: *Easy Rider* (Columbia Pictures / Photo12/Polaris); P. 158: (L) *Eyes Wide Shut* (Warner Bros. Pictures / Courtesy Neal Peters Collection); P. 158: (R) *Factory Girl* (MGM / Courtesy Neal Peters Collection); P. 159: *The Falcon and the Snowman* (MGM / Photo12/Polaris); P. 160: *Fear and Loathing in Las Vegas* (Universal Pictures / Courtesy Neal Peters Collection);

P. 164: The Good Girl (Fox Searchlight Pictures / Courtesy Neal Peters Collection); P. 166: The Graduate (MGM Home Entertainment / Photo12/Polaris); P. 171: Humboldt County (Magnolia Pictures / Courtesy Neal Peters Collection); P. 172: Hustle & Flow (Paramount Classics / Courtesy Neal Peters Collection); P. 175: Jacob's Ladder (TriStar Pictures / Courtesy Neal Peters Collection); P. 178: La Bamba (Columbia Pictures / Photo12/Polaris); P. 181: (L): Laurel Canyon (Sony Pictures Classics / Photo12/Polaris); P. 181: (R): Lenny (United Artists / Courtesy Neal Peters Collection); P. 182: Less Than Zero (20th Century Fox Film Corp. / Photo12/ Polaris); P. 184: The Man with the Golden Arm (United Artists / Courtesy Neal Peters Collection); P. 187: (L) Midnight Cowboy (United Artists / Photo12/Polaris); P. 187: (R) Midnight Express (Columbia Pictures / Photo12/Polaris); P. 188: My Own Private Idaho (New Line Cinema / Courtesy Neal Peters Collection); P. 191: Platoon (MGM / Courtesy Neal Peters Collection); P. 192: Head (Columbia Pictures / Courtesy Neal Peters Collection); P. 193: The Grasshopper (Warner Bros. Pictures / Courtesy Neal Peters Collection); P. 194: Psych-Out (MGM / Courtesy Neal Peters Collection); P. 195: Ray (Universal Pictures / Courtesy Neal Peters Collection); P. 196: Reefer Madness (Courtesy Neal Peters Collection); P. 199: River's Edge (MGM / Courtesy Neal Peters Collection); P. 201: Running on Empty (Warner Bros. Pictures / Photo12/Polaris); P. 203: Serpico (Paramount Pictures / Photo12/Polaris); P. 205: Sid & Nancy (The Samuel Goldwyn Company / Courtesy Neal Peters Collection); P. 208: Thelma & Louise (MGM / Photo12/Polaris); P. 209: Traffic (USA Films / Photo12/Polaris); P. 210: Trainspotting (Miramax Films / Photo12/Polaris); P. 212: (L) The Wackness (Sony Pictures Classics / Photo12/Polaris); P. 212: (R) Walk the Line (20th Century Fox Film Corp. / Courtesy Neal Peters Collection); P. 214: Y Tu Mamá También (IFC Films / Photo12/Polaris); P. 218: Barbarella (Paramount Pictures / Photo12/Polaris); P. 220: Wayne Coyne (J. Michelle Martin-Coyne); P. 222: Clash of the Titans (MGM / Photo12/Polaris); P. 223: Close Encounters of the Third Kind (Columbia Pictures / Courtesy Neal Peters Collection); P. 224: Conan the Barbarian (Universal Pictures / Photo12/Polaris); P. 225: The Dark Crystal (Universal Pictures / Photo12/Polaris); P. 226: Donnie Darko (Newmarket Films / Courtesy Neal Peters Collection); P. 227: Dr. Jekyll and Mr. Hyde (Paramount Pictures / Courtesy Neal Peters Collection); P. 229: The Faculty (Dimension Films / Courtesy Neal Peters Collection); P. 230: Flash Gordon (Universal Pictures / Photo12/Polaris); P. 232: Jason and the Argonauts (Columbia Pictures / Courtesy Neal Peters Collection); P. 233: Krull (Columbia Pictures / Courtesy Neal Peters Collection); P. 235: Labyrinth (TriStar Pictures / Photo12/ Polaris); P. 236: Legend (Universal / Photo12/Polaris); P. 237: Little Shop of Horrors (Warner Bros. Pictures / Courtesy Neal Peters Collection); P. 238: The Lord of the Rings: The Fellowship of the Ring (New Line Cinema / Photo12/Polaris); P. 241: The Princess Bride (20th Century Fox Film Corp. / Courtesy Neal Peters Collection); P. 245: Star Trek: The Motion Picture (Paramount Pictures / Photo12/Polaris); P. 248: THX 1138 (Warner Bros. Pictures / Courtesy Neal Peters Collection); P. 250: 2001: A Space Odyssey (MGM / Photo12/Polaris); P. 253: Willy Wonka & the Chocolate Factory (Paramount Pictures / Courtesy Neal Peters Collection); P. 256: The Cell (New Line Cinema / Courtesy Neal Peters Collection); P. 257: Children of Men (Universal Pictures / Photo12/Polaris); P. 258: Cleopatra Jones (Warner Bros. Pictures / Courtesy Neal Peters Collection); P. 260: Desperado (Columbia Pictures / Photo12/ Polaris); P. 264: Lords of Dogtown (Sony Pictures Entertainment / Courtesy Neal Peters Collection); P. 268: Sleeper (United Artists / Courtesy Neal Peters Collection); P. 270: Electra Glide in Blue (United Artists / Courtesy Neal Peters Collection); P. 271: Scarface (Universal Pictures / Photo12/Polaris); P. 273: Super Fly (Warner Bros. Pictures / Courtesy Neal Peters Collection); P. 274: True Romance (Warner Bros. Pictures / Courtesy Neal Peters Collection); P. 277: Aqua Teen Hunger Force (Cartoon Network / Courtesy Neal Peters Collection); P. 281: South Park: Bigger, Longer & Uncut (Paramount Pictures / Courtesy Neal Peters Collection); P. 285: Yellow Submarine (United Artists / Courtesy Neal Peters Collection); P. 287: Across the Universe (Columbia Pictures / Photo12/Polaris); P. 289: The Dukes of Hazzard (Warner Bros. Pictures / Photo12/Polaris); P. 291: Don't Look Back (Docurama / Courtesy Neal Peters Collection); P. 292: Gimme Shelter (Cinema 5 Distributing / Photo12/Polaris); P. 294: Hair (United Artists / Photo12/ Polaris); P. 298: The Last Waltz (United Artists / Courtesy Neal Peters Collection); P. 302: Pink Floyd The Wall (Warner Bros. Pictures / Photo12/Polaris); P. 304: Reefer Madness: The Movie Musical (Showtime Networks / Photo12/Polaris); P. 305: The Rocky Horror Picture Show (20th Century Fox Film Corp. / Photo12/Polaris); P. 306: Sgt. Pepper's Lonely Hearts Club Band (Universal Pictures / Photo12/Polaris); P. 308: Pulp Fiction (Miramax Films / Courtesy Neal Peters Collection); P. 309: The Big Lebowski (Universal Pictures / Photo12/Polaris); P. 310: Tommy (Columbia Pictures / Photo12/Polaris); P. 311: Wattstax (Columbia Pictures / Courtesy Neal Peters Collection); P. 312: Woodstock (Warner Bros. Pictures / Photo12/Polaris); P. 314: a/k/a Tommy Chong (Blue Chief Entertainment / Courtesy Neal Peters Collection); P. 317: (top) An Inconvenient Truth (Paramount Vantage / Courtesy Neal Peters Collection); P. 317: (bottom) Melissa Etheridge (JM James Minchin III); P. 321: Gonzo: The Life and Work of Dr. Hunter S. Thompson (Magnolia Pictures / Photo12/Polaris); P. 326: Richard Pryor: Live on the Sunset Strip (Columbia TriStar / Courtesy Neal Peters Collection);

Acknowledgments

Putting *Reefer Movie Madness* together was a huge undertaking that required the help of many friends and fellow writers. We would first like to thank our tireless intern, Daniel Haney, for all of his hard work over the last year and a half, as well as David Cashion, Leslie Stoker, Kathleen Go, and Kerry Liebling at Abrams Image for their patience. Our gratitude goes to Meg Handler, photo editor on this project and on *Pot Culture*. To our unofficial advisor, Mitch Myers: thanks for your ear and guidance. Thank you to Sarah Lazin and Danielle Young.

We are forever grateful to the musicians, actors, comedians, directors, and TV personalities who generously gave their time to be interviewed for this book: Tommy Chong, Cheech Marin, Doug Benson, Snoop Dogg, B-Real, Jason Mraz, Melissa Etheridge, Ray Manzarek, Margaret Cho, Danneel Harris, Taryn Manning, Nathan Followill, Andy Milonakis, Joe Trohman, P-Nut, Adrianne Curry, Method Man, Redman, Wayne Coyne, Robb Wells, John Paul Tremblay, Mike Smith, Andrew McMahon, Cisco Adler, Shwayze, Greg Proops, Austin Winkler, Jesse Hughes, Raul Malo, Jay Chandrasekhar, Greg Mottola, Selene Luna, and Jeff Dowd; and to the various managers, agents, and publicists who helped facilitate those interviews, including Stacey Pokluda, Ken Weinstein, Sheila Richman, Jeff Jampol, Cory Lashever, Ken Phillips, Lewis Kay, Carly Schencker, Kelly MacGaunn, Karen Wiessen, Adam and Peter Raspler, Rick Gershon, Kim Estlund, Greg Cortez, and Cary Baker. To Sarah Saiger at Bambu, Allen St. Pierre and Keith Stroup at NORML, Chang Weisberg and Veeda Armstrong at Guerilla Union: thank you for supporting our books.

To Chris Garrity and the folks at Netflix: This book could not have come together in any timely manner were it not for the amazing service that is Netflix. Thank you for providing it to us and millions of movie buffs.

Shirley Halperin would like to thank: All of the Halperins, but especially Rivka, Eli, and Shai. Thanks to Jeff Miller, Michelle Lanz, and Jessica Hundley for going the extra mile time and time again. The support of my West Coast crew has been invaluable; many thanks to Paul Bonanos, Jason Roth, Scott Igoe, Lori Berger, Charlie Amter, Roy Trakin, Mitch Davis, Heidi Wahl, Bob Berg, and Gina Orr, Super Dave, Bong Rip and Smokey at BongTVLive, and Farmer Dave. Same goes for my East Coast pals: Brian Mergentime, Andrew Whitman, Lori Majewski, Stu Zakim, Jenny Eliscu, Gabe Kirchheimer, Carleen Donovan, Katie Des Londe, Adam Siegel, and Liz Rosenberg. Special thanks to Lisa Taylor, Mary Patton, Alex Greenberg, Nick Lippman, and Steven Trachtenbroit for their help and professional advice. And to Jon Fishman, Alanis Morissette, Rob Thomas, and Dave Grohl: Your friendship over the years has meant a lot. To George Michael: thanks for being you. And last on this list but first in my heart: my husband, Thom Monahan.

Steve Bloom would like to thank: Lots of friends, family, and associates contributed immeasurably to this book with their advice, suggestions, and film picks. Thanks to my dad, Lenny, a huge movie buff; one of my oldest friends, David Smith; Brian Abrams, who took time away from his job as "Dreidel Hustler" at *Heeb* magazine to write some reviews; Mitch Myers, who also pitched in and provided welcome critical and publishing advice; former smuggler and raconteur Mel Zimmer; and my "best bud" and lawyer David Beame.

The starting point for this book, of course, is the seminal exploitation flick, *Reefer Madness*. Though he prefers to not take credit for unearthing the film in the early seventies (see page 197), I would still like to thank to Keith Stroup and NORML for his and the organization's tireless efforts to reform the nation's archaic marijuana laws.

Inspiration for *Reefer Movie Madness* also came from other authors and books, such as Peter Biskind's *Easy Riders, Raging Bulls: How the Sex-Drugs-and-Rock 'N' Roll Generation Saved Hollywood* (Simon & Schuster, 1998); John Hulme and Michael Wexler's *Baked Potatoes: A Pot Smoker's Guide to Film + Video* (Doubleday, 1996); *Marijuana in the Movies: The Complete Guide to Hollywood* (MediaGreen Press, 1999); *Addicted: The Myth and Menace of Drugs in Film* (Creation Books, 1999); *The Rough Guide to Cult Movies: The Good, the Bad and the Very Weird Indeed* (Penguin, 2001); Harry Shapiro's *Shooting Stars: Drugs, Hollywood and the Movies* (Serpent's Tail, 2003); and *Leonard Maltin's Movie & Video Guide* (Plume).

Lastly, thanks to all the stoners out there for inspiring us to write *Reefer Movie Madness* and *Pot Culture*.

The following people contributed reviews to *Reefer Movie Madness*. For a detailed list of credits, please visit www.reefermoviemadness.com.

Contributors: Brian Abrams, John Anderson , Steve Baltin, Jonathan Bernstein, Paul Bonanos, Rob Cantrell, Gregory Daurer, Kaitlin Fontana, John Fortunato, Andy Gensler, Nisha Gopalan, Guy in Tie, Daniel Haney, Shai Halperin, Jeremy Helligar, Jessica Hundley, Hal B. Klein, Michelle Lanz, Alexander Laurence, Rich Leivenberg, Jeff Miller, Joy Mitchell, Thom Monahan, Mitch Myers, John Rosenfelder, Jason Roth, Lisa Taylor, Roy Trakin, Ben Wener, Jeff Weiss, and Evan Winiker